Safari Rifles II

The author with his Botswana elephant, taken in April 2008.

Safari Rifles II

Doubles, Magazine Rifles, and Cartridges for
African Hunting

by
Craig T. Boddington

Safari Press

CAUTION!

Common sense needs to be used when handling and discharging a firearm. Keep the following principles of safety in mind so as to provide a safe environment for everyone: 1) Always point a firearm in a safe direction. 2) Never point a firearm at another person. 3) Treat all firearms as though they are loaded. 4) Wear eye and hearing protection at all times when handling firearms.

Do not attempt to handload your own ammunition using the bullet velocities and or loads listed on these pages. Your firearm may not be able to withstand the pressures generated by the loads and velocities listed in this book. If you aren't sure about your gun, consult a competent gunsmith.

The handloading of ammunition and the discharging of a firearm should never be attempted without the supervision of an adult experienced in both handloading and firearms. Do not attempt to handload ammunition without knowing how to read signs of (excessive) pressure in both guns and ammunition.

Boddington, Craig T.

Second edition

Safari Press
2009 Long Beach, California

ISBN 1-57157-329-1

Library of Congress Catalog Card Number: 92130104

10 9 8 7 6 5 4 3 2 1

Printed in China

Readers wishing to receive the Safari Press catalog, featuring many fine books on big-game hunting, wingshooting, and sporting firearms, should write to Safari Press Inc., P.O. Box 3095, Long Beach, CA 90803, USA. Tel: (714) 894-9080 or visit our Web site at www.safaripress.com.

DEDICATION

This one is for Donna,
a great hunting partner . . . and partner

Table of Contents

Author's Introduction to the Revised Edition

As impossible as it seems, eighteen years have passed since I put the finishing touches on *Safari Rifles*. I was much younger then, not nearly forty, and in the way of younger people I undoubtedly thought I knew more than I really did. Even back then, however, I had sense enough to understand that a book lasts a long time, and if I made a fool of myself in its writing, I would look a fool for many years. So *Safari Rifles* was a daunting task, treading on the heels of classics such as John "Pondoro" Taylor's *African Rifles and Cartridges*. Come to think of it, if you must know the truth, I'm not entirely certain *Safari Rifles* was even my idea. My longtime publisher and friend Ludo Wurfbain is a much better idea man than I am, and he was also a lot younger back in the late 1980s . . .

No book on a subject like this can be written without the help of good friends. Pondoro Taylor had depth of experience that I can never approach, but he drew heavily upon the experience of Fletcher Jamieson and others. In *Safari Rifles* I drew upon all the classic literature, and the experience of friends and mentors. I also had the prescience to conduct a survey of licensed African professional hunters. Well, OK, that probably wasn't my idea, either, but the response was overwhelming, and I have always believed that the data my respondents provided are the most valuable part of the book. (After all, my rule in African hunting is no different now than it was thirty years ago: When in doubt, trust your PH!)

Whether the book actually contained valuable information or, through blind luck, had fortuitous timing, since its actual publication in 1990 I have been both bemused and delighted by its acceptance. To date it is the most enduring, the best- and longest-selling, of my now twenty-odd books. Amazing, at least to me, is the fact that in total copies sold it closely rivals John Taylor's masterwork, which appeared clear back in 1948.

As stated, I will never have Taylor's experience with the dangerous game, nor do I consider myself as good a storyteller as he. However, I think several important factors influenced the success of *Safari Rifles*—most of which are related to timing. Taylor's book was (and is) comprehensive, but it focuses heavily on the thick-skinned game, primarily elephant, and naturally so because Taylor was a genuine ivory hunter.

Big-bore cartridges fascinate hunters and shooters alike, but by 1990 the landscape of the African safari had changed. The industry had moved south, average hunts had grown shorter, and the most common safari had become the plains-game safari. Although I endeavored to avoid giving short shrift to the dangerous game, I recognized this and attempted to present evenly the entire spectrum of rifles and cartridges for African hunting.

Too, Taylor's timing was unfortunate. In 1948 the British Nitro Express cartridges were at the top of the African food chain, but Taylor couldn't know that within a decade Kynoch would discontinue loading so many of the great old cartridges he wrote about.

And because he was based in remote Africa, he could not have extensive knowledge of American developments—or predict that during the 1950s and continuing to this day, American clientele would dominate the safari industry. But that doesn't make his information wrong, just outdated. So I still frequently refer to *African Rifles and Cartridges*, and recommend you do as well. Some of the cartridges he discusses have enjoyed a rebirth, but all are more or less available, some readily and others only with great effort. Most of the hunting bullets he discusses are obsolete, and today we understand better the critical importance of the hunting bullet. But the main problem is that anything developed after 1948 is missing.

Sadly, this is now the situation with the original *Safari Rifles*. There has been much development in rifles, bullets, cartridges, and optics since 1990. Many of you, and certainly my publisher, have been gently suggesting for some years that *Safari Rifles* needed to be updated. I have resisted. My excuse to my publisher, which he will confirm, is that the original was still selling steadily, so why compete with oneself?

My real reason, however, has been that although I really enjoy sitting down and writing a book, rehashing my own material sounded much more like work than fun! Note, please, that almost all of my books have been written "from scratch." I've never claimed to be a good writer, but I like writing, and I've never had a shortage of material. So, with the exceptions of *Fair Chase in North America*, which was always intended to be a collection of material from the Boone and Crockett Club's *Fair Chase* magazine, and *African Experience*, which was always intended to be a collected series of articles from *Safari* magazine, none of my books contain material adapted from magazine articles.

Nor, until today, have I ever set out to revise a previous work. Like writing one, this, too, is a daunting task! In any project some chapters will be much easier than others, so I avoid spoiling myself by tackling the easy ones first. I start a book with a tight chapter outline, and then I write it start to finish. Mind you, the outline usually morphs along the way, but I always have a plan. In this case the plan is the original chapter outline of *Safari Rifles*.

I must admit that until this project became inevitable, I hadn't actually studied *Safari Rifles* for a long time. I was totally shocked at its breadth and scope. Knowing my age and actual experience at the time I wrote it, I must say that Ludo (who has always provided invaluable input) and I reached far beyond ourselves. Over the years many of you have suggested that a "new" *Safari Rifles* should include various things such as discussion of scopes, expanding bullets, and solids. So I had notes to myself. Oddly, virtually all these suggested subjects were actually already right there on the table of contents and within the pages of the original book. I can only say that it's a big book, probably most often read in pieces rather than start to finish. And of course the additions cover subjects that have changed radically since 1990.

So this present volume is a true revision, top to bottom, page by page. I will keep that which is totally valid, update what I feel is missing, and add new chapters as required. From the objectivity of nearly twenty years, I can truthfully say that the original is pretty darn complete—but is clearly missing many new developments.

I was probably at the midpoint of writing *Safari Rifles* when Federal brought out .416 Rigby and .470 Nitro Express factory ammo. About the same time Remington introduced its .416 Remington Magnum and Weatherby its .416 Weatherby Magnum. But at publication in 1990 it wasn't clear that the .416s would become as popular as they have, almost sweeping from the field other "lower .40s" like the .404 Jeffery, .411 KDF, and .425 Express. Nor could I have envisioned the amazing revival of the double rifle. And, of course, there have been many other developments up and down the caliber scale.

No author can have a crystal ball, so it's likely that within my lifetime this volume, too, will become outdated. But there's another factor—the fundamental law that "you don't know what you don't know." By the late 1980s I had done a great deal of African hunting, but I had no idea that within another twenty years I would treble my experience. Back then I had plenty of basic experience, but no experience in specialized areas such as the forest, or the mountains of Ethiopia and the deserts of Chad. In the 1980s, too, I had relatively little experience with elephant. This didn't seem to matter at the time because it appeared almost certain that elephant, and the hunting of elephant, would follow the path of the black rhino. Times change. The herds have rebuilt (to the point of gross overpopulation in some southern countries), and the elephant is again an important part of African hunting. For that matter, even black rhino are now on very limited quota in South Africa and Namibia, and I never thought I would see this. So African hunting has continued to change, and my own knowledge of it has continued to expand. It's easy to add new rifles and cartridges to the text, but reflecting these factors will probably require the most work.

Having resisted—in fact, truly dreaded—this necessary project, I am now excited and ready to go to work. I know that I will be extremely embarrassed by some of the things I wrote twenty years ago, not having known any better. I will keep the good and excise the bad, and I believe the result will be of equal use to owners of the original volume and our next generation of African hunters.

Craig Boddington
Tafika Camp
Zambezi Valley, Zimbabwe
May 2007

Author's Note on Cartridge Nomenclature

This book will discuss capabilities and utility of many cartridges of American, British, and European origin. Each region has its distinct conventions and protocols for cartridge identification. However, just like the English language, especially in the case of British and American cartridges there are more exceptions than there are rules! Most Americans who grew up with the American system(s) probably understand them; likewise citizens of the Commonwealth grasp British cartridges while the rest of the world comprehend the metric system. But it is a confusing mess, so the publisher and I thought a bit of discussion on the subject might be in order.

American cartridges: Modern American cartridges are generally identified by bore or bullet diameter, usually expressed in hundredths (two digits, as in ".30") or thousands of an inch (three digits, as in ".257"). This information is customarily followed by the name of firm that introduced the cartridge. The bullet diameter given may be exact as in ".308 Winchester," or it may be approximate as in ".250 Savage" (which uses a .257-inch bullet) or ".30 Thompson/Center" (another .308-inch bore). Obvious exceptions in numbering occur when American manufacturers chose to use metric designations. This is inconsistent. For instance, .284 Winchester, 7mm Winchester Short Magnum, .280 Remington, and 7mm Remington Magnum are all 7mm (.284-inch bullet diameter) cartridges.

Cartridges that originated "off market" as wildcat or nonstandard cartridges but are later adopted by a manufacturer are often named in honor of the designer. Good examples are the .257 Roberts (named after designer Ned Roberts) and the .35 Whelen (named in honor of gunwriter Col. Townsend Whelen, who may or may not have actually had anything to do with the cartridge's design). The 7mm Shooting Times Westerner (STW) was designed by gunwriter Layne Simpson, who is a longtime contributor to Shooting Times magazine.

Some cartridges like the .220 Swift and .219 Zipper are identified with "buzzwords" rather than the name of the manufacturer, and as we've already seen the names of many cartridges are further modified, such as the ".308 Marlin Express" and ".300 Winchester Magnum." Today these words may help identify a cartridge, but guys in my business have long suspected they are added primarily for hype. At one time, however, both "express" and "magnum" had specific meaning. In the 1870s the British created bottleneck cartridges that pushed light-for-caliber bullets ahead of heavy charges of black powder, considerably increasing the velocity. These were called "express" loads, taken from the fastest thing they knew at the time, the express train.

Similarly, the British took the word "magnum" from an extra-large bottle of champagne and applied it to an extra-large cartridge case in the same caliber as another cartridge offered by the same company. Serious gun nuts who study this stuff thus take a modern "magnum" and wonder what, exactly, it is supposed to be a magnum version of. Winchester could argue that the .338 Winchester Magnum is definitely a magnum version of the old .33 Winchester Center Fire. Remington could argue that their 7mm Remington Magnum is a magnum version of their .280 Remington. Both firms, respectively, might have a little trouble explaining exactly what the .458 Winchester Magnum or the 8mm Remington Magnum cartridges are magnum versions of, however!

To make things even more confusing, hyphenated cartridge designations aren't uncommon—and can have significantly different meanings. In the black-powder era the second number in a hyphenated cartridge, as in ".45-70," denoted the charge weight. This was often further hyphenated to include the bullet weight, as in ".45-70-405." The convention of including the charge weight carried over to a number of early smokeless powder cartridges, including the .30-40 Krag, .25-35 Winchester, and .30-30 Winchester. By the way, not a few cartridges have more than one name. As denoted by the roll mark on early Winchester rifles so chambered, the .30-30 was originally called ".30 WCF" (for Winchester Center Fire).

Other hyphenations mean something altogether different. The "06" in ".30-06" is actually an abbreviation for the year of its design, the proper title being ".30 U.S. Government, Model of 1906." On the other hand, the "08" in 7mm-08 Remington doesn't stand for the year at all. Instead, it's an abbreviation for the parent case, which is the .308 Winchester. This hyphenation is not uncommon in nonstandard (wildcat) cartridges as in "6.5mm-06," a .30-06 case necked down to take a 6.5mm (.264-inch) bullet, and is also seen in Norma's 6.5mm-.284 Norma, the .284 Winchester case necked down to 6.5mm.

British Cartridges: As with American cartridges, the British cartridges loosely follow several different systems. Perhaps the most common is exactly the same as the American system: a two- or three-digit caliber designation, followed by the name of the maker, and perhaps with buzzwords added. Many, like the .375 Holland & Holland Magnum and .416 Rigby, are extremely straightforward. The .375 H&H uses a .375-inch bullet in a case designed by Holland & Holland, and it is definitely a larger and more powerful version of an earlier Holland & Holland .375. The .416 Rigby uses a .416-inch bullet and was designed by John Rigby. It was never designated a magnum because neither Rigby nor anyone else ever before used a .416-inch bullet.

Even with this simple and understandable system there are random anomalies. Americans tend to approximate bullet diameters, sometimes rounding up (the .460 Weatherby is actually a .458) and sometimes down (the .260 Remington is actually a .264). The British go a big step farther. There are two diameters in a rifle barrel, the larger groove diameter, which is approximately the same as the bullet diameter, and the land diameter, the distance between the raised portions between the grooves. Many British cartridges are named by the smaller land diameter rather than the larger groove diameter. For instance, the .318 Westley Richards uses a .330-inch bullet. The .404 Jeffery uses a .423-inch bullet. This would be understandable if it were consistent, at least in the offerings from a given firm—but the .333 Jeffery uses a .333-inch bullet.

At least to Americans, the most confusing nomenclature of British cartridges is for those that were based on an existing parent case necked down. In British parlance, the parent case is given first, followed by the bullet diameter of the actual cartridge. So a ".500/.465" is a .500 case necked down to take a (nominally) .465-inch bullet. This is also not consistently applied. Several cartridges had multiple versions, usually differing by case length. So case length is often appended, as in ".450/.400-3-inch" and .450/.400-3¼-inch." Although rim diameters aren't identical, both cartridges are based on a .450 case necked down to take a (nominally) .40-caliber bullet. As is the case with American cartridges, however, nothing is applied consistently. Like the .500/.465, the .470 Nitro Express is based on a .500 case—but it was named, simply, the .470 even though it uses a .475-inch bullet!

"Nitro Express," by the way, although catchy, actually has meaning. It denotes a cartridge designed for smokeless (nitrocellulose) propellant, and it certainly had a lot more velocity than its black-powder predecessors.

As we delved into the editing and proofreading of this volume, my publisher, Ludo Wurfbain, and I had a heated discussion over how the "style" of these cartridges should be handled. At some point undoubtedly the British had a consistent style for writing these designations, but in the past hundred years this has been corrupted to the point where almost no references display any consistency. Sometimes the ".450/.400" designation is written with hyphens (.450-.400) rather than a slash (.450/.400), and some references use decimal points and some do not (450-400 or .450-400). We noted with some dismay that there were inconsistencies in the original *Safari Rifles* as well! In this volume we have attempted to make the style consistent with decimal points and a slash, as in ".450/.400." This is because the numerals do refer to an actual caliber designation, first the parent case, and then the actual cartridge. I prefer the slash, because many Nitro Express cartridges are further modified with case length, as in ".450/.400-3¼-inch."

In many cases there were both rimless and rimmed versions of the same cartridge, the former for bolt actions and the latter for double rifles and single shots. The British designation for a rimmed cartridge is "flanged," as in ".375 Holland & Holland Flanged Magnum."

European Cartridges: Although we Americans have a terrible time wrapping our hands around the metric system, this is by far the world's simplest and most descriptive system of cartridge identification. The proper name for almost every European cartridge uses the bullet diameter in millimeters followed by the case length in millimeters. So, a 7x57mm cartridge uses a 7mm bullet in a case 57mm in length. Simple. A 7x64mm cartridge also uses a 7mm bullet, but clearly has a longer case. To this is usually added the name of the original designer, as in 7x57mm Mauser or 6.5x54 Mannlicher-Schoenauer.

Oh, yes, the exceptions. There aren't many, but there are a few. The original 8x57mm Mauser, often correctly referred to as a "7.9mm," used a .318-inch bullet. The cartridge was later redesigned to take a .323-inch bullet, which is the actual 8mm diameter. The original .318 diameter was designated "J" while the larger diameter was designated "S." So the 8x68S uses a .323-inch bullet. Another suffix often appended to metric cartridges is "R" as in 7x65R or 9.3x74R. This denotes a rimmed cartridge, which we Americans can easily understand, but it's pure coincidence that both "rim" and the German word for "edged cartridge," *randpatrone,* both start with an "R!"

It takes a lifetime of fascination with firearms to become fully conversant with the seemingly whimsical way so many cartridges are named—and there are still some out there that will stump almost anyone. This volume is much expanded from the original *Safari Rifles,* and we made an early determination that there were better and more current sources for precise case dimensions and exact bullet diameters, as well as ballistics tables, for the many cartridges mentioned herein. In most cases cartridge headstamps and firearm barrel markings will be clear, and it's a simple matter to consult standard references, either in print or on the Internet, to find out exactly what you're dealing with. However, there are some odd birds out there, so, if there is any doubt, the smart approach is to slug the barrel and/or make a chamber cast.

Part I
Big-Game Cartridges

The Ultralights:
.17 – .22

Chapter 1

"**S**afari" is a magical word that must stir the imagination of even the most apathetic among us. For the hunter, the soft Swahili word conveys the adventure, excitement, and even danger that are the essence of African hunting. The meaning of the word has continued to expand ever since Theodore Roosevelt's historic 1909 African expedition, but in truth the word "safari" simply means "journey." And every journey must have a beginning. This includes the safari we are now undertaking through the myriad sporting rifles and cartridges available and suitable for today's African hunting.

The Cape fox (a.k.a. silver jackal) is one of several small predators ideally taken with a very light rifle that minimizes pelt damage. This Marlin in .17 HMR was absolutely perfect!

Like many of you, I am fascinated by the heavy calibers intended for use on the largest game—and I'm certainly not alone. In the twenty years since I began the original of this work we have seen an amazing rebirth of double rifles, incredible popularity of the .416s, and a raft of other big bores—not to mention a confusing gaggle of Short, Super Short, and Ultra Magnums.

It would be tempting to start with some of the juiciest new developments. We aren't going to do that, though. We're going to start at the opposite end of the spectrum and work our way up, giving due consideration to cartridges as small as the .17 rimfires. Since Africa holds a greater variety of game than any other continent, the spectrum of useful arms and loads is very broad. There is indeed a wide array of large and dangerous game: two kinds of rhino, five varieties of buffalo, plus elephant, lion, hippo, and leopard. Nevertheless, what really gives Africa its flavor and provides the greatest part of its hunting thrills isn't the big stuff but rather the hundred-plus species and subspecies of plains game: zebras, wild pigs, and the antelopes great and small. These make Africa the world's greatest hunting ground. And we mustn't forget the smaller predators: jackals, foxes, and small cats.

On almost any safari today (except very specialized quests for big elephant), the majority of hunting hours and the vast majority of the cartridges expended will be devoted to members of the antelope clan. And a varied group it is. African antelope range from the jack-rabbit-size dik-dik, suni, and royal antelope up to moose-size eland. Between these extremes are many beautiful, interesting game animals that, in American terms, could be said to range from the size of javelina to the size of elk. These hundred-plus species, subspecies, and races of antelope occupy, in some combination, virtually all of Africa's diverse habitats. There are desert antelope, swamp-dwellers, true plains species, and brush-dwellers, species that have adapted to rugged mountains, and others that have found their niche in the dense forests.

These animals collectively are the heart and soul of African hunting, and the appropriate cartridges for them make a suitable starting point for our safari through rifles and cartridges. In the old days the British liked to characterize their cartridges as "small bores, medium bores, and big bores." As new cartridges developed, the definitions tended to change—and none are truly standardized. I believe it was John Taylor, for instance, who identified the cartridges between .40 and .45 caliber as "large medium bores." Big bores were over .45 in caliber, and the behemoth .577 and .600 (and now .700) were sometimes called "ultra-large bores." This is arbitrary, but a book like this requires organization, so I will arbitrarily create a new category from .17 to .22 that I will call "ultralight."

Keep in mind that this category reflects the African context, with those hundred-plus antelopes ranging from jack rabbit to moose in size. The North

Donna Boddington used the .17 HMR to take this exceptional steenbok. Though small, this antelope is at the absolute upper end of the little .17's capability. Her shot was perfect, but penetration was barely adequate.

American hunting most familiar to most of us tends to be specialized. We go pronghorn hunting or bear hunting, and a "combination hunt" might mean a deer tag included on an elk hunt. The most specialized of all African habitats holds more different native species than any like-size area in North America. You will always leave camp with a specific plan for that day, but you really don't know what you might actually encounter.

This is the fundamental challenge of choosing rifles and cartridges for African hunting. We could have great fun around the campfire selecting the perfect rifle and cartridge for each of the hundred-odd antelopes and more, but this would be a purely theoretical discussion with little practicality, because one cannot take a hundred rifles on safari. Or even ten. The practical limit is three, two is the most common choice, and in many cases the most sensible approach is just one.

This means that most rifles taken on safari should be chosen with an eye toward versatility. Given the size range of African game, my ultralight cartridges are not versatile. All would be very foolish choices for a one-rifle safari. On the other hand, the little guns are fun to shoot and can be extremely useful on the smallest game.

They are obviously at the opposite end of the spectrum from an open-sighted big-bore rifle but have in common that both the smallest and the largest cartridges are very specialized—so if an ultralight is chosen, extra care must be given to ensure great versatility in the other rifles taken on safari.

The .17s

The .17 Remington made quite a splash some years ago. Its little 25-grain bullet is amazingly fast, and it found much favor with hunters of small predators because the little bullet would rarely exit, thus doing little pelt damage. For instance, it became extremely popular among fox hunters in Australia. In recent years this cartridge fell into disfavor because of a reputation for being finicky and fouling the barrel very quickly. In 2006 it was essentially replaced (in the Remington line) by the new .17 Fireball, the old .221 Fireball case necked down to .17. The .17 Fireball is a bit slower and a bit less finicky, but indications are it hasn't caught on well.

On the other hand, one of the great commercial successes in recent cartridge history has been the .17 Hornady Magnum Rimfire (HMR), developed by Hornady by necking the .22 magnum case down to .17. Two hundred million rounds later the supply finally caught up with the demand! Also successful, but not quite so, is the .17 Mach 2, the .22 Long Rifle case similarly necked down to .17.

The little .17s have almost no recoil and tend to be incredibly accurate. They have their uses but are extremely rare in Africa because they are so specialized. Most serious American varminters find even the fastest .17 centerfires to be questionable on coyotes (which are very tough), especially as range increases. So the sensible limit for the .17 centerfires is probably animals weighing no more than forty pounds.

The .17 HMR, with great accuracy and relatively cheap ammo, is actually more useful—but is probably even more specialized. We used a Marlin .17 HMR in Namibia

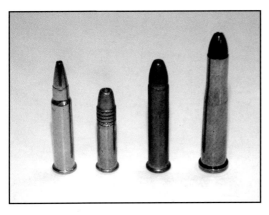

Left to right: .17 HMR, .22 Long Rifle, .22 WMR, .22 Hornet. All of these "ultralights" are useful in Africa, but because of their heavier bullets the .22s are probably more versatile than the .17s.

in 2006, and the same rifle again in 2007. It was wonderful for spring hares and foxes and would probably be perfect for genet and African wild cat. It is also perfect for the very smallest antelope, such as dik-dik, taken at medium ranges. However, results were questionable on antelope even as small as steenbok—questionable enough that I would not again use it on even a thirty-pound antelope.

.20s and .22s

With inexpensive, compact ammunition that makes little noise, the .22 rimfire has become a classic poacher's arm in Africa as well as elsewhere. For this reason, the "two-two" is not legal for game in some African countries, and its importation may not be allowed. Hunters who consider taking a .22 on safari should check the regulations carefully beforehand. Be advised that the regulations may simply state ".22," making the .22 centerfires just as illegal as a .22 Long Rifle.

Where legal, though, a .22 is not only useful on safari but also a lot of fun. In theory the .22 Long Rifle would be quite adequate for the smallest antelope—the dik-dik and smaller duikers—and in heavy cover would be an enjoyable stalking rifle for such game. In Ethiopia Joe Bishop and I used a well-worn Brno .22 owned by outfitter Col. Negussie Eshete to take dik-dik, and in the forest I've often used borrowed .22s for calling small duikers. Unfortunately, in practice, except in thick cover the smaller antelopes are often taken at ranges exceeding the sixty-yard limit placed on the .22 Long Rifle by its looping trajectory.

Its real use on safari is twofold—plinking and practice while in camp, and shooting for the pot. Neither should be scoffed at. Any shooting practice at all, even during the course of a safari, is to the good, and a .22 makes such practice enjoyable and relatively quiet. It isn't unusual, especially for relatively inexperienced hunters, to develop a bad shooting habit during the course of a safari. Flinching,

Left to right: .204 Ruger, .223 Remington, .22-250. The faster .22 centerfires are popular among local hunters in southern Africa, where they are used to take smaller antelopes as well as pests like jackals.

7

While slower cartridges like the rimfires may be more ideal for the smallest animals, you never know what shot you might get. I used Larry McGillewie's .222 Remington to take this bat-eared fox at 200 yards.

for example, can develop overnight if the hunter is unfamiliar with the heavier rifles. The best cure is to go back to the basics, relearning proper shooting through practice. The quiet, recoilless .22 is the best tool available. The late Finn Aagaard told me that in his Kenya days he always kept a .22 and plenty of ammo in camp, and if any shooting problems surfaced, the .22 provided the best cure.

Although Africa does have a small variety of rabbits much like our cottontail, most of the pot shooting consists of birds. If a change of diet is more desirable than a bit of sport, an accurate .22 is absolutely the best supplier of guinea fowl. With a shotgun, the flocks will often outrun you before taking flight; with a good .22, it's a simple matter to snipe two or three as they run straight away, just out of shotgun range. On several hunts in Central African Republic PH Rudy Lubin's Ruger 10/22 was always on hand. On these specialized safaris for bongo and Derby eland we often ate sniped guinea fowl for days on end. This wasn't altogether because other game wasn't available but because the quiet little .22 created such little disturbance.

The varmint shooting we enjoy in America is relatively unknown in Africa, perhaps because of the abundance of "legitimate" game animals. However, in southern Africa night shooting for spring hares (actually more like a kangaroo rat than a hare) is occasionally done. And in rocky kopjes the dassie, or rock hyrax (Africa's equivalent of a rockchuck), is occasionally shot. The .22 would be fine for the former but totally outclassed for the latter because of distance.

Because of practical limitations on the number of guns one can take on safari, I would probably not bring along a .22 rimfire, but I would be delighted if one happened to be in camp. If I were to take any rimfire on safari it would be not the .22 Long Rifle or any of the .17s but instead the .22 Winchester Magnum Rimfire (WMR). While the .22 WMR is a bit noisier and more expensive to shoot than the .22 LR, it has great advantages. Propelling its 40-grain bullet at 2,000 feet per second, the .22 WMR is effective on small game to about 125 yards, and shoots flat enough to let you hit at that distance, which is virtually impossible with a .22 Long Rifle.

The truth is that the .22 rimfires, whether Magnum or Long Rifle, are much more deadly than I'm allowing for. It has been rumored that an elephant was killed with a carefully placed between-the-ribs shot with a .22, and John Taylor himself said that he would walk from the Cape to Cairo with a .22 rifle and a heavy revolver and never go hungry. With precise shot placement, the .22 could certainly be used for impala, reedbuck, and a wide variety of similar game. Indeed, a resident hunter shooting for the pot might well use a .22 for such purposes.

But this book is primarily for the visiting sportsman, the hunter in search of the best trophy that can be found. Such a hunter can't always wait for the animal to stand just so and can't always get as close as he would like. For him, the .22, if used at all, is a fun gun only, for the pot and for a few practice shots in camp.

The high-velocity .22 centerfires are primarily an American institution, developed by and for the American varminter who needed to reach out considerable distances to dispatch small pests and small predators such as fox and coyote. Their British ancestor was the rook rifle, a class of cartridge typified by the .300 Rook and .310 Cadet cartridges. The former started life as a black-powder cartridge, firing an 80-grain bullet at 1,100 feet per second, while the .310 Cadet, a smokeless load, fired a 120-grain bullet at 1,200 FPS.

Rook rifles were used for target shooting and for shooting rabbits, hedgehogs, foxes, and such. "Rook," incidentally, is an English word for a type of crow. In the well-populated English countryside, long-range cartridges weren't desired, and the relatively large bullet diameter of the rook cartridges ensured quick kills without the need for velocity. In America, oldies but goodies such as the .25-20 and .32-20 serve the same purpose.

In America, however, the woodchuck hunter wanted to reach out across wide-open fields, and he needed the flat trajectory that only comes with high velocity. And, of course, there was also the early fascination with the incredible velocity made

In Ethiopia, outfitter Col. Negussie Eshete had a well-worn Brno .22 LR available. It was perfect for Cordeaux dik-dik, encountered in fairly thick brush where shots were close.

possible by smokeless powder. With actions and steels just making the adjustment to the much higher pressures of smokeless powder, initially the only way to achieve high velocity was to reduce caliber and bullet weight.

The .22 Savage High Power, designed by Charles Newton and introduced by Savage in 1912, is a classic example—and is certainly the first of the high-velocity commercial .22 centerfires. Firing a heavy-for-caliber 70-grain bullet at 2,800 FPS, it was a real sizzler and was actually intended for use not necessarily on varmints but on game up to deer. The large-caliber, heavy-bullet boys damned it, as they would today. But those who used it often swore by it. I recall a photo of a 1920s missionary in China posing with a very large tiger taken with his Savage 99 in .22 High Power. He thought the cartridge was perfectly adequate! Karamojo Bell himself, guru of smallbores, wrote of shooting buffalo with the .22 Savage High Power—but he mentioned that he was very, very careful!

Although a few single-shot rifles were chambered for it, the .22 High Power in typical lever-action form didn't have the accuracy needed for varmint hunting, and therefore wasn't a true forerunner of today's super-accurate, flat-shooting .22 centerfire. Those honors go to the 1920s-vintage .22 Hornet. With a 45-grain bullet leaving the muzzle at 2,690 FPS, the Hornet is relatively flat-shooting, and it was originally offered in accurate bolt-action and single-shot rifles. It achieved tremendous popularity early on; its muzzle blast wasn't too severe, and it could reach out to 150 yards and beyond with ease, even on the smallest of pests. As the decades passed, the Hornet was nearly abandoned in favor of much hotter .22 centerfires, but today it has enjoyed a rebirth, with several high-quality bolt actions and single shots again available for this fine old cartridge.

Before we go on to the modern .22s, for completeness we should mention two Winchester developments, the .218 Bee and .219 Zipper. They were designed for, respectively, the Model 92 and 94 Winchester lever actions. The former employed a 46-grain bullet at 2,860 FPS, the latter a 56-grain bullet at a very respectable 3,110 FPS. Both have been chambered in custom single shots, and the Bee has been offered in bolt actions. In those forms, they can be real tack-drivers, but in their original lever actions, just like the old Savage High Power, they don't normally offer the kind of accuracy desirable in a .22 centerfire.

The Hornet, in Winchester Model 54 and Savage 23-D bolt actions, really got interest going for .22 centerfires that would shoot flatter and reach out harder. In 1935 the .220 Swift answered that need with a commercial cartridge that's still at the top end of the velocity scale. The original loading boasted a 48-grain bullet at 4,110 feet per second, and our modern concept of the varmint rifle was born.

The Swift is still around, and with it are later developments such as the .222 and .223 Remington, and .22-250, and newer cartridges like the .204 Ruger (a true .20-caliber) and the .223 Winchester Super Short Magnum. Equally good .22 centerfires that have gone by the wayside are the .222 Remington Magnum, .224 Weatherby Magnum, and .225 Winchester.

Most writers tend to divide the .22 centerfires into three groups: the relatively low-velocity .22 Hornet; medium-velocity cartridges (3,000 to 3,250 FPS or so) typified by the .222 and .223 Remington; and the really fast numbers, which include .22-250, .220 Swift, .223 WSSM, and .204 Ruger.

For the sportsman visiting Africa, all three groups are limited in use. Of all the .22 centerfires, I would personally judge the .22 Hornet as the most useful on an average safari. Relatively quiet, with compact ammo, the Hornet can perform all the functions of the .22 rimfire. It can also perform like a champ on the smaller antelopes and furbearers such as jackal, especially in thornbush country where the shots rarely exceed 100 yards. And it would be a lot of fun to pack around in the hills to pot the occasional dassie or perhaps a klipspringer.

Although they're certainly more powerful, I see less practical use for either the .222–.223s or the red-hot centerfires. They make a bit too much noise, and the ammo is a bit too bulky, to allow for casual plinking and target practice. They're

An advantage to the .22 LR is that it is quiet. We were hunting bongo in the C.A.R. and we were meatless and hungry—but we didn't want to disturb the area with rifle shots. The good old .22 and some guinea fowl solved the problem.

also much too destructive to consider using on edible small game and birds. The Hornet with solid bullets is absolutely the upper limit for such use. The resident hunter who is willing to pick his shots could put these cartridges to good use on even very large antelope (and many do). Indeed, in southern Africa the .223 is extremely popular for springbok and other antelope up to blesbok and impala, but the visiting sportsman would be handicapping himself unnecessarily.

If I could manage a very light rifle in my kit, I'd take a .22 Magnum or a Hornet and forget the rest. In the days when it was much easier to take multiple rifles on safari, my mentors at the old Petersen Publishing Company, Robert E. "Pete" Petersen and Tom Siatos, always included a .22 Hornet in their battery. In Zambia in '96 Pete had his trusty .22 Hornet, and it accounted handily for impala and oribi for the pot. In 2003 I took a .22 Hornet barrel for my T/C Contender to Namibia. It was perfect for the little Damara dik-dik, which was one of the objects of that safari, and worked equally well on steenbok.

None of this is to say that the hotter .22s aren't effective on game. In Africa my only use has been limited to a couple of borrowed .223s, but I have taken numerous deer (where it was quite legal) with both .223s and .22-250s. These cartridges, and the rifles that chamber them, make precise shot placement a joy. With head and neck shots, the outcome is certain. And I've never seen one-shot kills more dramatic and instantaneous than behind-the-shoulder lung shots with a .22-250.

If one is a serious varmint shooter, and if the proposed African hunting menu will include such shooting along with a few species of smaller antelope, there's nothing wrong with packing along a favorite .223 or .22-250.

If you choose such a cartridge, pay attention to bullet selection. Until just a few years ago, virtually all the centerfire .22 cartridges were loaded with varmint bullets—thin-jacketed bullets designed to expand explosively on impact, virtually disintegrating in small varmints and reducing the potential for ricochet. Such bullets are not designed to penetrate at all; they will be too destructive on the very small antelopes and may fail to penetrate with body shots on game even the size of impala and warthog.

Readers of Africana will recall Ruark's trouble with the .220 Swift in *Horn of the Hunter*. He was undoubtedly using the original 48-grain bullets, very fast and very frangible, and he experienced classic failure to penetrate, caused by premature expansion. The same thing will happen today with typical varmint bullets.

Fortunately or foolishly, .22 centerfires are legal for deer in numerous American jurisdictions. Bulletmakers have recognized this problem and have responded with heavier bullets, up to 70 grains, designed for penetration. If I were to take one of the hotter .22 centerfires on safari, I'd use a mixture of these heavy-for-caliber bullets for the midsize antelopes and pests, and full-metal-jacket military-type or match bullets for the tinier antelopes. So loaded, the high-velocity .22 centerfires would indeed serve a purpose. As always, the number of rifles that can be taken on safari is sharply limited, so whether this is a good idea or not depends largely on the variety of game to be taken and the other rifle or rifles chosen.

Light Cartridges:
6mm–.270

Chapter 2

I have written previously about what I consider to be a myth regarding the toughness of African game, and it's appropriate that this subject be addressed right now. In many books and articles about African hunting we have all read that the game there is much tougher than North American game of similar size. Often this is carried to such an extreme that it would seem even a whitetail-size impala shouldn't be hunted with anything less than a .375. The toughness of African game is not pure bunk. Africa has a greater number of large and small predators than our domestic game must contend with, and I theorize that African animals are always on edge and alert, much closer to that surge of adrenaline that makes any animal appear super-tough.

A fatal shot will be just that: fatal. Pound for pound, African game has no tougher bones than American game, and the heart and lungs are in approximately the same places and just as vulnerable to perforation by a bullet. A bullet that reaches the vitals will be effective, period. However, a hit that is off by just a bit may well result in a longer tracking job than you would expect with similar-size North American game. And even a perfectly placed, fatal shot, such as a behind-the-shoulder lung shot that hits no heavy bone, may result in a longer death run than you might expect with, say, a white-tailed deer. The answer isn't heavier calibers; dead is dead. The answer is more precise shot placement!

There are wide differences in "toughness" among the hundred-odd varieties of plains game. To say that a ten-pound duiker or a twenty-five-pound klipspringer is tough is ridiculous. Pound for pound they may well be, but the point is moot with any centerfire rifle. Impala are particularly hardy animals. Once I had a fine ram run fully 200 yards after receiving a 162-grain softpoint from a 7mm Remington Magnum precisely behind the shoulder and through the lungs. He was dead, of course, but nobody bothered to tell him. The result would have been exactly the same, I suspect, if he'd been hit with anything from a .243 to a .375. If the shot had been four inches to the left, on the shoulder, the result probably would have been an animal that dropped in its tracks. My producer and partner in our DVD series, Tim Danklef, tells about

PH Larry McGillewie and me with a superb Cape grysbok, taken with a .243. I have never actually taken a .243 to Africa, but it's an extremely useful cartridge for small antelope, and I've borrowed a few. This is outfitter Rex Amm's .243, a rifle I've used more than once!

following a well-hit impala nearly to the top of Pfumbe, a very significant hill just west of the Chewore River in Zimbabwe's Zambezi Valley. Everyone knows, of course, that seriously wounded animals never go uphill, but nobody told this impala that, either. A favorite line of Tim's is that if impala were as big as buffalo we'd all be dead.

Among the larger African antelopes, there are indeed great differences in the relative toughness of one species versus another. Elk-size kudu, for instance, seem to me to be relatively soft. I wouldn't want to shoot at them with an inadequate cartridge, of course, and I wouldn't want to hit one in a nonvital place. (I did that once, and lost the best kudu I've ever had a chance at!) But even if the shot is off slightly, the chance of recovering the animal after a short tracking job is good. Although similar in bulk to the kudu, the oryx/sable/roan clan is a different story altogether. Like the American elk, these animals are sturdy—just plain tough. A powerful rifle won't make up for poor shot placement, and if the bullet isn't squarely in the vitals, plan on an all-day tracking job with slim chance of recovering the animal.

Wildebeest, too, are tough, and perhaps it's animals like these that have given African game the overall reputation for being well nigh bulletproof. They aren't, but they deserve to be shot properly with a cartridge powerful enough to do the job. We have just looked at what I call the "ultralights," which have their purpose. However, their great failure is a lack of versatility. You may be specifically looking for a steenbok, but you never know what any hunting day in Africa might offer up. This might be the day you encounter the greater kudu of your dreams. So now let's turn to lighter rifles for the more general run of African plains game.

The 6mms

When I wrote the original *Safari Rifles* I began with, "Three 6mms (.243 bullet diameter) are in common use today, and all three are American developments: the .243 Winchester, 6mm Remington, and .240 Weatherby Magnum." This remains true in origin, but both the 6mm Remington and .240 Weatherby, though fine cartridges, have nearly dropped by the wayside in the last few years. Among 6mms the .243 Winchester reigns nearly supreme, but the .243 Winchester Super Short Magnum must now be added to the mix. It would be easy to deduce that this bore diameter, so popular in the United States, was strictly an American concept. That's true, but not strictly. The 6mm Lee Navy was introduced as an experimental military cartridge in the Lee straight-pull bolt-action rifle clear back in 1895, and both sporting rifles and ammo were also available for some years. But the cartridge died out, and there was no commercial American 6mm until the advent of the .243 Winchester and the .244 Remington (the original designation of the 6mm Remington) in 1955.

Most of the credit for the 6mm's place as a sporting cartridge must be given to the British and Europeans, who developed at least eight 6mm sporting cartridges prior to 1925. Best known of these was the .240 Belted Rimless Nitro Express, a long-case cartridge that was loaded to push a 100-grain bullet at 3,000 FPS. It was a popular plains-game cartridge, and is still encountered occasionally.

Left to right: .243 Winchester, .257 Roberts, .25-06. The various .25s are not common in Africa, but the 6mms—especially the .243—are very popular with local hunters in southern Africa. All are very useful for smallish antelope in open country.

In Mozambique in 2006, Greg Rader's light rifle was his Ruger No. 1 in .25-06. It performed perfectly, as seen with this truly exceptional Chobe bushbuck.

In the 1950s American engineers went to work on a modern, domestic 6mm, certain that the older British round could be brought up to date. Winchester saw the .243 as a dual-purpose cartridge that could perform as an excellent varmint cartridge with light bullets and as a deer and antelope cartridge with heavier bullets. Remington, on the other hand, envisioned the .244 as a long-range varmint cartridge and gave the rifles so chambered a 1-in-12-inch rifling twist. This was great for light bullets but could not stabilize bullets over 90 grains. Winchester selected a compromise 1-in-10-inch twist to stabilize both 80-grain varmint bullets and 100-grain big-game bullets.

Apparently, the American public saw things the same way as Winchester; the .243 was instantly popular, while the .244, in spite of its longer case and slightly greater velocity, darn near faded away. Later, Remington realized its mistake and renamed the cartridge the 6mm Remington, at the same time changing the rifling twist to 1-in-9 and adding a 100-grain loading. The .240 Weatherby Magnum came along in 1968. Although offered only in Weatherby Mark V rifles, it's a true short magnum that will fit in any .30-06-length action. The .243 WSSM, using a shortened Winchester Short Magnum case, was introduced in 2003. It is significantly faster than the .243 Winchester, but at this writing (in 2007) it is still too early to assess its long-term popularity.

Although the 6mm was viewed as a dual-purpose varmint/deer round, I have a feeling that relatively few 6mm rifles (in any of the three calibers) are often used

I had a scope problem on my .30-06, so I borrowed Debra Bradbury's well-used pre-'64 Model 70 in .270 to take this bontebok. Bradbury has used this rifle almost exclusively on several safaris, cleanly taking game up to eland.

strictly as varmint rifles. That said, in the windy American West 6mm bullets carry in the wind much better than .22s, so many serious western varminters do have a heavy-barrel 6mm in some persuasion. However, I believe the 6mm's greatest popularity lies with America's deer and pronghorn hunters, and rightfully so. The .243 and 6mm Remington are very similar in performance; the .243 pushes a 100-grain bullet at 3,070 FPS, while the 6mm edges that by about 50 FPS in factory loads and as much as 100 FPS with good handloads. The .243 WSSM edges the .243 by a solid 100 FPS, while the .240 Weatherby is much hotter, pushing a 100-grain bullet at nearly 3,400 FPS. All are flat-shooting, mild-recoiling cartridges that are extremely efficient on game up to the size of large deer. Most popular by far is the .243 Winchester, the perennial favorite as a "first deer rifle" for American youngsters.

With the incredible size range of African antelope, the 6mms are limited. They aren't kudu cartridges, much less cartridges for the hardy oryx tribe. On the other hand, they're nearly ideal for a tremendous range of game: gazelle, springbok, impala, bushbuck, reedbuck, and the list goes on. A good, accurate .243 would be extremely useful on many African safaris that involve such species—but such safaris also generally include larger game such as kudu, oryx, zebra, wildebeest, hartebeest, sable, and such, so a 6mm could not be the only accurate, flat-shooting rifle chosen.

As to which of the 6mms is best, well, it doesn't make much difference. The 6mm Remington and .243 WSSM are both slightly better cartridges than the .243, and the .240 Weatherby Magnum is clearly the most powerful of all. But all are accurate and flat-shooting, and no amount of added velocity will turn any 6mm cartridge into an all-purpose plains-game rifle.

18

Unlike the others, the .243 Winchester has achieved universal acceptance. This says nothing about its comparative worth, but is a factor in ammo availability. The .243 is one of the most popular sporting cartridges in both South Africa and Namibia, used extensively for hunting the pronghornlike springbok and also used without reservation on game up to kudu. However, there is a wide gulf between the local meat hunter, who goes out of his way to position for a head or neck shot, and the safari hunter, who tends to avoid such shots because of potential damage to the trophy. I will admit I have never taken any 6mm to Africa, but I have borrowed a .243 on numerous occasions for impala, bushbuck, springbok, and such. In this country, my own .243s have worked wonders on antelope and deer. Over there, the fast, efficient 100-grain slug has worked just as well.

I have never used the .243 on American game such as black bear and elk, though some hunters do. Nor have I used it in Africa against the largest plains game. With precise shot placement, it would do just fine—but there are much better tools available for the bigger jobs.

The .25s

Bore designations become extremely confusing because there are no hard and fast rules to govern what the makers call their cartridges. Americans, for example, are very likely to use the bullet diameter to name a cartridge, as is the case with the .257 Roberts and the .308 Winchester. Failing that, the approximate groove diameter is often used. The British have used these systems, but out of what seems sheer perversity they quite frequently use the smaller land diameter. So they have often called a 6.5mm cartridge (.264-inch bullet diameter) a .256. That's really misleading, because neither the British nor the Europeans have any history of true ".25-caliber" sporting cartridges. This bore diameter is American, and it goes back to the very beginning of the smokeless era with lever-action cartridges such as the .25-20 and .25-35, and Remington's rimless .25 Remington for its turn-of-the-century semiautos.

In terms of general-purpose hunting cartridges, there are just five .25s, and three of them are real old-timers. The .250-3000, or .250 Savage, was a Charles Newton cartridge introduced by Savage in the Model 99 before World War I. Its original loading, with an 87-grain bullet, was the first commercial cartridge to break the 3,000-FPS barrier. The .257 Roberts, based on the necked-down 7x57 case and offering a good deal more powder capacity, came along as a wildcat cartridge in the 1920s and was legitimized as a factory cartridge in 1934. The .25-06 is, as its name indicates, a .30-06 case necked down to take .257-inch bullets. In wildcat form it's been around for decades, but it didn't become a factory cartridge until Remington adopted it in 1969. Hottest of all is the .257 Weatherby Magnum, developed by Roy Weatherby in

Over the years I've used an eclectic array of rifles in Africa. This is a pretty little .250 Savage built on a Mexican Mauser action. It worked well on light plains game in Zimbabwe's thornbush, where ranges are usually fairly close.

1944. Newest is the .25 Winchester Super Short Magnum, introduced in 2003 as the last (to date) of Winchester's Super Short family (.223, .243, and .25 WSSM).

All five are extremely fine hunting cartridges. The .250 Savage and .257 Roberts are relatively mild cartridges, pushing 100-grain bullets at, respectively, about 2,800 and 3,000 FPS. The .25-06 and .25 WSSM are nearly identical ballistically, both adding about 200 FPS; the .257 Weatherby adds another 200 to 250, making it very fast and very flat-shooting. The .250 Savage lacks the powder capacity to push 117- and 120-grain bullets at useful velocities, but in ascending order the three others can handle the heavier bullets nicely.

I have never been a heavy user of any of the .25s, but it certainly isn't for lack of respect. All are fine game-getters, and although the bore diameter lost much of its popularity when the modern 6mms came along, the added bullet weight and increased frontal area of the .25s make them extremely efficient game cartridges.

The little .250 Savage fills approximately the same niche as the 6mms, but the three others almost reach into the general-purpose plains-game category. I took a lovely .250 Savage on a Mexican Mauser action to Rhodesia in '79 and had a wonderful time with it. I used it to take a number of impala for the pot, plus warthog, duiker, and such. In that role it was pure joy, but I didn't attempt to take any of the larger antelope with it. The four other cartridges have enough going for them to be used for somewhat larger game.

The .257 Weatherby Magnum was Roy Weatherby's personal favorite, and he used it on game up to Cape buffalo on several African safaris. I don't think I would go that far, but I have used the .257 on enough game to agree that its extreme velocity gives it a lightning-bolt effect on fairly good-size plains game. Ken Elliott, the longtime publisher at *Petersen's Hunting* (and thus my boss during our day there) has taken a .257 to Africa twice now and reports incredible results on plains game up to the hefty lechwe.

I have used both the .25-06 and .25 WSSM on quite a bit of North American game, although mostly deer-size, and must admit that their capabilities are wonderful. Even with the heaviest bullets I wouldn't recommend any .25 for the largest plains game, but if you're a fan of the caliber, your favorite .25 will serve you well for a wide range of plains game up to maybe 350 to 400 pounds.

The bottom line? If you have a good, accurate .25 you're comfortable with, don't leave it at home. But, like the 6mms, it should not be the only scoped, flat-shooting rifle you have if your game list includes the larger or tougher plains species.

The 6.5s

The 6.5mm, shooting a bullet of .264-inch diameter, has never been popular in America, despite the fact that a number of very fine European 6.5s have attained tremendous popularity over there. I will cover some of these in the chapter on metrics, and here we'll address just the American 6.5s. There aren't many. The .256 Newton, really a 6.5, was a fine cartridge on the order of the .270 Winchester. Although loaded commercially, it never really made the grade . . . and there wasn't another 6.5 until Winchester introduced the .264 Winchester Magnum in 1958. A short magnum able to function through .30-06-length actions, the .264 was a very hot number. It arrived in—and to some extent heralded—the magnum mania that extended through the 1960s, and it achieved almost instantaneous popularity.

The original factory specifications suggested a 100-grain bullet at 3,700 feet per second and a 140-grain bullet at 3,200. Velocity was enhanced by the 26-inch-barrel Model 70 "Westerner," the rifle in which the cartridge was introduced, but those original figures were somewhat inflated. Even so, with the 140-grain bullet the .264 was and is extremely flat-shooting and tremendously effective. Shortly after its introduction, several writers took the new cartridge to Africa, wrung it out on a variety of species, and wrote glowingly of it. (And the reports of .264 performance in the western United States and Canada were equally impressive.)

I'm not surprised. I got my first .264 in 1965, and I believed it to be a death ray. Never mind that the 24-inch barrel on my rifle never approached the velocities I thought I was getting in those innocent pre-chronograph days! I really believed in that .264, and

This is my new .264 Winchester Magnum, built by Serengeti Rifles on a P.O. Ackley Mauser action with a 26-inch barrel. On the Serengeti or the Kalahari—or any other open country—I can't imagine a better setup.

it performed magnificently on a wide variety of North American game. Even though today's factory ballistics have been adjusted to reflect more accurate figures, the .264, in ascending caliber progression, would be the first American cartridge I would consider as an all-round rifle for African plains game—or, to put it another way, the lightest rifle I would choose to handle all the nondangerous species.

I have had a couple more .264s since that 24-inch-barrel Remington, and these have been original Winchesters with 26-inch tubes. I worked up a load with a 129-grain Hornady spire point that yielded more than 3,300 feet per second (over a chronograph!), and ballistics like that do indeed make the .264 one of the very best cartridges for wide-open country. I hadn't had a .264 for years, but I just took delivery on a .264 built for me by Serengeti Rifle Works, based around an old Parker Ackley left-hand Santa Barbara action and a good Obermayer 26-inch tube. I honestly don't know if that rifle will ever see the Serengeti. It would be just fine there, and equally good in the Kalahari or Ethiopia's Danakil, but what I really have in mind for the rifle is mountain hunting for sheep and goats.

Optimally I'd like a bit more caliber and a bit more bullet weight for game such as zebra, sable, and gemsbok—and certainly for eland—but the .264 will do the job.

Unfortunately, whether I like it or not the .264 is just about a dead duck. It had a short blaze of glory, and then the introduction of Remington's 7mm magnum blew it out of the limelight and it has never come back. The 7mm is indeed a more effective all-round cartridge, but with careful selection of loads and that longer barrel that the .264 needs, it remains one of the finest long-range cartridges for open-country hunting.

Come to think of it, none of our domestic 6.5s is faring well. The 6.5mm Remington Magnum was, for its day, an ultra-short magnum able to work through .308-length actions. Together with the .350 Remington Magnum, it should be considered the forerunner to today's short magnums. Introduced in Remington's short, light Model 600 carbine, it was and is a decent cartridge, propelling a 120-grain bullet at 3,200 feet per second. It just plain didn't catch anyone's eye, and although Remington has made a halfhearted attempt to bring it back, it must be regarded as one of the great losers in recent gunmaking history.

Much more recent is the .260 Remington, a wonderfully mild and effective cartridge based on the .308 Winchester case necked down to 6.5mm. The brainchild of Jim Carmichel, it came out amid much fanfare about its marvelous inherent accuracy. This I can't speak to; the two .260s I have owned were quite accurate but not spectacular. Ballistically, it's about the same as the great old 6.5x55 Swedish, meaning a 140-grain bullet at 2,700 FPS. This makes it mild in the recoil department, and at its modest velocity bullet performance tends to be routinely spectacular. We used it in South Africa and Namibia in 1999, where it performed wonders on plains game all the way up to blue wildebeest.

Unfortunately, the .260 is still a 6.5mm, a bullet diameter that seems almost impossible to sell in the United States. I'm told that after considerable initial success, sales of the .260 are slipping badly. This is regrettable, but I can't say it's a big surprise. Still, as the Europeans have long known, the high sectional density of the 6.5mm bullet has tremendous advantages. In open country an aerodynamic 6.5mm bullet holds its velocity extremely well and bucks wind about as well as anything available. On game, that high sectional density offers exceptional penetration. For a light rifle that offers performance without pain, I wouldn't hesitate to use a .260, 6.5x55, or 6.5mm Remington Magnum. In big country, well, I might wind up going full circle and coming back to the .264.

The .270s

The .270, bullet diameter .277, is another uniquely American development. There are just four factory cartridges that use this bullet: 6.8mm Special Purpose, .270 Winchester, .270 Winchester Short Magnum, and .270 Weatherby Magnum.

The little 6.8mm was designed by Remington as a military cartridge that would offer more punch in the AR/M-16 receiver. As a military cartridge it hasn't yet gotten a lot of play (and may or may not in the future), but as a sporting cartridge it has proven very effective on deer-size game with very little recoil. Its problem is that it was designed around relatively light-for-caliber 120-grain bullets. Velocity falls off quickly with heavier .277 hunting bullets, so I have a bit of trouble fitting it into the African scenario.

I have no such problems with the .270 Winchester! It was, as everyone knows, one of Jack O'Connor's favorites. To some extent he created its popularity, and to some extent it created his. Jack was undoubtedly the finest gunwriter America ever produced in terms of literary skill, and he was also one of the most experienced hunters in the outdoor-writing field. He didn't need a gimmick, so I'm not being derogatory when I say the .270 was his gimmick. He liked it, to be sure, but he privately admitted that the .30-06 was more versatile. But lots of folks, including the great gunwriters of O'Connor's youth, were .30-06 fans. So Jack hitched himself to the .270's star, and it hitched itself to him. Proof of this could be seen in the fact that the .270's popularity dropped considerably in the dozen years after Jack passed away. But nearly twenty years have passed since I penned this last line, and in recent years the .270 seems to have made a considerable comeback. Certainly it has with me!

I have used it a great deal in recent years, in Africa and elsewhere, and I must admit that O'Connor had it right: The .270 Winchester is a magnificent cartridge. Introduced by Winchester in 1925, it offered a 130-grain bullet at 3,060 FPS and a 150-grain bullet at 2,850 FPS. Both are extremely flat-shooting and extremely effective. O'Connor preferred the lighter bullet; although I'm not one to dispute the master, I personally prefer the 150-grain bullet, and have had very good results with it on a variety of African game up to kudu. One of the attributes of the .270, besides its flat trajectory, is its effectiveness with light recoil.

I must admit that in Africa I'm more of a 7mm or .30-caliber fan. However, there is nothing wrong with the .270 in Africa. My old friend Debra Bradbury, widow of Weatherby Award winner Basil Bradbury, uses almost nothing other than her old Model 70 in .270, including on several African safaris. Using the compromise 140-grain load with tough Winchester Fail Safe bullets, she has cleanly taken plains game up to eland. Her confidence in the cartridge and load are such that she would have taken a buffalo with her .270 had her professional hunter allowed it—but he wisely insisted she use a borrowed .375!

The .270 has been used extensively on African game from one end of the continent to another. O'Connor himself used it as his light rifle on numerous safaris, and it worked for him on game up to greater kudu and eland just as well as it worked in North America on game up to elk and moose. My first professional hunter, Kenyan Willem van Dyk, had an old Model 70 in .270 that he swore by, and in recent years I've seen more and more .270s in both South Africa and Namibia. It is not anywhere near as universal as its parent cartridge, the .30-06, but has truly become a worldwide standard.

The new kid on the .270 block is the .270 WSM. Capable of pushing a 140-grain bullet to 3,200 FPS, it is considerably faster than the .270 Winchester, yet its short case allows it to be housed in a .308-length action. I must admit that the .270 WSM has become my personal favorite among the several new short magnums. I have not used it in Africa and don't particularly intend to (for no good reason), but I have used it on game up to elk and have done quite a bit of sheep and goat hunting with it. The extra velocity flattens the trajectory a bit, but since so little genuine long-range shooting is done

Left to right: .264 Winchester Magnum, .270 Winchester Short Magnum, .270 Winchester, .270 Weatherby Magnum. Although only the .270 Winchester is truly popular in Africa, all four of these cartridges are ideal for midsize game in open country.

An exceptional Chobe bushbuck, taken with a Dakota in .270 Winchester. In Africa I generally load a .270 with a good 150-grain bullet.

in Africa, this is not extremely significant. More important is that I believe the increased energy yielded by the higher velocity offers noticeably increased impact on game.

Depending on exactly whose loads you're using, the .270 Weatherby Magnum is a bit faster than the .270 WSSM. Obviously it is at least the equal of the .270 WSSM, plus a bit more. I used one in Namibia in the early 1990s and it flattened game up to gemsbok and hartebeest. The .270 Weatherby Magnum is largely an unsung cartridge, but to my mind it's one of Roy Weatherby's best. Again, in Africa the ultra-flat trajectory is rarely of great value, but any of the three fast .270s will reach out as far as is needed, and with good bullets will be effective on the majority of antelope up to perhaps 500 or 600 pounds. I'd rate the .270s, together with the .264, as the lightest rifles that make sense for the full range of African plains game—but unlike O'Connor and my friend Ms. Bradbury, I would personally draw the line long before I got to eland! The visiting sportsman or woman generally wants the best representative of a given species that can be found. Time is not unlimited, and it's impossible to predict the shot you might get. One simply must not be undergunned, which means that at least some of the time one will almost certainly be overgunned. Later in this book we will look at how the light rifles from 6mm to .270 might be combined with other calibers to be an effective part of a battery, but now let's take a step up in both caliber and versatility to the 7mms.

The Versatile 7mms

Chapter 3

We weren't hunting kudu. In fact, we weren't hunting anything at all; high noon was approaching, and we were simply checking leopard bait in the heat of the day. But the greater kudu is a show-stopper of an animal. With his lovely white-striped gray hide, white nose chevron, and salt-and-pepper neck ruff, you'll stop to look at him under any circumstances. And if his ivory-tipped, spiraling horns are big enough, you'll be tempted to forgo whatever else you're planning so you can possess those wonderful spirals.

This kudu was big enough, and he wasn't in southern Africa, where kudu are exceedingly common in many areas. He was in the hills of Masailand, where professional hunters prize him above all else and where an entire season can pass without the sighting of a good bull. He was in the company of a much younger bull, and together they flashed across a clearing. We saw the youngster first, and he drew our attention, as a greater kudu always will. Then we saw his traveling companion. This one took our breath away, and then was gone—and I knew I'd not see his like again on this trip. I followed up quickly, and the miracle continued. Both bulls had stopped over a low rise, just on the edge of the donga's thick thornbush. They paused for an instant only, for one backward look to see if they were being followed.

At sixty yards my scope found the shoulder of the big bull. I could see his muscles tense for the one leap to safety, and see the beginning of movement just as the rifle went off. The bull had hesitated less than a second too long; the huge antelope crumpled on the spot and never moved.

Although not so tough, pound for pound, as smaller antelope such as sable and oryx, the kudu is a large animal. A very big bull may weigh six hundred pounds and more. In other words, he is quite similar to the American elk in size. In some parts of the kudu's range, such as the northern Transvaal, northern Namibia, and much of Zimbabwe, the species is exceedingly common. Elsewhere, in Kenya, Tanzania, and

Ethiopia, a good bull is a most rare prize. His beauty and his cover-loving craftiness are such that he is never taken lightly. Over the years, I have taken most of my kudu with .375 H&H or similar cartridges, but this Tanzanian kudu—folded in his tracks—was taken with a little .284-caliber bullet weighing only 162 grains.

The rifle is a lovely custom bolt action by Tucson gunmaker David Miller, chambered for the 7mm Remington Magnum, one of America's most popular hunting cartridges. The rifle could well have been chambered for any of some two dozen American, British, or European factory rounds, current or obsolete, using the .284-inch bullet, and chances are the results would have been exactly the same: a well-placed, well-performing bullet and a very dead kudu.

As I review these words from the perspective of twenty more years of intensive African hunting, I'm pleased with them, but I must admit that I have mellowed somewhat over time. That kudu, taken in 1988, was the first kudu I shot with any 7mm, and in those days I considered it a fairly light rifle for game of such size. I recall another kudu, taken in 2005 in Namibia with another 7mm rifle. This bull stood in dense thorn quartering very slightly away, ready to bolt. I shot him just behind the on-shoulder, angling to the off-shoulder, and it happened so fast that my professional hunter and friend, Dirk de Bod, thought I must have caught brush and missed. I had not. The big-bodied bull went forty yards and piled up to a perfect heart shot.

This rifle is another beautiful custom job, easily the finest rifle I own, made by Texas riflesmith Todd Ramirez on the lines of a British "stalking rifle" of the 1920s. Appropriately, its chamber is cut to the mild and historic 7x57 Mauser, and the bullet lodged against the hide on the far side of this animal was a 139-grain Hornady InterBond.

Left to right: 7mm-08 Remington, 7x57 Mauser, .280 Remington. The milder 7mms are wonderfully effective, yielding consistently good bullet performance and surprising power.

The first animal I took with the Ramirez 7x57 was this Cape hartebeest. It was also the longest shot I've taken with the 7x57, a bit over 300 yards.

It's a metric world today, and America is one of the very few countries still clinging to the old English system of weights and measurements. In the shooting world, we've not only clung to it but we thumb our noses at the rest of the world. We measure our powder and bullets by the relatively complex system of grains and pounds; the rest of the world uses grams. We use caliber designations in hundredths or thousandths of an inch, not millimeters, and rare is the bore diameter that's been able to overcome this bias. The 6.5s, ever so popular in Europe, have never done well in America, nor has the 8mm (.323-inch), Europe's equivalent of our .30-caliber. But the 7mm has broken all the rules—and is so entrenched in America and has so many cartridges and so many component bullets that it becomes hard to remember it's not really a domestic caliber.

It was that 7x57, also called 7mm Mauser and .275 Rigby, that started the 7mm on its way. It is still with us and still wonderful. The 7x57, introduced in 1892, was one of the first cartridges designed exclusively for use with the brand-new smokeless propellants. The original loading used a very long 173-grain roundnose bullet at a velocity of about 2,300 feet per second—not very impressive by today's standards but red-hot in comparison to the black-powder cartridges it replaced.

Americans got their first taste of the 7mm Mauser in Cuba in 1898. The battle of San Juan Hill is remembered for the charge of Roosevelt's Rough Riders (who

Jim Morey and PH Dirk de Bod with a superb greater kudu, taken with a single shot from Jim's 7mm Remington Magnum. The magnum 7mms are wonderfully versatile and handle heavier bullets much better than the smaller-cased 7mms.

were afoot in the battle)—and we tend to forget that the disastrously outnumbered Spanish defenders, using their 7mm Mausers, inflicted enormous casualties on the attacking Americans before the hill was taken. The British were introduced to the high-velocity Mauser about the same time, during the Boer War. A whole generation of Englishmen learned healthy respect for the little 7mm, especially in the hands of skilled marksmen like the Boer hunters. The cartridge was widely used in America, not only in surplus Mausers but also in the unlikely Remington rolling-block single shot, as well as factory and custom bolt actions of many types. It had its strong supporters, including the likes of Jack O'Connor, who used it both before and after the introduction of "his" .270. But it would be stretching a point to say that the 7x57 achieved tremendous popularity in the States.

It had much more success in the far-flung British Empire. As early as 1907, John Rigby adopted it, calling it the .275 Rigby after the English fashion of naming cartridges by land rather than groove or bullet diameter. Rigby loaded it with a 140-grain spitzer softpoint at fully 2,800 feet per second. In this guise, the cartridge became a British standard for light to medium game. It was one of Bell's favorites for elephant—but not with the 140-grain pill. He used the 173-grain roundnose in Kynoch's superb steel-jacketed-solid form. That long, heavy bullet at moderate velocity would penetrate an elephant's skull and find the brain from almost any angle—as it would today, of course. But the days are long gone when elephant stood in the open and allowed the kind of precision shooting that was Bell's strong suit.

The 7mm bullet diameter has a great deal going for it. Bullets of this diameter tend to have excellent sectional density—the relation of the bullet's weight to its cross-section—without tremendous weight. This fact, combined with an aerodynamic design, means they hold their velocity extremely well and thus tend to have flat trajectories. Whether spitzer or roundnose, that sectional density gives excellent straight-line penetration in game.

The smokeless era opened up a whole new world of velocity, and if fast was good, faster must be better. The early years of the century saw the British develop some half-dozen large-case 7mm cartridges, all of which approach the performance of today's 7mm magnums. These include the .275 Belted Rimless Magnum Nitro Express and its .275 Flanged Magnum counterpart, both Holland & Holland developments; the .280 Jeffery; and, of course, the .280 Ross developed for the Canadian straight-pull Ross rifle. The Ross pushed a 140-grain bullet at 2,900 FPS; the Jeffery went a step farther and was listed at 3,000 FPS for the same bullet weight.

Early African hunters were just as beguiled by high velocity as Americans were during the magnum mania of the late 1950s and 1960s. They found that the explosive little bullets at such unheard-of velocities dropped game like lightning, and the flat trajectory was a whole new world. Unfortunately, there were two problems.

First, bullet development hadn't yet caught up with cartridge development. A bullet's expansion properties at impact velocities of 2,200 to 2,400 feet per second differ considerably from expansion at 2,600 to 2,800 FPS. Bullet makers still have trouble with this today, but at the turn of the century our concept of controlled expansion was unknown. In other words, bullet blow-up was relatively assured at closer ranges, especially if heavy bones were struck.

The other problem was that too much reliance was put on the lightning-bolt effect of all this new velocity—and the new, ultra-velocity cartridges were employed against animals that were beyond their capabilities. One of the early casualties was George Grey, a universally liked and highly respected soldier and gentleman. He was galloping for lion on the Athi Plain in Kenya Colony, a very dangerous pastime. Typically, a lion would be "tally-hoed" on horseback until it turned to charge, whereupon the rider would dismount to shoot. Grey used a .280 Ross, and died a lingering death from infection when he failed to stop the charge. By some accounts he shot five times, and by all accounts the bullets broke up on the outside and failed to penetrate.

Joe Bishop has used his battered Sako 7mm Remington Magnum all over the world, and it serves him just as well in Africa as everywhere else. He dropped this fantastic Chobe bushbuck in Mozambique with the finest running shot I've ever seen.

Hunters today would hardly consider a fast-moving 7mm the ideal choice to stop a charging lion—or a charging anything else. Obviously, that isn't the caliber's purpose, let alone strong suit. Karamojo Bell, who took many of his 1,013 elephant with the 7x57, would probably agree. If he were here today, he might or might not concede that he hunted unsophisticated, unalarmed animals. But I trust he would agree that the methodical, precise marksmanship he practiced with his 7mm is a far cry from having to stop a charge at close quarters.

By the way, again from the perspective of nearly twenty years, it's true that I lean toward larger calibers and heavy-for-caliber bullets. But I am tired of answering reader mail that cites Bell's taking of a thousand elephant with his 7x57. He did not, and never claimed that he did. Bell was the king of the smallbore fans, but let's get the facts straight. He used the 7x57 quite a bit, but he took far more of his elephant with the .303 British and .318 Westley Richards. I submit that there is a difference between a .284-inch 173-grain bullet and the 215-grain .311-inch bullets of the .303 and the 250-grain .330-inch bullets of the .318. Bell actually agreed with this. His last story, written for *American Rifleman* in the mid-1950s, conceded that the

160-grain 6.5mm bullets were too slender and tended to bend, and that the 173-grain 7mm bullets were minimal. Smallbore man to the end, he wrote that if he were starting over, his ideal elephant cartridge would be the new .308 Winchester with its short case and resultant short bolt throw, loaded with 220-grain solids.

A few horror stories similar to that of George Grey prevented the true high-velocity 7mms from achieving great popularity for nearly fifty years, but the 7x57 kept rolling along. It remains a marvelously efficient killer on all but the largest of plains game, with the bonus of a relatively soft report and low recoil even in a very light rifle. I have used my 7x57 quite a lot in the last few years, and it remains a wonderful cartridge for Africa and anywhere else, provided shooting ranges are within 250 yards or so (which describes almost all African shooting). The modern bonus is that our hunting bullets are so good today that the heavier, slower bullets are no longer essential. My results have been so good that, in mild 7mms like the 7x57 and 7mm-08, I no longer use the 160- to 175-grain bullets I might have used once, instead relying on bullets from 139 to 154 grains, out of which I can get a bit more velocity.

Today, excluding innumerable wildcats and proprietaries and a few custom rifles built for old-timers like the .275 H&H and 7x61 Sharpe and Hart, there are twelve commercial 7mm rifle cartridges. These are the 7x57, 7x64 Brenneke, 7x30 Waters, 7mm-08 Remington, .284 Winchester, .280 Remington, 7mm Remington Magnum, 7mm Weatherby Magnum, 7mm Winchester Short Magnum, 7mm Remington Short Action Ultra Magnum, 7mm Shooting Times Westerner, and 7mm Remington Ultra Magnum. This total is raised to fourteen if you add the rimmed 7x57R and 7x65R that are loaded in Europe. This profusion of .284 cartridges exceeds even America's darling .30-caliber.

Of these, it's interesting to note that only the two European numbers go back a long way—the 7x57 clear to the beginning and the excellent 7x64 to 1917. All of the early "magnum"-velocity 7mms fell by the wayside. Interesting, too, is the fact that with the lone exception of the 7x30 Waters, developed for the Model 94 Winchester lever action by necking the .30-30 down to 284, all of these 7mms are more than just acceptable for a tremendous variety of African hunting.

Although it's easy to oversimplify, there are basically three power levels among the 7mm rifle cartridges, excluding the somewhat anemic 7x30 Waters—which is further handicapped by the necessity to shoot flat-point bullets in the tubular-magazine rifles for which it was designed.

The first level is that of the good old 7x57 and the newer 7mm-08 Remington. The 7mm-08 factory load uses a 140-grain bullet at 2,860 feet per second—almost the velocity that was said to have gotten George Grey killed! Current factory loads are listed with that bullet weight for the 7x57 at 2,660 FPS—and that makes the

There are many fine 7mm cartridges in the "fast to ultra fast" velocity range. All are excellent for African plains game in open country. Illustrated are the 7mm Remington Short Action Ultra Mag, .280 Remington, 7mm Remington Magnum, 7mm Weatherby Magnum, 7mm Shooting Times Westerner, and 7mm Remington Ultra Mag.

7mm-08 look pretty good. The 7mm-08 is indeed a fine cartridge. It's based on the short .308 Winchester (or .243) case, so it can be used in a true short bolt action, and in factory loads it has the advantage of being a recent development and therefore loaded to modern pressure levels.

My elder daughter, Brittany, went through a teenage antihunting phase, which, considering the options available to kids today, is a fairly harmless rebellion. At seventeen she returned from the dark side and decided to give this hunting thing a try. She's right-handed and I'm left-handed, so none of my rifles were useful. I settled on the 7mm-08 as the best combination of power with modest recoil, but I was (and continue to be) shocked at the incredible performance of this little cartridge. Brittany has now taken nearly the full range of plains game, including tough stuff like wildebeest and zebra, with this little cartridge. We settled on a 150-grain Swift Scirocco bullet at 2,700 FPS, which expands and penetrates wonderfully at this velocity. It has worked so well there has been no incentive to experiment much!

The 7x57 is a very old cartridge, and the factories exercise extreme caution in producing such loads since they may be used in very old rifles. However, the 7x57 can be loaded to give performance well beyond today's factory ballistics. You'll remember that the .275 Rigby (dimensionally identical to the 7x57) used a 140-grain bullet

Brittany Boddington took this fine eland with a single 140-grain Nosler Partition from her 7mm-08. This is really pushing the capability of any 7mm, but confidence, shot placement, and bullet performance are always more important than raw power.

at 2,800 FPS, and I've gone well beyond that with carefully worked-up handloads in a modern action. The 7x57 offers more case capacity than the 7mm-08, and, all other things being equal, it must be—and is—capable of more velocity. But not in domestic factory loads. Essentially, then, unless you handload and thus can get the utmost in performance out of your 7x57, the 7mm-08 would be the best choice for a low-recoiling, extremely efficient .284-caliber rifle. That said, for myself I tend to stick with the 7x57. Nostalgia and tradition must be worth something, right?

The 7mm-08, too, can benefit from judicious handloading, and of course it has available the full spectrum of 7mm bullets. But, as we shall see when we look at the .308 versus the .30-06, it lacks the case capacity to be efficient with bullets weighing over 150 grains. Beyond that point, achievable velocity is greatly reduced. Thus the 7x57 is the logical choice for the handloader—unless one is building an ultralight rifle and simply must use a short action. In recent years the 7mm-08 has become well entrenched and reasonably popular, and is now available in a considerable array of factory loads, which was not the case twenty years ago. In the same period the 7x57 seems to have gone into another of its periodic slumps in popularity, resulting in a more limited selection of factory loads. So unless you handload—or value tradition as I do—then the 7mm-08 is probably the sensible modern choice.

The first animal I ever took with a 7mm Remington Magnum was this ostrich, in 1979 out in the Namib Desert. I borrowed the rifle from PH Ben Nolte, and it performed wonderfully on a tough running shot.

The next power level is occupied by the nearly obsolete .284 Winchester, the .280 Remington, and the nearly identical European 7x64 Brenneke. All three are very fine cartridges, but unless one handloads in the United States, the .280 is the only sensible choice—and even then selection of factory loads is limited. Remington introduced the .280 in the late 1950s, and it was very slow to catch on. In 1979 it was renamed the 7mm Express Remington and reintroduced. That proved to be a real disaster. When 7mm Express ammo was fired in several 7mm Remington Magnum rifles, catastrophic blowups ensued. Since 1980 it has again been the .280. Essentially the .30-06 case necked down to .284 with the shoulder moved slightly forward, it's also nearly identical to (though not interchangeable with) the popular European 7x64 Brenneke. It offers very high velocity with the lighter bullets, and has the case capacity to push bullets up to 175 grains very respectably. Twenty years ago I wrote that the .280 seemed finally to be gaining in popularity, but at this writing that really isn't true. It is chambered in few factory rifles, with limited factory loads. It sort of rolls along with a small but dedicated following, and despite its lack of popularity, it may well be the very best of our factory cartridges based on the .30-06 case. Certainly its most staunch proponent, Jim Carmichel, would agree with that!

The next power level is the magnums 7mms, which range from fast to very fast. First was the 7x61 Sharpe & Hart, a great cartridge that, regrettably, should be considered a dead issue. It was developed in the United States and was chambered in the Danish Schultz & Larsen rifle in the 1950s. Dimensionally and ballistically it's very similar to the old .275 H&H. It achieved some following but was blown completely off the market when Remington introduced the 7mm Remington Magnum in 1962.

The other major American manufacturers quickly adopted the 7mm Remington Magnum, as did the public. Before long it became a world-standard hunting cartridge, and despite all the competition, it remains the most popular "magnum" in the world.

As we have seen, a fast 7mm was far from a new idea. Cartridges of its performance level go back to the turn of the century, and in the post-World War II years there was a proliferation of high-performance 7mm wildcats. The late Warren Page, shooting editor of *Field & Stream,* was a tremendous advocate of the fast 7mm. Page, it's worth noting, was more than a passable African hand with a tremendous breadth of experience—considerably more African experience than any gunwriter of his generation. He was the first gunwriter who could lay claim to having taken all of Africa's nine principal spiral-horned antelope. Some forty years after he accomplished this feat, I remain the second, which says something about its difficulty.

Remington's "big seven" offered an inexpensive, over-the-counter, high-performance 7mm, and immediately proved there was a market for it. But it didn't exactly fill a vacuum in the ranks of .284-inch cartridges. The 7mm Weatherby Magnum had been introduced in 1944 and was (and is) an important part of the Weatherby line. Only slightly longer than the Remington, the Weatherby is also a short magnum with the characteristic double-radiused shoulder and a slightly greater case capacity than the Remington. The 7mm Weatherby is a fine cartridge, and was quite popular until Remington's entry appeared. The 7mm Weatherby will edge the Remington by as much as 200 feet per second with handloads, and that's significant.

Similar in power to the 7mm Remington Magnum are the two relatively new short magnums, the 7mm Winchester Short Magnum and 7mm Remington Short Action Ultra Magnum (RSAUM). They are frighteningly similar, but not interchangeable. The WSM case was designed to offer "standard belted magnum" performance in a short (.308 Winchester length) bolt action. This left Remington in a bit of a pickle, since the WSM case was a bit too long for its slick little Model Seven action. The .300 WSM was introduced in 2000, the .270 and 7mm WSM in 2001, with the 7mm and .300 RSAUMs following a short time later. This obviously created not only confusion but also a surfeit of short-magnum cartridges.

This confusion is still sorting itself out, and I do not believe that all the Short, Super Short, Ultra, and Short Action Ultra Magnum cartridges will prove commercially

PH Cliff Walker and I with an impala taken in the Selous Reserve in 2000 with the then-new 7mm Remington Ultra Mag. With the fastest 7mms you should be careful to select tough bullets to avoid premature expansion. We used 140-grain Nosler Partitions with consistently excellent results.

viable in the long run. But for the purposes of this discussion, any of the fast 7mms is a fine choice for the general run of African plains game excluding eland. The two short magnums are essentially the equal of the 7mm Remington Magnum with bullets from 140 to perhaps 160 grains, which, given our wonderful modern bullets, is plenty of bullet weight for everything up to zebra, but all 7mms are on the light side for eland. The advantages to the short-magnum concept are: First, this power level can be housed in a shorter, lighter action. Second, the shorter, wider case achieves considerable burning efficiency that actually yields greater energy per grain of powder burned relative to longer, slimmer cases. This is why such velocities are attainable from such a short case with somewhat less powder capacity. Third, the short magnums tend to be very accurate. This comes from a combination of more precise shoulder headspacing from the unbelted case; burning efficiency is conducive to accuracy; and the shorter action tends to be more rigid. One disadvantage is that, with any new cartridge, factory loads will tend to be very limited until the cartridge has proven popular. Another disadvantage is that it is much more difficult to make these short, fat cartridges feed smoothly and consistently.

There are two factory 7mms that are considerably faster yet—the 7mm Shooting Times Westerner and the 7mm Remington Ultra Magnum, both currently loaded only by Remington. The former is a belted cartridge developed by gunwriter Layne Simpson, based on the 8mm Remington Magnum case necked down; the latter is Remington's big, fat, full-length unbelted Ultra Magnum case necked down to 7mm. Both are considerably faster than either the 7mm Remington or Weatherby Magnums, able to push 150-grain bullets to 3,400 FPS and beyond. I've used both the 7mm STW and 7mm RUM here and there, and when it was just introduced I used the 7mm RUM in Tanzania in 2000. Load selection is very limited, and these cartridges are extremely finicky to handload for. However, they shoot amazingly flat, yet deliver surprisingly mild recoil for the level of power. Personally, I think they are better suited for country where shooting ranges are a bit longer than is normal for Africa, but they are certainly deadly open-country cartridges.

Some things never change. The magnum 7mms aren't any better suited for stopping charging lion than they were in George Grey's day, although the bullets are inestimably better. Today's bullets, if chosen wisely, will hold together at high velocities and give outstanding penetration as well as the flat-shooting capabilities that the velocity offers. The magnums 7mms will deliver well in excess of 3,000 foot-pounds of energy, which is impressive, but frontal area and bullet weight are needed when it's time to stop a charge, and that's no different now than it was in George Grey's day.

So where do the 7mms fit in for African hunting? Well, almost anywhere. With apologies to Bell, the 7mms are not elephant cartridges, nor are they suited for buffalo, rhino, or lion. I would also prefer not to tackle the largest of the plains game, most specifically eland, with any 7mm cartridge. With proper bullets and proper shot placement, of course, all of the various 7mms could handle all of these animals (and have many times)—but if the slightest thing goes wrong, no 7mm cartridge can reliably clean up the mess.

With these exceptions, the 7mms are adequate for the full range of African plains game—given, again, proper bullet selection and careful shot placement. In thornbush country, where shots rarely exceed 150 yards, a light 7x57 (or 7mm-08) loaded with 140- or 150-grain bullets would provide excellent service on most plains game, and would be ideal for leopard over bait.

Personally, I'm not sure there is a significant difference between the .280 Remington 7x64 and the magnum 7mms. Careful handloading can wring a very slight velocity edge out of the Remington magnum, and a bit bigger edge from the Weatherby—but hardly a significant one. The 7mm STW and RUM are clearly much faster, but the long-range shooting these cartridges excel in is rare in Africa. Hunters who shoot factory ammo would probably be best served by the 7mm Remington Magnum, since it offers far and away the widest selection of loads.

By the way, although the 175-grain heavyweight is often touted for African hunting, only rarely have I used this bullet in 7mm. Over the years, in a wide variety

I used my David Miller 7mm Remington Magnum all over the world with very good results. In Africa I leaned toward heavier, tougher bullets like the 160-grain Nosler Partition, just fine for smaller antelopes like this Grant gazelle, and tough enough for wildebeest and greater kudu.

of 7mm rifles, I have observed and achieved wonderful results with lighter bullets. These have the obvious advantage of higher velocity and, with modern controlled-expansion bullets, have offered all the penetration I have ever needed.

When choosing among the various 7mms, consider the country to be hunted as well as the game. In effect on game, the only real difference in the big-case cartridges is that they'll reach out just a bit farther. Choose a bullet weight that will maximize the performance of the cartridge you choose. I like bullets from 139 to 154 grains in the 7x57; from 150 to 165 in the .280; and from 160 to 175 in the magnums. Any of the 7mm cartridges we've discussed would make a fine choice for an all-purpose African rifle, the rifle that will be carried the most and shot the most. None is suitable for lion and the thick-skinned game, but those aren't jobs one should ask the 7mm to perform. The jobs you should ask it to perform—light, medium, and even heavy plains game at short, medium, or long range—it will handle perfectly—just so long as you do your part and put that little .284-inch pill in the right place.

The All-American
.30-Caliber

Chapter 4

As with so many Americans of the past few generations, one of my first centerfire rifles was a 1903 Springfield, caliber .30-06. And like so many millions of Americans, I've found the caliber so useful that one of my favorite hunting rifles remains the .30-06, a cartridge I've hunted with in bolt actions, single shots, slide actions, semiautos, and even doubles. Theodore Roosevelt's "sporterized" Springfield was one of the first .30-06 rifles to see use in Africa, and ever since then it has remained a standard choice as a light or all-purpose safari rifle. As we have seen, it isn't the only choice—but after 100 years it's a choice that's hard to argue with.

The .30-06 isn't the only good .30-caliber cartridge, nor was it the first or last to capture the hearts of American hunters. It may not even be the best of its kind, but it certainly is the most common throughout the world. I promised myself I wouldn't pick favorites in this book, but it's difficult not to pick one in the .30-06. Like Hemingway, Ruark, and Roosevelt—perhaps because of them—I chose the .30-06 for my light rifle on my first safari to Kenya. On game ranging from the tiny dik-dik to the tough zebra, it accounted for something like fifteen animals with fifteen shots, quite possibly the best run of shooting I've ever had in Africa. I haven't always taken a .30-06 on safari, but in 2007 I can honestly say that it is the light rifle that I have used most often, has accounted for more African game than any other cartridge, and has never let me down. Most fans of the .30-06—and there are millions of them—would echo this last.

Americans' love affair with the .30-calibers didn't start with the .30-06. That credit must go to its predecessor, the .30-40 Krag. Adopted as the U.S. military cartridge in 1892, chambered in the Norwegian-designed Krag-Jorgensen rifle, the .30-40 was America's first smokeless-powder military cartridge. Firing a long 220-grain roundnose bullet at 2,200 feet per second, it seemed a real flat shooter compared to the .45-70 black-powder cartridge it replaced.

The .30-40 was quickly chambered in the Winchester high-wall single shot, and became the most popular chambering for the same firm's Model 1895 lever action. A later factory loading of a 180-grain bullet at 2,470 FPS flattened the trajectory significantly. The .30-40 was an extremely popular hunting cartridge in North America, and quite a number of rifles so chambered were carried to Africa by early American adventurers. Its long, heavy bullet traveling at moderate velocity was indeed effective, and I suspect that those who used it never found it wanting on midsize African game. An unusually short duration as the American service cartridge (1892–1903) precluded its long-term popularity—that plus the fact that it was replaced by the .30-06, a better cartridge in virtually all respects.

It did, however, have a contemporary rival that has had more lasting impact in Africa. Although not a true .30-caliber, the .303 British, using a bullet with a .311-inch diameter, was ballistically almost identical to the .30-40. Amazingly, the .303 started life in 1887 as a black-powder cartridge, using a compressed load that propelled a 215-grain bullet at 1,850 FPS. In 1892, the same year America adopted the Krag, the .303 was converted to a smokeless load. The velocity was boosted to just under 2,000 feet per second, not too flashy but miles ahead of the black-powder competition.

At the start of World War I, the British changed to a spitzer 174-grain bullet at 2,440 FPS, a cartridge that remained the Empire's standard for more than forty years. The old Short Magazine Lee Enfield [SMLE] and its predecessor, the Lee-Metford, chambered in .303, became a fixture throughout the British Empire. This was the rifle carried by Cecil Rhodes's Pioneer Column into the Rhodesias, and the rifle the British used in the Boer War. It was chambered in a number of sporting rifles; and since it's a rimmed cartridge, many double rifles and single shots have been built

Left to right: .30-30 Winchester, 7.62x39, .308 Winchester, .30-06. Any .30-caliber you can think of has a place in Africa. The grand old .30-30 still has some following in thornbush, and these days the 7.62 Russian is carried by game scouts and poachers alike. For most of us, though, the versatile .308 and .30-06 are among the most useful of African cartridges.

PH Dirk de Bod and Matt Morey with a blue wildebeest taken with a .300 Winchester Short Magnum. Like all the fast .30s, the short magnums are effective and versatile under a wide range of conditions.

around it. Selous used the .303 extensively, as did Bell. With the heavier bullet, it offered adequate penetration on elephant, but it was no more ideally suited for such game than was the 7x57mm.

To this day, battered old SMLEs may be encountered throughout Africa, and to this day they undoubtedly account for a tremendous variety of game. But the .303 was never a flat-shooting cartridge, and in spite of its long-lived popularity it is one of the least useful of the .30-calibers. In a vintage double or even a Lee-Metford, those with a taste for nostalgia would find it satisfactory as a medium-range, medium-game rifle. But it's really a part of history today.

A number of other American .30-caliber cartridges were developed over the years, primarily for use in lever actions and early pumps and semiautos. Some of these have died away while others remain incredibly popular. A partial list would include the .30-30, .30 Remington, .303 Savage, .307 Winchester, and .300 Savage. The .300 Savage is the most powerful of these, nearly duplicating the ballistics of the .303 British. All of these moderate-velocity .30-calibers are outstanding short-range deer cartridges, and as such would be well suited for hunting midsize African plains game in brushy or forested country.

PH Russell Lovemore and Derek McDonald with a fine Cape kudu taken with the .300 Winchester Magnum and 180-grain Hornady bullets. Today the .300 Winchester Magnum rivals the .30-06 in popularity.

I have actually seen a number of Winchester Model 94 .30-30s in use in Africa—and they do just as well over there as they do in America's whitetail woods. Tubular magazine lever actions, however, are not sensible choices for the safari hunter who will encounter a wide range of plains game at varying ranges under varying conditions. The exception could be the brand-new (at this writing) .308 Marlin Express, introduced in 2006. Using Hornady's Lever Evolution bullet, a "compressible" spitzer bullet that for the first time allows an aerodynamic bullet to be used in a tubular magazine, the .308 Marlin essentially duplicates .308 Winchester performance in a tubular magazine rifle. It will do almost anything the .308 Winchester will do, which makes it a viable choice as a general plains-game rifle.

The cartridge that replaced the .30-40 Krag took .30-caliber performance to an entirely different level. Originally introduced in 1903 with a 220-grain bullet at 2,300 feet per second, the case was shortened slightly in 1906 and the loading changed to a 150-grain spitzer at the unheard-of velocity of 2,700 FPS. Today the original version is called the ".30-03," while the 1906 version, officially "caliber .30, model of 1906," is our beloved .30-06. It is a rimless cartridge originally designed for a Mauser-type action, and over the years its loadings have changed markedly—usually for the better.

Current factory loadings for the .30-06 run from 110- to 220-grain bullets. The most interesting loadings for the hunter are a 150-grain bullet at 2,910 FPS, a 165-

grainer at 2,800, and the standby 180-grain load at 2,700. There remain a few 200- and 220-grain loads, but velocity starts to flag, and modern bullets are so darned good I am no longer convinced the additional weight is useful at the .30-06's modest velocity. Both Hornady (Light Magnum) and Federal (High Energy) offer loads that, using new propellants, significantly increase the velocity. Handloaders can also beat standard velocities by some margin, and can also select from an incredible range of outstanding bullets in all of these weights. Truthfully, however, factory .30-06 ammunition is hard to beat in all respects. The cartridge has remained popular for so long that tremendous amounts of development have gone into today's .30-06 ammunition. And, of great importance, the majority of .30-caliber bullets available today have been developed to perform at .30-06 velocities—and most of them perform well.

The 165-grain bullet is a relatively new development in the .30-caliber field, and it just may be the best choice for open-country work on midsize game. Its greater sectional density, when compared to the more common 150-grain bullet, allows it to hold its velocity better, and of course its greater weight and length give it better penetration. However, for African hunting, where one never knows what one might encounter next, the 180-grain bullet is probably the best choice for all-round plains-game hunting. In spitzer design it shoots plenty flat enough for almost all purposes, and can be relied upon for all African game up to kudu, zebra, and such.

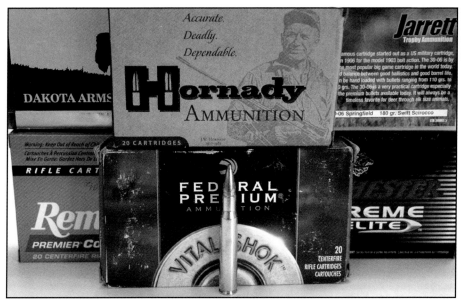

One of the great advantages to the .30-06 is, with its 100-year legacy of popularity, a rich diversity of loads and loading data.

I used my Ruger M77 in .30-06 to take this fine nyala in South Africa's Eastern Cape. I have taken more plains game with the .30-06 than with all other cartridges combined.

On his 1935 safari Hemingway had excellent success on lion, buffalo, and rhino with 220-grain bullets from the .30-06. It would give the same results today; in terms of penetration, there's just no stopping that long 220-grain bullet at moderate velocity. Personally, I have shot nothing larger than zebra, wildebeest, and kudu with the .30-06. But if I happened to have that rifle in my hands, and if it was loaded with a heavy bullet, I wouldn't hesitate to tackle undisturbed Cape buffalo with the .30-06. I must add that I'd sure want a bigger rifle handy to tidy up the mess in case I screwed up.

The late George Parker—war hero, border patrolman, gunfighter, and one of the unsung greats in the hunting world—was a .30-06 fan. In those pre-chronograph days he preferred an Improved version with the case blown out. Today we know that most Improved versions of the .30-06 do indeed burn more powder but actually achieve little velocity edge. Parker used his '06 exclusively on a 1952 Angolan safari, during which the bag included not only large plains species such as roan, kudu, and giant sable but also hippo and the mean little dwarf forest buffalo.

In the middle years of my African career I strayed from the .30-06, but on recent safaris I have come back to it in a big way. These days I'm hunting more and shooting less, and my wife, Donna, has been doing a lot of the shooting. She shares my left-hand affliction, so we've been swapping back and forth with a left-hand Ruger M77 in .30-06, fed a steady diet of 180-grain Hornady InterLocks. Performance has been routinely spectacular in both of our hands, just like it was for me thirty years ago with another Ruger M77, and just like it was for the great hunters of years gone by.

Fed a steady diet of 180-grain spitzer of good construction, the .30-06 will do anything on safari you ask of it short of handling the dangerous game. With a handful of heavier bullets, both solid and soft, "just in case," it remains what it was when Roosevelt used it in 1909: an ideal plains-game rifle.

Its little brother, the much more recent .308 Winchester, was developed as a military cartridge in the years following World War II. The .308 has a shorter case, better suited for use in semi- and fully automatic military rifles. It quickly caught on as a sporting cartridge, being equally suited for use in lever actions such as Browning's BLR and the Savage 99, and of course in short bolt actions.

Up to a point, everything I've said about the .30-06 applies to the .308 Winchester. With bullets up to 180 grains, it lags about 100 feet per second behind the .30-06, hardly a significant difference. With heavier bullets, though, case capacity starts to tell and the gap widens considerably.

I do have a prejudice in favor of the .30-06, but the .308 is a fine cartridge. In a bolt action it can be built a few ounces lighter on a shorter action—but I've never seen any reason for owning a bolt-action .308 when a .30-06 gives so much more versatility with heavier bullets. There are, however, lots of good reasons for owning and using a slick lever-action .308 like the Browning, or the Savage 99 or Model 88 Winchester (both long discontinued). I used a Savage 99 .308 in South Africa many years ago; such a rifle is just as suitable on African plains game at moderate range as it is in America. An interesting new development in "standard .30s" is the brand-new .30 TC, a shorter case than even the .308, but with modern propellants developing velocities approaching the .30-06. Time will tell where this cartridge goes, but it would be ideal in a lever action or very short, light bolt gun.

The Magnum .30s

High-performance .30-caliber cartridges are hardly new. The first successful cartridge of this type was the .300 Holland & Holland Magnum, originally called the "Super .30." Introduced in 1925, it is essentially the 2.8-inch .375 H&H case necked down to .30, retaining the belt that for so many years seemed to define

Provided local laws don't stipulate a larger caliber, I think the .30s are absolutely ideal for leopard. I used a Miller Arms single-shot .30-06 with 180-grain Swift Scirocco bullets to take this Zambezi Valley tom with professional hunter Andrew Dawson.

"magnum" performance. However, it's worth noting that this Holland & Holland development wasn't the first high-performance .30-caliber. Those honors go to the .30 Newton, an unbelted cartridge designed by Charles Newton around 1913. Western loaded factory ammo for it, but only Newton offered rifles so chambered. It wasn't quite as hot as the .300 H&H, but it did offer significant improvement over .30-06 velocities with all bullet weights.

Holland's Super .30 enjoyed much more success and retains a significant following to this day. It caught on rather slowly—until Ben Comfort used it to win the Wimbledon 1,000-yard match in 1935. Two years later the then-new Model 70 Winchester was chambered for it, and it quickly gathered a large following.

Today no new factory rifles are chambered for the .300 H&H, and the few modern factory loads for the .300 H&H are downright anemic: just 2,880 FPS with a 180-grain bullet, which, despite the H&H's wonderful case capacity, doesn't equal the hottest loads available for the .30-06. Handloaders can raise these velocities considerably. I have used the .300 H&H quite a bit in recent years, and although many modern cartridges have eclipsed it, it is still a great old warhorse. For sheep hunting I've been loading a 150-grain at nearly 3,400 FPS, a velocity I have trouble reaching with the .300 Weatherby case. In Africa I've used a 200-grain Sierra at 2,900 FPS for a variety of plains game. Performance has been awesome, but, realistically, if you don't handload, there's little reason to choose a .300 H&H today. But if you run into a clean old rifle in that chambering, don't overlook it. With good handloads it will really come to life. That long, tapered case provides wonderful feeding, and despite its archaic design, accuracy can be astounding. My own .300 H&H is a very simple rebarreling of a Remington M700 action by Rigby's Geoff Miller. Well, OK, it wasn't so simple. The barrel is a match-grade Pac-Nor, and Geoff cut a tight chamber and put it together right. Its best group to date is a 1½-inch cluster at 400 yards.

The .308 Norma Magnum, introduced in 1960, was a fine cartridge that really never had a fighting chance. Extremely similar to the .30-338 wildcat once popular among 1,000-yard benchresters, it's an extremely accurate cartridge whose only factory load propels a 180-grain bullet at a fast, effective 3,020 FPS. Unfortunately, it came out just behind the commonly chambered .300 Winchester Magnum and was made available in very few rifles. Although still a fine cartridge, the .308 Norma is something of an oddity today.

The 1963-vintage .300 Winchester Magnum is a whole different story. Unlike the 2.8-inch .300 H&H, the .300 Winchester is a short magnum with a case length of 2.62 inches, meaning it will function in .30-06-length actions. With a 150-grain loading at 3,290 FPS, 180 grains at 2,960, 200 grains at 2,830, and 220 grains at 2,680, the .300 Winchester Magnum clearly offers a tremendous improvement over .30-06 velocities, with significant resultant advantages in both trajectory and striking energy.

At this writing the .300 Winchester Magnum is the most popular "fast .30," but it has tremendous competition. The .300 Weatherby Magnum is the flagship of the Weatherby line, by far the most popular Weatherby cartridge. It has been available in commercially loaded ammo since about 1948, but in the years since I completed the original of this volume several companies have "broken" Weatherby's proprietary hold on this cartridge. Today both loaded ammo and rifles are available from other makers. I believe the .300 Weatherby Magnum is generally more popular among sheep hunters than on the African scene, but it is definitely a world-standard cartridge and, short of thick-skinned dangerous game, a wonderfully versatile choice. Essentially it is one of several "improved" or blown-out versions of the .300 H&H, using the full-length case with the body taper removed, and carrying the Weatherby hallmark of the double-radiused "Venturi" shoulder.

Published velocities for Weatherby factory ammo include a 150-grain bullet at 3,545 FPS, a 180-grain bullet at 3,245, and a 220-grain at 2,905. Velocities like

Remington's Eddie Stevenson and me with a gemsbok taken with the .300 Remington Ultra Mag. The fastest .30-calibers mated with tough bullets are wonderful for plains game in open country.

these put muzzle energies above the 4,000-foot-pound level with all bullet weights, rivaling energy figures for the .375 H&H. The .300 Weatherby is clearly extremely powerful and just as clearly extremely flat-shooting, and it's been the choice of many of the top modern hunters.

Both Herb Klein and Elgin Gates used almost no other cartridges to hunt the world. In both cases their .300 Weatherby rifles, with heavy bullets, were used for game up to and including elephant and rhino. I haven't used the .300 Weatherby for such heavy game, but I have used it on a variety of game in Africa, Asia, and North America. It's a long-range cartridge without peer, and most certainly an efficient killer of almost anything that walks.

My, how times change. In 1989 I could conclude the discussion of fast .30s at this point. No longer! So many new cartridges are out and about today that I am trying to limit most discussion to commonly available factory options. However, in the late 1980s and through the 1990s, with brass readily available from Jim Bell (Brass Extrusion Laboratories, Ltd.) and others, we seemed to be entering a period of "proprietary cartridges" in which smaller gun companies developed their own cartridges and offered ammo as well as rifles. In the late 1950s we entered what I call the "first magnum craze," a time when almost all new cartridges used a belted case and carried the word "magnum" in their title. It's hard to say when this trend stopped, but by 1980 a few commercial failures had apparently proven that the word "magnum" was no longer a sure recipe for commercial success. And now came proprietaries that provided high performance without the belt: the Imperial Magnum line from Canada, based mostly on the fat, unbelted .404 case; Don Allen's family of Dakota Magnums, also based on the .404 Jeffery (except for the .416 Rigby-based .450 Dakota Magnum); and John Lazzeroni's extensive line of fat-case, unbelted magnums. Lazzeroni's line included not only full-length magnums in several bullet diameters but also the same fat case cut down to .308 Winchester length. Personally, I give John Lazzeroni full credit for today's rash of unbelted magnums, both short and long.

The major manufacturers must have been worried about the publicity surrounding these new unbelted magnums, especially considering the huge publicity blitz that John Lazzeroni orchestrated. Life would have been simpler if the majors had joined "Lazz" and chambered to his cartridges, but the problem was that his cartridges used a really fat case, too fat to fit into many commercial actions without considerable re-engineering. But the public has discovered what Charles Newton knew back in 1913: Performance has nothing to do with a belted case, and the belt was not needed either for case strength or positive headspacing.

As might be expected, factory unbelted magnums started with America's darling, the .30-caliber. First came the .300 Remington Ultra Magnum in about 1998, essentially a full-length unbelted magnum based (loosely) on the .404 Jeffery case necked down, and with the rim rebated. By 2000 the Remington Ultra Magnum, or "RUM," family included 7mm, .338, and .375—but the .300 RUM remains the most popular. Its wide, unbelted case is a sound design, and it actually has a bit more case capacity than the .300 Weatherby. Norma, which has long loaded Weatherby factory ammo, tends to load to a bit higher pressures than American manufacturers. So, on paper and with factory ammo, the .300 Weatherby Magnum slightly exceeds .300 RUM performance. With handloads this will be reversed. Worth noting (and breaking my rule about discussing proprietaries) is that almost equaling .300 Weatherby/.300 RUM performance is Lazzeroni's short .30-caliber, his 7.82 (.308) Patriot.

Legend has it that Remington had on the drawing board both a short and a long version of its Ultra Magnum case, but the company chose to release the long version first. Winchester thus stole a march when it came out in 2000 with the .300 Winchester Short Magnum, using a short, fat, unbelted case to essentially duplicate .300 Winchester Magnum performance in a .308-length action. As stated in the chapter on 7mms, Remington was essentially left holding the bag because the Winchester case was just a wee bit too long for its Model Seven action. So the firm followed with the .300 and 7mm Remington Short Action Ultra Mags, while Winchester expanded its Short Magnum family to include 7mm and .270 WSM, and later the .325 WSM.

I really thought we were done, and I still think the market has more short magnums than it can absorb. The latest development, however, is that late in 2007 Hornady shortened and necked down its .375 Ruger case, creating the .300 (and .338) Ruger Compact Magnums (RCM). The .375 Ruger case isn't quite as fat as the RUM or WSM case. In fact, it's the same .532-inch as the rim and belt of a belted magnum. This makes it easy to manufacture and easy to make feed. Using new propellants not available to handloaders, the .300 RCM achieves, in Hornady factory loads, about the same ballistics as the .300 Winchester Magnum (and .300 WSM), and, like the .300 WSM, it fits into a .308-length action.

Until the early 1990s the .300 Weatherby Magnum was at the top of the .30-caliber velocity heap, at least among factory cartridges. This, too, has changed. The .300 RUM is potentially a bit faster, but the big .30-378 Weatherby Magnum is quite a lot faster, and Lazzeroni's flagship cartridge, the 7.82 (.308) Warbird, is faster yet. These cartridges are, in my view, among the finest in the world for serious long-range work. Just keep in mind that there is relatively little long-range shooting in Africa. These ultra-fast .30s do harness vast amounts of energy, but if they are to be used, great care must be taken in bullet selection so as to avoid premature expansion at close range. Alain Lefol has one that he kept in Chad, where it was used by several clients for aoudad and such (which can be long-range shooting). He also used it for buffalo (the smaller Central African savanna buffalo) and reported no problems.

We now have a complex multiplicity of new magnums, especially in .30-caliber and 7mm. To keep things simple, let's look at it like this: Any .30-caliber

Left to right: 300 Winchester Short Magnum, .300 Winchester Magnum, 7.82 (.308) Patriot, .300 Weatherby Magnum. Today the .300 Winchester Magnum is the most popular of the fast .30s, but all are extremely useful for African plains game.

The first time I ever hunted with the .30-06 was in Kenya in 1977. Using 180-grain Nosler Partitions, it performed flawlessly on a wide variety of plains game, including this hartebeest, at distances from very short to very long. I have been a .30-06 fan ever since!

from .308 Winchester or .30-06 on up, if mated with a well-constructed 180-grain bullet, will perform extremely well on almost the full spectrum of Africa's nondangerous game. I do not think any .30-caliber is ideal for eland, but, where legal, a 180- or 200-grain .30-caliber bullet of tough construction would be just fine. This may seem heresy, but I have not personally found the .300 magnums to be noticeably more effective on game than the .30-06. They do indeed make hitting game at longer ranges much easier, and they certainly extend one's practical range a fair measure. Bullet performance, however, is a concern with all of the .30-caliber magnums—especially at short to medium ranges, which encompass most African hunting.

At .30-06 velocities, the velocities for which most .308-inch bullets were designed, penetration is sure and expansion is reliably controlled. Push those same bullets as much as 500 FPS faster and the results are much less predictable. In fact, most lighter .30-caliber bullets—and many medium-weights—become virtual bombs at .300 magnum velocity. Obviously, one mitigates this by choosing ever-tougher bullets as velocity increases. At the mild velocities of the .30-06 I have seen little reason to use extremely tough bullets like the Swift A-Frame and Barnes Triple-Shock—but in the really fast cartridges this is exactly what I choose!

I used my .300 H&H with 200-grain Sierra bullets to drop my best waterbuck with a frontal shot. I still like the great old .300 H&H, but its popularity has definitely slipped in recent years.

This is also mitigated by range, because at longer distances velocities are reduced. Again, there is relatively little genuine long-range shooting in Africa—but there are places where a bit of reach is often required. So in areas like the Kalahari, the great Karoo, perhaps the short-grass plains of East Africa, and definitely the mountains of Ethiopia, any fast .30 will be superior to the .30-06, not only in ranging capability but also in energy delivered at the target. But for general African use, forget the fancy ballistics and stay away from the lighter bullets in the magnum 30s.

In any .30-caliber cartridge a stoutly constructed 180-grain bullet is a good choice. Some years ago I would have suggested a heavier bullet in the faster .30s. I still like 200-grain bullets in the magnums, but these days hunting bullets have gotten so good that you're just as well off to stick with 180-grain slugs. Just use tougher bullets as velocity increases. As for the 220-grain bullets and the heavier .30-calibers (like the 250-grain bullets Barnes used to make), today I tend to think they're an anachronism. Just maybe they have their uses if one insists on taking on thick-skinned game with a .30-caliber, and certainly they would be useful under specialized circumstances such as forest hunting. However, I believe I'll stick with 180s and occasional 200-grain bullets in my .30-calibers. If I think I need more, then what I really need is a bigger gun!

Among American deer and elk hunters we have outspoken proponents of bullet diameters .270, 7mm, and .30-caliber. I like them all, but in Africa I have a definite preference for the .30-caliber. I agree that the 7mm's long-for-caliber bullets tend to penetrate a bit better, but because of the great size variance among African game animals I prefer the heavier bullets and greater frontal area of the .30-caliber. As to which .30, I don't think it matters much, except in specialized circumstances. For most hunting the .308 and .30-06 are wonderful, and these two cartridges are by far the most popular among professional hunters and local African hunters—partly, admittedly, because of availability. Any of the .30 magnums will work just as well, and in more open country will work better. The drawbacks of the magnum .30s, compared with the .30-06, are increased recoil and muzzle blast, increased gun weight, and length (a .30-06 is just fine with a 22-inch barrel, but all the magnum .30s really need a 24-inch tube and the extra-fast cartridges strut their stuff best with a full 26 inches of barrel), and a greatly reduced selection of bullets that can be relied upon to perform at the increased velocities. The advantages are increased practical range and easier shooting at longer ranges, plus an across-the-board increase in raw energy.

Those energy increases are significant. However, in spite of what many experts have accomplished with .30 magnums, they are still not suitable charge-stopping cartridges for lion and the thick-skinned African game. No .30-caliber bullet yet designed, at any velocity, is. In terms of performance on game, none of the magnum .30s will display a noticeable advantage over the .30-06 (or, for that matter, the .308 or .303 British) under most African hunting conditions. However, in the African deserts, open savannas, and mountains, the ranging abilities of the magnum .30s do offer tremendous advantages.

Whether a magnum or a "standard" .30 is chosen, it's a cartridge that will provide yeoman service on a tremendous range of African game. It is ideal on game from impala up through kudu and zebra, and in a pinch, with proper bullets, it will do the trick even on massive eland. It will turn the lights out on a leopard much more quickly than a heavier rifle. And it's been used with success against lion and buffalo much too often to say it can't be done. I used a .300 RUM with 200-grain Swift A-Frames when I got a surprise "problem lion permit" in Namibia in 2007. It was what I had, and it worked just fine—but I don't think it's a particularly good idea. To find sensible absolute minimums for such game, we'll need to take another step up in caliber.

The Light Mediums

Chapter 5

There has been some confusion about the capabilities of those cartridges falling between the .30s and the .375, that broad and useful spectrum of cartridges from 8mm, or .323-caliber, to 9.3mm, or .366-caliber. There is a tremendous variance in velocity, bullet weight, and power among this group, so it's most unwise to make broad statements. Generally, though, these cartridges can perform duties above and beyond what you would expect from a "light" safari rifle—but they won't stop a charge the way a "heavy" rifle will or as reliably as the classic "medium" bore, the .375 H&H. They're sort of in-betweeners, either "light mediums" or "heavy lights." Whatever you choose to call them, the group includes a number of wonderful hunting cartridges.

Good ones in this class are America's medium magnums, the 8mms and the fast .33s. I have a longstanding "thing" with the 8mm Remington Magnum, and in the last couple of years I've spent quite a lot of time with its new little brother, the .325 Winchester Short Magnum. It's true that no 8mm has ever achieved lasting popularity in the United States, but I like both of these cartridges very much, and I swear to you that they hit noticeably harder than any .30-caliber, and come very close to the .33s in practical performance on game.

The .33s are popular in this country, and there are plenty of good ones to choose from. Most popular by far is the .338 Winchester Magnum, but there are still faster and more powerful .33s, to include .340 Weatherby Magnum, .338 Remington Ultra Magnum, and still faster and more powerful cartridges like the .338 Lapua and Lazzeroni 8.59 (.338 Titan).

The .338 Winchester Magnum, introduced in 1958, was slow to catch on, but it has become the archetypical elk cartridge. It is popular enough that, as Americans are prone to do, we have come to believe we created this class of cartridge. Actually, we Americans, the British, and the metric-minded Europeans all have a long history of cartridges in this class. More to the point, the British and Continental cartridges

I used the .325 Winchester Short Magnum to drop this gemsbok bull in its tracks. The .325 is essentially an 8mm cartridge, faster than the 8x57, slower than the 8mm Remington Magnum, and very close to the .338 Winchester Magnum in performance on game.

have a long and glorious history in Africa, while the American "light mediums" are new to that scene.

For the sake of simplicity, the metric cartridges will be covered in detail in a separate chapter. To keep things in perspective, though, the 8mm Mauser, or 8x57, dates back to 1888 and remains a European standard. Although it's a fine hunting cartridge, its limited case capacity keeps the velocity down, especially with heavier bullets. It offers no real advantage over .30-06-class cartridges. The 1912-vintage 8x64 Brenneke, essentially the same as our wildcat 8mm-06, will keep pace in the velocity department—and do it with heavier bullets with larger frontal area. Better still is the 8x68S Magnum, a true rimless magnum developed in 1940. This one is extremely popular among savvy Europeans, essentially filling the niche occupied by our .338. Ballistically it is very similar to the 8mm Remington Magnum.

There have been a number of 9mm rifle cartridges, but only the 9x57 has survived (and only in European loadings). It is essentially similar to, but a bit less powerful than, our .358 Winchester. More popular and more lasting among European hunters is the 9.3mm, caliber .366. Frank Barnes's *Cartridges of the World* lists fully fifteen cartridges in 9.3mm, most of which are long gone. The most common survivors are the 9.3x62 Mauser, the 9.3x64 Brenneke, and the 9.3x74R. All have been available with excellent bullets ranging from 232 to 293 grains. The 9.3x62 goes clear back to 1905, and it was the most popular general-purpose cartridge in the portions of Africa settled by the Germans. Although it uses heavier bullets, it's actually very similar to the .35 Whelen. Much newer and a bit more powerful is the .370 Sako, a long, slender cartridge that has a following among Scandinavian moose hunters. In 2007 Federal announced a factory load for this rifle, but at this date (late 2007) no U.S. rifles are so chambered.

The 9.3x64 Brenneke is also not chambered (or loaded) in the United States, but it's another story altogether. Actually an unbelted magnum, the 9.3x64 gives up nothing to the .375 H&H, propelling its heaviest 293-grain bullet at 2,570 feet per second. Because of ammo availability, an American probably wouldn't choose it over the .375—but a European might, and he wouldn't be wrong.

The 9.3x74R is a very long, very trim rimmed cartridge for use in doubles and single shots. It can't compete with the .375 H&H, but it's very close to the .375 Flanged, and much more available. Its 286-grain bullet at 2,360 FPS has been used on all African game, including elephant, with much success. Personally, I'd want a bit more gun, but the 9.3x74R does have a great advantage in that its slim, pencil-like profile allows it to be built into a double of incredible trimness and light weight. Just this past year Hornady announced the first American factory load for the 9.3x74R, and Ruger added it to the extensive lineup of No. 1 single-shot chamberings. I used one of the prototype No. 1s in 9.3x74R in Namibia in 2006, and although that cartridge's arcing trajectory probably wasn't the most ideal match to Namibia's open thornbush, it sure thumped the heck out of gemsbok and kudu!

Left to right: .358 Winchester, .350 Remington Magnum, .35 Whelen. The various .35s have never been especially popular, but I like them very much, especially these three. All would be superb for the full run of plains game at moderate ranges.

My long-barrel 8mm Remington Magnum is one of my favorite rifles for plains game in open country. This is a red Cape hartebeest, taken in central Namibia.

The English, too, had a proliferation of medium cartridges, though not as many as the Europeans. Some, like the .360 Nitro Express, were simply smokeless adaptations of black-powder cartridges, offering little. Others were indeed fine cartridges. Unlike their European counterparts, all of the British over-.30-and-under-.375 cartridges can be considered obsolete today—but several of them left their mark.

The first smokeless cartridge in this class was the .400/.350 Nitro Express, a rimmed cartridge introduced by John Rigby in 1899. It fired a 310-grain .35-caliber bullet at just 2,000 FPS—but that long, heavy bullet at such a modest velocity penetrated like crazy, and the cartridge had a tremendous following. A friend of mine, South African diplomat Vic Zazeraj, has a Greener .400/.350 on a Martini-type single-shot action, and he swears by it for game up to, but not quite including, buffalo.

Under the British proprietary system, other companies soon followed with the slightly less powerful .400/.360 Nitro Express, but it never achieved any following to speak of. Better was the 1905-vintage .360 Nitro Express No. 2, a larger-case cartridge that propelled a heavy-for-caliber 320-grain bullet at 2,200 FPS. This was really a fine cartridge; a double so chambered could be put to good use today.

Farther down the caliber scale were more interesting developments. John Rigby developed the .350 Rigby Magnum, also called .350 Rimless Magnum, for use in Mauser actions in about 1908. It remained popular clear up to the collapse of the

Left to right: .325 Winchester Short Magnum, 8mm Remington Magnum, .338 Winchester Magnum, .340 Weatherby Magnum, .338 Remington Ultra Mag. To my thinking all of the faster medium magnums are simply outstanding for the wide variety of antelope that might be encountered in Africa. One caution: The fastest .33s have a lot of recoil!

British Empire in Africa, and is still seen occasionally today. I had a left-hand .350, one of the last London Rigby rifles, and I used it a bit in Africa. It's one of the many rifles over the years that I probably should have kept, but the accuracy of this particular rifle just wasn't what I expect from a bolt action. Factory ballistics suggested a 225-grain bullet at 2,600 FPS, yielding 3,380 foot-pounds of energy. For its day, that was good velocity, and even heavy-rifle king John Taylor had nothing but good things to say about the .350 Rigby Magnum. Ballistically it is actually just about identical to the .35 Whelen, at least with factory loads. Its fatter case does have more capacity, and it had been my intention to see what could be done with that case. Regrettably, I never got around to it. My friend Marv Quillen built a rifle to this cartridge and worked up some good loads, and he has had excellent results with it. The .350 was used rather extensively for buffalo and even elephant, with darn few complaints. I would personally use such a cartridge on buffalo only in fairly open country, which is the way they were typically hunted when this cartridge was in its heyday.

Another fine cartridge that came out just a couple of years later was the .333 Jeffery, or .333 Rimless Nitro Express. Its companion rimmed cartridge was the .333 Flanged. Firing a 250-grain bullet at 2,500 FPS and a very long 300-grain bullet at 2,200, this one was also considered a deadly killer on game up to buffalo.

A Hartmann zebra, taken with a .338 Winchester Magnum. No matter what you run into, there are few things in Africa a .338 can't handle.

John Taylor apparently thought little of the copper-capped 250-grain bullet, but believed in the heavy 300-grain slug. I can appreciate that; we know today what a good 250-grain .338 bullet will do, and I would suspect that the much longer 300-grain slug would be darn near unstoppable. (Note: This was a campfire discussion in Tanzania just the other day. There used to be a 300-grain load for the .338 Winchester Magnum, and a couple of PHs with some experience with this bullet maintained that it was just plain too long for caliber and tended to bend. So maybe it is possible to have too much of a good thing!)

The .333 Jeffery was the inspiration for the .333 O.K.H. wildcat developed by the legendary team of O'Neil, Keith, and Hopkins, based on the .30-06 case. Later they developed the .334 O.K.H. using the .375 H&H case blown out. Carrying it a step farther, you could say that it was therefore the inspiration for the .338 Winchester Magnum.

True .333 bullets are available from the Australian firm of Woodleigh, or .338 bullets can easily be swaged down. Enough .333 rifles were built that they do come up for sale every now and again—and they're worth having. In power the .333 is very close to our popular wildcat cartridge, the .338-06.

61

I had a last-light opportunity at this exceptional blue wildebeest. This is one of Africa's toughest antelope, and I wouldn't have taken the shot with a light cartridge. With a .338 Winchester Magnum I was in good shape!

Virtually the only cartridge in this class that failed to build a good reputation was the .33 Belted Rimless Nitro Express, a Birmingham Small Arms development. This one uses a .338-inch bullet, so its ills would be easy to cure with modern bullets. It was a belted cartridge and thus was quite similar to the .338 Winchester Magnum—except that it was offered only with a much-too-light 165-grain bullet, obviously of poor sectional density and just as obviously offering dismal penetration on game. It didn't last very long.

Saving the best, or at least the most popular, for last, that brings us to the .318 Westley Richards, or .318 Rimless Nitro Express. Never as readily available or as commonly used as the 9.3x62, the .318 was nevertheless the most popular and most popularized British medium bore. Introduced in 1910, it has been called the British equivalent of the .30-06, and indeed it's similar; when I had a .318, I made brass from .30-06 cases. However, its .330-inch bullet has much more frontal area, and it was blessed with tough, deep-penetrating 250-grain softpoints as well as the excellent Kynoch solids.

Factory ballistics listed the 250-grain bullet at 2,400 FPS and a 180-grain bullet at 2,700. That makes it almost the equal of the .333 Jeffery, and about the same as our current .338-06 wildcat—provided, of course, that the factory figures published nearly eighty years ago were accurate. I had a .318, a beautiful Westley Richards Mauser, for some time and shot it extensively. I chronographed several batches of old Kynoch ammo, and the velocities I got weren't even close: The 250-grain loads didn't come up to 2,200 FPS. One has to wonder if that was because the ammo was half a century old, or if it ever reached published velocities.

It doesn't really matter; the .318 was widely used and widely sworn by. Taylor rated it extremely effective, saying, "I have the highest possible opinion of it provided it's kept in its place and not abused by being taken alone against dangerous game in thick cover." Amen.

My own experience with the .318 was limited to plains game; I took it to Botswana and South Africa in 1987 and used it to take a variety of animals up to wildebeest and zebra at various distances. I was using old Kynoch 250-grain solids and softs and Barnes 250-grain .338 bullets swaged down (in two steps) to .330. It

Tracker Mavros, PH Pete Kibble, and me with a beautiful cheetah. This was a chance encounter, a difficult shot at over 250 yards. The .338 Winchester Magnum can easily handle such situations.

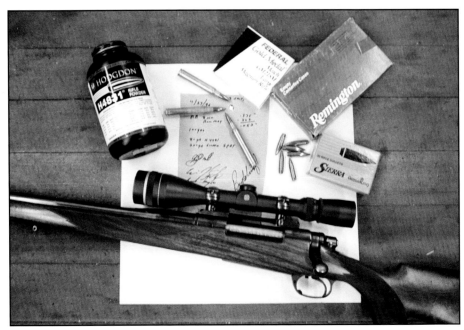

Aside from its velocity and hard-hitting capabilities, what I really like about my 8mm Remington Magnum, built by Rigby's Geoff Miller, is its incredible accuracy. A rifle that produces groups like this gives one tremendous confidence.

was, quite simply, one of the deadliest rifles I have ever used. There seemed to be no stopping that long, heavy bullet at its moderate velocity.

I shot a big blue wildebeest, a very tough antelope, at quite a long distance— some 225 yards. The big bullet penetrated completely through both shoulders and literally flattened the bull in his tracks. I would not hesitate to use the .318 on an unwounded, undisturbed buffalo, and I intended to do so. It just didn't happen; we could find our buffalo only in the heaviest cover, and that was what my other rifle—a .470 double—was there for.

The .318 is a charming, charismatic cartridge with little recoil. I wish I still had that rifle, but I'm a lefty and of course it had a right-handed bolt—and, to be honest, somebody else wanted it more than I did. I found it in a gun shop in Los Angeles, and it had had quite a checkered career before it got to me. Built in 1927, it had been shipped to New Brunswick originally. From there it somehow got to Australia— the "broad arrow" stencil on the stock showed it had been commandeered by the Australian military during World War II. Westley Richards had reconditioned it fifteen years before I bought it. After all that, it still shot well. New brass and Woodleigh .330-inch bullets are now available, and Westley Richards has made a few .318 rifles in recent years. We have so many fine cartridges today that I'm not sure it really deserves a comeback, but it is one of the old-timers for which I will always have a soft spot.

On the American side of the Atlantic there were several cartridges in this class. We had a whole slew of them from .32 to .35 designed for the pump, lever, and early semiautos that were in vogue in the early days of smokeless powder. Most were low-power rounds very similar to the sole survivor, the .35 Remington. A couple are worth mentioning. The .35 Winchester, designed for use in the big Winchester 1895 lever action, fired a 250-grain bullet at almost 2,200 FPS, so it was no pipsqueak. It was loaded by Kynoch for some time and saw some use in Africa. It died along with the Model 1895, and is a real rarity today. Also worth mentioning is the .33 Winchester, the last chambering for the great Model 1886 Winchester. It was widely used as a bear and moose cartridge, but its real claim to fame is that it used a .338-inch bullet, making it the American ancestor of the .338 Winchester Magnum and all the rest of our fast .33s.

A cartridge that really could have gone places is the .35 Newton, one of Charles Newton's excellent rimless magnums. It was offered in factory loads for a time, and they were red-hot—not just for their day but for any day! It's said that a 250-grain bullet could be pushed in excess of 2,900 FPS. I have trouble believing that, but I have no trouble with the last listed factory load, a 250-grain bullet at 2,660. That makes the cartridge faster than the .35 Whelen or the .350 Rigby Magnum, and pushing the .358 Norma, a belted magnum. It must have been really something, but it died with the Newton Rifle Company during the Depression. Charles Cottar, the first American professional hunter in Africa, was one of few recorded .35 Newton fans.

All this has been background; as great as the British cartridges were, they're long gone today. And as great as some of the metrics are, ammunition for most of them is scarce as hens' teeth—not only in America but also in much of Africa. Now let's look at the commonly available cartridges in our "light medium" class.

Lever-Action Cartridges

These need to be mentioned not only because of Americans' love for their lever guns but also because they're fine cartridges. In this group we'll lump together the .348, .356, and .358 Winchesters. We'll ignore the .35 Remington, a great cartridge in the whitetail woods but underpowered for larger game. The .348 is the oldest of these. It was only chambered in the Model 71 Winchester, the last incarnation of the old 1886 lever action. The .348 was dying, not easily or quickly but steadily, until Browning brought out a modern replica. With a 200-grain

I took a nice gemsbok bull on the same day as I shot a kudu, shooting my 8mm Remington Magnum

20-grain Sierra bullets.

The .338 Winchester Magnum isn't especially fast or flat shooting, but it is capable of handling considerable range if you know the trajectory. I shot this Vaal rhebok at something over 300 yards with a .338 firing a 210-grain Nosler Partition, easily one of the best (or luckiest) shots I've ever made.

bullet at 2,530 FPS, the .348 is a powerful and effective hunting cartridge. Its discontinued 250-grain load, with a muzzle velocity of 2,350, was even better. I have not taken the cartridge to Africa, but I have used it extensively on black bear and wild hogs. With handloaded flat-point 250-grain bullets, it's simply deadly. I don't see it as an African cartridge; the only rifle ever chambered for it doesn't lend itself to scope use, and it certainly isn't a dangerous-game cartridge. But it would be deadly in thornbush.

The .358 was introduced to replace the .348. It's a short rimless cartridge based on the .308 case, and with the 200-grain bullet its muzzle velocity is identical to that of the .348. With the 250-grain loading, also discontinued, it lagged about 100 FPS behind because of its smaller case capacity. However, it was offered in the box-magazine Model 88 Winchester and the rotary-magazine Savage 99, and is still available in the slick little Browning BLR. All of these guns can be scoped. They can also use sharp-pointed bullets, which a tubular-magazine gun cannot. The flatnose slugs hit like a freight train, but they shed their velocity like a thrown rock.

James Mellon mentions using a .358 in *African Hunter,* and he had good luck with it. I took a Model 88 in .358 to Zambia in 1996, and it worked just fine. It would be a slightly different but very good choice for any and all plains game in thornbush, but unfortunately the .358 seems almost a dead duck today. Likewise the .356 Winchester, a cartridge that was designed, in turn, to replace the .358 (but in tubular-magazine rifles).

Mainstream Mediums

At this writing the newest kid on the medium-cartridge block is yet another .33, the .338 Federal. Based on the .308 Winchester case necked up, it is obviously very similar to my much beloved (but apparently only by me) .358 Winchester, but has the advantage of using the greater range of .33-caliber bullets. It also has the advantage of being "new," so perhaps it has a chance for success in the fickle gun market that has long bypassed the .358! With its limited case capacity it cannot approach any of the faster .33s, especially with heavy bullets, but it's a very speedy little cartridge, propelling a 210-grain bullet at more than 2,600 FPS. Able to be housed in a short bolt action (or a modern lever action like the BLR), it would be a great rifle for hunting plains game and such in heavy thornbush.

Twenty years ago the .338-06 (.30-06 necked down to .338) was a popular wildcat, and I really believed it would be a successful factory cartridge someday. Today it remains a fairly popular wildcat, but although both A-Square and Weatherby made efforts to legitimize it, it just hasn't gone anywhere. With the new .338 Federal on the street, I now believe the .338-06 will remain an occasionally encountered wildcat, and that it will slip into obscurity. But I'm fully prepared to be wrong, because the .338-06 is a great cartridge.

It is not necessarily better (or worse) than the .35 Whelen. Realistically, however, I'm not sure we need both! Most of the time we Americans tend to prefer .33s to .35s. Given that available weights are about the same for both calibers, the .33 offers more sectional density and thus, all things being equal, greater penetration. The .35 offers more frontal area and thus more initial energy transfer. Take your pick! The .35 Whelen languished as a fairly popular wildcat for sixty-five years, and then in 1988 Remington finally adopted it as a factory cartridge. Initial results exceeded the company's wildest expectations, but in recent years I'm told sales have slipped considerably. This is probably true, since .35-caliber cartridges have been perennial losers among American hunters.

In the Selous Reserve in 2000, we used all the Remington Ultra Mag cartridges, including the fast, powerful .338 Remington Ultra Mag. It worked perfectly on a longish shot on this Lichtenstein hartebeest.

Popular or not, however, the .35 Whelen is a great cartridge. I have used it on quite a bit of North American game, including elk, moose, and bear, and have tremendous respect for its capabilities. Shame on me, to this day I have not taken a .35 Whelen to Africa, but I haven't changed my opinion: Loaded with 250-grain bullets, it would be one of the very best choices for thornbush hunting. Factory ballistics put that bullet at a very respectable 2,400 FPS; handloading could beat that by some measure. The wonderful thing about the Whelen, though, is that it does what it does with very little recoil and muzzle blast. Of course, exactly the same can be said about the .338-06.

Medium Magnums

Remington's "Big Eight," the 8mm Remington Magnum, was introduced in 1978. It is based on the .375 H&H case, necked down with the body taper removed. In 1988 I wrote the following about this wonderful cartridge: "Although there was much initial fanfare, the public didn't seem to care; the cartridge has languished since the very beginning, and I seriously doubt if rifles will be chambered for it much longer."

I was wrong, but not by much. The 8mm Remington Magnum continues to hang on, but just barely. I think this is a real shame. I used it quite a bit when it was new, but in recent years I've had quite a fling with the 8mm Remington Magnum. I have used it in Namibia, South Africa, and Zambia as part of a battery, and it was the only rifle I used in Ethiopia in 2000 and Chad in 2001. I use the heavy 220-grain bullets. I am not going to suggest that a 220-grain .323 bullet beats (or even equals) a 250-grain .338 bullet. However, the 8mm definitely hits harder than any .30-caliber bullet. And you can get more velocity with less recoil than you can from a .33.

My particular 8mm has a long 28-inch barrel put together by Rigby's Geoff Miller. I don't think of it as an all-purpose rifle, but that 220-grain bullet at nearly 3,100 FPS has performed marvelously on sitatunga, mountain nyala, kudu, aoudad, gemsbok, and even eland. I seriously doubt that all the ink I have spilled over the 8mm can save it—but it deserves to be saved.

The new .325 Winchester Short Magnum is also, technically, an 8mm, since it shoots the same .323-inch bullets. It obviously cannot do what the 8mm Remington Magnum can do, but to my thinking it is one of the most appealing of all the new short magnums, and especially for African hunting. It propels a 200-grain bullet up to 2,900 FPS, and although my use of it in Africa has been limited, I believe it may prove the most useful of all the new short magnums. Again, the 8mm hits harder than a .30-caliber but, especially in .325 WSM form, offers considerably less recoil than the fast .33s.

By the way, one argument often leveled against the 8mm is a shortage of good bullets. It's true that the selection is much more limited than with the .338, but how many good bullets do you need? In my 8mm Remington Magnum I'm pretty well stuck on 220-grain bullets, and I've used Hornady, Sierra, Barnes X-Bullet, and Swift A-Frame in that weight. The little .325 probably struts its stuff best with 200-grain bullets, and there are Nosler Partitions, Barnes Triple Shock, and Hornady (among others) in addition to perfectly good factory loads in that weight.

Introduced in 1958 in a version of Winchester's pre-'64 Model 70 called "the Alaskan," the .338 Winchester Magnum is probably, worldwide, the "top gun" between .30 and .375. It had a great deal going for it from the start. Obviously, it had the backing of what was then America's premier gun company, in a day when the Model 70 was *the* bolt-action sporter. It was also a true short magnum, able to fit into any .30-06-length action. And it had the excellent legacy of the British .33s to trade on—plus the backing of Elmer Keith, who had been championing his O.K.H. .33-caliber wildcats for decades.

Surprisingly, in spite of all these advantages, the .338 was very slow to catch on. No, it has never teetered on the edge of disaster like the 8mm Remington, but it was a slow starter. I think it was acceptance by American elk hunters that finally got it going, and indeed the .338 is one of the finest of all elk cartridges. It is also a wonderful bear cartridge, and in Alaska it is now more popular than the .375 H&H. Chances are it will always be more of a North American cartridge than an African cartridge, but slowly and surely it's working its way into the Dark Continent as well. As it should—it's everything the old-time .33s ever were plus a lot more.

One of its prime attributes is that, with its fifty-year history, it has a wonderful selection of superb bullets available, with weights ranging from 180 to 300 grains. The most popular weights, and the weights in factory loads, run from 200 to 250 grains. For African use I recommend 225 or 250. Some are tougher than others, but in these weights you really can't go wrong.

The .338 is not exceptionally awesome when you study the ballistics. Factory figures list a 225-grain bullet at 2,780 FPS at the muzzle, which yields 3,862 foot-pounds. The 250-grain bullet is listed at 2,700 FPS for 4,046 foot-pounds. The .338 can't be considered as powerful as the .375 H&H. Its bullets have a higher sectional density and are generally more aerodynamic, so it will reach out a bit better. But they don't have the frontal area or the weight. That said, because of higher sectional density (and less resistance because of its smaller diameter) a 250-grain .338 will outpenetrate a 300-grain .375 all day long. I have dropped Cape buffalo square in their tracks with .338-caliber 250-grain Swift A-Frame bullets.

Several comments on this: First, it can be done. Second, game laws usually exist for good reason, and there is good reason why the .338 is not legal for buffalo in most African jurisdictions. This reason is very simple: The .338 will do a bang-up job for 95 percent of all African shooting, and it has bullets available that will handle the rest if necessary. But it still isn't a charge-stopper, and shouldn't be considered as such.

What it is is a general-purpose safari cartridge with few equals—especially in country where some reach is required. The .338 Winchester Magnum is one of my favorite cartridges, a most useful safari caliber. Except in some very specialized circumstances, it is not a sensible one-gun battery, but it makes a fine choice as the lighter rifle of a two-gun outfit, or the heavier rifle on a safari that does not include thick-skinned game.

The newest .33 is the .338 Ruger Compact Magnum (RCM), developed by Hornady by shortening and necking down its .375 Ruger case. A companion introduction to the .300 RCM, the .338 RCM essentially duplicates .338 Winchester Magnum performance but fits in a .308-length action.

Everything that can be said about the .338 Winchester Magnum (and the .338 RCM) can be said in spades about the faster .33s. Introduced in 1962, the .340 Weatherby Magnum is one of Roy Weatherby's later creations—and in my view one of his best. Based on the .375 H&H case, it requires a full-length action, but that case capacity enables it to do wonderful things with heavy bullets of great sectional density and superb aerodynamics. And Lord, is it fast! A reference quotes the 250-grain factory .340 at 2,850 FPS muzzle velocity. (Another reference quotes that load at 3,000 FPS, which is a bit optimistic!) Some time back I chronographed a fresh batch of Weatherby ammo out of a Mark V with 26-inch barrel. Actual velocity was a full 2,900 FPS and a bit of change—which translates to muzzle energy of 4,668 foot-pounds.

The .338 Remington Ultra Magnum offers performance very similar to the .340 Weatherby Magnum, with the same comparison as the .300 RUM versus the .300 Weatherby Magnum. In factory loads, at least as published, the Weatherby wins. But the RUM has more case capacity, and so with carefully worked up handloads is theoretically capable of slightly greater velocity. Monstrous-cased .33s like the .338 Lapua and Lazzeroni's Titan will win the velocity races hands down. Just keep in mind that recoil goes up dramatically!

I'll stand on what I said regarding the .338 Winchester Magnum: Regardless of energy figures, no .33 will match a .375 when it comes to stopping a charge, and it certainly can't take the place of a heavier rifle. However, fast .33s are wonderful for hunting large plains game in big country. I have used a .340 Weatherby on several safaris, and it was the only rifle I took on my first Ethiopian hunt in 1993. When it was brand-new I used a .338 Remington Ultra Mag in Tanzania in 2000, and it was just wonderful. Again (this is a foot-stomper!): When velocity goes up, so does energy. And so does recoil, at the same exponential rate as energy. Most people can handle a .338 Winchester Magnum, while the really fast .33s are much more difficult to shoot. Over time I decided the fastest .33s were a bit too unpleasant to shoot for my taste. Love their capabilities, but I've downgraded back to the .338 Winchester Magnum!

Missing from the modern selection of light mediums is a fast .35-caliber. The hot little .350 Remington Magnum has made somewhat of a comeback. I have one on a short left-hand Remington action that Kerry O'Day of Match Grade Arms built for me, and I love it. (As you've noticed, I like .35s!) However, I have to admit that it doesn't really do anything that a .35 Whelen won't do—it just does it with a shorter case that fits into a shorter action. Twenty years ago I predicted (wishful thinking?)

that the .358 Norma Magnum might make a comeback. As we know, that hasn't happened. It's a great cartridge, but today it is really a footnote to cartridge history.

For a time it appeared that the .35 Shooting Times Alaskan, the 8mm Remington Magnum case necked up to .358, might have a chance as a factory cartridge. But today unbelted cartridges are "in," so I don't see any major manufacturer taking a chance on any belted cartridge. The new unbelted .375 Ruger case would be wonderful necked down to .35. Realistically, however, that's almost a step beyond wishful thinking. The .35-caliber has fared so poorly that, as much as I'd like to see it, a new fast .35 seems most unlikely. And if one should come along, where would it fit? Actually, no differently than the fast .33s.

This has been a long chapter because so many cartridges in this group have a real purpose in African hunting—but not in close cover after dangerous game. John Taylor had it pegged a generation ago, and although the cartridges have changed, their purposes and limitations remain unchanged. "Always provided that there is a more powerful rifle at hand for use in thick cover, you could not wish for a more satisfactory general-purpose medium bore than Westley Richards's .318," wrote Taylor. Instead of the .318, he could well have applied those words to any of the cartridges we've discussed in this chapter—whether of his day or ours. All of them will provide yeoman service on the vast majority of game. And under the right conditions, with the right bullets, all of them could be used on anything that walks. But none of them will provide the margin you must have for dangerous game at close quarters.

The "magnums" in this group extend the reach, the practical shooting distance—and that's desirable in open country. But even the fastest of this group, with the flashiest of trajectories, will fail to carry these cartridges into the realm of charge-stoppers for lion, buffalo, and elephant. That's why so many African game departments have made their use on such game illegal.

The Great .375

Chapter 6

It seems in vogue today to malign the .375 H&H in favor of more modern cartridges—whether bigger or smaller, faster or slower. Introduced clear back in 1912, the .375 H&H is an archaic design—a long, sloping body with a minimal shoulder—and generates velocities that are hardly red-hot by today's standards. A variety of smaller-caliber cartridges shoot flatter and hit almost as hard. And a number of larger cartridges hit harder and shoot almost as flat. All of these cartridges have their places—and under certain circumstances they might be more useful than the old warhorse .375. These words were true in 1988, but they are far truer today. The incredible resurgence of the .416 (and its ilk) has dipped deeply into the traditional .375 market.

On the other hand, since 1988 we have seen several new .375-caliber cartridges. They are good, and the .416s are good . . . but none of this has suggested to me that the patriarchal .375 H&H is no longer good. As we shall see later on in this volume, the .375 may not have a place in every safari battery today. But whether in .375 H&H or some other configuration, the .375-bore remains what it was nearly a century ago: the single most useful rifle any African hunter could carry.

Now I'm really embarrassed. If you compare these lines to the original, at the time I was writing this chapter I had made just eighteen African hunts. At this writing my total is triple that and more, but the results are pretty much the same. I have not taken a .375 on every African hunt, but I've taken one more often than not. I'm actually writing (or revising, your choice) this chapter in the Victoria Falls Hotel, and one of the rifles in the hotel's vault is my .375 Ruger. This also reflects a change in the last twenty years.

I don't have a "problem" with any of the various .375 cartridges—all are darn good—but there was a point at which I had personally used only the .375 H&H. This point has long been passed. I have not used all the .375 cartridges, but I have hunted buffalo and other suitable game not only with the .375 H&H but also with the .375 Dakota, .375 Weatherby Magnum, and .375 Ruger.

This is my old—and very weird—left-hand-converted, pre-1964 Winchester Model 70. Now on its second barrel, it shoots 300-grain solids and softs to the same point of impact.

My uncle, Art Popham, used a .375 Improved on his 1956 Tanganyika safari. It worked well on this buffalo, and on lion and elephant as well.

Well, OK, I do have a problem with one .375 cartridge, and that's the .376 Steyr. It is an effective, low-recoiling, deep-woods or thornbush cartridge for large plains game, and I suppose it would be fine for lion. But it is not anywhere near as powerful as the .375 H&H. Since it is .375 in caliber, it may be technically legal for dangerous game, depending on how the local laws are written. But the intent of these laws was generally to make the .375 H&H the minimum, and the .376 Steyr doesn't measure up. In my view it should be considered much the same as the 9.3x62. This is not damning with faint praise—but it should also not be considered in the same league as the .375 H&H.

A .375 has not always been my primary arm. On many occasions I have personally carried an open-sighted heavy rifle—but I've asked a tracker to carry a scope-sighted .375 "just in case." Several times, on buffalo, I've traded the heavy rifle for the .375 so I could be absolutely certain of the shot placement I knew I must have. Yes, I've said in print that the .375 is marginal for buffalo. It is, but it's on the right side of the margin. I've hunted buffalo with the .450/.400, .500/.416, .416 Taylor, .416 Rigby, .416 Hoffman, .416 Weatherby, .458 Lott, .450-3¼", .450 Ackley, .458 Winchester Magnum, .460 Weatherby, .470 Nitro Express, and .500 Nitro Express—but I've shot more buffalo with .375s than with all the others combined.

And yes, I've said in print that the .375 is only marginally flat-shooting enough for open-country hunting. But I have a big Kafue lechwe that I shot at well over four hundred yards with a .375 H&H. If you choose your loads well and understand them, the .375 H&H shoots plenty flat enough for most hunting in the world, and especially flat enough for most African hunting. But if you need that little bit more confidence that a flatter trajectory offers, there are faster and flatter-shooting .375 cartridges available.

The .375 is believed to have been a British development. Maybe, but only in retaliation to Continental gunmakers. The inspiration for the .375 H&H can probably be found in the 9.5mm Mannlicher-Schoenauer, called in Britain the .375 Nitro Express Rimless. Chambered in light, inexpensive Mannlicher rifles, it wasn't much more powerful than the 9x57, but in the years before 1910 it was growing too popular for the British gun trade's peace of mind. Holland & Holland countered with the .400/.375, or .375 Velopex. Almost identical in power to the 9.5, the .400/.375 was probably the first belted cartridge.

The .400/.375, besides being anemic, apparently also suffered from bad bullets. It didn't make the grade. Its successor, introduced in 1912, is still going strong. The .375 Belted Rimless Nitro Express was first introduced with 235-, 270-, and 300-grain bullets. Initial loadings are listed with the light bullet at 2,800 FPS; the 270-grain slug at 2,650; and the 300-grainer at 2,500. The .375 Flanged Magnum Nitro Express, its rimmed counterpart for doubles and single shots, was loaded slightly slower to keep the pressures down. Ballistics for this version were quoted as 2,600 FPS for a 270-grain bullet and 2,400 FPS for a 300-grain bullet. This was actually a very flat-shooting load for a double rifle, and it remains a good choice today—except that no double can be regulated for two different bullet weights at the same time!

The .375 H&H has long been blessed with great factory loads for any occasion. Left to right: Hornady's fast, aerodynamic 270-grain Spire Point; Federal's 300-grain TBBC; and Hornady's new DGS.

I used a 300-grain solid from the Kimber Caprivi to take this steenbok in northern Namibia. For both the smallest and largest game, the 300-grain solids are marvelous.

In those pre-World War I days, it would be an overstatement to call anything an overnight success, but successful the .375 Holland & Holland was, and it became so very quickly for its day. Then, as now, the wonderful thing about the .375 was that it seemed to be effective far beyond its bullet weight, energy, and recoil. Even John Taylor, who created his own "Knock-Out" values to quantify the hitting power of a rifle, wrote regarding the .375 that his "Knock-Out value of 40 points . . . does not really do full justice to it."

Ivory hunter Pete Pearson started his career as a staunch .577 fan but eventually switched to the .375 and never went back. Harry Manners, another of the all-time great elephant hunters, swore by his over-the-counter Winchester Model 70 .375. And, of course, the number of professional hunters who to this day rely on the .375 as their backup rifle is overwhelming.

Some cartridges, quite possibly through accident, achieve a happy, near-perfect combination of bullet weight, bullet construction, velocity, and frontal diameter. I suspect the .318 Westley Richards, with very modest ballistics, was such a cartridge. In its class, the .30-30 Winchester is another. Certainly this holds true for the .375.

While many British cartridges remained purely proprietary rounds—and were thus eventually doomed when the I.C.L. conglomerate discontinued Kynoch ammunition—the .375 Belted Rimless Nitro Express was eventually released to the gun trade, and many rifles of many makes were manufactured. As far as I can tell, this was not as true of the .375 Flanged Magnum; I have personally seen few older rifles that weren't made

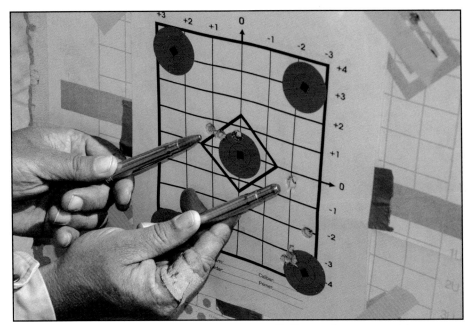

Legend has it that the .375 H&H will "always" put a variety of bullets into the same group. This is not true, so if you're using both solids and softs or any other combination, always check to make sure.

by Holland, while its closest competitors in doubles, the .400/.350 on one side and the .450/.400 on the other, were made by nearly everyone. This, of course, holds no water today. Anybody making doubles can make them to any desired cartridge, needing only appropriately rifled barrels and a reamer. Still, very few new doubles have been made for the .375 Flanged Magnum, and I'm darned if I understand why that is so.

The .375 crossed the Atlantic to America quite early, and by the mid-1920s Western was loading ammunition. The first factory American rifle so chambered was the new Winchester Model 70, introduced in 1936 and offered in .375 in 1937. Prior to that, a number of American custom shops, led by Griffin & Howe of New York, had built custom .375s.

The 235-grain loading dropped by the wayside, while 270- and 300-grain bullets have remained the traditional loads. That 235-grain bullet started very fast, but, lacking in sectional density, it shed its velocity quickly. Still, I suspect it was a useful load for light game, with the advantage of much-reduced recoil. Speer still offers a 235-grain semi-spitzer, a bullet I've used on a fair amount of African game. It was extremely effective for me on animals up to the size of kudu—and that's just what it was meant for. When Jack Carter was alive, he offered a 240-grain Trophy Bonded Bear Claw, and I used that one as well. With my handloads pushed to

A beautiful eland taken in Eden in northern Namibia with a .375 H&H firing 300-grain Trophy Bonded Bear Claw bullets. The .375 is an ultimate compromise caliber, perfect for few animals—but the eland is one animal it is truly perfect for.

2,900 FPS, it was a real screamer, and with that wonderful bonded-core construction, it performed extremely well on game up to kudu and elk. Barnes also makes light .375 bullets in its homogeneous alloy Triple-Shock X-Bullet. That bullet changes the rules, and you just don't need as much weight as we once thought mandatory. Nosler offers 260-grain .375 bullets, another fine choice for lighter game.

Even so, the mainstays for the .375 remain the traditional 270- and 300-grainers. Of these, I have always preferred a 300-grain bullet. There are some good 270-grain bullets around—Hornady's 270-grain Spire Point and Winchester's Power Point, to name just two. However, the standard .375 solid is 300 grains, and it always made more sense to me to have both bullets the same weight.

There's a myth that the .375 will print all its bullet weights to the same place at 100 yards, and it's a myth perpetuated by the best of writers. The occasional rifle will do so, it's true—but most won't. Mine won't. Don't count on this until you've checked it out!

The primary advantage to the 300-grain bullet is its greater sectional density, which means greater penetration on game—and just as importantly, given equally aerodynamic shapes, better long-range ballistics. The 270-grain slug may start faster, but a 300-grain bullet, if also of spitzer design, will be going faster at 250 yards and will drop less as well as carry more energy. Note: This is not meant to imply that the

270-grain bullet is inadequate. Last year, in Mozambique, I saw several buffalo well and truly flattened with the first run of Hornady's .375 Ruger ammo loaded with plain old 270-grain InterLock Spire Points. That is not an "extra-tough" bullet, but apparently it was tough enough. I have also seen dramatic one-shot kills with other 270-grain bullets, including Barnes X-Bullet and Winchester Fail Safe (which one might expect to perform wonderfully) and Winchester Power Point (which, in theory, was not designed with buffalo in mind).

The .375, with its long history, has a wealth of wonderful bullets available. And today more factory loads exist for the .375 H&H than ever before. The handloader has even more available, with Swift A-Frame, Nosler Partition, Woodleigh Weldcore, and more. One advantage to the .375 H&H is its universality, with plenty of factory loads and nearly a century of handload recipes. There are also some extra-heavy bullets of 350 and even 370 grains. I went through a phase in the 1980s when I had, through my own fault, a lack of confidence in the .375. I tried 350-grain bullets. They work just fine, but today I personally have no use for them. Standard 300-grain bullets penetrate adequately, and the heavier bullets are too slow, thus robbing the .375 of its primary attribute, which is versatility. Also, in my experience, point of impact with the extra heavyweights is radically different, so it isn't practical to use both.

If the .375 H&H has a disadvantage, it's that it requires a full-length action; it will not fit into a .30-06-length action. Wildcatters recognized that long ago, and there have been a number of wildcats based on the .300, .338, and .458 Winchester Magnums necked up or down to .375. Most of these cartridges will duplicate .375 H&H performance in a short action—but none has come particularly close to appearing in factory form. The .376 Steyr was, I suppose, an effort to house the .375 in a shorter action. Unfortunately, its smaller case cannot come close to

Left, .375 H&H; right, .375 Ruger. I actually like the new .375 Ruger just as much as the great old .375 H&H, which is saying quite a lot. It is a wee bit faster but, perhaps more important, it achieves velocity in a shorter barrel and can be housed in a shorter, handier action.

The .375 with a good 300-grain solid is definitely adequate for elephant, though perhaps not ideal. I used a 300-grain Sledgehammer solid to take this "problem elephant" in northern Namibia.

.375 H&H performance, and it was a stunning flop as a commercial cartridge. The .375 Ruger is altogether different. A joint development by Hornady and Ruger, the .375 Ruger surprised a whole lot of us, me included. Instead of using any existing case, the engineers created a new unbelted case by taking the .532-inch rim and belt diameter of the belted case and going straight forward, without a belt. The result is a .30-06-length case that can easily be adapted to any belted magnum bolt face or magazine box.

The intent behind the design was to develop a case that would fit into a .30-06-length action and yet produce about the same velocity as the .375 H&H. The engineers didn't figure in the added efficiency from a shorter, fatter, straighter case, so the bonus came as a surprise. The .375 Ruger develops a solid 100 to 150 FPS more velocity than the .375 H&H with any bullet weight. So it offers a shorter case that can be housed in a cheaper, lighter action, plus a bonus in flatter trajectory and greater downrange energy. Not a bad deal.

As I said, we used some of the prototype .375 Rugers in Mozambique in 2006, and a couple weeks ago I shot a nice old *dagga* bull with the first left-hand version. I like the cartridge, and I like the new version of the Ruger M77 that houses it. I especially like the fact that it will be available in left-hand without a premium. All said, it still isn't a perfect world. Factory loads for the .375 Ruger will always be more limited than for the H&H, and I don't know that any cartridge on Earth will ever have the name recognition or panache of the .375 H&H.

Another complaint about the .375 H&H is that the cartridge is inefficient; if all that body taper were removed and the shoulder changed, significant improvements

A nice Zambezi Valley dagga bull, taken in 2007 with the .375 Ruger. The last couple of seasons I hav

used the .375 Ruger a great deal, with wonderful results.

Left to right: .375 H&H, .375 Ruger, .375 Weatherby Magnum, .375 Remington Ultra Mag, .378 Weatherby Magnum. I have used most of the various .375 cartridges, and all have performed very well. The faster .375s hit extremely hard, but recoil goes up sharply as you increase velocity.

in velocity could be achieved. That's quite true. The .375 Improved was a very popular wildcat fifty years ago, and it did indeed improve the velocities of the .375. So did Roy Weatherby's .375 Weatherby Magnum, very similar to the Improved but with Weatherby's distinctive double-Venturi shoulder.

An uncle of mine, Art Popham, has had a .375 Improved since the early 1950s, and he swears by it. He took it to Tanganyika in 1956, where it accounted for buffalo, lion, and elephant, no problems. Gunwriter Jon Sundra has a .375 JRS, essentially a .375 Improved but based on the 8mm Remington Magnum case. Art Alphin's A-Square Company brought back the .375 Weatherby in both rifles and factory-loaded ammo, and in 1999, after a forty-year lapse, Weatherby reintroduced the .375 Weatherby Magnum.

I actually have two .375 Weatherby rifles, an A-Square and a Weatherby Mark V. With a 300-grain bullet, 2,750 FPS is a breeze, and 2,800 is touchy but possible. This is a significant velocity advantage over the H&H, but it's only fair to compare apples with apples. My regular handload for the standard .375 H&H chronographs an honest 2,600 FPS with a 300-grain bullet. For open country, I use the most aerodynamic of the .375s, the 300-grain Sierra boattail or the Hornady 300-grain Spire Point boattail. The computer indicates that when it's sighted 2.14 inches high at 100 yards, it's dead-on at 200 yards and 8.67 inches low at 300 yards. Supposing I could get my .375 Weatherby up to 2,800 FPS with the same bullet (I can, but it's not easy, and not for warm weather!), the computer tells me I should sight 1.73 inches high at 100 yards to achieve that 200-yard zero—and I'd be just 7.32 inches low at 300 yards. Is a 1.35-inch difference at 300 yards worth all the fuss? Not really.

Remington's Art Wheaton with a fine Selous Reserve buffalo taken in 2000 with the then-new .375 Remington Ultra Mag. We used 300-grain Swift A-Frames, and performance was wonderful.

Energy differences are more significant—4,300 to 4,500 foot-pounds for the .375 H&H, depending on the load, versus well over 5,000 to as much as 5,500 for the faster .375s. To my thinking this is a better reason to consider the fast .375s. As I said, I've used most of 'em. The .375 Remington Ultra Magnum will also provide an honest 2,800 FPS with a 300-grain bullet. In recent years I've shot a lot more buffalo with a .375, but I've also shot buffalo with the fast .375s. Honest, there is a difference. The great old .375 H&H kills buffalo plenty dead, but add something close to a thousand foot-pounds of energy and you can actually see the difference. Given equally good shot placement with good bullets, the fast .375s seem to hit more like a .416, and indeed have the same energy as the .416 Rigby and .416 Remington Magnum.

That said, please understand that the .375 H&H has proven itself for almost a hundred years. It has enough energy as it sits. And yet I have not one but two .375 Weatherbys, and I rather like them. And now I have a .375 Ruger, and I like it, too. The extra velocity does make a difference, but you really don't need it. Pretty much the same thing goes for the biggest .375 of all, the .378 Weatherby. With careful handloading, you can get its 300-grain bullet clear to 2,900 FPS, about the level reached by Weatherby's factory loads. Friends of mine swear by the .378—while others curse it. I have never hunted with it, so I can't draw a conclusion, but I will make some observations. First, when you get to 2,900 FPS with a 300-grain bullet, you're starting to pay a vicious price in recoil. Come to think of it, anytime you increase velocity you will increase energy

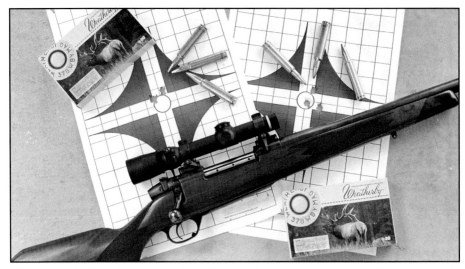

The mighty .378 Weatherby Magnum is incredibly hard-hitting and flat shooting, and this rifle was superbly accurate. Today's tougher bullets will hold up under the extreme velocity, but the recoil is ferocious.

exponentially, but you will increase recoil at the same rate. The .375 Ruger kicks more than the .375 H&H, and the .375 Weatherby and .375 RUM kick more than the .375 Ruger. The mighty .378 Weatherby Magnum kicks the most of all and, because of its velocity, may be one of the hardest-kicking rifles on this planet.

Some people can take it and some can't. However, the .378 Weatherby has a longstanding bad rap because of bullet blowup. I'm sure this was true in 1960, when all .375 bullets were designed for .375 H&H velocities, and I'm sure it's still true with many bullets. Today, however, there are plenty of extra-tough bullets that will hold up at .378 Weatherby Magnum velocities. If you can hold up under the recoil, this cartridge is suitable for any dinosaur that walks.

Since dinosaurs are fairly scarce out there, what are a .375's normal chores? Just about anything, at anytime. The .375 will not reach out over the short-grass plains like a smaller-caliber, higher-velocity cartridge will—but it will do the job in a pinch, albeit with a good deal more punch than is needed on the smaller African antelopes. It will also drop buffalo and even elephant with deadly efficiency, given reasonable shot placement. It will not do this as effectively as something over .40-caliber, but it will do it. On the upper and lower ends of the African game spectrum—impala, reedbuck, bushbuck, etc., on one end, and buffalo, rhino, and elephant on the other—it's the ultimate compromise caliber.

For the largest of plains game—eland, bongo, and tough smaller animals such as gemsbok, sable, and roan—it's an ideal cartridge. And its real forte is lion. An unwounded lion may be taken most readily with a .30-06, 7x57, even a .270. A wounded lion may not be stopped by a big double. Taking the average of all circumstances, the .375 remains the perfect lion gun, and for that matter it's just as perfect for brown, grizzly, and polar bear.

The beauty about the .375 is that you never know exactly what you might run into next in Africa, and with that .375 you are ready, if not exactly perfectly armed, for anything. With a big double, you're ready for a charging buffalo, but are you ready for the 65-inch kudu that appears across a wide ravine? With a scope-sighted 7mm, you're quite ready for that kudu, but are you ready for the buffalo that waits around the next bend, the same buffalo a poacher wounded the day before? With a .375, you're just fine.

Over the years I've shot a tremendous amount of game with a .375. Obvious animals like eland, kudu, elk, bear, moose, and lion . . . and not so obvious ones like tiny grysbok. No matter what pops up, you can handle it with a .375. Some opportunities have come at long range, and I never found a .375 wanting. I mentioned the lechwe I shot at extreme range. Last year I used a .375 Ruger on a big waterbuck in open flood-plain country, and the year before that I made the most difficult shot I can remember. The rifle was my old .375 H&H, the bullet that same 270-grain Hornady that put paid to the waterbuck. The distance was only seventy or eighty yards, but the animal was a huge crocodile, and I had to hit the walnut-size brain. The .375 can do these things—and stop a charging elephant as well.

The .375 is not a true heavy rifle, not by any means. Nor is it a light rifle. Taylor differentiated between the "large bores" and the "large medium bores," making the separation at, I believe, .450. Clearly the .375 falls far short, and thank God for that! The .375 is the ultimate medium, fully able to stand in for the heavy—not just in a pinch, as the .33s to .35s can, but with deadly efficiency. Yet it's flat-shooting, accurate, deserves the benefit of a good scope sight, and the man who knows how to use it gives up nothing to any high-velocity light rifle.

On many occasions in the African bush, I have carried a heavy rifle and wished for something with more accuracy or more reach. On several occasions I've carried a light rifle in search of smaller game and wished for the weight of a double in my hands. I've never carried a .375 and switched it for something else, at least not for the first shot—nor have I ever wanted to. In its original form, or in one of its more compact or faster versions, since 1912 it's been *the* medium bore, one of the most useful of all African calibers.

The .416 Revolution

Chapter 7

I suppose I saw it coming in the late 1980s, but in those days it was unclear just how far it would go. Would the spate of factory .416s that appeared in 1988–89 be a passing fancy, or would they have real impact on the African scene? Obviously the .416s are here to stay, and this bullet diameter has achieved almost complete domination in that huge gap between the classic medium bore, .375, and the true big bores, which I believe properly to be .450 and upward.

John Taylor called this class of cartridge, above .375 and below .450, the "large medium" bores, and I think that's extremely apt. Historically there weren't very many cartridges in this class. Heck, there are more now than ever! The .416 Rigby was one of them, but just one. It was not the most popular, and it was the only cartridge to use the .416-inch bullet diameter. It wasn't even the first "large medium" designed for bolt-action repeaters. The .404 Jeffery, bullet diameter .423-inch, preceded the .416 Rigby, as did the .425 Westley Richards, bullet diameter .435. It was 1912 when John Rigby introduced his .416 Rigby. Unlike the .404 Jeffery, put out by numerous makers, John Rigby retained his .416 as a proprietary cartridge. Unlike both the .404 and the .425, no colonial game departments adopted the .416. So John Rigby's .416s were to-order custom rifles, and in actual fact relatively few were made—far fewer than .404s and .425s.

Despite its relative scarcity, the .416 Rigby achieved a tremendous reputation— partly because it was a very sound design and a very good cartridge. Its original 410-grain bullet had wonderful sectional density and, for its day, very high velocity at 2,370 FPS. The energy yield was right at 5,000 foot-pounds. Is it a coincidence that this is the same energy developed by John Rigby's .450-3¼" Nitro Express developed for double rifles and single shots in 1898? I doubt it.

Almost a century old today, the .416 Rigby case looks as modern as tomorrow, a fat, unbelted case with minimal body taper and a relatively sharp shoulder. It is

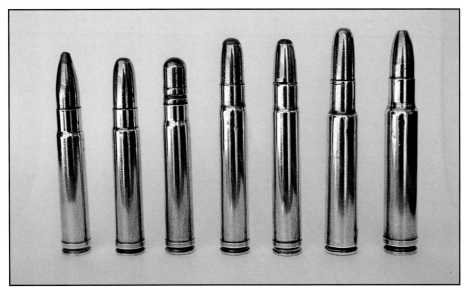

Left to right: .411 KDF, .416 Taylor, .425 Express, .416 Hoffman, .416 Remington Magnum, .416 Rigby, .416 Weatherby Magnum. The four wildcats on the left kept interest in the "lower .40s" alive through the 1980s. Then, in the space of a year, the three at right all became available around 1988.

considerably more powerful than the .404 Jeffery, which was traditionally loaded very mild to keep pressure down and to match the ballistics of the .450/.400 double rifle cartridges. It is not more powerful than the .425 Westley Richards, but its .416 bullets have better sectional density than the .425's .435-inch bullets, and, let's face it, the .425 Westley Richards is a weird-looking cartridge. It was designed to get around Rigby's then-exclusive on magnum Mauser actions, so it has the first rebated rim and a long, tapering neck—sort of the Ichabod Crane of cartridges.

So the .416 Rigby achieved its reputation not by numbers but partly by merit, partly on good looks, and at least partly by sheer luck. It was used, and used well, by some great names who happened to write about their exploits, like George Rushby and Commander David Blunt. Perhaps its greatest stroke of fortune came in the 1940s when a lorry backed over Harry Selby's double rifle. He made a quick run to Kenya Bunduki and purchased a .416 Rigby off the shelf. A few years later Selby's .416 was mentioned in Robert Ruark's *Horn of the Hunter*. In turn, Selby became the real-life model for fictional professional hunter Peter McKenzie in Ruark's blockbuster *Something of Value*—and McKenzie's .416 Rigby was itself almost a character in the novel. Selby's .416 is now owned by American Frank Lyons, and it is my opinion that, absent this rifle and Ruark's writing about it, the .416 Rigby could have been just another obsolete British cartridge.

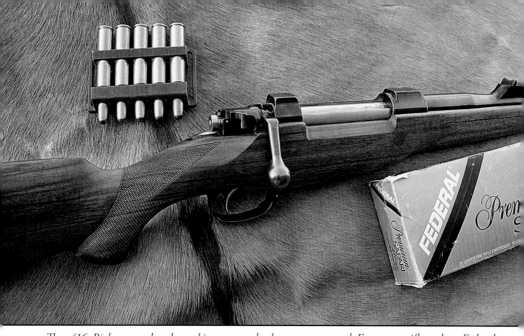

The .416 Rigby was already making a comeback on custom and European rifles when Federal introduced their factory load in 1989.

In the 1960s Kynoch discontinued loading for all the big Nitro Express cartridges, including the .416 Rigby—but by then its fame had far outstripped its actual popularity. The great Jack O'Connor used few heavy rifles, but he owned a .416 Rigby and used it in Africa. It is probably not altogether coincidental that the .460 Weatherby Magnum case is simply the .416 Rigby case with a belt added. Roy Weatherby, of course, vehemently denied that he had pirated Rigby case dimensions, but during the dark period when .416 Rigby brass was unavailable, by sheer happy coincidence it was simple to make .416 Rigby brass by turning the belt off of .460 (or .378) Weatherby brass.

During that dark period, thanks to Weatherby brass the .416 Rigby was actually one of the easiest of the big British cartridges to keep going. Fred Huntington at RCBS made dies, and Barnes made bullets. One of the only drawbacks to the .416 Rigby was (and is) its sheer size. With a case length of 2.9 inches, it's too long and too fat to fit into most bolt actions, requiring a genuine magnum action. These have always been in short supply and very expensive.

Of course, the .416 Rigby was designed for Cordite powder, using a great big case to reduce pressure. With modern propellants the same ballistics—400-grain bullet at roundabout 2,400 FPS—can easily be achieved with a much smaller case. Over the years there have been many wildcat .416s, but two were probably most responsible for keeping the .416 bore alive and sparking the revolution: the .416 Taylor and the .416 Hoffman.

Robert Chatfield-Taylor was an American gunwriter. He achieved some prominence in the 1960s, and had a heart attack not taken him early, he would probably be among the greats in our business. He introduced the .416 Taylor in the pages of *Guns & Ammo*. Based on the .458 Winchester Magnum case necked down to accept a .416 bullet, it will fit into standard .30-06-length actions and yet is fully capable of at least approaching original .416 Rigby ballistics. This makes it a wonderful cartridge, and given that Chatfield-Taylor was writing about it in that euphoric first magnum craze, it's amazing it never made it into factory form. Bill Ruger definitely considered it, as did Winchester. When Chatfield-Taylor died, others took up the flag, including John Wootters. The .416 Taylor never made it into factory form—but it was, and is, a popular wildcat, and through the 1970s and early 1980s it helped keep .416 interest alive. A-Square made ammunition for the .416 Taylor, and today it is readily available from Superior ammo.

American professional hunter George Hoffman created the .416 Hoffman, a .375 H&H case necked up to .416 with most of the body taper removed and a fairly short neck. When the .416 Taylor was in its heyday the .458 Winchester Magnum was under heavy criticism because it had just barely enough powder capacity to achieve full velocity. It was this lack of powder capacity that led Jack Lott to his .458 Lott, Hoffman to his .416. George used it personally in Sudan, Zambia, and Botswana, and swore by it. I lay no personal claim to the .416 revolution; I was still pretty much a junior gunwriter when all this was going on. However, I was certainly in the middle of it. George Hoffman, now departed, was a really good guy. At his insistence I got a .416 Hoffman in about 1985, a fiberglass-stocked "swamp rifle." It was my first .416, and it pushed a 400- or 410-grain bullet at 2,400 FPS. George reported achieving somewhat higher velocities, but in my particular rifle I started to get pressure above that level. It doesn't really matter; 2,400 FPS is plenty. I shot a number of buffalo with that rifle, and also my first elephant, a big Zimbabwe bull. I took him with a side-on brain shot with one of the first Barnes homogeneous-alloy "Super Solids," a 400-grain roundnose. The elephant was down before the rifle came back from recoil; the bullet whistled through the skull in a straight line, and as far as I know it's still going.

A couple of years later I got my first .416 Rigby, a Belgian-made Dumoulin on a big magnum Mauser action. By this time things were starting to happen fast. Jim Bell was making ammo, as was A-Square. Norma was making brass, and the .416 Rigby was clearly back in business. It was long known that Bill Ruger wanted to make a big bolt action that would house the .416 Rigby, and rumor had it Federal was going to load ammo.

Professional hunter Mike Payne and Mike Schoby with a Zambezi Valley buffalo taken with Ruger's big .416 Rigby bolt action.

With no rumors and little fanfare, Remington beat everybody to the punch with its .416 Remington Magnum. The firm did it fast, with efficiency, and with few leaks until it was a reality. The .416 Hoffman was a natural for the company, since its standard Model 700 action would handle the full-length .375 H&H case. Company officials consulted heavily with George Hoffman but chose to use their own 8mm Remington magnum case necked up rather than the .375 H&H case. This effectively killed the .416 Hoffman, but they're virtually identical, differing primarily in neck dimensions. For those left with .416 Hoffman rifles, .416 Remington ammo will fit and can be safely fired in the Hoffman chamber—but not vice versa.

The .416 Remington's ballistics are no great surprise, nominally a 400-grain solid or soft at 2,400 FPS, yielding 5,117 foot-pounds of energy. Initially Remington sourced Swift A-Frame bullets and the Barnes Super Solid, these great bullets definitely helping to jump-start the new cartridge. Some years passed before I had the opportunity to use a .416 Remington Magnum in Africa, but I did have the honor of shooting the very first head of game with a factory .416 Remington firing factory Swift softpoint loads. It wasn't a buffalo, but it was a very fine record-class Alaska-Yukon moose. Of course the big bullet did its job, retaining 97 percent of its weight in the process.

From there things happened very quickly. Within the year Ruger's big Model 77 Mark II action was on the street in .416 Rigby, as was Federal's .416 Rigby ammo. With ammo available, there were more actions and more bullets, and suddenly the .416 was back in business—but the revolution wasn't over. In the late 1980s, the time couldn't have been more ripe for a new Weatherby Magnum. There had been no additions to the line since the .240 Weatherby Magnum was introduced in 1968, and the company's founder, Roy E. Weatherby Senior, had effectively turned over the reins to his son, Roy E. Weatherby Junior (Ed, as he prefers to be called), before he passed away in 1988. Although some thought was given to a 6.5mm Weatherby Magnum, the only major caliber gap in the entire line lay between the .378 and .460 Weatherby Magnums.

The case used by these two cartridges was also ideal, essentially a belted version of the .416 Rigby case. Clear back in the 1950s Roy Weatherby himself had considered necking the .378 up to .416. But in those days there were no readily available American .416 bullets, and the mark he wanted to beat was the .458 Winchester Magnums. So he created the .460 Weatherby instead, and another thirty years passed before the time was right for the .416 Weatherby.

In 1989, the time was right. Good bullets were available from multiple sources, including indestructible Swift softpoints and monolithic solids that could handle Weatherby velocities. And interest in the .416-bore was at an all-time high.

I borrowed Marc Watts's beautiful Rigby double in the Krieghoff-developed .500/.416 to take this buffalo cow. The .500/.416 is almost as fast as the .416 Rigby, and thus just as versatile.

My left-hand Ruger M77 rebarreled to .416 Taylor was the only rifle I took to the Cameroon forest in 2006. I used it to take this yellow-backed duiker at 200 yards, an impossible shot with an open-sighted big bore, but just fine for a scoped .416.

The .416 Weatherby Magnum was announced at the S.H.O.T. Show in January 1989, but it was late spring before the first rifles were available. In fairness, it must be stated that little is new about this hottest of the .416s. It's a belted version of the .416 Rigby, with case capacity virtually identical to the Rigby cartridge. However, right from the factory it's loaded to the absolute upper limit of velocity that even the most courageous handloader would try to wring from a .416 Rigby. The goal was to push a 400-grain bullet at 2,700 FPS, and the first batch of handloaded ammo sent to me by Weatherby's Larry Thompson beat that by some 50 feet per second. That was actually too close to the limit; extraction was sticky and the cases showed signs of excessive pressure. Backed off to 2,700 FPS, the energy figures for the .416 Weatherby are stunning: nearly 6,500 foot-pounds at the muzzle. The price is fierce recoil, over 100 foot-pounds in a 9½-pound rifle, whereas the Rigby and Remington are down in the 60s.

In late May 1989, Ed Weatherby and I took the new .416 to Botswana's Chobe area to try it out on Cape buffalo. The cartridge obviously had the bullet weight, bullet diameter, and energy to be effective on buffalo, but the concern was equally obvious. Would the bullets hold up under such high velocities, fully 300 FPS above the .416 Rigby for which they were designed? We took several buffalo, shooting Swift softpoints, and indeed they did hold up. Recovered bullets were few and far between, but those we found had retained over 95 percent of their original weight, with the classic Swift mushroom.

In 1987 any .416 was a very specialized tool, fed only by handloads or custom ammo. Just two years later we had three factory .416s, all with both rifles and ammo readily available. To keep things simple, the .416 Rigby and .416 Remington are ballistic twins. It is true that the Rigby has much greater case capacity, so with handloads you can wring a lot more velocity from it. On the other hand, with standard loads (400-grain bullet at 2,400 FPS) the Rigby produces considerably less pressure than the .416 Remington.

In recent years I have heard whispers about pressure problems with the .416 Remington. Yes, as just stated, standard .416 Remington ammo is loaded to higher pressure than standard .416 Rigby ammo. This is not a "problem," just a statement of fact. I have tried really hard to ferret out some genuine incidences of pressure problems, meaning sticky extraction or failure to extract with the .416 Remington, and I have been unable to find any documented incidents. Perhaps there are some. Again, starting pressures are higher, so I'd be a bit leery about leaving .416 Remington

My .416 Taylor with 400-grain Hornady bullets accounted for this Mozambique buffalo in 2006. I built the Taylor because I needed a "big gun" on the left-hand Ruger action, which is limited to .30-06-length cartridges.

ammo (or any ammo) to roast in direct sunlight, especially in African heat. But I can honestly say that I have never seen a problem or heard a direct complaint about the .416 Remington, and I have used it in extreme heat, including in the Cameroon forest and the Zambezi Valley.

So, to my thinking, the Rigby case offers the utmost in nostalgia and tradition, while the Remington is the more economical choice—but they are identical. Obviously the .416 Weatherby is much faster, not only producing more energy but shooting considerably flatter—though at a high price in recoil. All three are wonderful for buffalo and plenty adequate for elephant. On the lower end, meaning plains game, the .416s are not as versatile as the .375, but on the upper end, for the really big stuff, they are much more capable.

Missing from the .416 lineup was a rimmed cartridge suitable for double rifles. Krieghoff fixed this with the .500/.416-3¼" Nitro Express, the first "new" Nitro Express cartridge in many a year. It is simply the 3¼" .470 (or .500 basic) case necked down to accept a .416 bullet. It is faster than most double-rifle cartridges, propelling a 400-grain bullet at 2,350 FPS, and thus only slightly slower than the .416 Rigby. I used it in Australia in a Krieghoff double, and I also used a borrowed Rigby .500/.416

Terry Moore and PH Ian Gibson with a big Zambezi hippo taken with Moore's .416 Rigby built by Rifles, Inc. Today big actions that will house the .416 Rigby are relatively common, with many custom makers building them.

PH Ivan Carter congratulates Jim Hall on his tuskless elephant, taken with a frontal brain shot from a distance of five yards with his A-Square-built .416 Remington. With higher velocity and less resistance (frontal area), the .416s actually penetrate better than most big bores.

on a Cape buffalo hunt. No buffalo (or elephant) that walks will ever notice the lack of fifty feet per second. On the other hand, what really surprised me about the .500/.416 is that recoil is about the same as a .470. Five thousand foot-pounds are five thousand foot-pounds, and recoil is an equal and opposite reaction. Duh. So the .500/.416 offers more versatility than the big bores, and about the same level of versatility as a bolt-action .416, but it is not the lower-recoil option that I'd expected, or, I suspect, that many buyers expect when they choose it.

In addition to the factory cartridges and wildcats, there are also several proprietary .416s, including the .416 Dakota Magnum (based on the .404 Jeffery case, which is slightly smaller than the .416 Rigby case) and a big Lazzeroni .416. As is the case with all Lazzeroni cartridges, the brass is made extra-heavy to John Lazzeroni's specifications, and he loads it to the gills. Lazzeroni cartridges will always be the fastest in their class, in this case his .416 Meteor actually exceeding the .416 Weatherby Magnum.

The .416-bore is extremely popular today, and there is no doubt in my mind that it has cut into both the .375 market and the big-bore market. I tend to believe we have about all the .416 cartridges we really need, but these things aren't up to me. I sort of expected Remington to neck its Ultra Magnum case up to .416, but it has not. Come to think of it, since the .416 Remington Magnum is the company's, why would they want to kill it? Now I sort of expect Ruger and Hornady to neck their .375 Ruger case up to .416, which would create a .416 cartridge with .416 Rigby/Remington capabilities but sized to fit a .30-06-length action.

That would actually suit me just fine. Sometimes I find myself going full circle. I was among the first to write about the .416 Hoffman, I was an early (pre-Federal) user of a .416 Rigby, and I was the first to write about both the .416 Remington and .416 Weatherby. These days it's no secret that Ruger is a sponsor of the *Tracks Across Africa* TV show that I host—but Ruger's big bolt action is right-hand only and I'm disastrously left-handed. So, without knowing about the .375 Ruger project, I had gunsmith Don Golembieski rebarrel a left-hand Model 77 in .300 Winchester Magnum to the nearly forgotten .416 Taylor. It shoots wonderfully and feeds like a dream, and it convinced me that despite our multiple .416 offerings, there just might be room for a .30-06-length .416. My guess is the .416 Taylor is a dead issue. The public has spoken: Belted cartridges are "out" and unbelted cartridges are "in." But that's OK. For now my little .416 Taylor is just wonderful (and Bob Chatfield-Taylor and John Wootters were right about it all along). But if my guess is right and the .375 Ruger case is necked up to .416 as a factory round, it will be a very simple matter to clean out that chamber with a reamer.

Other Lower .40s

Chapter 8

At the time I completed *Safari Rifles* the .416 revolution was well under way, but it was hardly clear exactly where it was going. There was definitely a market for viable cartridges somewhere between .375 and the true big bores over .45 in caliber, but it was impossible to predict how large this market would actually become or which cartridges would be winners and which would be losers. I think the demand for the large mediums came about partly because in the Africa of the 1980s there was still a lot of buffalo hunting, but the world of elephant hunting was shrinking very quickly. As I have said, and will say again, any of the .375s from .375 H&H on up are absolutely adequate for buffalo and offer tremendous versatility for a wide range of plains game. Although over the years I have gathered that this is a confusing concept, the large mediums, between .375 and .450, are "more adequate" for buffalo but somewhat less versatile for plains game.

Let me try to explain this seeming contradiction. A buffalo properly hit with a good, modern bullet from a .375 will certainly die, and almost as certainly will die before it can wreak havoc on its tormenters, at least if due caution is used in the approach. However, I believe very strongly that a buffalo equally well hit with an "over .40" loaded with a modern bullet of equal construction will succumb more quickly than is the norm with a .375. Dead is dead, but the large mediums give more dramatic results and quicker gratification than a .375 if shot placement is similarly ideal. If shot placement is poor, I am not prepared to say that anything short of an anti-tank round will prevent an extremely long day, although I do believe that with animals as big and as strong as buffalo, the bigger the gun the more likely eventual recovery.

Against this you have the simple fact that the large mediums in general tend to have more recoil than the .375s and also tend to have a more arcing trajectory. There are exceptions, of course. Few cartridges kick as hard or as fast as the .378 Weatherby Magnum, and certainly some of the slower large mediums, like the old .404 Jeffery (as originally loaded) offer less recoil than any of the fast .375s.

This is a John Wilkes .450/.400-3¼". Both the 3" and 3¼" versions were quite common, both made by numerous makers. To my thinking the .450/.400s are just perfect for buffalo—and minimally adequate for elephant.

But absent extreme velocity, the versatility on plains game is reduced, and of course recoil is always mitigated by gun weight and stock fit.

Regardless of rationale, through the 1980s it seemed to me that interest in large mediums continued to increase. At that time several viable candidates were out there. These included the various .416s covered in the previous chapter, but at least until 1988, "The Year of the .416," it wasn't at all clear that .416 would be the winning caliber. My old friend Cameron Hopkins and his buddy, gunwriter Whit Collins, developed the wildcat .425 Express and proposed it as the ideal large medium. Their cartridge used a 400-grain .423-inch bullet at 2,400 FPS. This is the bullet diameter of the older, larger-cased, but slower .404 Jeffery. Obviously this cartridge was the ballistic equal of the .416 Taylor and/or .416 Hoffman. I remember a lively discussion with Cameron in that era, he espousing the "larger frontal area" of the .423-inch bullet while I argued for the greater sectional density of the 400-grain .416-inch bullet. Obviously this was a silly discussion, as the bore diameters are too close to matter much.

In any case, the .425 Express got some play and was offered for a brief time in the Savage 110. The original .404 Jeffery was a candidate in those days, and it remains viable today. With a case length of 2.87 inches and case diameter of .544, it can be crammed into more modern actions than the longer and thicker .416 Rigby (length 2.90 inches, diameter fully .589-inch). The .404 Jeffery was actually announced as a chambering for the big Ruger Model 77 Express rifle at the same time the .416 Rigby was announced, but to my knowledge no rifles were actually manufactured. More about this cartridge later.

In those days Phil Koehne's KDF firm (Kleinguenther Distinctive Firearms) was a significant player, and his large medium was the .411 KDF, also the .458 Winchester Magnum case necked down to accept a—you guessed it—400-grain bullet at 2,400 FPS. I guess one could extend the argument farther and project that, velocity and bullet performance being equal, a 400-grain .411 bullet would penetrate better than either a 400-grain .416 or a 400-grain .423 . . . but that, in ascending order, the increased frontal area of the larger calibers would transfer more energy and leave a larger wound channel. Again, in this caliber range the difference isn't enough to argue about. The .411 was (and is, if you happen to have one) a good cartridge. I used it in the 1980s, and it offered wonderful penetration. However, like the .425 Express, it lost the war to the various .416s.

There are, however, some other non-.416 "large mediums" that seem to have current following and future promise. Interestingly, both historically and currently these cartridges seem to start at .400. I've always found it fascinating that in Europe, America, and England, almost no smokeless cartridges have ever existed that use bullets between .375 and .400. This is virtually the only .025-inch gap in the entire world of sporting cartridges between .17 and .500. Perhaps it's because the .375 H&H came so early and was so good. Or perhaps it's because the next number up from the .375, which preceded it by a good fifteen years, was also so good. This was the .450/.400.

The .450/.400-3¼" Nitro Express was based on a black-powder .450 case necked down to take a nominally .40-caliber bullet. In the early years of smokeless powder there were quite a few incidences of sticky cases, generally caused not exactly by pressure but by brass designed for lower pressure. In 1902 W. J. Jeffery designed its own version of the .450/.400 using a heavier case with a thicker rim, shortened by a quarter-inch. This cartridge, the .450/.400-3", also known as the .400 Jeffery, was the first large-caliber cartridge specifically designed for smokeless powder. Both versions were popular, and together they emerged as a classic "all-round" cartridge for the day.

The two case lengths are not interchangeable but offer identical ballistics: 400-grain bullet of excellent sectional density at between 2,100 and 2,150 feet per second, giving penetration unequaled by many heavier calibers. The .450/.400

remained popular until the end of Britain's colonial era, but as effective as it was, it had a problem: Its long, rimmed case was best suited for use in double rifles and single shots. However, it was chambered in a few early bolt actions, using a slanted magazine so that the rims wouldn't catch. A Canadian guide I hunted with in 1973 had a turn-of-the-century .450/.400 bolt action, a strange-looking affair. I'd give anything to have recorded the make and taken some photos of that odd duck. I could have, but at that time it didn't seem important.

Such rifles must have been uncommon, and are virtually forgotten today; like the other big rimmed Nitro Express cartridges, the .450/.400 was an ill fit in a bolt action. It is, however, an extremely useful cartridge for double rifles and single shots. Pondoro Taylor, a staunch big-bore (and double-rifle) man, wrote that the .450/.400 delivered the greatest penetration of any of the big Nitro Express cartridges. Karamojo Bell, an equally staunch smallbore and bolt-action man, actually used a .400 Jeffery double on his final safari after World War I. To my thinking the .450/.400 remains extremely useful today. Delivering about 4,000 foot-pounds of energy, it might be considered a bit on the light side for elephant (though better than any .375), but it is perfect, perfect, perfect for buffalo, and has the tremendous advantage of much lighter recoil than the true big bores.

The two .450/.400s together, though not interchangeable, were almost certainly the most popular double-rifle cartridges. For many years .450/.400 doubles were considered "less desirable" than the plus-.450s, and prices were very reasonable. This isn't true today; as supplies of good British doubles have dwindled, prices have skyrocketed for all calibers. However, I have long thought that the .450/.400, with its light recoil and great penetration, deserved more than the dustbin of cartridge history. It is a perfect fit for the Ruger No. 1 Single Shot, and in 2006 Ruger

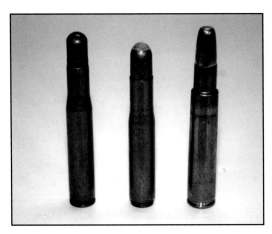

Left to right: .404 Jeffery, .425 Westley Richards, .416 Rigby. Truthfully, both the .404 and .425 were far more common than the .416 Rigby, but for some reason never achieved the charisma. The .404 still has some following, but the .425 has become a rare bird.

announced a run of its lovely "Tropical" No. 1s in .450/.400-3", with Hornady loading new ammo in 400-grain solids and softs.

I will freely admit that I had a bit of influence on this project. Two decisions were required, one seemingly easy and the second very difficult. The first, obviously, was which version of the .450/.400 to resurrect. The .450/.400-3" Nitro Express, or .400 Jeffery, was chosen. To me this seemed obvious, but colleague Ross Seyfried bitterly attacked Steve Hornady for choosing the shorter instead of the longer case length. Ross is definitely one of the top authorities on latter nineteenth-century and early twentieth-century British firearms, and he believes that the 3¼" version was overwhelmingly more popular than Jeffery's 3" case. Honestly, most of the guys in my business get along well, but Ross' long-standing problem with me is such that if I said the sky was blue on a clear day, he would be compelled to disagree just because I said it. However, I think he really believes the 3" version was the wrong choice. I don't agree.

I think the two were pretty close in numbers of guns produced, and I have personally encountered far more 3" guns than the older, longer version. Jeffery made many, mostly for the Indian trade, but so did a lot of other makers. I had a Thomas Turner .450/.400-3", and my friend Mike Box had a lovely Jeffery in the 3" case that I had my eyes on. Unfortunately I let it slip away. And so it goes. However, a choice between the two needed to be made. It seemed unlikely that there were enough old guns in use to be worth Hornady's trouble, so newly manufactured rifles must support the choice. The 3" version was the best choice because, with modern powders, the longer case isn't necessary, and the shorter case achieves much better load density. (Having already done most of the manufacturing effort, it now seems likely Hornady will also offer the .450/.400-3¼", which would then make everybody happy.)

The second decision was more difficult: What bullet diameter? Unlike many of the Nitro Express cartridges, many manufacturers made the .450/.400s, and there is considerable variance in bore diameter. Some run as tight as .408, while a few are as loose as .412. I could be wrong, but it has long been my opinion that .410-.411 was most common, so when I proposed the project, it was my hope that the .411 bullet of the .405 Winchester, which Hornady was already making, would work. This proved too risky. A thousandth or so oversize probably doesn't matter, especially with a "compressible" lead-core bullet at the .450/.400's modest pressure and velocity. However, you don't want to overdo it, especially in older guns that often had thin barrel walls. So Hornady settled on a .410-inch bullet diameter, which was both a consensus and a compromise.

A few modern doubles have been made in .450/.400-3", and all that Hornady could find had been barreled to .409 or .410. Unless otherwise specified, Larry Barnett of Superior Ammunition always loads .409-inch bullets in .450/.400 ammo. So .410 seemed the best compromise, and it would work OK through a .409-inch barrel without too much pressure. It also seems to upset well enough into .411-inch barrels to provide acceptable accuracy . . . and nobody I've talked to has yet found a .412-inch barrel to try.

Steve Hornady shared the first Ruger .450/.400-3" with Donna and me in Zimbabwe in 2006. Accuracy was superb, recoil wonderfully mild, and performance absolutely awesome. Steve shot a big hippo and we took several buffalo, all with no problem whatsoever. Unfortunately, Ruger was a bit behind the power curve in getting the rifles to the market. The first production rifles were delivered in June 2007, while Hornady had the ammo on the market at the first of the year. There must be a few more vintage and custom .450/.400-3" rifles than we suspected, because in the first few months Hornady sold 100,000 cartridges—without any new rifles on the market. It is my understanding that most of the makers of new double rifles will be chambering for this cartridge and regulating with Hornady ammo, so I think the .450/.400 will make the comeback it deserves. As far as older rifles go, well, no double rifles made before 2006 were regulated with the Hornady ammo. It is intended to match the original Kynoch specifications, but it's still a slightly different load. This means it will regulate well in some doubles and poorly in some others—and probably reasonably acceptably in most.

The Mauser and Mannlicher sporters—dependable, accurate, offering repeat firepower, and available at a fraction of the cost of a double—were selling like

On the left is an original .405 Winchester cartridge, Teddy Roosevelt's "lion medicine." Center is Hornady's new 300-grain factory load, and on the right, also from Hornady, a heavy load they cooked up for the Ruger No. 1 with a 400-grain bullet at 2,150 feet per second.

Brittany used 400-grain solids in the Ruger No. 1 in .405 Winchester to take this excellent old buffalo on the Lemco concession in southern Zimbabwe.

hotcakes among British sportsmen in the first years of this century. Light rifles such as the 6.5x53R Mannlicher-Schoenauer and the 7x57, delivering unprecedented penetration with their very long bullets, were the darlings of the smallbore crowd. The 8mms, 9mms, 9.3s, and 9.5s filled the medium niche. Clearly the British gun trade had to respond, and a logical avenue was with magazine rifles that approximated the ballistics of the .450/.400.

The redoubtable .450/.400 originated as a black-powder cartridge. This round, its black-powder cousins, and the straight-case, much more obscure .400 Purdey were virtually alone in the British field of cartridges between .375 and .450. Surprisingly, the Americans had a great many black-powder and early smokeless cartridges in this caliber range. *Cartridges of the World* lists some forty American black-powder cartridges in the upper .30s and lower .40s. Many of these were Sharps, Maynard, and Remington cartridges for single-shot rifles, and Winchester and Marlin rounds for lever actions. A few of the black-powder cartridges survived into the smokeless era, if briefly, and a couple are now seen in Cowboy Action Shooting, but only one had any impact in Africa.

This lone American was, of course, the .405 Winchester, Teddy Roosevelt's "lion medicine," developed for Winchester's Model 1895 lever action. The rifle

In the heavy-barreled Ruger No. 1, recoil from the .450/.400-3" is wonderfully mild. Accuracy was superb, and performance on game spectacular.

itself was nearly ten years old when the cartridge made its appearance. It fired a 300-grain bullet that was a bit light for its caliber, but it produced 2,200 FPS velocity for well over 3,000 foot-pounds of muzzle energy. Roosevelt found it marvelously effective on game up to lion, but lacking penetration on heavier game. Old Charles Cottar, the first American professional hunter, used the .405 extensively throughout his long career—and he was killed when his .405 failed to stop a black rhino. The rifle was a heavy kicker and was considered needlessly powerful for American game; thus the .405 chambering was never a big seller, and it died with the Model 1895 during the Depression.

Browning brought back an exact copy of the '95, initially in .30-40, and then came a run in .405. I was interested in Theodore Roosevelt's lion medicine, but I never got around to taking one to Africa. A few people did, including Larry Potterfield of Midway U.S.A. Using Woodleigh bullets, which are far better than the bullets available to Roosevelt and Cottar, Potterfield had no problem taking Cape buffalo as well as lion with his '95.

Even so, the problem remains: The .405 Winchester cartridge with its original 300-grain bullet "maxes out" the 1895 action, and it is very difficult to load heavier bullets without intruding into the powder space. Which is why the .405 Winchester was originally loaded with the short, light-for-caliber 300-grain bullet. In 2003 Ruger added .405 Winchester to its chamberings for the No. 1 single shot. The company sent me one as a test rifle, sort of out of the blue, and I honestly didn't have a clue what to do with it. I should have returned it, but I hadn't gotten around to it. And then my daughter, Brittany, suddenly became interested in hunting (at the advanced age of seventeen, after a considerable stint as an anti!). She shoots well but hates recoil, so I needed a low-recoil option that had a punch. Suddenly I spied the Ruger in .405. We took it to Australia in 2004, and after experimenting a whole bunch on wild hogs with Hornady's 300-grain loads, we each took a water buffalo with no problems.

Penetration was such that, with careful shot placement, I would have no qualms about using these bullets on Cape buffalo. By caliber they would be legal in most African countries, but Zimbabwe actually has an energy requirement. Expressed in kilojoules, which no Americans understand, the minimum is about 4,000 foot-pounds at the muzzle. Fortunately, the Ruger No. 1 action has neither strength nor cartridge-length limitations, so I asked the Hornady boys to put together some "Brittany Boddington" 400-grain loads, essentially duplicating the .450/.400's 2,150 FPS and 4,000 foot-pounds of energy. We have taken buffalo and a bunch of other stuff with this load, and it works wonderfully. With solids it would be a good minimalist choice for elephant, and since Brittany thinks it's magic, I assume that is what she will use if she ever hunts elephant. However, now that the .450/.400 is available, there isn't as much utility in heavy loads for the .405—except that the standard 300-grain loads are wonderful for lighter game and practice, and offer very little recoil in the heavy-barreled Ruger.

The Europeans also had a few entries into the lower .40s-caliber spectrum, in both black-powder and smokeless form. The 10.75x57 was the largest variant of the 7x57 case, using a .424-inch bullet at understandably low velocity from so small a case. A bit better was the 1910-vintage 10.75x63 Mauser, which suffered more from a light-for-caliber bullet than from lack of power. Both undoubtedly saw use in the German colonies before World War I. Later developments were the 10.75x68 Mauser and the big 11.2x72 Schuler (using a .440-inch bullet). These cartridges did have an impact in Africa, but the lasting glory was to go to the British cartridges, at least up until today.

The British gunmakers had a problem: fitting enough cordite to generate the desired power into a case that would fit the available bolt actions. Until around 1910, John Rigby was Mauser's British distributor, and no magnum Mauser actions were made available to other makers. Westley Richards solved this dilemma with

Donna took her first buffalo with the Ruger No. 1 in .450/.400-3". It was a quartering shot, with the 400-grain solid entering the point of the on-shoulder and exiting the opposite flank. This is the kind of penetration John Taylor claimed for the .450/.400, and of course he was right.

the .425 Westley Richards, which it introduced about 1909. This unusual cartridge could be called the first of the "short magnums" since it did indeed fit into a standard-length Mauser action, although not without some unusual dimensions.

Case length is 2.64 inches, a tight fit. The head diameter is a very fat .543-inch, but the rebated rim was turned down to just .467 to fit a standard Mauser bolt face. It wore an amazingly long neck, making it quite possibly the oddest-looking cartridge ever developed. Under England's system of proprietary cartridges, it was made by almost no one else, ever, yet it was quite a success for Westley Richards. And well it should have been; firing a 410-grain bullet of .435-inch diameter, it had a muzzle velocity of 2,350 FPS for energy of 5,010 foot-pounds—in other words, the same energy delivered by double-rifle cartridges from .450 to .475.

The standard Westley Richards bolt-action .425 sported a 28-inch barrel. This was a common length for early double rifles, but, added to the action length of a bolt gun, it made the rifle most unwieldy. Still, the cartridge retained a following for many years, and was the standard game-department issue in Uganda. The .425 was also chambered in a few doubles and, as unlikely as it seems, was said to be satisfactory. Westley Richards continues to offer the .425, with new ammo available as well.

The .404 Rimless Nitro Express, better known as the .404 Jeffery (or, in Europe, the 10.75x73mm) came along just a year later. The .404 Jeffery can also be housed in a standard action, although not easily; it takes quite a bit of work to cram it in. Introduced by Jeffery but released to the gun trade, it achieved much more lasting popularity than the .425 and, in terms of rifles made, the more famous .416 Rigby. The point? Kynoch discontinued the .416 Rigby along with all the other Nitro Express cartridges, but .404 Jeffery ammo continued to be made in Europe. Perhaps this was because several makers offered it. Certainly it isn't because of its flashy ballistics. Although it fires a fatter .423-inch bullet (and thus one with less sectional density and penetrating abilities), the .404 basically duplicates the .450/.400's ballistics— a 400-grain bullet at 2,125 FPS for 4,020 foot-pounds.

The .416 Rigby is the most famous of the big British bolt guns, but the .404 was unquestionably the most popular. God only knows how many thousands were made by Jeffery, Westley Richards, Cogswell & Harrison, and numerous other firms in England and on the Continent. The .404 was the standard game-department issue in Kenya, Tanganyika, and the Rhodesias (Uganda was a notable exception). The German firm of RWS continued loading ammunition after Kynoch dropped the .404, and indeed loads it to this day.

An amazing number of old .404s are still in service in Africa. When I hunted Rhodesia in the late '70s, my host, Roger Whittall, had a battered Cogswell & Harrison .404, undoubtedly a game-department rifle. I didn't use it, but my partner, Ron Norman, used it on both hippo and buffalo with good results. In the late 1980s I saw the same rifle, even more battered, in Mozambique in the hands of Roger's tracker, Chinkengiya. The game scout who accompanied me in Masailand in 1988, Julius Sayo Mahoo, was armed with a lovely Westley Richards .404, and although he never had to use it in my behalf, I never questioned whether he or it could do the job. There are some new ones out there as well. Just a couple of weeks ago PH Andy Wilkinson (from Zimbabwe, but hunting in Tanzania) proudly showed me his custom American-made .404 Jeffery.

Today neither the .404 nor its .423-inch bullets are nearly as popular as the several .416s, but the .404 isn't a dead duck. RWS ammo is still available, as is Superior, and I continue to believe that either Hornady or Federal will introduce an American factory load. There are small numbers of new rifles,

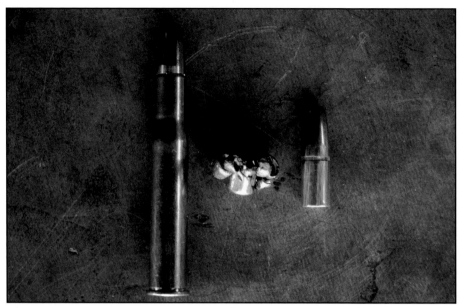

Hornady's new factory load for the old .450-400-3", or .400 Jeffery, shown with a recovered solid and softpoint, both 400 grains.

but I think this could expand. To this day I have never used a .404, but I have always wanted to, and am currently having one built by James Mills at Gun Creations in Lubbock, Texas. As factory-loaded, it isn't as powerful as the .416 Rigby, but it kicks less and, like the .450/.400, is truly perfect for buffalo. Its slightly smaller case can be adapted to more actions than the .416 Rigby, and with modern powders can be loaded to considerably higher velocity if desired.

In the old books you'll find the occasional whispers of .404 bullet failure. However, considering its wide use by so many game departments as well as private individuals, it's quite possible that more heavy game was shot with the .404 than any other British cartridge. If that's true, and it's at least close to the truth, then there must inevitably have been a few failures along the way. In all probability, most problems with the .404 resulted from using not the 400-grain bullet but rather a light, short 300-grain copper-capped bullet also offered for some years. With a muzzle velocity of 2,600, this bullet was designed for rapid expansion on thin-skinned game. It did that, possibly all too well; it had a reputation for explosive expansion, and was probably downright hazardous to use against dangerous game. Fortunately, the .404 has outlasted this loading by decades.

Today the bullet selection in .423-inch isn't as robust as .416, but there are plenty enough to go around, including "good stuff" like Woodleigh and Barnes.

There remains considerable interest in the .404 Jeffery. A few years ago Federal told me it intended to load it, but to date it hasn't done so. Hornady has also shown me sample cases, which suggests that Hornady will be offering .423-inch bullets as well as loaded ammo. Norma has included the .404 Jeffery in its new line of safari ammo, including a load with an extra-heavy 450-grain bullet. This would definitely be a better choice for elephant, but I think the standard 400-grain bullet remains just fine for buffalo.

Careful readers will note that this chapter is already longer than the original *Safari Rifles* chapter on the large mediums, which included the .416! So obviously my own interest in this class of cartridge has expanded, as has current availability. In addition to the cartridges mentioned, there are innumerable wildcat and proprietary cartridges that more or less duplicate the performance of the .404 Jeffery, .416 Rigby, and, less frequently, the .425 Westley Richards. Most of these are long forgotten, but their common goal was to achieve the ballistics of these famed cartridges in modern cases that would fit in either .375 H&H or .30-06-length actions. Most of them use either the .375 H&H case or the .458 Winchester Magnum case, necked to appropriate diameter with various shoulder conformations.

I mentioned the .411 KDF, the .416 Taylor, .416 Hoffman, and the .425 Express. This development has continued, and will continue. A couple of years ago Holland & Holland announced the new .400 H&H, which I have not seen but understand to be a .375 H&H case necked up to take a more-or-less .400-caliber bullet. I'm sure it's a most effective cartridge, with the advantage of being housed in a .375-length action. I have used the .404 Dakota, which is a shortened .404 Jeffery case, easily able to fit into a .30-06-length action but propelling a 400-grain .423-inch bullet at 2,400 FPS and more. There are others, and will be more. I suspect we will see the .375 Ruger case necked up to ".40-something," and with a major manufacturer behind it, such a cartridge could become popular. I'm sure the .450/.400 and .404 Jeffery will make a considerable comeback, but my opinion is the .416 bullet diameter will continue to rule the cartridge spectrum between .375 and .450.

Big Bores for Repeaters

Chapter 9

The very term "big bore" is hard to define. In North America it could easily be argued that the .375 is a big cartridge. Africa is different, so for our purposes we'll say that modern big bores begin at .450. This is admittedly arbitrary; the .416 Rigby and its progeny all develop energy levels comparable to the Nitro Expresses from .450 to .475. In fact, it wasn't until 1956, with Winchester's introduction of the .458, that a cartridge designed for repeating rifles existed at the lower end of the "big bore" scale. Because of the proprietary system, a proliferation of nearly identical .450-caliber-plus cartridges evolved in England, but with very few exceptions they were rimmed cartridges for double rifles.

Historically, there have been almost no big-bore developments, period, on the Continent. The one exception, the 12.7x70mm, is a good one, but European gunmakers don't have a rich history with big cartridges.

Given all the rimmed cartridges for doubles, it's interesting to speculate why big-bore cartridges for repeaters have been so scarce. Obviously, the heavies have a limited market, but just as obviously there is a market, and the sales potential would have been especially good back in the pre-World War I days when most of the big-bore development was under way.

It seems likely that the .425, .404, and .416 were considered so effective that a really big jump upward in caliber was needed to gain any benefit. In effect, that's what happened; no British rimless or belted cartridges existed between this trio and the two big .50s, the .500 Jeffery and .505 Gibbs. The Europeans had a pair of 11.2mm cartridges, caliber .440, and then nothing until you get all the way to the 12.7x70mm Schuler mentioned above. Firing a .510-inch bullet, it just happens to be identical in all respects to the .500 Jeffery. Today it is uncertain whether this cartridge was actually a Schuler cartridge adopted by Jeffery or vice versa. But whichever, it stands as the lone European big bore.

From the black-powder era until 1956, there was no factory American big-bore cartridge designed for smokeless powder, although there were smokeless versions

The fast .460 Weatherby remains one of the most powerful cartridges available and retains a following. Stephen Bindon used a .460 to take this desert elephant in northwestern Namibia.

of several black-powder cartridges. The .45-70 Government cartridge is the last of these, and it looks as if it will survive as long as metallic ammunition is loaded!

Starting with Winchester's Model 1876 lever action, then continuing with the Model 1886 and comparable Marlins, we Americans had a long succession of lever-action rifles chambered for powerful, large-caliber black-powder cartridges: .45-75, .45-70, .45-90, .50-95, even the big .50-110 (which survived briefly into smokeless loading). Such rifles indeed saw some service in Africa; H. Rider Haggard included Winchesters in the armament of Allan Quatermain's party in his turn-of-the-century *King Solomon's Mines*, and the other Quatermain novels as well. Stanley's party actually carried big Winchesters, which is perhaps where Haggard got the idea. However, it must be remembered that such rifles were smallbores in the black-powder era.

It wasn't until 1898 that John Rigby redefined a .45-caliber rifle as a big bore. He did it with his .450-3¼" Nitro Express, and the world has never been the same. Prior to the introduction of this smokeless cartridge, which fired a 480-grain jacketed bullet at 2,150 feet per second, a .450 was a light rifle in Africa. A .577 black-powder rifle was a sort of heavy medium, and the standard heavy rifle was an 8-bore, the same designation we use in shotgun gauges: 8-bore or 8-gauge means, roughly, that eight

115

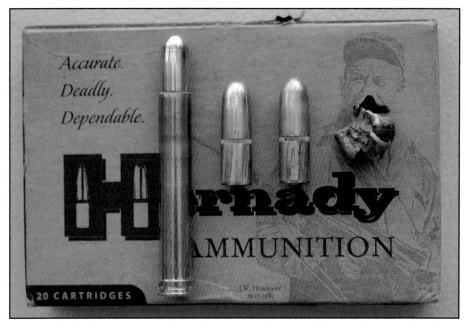

Jack Lott developed the .458 Lott in the early eighties, now legitimized by Hornady. Powerful, effective, and able to be housed in .375-length actions, this is now the preeminent big-bore cartridge for repeaters.

round balls fitted to that bore diameter weigh one pound, so its round ball weighs two ounces. The big 8-bores varied somewhat in exact bore diameter and case design, but a bullet of conical shape weighing 1,250 grains with a diameter of .875-inch was fairly common. Velocity, with a load of 10 drams of black powder, was about 1,500 FPS, and energy was just over 5,000 foot-pounds. During the forty-year reign of the black-powder breechloader in Africa, this was the standard formula for stopping a charge.

It hardly seems coincidental that Rigby's .450-3¼" would achieve the same energy figures, or that the .458 Winchester Magnum would strive to do so another half-century down the road. Rigby's .450-3¼" Nitro Express seemed to kill every bit as well as the big 8-bore. It was perhaps not quite so reliable a charge-stopper, but it penetrated better and could be built into a rifle that could actually be carried, whereas the 8-bores weighed 16 to 18 pounds.

It is probably no coincidence, either, that both the .425 Westley Richards and the .416 Rigby develop energies just over 5,000 foot-pounds. Like the .450-3¼" compared to the 8-bore, the .425 and .416 achieved that level with the increased velocity of a lighter bullet. And, as I said, perhaps these were so effective that no demand was perceived for a rimless version of John Rigby's .450. At the turn of the century, a few magnum Mauser actions were barreled to the .500-3" Nitro Express.

I used Ruger's big-bolt action in .458 Lott to take this hippo in Zimbabwe's Zambezi Valley. I missed the brain with the first shot—and that's when you need a big bore with good solids to clean up the mess!

A slant-box magazine was used so the rim of a cartridge rode ahead of the rim of the cartridge below it in the magazine. As mentioned, I saw a .450/.400 bolt gun once as well. In recent years this idea has resurfaced in a few bolt actions chambered for big rimmed cartridges. Heym, for instance, has made a few behemoth bolt guns for the .600 Nitro Express. These work perfectly so long as the rims are stacked back-to-front, bottom-to-top, when loading. Realistically, however, rimmed cartridges are for doubles and single shots, and rimless and belted rimless cartridges are for bolt actions. The early bolt guns for rimmed cartridges fell by the wayside with the development of the .404, which became the standard chambering for a big-bolt gun. Rigby, of course, kept its .416 for itself, as did Westley Richards with the .425. And then the big .50s arrived on the scene.

It is generally believed that the .505 Gibbs predates the .500 Jeffery, so we'll look at it first. It may go back as early as 1913, and was almost certainly actually introduced by George Gibbs. Original .505s are rare and quite valuable today. George Gibbs apparently made just seventy-odd rifles. Interestingly, Zimbabwe's great PH Barrie Duckworth learned elephant hunting from another good friend of mine, legendary elephant hunter Richard Harland. Duckworth and Harland, both staunch bolt-action men, own original Gibbs .505 rifles with consecutive serial numbers.

Left to right: .458 Winchester Magnum, .458 Lott, .450 Rigby Rimless Magnum, .460 Weatherby Magnum, .500 Jeffery, .505 Gibbs. These, together with the .450 Dakota (which is almost identical to the .450 Rigby Rimless) are probably the most commonly encountered big bores for bolt-action rifles.

The .505 Gibbs is one more cartridge whose reputation outweighed its actual use, another legendary British big bore with a charisma that lasts to this day. It was written about widely, even by Ernest Hemingway, who chose it as the backup rifle for his fictional professional hunter in *The Short Happy Life of Francis Macomber*. Tony Sanchez-Ariño wrote that it was J. A. Hunter's favorite, especially for elephant cropping. (Hunter's own writings are not quite so clear on that.)

Ballistics were extremely impressive: A 525-grain bullet of .505-inch diameter left the muzzle at 2,300 FPS for 6,180 foot-pounds of muzzle energy. It was obviously effective on anything that walks, and friends who have shot the original Gibbs rifles rate them as the hardest-kicking firearms they've ever handled.

Original ammunition was available well into the 1950s, and a number of custom .505 Gibbs rifles were built in this country, especially by long-defunct Hoffman Arms. Like the .416 Rigby, this is another cartridge that is seeing a rebirth today, though on a much smaller scale than the .416. The original Kimber firm offered its magnum bolt action in .505. European firms such as Heym and Henri Dumoulin have chambered to it, and today the big (and amazingly affordable) CZ rifle is chambered to .505 Gibbs. A-Square and B.E.L.L. made the ammunition, and today it's readily available from Superior and Kynoch, and will be included among the offerings in the new Norma line of big-bore ammunition. A variety of good bullets is available, and it has experienced more of a renaissance than its big brother, the .500 Jeffery.

The .500 Jeffery offered several advantages over the Gibbs. It had a much shorter case, 2.74 inches versus 3.15, with a rebated rim, making it much easier to fit into a bolt action and allowing bullets to be seated much farther forward. It was also loaded hotter, using a .510-inch 535-grain bullet at 2,400 FPS for 6,800 foot-pounds of energy. The cartridge is believed to have been developed by the German firm of Schuler, which made rifles chambered for the metric version, the 12.7x70mm Schuler. It was clearly a great thumper for the largest of game, but it never achieved the reputation of the Gibbs. Perhaps it came along too late; it is believed to have been introduced in the 1920s, after most of the Nitro Express cartridges were well established. Jeffery only made twenty-three rifles. Schuler may have made more, but because of Germany's turmoil between the world wars, this is unknown.

This is actually one of the rarest of the Nitro Express rounds, and ammunition has long been a massive problem. According to the references I could find, original ammunition was made in Germany, not in England, and it was not available after World War II. In the 1980s Harald Wolf started making both ammunition and rifles in Belgium on a limited basis, but his version differs from the original in that his rim isn't rebated. This variance creates massive problems for the cartridge and, unfortunately, essentially precludes any serious resurgence on anything other than a pure custom basis. Tony Sanchez-Ariño used one of Wolf's rifles for backing up his clients and reported marvelous results on elephant. American Bill McBride has a Krieghoff .500 Jeffery. Johan Calitz has a custom .500 made by a South African custom gunmaker.

Other makers, including Rigby, have made a few. In October 2006 I hunted elephant in southern Tanzania with Jim Crawford. Then in the process of acquiring Rigby, he used a beautiful Rigby in .500 Jeffery, and of course it worked wonderfully. C. Fletcher Jamieson's .500 Jeffery, the most famous rifle made in that caliber and referred to often by John Taylor, still exists and was recently sold by Jamieson's son. The obvious problem is twofold. First, when having a .500 Jeffery made, you must be careful which case dimension to specify—and when acquiring ammo, you must know what you have and what you are getting. But, like almost any scarce cartridge today, there are sources, including Superior.

When World War II ended, the .500 Jeffery was dead and the Gibbs, like all the other British Nitro Expresses, was dying slowly. There was a real gap in powerful cartridges for repeaters, and it was not to be filled until the .458 Winchester cartridge came along in 1956. In the meantime, handloading Americans got busy.

Wildcats and Lever Actions

The first important big-bore wildcat was not a bolt-action cartridge at all; it was a lever-action cartridge designed by Alaskan outfitter Harold Johnson. Called the .450 Alaskan, it was based on the .348 Winchester case, introduced along with the

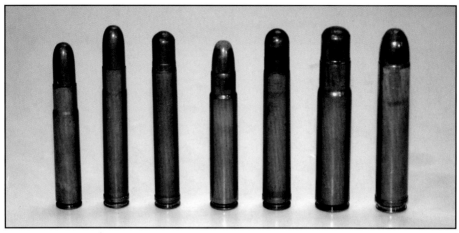

Left to right: .460 G&A, .450 Ackley, .470 Capstick, .475 Bibamofu, .500 A-Square, .577 Tyrannosaur, .600 Overkill. Big-bore wildcats and proprietary cartridges are legion and range from sensible to downright whimsical. When you get much above the power level of the .458 Lott, recoil becomes too ferocious for most of us to handle.

Model 71 Winchester in 1936. The rifle was (and is) a big, strong lever action, the last incarnation of the great Model 1886. The .348 proved extremely effective on elk, moose, and midsize bears, but Harold Johnson wanted a bit more gun to take into the alders after brown bear.

He developed the .450 Alaskan in the late 1930s. It had quite a following, and is still occasionally seen today. Because of the tubular magazine, flatnose bullets are required; and because of limited case capacity, a 500-grain bullet starts to sacrifice velocity. But with a good flatnose bullet like Speer's 400-grainer, made for the .45-70, the .450 Alaskan is quite a cartridge. Velocity figures given go as high as 2,200 FPS, and of course velocities in that range with a 400-grain bullet yield over 4,000 foot-pounds of energy.

There were several other versions of Johnson's cartridge, including the .450 Fuller and .450/.348 Ackley Improved, both of which removed more of the body taper and gave additional powder capacity. My own "Alaskan" was actually the Ackley version, and I chronographed 405-grain bullets at 2,270 FPS from my rifle! That proved a bit too hot. And, to be honest, given the stock style of a Winchester lever action, the recoil was frightful. I backed off a bit, but even so, a good, honest 2,150 FPS was no problem. That's a 4,000-foot-pound load, essentially the same as the .450/.400. I haven't read any accounts of the .450 Alaskan or its brethren being used in Africa, but there's no reason it wouldn't be darn near perfect for lion and acceptable for buffalo.

PH Paul Smith, Wayne Holt, and I with Holt's amazing Zambezi Valley buffalo, 45 inches in horn spread. This bull almost gave us the slip, but Holt's .458 Lott literally stopped him in his tracks.

These days, with strong modern actions and heavy loads readily available for the .45-70, and with the advent of the .450 Marlin, I am often asked about the suitability of these cartridges for buffalo. This depends on the load, which in turn depends on the rifle. The Marlin lever action is much stronger than the old trapdoor Springfield, and in the Marlin you can safely get a 400-grain bullet up to something approaching 1,900 FPS. Given a well-constructed bullet that will penetrate, this load would be adequate for buffalo. The .450 Marlin, developed by Hornady, is essentially just a hopped-up .45-70 with a belt ahead of the rim, this to preclude its chambering in any .45-70 chamber. Adequate, yes, but not legal in all venues. I think it is very difficult, though not always impossible or unsafe, to produce Zimbabwe's legal minimum of about 4,000 foot-pounds in any lever action.

Modern single shots are something else. The Ruger No. 1 and other modern actions are among the strongest actions in the world, and a single shot has no issues with overall cartridge length. So, in the Ruger No. 1, a .45-70 case can be stuffed with a 500-grain bullet to velocities at least approaching 2,000 FPS, essentially the equal of some factory loads for the .458. This means that in the right rifle, a .45-70 could be loaded so as to be adequate for elephant . . . but I think there are more suitable tools!

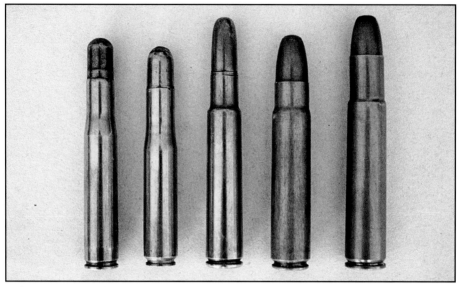

Left to right: .404 Jeffery, .425 Westley Richards, .416 Rigby, .500 Jeffery, .505 Gibbs. These are the traditional British bolt-action cartridges above .40-caliber, dating to the early 1900s. Our current raft of .450+ cartridges for bolt actions started with the .458 Winchester Magnum in 1956.

In the years following World War II, a number of wildcats were developed around the full-length .375 H&H case, necked up to take .458 bullets and blown out to remove most of the taper. The .450 Mashburn and .450 Watts were nearly identical, being straight-walled cases with slight body taper. The .450 Ackley, still seen today, has almost no body taper and a slight shoulder.

After the development of the .458 Winchester Magnum, the .45 wildcats died out for a while, but came back strong when rumors started to fly about .458 Winchester Magnum performance. The issue was that the .458 was designed to fit into a .30-06-length action. This is inexplicable, since it was introduced in the Model 70 Winchester, which easily accommodates the full-length .375 case. Original velocity was claimed to be a 500-grain bullet at 2,150, yielding about 5,000 foot-pounds of energy, suspiciously duplicating the formula of the Nitro Express cartridges between .450 and .475. The challenge was that with propellants then available the .458 was very hard-pressed to reach this level, and required a significantly compressed powder charge.

There were stories about lack of penetration, probably caused by improper ignition. Jack Lott reported seeing a 500-grain bullet from a .458 bounce on the ground between him and a fifty-yard target—with unburned clumps of powder remaining in the barrel. And then there were the "urban legends" about finding .458 solids just a couple inches inside elephants' heads. The old .458-caliber wildcats

I used a very early .458 Lott in Zambia back in 1984. Jack Lott developed the cartridge because of concerns over the .458 Winchester Magnum's penetrating abilities, but his gently tapering case allowed use of then-common .458 Winchester ammo.

were resurrected, and there were new ones on the .375 cases, including the .450 Barnes Supreme, straight-cased with a slight shoulder and short neck. Then came the winner and still champion, Jack Lott's .458 Lott, a straight-walled case with a tiny bit of body taper. The Lott was designed so that a hunter short on ammo could fire .458 Winchester Magnum ammo in his Lott chamber with no problems. As we now know, it was brought to factory form by Hornady, with inexpensive factory rifles from Ruger, CZ, and others readily available.

All of the .458-caliber wildcats based on the .375 case are ballistic equals. With modern powders and plenty of case capacity, it's a breeze to achieve about 2,300 FPS with a 500-grain bullet, which yields 5,870 foot-pounds. With most of these cartridges in most rifles it's possible to reach 2,400 FPS without undue pressure. That load yields well over 6,000 foot-pounds, more than enough for anything.

Please note, however, that recoil goes up sharply as velocity increases. Hornady's factory load for the .458 Lott is actually quite mild at 2,250 FPS, but that is still enough velocity to put a good solid through an elephant's brain from any angle, and for me is a great compromise between performance and recoil.

I had a lovely .458 Lott clear back in 1984, when it was a relatively new wildcat. I took it to Zambia on a hunt with Geoff and Russ Broom. Midway through the hunt, Geoff and I decided to take a short holiday and go to his home at Matetsi, in Zimbabwe. Because of the gun permits, I left my .458 Lott in Zambia, but he had a .450 Ackley with no ammunition—so I packed along some ammo to help him clean

Paul Roberts, then proprietor of Rigby's in London, tinkering with one of the first .450 Rigby Rimless Magnum rifles in the Selous Reserve in 1993.

up some leftover buffalo permits. The ammunition fed and functioned perfectly, just fireforming slightly to attain the Ackley shoulder in the process. I don't recommend such haphazard interchange, but the point is that all of the .458 wildcats are very similar—but today the .458 Lott is the one that makes the most sense, and I think it is now the preeminent big-bore cartridge for a bolt-action rifle.

The .404 Jeffery case has been another basis for .458 wildcats. The best known of these is the .460 G&A, for *Guns & Ammo* magazine. The brainchild of *Guns & Ammo's* Tom Siatos and Jack Lott, the cartridge is essentially the .404 Jeffery necked up to .458, with the shoulder moved forward and most of the body taper removed. Again, it achieves about 2,300 to 2,350 feet per second with a 500-grain bullet. Tom Siatos, Bob Petersen, and longtime Central African Republic outfitter Jan Schallig used the .460 G&A with great success. Ian Henderson, one of the pioneers of safari hunting in what is now Zimbabwe, used one of the first .460 G&A rifles, built by Californian John Pollon on a .404 Jeffery that had belonged to Ian's father. He wrote to me about it: "I used it during a cull and found the penetration superb. In fact, all the shots went clean through and we did not recover one bullet, which was a pity. My experience was hardly a true test, as we were taking head shots in mixed herds with no large bulls, so were not able to fully test the knock-down effect.

I would class this rifle in the same category as the .505 Gibbs." On our Zambian safari in 1996 Bob Petersen used his famous old George Hoffman .460 G&A to roll a lovely buffalo. Regrettably, this was Petersen's last African hunt. Johan Calitz, one of the few professional hunters I've run into who is a real rifle nut, also has a .460 G&A, his built in South Africa.

In a later development, Jack Lott cooked up the .450 G&A Short Magnum, again using the .404 case but shortening it so the cartridge would fit in a .30-06-length action. Ken Elliott, longtime publisher of *Petersen's Hunting,* has a Model 77 Ruger .458 rechambered to this cartridge, and he used it to stop a buffalo charge cold in the Zambezi Valley. In the shortened form, velocity runs about 2,200 FPS, still plenty. Ken had this rifle on the same Zambian safari in '96, and used it to take a spectacular buffalo.

After the big .378 Weatherby was introduced in 1953, the wildcatters had a new, big, and readily available case to play with. John R. Buhmiller wildcatted the .450 Buhmiller on the .378 case, taking it to Tanganyika in 1955. Ultimately, this cartridge was the basis for the .460 Weatherby. Other wildcats based on this case include the .475 A&M, designed by the team of Atkinson & Marquart, using the .475-inch .470 Nitro Express bullet; and Gil Van Horn's shortened-case .475 Van Horn. Another shortened version is the .460 A-Square Short Magnum, for which A-Square offers factory ammo.

The .460 case has been necked up farther into a variety of .50-caliber wildcats using both .505- and .510-inch bullets. A-Square has both a short version, the .495 A-Square (.375 H&H-length), and a full-length version, the .500 A-Square, for which it offers factory loads. Then there's a .500 Barnes Supreme featuring a straight, tapered case with no shoulder. The most publicized of these is the .510 Wells, designed by Arizona riflemaker Fred Wells. Using a relatively straight case with a slight shoulder, the .510 Wells is an extremely powerful cartridge pushing a 600-grain bullet at over 2,400 FPS. Tanzanian professional hunter/rancher Gary Hoops proudly showed me his .510 Wells when we pitched up at his farm in the middle of Masailand to get a truck spring welded.

In the 1980s, as brass became more readily available, the .416 Rigby case became another favorite for wildcats and proprietary cartridges. Most of the Dakota proprietary magnums are based on the .404 case necked up. The exception is the .450 Dakota Magnum, which is based on the .416 Rigby case necked up. It is essentially identical to (though not interchangeable with) the .450 Rigby Rimless Magnum, which was developed by Rigby's then-proprietor, Paul Roberts. We used it in Tanzania in 1994, and with a 500-grain bullet at 2,400 FPS it is a real killer. On both ends! This level of performance, however, has achieved a significant following among several professional hunters that I trust. Geoff Broom uses a .450 Dakota, but with 600-grain bullets. So does Michel Mantheakis. Both swear by them for backup on elephant, where they can count on a going-away shot to penetrate fully.

Gunwriter Ross Seyfried experimented with an "ultimate" wildcat, a rimless .577 that pushed a 750-grain bullet in excess of 2,250 FPS. He rated it a killer on both ends. Later Art Alphin came up with the .577 Tyrannosaur. There are others, some sensible and some bordering on insanity. George Sandmann at Empire Arms is just now developing the .505 Empire, essentially a .460 Weatherby case necked up to accept a .50-caliber bullet. I haven't yet seen the exact cartridge or the specifications, but the concept is sound: using a modern, available case to achieve essentially .505 Gibbs performance.

Factory Choices

The drawback to all wildcats and proprietaries is the relative unavailability of ammo. Today this is nothing like the problem it used to be. Jim Bell's Brass Extrusion Laboratories, Ltd. is long since sold, but between Bertram, Norma, Hornady, A-Square, and others there is now brass for darn near anything, and so long as there is brass, custom suppliers like Superior will load the ammo. Of course, the point with a proprietary is that the rifle's maker will also supply the ammo, which works just fine so long as the maker remains in business. But the less common the cartridge the greater the ammo resupply problem can be.

Some Africa-bound hunters worry about this and some do not. Personally, I don't worry about it unduly. I just accept that if I'm carrying an uncommon cartridge and I get separated from my ammo I will probably have to borrow a rifle as well as ammo! Honestly, over the course of now seventy-odd separate African hunts, involving at least half that many round-trip overseas plane tickets, I have never once (touch wood) not received my rifles (though sometimes only after a few days' delay). Only once was I genuinely separated from rifle and ammo. This was in Mozambique in 1989. On arrival in Johannesburg I knew that my rifles had made it, but my duffel bag did not. I had a five-hour layover in which to acquire underwear and outerwear and ammo. Cartridges for my .375 H&H were no problem, but back then .500 Nitro Express for the Heym double was a challenge. A friend at a gun shop pried five old Kynoch rounds from a collector, and I went elephant hunting.

Another concern with any wildcat cartridge is that in some African countries you can expect your cartridges to be inspected and the headstamp had better match the rifle. In other words, if you have .458 Lott ammo made from necked-up .375 H&H cases, you could run into problems. This is a possibility in any

A scoped big-bore, bolt action offers considerably more versatility than an open-sighted rifle of similar power. I used the .450 Rigby Rimless Magnum to take this eland from about 200 yards. I couldn't have made the shot with an open-sighted rifle.

African country for which rifle and ammo permits are required (and they are just about universal today), but in my experience the most rigorous inspections have been in Ethiopia and Zambia.

The wildcatting will go on, and for several reasons. First, powerful cartridges are fascinating—and it's always interesting to see how much power can be obtained from a shoulder-fired rifle. Witness the huge bolt actions currently being built around the .50 Browning machine-gun cartridge! But if the .458 Winchester had done what it was designed to do and was publicized as being able to do, I doubt if we'd have nearly as many wildcats, and possibly not the current .416 craze, either.

Introduced in 1956, the .458 Winchester Magnum is the largest of Winchester's family of short magnums, which also includes the .264, .300, and .338 Winchester Magnums. All, introduced between 1956 and 1962, were designed to function in .30-06-length actions. The original ballistics listed a 500-grain solid and a 510-grain softpoint, both at 2,130 FPS for just over 5,000 foot-pounds of energy. Initial loadings did come very close to published figures, but ignition problems were apparently common enough that the powder charge was reduced and factory figures were quietly downgraded. Current figures are generally quoted at 2,040 FPS for 4,622 foot-pounds of energy. That is still respectable, but it isn't what the cartridge was designed to produce. Is it enough? Sure it is, especially with the excellent bullets Americans have available. But it won't equal the old .470 or its kin. Nor will it equal the modern

127

.416s. In fairness, the .458 retains a tremendous following, including among many top hunters. These include the likes of the late Finn Aagaard and my old friend Barrie Duckworth, who shot his thousandth elephant with a Mannlicher .458.

Today the .458's bad rap is really quite unnecessary. We have a lot of better propellants available today, so handloaders can easily get the .458 back to at least 2,100 FPS and a bit more with carefully selected powders and judiciously compressed loads. There are also a few factory loads that, using newer propellants, equal or exceed initial velocities without ignition problems. Hornady has a 500-grain factory load at 2,200 FPS that will certainly do anything anybody needs to do. Another option, thanks to the great modern bullets we now have available, is to simply drop bullet weight. There are 400- and 450-grain bullets that will work just fine, at least as well as the 500-grain bullets available in 1956.

The beauty of the .458 has always been the proliferation of relatively cheap, available ammo. It came about at a time when the Nitro Expresses were being discontinued, and of course the American mass-produced rifles were serviceable and available at a fraction of the cost of even a British bolt gun. It took Africa by storm, and although it is not nearly as popular now as it was just twenty years ago, it is unquestionably the single most common big bore in history. Today I would suggest a .458 Lott as the most sensible choice, since both Lott ammo and lower-recoiling .458 Winchester Magnum ammo can be used.

The big daddy of factory American cartridges needs no reloading to boost up its performance; it's just fine right out of the box. The .460 Weatherby Magnum, based on John Buhmiller's wildcat, was introduced by Roy Weatherby in 1958. Its stated purpose was to give Roy Weatherby the world's most powerful cartridge, and so it was (and is, at least in terms of factory cartridges). A subtler reason was the East African Professional Hunters' Association's banning of cartridges under .40-caliber for use on elephant, buffalo, and rhino. His .378 Weatherby Magnum was suddenly out of the running; Weatherby needed a cartridge that would compete in that arena with the new .458 Winchester Magnum.

The .460 can do that in spades. Factory velocity is quoted at 2,700 FPS, yielding a stunning 8,095 foot-pounds of energy. In all of my testing, actual velocities have run a bit lower, but with factory loads or handloads 2,600 to 2,650 is about right, and they are hardly figures to sneeze at. The .460 Weatherby has been widely maligned, and indeed with a softpoint designed to perform properly at a velocity 500 FPS slower, it may not give the desired penetration. But with a good solid or a tough softpoint, it's just plain magnificent.

A good friend of mine, Bruno Scherrer, was on a hunt in Sudan many years ago, carrying his .460 Weatherby. He had been working his tail off to get a decent elephant. Tracks, small bulls, cow herds, but nothing big. The wind shifted when they were working a very large herd, and the game was over . . . almost. The forest opened into a broad clearing, and they reached it just in time to watch the herd pass on the far end, much too far to shoot at an elephant. The last bull to pass was a dream elephant with long, heavy ivory. Against his professional hunter's wishes, Bruno took the shot. It was easy, really—a single lung shot with a scoped .460 Weatherby at very close to 200 yards. At that distance it had what the .458 has at the muzzle, and the ivory weighed out at 98 pounds per side. It was also the kind of shot that is never attempted at an elephant, and should not be attempted. But the .460 Weatherby is darn near the only cartridge that makes it remotely practical.

The .460 Weatherby does bring some excess baggage with it. Recoil is fierce enough that recovery for the second shot is slowed, and the big belted case is so bulky that its Weatherby Mark V rifle holds but two shells in the magazine. (That capacity is the same for the .378 and .416 Weatherby as well.) It's a price to pay; I've always been more comfortable with the added capacity and somewhat lower recoil of something like a .416 Rigby or a .458 Lott. Still, the .460 Weatherby does fill a valuable niche as a magazine rifle that is unexcelled in sheer stopping power. A professional-hunter friend of mine told me the .460 was the deadliest rifle he'd ever seen on buffalo. I don't doubt that for a minute; on the occasions I have used it, it's been devastating.

As we've discussed, options in big-bore cartridges seem to be increasing. Norma ammo will now be available in several big-bore cartridges, including .505 Gibbs, and although you won't find any big-bore cartridges on the average dealer's shelves, almost anything can be obtained today provided you plan ahead. Unlike all the cartridges we've discussed heretofore, these big bores are not multipurpose rifles. They're stopping rifles, designed only for the largest of game: elephant, buffalo, rhino, and hippo. In bolt-action form, they do offer exceptional accuracy, and will reach out to a couple of hundred yards on lesser game. But lighter cartridges are much better suited. With softpoints, they're also devastating on lion, especially if things go sour with the first shot. But their strong suit, what they're made for, is getting a heavy bullet deep into the vitals of the largest game on Earth. They're special-purpose cartridges, not jacks-of-all-trades. And in that special role, together with their Nitro Express cousins designed for use in doubles, they're irreplaceable.

Big Bores for Doubles and Single Shots

Chapter 10

It's more than possible that the likes of the .303 British and 9.3x62 Mauser accounted for more game than all the large-caliber Nitro Express cartridges put together. Double rifles, and the cartridges they fired, were always expensive and somewhat unusual. Many professionals, whether professional guides or professional poachers, did carry them in the old days. A few, darn few, clung to them during the dark days when Nitro Express ammo was unavailable. Many more carried cheaper, lighter, higher-capacity magazine rifles. The game rangers rarely carried doubles; they couldn't afford them. Neither could the ranchers and farmers who, as a group, undoubtedly accounted for more game than all the rest. But facts be damned: The British Nitro Express cartridge is more than just part of the legend of safari. As a pervasive symbol, the big cigar-shaped cartridge *is* African hunting.

I succumbed to the legend early on; at about thirteen I discovered J. A. Hunter and his double .500 in the school library, and it wasn't long after that I discovered Robert Ruark and his Westley Richards .470. From those days onward I coveted a big double, something every Kansas schoolboy really needs. Eventually I traded around and got my hands on one, and in the years that have followed I've owned a variety of big doubles and shot many more. The big doubles and the cartridges they fire are indeed wonderful; pressures are kept very low by the huge cases, and although unhandy, those big cases offer a tremendous psychological lift.

Their sole job is to stop the largest and most dangerous game, whether it's inbound, outbound, or standing still. And this they do, all of them, and in nearly equal measure. Thanks in part to the British proprietary system whereby a gunmaker could have an exclusive right to sell both rifles and ammo for a cartridge he designed, there exists a bewildering array of Nitro Express cartridges ranging in caliber between .450 and .500. Many use the same basic case, and although bullet diameters may differ by a few thousandths, bullet weights and velocities are generally very close, if not identical.

Cartridges for double rifles, and to a slightly lesser extent single shots, should have rimmed cases. The extraction system is relatively weak compared to the camming power of a turnbolt, and the big surface of the rim is essential to ensure positive extraction/ejection.

In John Taylor's day good copy could be had by comparing in depth one of these cartridges to another, much the way modern scribes pit the .280 Remington against the .270 Winchester. Back then, there might have been some limited validity in such a comparison; most of the cartridges were available then, and the bullets some of them fired were also exclusive with one or another maker. Today it borders on the ridiculous to attempt to compare the .470 with the .475 No. 2 or the .450-3¼" with the .500/.450. Original ammunition for all of them is now too old to rely upon, as are many of the original rifles. On the other hand, more new double rifles are being built right now than ever before, and double-rifle ammo is more available than ever before. Right now good brass and better bullets are readily available, so none of the old rifles still in sound condition need be shelved—but some Nitro Express cartridges have experienced a rebirth, and some have not.

John Rigby started the Nitro Express race with his .450-3¼" Nitro Express in 1898. Holland & Holland soon countered with the .500/.450, a basic .500 case necked down with a 3¼-inch case. Then came the .450 No. 2, using a massive 3½-inch case to reduce pressure just a bit. The .450 No. 2 was developed by Eley, an ammunition manufacturer, so it was released to the trade and chambered by numerous makers. Then, in 1907, caliber .450 was banned in both India and Sudan. The old British black-powder military round for the Martini-Henry, the

Over the years I owned and used several .470s. It was and is a great cartridge—although I no longer believe it is the "best" double-rifle cartridge. This was a great boxlock by C.W. Andrews, one of many rifles I have owned that I should have kept!

.577/.450, was the weapon of choice (because of availability). It used a .45-caliber bullet, so let's keep ammo out of the hands of the bad guys by banning all .45-caliber cartridges. Apparently gun laws could be draconian even in the Victorian era!

This is what caused the avalanche of .470 and .475 cartridges. Holland & Holland introduced the .500/.465. Joseph Lang gets credit for the .470. Westley Richards introduced the .476. There was a straight-case .475 Nitro Express, and there were two versions of the .475 No. 2, using the big 3½-inch case: the .475 No. 2 Nitro Express, most often using a .483-inch bullet, and the .475 No. 2 Jeffery, using a .488- or .489-inch bullet.

All of these cartridges, plus the three .450s that preceded them, should be considered ballistic equals. Original specifications all called for bullets between 480 and 520 grains at velocities of around 2,150 FPS, all yielding plus or minus 5,000 foot-pounds of energy, all producing about the same level of recoil. Depending on the exact bullet diameter, the modern selection may be robust, as it is for .458 and .475 (.470 NE), or it may be limited to Woodleigh bullets—but the bullets will be

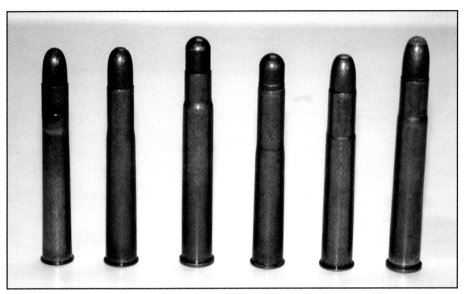

Left to right: .450-3¼", .500/.450, .450 No. 2, .500/.465, .470, .475 No. 2. These cartridges (and a few that are missing) are essentially identical in ballistics and performance, all firing bullets from 480 to 500 grains at velocities between about 2,100 and 2,175 feet per second.

better than those available in 1907! So, in terms of performance, there is little to pick from among the .450 to .475 group.

Legend has it that the .470 Nitro Express was the most popular. I'm not at all certain this is true. Unlike proprietaries like Holland's .500/.465, Westley Richards's .476, and the .475 No. 2 Jeffery, the .470 was released to the trade and became standard among several makers, including Rigby. However, the older guns encountered today are really a potpourri of the various cartridges. I believe the .450/.400, a step down in both power and recoil, was the most common double-rifle chambering. The .500-3" Nitro Express was also very standard and made by numerous makers.

Personally, I think Robert Ruark made the .470 the winner that it definitely is. It became the best-known, if not actually most popular, of the big-bore Nitro Express cartridges, and it was definitely the .470 that was chosen for a renaissance. Right now it is far and away the most popular chambering for new rifles, and, of course, Federal has been loading .470 ammo since 1988. However, Federal's .470 isn't the only option. Virtually all the old Nitro Express rounds are available from both Superior and Kynoch. Norma is offering several of these old-timers in its new line of safari ammo. Hornady took a big plunge with the reintroduction of the .450/.400-3" and has just announced the .400-3¼". The company also

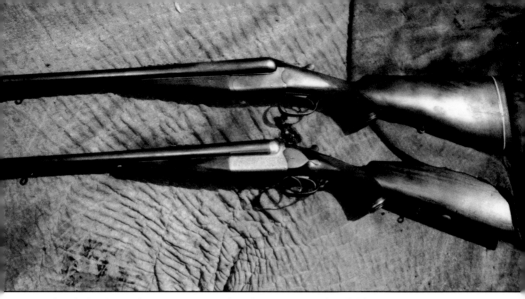

Though the .470 is the most common today, there are quite a lot of older guns still in service. On a Zambezi Valley safari a few years ago, my partner Tim Danklef and his PH, Andre Van Eeden, carried nearly identical Jeffery rifles in .475 No. 2 Jeffery, one of the more obscure Nitro Express cartridges.

announced the .450-3¼", and it isn't done yet. I'm sure it will eventually be offering .500-3" along with .470, probably by the time you read these lines.

So things are a whole lot brighter today, and there are a whole lot more choices, than was the case just twenty years ago. For many years the value of a vintage double was predicated on whether the sale was accompanied by a supply of ammunition. Forget it. One way or another, today ammo can be had, and original ammunition is now much too old to rely upon, especially if the chips are down. Twenty years ago I had misfires with old Kynoch ammunition, as have most hunters who dare to use it. As of 1988 I'd heard of two different failures of old Kynoch on lion—and one of them resulted in a mauling. I also heard about a professional hunter who was nearly killed by a buffalo after old Kynoch ammo misfired. The horn went in under the third rib. After stuffing his right lung back into the wound, he drove himself to the hospital.

Consider old Kynoch cartridges the collectibles they are, but don't overlook any old rifle in good condition, no matter what the chambering. New ammunition is probably available from multiple sources, but even with some of the real rare birds, like .475 Nitro Express and .500-3¼", cases, bullets, and dies are available, so you can load your own or have a custom outfit like Superior do it for you.

So why do we worry about these big, expensive rimmed cartridges when there are slim, trim, and readily available cartridges like the .458 Winchester Magnum and .458 Lott? In those dark days between Kynoch's discontinuance of the big Nitro Express cartridges and Federal's reintroduction of .470 ammo, there were indeed quite a few double rifles chambered to .375 H&H and .458 Winchester Magnum. Over the years a few doubles have been chambered to rimless cartridges like the .416 Rigby, and I have heard of at least one double rifle chambered to .460 Weatherby Magnum.

For all of its attributes, the double rifle has two major limitations. First, it is not nearly as strong as a bolt action. Primary lockup on a double is achieved by massive underbolts. With modern steel and today's precise machining capability, there is debate among double-rifle men about the real utility of a third (top) fastener, such as a doll's head or a Greener crossbolt. Regardless of the precise lockup mechanism, the natural force of any break-open rifle (double or single shot) is to attempt to unhinge during firing. This is called "coming off the face." The more pressure you have, the more difficult it is to control this action. The large-case Nitro Express cartridges were initially made large to reduce pressure with the volatile cordite propellant. I don't personally believe the biggest cases are desirable with modern powders, but that initial expansion within the case does reduce pressure. The big Nitro Express cartridges have working pressures of around 40,000 PSI. Most modern rimless and belted rimless cartridges have standard working pressures in the 50,000-PSI range. Well-made modern doubles can handle these pressures, but you're pushing it. Some modern magnums, like the Weatherby Magnums as loaded by Norma, have standard working pressures up into the 60,000-PSI range. This is looking for trouble.

The second issue with double rifles and most single shots is they lack the camming power of a bolt action for extraction. Many doubles have been made for rimless and belted cases, but the extractors are truly a Rube Goldberg affair, with spring-loaded plungers that must fit into the extractor groove. This has always been a questionable compromise. All double rifles chambered to rimless or belted rimless cartridges will eventually, even occasionally, have failures to extract. Mr. Murphy being the optimist that he is, this will invariably happen when you least want it to!

Today, with ammo readily available, there is simply no reason to chamber any double rifle to anything other than a rimmed cartridge. This also applies to single shots, although perhaps not quite as strongly. The extraction/ejection system of the Ruger No. 1 works extremely well, too well for me to knock it. It also has more power than a break-open gun. Even so, I would prefer a rimmed cartridge in any single shot. Some years back I shot several buffalo with a Dakota Model 10 chambered to the rimless .375 Dakota Magnum. The Model 10 is a lovely action, but extraction wasn't positive at all with that rimless case. It was truly a one-shot single shot, and I'd best not be in any hurry for a follow-up. A rimmed case would have helped a lot.

So, with the resurgence of the double rifle I think there is still a need for rimmed—or, as the Brits would have said, "flanged"—cartridges. In larger calibers intended for dangerous game, I think this applies to all single shots as well. On the lower end of the caliber/power scale there actually aren't many rimmed cartridges to choose from. Rigby's Geoff Miller has made a couple of new doubles in .22 Hornet and the (inexplicably rimmed) .225 Winchester. European rimmed cartridges like the 7x65R are hard to get in the United States. The British offered flanged versions of many small- and medium-bore cartridges, from .240 H&H on up, but these are all rare birds today. Miller and I have wracked our brains trying to come up with sensible modern options for a rimmed, versatile, medium cartridge, and there just isn't anything out there. Nobody wants a .303 British or .30-40 Krag in a modern double. Brass is hard to find for the flanged version of the .300 H&H (forget loaded ammo). The .348 Winchester doesn't make much sense because of a dearth of bullets. Rigby has made a couple of doubles on the .348 case necked up to .358, which solves the bullet problem—but an expensive double on a wildcat cartridge is a questionable project. The 9.3x74R is readily available, but its velocity is so low that it isn't all that versatile a cartridge. There isn't much at all until you get to the .375 H&H Flanged.

Essentially just a rimmed version of the .375 H&H, the .375 Flanged is usually loaded a bit lighter to keep the pressures down, but it will do everything the .375 H&H will do and, unlike the 9.3x74R, is "street legal" in any country with a .375 minimum for dangerous game. The problem with the .375 Flanged is that it remains, and very probably will remain, a specialty cartridge, with brass and ammo available only from smaller suppliers. It is not, however, a dead cartridge. Quite a few new doubles have been so chambered, including from American

Left to right: 500 Nitro Express, .577 Nitro Express, .600 Nitro Express. The .500 offers a noticeable increase in power over the .450 to .475 crowd, while the .577 and .600 are clearly much more powerful. The problem with the latter two is the rifles must of necessity be awfully heavy, and of course recoil is dramatic.

Left to right: .405 Winchester, .45-70, .375 Flanged, .450-400-3", .500-416. Historically, doubles have been built for the .405 and .45-70, and the .375 Flanged and .450-400 were once very popular. The .500-416 is a new cartridge developed by Krieghoff, lagging just behind the .416 Rigby in velocity.

makers like Butch Searcy and Rigby. Heym offers it in its new, stripped-down "PH" double rifle. It remains a sound option for a light, versatile double offering less recoil than the big bores.

Accepting that, right or wrong, we consider the double rifle to be a relatively short-range tool, I think Hornady's reintroduction of the .450/.400-3" fills the same niche very effectively. It is not only street-legal but also effective for game up to elephant, yet recoil is wonderfully mild. With ammo now available, it is my understanding that most modern makers of doubles, including Dumoulin, Heym, Krieghoff, Merkel, Rigby, and Searcy, will now chamber for the .450/.00-3". As stated earlier, the three-inch case offers good load density with modern powder, plus it can be built on a lighter, trimmer action than the group of cartridges based on the .500 case, which includes .470 and .500/.416.

A legitimate problem with many older .450/.400s is that they were built on actions that would accommodate larger cartridges, thus ending up at a weight of eleven pounds or more. Recoil is greatly reduced, but these guns have more weight than needed. I can't imagine anything more pleasant to carry and shoot than a .450/.400 double, at no more than ten pounds. Especially in today's Africa, when so few safaris include elephant, a .450/.400 would be a particularly sensible choice

Jim Fullerton's double is a classic prewar Rigby in .450-3¼". This cartridge is fairly common, and would have had more lasting popularity except for the weird regulation in about 1907 that banned .450-caliber cartridges in both India and the Sudan.

for buffalo and tracking hunts for lion, but if you have one built, insist on keeping the weight down just a bit.

Moving up a step, there are actually lots of choices. The top three at this writing are without question the .470 Nitro Express, .500-3" Nitro Express, and .500/.416-3¼" Nitro Express, probably in that order. Whether or not the .470 was really the most popular big-bore Nitro Express "pre-Ruark" is questionable, and whether or not it's the "best" big-bore Nitro Express is, to me, equally questionable. But it is the most popular and the most available, both in new ammo and new rifles. The .470's .475-inch bullet is relatively available, and certainly it is effective on anything that walks this Earth.

Interestingly, the older .500-3" Nitro Express has also enjoyed a considerable resurgence. It is not as popular as the .470, but all modern makers of double rifles also manufacture it. In older rifles it was generally accepted by the trade, so it is seen in a wide array of makes and grades. Note that there were two versions, the .500-3" and the longer .500-3¼". The latter is very rare but does exist; my old friend Sherwin Scott has a lovely sidelock Holland & Holland in the longer-case .500. Today, because of better load density with modern propellants, the 3" case is actually preferable, and it was and is the most common. Both versions originally used a 570-grain bullet in front of 80 grains of cordite, producing 2,150 FPS for 5,850 foot-pounds of energy. This cartridge is thus the first genuine leap forward in power from the .450 to .475 group of cartridges.

I have used the .500 off and on over the years, including on elephant. Unfortunately, I just don't have enough experience with elephant to properly judge whether it is truly more effective than the .450-to-.475 class. Those who do have such experience, however, tend to swear by it. Over the years, I have owned more .470s, and have taken more game with .470s, than any of the other double-rifle cartridges, but with today's availability of ammo, if I had to choose between the .470 and the .500, I would choose the .500. Gun weight and bulk will be about the same. Recoil will be similar. Effect, especially on elephant, is probably enough greater to be worth the slight difference in ammo availability.

The .500/.416 is obviously a step down. This cartridge is a recent development by Krieghoff, and is actually the only "new" Nitro Express cartridge. Officially designated .500/.416-3¼" Nitro Express, the .500/.416 is thus actually the .470 case (which is based on the .500-3¼" case) necked down to accept a .416-inch bullet. Velocity is reduced a wee bit (from the .416 Rigby's 2,400 FPS), to 2,350 FPS with a 410-grain bullet, to keep pressures down. This is still a 5,000-foot-pound cartridge. Note, please: If you want a double rifle in a .416-caliber cartridge, this big rimmed case is the only one to choose. It is obviously not available in older rifles, but all current makers of double rifles have made at least a few rifles in this cartridge, with Krieghoff undoubtedly leading the pack. Krieghoff offers European ammo, but Superior also loads .500/.416 and will load it with any .416 bullet the customer prefers.

I took a Krieghoff .500/.416 to Australia a few years ago, using it on banteng as well as buffalo. I also used Marc Watts's Rigby .500/.416 on a Cape buffalo a couple of years ago. It is a great cartridge. The first animal I took with it, a very large-bodied water buffalo, was rocked back on its hocks by the first barrel and flattened by the second. In a scoped double it probably offers the utmost combination of power and versatility, shooting considerably flatter than the big bores but offering similar energy. It does have drawbacks, at least to my thinking. Since it is based on the same case head, rifle weight and mass will be much the same as a .470 or .500. In some ways this is just as well; because the velocity is higher and energy is similar, felt recoil is much the same as with a .470 or .500! So it should be chosen for its versatility, but not as a step down in recoil from the big bores. If that's what you want, go to the .450/.400-3" now that it's again available.

In the .450 to .475 class it is pretty much a .470 Nitro Express world insofar as new rifles are concerned. A different cartridge is just a reamer, and ammo is available, so I suppose anything can be made, and perhaps has been. I have heard of a couple of new doubles in .450 No. 2, and I think Simon Clode at Westley Richards has made some new doubles in .476 WR. Rigby currently has an order for a .475 No. 2 (God knows why, except for the obvious: The customer is always right!). Holland & Holland continues to make .500/.465 doubles, which of course is the company's own traditional cartridge.

Realistically, the .470 is the simplest and most available choice, at least at this writing. I have owned and used several .470s with no issues whatsoever. However, my personal favorite in the .450 to .475 class is the old 1898 John Rigby .450-3¼" Nitro Express. Old-timers often refer to it as the ".450 Straight" because of its very straight case, and to me this is one of its great advantages. The straight case gives better load density with modern powders than the .470's bottleneck case, and that same narrower case also allows it to be housed in a trimmer, lighter action. As a traditional Rigby cartridge, Rigby has made a few (very few) modern doubles in this chambering (as Holland has made a few new .500/.465s). One of them is a very plain boxlock made for me, but it's on a wonderfully slim action weighing just a bit over ten pounds. Recoil is surprisingly mild, but I think that's because its left-hand stock fits me well.

At this writing I've had it just a year, but I've carried it for nearly three months of elephant hunting. Please note that rifles are carried a whole lot more than they are shot, so as I get older "carryability" seems to be gaining in importance. The other advantage to this (or any other .450 cartridge) is its ability to use standard .458-inch bullets. Mine is regulated with plain old Hornady 500-grain solids, but point of impact differs very little with the more traditional 480-grain Woodleigh bullets. My friend and elephant hunting guru Ivan Carter also uses a .450-3¼". Carter's is a lovely rifle custom-made for him by Heym, but Heym also offers its PH model in .450-3¼". I expect at least a slight resurgence of interest in this cartridge, with new factory loads from Hornady and a potential run of Ruger No. 1 single shots in .450-3¼". You see, with its basic .450 case head, the .450-3¼" is the largest-diameter cartridge that can be readily housed in the Ruger No. 1 single shot. The Ruger action can harness a .470 or .500, but only with fairly extensive work; the .450-3¼" drops right in with minimal modification. Quite a few No. 1s have been customized to this cartridge, and a run of factory rifles is contemplated. If it happens, it will be a huge shot in the arm for this excellent old cartridge.

The other big Nitro Express cartridge that has seen a bit of a rebirth is the .577-3" Nitro Express. Honestly, above .500 all the big bores are fairly unusual and today command significant premiums in both new and used rifles. However, the mighty .577 is truly a magnificent cartridge. This one was the real tool of the

PH Brent Leesmay and Jeff Wemmer with a tuskless elephant taken with Wemmer's new American-made .470. Without question the .470 is the most available double-rifle cartridge today.

ivory hunter. It was and is too much gun for the casual sportsman and too heavy for most professional hunters to carry, but the .577 is still wonderful for serious business with big elephant.

A smokeless version of an existing black-powder cartridge, the .577 Nitro Express, like the .500 and .450/.400, occurs in two case lengths, 3" and 2¾". But unlike the two others, there is a huge difference between the short case and the long one. The .577-3" used 100 grains of cordite and a 750-grain bullet, reaching 2,050 FPS and 7,020 foot-pounds of energy. Even today, it stands as one of the most powerful cartridges the world has known. The 2¾" case is a totally different cartridge, and they must not be confused; the shorter version used a reduced charge of cordite to propel a short-for-caliber 650-grain bullet; velocity was low and energy just 5,500 foot-pounds.

Rifles for the 2¾" version could be built relatively light, and in this guise it had some popularity in India. However, the strong suit of the .577's 750-grain bullet was not only power but also penetration, and the 650-grain bullet does not stack up. Take a close look at the proof marks if someone offers you a good deal on a .577.

The .577 in black-powder form was extremely popular throughout the British Empire in the last quarter of the nineteenth century. The transition to smokeless

141

came early, and many of the great ivory hunters relied on the big .577. James Sutherland used the .577; F. G. Banks used one; George Rushby used one; Tony Sanchez-Ariño still uses one; and the list goes on. American professional hunter Owen Rutherford, a good friend of mine, regrettably was killed in a freak accident in 1989. One of very few Americans to have killed a hundred bull elephant, Rutherford did it in his later years with a .577. A tough young Zimbabwe PH I know, Cliff Walker, carries a .577 every day and wields it like a toy. He wasn't carrying it the day he got mauled by a lion in Ethiopia; it had been left home because of gun-permit issues. Cliff figures he might have been saved a bunch of stitches if he'd had his .577.

The problem is most of us aren't quite as tough as Cliff Walker or Owen Rutherford, and a (minimum) fourteen-pound .577 is too much gun to lug around all day. I couldn't do it, and few men can. Taylor recommended the .577 (and the .600) as a second rifle, to be carried by someone else while the hunter saves his strength and carries something in the .450 class. But in the modern world of sport hunting, if there's a second rifle to a .450 or .470, it's probably a .375, not something bigger! The other drawback of the .577 is pure, unadulterated recoil. The .577 isn't for everyone, but it remains surprisingly popular with current makers. If you can handle it, man, does it work!

Many current makers of double rifles have made .600s as well. In original rifles it was actually quite rare, another example of a British cartridge with a reputation that far exceeded its actual use. Firing a 900-grain bullet at a relatively slow 1,950 FPS, it produced 7,600 foot-pounds of energy. This obviously delivered a tremendous blow, but with the greater frontal area and lower velocity,

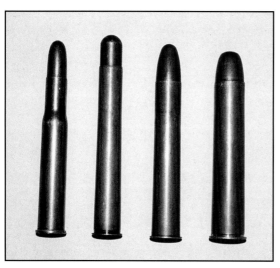

Left to right: .450-400-3", .450-3¼", .500-3", .577. Admitting the .470's greater popularity, I think these are the "best" double-rifle cartridges. The .450/.400 offers great performance with little recoil. The .450-3¼" fits into a trim action and uses common .458-inch bullets. The .500 is a genuine upgrade in power, and if you can handle the recoil and you're willing to carry such a heavy rifle there is nothing like a .577!

*Zimbabwe PH and elephant specialist Ivan Carter and I both like John Rigby's original .450-3¼"
Nitro Express, used to take this fine Botswana tusker in 2008. Carter's rifle is a Heym he had custom
made in the cartridge some years ago; mine is a new Rigby.*

all reports indicate that it never penetrated as well as the .577. Still, the .600 did
see use. Taylor wrote glowingly of a .600 he owned, and so did Major P. H. G.
Powell-Cotton, both Jeffery rifles. Powell-Cotton, however, relied more heavily
on a .450/.400, and, as mentioned above, Taylor recommends the big guns only
for closing the final deal.

Few well-known ivory hunters seem to have relied extensively on the .600.
One was Bill Pridham, who used the .416 Rigby as his main rifle but backed
it up with a .600 for the tough stuff. Another was Carl Larsen, a Dane who

During the sight-in before a Botswana safari, Bill Jones takes a bash from his Marcel Thys .577. Nobody ever said the .577 was fun to shoot, but many of the old-timers considered it the ultimate cartridge for the largest game.

hunted Portuguese East Africa in the early years of the century. His rifle was also a Jeffery, probably the underlever hammerless design most frequently seen.

The problems with the .577 are compounded in the .600; the rifles weigh 16 to 18 pounds, recoil is fierce, and, of course, the ammunition is very heavy and bulky as well. On the other hand, one shouldn't need a lot of cartridges!

The .700 Nitro Express, inspired by American Bill Feldstein, goes yet a step farther. When *Safari Rifles* went to press, the first .700 was still "in the works." Since then several have been made, but honestly, I have to regard this as a stunt rather than a practical hunting arm. The .700 has a 3½-inch case and its 1,000-grain bullet requires 215 grains of smokeless powder to develop 2,000 FPS. Energy is 9,050 foot-pounds. This is all very impressive, but the rifle that houses such a monster (and can be fired from the shoulder) must weigh about 22 pounds. You might as well try to lug around a Barrett rifle chambered for the .50 BMG cartridge.

The big, rimmed Nitro Express cartridges go hand in hand with double rifles, and today both have made an amazing resurgence in popularity. This certainly doesn't apply to all of them, but in modern rifles we don't need all of them! A big change since I wrote *Safari Rifles* is not only the increased popularity of doubles but also where they come from. In 1990 plenty of old doubles were available, but few new ones. Today the supply of old doubles in shootable condition has evaporated and prices for vintage guns are skyrocketing—but more new doubles are being built than ever before. Most of these will be built in just a few chamberings, but modern popularity doesn't necessarily equate to effectiveness.

With brass and bullets more readily available than ever before, don't overlook an older gun in good shape just because of its oddball chambering—especially if the price is right. But be careful. Most of the big Nitro Expresses were derived, at least initially, from black-powder Express cases. Obviously, they are not interchangeable. If you have any questions about the exact chambering of a rifle you're considering buying or using, find an expert. A number of black-powder rifles were made well into the smokeless era, and in rare instances only the proof marks on the "flats" of the barrels will tell you whether the rifle was proofed for black powder, Nitro, or both. If it seems too good a deal to be true, it probably is!

A second word of caution: Slug the barrel of any older double to determine exact caliber. For unknown reasons, the bore and groove diameters of British double rifles vary widely, with some calibers and cartridges much worse than others. Some of the most respected references on the subject are just plain wrong regarding bore and bullet diameters for Nitro Express cartridges, so check to make sure, but don't panic. The popularity of doubles is such today that no matter how oddball the dimensions, ammo can be obtained, one way or another.

Some Useful Metrics

Chapter 11

They say America will eventually make the transition to the metric system, abandoning our antiquated and complex English system of weights and measures. Perhaps we will someday; the metric system makes a lot of sense once you understand it. But that's the rub: Americans don't understand it, and few and far between are the metric cartridges that have received any acceptance among American shooters.

The lone exception seems to be the 7mm group; the various 7mms have darn near eroded the .30-caliber's position as America's favorite. But then, they had a head start, since the 7x57 predates even the .30-40 Krag and the .30-30. But the 8mm Lebel was the first successful smokeless cartridge, and the 8x57 goes back almost as far as the 7x57. Regardless of lineage, 8mm cartridges haven't done well in America. Remington's 8mm magnum has been a dismal failure in terms of sales, just barely hanging on. It's too early to tell how the .325 WSM will eventually fare. Like the "Big Eight," it's another great cartridge—but I fear it will suffer from the curse of the 8mm. The 6.5mm is a European standard, but the 6.5mm Remington Magnum went nowhere fast, and the .264 Winchester Magnum, even with its English designation, had but a short day in the sun.

The examples are endless. In spite of being an unquestionably better cartridge, the 6mm Remington is nowhere near as popular as the .243.

If our homegrown metric cartridges suffer so badly on the American market, it should be clear that European metric cartridges have no chance at all, and this is generally true. But it doesn't mean there aren't a number of really excellent European cartridges, past and present, that have made their mark in Africa's game fields.

In truth, an American who wishes to own and use a currently manufactured European cartridge lets himself in for almost as much hassle as he would in choosing an obscure and obsolete Nitro Express, or even a wildcat. If he latches onto a rifle chambered for an obsolete metric, he may inherit virtually unsolvable ammunition problems.

However, there are good sources for the most common metrics in the United States. RWS's excellent ammunition is imported, albeit in small quantities. Norma ammunition tends to be a bit more available. Not all of Norma's offerings are imported, but it loads a wide variety of common (and some obscure) metrics. Among R.C.B.S., Huntington, and Hornady you can find (or have made) dies for almost anything, and bullets can be had for most of the more common metric designations. But under no circumstances, as with the Nitro Expresses, will it be as simple as going to the corner store and purchasing a box of .270, .30-06, .375, .458, or even .416 Remington.

In spite of the frustrations, there are good reasons for owning some of the metrics. For one thing, many of them were and are chambered in excellent rifles that just beg to be taken to Africa and used. For another, a few metric cartridges occupy niches unfilled by domestic offerings. OK, that's stretching a point. We have incredible redundancy in the wide spectrum of modern cartridges. But whether it's real or not, we rifle nuts can always find an excuse to own and use a particular cartridge. Let's take a look at some of the most useful metrics that might be encountered.

6.5mm

The 6.5mm, bullet diameter usually .264, is a European standard and has been since smokeless powder came into being. Perhaps the most famous of all the 6.5s is the 6.5x53R Mannlicher-Steyr, originally a Greek military cartridge and sold all over the world in the fine Austrian Mannlicher sporters. The English called it the .256 Mannlicher after their manner of calling a cartridge by the land diameter of its bore rather than of the groove or bullet.

Firing a very long, well-constructed 156-grain bullet at 2,300 feet per second, this little cartridge gave incredible penetration. The 6.5x53R sparked the smallbore craze that swept Africa, and it was widely used by many turn-of-the-century hunters. The near-identical 6.5x54 Mannlicher-Schoenauer that followed it in 1903 (and was soon called the "new" 6.5 or .256) shared its ballistics and reputation. Sometimes it's unclear who used which cartridge. Philip Percival loved the .256, and so did the great lion hunter Leslie Tarlton. Bell used it some, and Powell-Cotton, John Millais, and Blayney Percival swore by it. It was the favorite rifle of the great hunter/soldier Maj. C. H. Stigand.

The 6.5x54 M-S is still available today, but the rimmed 6.5x53R cartridge is strictly a piece of history, and most of the rifles still in existence have been shelved for lack of ammo. Roger Whittall retired his for that reason, a grand old rifle that he learned to shoot with. It was given to his grandfather by F. C. Selous himself.

The .256 wasn't a giant killer, but it was light, quiet, and gave unprecedented penetration, much appreciated by hunters who had grown up with black-powder, low-velocity arms firing hardened lead bullets. The 6.5x54 Mannlicher-Schoenauer remains with us today, though no longer as popular as it once was. Today it is rarely considered as a cartridge for really large game. There are several very similar 6.5s, including the 6.5x55 Swedish, 6.5x58 Portuguese, 6.5 Carcano, et al. (And, for that matter, our own .260 Remington.) All of these metrics originated as military cartridges, and the lifespan of each was more or less tied to the rifles that were chambered to them. Today the 6.5x55 Swedish is probably the most popular, and with its modern loadings, it—or any of the others—is certainly an efficient, viable choice for a wide range of plains game.

More interesting is the 6.5x68, a Schuler cartridge that is a true rimless magnum. Dating back to just before World War II, it's essentially the 8x68S necked down to 6.5, and the velocities are wonderful, about the same as or better than the .264 Winchester Magnum without the magazine-capacity-devouring belt. As with many of the 6.5s, the Europeans also load a rimmed version for single shots and the popular drillings.

7mm

The 7mms have been covered in chapter 2. However, it should be noted here that the 7x57, 7mm Mauser, or .275 Rigby—whatever you choose to call it—remains one of the world's great sporting cartridges. It was one of Bell's favorites with the

Europeans and Americans alike love their 7mms—but they have a lot of 7mm cartridges that are fairly rare in North America. The 7x57, left, remains quite popular over there, but the 7x64, center, and its rimmed version, the 7x65R, are also quite popular. The latter two are very similar to the .280 Remington in performance.

long, stable 173-grain solid; he once said that the barrel of his .275 had never been "polluted" by a softnose bullet. Today it would be generally illegal, and most folks would at least consider it unwise, to use the 7x57 on the kind of game Bell shot with it. But it must not be forgotten that it did the job, and it still could. While modern loadings push lighter bullets fast enough to give quite flat trajectories, Bell's experience might well be remembered today. The long 175-grain loadings that are still available may well be slow, but at moderate ranges they'll outperform the short, light, fast bullets all day long.

There is, of course, a rimmed version of the 7x57, and likewise for the 7x64 Brenneke mentioned in chapter 3. The 7x64 is virtually identical to, although not interchangeable with, the popular American .280. Its rimmed counterpart, the 7x65R, makes a wonderful light rifle in double or single-shot form, or as the rifle barrel in a versatile drilling, two shotgun barrels over a rifle barrel (or, rarely, a double rifle with a third, smoothbore, barrel underneath). The Europeans, too, have had their share of high-velocity 7mms, but the 7mm Remington Magnum has become a universal choice.

8mm

The 8mm bore has always been popular in Europe, and among Europeans who travel to Africa it pretty much occupies the niche the .30-caliber fills with American hunters. The good old 8mm Mauser or 8x57 dates clear back to 1888, making it one of the oldest cartridges still in use. Originally, it had a bullet diameter of .318, but in 1905 this was increased to .323. Since then, the earlier bore has been called "J" and the later version is designated "S." The English called the "J" bore a 7.9mm Mauser, and it was extremely popular. H. C. Maydon used his almost exclusively, as did literally thousands of sportsmen. Although the "J" bore is rare today, in the .323 configuration the 8x57 remains extremely popular to this day, and anything you say about the .30-06 could well be said about the 8x57. What it gives up in velocity it gains in frontal area, and the effect on game is about a draw.

A great many other 8mm cartridges were developed over the years. A few of them have hung on while many have died away. The most powerful, and the most interesting, is the 8x68S, a magnum-length cartridge with a case length of 2.658 inches. This is a cartridge a European might have instead of a .300 magnum, 8mm Remington, or .338. And it's every bit as good as any of them. RWS loadings range from 180 to 224 grains, and velocities and energies are quite high, the latter well above the magic 4,000-foot-pound level. I am a big fan of the 8mm Remington Magnum and have used it a great deal in Africa and around the world. The 8x68S is at least as good.

Flat-shooting and said to be extremely accurate, the 8x68S was introduced about 1939, and then reintroduced after the war. It has never been loaded in America but is a favorite of European big-game hunters. Like so many European cartridges, the really wonderful thing about it is the fine bullets RWS loads it with, from controlled-expansion H-Mantels to full-metal-jackets to aerodynamic "cone-point" bullets; available ammunition runs the full gamut.

9mm

There were some half-dozen European 9mm rifle cartridges, bullet diameter generally .356 instead of our more common American .358. Of them, the 9x57 Mauser enjoyed a degree of popularity, even in America. Although the bore diameter has potential, the European cartridges had generally low velocity. The best of them was no better than the .358 Winchester, and most were in a class with the .35 Remington. Rather than spend more time on the 9mms, let's turn to some metrics that still have real importance in African hunting.

9.3mm

The 9.3mm is a traditional European caliber with a rich tradition of excellent cartridges, some quite slow and primarily useful for driven boar, some a bit faster and more versatile, and a couple very fast and very useful indeed. In the English system, the bullet diameter is .366, making it quite close to the .375. The first smokeless 9.3mm cartridge, still loaded and occasionally seen, is the 9.3x57, based on the 7x57 necked up. The 9.3x57 is a bit of a wimp, but the 9.3x62 that soon followed makes good use of its greater case capacity and is a fine cartridge.

Introduced around 1905 in Mauser sporters that were far less expensive than the various English guns, it was at one time the most popular all-round African cartridge—and it's a good one to this day. I have a left-hand Tikka in 9.3x62. It's one of my favorite pig rifles, but for no good reason I have never taken it to Africa. The 9.3x62 is, however, an African cartridge of note, and it is still frequently encountered.

The best of the modern loadings propels a long, stable 293-grain bullet at 2,430 fps for 3,843 foot-pounds of energy, a deep-penetrating load that is available in Brenneke's TUG dual-core and H-Mantel bullet, the latter similar

Left to right: 8x57, 8x68S, 8x75R, 9x57, 9.3x62. There are some metric cartridges that have some following in the U.S., others we've perhaps heard of—and some we've never laid eyes on. Just like in the U.S., there are a lot of different cartridges in use by European hunters, and most of them do exactly what they're supposed to do.

to Nosler Partition and extremely effective. Full-metal-jacket bullets and more conventional softpoints are also available.

Few Americans have played with this cartridge in recent years, but it has some interesting advantages. First, it's a relatively small, rimless case, so it can be built into a light, compact magazine rifle with a full five-round capacity. That 293-grain .366 bullet also offers better sectional density, and thus better penetration, than even the 300-grain .375. Thanks to the European market, most major American bullet makers now offer .366 bullets, including Barnes, Hornady, and Nosler, so a full range of familiar bullets is available. The 9.3x62 is not a giant killer, but it is sort of like an upgraded .35 Whelen or .376 Steyr.

The 9.3x62 remains an excellent African cartridge today, especially for someone seeking performance with little recoil. Where its caliber is legal to use, I'd rate it as the minimum sensible caliber for buffalo and cats, made so as much by its excellent bullets as by its power level.

Better yet is Wilhelm Brenneke's largest cartridge, the 9.3x64, using a fatter, longer case to drive a 285-grain bullet at 2,690 feet per second for 4,580 foot-pounds of energy, and a 293-grain bullet at 2,570 FPS and nearly 4,300 foot-

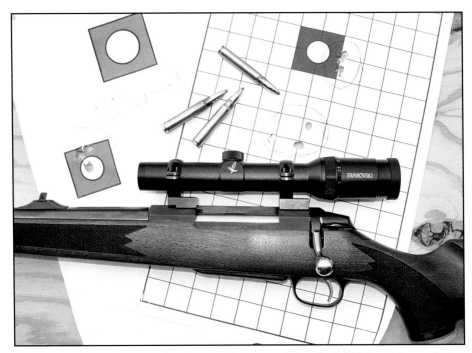

My left-hand Tikka 9.3x62 produced very good groups with handloaded Nosler 286-grain bullets. Bullets in 9.3mm are readily available in the U.S. because U.S. bullet makers also sell to European outlets, but this cartridge, like many of the metrics, is primarily a handloading proposition.

pounds. Although never popular among English-speaking hunters, the 9.3x64, in terms of trajectory, penetration, and bullet performance, must be considered every bit as good as the .375 H&H—and just possibly the only cartridge in the world that's better for all-round African use. Somewhat inexplicably, Federal has recently announced a loading for the 9.3x66, dubbed the .370 Sako Magnum. Based on a long, slender case, this cartridge must not be confused with the 9.3x64. At this writing I haven't had a chance to check this cartridge out, but my understanding is the .370 Sako Magnum is more akin to the 9.3x62 or the .376 Steyr, while the 9.3x64 should be lumped with the .375 H&H and newer developments like the .375 Ruger.

Ammo for 9.3x64, though currently all European, is readily available, and several European firms still make the rifles. It's amazing how strong the charisma of the .375 H&H really is; here's an equally good, currently available cartridge that is forgotten and ignored throughout much of the hunting world. But it's hardly forgotten by the hunters who swear by it, and many have—for all game up to elephant.

The European metric calibers are not seen nearly as often in Africa as in the old days, not even with European hunters. PH Justin Seymour-Smith of Zimbabwe and nine-year-old Rory Wurfbain are pictured with a Franz Sodia 9.3x74R that was used to take this eland.

The long, slender, rimmed 9.3x74R is probably the 9.3mm cartridge most familiar to Americans. A perfect choice for a light, fast-handling double in either the European-preferred over/under configuration or side-by-side, 9.3x74Rs in great numbers have made their way into the United States. It's also a common rifle-barrel chambering for a drilling. A gun with two 12-gauge barrels and a 9.3x74R is ready for just about anything. Just recently Hornady introduced the first American loading for the 9.3x74R, with Ruger chambering it to its No. 1 single shot, respectively the first American-made factory rifle so chambered.

In Namibia in 2006 our party had the chance to use one of Ruger's first 9.3x74R single shots with the first run of Hornady ammo. Performance was marvelous on plains game, provided we could get close enough. In a pinch I would use this cartridge on buffalo, and it would be just fine for lion, but it really is a bit too light for elephant even with the best solids.

The 9.3x74R goes back nearly to the turn of the century, but must not be confused with the still-older and much less powerful 9.3x72R, still loaded

My buddy Chub Eastman with a New Mexico bull elk taken with a custom Model 70 chambered for 9.3x64 Brenneke. Chub, himself a fine writer, has a "thing" for the 9.3s and uses several 9.3mm cartridges. (Photo courtesy of Chub Eastman)

and seen occasionally. The traditional loadings for the 9.3x74R today are a 285- or 293-grain bullet, both at 2,280 FPS, for 3,291 and 3,383 foot-pounds, respectively. Hornady's load is a 286-grain bullet at a slightly faster 2,360 FPS, yielding 3,536 foot-pounds. That puts the 9.3x74R on a par with, although slightly less powerful than, the rimmed version of the .375 H&H, the .375 Flanged Magnum.

Thanks to its excellent bullets, the same ones loaded in the other 9.3s, it has been used with success on game up to elephant. Again, for my money it's a bit light for such work, but it has certainly proven itself adequate for cats, buffalo, and all manner of plains game. Its strength is that it can be built into a very light, very responsive double rifle. Its weakness is its low velocity, giving it an arcing trajectory and a very limited range.

Given a choice, I'd prefer a .375 Flanged. However, most vintage .375 Flanged Magnum rifles were made by Holland and thus are extremely valuable. A great many 9.3 doubles were made, and do not command the same prices as the larger Nitro Express rounds. I once had a set of 9.3 barrels on the Valmet system for literally the cost of a common over/under shotgun. The 9.3x74R offers one of the best opportunities to find an affordable double that is more or less adequate for at least some dangerous game.

10.75mm and Larger

The Europeans had several 9.5mm cartridges, essentially a .375 that just didn't make it. Perhaps if either World War had turned out differently, those cartridges would have achieved wider use, but I have personally never seen a 9.5mm rifle. The next metric bullet diameter that sparked a lot of cartridge development—and still has impact on African hunting—was the 10.75mm, caliber .423. There were nearly a half-dozen 10.75mm cartridges, including a straight-case 10.75x57, the ultimate necking-up of the 7x57 case. Of these, just two achieved some level of popularity: the 10.75x68 and the 10.75x73. This latter cartridge is identical to the .404 Rimless Nitro Express, or .404 Jeffery.

The older 10.75x68 has the caliber and the case capacity, but it was loaded with a too-light-for-caliber 347-grain bullet at 2,230 FPS for 3,830 foot-pounds of energy. It obviously has the energy as well as the frontal area, and since it was available in inexpensive Mauser rifles, it was widely used. However, it was also widely mistrusted and is rarely seen today. That short, light bullet wasn't long in the penetration department and gave unsatisfactory results on thick-skinned game. Chances are it was just dandy for plains game and lion, but that isn't usually what one seeks in a .423-caliber cartridge.

Handloading with good bullets might cure its ills, but the 10.75x68 is probably best forgotten, and should not be chosen over any of the 9.3s with their long, well-constructed bullets. The 10.75x73, of course, is a marvelous cartridge, as it always was. Everything said about the .404 Jeffery in chapter 8 applies, and with it should be added thanks to RWS for keeping the cartridge alive long after the British gave up on it. As noted, the 10.75x73, a.k.a. .404 Jeffery, seems to be enjoying a bit of a revival. Norma has introduced a new factory load in its Safari line of ammo, and at this writing both Federal and Hornady are considering new American factory loads.

There were, additionally, a couple of 11.2mm (caliber .440) cartridges, the anemic 11.2x60 Mauser and the powerhouse 11.2x72 Schuler. Both vanished during World War II, probably never to be seen again. As mentioned in chapter 9, the famed .500 Jeffery was probably a European development, called on the Continent the 12.7x70 Schuler. It's likely that more German rifles were made than English, and Taylor mentions that the only ammo available was actually made in Germany, probably by Krieghoff-Schuler.

Mike Boileau and his leopard collected in Namibia with a pre-WW II double rifle made by Beissel-Winiecki, chambered for 9.3x74R using 250-grain Ballistic Tips. (Photo courtesy of Chub Eastman)

Now here's a bit of pure speculation, so please take it as such: History tends to be written by the folks who won the wars. If it's true that the .500 Jeffery (a.k.a. 12.7x70 Schuler) was a German development, is it also possible that the 10.75x73 (a.k.a. .404 Jeffery) was as well? The point to the .404 Jeffery was said to be to duplicate .450/.400-3" Nitro Express ballistics in a rimless case designed for bolt actions. To fit such a cartridge, this meant Mauser bolt actions. And why the seemingly inexplicable jump from the .450/.400's nominally .409 bullet diameter to the .404 Jeffery's .423-inch bullet? 10.75mm, bullet diameter .423, was already an established European bullet diameter. Again, this is pure speculation, but it makes sense. In those pre-World War I days Rigby was tied in with Mauser, and apparently Jeffery was tied in with Schuler. Why not?

In the realm of large, powerful cartridges there haven't been many metrics, but several made their mark and shouldn't be ignored by modern hunters. The German hunters of today tend to be knowledgeable and demanding of their rifles—and they're more likely to carry an 8x68S than a .300 Weatherby, or a 9.3x64 rather than a .375. They know what they're doing.

Smallbore vs. Big Bore

Chapter 12

Campfire arguments are part and parcel of the sport of hunting. It isn't that hunters are by nature particularly argumentative. But we do tend to be a bit self-righteous, and are certainly convinced that our own views are the proper ones. And, after all, since hunters love their rifles as much as they do their game, what better subject for campfire discussion—with each party certain that his own choice is the only sensible one?

The controversies are endless. Double rifle or magazine? Long barrel or short? Solid bullet or soft? Long Mauser extractor or the modern type? Even the heavy-caliber double-rifle crowd can argue endlessly over the choice of extractors or ejectors, hammer or hammerless. But few such campfire discussions are as fundamental as the one that rages between those who prefer small-caliber rifles and those who prefer the big bruisers.

The discussion has raged since there were hunters, and I suspect our ancestors discussed heatedly what size rock was the most effective: a huge stone that had to be dropped from above or a light, round stone that could be hurled with both velocity and accuracy? In America the argument was characterized by the fifty-year war of words between Jack O'Connor and Elmer Keith. For general hunting, Jack loved his .270 with 130-grain bullets, rarely using anything heavier than a .30-06. Elmer wanted more, and felt more was needed; he developed his .333 (and later .338) wildcats, believing that his 250-grain .33-caliber bullet was perfect medicine not only for elk but also for deer-size game.

It should be immediately obvious that such a discussion is relative to the size of the game being considered; what is "small" for an elephant is not small for a white-tailed deer. Nor can there be any absolutes about just what is "small" or "large." In the final analysis, although Keith and O'Connor remained bitter rivals, if not actual enemies, to their deaths, they weren't really all that far apart. (OK, that's an exaggeration. Keith genuinely hated O'Connor, but O'Connor

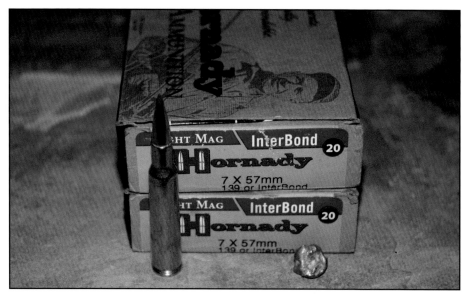

The 7x57, also known as the .275 Rigby, was one of the favorites of the "smallbore clan." I am extremely impressed by its performance on very large game, but I'm talking softpoints on kudu and zebra and such, while they were talking about solids used against elephant. Sure you can, but over time the majority opinion turned toward larger calibers.

seemed more mildly amused than aroused!) When Keith eventually got to Africa, he relied on his .33s for plains game but used a .375 for lion and a double in .476 or .500 for the really big stuff. O'Connor, too, hunted Africa extensively, actually acquiring considerably more African experience than Keith. He did indeed rely on a .270 or .30-06 for plains game, but the .375 was his minimum choice for dangerous game, and he also used a .416 Rigby. No one ever called the .416 a light rifle!

In Africa, the small-versus-large-bore discussion may not have been as heated, but the lines were more clearly drawn. King of the smallbores was Walter Dalrymple Maitland "Karamojo" Bell, unquestionably one of the great early ivory hunters and also an excellent storyteller who left behind a fine record of his exploits. Bell concentrated on elephant in a time when the great beasts were relatively undisturbed, and by all accounts he was one of the finest rifle shots of his day.

Bell used a number of rifles, including the .303 British, .256 Mannlicher, .318 Westley Richards, and even a double .450/.400. His greatest one-day bag was with the .318: nineteen bulls. He started with thirty-five cartridges, had eight misfires, and wrote that he had a couple of shells left over. Another favorite of his was the .275 Rigby, the old 7x57 Mauser, firing a long, beautifully shaped, 173-grain steel-

The big-bore boys were likely to go all the way up to the .577. This was a familiar "medium bore" in the black-powder days, but in a Cordite load it was (and is) a real powerhouse. The rifles were heavy and recoil was ferocious, but many serious ivory hunters, including Jimmy Sutherland and George Rushby, preferred the .577.

jacketed solid at a modest 2,300 FPS. With it, he shot a great many of his thousand-plus elephant, and his oft-quoted and most succinct analysis (from *The Wanderings of an Elephant Hunter*) goes like this:

> I have never been able to appreciate "shock" as applied to killing game. It seems to me that you cannot hope to kill an elephant weighing six tons by "shock" unless you hit him with a field gun. And yet nearly all writers advocate the use of large bores as they "shock" the animal so much more than the small bores. They undoubtedly "shock" the firer more, but I fail to see the difference they are going to make to the recipient of the bullet. If you expect to produce upon him by the use of large bores the effect a handful of shot had upon the jumping frog of Calaveras County, you will be disappointed. Wounded non-vitally, he will go just as far and be just as savage with 500 grains of lead as with 200. And 100 grains in the right place are as good as ten million.

Truer words have never been written; shot placement is everything—but Bell was an extraordinary shot who hunted in times that were, if not extraordinary, certainly much different from the years that followed. Many of Bell's contemporaries

In order to fully understand the smallbore versus big-bore argument, you simply must stand your ground while a six-ton elephant bears down on you. No rifle will feel particularly large! (Photo by Ivan Carter)

started with the light rifles—but few continued with them, and he is one of few hunters of his era who actively advocated them. Note, too, that even Bell had his limits. Later in his life he admitted that the long, slender 160-grain bullets of the 6.5s tended to bend. He wrote that the 173-grain 7mm was perhaps the minimum. I get a lot of letters reminding me that "Bell shot a thousand elephant with his 7x57." No, he did not, and he never said that he did. He shot many elephant with his .275 Rigby, but he also shot many with the .303 British, 215-grain .311-inch bullet, and remember that his greatest bag was with the .318, a 250-grain .330-caliber bullet. On elephant, that's still a smallbore, but it's a whole lot bigger than a 7x57!

John Taylor, author of *African Rifles and Cartridges* and *Big Game and Big Game Rifles,* was another marvelously entertaining writer who knew what he was talking about. One hears the occasional rumor that Taylor, unlike Bell, shot better with his typewriter than his rifle, but who doesn't? Taylor is considered the champion of the big-bore advocates, but he was nothing of the sort. He did use .577s and .600s, the ultimate big bores—but he rated them useful only as a second rifle for the professional elephant hunter. As you read his books, you quickly note that he was a double-rifle man, preferring the .450-.475 class. And in spite of that, he was lavish in his praise for the .375 H&H, .400/.350, .333 Jeffery, and certainly the .425 Westley Richards and the magazine-rifle cartridges of similar power. His "thing," if you will, was bullet performance, whether from large bore or small: "There were many occasions that convinced me of the excellence of these long heavy bullets of moderate velocity thrown by the .333 and .350."

If a bottom line is to be found in Taylor's works, he recommends something on the order of a .450 to .475 for the largest game, and few people have ever disputed such advice. Oddly enough, Bell himself might have made the same recommendation. In a letter to Denis Lyell, he wrote:

> The ordinary average city man (which we all are today when it comes to elephant and such, like it or not!), out for rhino say, will undoubtedly feel better about it when carrying a double .470 or .577 than he would with a .256 or .275. We must not forget that he has not had the opportunities of knocking rhino spinning with a .256. Therefore I take it the novice is behaving in a more sportsmanlike way when he arms himself with the deadliest weapon he can obtain, i.e., a heavy double.

A great many of the early hunters started with the great black-powder guns, changed to smallbores—and eventually went full circle to the largest of the Nitro Expresses. Selous himself started with muzzleloading 4-bores, later giving them up

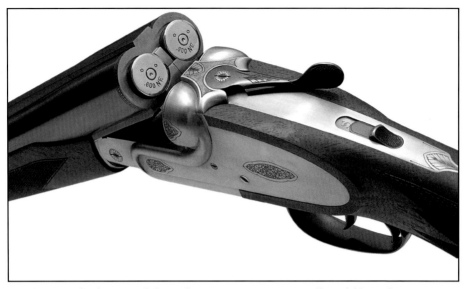

For the serious big-bore crowd the mighty .600 Nitro Express is still available, and I suppose some makers will put together a .700 if your pockets are deep enough. Because of gun weight, however, sensible cartridges probably stop at .577—and always did.

in favor of a single-shot .461 by Gibbs, which he used well into the smokeless era. However, he also used the .256 Mannlicher and the .303, and he finished his career a great fan of the then-new .375 H&H.

Arthur Neumann is believed to be one of the three greatest elephant hunters of the old days. The two others are Bell and Capt. James Sutherland. Neumann started with black-powder 10-bores and black-powder .577s, all breechloaders. At the end of his career, he used a .303 British, .256 Mannlicher, and a .450-3¼" by Rigby. He reckoned the .256 too light for elephant, but used the .303 on the great beasts.

Capt. James Sutherland hunted from 1896 to 1932, and might have been the greatest elephant hunter of all. Starting in the smokeless era, in his early years he used a .303 Lee-Metford, and later on a .318 Westley Richards. He gave up on them, eventually shooting a pair of .577 Nitro Expresses. In *The Hunter is Death,* Bulpin quotes Sutherland as saying to George Rushby:

> After all, we are in the business to kill elephants and the more efficiently and humanely we do it the better. All the hunters I know, particularly the young and cocky ones, who use smallbore weapons and consider themselves such stylish shots that they cannot possibly miss a vital point, invariably litter the bush with wounded animals, or get themselves killed before they learn any better. Common humanity demands that if we are to kill, we at least do so with maximum dispatch.

I have seen enough failures to penetrate with perfectly adequate elephant calibers that I have no desire to test the smallbore versus big-bore argument personally. I think the .375 is adequate, but marginally so, and a .40-plus with a heavy bullet and adequate velocity is a whole lot better.

George Rushby, too, was an early fan of the .318. He was shooting elephant from a ladder, and that 250-grain bullet was just the ticket, allowing precise shot placement with little disturbance and little recoil. He tried it with a double .450 and the recoil knocked him off the ladder! In general, though, Rushby, like Sutherland, was a .577 man. In his own book, *No More the Tusker,* Rushby wrote that for elephant, "All rifles from .400 cal. downward should be considered smallbores and from .400 cal. up to .475 cal. as medium bores and from .475 cal. up to .600 cal. as large bores."

By Rushby's classification, there were several "medium-bore" advocates. Commander David Blunt used almost nothing but a .416 Rigby. "Samaki" Salmon and William Pridham shot several thousand elephant between them, largely with .416s, although each also had a big double for backup—Salmon a .470 and Pridham a .600. And yet Bell wasn't alone with his smallbore. Maj. C. H. Stigand, who shot in Somaliland and Central Africa between 1899 and 1919, was a true smallbore fan; although he had a double .450, he much preferred the .256 Mannlicher for virtually everything.

163

Walter Bell in 1951 at Corriemoillie, his estate in Scotland. No other hunter has ever been identified more closely with smallbores for large game than W.D.M. Bell. He shot the majority of his 1,000-plus elephants with a .318 and a 7x57.

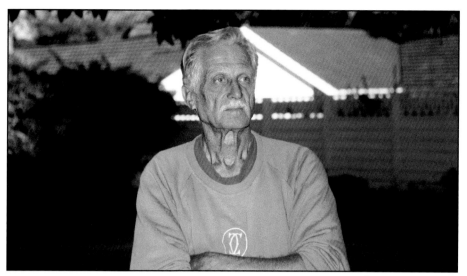

Famous elephant hunter Ian Nyschens shot most of his elephants with a .450-3¼″ double rifle by John Rigby. He used it so much that the barrels eventually separated at the ribs, and he had to send it back to London for repairs. Not many people shoot a double rifle that much! This picture was taken in 1985.

When Oklahoma lawman Charles Cottar fetched up in East Africa at the turn of the twentieth century, he had his Winchester .32 Special with him. Apparently nobody told him it wasn't enough gun, and he used it well until, later on, he obtained a Model 95 in .405. It could be argued that even his .405 was downright marginal for the largest game: Eventually a rhino did, indeed, kill him.

With a current bag of well over a thousand elephant, Tony Sanchez-Ariño is one of the greatest living elephant hunters. Regarding Bell's bag of over a thousand elephant with smallbores, Sanchez wrote:

> This fact has been intensely discussed by others far more knowledgeable than me, but I would like to say that if all his elephants were killed with the smallbore, and, in addition, several hundred buffalo and plenty of lion, then he was very lucky to have survived to tell the tale.

The smallbore men relied on precise shot placement, which they were capable of delivering, plus excellent performance from long, heavy-for-caliber bullets. The large-caliber advocates relied on nothing different; they also demanded topnotch bullet performance, and they staked their lives and fortunes on their ability to place those bullets. On the other hand, they wanted the large-caliber, heavy bullets as a hedge against human error and occasionally less-than-perfect bullet performance. That's the

Ivory hunter James Sutherland could be considered the direct opposite of Walter Bell, for he shot a .577 double and considered it a necessary tool of his trade.

difference, pure and simple. Given shot placement, a good bullet from a smallbore will work wonders.

As I mentioned, I'm incredibly impressed by the 250-grain bullet from the .318 Westley Richards, and also the 220-grain .30-caliber and 175-grain 7mm bullets. In a pinch I'd use them on darn near anything—but I'd prefer not to have to. Our little .30-06 has a wonderful reputation in Africa, going back to Teddy Roosevelt's 1909 safari. The old Kenya hand, Leslie Tarlton, may have held one of the highest all-time bags for lion. In a letter to Denis Lyell in 1926 he wrote, "I also think a great deal of the American Springfield, which with a 220-grain bullet is, I rather fancy, the best all around smallbore in the world."

On his 1934 safari Hemingway did wonderful work on buffalo, lion, and rhino with his Springfield—which he understood and shot extremely well. He did not do so well with his double .470; he hated the trigger pull, didn't know the rifle, and just plain couldn't shoot it. Therein is the crux of the matter. Whatever rifle is chosen, whether .30-06 or .600 Nitro Express, the bullet must be constructed so as to get into the vitals—and the shooter must be able to put that bullet there.

There is also the experience factor, which, human nature being as it is, the inexperienced among us are loath to take into account. The old-timers we are discussing hunted every day for periods of weeks and months and, when the hunting

Harry Manners with Eleanor O'Connor in Mozambique. Manners was a great proponent of the classic .375 H&H and shot most of his elephants with it. He was one of the few ivory hunters who was neither a strong proponent of a large bore nor a proponent of the smallbore. Eleanor herself took most of her game with a 7x57.

was good, shot elephant every day. They got good at it or they went broke. Or they were killed. Despite serious elephant overpopulation in several southern African countries today, little "culling" is being done, partly because of cost but mostly because, despite the growing necessity, it is politically incorrect. But culling was widely practiced in the post-World War II years, and there are some hunters alive today who have more experience with elephant than any of the old ivory hunters. Note that culling is different from ivory hunting. Cow elephant are considerably smaller than bulls, with lighter skull structure. Even so, Paul Grobelaar, still alive today, has shot more elephant than any other man who ever lived. He did a lot of it with an FN-FAL using full-patch 7.62 NATO ammo.

During their time together at the department of Rhodesia National Parks, Grobelaar mentored my friend Richard Harland, who refuses to quote the number of elephant he took. Early in his career Richard used what was available, from a .30-06 with 220-grain solids to big doubles, but he settled on the .458. In turn, he taught Barrie Duckworth how to hunt elephant. Duckworth, just a few years older than I, is another man who has taken a thousand elephant. Barrie settled on a pair of

Mannlichers in .458. Again, culling is different. It is worth noting that today Harland and Duckworth, confirmed bolt-action men, now own original .505 Gibbs rifles with, by pure coincidence, consecutive serial numbers.

When I started hunting in Africa it wasn't uncommon to have two or three buffalo on license. Today it is more usual to have just one buffalo available on a safari. On one safari in five, today's hunter may have the opportunity to shoot one elephant. At today's prices, few of us will have the opportunity to take more than one lion in our lifetime, and many will acquire considerable African experience but never take a lion. In almost all cases in modern Africa, a wounded animal goes on your license. The capability of the smallbores to take game far beyond what might reasonably be expected is there, but it seems ridiculous in this day and age to take any risk whatever that could result in a wounded and lost animal.

The old East Africa Professional Hunters' Association, which counted as members several of the old smallbore gang, established .40 as the minimum caliber for elephant, buffalo, and rhino. In other countries the .375 H&H is often the stated minimum for lion, eland, and larger game. Even the most recoil-shy hunter should be able to learn to handle a .375—and remember that George Rushby called the .375 a "smallbore" when it came to elephant. It is a game of shot placement and bullet performance, but both the large-bore and the smallbore camps always recognized that. It's just that the large-caliber advocates realized that neither would always be perfect, and they wanted the slight edge that a larger bullet of greater diameter does unquestionably offer.

It's also very important to understand that times have changed. In the days of Stigand and Bell the occasional loss of a wounded animal was, though regrettable, acceptable. Both of their writings include mentions of such events, matter-of-factly and with little recrimination or apology. Ethically, we no longer willingly accept such losses. Pragmatically, we can't afford them!

The Modern Softpoint

Chapter 13

The jacketed bullet was a parallel development with smokeless powder. Even hardened lead projectiles, which worked fine at the velocities black powder was capable of, skidded down the barrel and were unable to "take" rifling grooves when smokeless powder jumped velocities forward. It seemed a simple expedient to cover the lead with a "jacket" of gilding metal or copper. That allowed the harder metal (at a higher melting point) to take the friction and engrave into the rifling. Early developments were for the military, and the design the military settled on was a lead core completely encased in harder jacket material. Thus, a by-product of smokeless powder and jacketed bullets was unprecedented penetration. Higher velocity and less bullet deformation were the primary factors, but the greatly reduced bullet diameter of the new smokeless-powder cartridges (compared to the older black-powder cartridges) also contributed, because bullets of smaller diameter meet less resistance and tend to penetrate deeper.

In any discussion of modern bullets and bullet performance, it is important to keep these things in mind. Newer propellants and case designs have increased velocities since the first smokeless-powder cartridges, but the rules haven't changed. Penetration on game remains primarily a function of velocity versus resistance. Long before bullets were jacketed, it had been learned that bullet expansion—upset—on impact transferred more energy, created a larger wound channel, and did more damage to vital organs. There are plenty of examples of lead projectiles with hollow nose cavities, split noses (as from the Dum Dum arsenal in India), and even nose cavities filled with explosives. Long before smokeless powder it was known that such projectiles created horrible wounds in combat and on lighter game, but experienced hunters of really large game learned that to get the penetration required, they needed harder bullets that would hold their shape as they penetrated.

It wasn't a huge leap to transfer this knowledge to early jacketed projectiles intended for the higher velocities of smokeless powder. In fact, expanding bullets were much easier to make than full-metal-jackets: A cup of soft copper with a solid base could be drawn and filled with softer lead, with the lead exposed at the nose. To this day many hunting bullets are still made with this simple cup-and-core construction. Upon impact the exposed lead at the nose flattens and the jacket peels back. When we say a bullet "expands," we mean that it increases not in mass but rather in frontal diameter. Increased diameter means a larger wound channel—but also more resistance.

I still use the term "softpoint" as a generic for bullets designed to expand on impact, so coined because the tip was soft lead. Bell and his contemporaries called them "soft-nosed" bullets, as in his famous quote: "The barrel of my .275 Rigby has never been polluted by the passage of a soft-nosed bullet." Various tip designs and materials have been used on bullets designed to upset on impact and during penetration, and some of these bullets now contain no lead at all. So the proper term really is "expanding bullet." But whatever name we may use, in his day Bell was correct: Early expanding bullets were, if not erratic, extremely inconsistent. Bell saw it on African game. In his youth Elmer Keith guided elk hunters and saw numerous failures of early softpoints in .30-06s and .30-40 Krags. For a time he went back to black-powder single shots, and throughout his life he advocated relatively heavy calibers with long, heavy-for-caliber bullets—even on fairly light game.

Over the years expanding bullets got a whole lot better. It didn't take long to figure out that bullet expansion was good, at least on lighter game, but not if too much expansion occurred too quickly upon impact. The expansion of even the simplest cup-and-core bullet could be retarded, if not actually controlled, by jacket thickness and material, and by the amount of lead exposed at the tip, and even the shape of that tip. And, as Elmer Keith figured out, sheer bullet weight covers many sins in bullet construction!

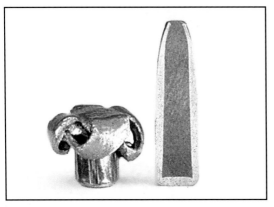

The Australian-made Woodleigh Weldcore bullet uses a thick jacket and a bonded core. They are ideal at moderate "Nitro Express" velocities, and are excellent choices for double rifles and cartridges up to about .416 Rigby in velocity.

Gary Williams took this buffalo very cleanly with a single 270-grain Winchester Fail Safe from his .375 H&H. In the old days the majority of professional hunters preferred "solids only" for buffalo. Today the majority prefers good softpoints, at least for the first shot.

Long before I started hunting, expanding bullets had become the norm throughout North America, with nonexpanding bullets specifically illegal for hunting big game in most jurisdictions. Even in Africa expanding bullets had become the norm for most thin-skinned animals. This is simply because they work better and faster. Well-designed solids do provide deeper, straight-line penetration. On lighter game they will almost always provide the exit wound that proponents of through-and-through penetration cite as making tracking easier. On the other hand, the disruption of tissue and vital organs caused by an expanding bullet is much greater, generally resulting in a quicker death and less tracking in the first place.

For larger game, however, the distrust of softpoints continued well into my own hunting career. In the 1970s it was still relatively common for professional hunters to recommend solids for eland, and almost universally to insist on solids for buffalo. This changed through the 1980s. Today it is very unusual to hear a modern PH recommend a solid for the first shot on buffalo, and it's almost unheard of with the largest plains game.

This is because our modern expanding bullets are really, really good. A few are so good and so tough, and their expansion is so controlled, that it's whispered now

It is often said that a buffalo's horn will turn a softpoint bullet. This is simply not true. A modern softpoint will cut through buffalo horn like it was butter. This was a finishing shot made with a standard .375 Power Point, not even a premium bullet!

and again that you can even use them for game up to elephant. Yes, maybe, under perfect conditions. In the Selous Reserve in 1988 we had an incident where a young bull was on the rampage and had essentially trapped my hunting partner, Bill Baker, and his PH and trackers against a patch of impenetrable thorn with no place to go. It is possible the bull needed to be shot, but more likely he was demonstrating, since his head was up. The PH was Luke Samaras, an extremely experienced elephant hunter. He probably would have let things develop for a few more seconds, but the game scout preempted that option by firing almost straight up into the elephant's throat. The bull spun away and fell over dead after a few steps.

The game scout had an old game-department Mauser converted to .458 Winchester Magnum, and the only ammo he had was Winchester's 510-grain softpoint. This is not and never was an elephant bullet, but it killed an elephant very dead with that shot on that day. So if it could be done with a conventional softpoint bullet, then there is no doubt in my mind that some of our really tough expanding bullets like the Swift A-Frame and Barnes Triple Shock could be used on elephant with some shots some of the time. Even so, I draw the line on softpoints

The Modern Softpoint

versus solids before you get to elephant. I want a bullet that will do the job all the time, regardless of the shot presentation offered.

Expanding bullets are not for use on elephant. A really tough modern expanding bullet could probably be used for the first shot on rhino. If the intention is to brain a hippo, then any decent expanding bullet will work just fine; the hippo's skull is like an eggshell, especially from the frontal presentation. But with body shots the hippo is a massive bullet sponge, and this is a game for solids only. We will leave buffalo for a final discussion in this chapter. Let's turn to modern softpoints as they relate to African game.

Bullets for Plains Game

The catchall term "plains game," as Jeff Cooper pointed out, is probably nonsensical. We use it to refer to the vast run of nondangerous African animals from dik-dik and duiker on up to eland. We can't use "antelope" because this group also includes zebras and pigs. We probably shouldn't use "plains game" because some of these animals are found in swamps, forests, deserts, mountains, and thornbush, not just on the plains! But I'm sure you get the idea.

The problem with selecting bullets, as well as cartridges, is the great variety of game Africa presents. However, bullet selection is really more complicated than selection of cartridges. You can carry two or even three rifles on safari and thus have a lot of flexibility and versatility—but I think you are pretty much obligated to choose just one bullet. The obvious exception is that with a heavier rifle, you probably want both solids and softs, but the former are for very specific purposes. Yes, I hear guys say they're taking two or three different bullet types so they'll have the perfect performance for various classes of game. I've tried this. Actually, I've tried it often, because part of what I do on many safaris is try out different bullets.

In practice this just doesn't work very well. You will probably have specific intentions on any given hunting day, but you just don't know what Africa will offer up. Even if you have two other rifles available, there will be times when an opportunity comes along and you will use the rifle in your hands. It is simply too complex to attempt to fumble for the right bullets for the right game and switch them out when you're in the presence of game and excited. If you try to do this, sooner or later you will rob yourself of great opportunities.

Perhaps the classic example of this is what so many of us do: Carry a few solids so that if a small antelope is seen, we can switch out and take it cleanly without undue damage to the cape. I tried this in the very beginning. On my first hunt in Kenya I used 180-grain Nosler Partitions in my .30-06. I had a handful of 180-grain FMJ Match bullets for dik-dik, duiker, and such, carefully loaded to the exact same point

173

of impact. By their very nature these animals are often taken in chance encounters. On that hunt I took very fine specimens of Kirk dik-dik, East African bush duiker, and steenbok—but I never once managed to switch loads. Since then I've tried a few more times, and once in a while I've had both the time and the presence of mind to purposefully switch out loads and take a small antelope with a .375 solid. But not very often! The best answer on the very smallest antelope is not to even consider switching loads, but instead change your hold and consciously shoot a bit behind the shoulder. How much more complex would it then be to have quicker-expanding bullets for deer-size antelope and warthog, and tougher bullets for the larger stuff?

To my thinking the only proper choice for Africa's nondangerous game is to use bullets that are tough enough to hold together and provide deep penetration on the largest game you intend to hunt with that rifle. Period. Provided you stay off the shoulder, appropriately tough bullets shouldn't do much more damage than a solid on the smallest antelopes. It is true that you may have to track impala-size animals a bit farther than with quicker-opening bullets that are more ideal, but on African game in general it's best to change your thinking a bit. We Americans love our behind-the-shoulder lung shot. Except for the pygmy antelopes, shoot instead for the center of the shoulder rather than behind it. Concentrate on the shoulder and you won't do nearly as much tracking!

Today we have wonderfully tough bullets available, the most classic current examples being the Swift A-Frame and Barnes X-Bullet or Triple Shock. So much hype surrounds these bullets that many hunters use them for everything. They work (oh, boy, do they work!), but in my view they are tougher than necessary for deer-size game. Obviously, caliber and velocity are factors. Velocity is the great enemy to bullet performance, and it works both ways. At very low velocities the toughest bullets may not expand as much as you'd like, sometimes acting almost like solids. On the other hand, at very high velocities bullets tend to expand quicker. Bullets that might perform very well at .308 Winchester and .30-06 velocities can become unreliable bombs at .300 Weatherby velocities. This is especially true if you draw a close shot; well, guess what—in most African areas shooting tends to be closer rather than farther. So with really fast cartridges you probably want tougher bullets that will absolutely hold together no matter the distance.

Caliber also counts. If you are pushing your power envelope—for instance, in North America using a .243 or a .25-06 for elk or in Africa using a .270 for the full run of plains game—you better choose a really good bullet. As I wrote earlier, my old friend Debra Bradbury has used almost nothing other than her battered old .270 for an incredible range of African game on several safaris. But she uses the now-discontinued Winchester Fail Safe, a really tough bullet that will absolutely penetrate.

I have come full circle on this. I used to advocate somewhat heavier calibers and somewhat tougher bullets than I do today. I also used to prefer through-and-

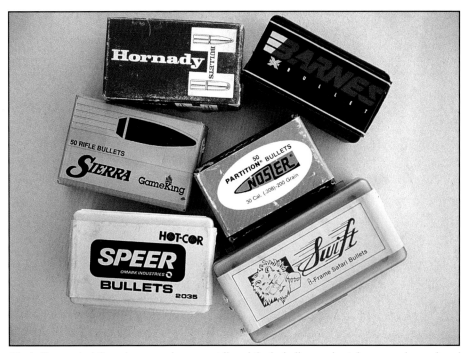

The bullets on the left tend to expand more rapidly, while the bullets on the right are tougher and tend to provide more penetration. All are good depending on what you want them to do. Also, never forget that impact velocity has much to do with how any given bullet performs on game.

through penetration across the board. This level of performance is still good, but over the years I have come to believe that, provided the bullet will reach the vitals from any sensible shot angle, a bit more bullet expansion is wonderful, and energy expended within the animal is just fine. There are some very good hunting bullets that will do these things consistently, provided there isn't too much velocity, too close a shot, or game animals larger than the bullet was intended for. So on game such as deer, sheep, goats, pronghorns, and even caribou, I am very likely to use a quick-expanding bullet design like Nosler's AccuTip, Hornady's SST, or even a conventional softpoint that I know will expand fairly quickly.

Such bullets would be perfect for impala and reedbuck, and probably equally effective on slab-sided antelope like hartebeest. The problem in Africa is that the game list usually includes multiple animals of varying size and toughness, so I think tougher bullets suitable for the largest and toughest game on your list are the best choices. If your list includes really big and really tough stuff like wildebeest, zebra, oryx, roan, and sable, you might well go straight to the extreme end of the toughness spectrum and choose bullets like the Swift A-Frame and Barnes Triple Shock.

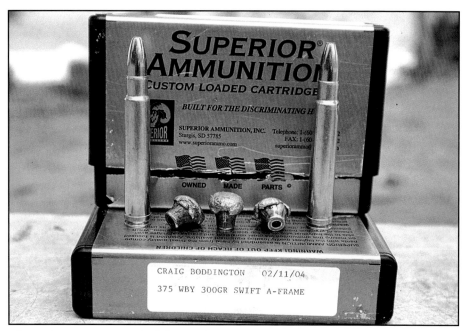

The Swift A-Frame is a wonderfully tough bullet, essentially combining a bonded core with a thick, tough jacket and a Nosler-like partition of jacket material. Characteristic of the Swift A-Frame is slight "squashing" of the shank and almost complete weight retention.

They will do the job, but they are not the only good choices. Back in 1948 John Nosler created a bullet that offered a truly reliable combination of both shock-inducing expansion and deep penetration. His Partition had a dual core separated by a wall or partition of jacket material. The front part expands quickly, and during penetration much of it is often wiped away. The back part, behind the partition, acts sort of like a mini-solid and keeps driving. The Nosler Partition was and is a benchmark bullet, and (always in calibers and weights appropriate for the game) it remains a fine choice for Africa. Note that there is little new under the sun. The Nosler Partition is not the only "dual-core" bullet. The German H-Mantel preceded it, with a front core of soft lead and a rear, harder core. The Swift A-Frame also has a partition separating two cores, but the magic of the A-Frame is that the front core is chemically bonded to the jacket so it cannot be discarded as the bullet expands and penetrates.

The initial "tipped" bullets tend to expand a bit too quickly for use on really big game. The polymer tip is relatively new, but the concept is not. Remington's old Bronze Point, still a great deer/sheep/pronghorn bullet, used a cap that was driven down into the bullet's nose on impact, initiating violent expansion. Likewise the Westley Richards capped bullet of a century ago. Canadian Industries Limited (C.I.L.) had a "saber-tip" plastic-tipped bullet forty years ago! But let's add bonded-core technology. This was started by Bill Steiger's Bitterroot Bullet, legendary but always in very limited supply and hard to obtain. Jack Carter popularized the bonded bullet with his Trophy Bonded Bear Claw, and of course now there are many bonded bullets. Bonding keeps jacket and core together no matter how radical the expansion, so weight retention and bullet integrity are increased dramatically. Retained weight, by the way, is an important factor not only in sheer penetration but also in the bullet's ability to hold its course as it penetrates.

Now let's combine the expansion-inducing polymer tip with the weight retention and integrity of a bonded core. The first of these were Nosler's AccuBond and Hornady's InterBond, followed by Swift's Scirocco. The latest, just now coming on the market, is Federal's "tipped and bonded" version of the Bear Claw, the "Trophy Tip" bullet. All these bullets are truly excellent for African plains game. I have used them all, in a variety of calibers, on a wide variety of game. They are wonderful, just provided you use common sense in their application.

Again, if you are pushing the caliber envelope or using the fastest cartridges, you might consider the toughest bullets. For instance, in 2005 I used 180-grain Swift Scirocco bullets in a .30-06 on a wide variety of game, with magnificent results. My daughter insists on 150-grain Swift Scirocco in her 7mm-08, and she works miracles with it. I often use 139-grain Hornady InterBond in my 7x57, and it has worked perfectly well on game up to kudu and zebra. In 2007 the first use of Federal's new bullet was on a wide variety of Namibian plains game. We were using 180-grain .30-calibers in a .30-06, and they performed magnificently on plains game up to eland and even giraffe, equally well on a host of lesser game.

Note that these are all examples of cartridges that have fairly mild velocities, which tend to produce consistent bullet performance, and the bullet weights were at least medium for caliber. Provided bullet weights are in that medium range, I'm not sure there is such a thing as "bad bullet performance" in mild cartridges like the 7mm-08, 7x57, and .30-06! No matter what bullet you choose, you can expect pretty darn good performance from any 180-grain bullet from a .30-06 at 2,700 feet per second. Go up 500 FPS, and you must be much more careful about your choice of bullet!

But as I said earlier, bullet weight can cover a lot of sins in bullet construction. I still like the plain old Hornady InterLock, and in the past couple of years both Donna and I have taken all manner of African game with 180-grain Hornady InterLocks from the Ruger M77 we share. Performance is consistently wonderful, and results are routine. I am also a big fan of plain old Sierra GameKings. They expand fairly quickly, true, but the accuracy is fantastic. It's just a matter of matching the bullet to the game. In my .300 H&H I go up a step for African game, using the 200-grain

Sierras that this rifle loves. My 8mm Remington Magnum also loves Sierra bullets, but the 8mm bullet I use is a relatively heavy 220-grain slug. This was the only rifle and bullet I took to Ethiopia in 2000 and Chad in 2001. It has accounted for kudu, mountain nyala, and even eland without a hiccup.

So, in sum, today the classic bullets for African plains game are probably the toughest bullets. If in doubt, by all means err on the side of a bullet that is too hard rather than too soft. Because of the range of game, bullets that are medium- to heavy-for-caliber are certainly better than light-for-caliber bullets. We Americans tend to be obsessed by velocity and accuracy (probably in that order), but neither is of utmost importance in African hunting, because shooting at really long range is rare. Bullet performance should be the most important criterion, and you definitely must choose a bullet tough enough to provide the penetration you need on the largest game you intend to hunt. But the toughest bullets are not the only choices. The goal is still to obtain an effective combination of expansion and penetration. Depending on your caliber and velocity, chances are there are many fine choices.

Bullets for Leopard

The leopard is a special case. He is properly considered dangerous game, and indeed can be very, very dangerous—but even a big leopard is only half the size of a lion, and perhaps just 10 percent the size of a buffalo. Because he is dangerous, and probably because relatively few Americans have a lot of experience with genuinely dangerous game, all too many of us go leopard hunting armed with too much gun and too much bullet. We'll address the gun issue later, but I think bullet selection is the more important of the two.

A really big leopard might weigh two hundred pounds, but the average normal shootable tom weighs considerably less. An average leopard is about the size of a medium-size white-tailed deer. Deer are taken more quickly and cleanly with a relatively fast bullet that expands and does damage than with a slower, heavier bullet designed for much larger game. There's nothing wrong with taking a leopard, or any other African animal, with a .375, but here's a good example of what will often happen: In Namibia's eastern Bushmanland in June 2007 I had a lovely tom come onto a bait at exactly 5 P.M. in beautiful light. It wasn't a big leopard, just a nice, normal, mature tom, body weight about 140 pounds. I had plenty of time and good light, unusually good conditions for shooting a leopard, and the shot was almost dead broadside at fifty-three yards. I came up the rear line of the foreleg one-third up into the body, moved the cross hair a couple of inches into the shoulder, and fired. The rifle was a .375 H&H, the bullet a 300-grain Trophy Bonded Bearclaw.

All of these softpoints were recovered from game. Some look better than others, and (characteristically) the boattails shed their core as they slowed down and upset. Remember, all were recovered from game, so all of these bullets did their work.

I expected the leopard to collapse on the branch and be dead under the tree. Instead, as I came out of recoil I saw that the cat had launched high and left, and I caught just a quick glimpse of it at the top of its trajectory. It isn't a good sign when a leopard exits the tree under its own power, so this didn't look good. With the rare luxury of good light, we waited a few minutes and then advanced carefully. I was sure of the shot, so I still expected the leopard to be crumpled dead at the end of his parabolic leap. Nothing doing, and suddenly the light seemed to be fading very, very quickly and the sere grass that had seemed so sparse looked thick and forbidding. We found deep tracks where the leopard had landed, but we missed the line of his retreat. Then the trackers joined us, and we found the leopard dead just thirty yards away. The entrance hole was exactly where I'd wanted it, and exactly where it should have been. The caliber-size exit hole was exactly on the other side, and the leopard had died in mid-stride.

No two animals react exactly alike upon receiving a bullet. That leopard was shot well and died quickly, so there were obviously no problems. However—and I'll admit there is no way to prove this—I firmly believe that with that shot placement this leopard would have been dead under the tree had I shot it exactly that way with any quicker-opening deer bullet from any deer caliber, perhaps from .243 on up. In 2005, when we did the leopard hunt for *Boddington on Leopard,* I used a .30-06.

This is Federal's newest bullet, the "Trophy Tip" with polymer tip and a small lead core up front bonded to the jacket. So far every bullet I've recovered has looked like this, with a long shank and nearly total weight retention. Hunting bullets just get better and better!

Swift Bullets was a sponsor of that film, so of course I used Swift bullets, but instead of the tough Swift A-Frame I used the quicker-opening Swift Scirocco. The light was terrible, so I used the safer lung shot rather than the more dramatic shoulder shot. As a result the leopard ran forty yards and gave us a scary follow-up in the dark, but the bullet entered where it should have and the exit wound showed good expansion.

There are some places where the .375 is still the legal minimum for all dangerous game, including leopard, and there are probably more occasions when the .375 is the scoped rifle that is available to take into the leopard blind. This is not a problem, but if you know going in that you're going to use your .375 for a leopard, this is one situation where you might consider taking a handful of cartridges with bullets that are lighter, quicker, and faster-opening than the bullets you might prefer for buffalo and other game for which the .375 is really designed. This shouldn't be a problem, because before going to the leopard blind you will almost certainly check zero at the exact measured distance from blind to bait. Good choices would include light bullets like the old 235-grain Speer or 265-grain Nosler AccuBond, or a common 270-grain bullet like the Hornady Spire Point. Or, if you want to stay consistent and use 300-grain bullets across the board, I've had great luck with 300-grain Sierras.

The beauty of the .375 is, of course, its marvelous versatility, and you can use any .375 bullet and have more than enough gun for leopard. Leopard are not only not large but also not particularly tough. And yet I have personally seen more of these cats wounded with .375s than with all of the smaller cartridges put together. I believe this is because most .375 bullets are designed for optimum performance on much larger game. Keep this in mind. If you have a choice, use a deer caliber with a deer bullet. If you don't, be very careful of your shot.

Bullets for Lion

It's funny how often we hunters exaggerate the size of the game we hunt. Buffalo are often quoted as "two thousand pounds of fury" or some such malarkey. This is probably 25 percent inflation, although 1,500 pounds of upset buffalo is still a lot of bull. Similarly, lion are often described as weighing 500 pounds. I'm sure captive-reared lion reach this figure, but a wild lion weighing anything close to 500 pounds would be extremely rare, if even possible. A good weight for a fully mature male is close to 375, maybe 400 if he has just fed heavily. This is still a lot of cat, but cats are thin-skinned and relatively light in the shoulders, offering nothing like the resistance to a bullet that a buffalo presents.

In most jurisdictions the .375 is the legal minimum for lion, and it's a wonderful choice. You could argue that this much power isn't needed for a 400-pound animal, and you'd be exactly correct. Except you mustn't forget what a lion can do to you and your hunting companions if you don't do things right! So I agree with the .375 for lion, and any good .375 expanding bullet will do the job. But there's a qualifier: If lion is the goal, the toughest bullets designed for optimum performance on really big game may not expand as much as is ideal on lion. With a .375, and especially with anything larger than a .375, you will get plenty of penetration no matter what bullet you choose, so the ideal would be a softer bullet that will open up. On lion you want and need bullet expansion. Wonderful choices include the same bullets mentioned for leopard, and also modern bullets designed to hold together and expand, like the Trophy Bonded Bear Claw and Woodleigh Weldcore.

Following up a wounded lion is obviously different from the first shot at an undisturbed lion, and the .375 isn't always the legal minimum. In July 2007 I got an unexpected opportunity to take a problem lion on the edge of Namibia's Etosha National Park. The most powerful rifle I had was a .300 Remington Ultra Mag, and .30-caliber is the legal minimum for lion in that country. I could have borrowed an open-sighted .375, but I thought I'd be better off with my scoped .300. This decision was aided by the 200-grain Swift A-Frame ammo I was using! If you intend to take a lion with anything less powerful than a .375, then you'd better be sure you have tough bullets that will absolutely penetrate. My first shot was quartering to; the bullet entered the point of the on-shoulder and exited just behind the opposite shoulder. Lion often die hard and this one did, so additional shots were fired. This was appropriate because of the potential danger, but that first shot was all that was really needed.

Bullets for Buffalo

Now we're talking about an animal that is not only potentially dangerous but also very large and very tough. But even the toughest buffalo isn't tough enough to stand up to a modern softpoint, given good shot placement and adequate weight and caliber. I never recommend that anyone go against the recommendations of his professional hunter, and there are still a few "solids-only" diehards out there, but I am absolutely convinced that a good softpoint will take a buffalo down more quickly than any solid. There is also much less risk of overpenetration. In any herd situation you must be very careful of what might be behind your buffalo, and you simply cannot use a solid in a herd. With some shot presentations (as in frontal), you can safely take a shot with a softpoint.

Most of the time I still hedge my bets, using a softpoint for the first shot and backing myself up with solids. On a follow-up I will generally use solids all the way. However, I freely admit that this is not an absolute necessity but rather just me becoming a bit of an old-timer myself. If you are using some of our really good and really tough modern "super softpoints" like the Swift A-Frame and Barnes Triple Shock, you probably don't need solids at all for hunting buffalo. I just feel better using solids for backup, and probably always will.

The rules are essentially the same as with choosing bullets for plains game; you just move up the scale a bit. The legal and practical minimum is probably .375, but appropriate bullets are still caliber- and velocity-dependent. Let's put it another way: At .375 H&H velocities there are no "bad bullets" that I know of. The really tough bullets work wonderfully, but so do bonded-core bullets like Trophy Bonded Bear Claw, Woodleigh, and Hornady's new "DGX" (Dangerous Game Expanding). Nosler Partitions are also superb, and so are the many specialty bullets like the North Fork and so many others. Nobody can claim adequate experience with all the great bullets we have today! It is also important to mention that over the years, I have taken a lot of buffalo with plain old Hornady InterLocks (both 270- and 300-grain in .375, and 400-grain in .416), and several with 300-grain Sierra boattails. Sure, the more conventional designs will shed some weight—but I have never experienced inadequate penetration.

Things change a bit when you move up to .375 Remington Ultra Mag, .375 Weatherby, and .378 Weatherby velocities. Most .375 bullets were designed to perform their best at .375 H&H velocities, and it takes a very tough bullet to hold together if you increase velocity a few hundred feet per second. The exact same situation applies with larger calibers. Bullet performance is routinely wonderful at the .416 Rigby's 2,400 feet per second. I have used great bullets like Barnes X-Bullet and Swift A-Frame and had great results—but I've also had great results from Nosler Partition, Trophy Bonded Bear Claw, Woodleigh, and plain old Hornady roundnose bullets. Go up to .416 Weatherby Magnum velocity, and you will have the best results with the toughest bullets.

I suppose this is equally true with the true big bores of .450 caliber and larger. At the standard old Nitro Express velocities of 2,150 feet per second or so, bullet performance is routinely wonderful. Increase that to .458 Lott and .460 Weatherby Magnum velocities and you have to be a bit more careful with bullet selection, but here the sheer size of the bullet relative to the animal starts to come into play. The .375 is not a really big gun on buffalo, but anything .450 or larger is a big gun on buffalo. You wouldn't want to be silly and use a 350-grain .45-70 bullet pushed very fast, but I don't know of any 500-grain .458 bullets that are likely to cause a problem.

Note that I prefer to stick with bullet weights that are more or less standard for caliber. I have read some pundits recently who recommended extra-heavy bullets like 350- and even 370-grain in the .375 and 450-grain bullets in the .40-calibers. More than twenty years ago I went through a phase where I tried extra-heavy bullets, and today I am very much opposed to them for reasons that I think are valid.

First and foremost, our modern expanding bullets are so good that there is no buffalo that walks that cannot be killed cleanly with a well-placed 300-grain bullet from a .375, or a 400-grain bullet from a .404 or .416. And if a charge can be stopped, it can be stopped by these bullets in the right place. Certainly the extra-heavyweights will work, and, specifically for hunting elephant, extra-heavy solids might have a place. But, the foregoing being true, the second reason I don't like them is they rob these cartridges, especially the .375s, of their great virtue of versatility. The weight difference from the norm is so great that, while actual accuracy may or may not be OK, the point of impact will probably vary wildly from standard bullets. These extra-heavy bullets do penetrate, but the velocity is so much slower that the .375 is no longer the all-round rifle that it should be, and the over-.40s lose their versatility as well. I suppose they would be OK if you knew you were only going to hunt buffalo in thornbush. But what if, on the way back to the truck, you saw the kudu of a lifetime 250 yards across a *korango*? What I love most about the .375, and to a lesser extent the "lower .40s," is the simple fact that you can do almost anything with them. So I'll stick with standard bullet weights that I know work, thank you!

Solids Today

Chapter 14

I n the old days they called these bullets "full patch." We tend to call them "full-metal-jackets" or "solids." Depending on the bullet, some of these terms may be descriptive—or altogether inaccurate. The best term is probably "nonexpanding hunting bullets" because some modern designs still have a lead core within a jacket of harder metal, while others are true "solids" of homogeneous alloy. Whichever, the purpose to these bullets is not to expand but rather to provide deep, straight-line penetration, usually on the largest and heaviest game.

That being the case, the actual utility for this kind of bullet is limited today. This is not only because hunting of the largest game is more limited than in bygone days but also because, as discussed in the previous chapter, modern expanding bullets are so good and so reliable. On the other hand, we do need solids, and when you need one you need one badly. There is no substitute, and I doubt there ever will be!

As I said, I am personally most comfortable using a softpoint for just the first shot on buffalo, and then switching to solids for backup shots and the follow-up. But I've admitted that you can forgo solids for buffalo altogether, especially if you're using the best and toughest modern expanding bullets. Nobody today has extensive experience actually shooting rhino—I certainly don't—but the sheer size of the beast and the angles presented during a charge suggest that the rules haven't changed: You need a good solid to reliably stop a rhino. I do have enough experience with hippo to have a firm opinion. An expanding bullet is just fine for a brain shot, but for body shots there is no substitute for a solid.

On elephant there should be no discussion, but, almost inexplicably, sometimes there is. The thing is, the demand for solids is limited, and not every bullet manufacturer offers a solid to fill this limited demand. In recent years the representatives of some bullet manufacturers have suggested that modern softpoints are so good that solids are no longer necessary, but these manufacturers invariably are the ones that do not make solids and who have little or no actual experience with

When you need a solid, you need it badly! One can argue whether you need a solid for the first shot on buffalo. Most feel you don't. But if you must stop an outbound wounded buffalo or, worse, stop a charge, there's no question. You want a good solid.

thick-skinned, dangerous game. As discussed, this might be true with buffalo, and in some circumstances you can get away without a solid for rhino or hippo. It is even possible to kill an elephant with a perfectly placed modern expanding bullet. But if you try it often enough, somebody will get killed.

Taking an elephant is no different today than it was in Bell's day. It is not a matter of raw power, because Bell was right: You cannot shock an elephant with anything less than a pack howitzer. It is a matter of deep, straight-line penetration that enables the bullet to reach the vitals. This means a *minimum* of perhaps eighteen inches of penetration through bone, gristle, and heavy muscle—and, depending on the angle and the shot desired, as much as four feet of penetration. Only a solid will provide this level of penetration on a consistent, reliable basis, and it had better be a damn good solid that will not bend, rivet, flatten, or deform. Bell and Taylor would

Modern softpoints are so good today that under most circumstances you could probably hunt rhino with the very best modern bullets. But what if you get a charge? Better load up with solids!

have been in complete agreement on this; their only disagreement would have been in the optimum caliber and weight of that solid.

There are actually relatively few nonexpanding solids currently available. That's the bad news. The good news is that, at least in my experience, all of them are pretty darn good. The major players available in the United States are Woodleigh and Hornady, both offering traditional steel-jacketed solids, and Barnes and A-Square, both offering homogeneous-alloy ("solid solids") solids (Barnes Super Solid and A-Square Monolithic). Then there's the Jack Carter-designed Sledgehammer Solid, long made under license by Federal; smaller suppliers such as North Fork; and also some excellent South African bullets, mostly lathe-turned solids, that work extremely well but are little known in the United States.

When recovered, the perfect solid can be reloaded and fired again. The imperfect solid may bend, flatten, or squirt some of its core out the base. So long as adequate penetration was obtained, this doesn't bother me so much. Bullet performance isn't necessarily a beauty contest, but if a solid breaks up, shatters, or expands like a

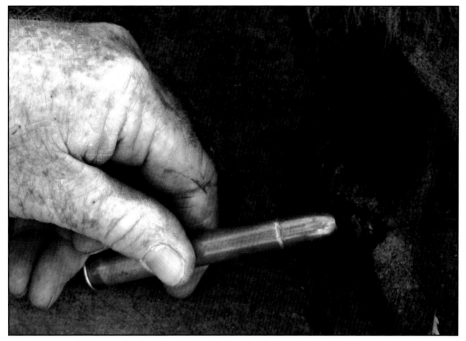

A .450-3¼" cartridge with a solid shown next to an entrance hole on an elephant. Always remember that a solid kills only by penetration through the vitals, with very little shock. Shot placement must be perfect.

softpoint, then it can be said to have failed. These conditions are extremely rare with modern solids, but they do occur. As with softpoints, this can be a simple matter of more velocity than the bullet was designed to withstand . . . usually coupled with extreme resistance.

The toughest solids out there are, at least in my opinion and experience, the homogeneous-alloy solids, whether of Barnes, A-Square, or other manufacture. Some years ago Paddy Curtis and I apprehended a poacher in the Selous Reserve. His rifle was a badly abused Brno .375, and he was using lathe-turned .375 bullets that he would recover, hammer back into shape, and reload into his fired cases. His primers and propellant came from AK-47 cartridges!

The problem with these projectiles is they don't compress much as they take the rifling, so you do get a major pressure spike. They can be used in some modern doubles . . . and some older doubles, especially guns with eroded throats and worn rifling, can handle them very well. Realistically, however, the double rifle is the weakest action type in common use today. Many vintage doubles were made with extremely thin barrel walls, and the steel in older rifles is, well, as old as the rifle. I don't shoot this kind of solid in any double rifle, new or old.

This is a "Bullet Test Tube," part of a bullet-testing system. These two blocks were end to end when a solid was fired. A softpoint wreaks havoc in this plasticlike test medium, leaving a huge "wound channel," but a solid will penetrate with the hole little more than caliber-size.

The good news is you don't have to. Double rifles are almost always chambered to cartridges that deliver lower pressure and lower velocity. At standard Nitro Express velocity, rarely higher than 2,200 feet per second, Woodleigh solids, designed to replicate the original Kynoch bullets, will hold up just fine. Move on up to the higher velocities of cartridges like the .458 Lott and the Weatherby Magnums, and I have seen some jacketed solids come unglued—but these cartridges are chambered in stronger actions, either bolt actions or modern single shots. You should have no qualms about using homogeneous-alloy solids if that is what gives you the most confidence.

Personally, I have complete confidence in good old Hornady solids, because that is what I have used the most. The traditional Hornady solid was a lead core encased by a copper-gilded steel jacket. The jacket material was obtained in a huge sheet, and there was a time in the early 2000s when this material was not obtainable. During this period Hornady used a thick alloy jacket, but no steel underlayer, with their solids. At high velocity this bullet may have caused some problems. I can't say because I never saw any problems; I just heard the rumors.

A Hornady solid (left) and flat-point North Fork solid (right), both 300-grain .375s recovered from a Bullet Test Tube medium. The perfect solid can be loaded and fired again after recovery, and both of these could be.

I shot several elephant with this bullet, using my .450-3¼" at the original 2,150 feet per second, and I had no problems at all. We shot others with this solid in the .375 Ruger, again with no problems; and we shot a lot of heavy game with this type of solid in Hornady's .450/.400-3". Again, no problems. However, this is now a moot point. After a couple of years of experimentation Hornady was again able to source copper-coated steel, this time in Germany, and that is the material now used for the company's solids, now redesigned with a flatter nose and called DGS (Dangerous Game Solid).

Two Woodleigh solids with two Woodleigh softs, all recovered from buffalo. The Woodleigh, like the Hornady, is a traditional steel-jacketed solid.

These days much fuss is made over the nose shape. Jack Carter pretty much started this with his flatnose Sledgehammer Solid, now made by Federal and still a very good bullet. I have read "authoritative" reports that state that you get better penetration with a flatnose bullet than with a roundnose design. I am very certain that a blunt-nose bullet transfers more energy on impact, and this is definitely a virtue of the Sledgehammer Solid (and other blunt-nose solids), and why it was so named. I have not yet seen any tests thorough and definitive enough to convince me that a flatnose solid penetrates better. As the theory goes, the flatnose develops a "bubble" of air that is pushed in front of the bullet, somehow aiding in penetration. At this writing this theory has not been definitively proven. Some bullet makers believe it and some do not.

With my military background, I am a skeptic. If this were true, then it seems to me our armor-piercing ammunition would be flatnose to aid in penetration. Actually, part of the reason elephant cullers in old Rhodesia often used FN assault rifles in 7.62 NATO was not just because the ammo was cheap and available but because of the wonderful penetrating abilities of the military spitzer "FMJ" bullets. However, there is a big difference between culling in mixed herds

This is the South African Dzombo homogeneous alloy solid. The homogeneous alloy solid is virtually indestructible, and is preferred by many professional hunters.

An elephant's skull is honeycombed bone with all sorts of odd angles that can turn a bullet off course. Only a solid can be relied upon to penetrate reliably, and only a solid should be used.

I used 500-grain Hornady solids in my Rigby .450-3¼" to take this Botswana tusker. These solids Johan Calitz with his Butch Searcey sidelock double.

have provided consistently excellent performance in several different calibers. Also shown is outfitter

Anthony Acitelli with a young Namibian "problem elephant" taken with a frontal brain shot from about a dozen yards. Anthony used a 300-grain Sledgehammer solid, perhaps the first "flat-pointed" solid and still a very fine choice.

and trophy hunting, so I don't recommend the 7.62 with military ball. Nor do I recommend spitzer bullets, because while I believe they probably penetrate better than blunter shapes, they transfer very little energy.

Over the years I have been perfectly happy with the penetration of roundnose solids. I do want lots of sectional density (weight for caliber), and I want long, parallel sides. Take these things, plus adequately strong construction, and you will get the penetration you need. On the other hand, I have no problem with the flatnose design that more and more bullet makers are shifting to (including Hornady). I am not convinced penetration is enhanced, but you do get better energy transfer. In my opinion, this means nothing on elephant. An elephant is just too big to be impressed by anything other than the very largest of hand-held firearms—and even then the only lasting effects will be dealt by bullet performance and shot placement. But there is a difference with buffalo. Flat-point or very blunt roundnose solids do hit noticeably harder than gently rounded designs. So I'm all for them, provided their construction is such that they will penetrate without deforming.

All said and done, a solid bullet is about penetration. This is not just a function of construction. Penetration may or may not be enhanced by nose design, but this I can tell you: Bullet weight, caliber, and velocity are extremely important. Sixty years ago John Taylor wrote that the .400 Jeffery (.450/.400-3") penetrated better than the true big bores. When Hornady reintroduced this cartridge in 2006, we took a few elephant and quite a few buffalo with it. We found exactly the same thing: unbelievable penetration with 400-grain solids. Let's examine this. The sectional density of a 400-grain .409 bullet is similar to that of a 500-grain .458 bullet. The .400 Jeffery is quite slow, no more than 2,100 feet per second, so this is comparable to many .458 Winchester Magnum loads and a bit less than .450-3¼" velocity. The .400 Jeffery absolutely penetrates better than a .458 or my .450-3¼", and it does this because its .409-inch bullet has less frontal area and less resistance.

Now, if you were to add velocity and could maintain consistent bullet performance (actually, the performance of a solid bullet should be called nonperformance, because what you want is a bullet that is recovered intact and unchanged except for engraved rifling marks), you would get more penetration. I am absolutely certain that the .416 Rigby and .416 Remington at 2,400 feet per second out-penetrate all the old Nitro Express cartridges at nominally 2,150 feet per second. This is because of higher velocity and less resistance. Now, if you step up from the .458 Winchester Magnum to the .458 Lott, you will definitely get more penetration. But a .458 Lott at 2,400 feet per second (possible velocity with handloads) will not penetrate as well as a .416 at the same velocity, because of the greater resistance. On the other hand, the 500-grain .458 bullet clearly delivers more energy than the 400-grain .416 bullet.

So it's always a compromise between adequate penetration and hitting power, both delivered from a package producing recoil that is acceptable to you. Velocity does increase energy and may increase penetration, but velocity also increases recoil, and (as with energy) this increase is exponential because the formula used to derive kinetic energy requires the square of velocity but takes the bullet weight "as is." Adequate penetration is essential and hitting power is nice, but ultimately it's still about shot placement, so we all have to stay within recoil limits that still allow us to place our shots.

With solids, always keep in mind that penetration is the goal; delivering energy is secondary. All things being equal, velocity does indeed increase penetration, but only if the bullet is able to stand up to that velocity and remain intact. In this regard the rules are the same as with expanding bullets: Resistance limits penetration. In the case of an expanding bullet, the more the bullet expands, the quicker it slows down and the less it penetrates. Solids aren't supposed to expand, but if they bend or squish or flatten they will slow down and/or deviate from their course. Modern solids, all of them that I have experience with, are really good—but the rules aren't different. Velocity enhances penetration if the bullet remains inviolate, but velocity is the great enemy of bullet performance, whether soft or solid.

If you have any questions about how a solid is performing at your velocity, try it in test media. Not too long ago I used "The Bullet Test Tube," ballistic wax tubes that can be laid end to end. Ballistic gelatin or even telephone books also offer a good opportunity to see what any given bullet is doing. Just keep in mind that no test medium properly replicates muscle and bone. Some test media are actually harder on bullets than the real thing, while some are easier—and this may depend on the shot you draw. Because of this I don't personally take great stock in supposedly definitive penetration tests, but checking penetration in any medium does give you a chance to compare bullets against each other and really see how a bullet is performing at the velocity of your load. Just be prepared: With modern solids you need an awful lot of test media stacked end to end!

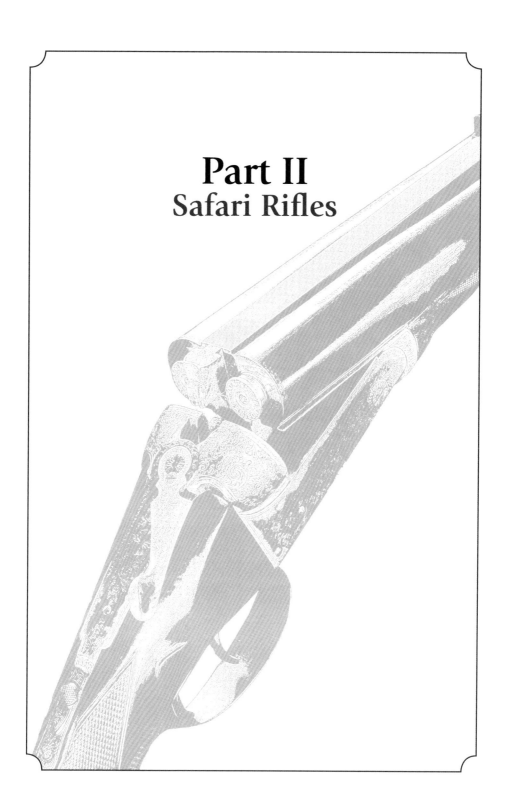

Part II
Safari Rifles

The Double Rifle:
A Historical Perspective

Chapter 15

When Cornwallis Harris headed inland from the Cape Colony in 1836, the firearms he had at his disposal were woefully inadequate. The only choice was a muzzleloader, and even percussion ignition was a few years away from common use. Heavy-for-caliber conical bullets were unusual, but at least it was known that pure lead balls could be hardened with tin or pewter for better penetration.

Even rifling, though widely used, was only partially understood at this time; rifled sporting arms were likely to have but two grooves, and the ball would often be cast with a "belt" to take the rifling. Accuracy was perhaps a bit better than a smoothbore musket could offer, but not much. Many concepts for repeating firearms had been tried, but until the self-contained metallic cartridge came along, the need to use loose powder, bullet, and priming separately made repeaters impractical. Multiple-barrel arrangements—usually two but occasionally three and even four—were the only way to obtain additional shots. Doubles were obviously the most practical; two locks and side-by-side barrels made an attractive, well-balanced arrangement, while additional barrels made the whole affair too heavy and unwieldy.

Calibers were large, but even so penetration was sketchy. On the really large game, first encountered by Englishmen such as Harris, William Cotton Oswell, and Roualeyn Gordon Cumming, multiple shots were normal. These early adventurers hunted on horseback, galloping close to fire and then dashing away—sometimes, according to their accounts, charging their muzzleloaders at the gallop from a bag of loose powder! With our modern concept of sportsmanship and the humane one-shot kill, the accounts the early hunters left behind seem barbaric. With game such as buffalo, giraffe, rhinoceros, and elephant, it wasn't unusual for dozens of balls to be fired before the game was finally brought down. It was exciting, dangerous sport, and many of the early hunters paid for it with their lives.

Velocities were quite uniform, somewhere between 1,300 and 1,600 feet per second. Conical bullets were occasionally seen, but they tended to be relatively

In the great (and waning) days of Empire there were literally dozens of small shops making double rifles. Some became famous, but most did not. Of course, the larger firms had their own cartridges, which complicates things to this day. This is a .475 No. 2 Jeffery (with its odd .488-inch bullet diameter).

stubby and light-for-caliber; the aerodynamic and penetrating potentials of a long, parallel-side, heavy-for-caliber bullet weren't yet known. In other words, the only way to increase killing power was to increase caliber. Bore diameters were expressed in gauge, or balls to the pound. For instance, the first British military rifle was a round-ball gun bored "20 to the pound," or 20-gauge, caliber .615.

In common use as sporting rifles during the middle years of the nineteenth century were 10- and 12-bores, both considered "general-purpose" rifles. For larger game, the 8-bore was most common. However, 4-bores (quarter-pound round balls) were relatively common as a "big bore," and 2-bores were occasionally seen. Sir Samuel Baker's "Baby" was a gargantuan single-shot 2-bore. Weighing twenty pounds and firing a half-pound explosive shell, "Baby" was indeed awesome. Baker confessed to being afraid of it, and reckoned he fired it altogether just twenty times. "I very seldom fired it, but it is a curious fact that I never fired a shot with that rifle without bagging . . ." Curious, because in those days the really large game was often brought down by sheer weight of lead.

Ballistics of these rifles were nothing to sneeze at, even by today's standards. The 10-bore generally fired an 875-grain ball at 1,550 FPS, yielding 4,660 foot-pounds. The 12-bore fired a 750-grain ball at the same velocity for about 4,000 foot-pounds. Both were used on dangerous game, and obviously they possessed the foot-pounds—but not the penetration. The 8-bore, with a 1,257-grain bullet at 1,500 FPS, could do the job. In foot-pounds it delivered just fewer than 5,300, the same energy level

Lou Hager took this buffalo with his William Evans .450/.400 3¼" double. There were probably more .450/.400 double rifles made than all the big bores put together.

that "elephant cartridges" produce to this day. The 4-bore, just for comparison, fired its 1,880-grain bullet at some 1,330 FPS. It produced 7,400 foot-pounds of energy, a level unmatched in the smokeless era until Weatherby's .460 came along!

The 4-bores were almost invariably single-shot arms; the weight was far too excessive if built into a double. The 8-bores and smaller bore sizes could go either way, in single shot or double form. By the middle of the nineteenth century James Purdey, Westley Richards, and Holland (singular at that time) were all building double-barreled percussion rifles. William Cotton Oswell, who hunted from 1837 to 1852, had a smoothbore Purdey double 10-bore as his favorite arm. Gordon Cumming hunted for five years, from 1843 to 1848, and his favorite also was a Purdey, a double 12-bore. But for larger game he had better luck with a single-shot 4-bore.

Although beautifully made, the muzzleloading double rifles were not doubles as we know them; they were in essence two rifles—two barrels and two locks—put together on one stock. For a double rifle's barrels to shoot together, the first essential criterion is consistent ammunition. This would not be fully practical until the invention of the metallic self-contained cartridge.

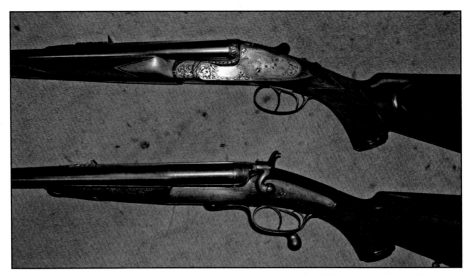

Bottom, a Rigby underlever hammer gun, circa 1880s; top, a new Rigby sidelock. Except for small advances, the double rifle was fairly complete before smokeless powder—and in many ways modern double rifles are still made with 1880s technology.

British gunmaker Joseph Lang saw the French pinfire self-contained cartridge as early as 1851, and was impressed. But this system was fragile and unsuited for powerful arms. The centerfire cartridge developed by George Daws, circa 1861, was the answer. By 1870 brass cartridges in 4-, 8-, 10-, and 12-bore were readily available—and so were double rifles very much as we know them today.

These big-bore, black-powder, breechloading doubles were exposed-hammer underlever guns, opened by a lever surrounding the trigger guard. When the lever was swung to one side, the barrels were released and dropped open. Underlever doubles were made well into the smokeless era, including a few hammerless guns. Jeffery's underlever design is one of the most common versions of that firm's .600 Nitro Express rifle.

James Purdey himself invented the top lever, and in 1875 W. Anson and John Deeley, both employees of Westley Richards, patented the Anson & Deeley hammerless action, to this day easily the most common hammerless boxlock action in the world.

By 1890, just before smokeless powder came into widespread use, hammerless double rifles were starting to take over. To this day, however, a few double-rifle men (their numbers are constantly decreasing!) will argue in favor of exposed-hammer guns. Indeed, a sound argument can be made; a hammer gun can be carried in greater safety, since a hammerless gun is always cocked and ready and must rely on a mechanical safety. The exposed hammers on the older variety can be lowered to the

A nice Tanzanian buffalo that I took with my C.W. Andrews boxlock back in 1988. At that time there were still reasonable supplies of vintage doubles, but today such rifles are very hard to find and extremely expensive.

safety position. On the other hand, absent a mechanical hammer-blocking safety (occasionally seen), they are exposed and there's always the possibility that a chance blow to the hammer could cause an accidental discharge. A nonejector hammer gun is also said to be, and undoubtedly is, the most silent of all rifles to get into action. By holding the trigger back while the hammer is cocked, total quiet can be maintained. But by the time the cordite Nitro Express cartridges were introduced, hammer guns were already an anachronism. Though rare, nitro-proofed hammer doubles do exist. Jack Lott had a wonderful .577 hammer gun, and Zimbabwe professional hunter Steve Alexander uses an Army & Navy .450 No. 2 hammer gun. Vintage hammer guns are much less expensive than hammerless, and every year a few hunters take these old rifles to Africa and do just fine with them.

In its heyday the underlever black-powder hammer gun could have been a big bore, an 8-, 10-, or 12-bore, or, rarely, even a monstrous 4-bore; or it might have been more of a general-purpose rifle chambered for something like the .577, .500, or one of the .450s.

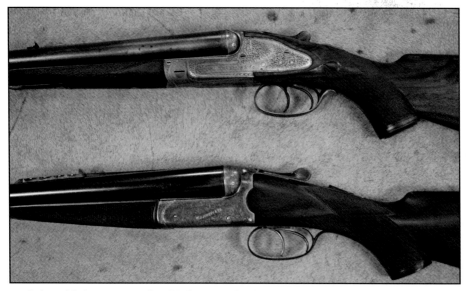

Boxlock or sidelock? At one time the sidelock was considered stronger, but today there is no practical advantage either way. Historically and today, however, sidelocks are considered "fine guns" while boxlocks were and are thought of as "working guns."

Bullets had changed; conicals had almost universally replaced the round ball, and hunters were well aware of the conical's increased penetrating qualities. In the 1870s the black-powder "express" cartridges began to make their appearance, possibly the first velocity fad to hit the world's hunters. The black-powder expresses, another development credited to James Purdey, took their name from the then-new "express train." Inserted in a bottleneck cartridge such as the .500/.450, a very heavy charge of black powder was used to drive a light-for-caliber conical bullet at unprecedented velocities. The bullets were often made light by a cavity in the nose, thus also inducing rapid expansion, especially in the soft, unjacketed lead. The weight of a caliber .450 "express" bullet might be as light as 270 grains, and velocities ran just shy of 2,000 feet per second, approaching the practical limit for black powder.

These expresses flattened trajectories tremendously, and they became very popular for light game. On large game, as would seem obvious, the bullets failed to give needed penetration. As the century wound down, serious hunters of large game clung to their 8-bores. The smallbore fans, of which there were many, stuck with black-powder .577s.

In 1876, when gunmaker Harris Holland took his nephew, Henry Holland, into the business, Holland became Holland & Holland. In 1886 they introduced a new wrinkle in double guns: Paradox rifling. The Paradox was essentially a smoothbore

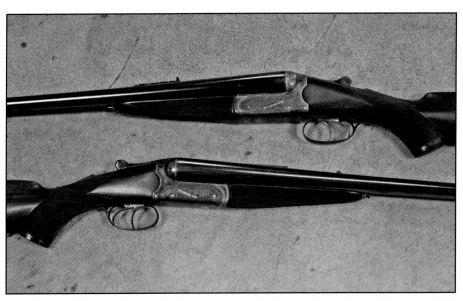

Though not widely known, far more double rifles went to the India trade than to Africa. This is a pair of .475 No. 2 Jeffery rifles from a maharajah's estate, now owned by Bill Jones. This pair is unusual in that these are boxlock guns, which weren't often paired up. Speculation is that this was a gift, or perhaps an extra pair for guests. Those were the days!

gun except that the last few inches of the barrel were rifled. And you thought a rifled choke tube for slugs was a new idea? The idea was to give an instant choice between ball and shot, with the recommendation that one barrel be loaded with each. Powder charges were fairly light, as were the guns. Although Paradox guns were made in 8-, 10-, and 12-bore, their cartridges for big-game rifles of the same bore size were generally not interchangeable with Paradox guns. The concept was popular. Before the Paradoxes vanished, other companies brought out their own versions under such fanciful names as Explora, Colindian, Jungle Gun, and so forth.

Although the Nitro Expresses were yet to come, the double rifle was in its final stage of development by the mid-1890s. When, in 1898, John Rigby introduced the .450-3¼", the complete, fully developed rifle was ready and waiting. From this point to the present, the few changes that would occur would be minor refinements—for instance, the shift to the Anson push-rod system to remove the fore-end, as opposed to the older lever system. By the time the switch to Nitro was made, the process of regulating the barrels was fully understood. This was and is an art, always costly and time-consuming, and mastered by very few artisans. On the surface, it would seem quite simple; surely if the barrels were exactly parallel, the accuracy would be all anyone could ask for. It isn't that easy.

To some degree the fore-end lever dates older rifles. The swing-out lever is the oldest, followed by the Anson push-rod, center (more frequently seen on shotguns than rifles). The most recent was the Deeley latch, which came in around 1920.

The problem is that one barrel lies to the right of the center of gravity, the other to the left. If the barrels were exactly parallel, during firing the forces of recoil would pull the right barrel off to the right and the left barrel off to the left. To combat this, the barrels must have a very slight angle of convergence. Too little and they will never shoot together; too much and they will crossfire at close range.

To this day, although modern technology can help, the only way to regulate a double is by hand, through trial and error. The craftsman starts with the barrels' axes converging very slightly, and the barrels firmly joined at the breech, soldered together at the muzzle, and traditionally wrapped with wire to hold them in place. Now begins the trial and error. Shoot, and then adjust the convergence or divergence by heating the barrels to melt the tin holding them together and moving an adjusting wedge at the muzzles. Shoot again, reheat, and move the wedge until an acceptable degree of accuracy is achieved.

Considering the inexact nature of this procedure, it's simply amazing the degree of accuracy that a double rifle can offer. In general, two shots from each barrel within a four- to six-inch circle at one hundred yards are just fine. Call it "grapefruit accuracy"—but I've seen doubles that would cut that in half, and once in a while you'll run into "tennis-ball" or even "golf-ball" accuracy. Regulating a double is a frustrating,

If rifles could tell tales! This is Andrew Dawson's William Evans .470, a plain working boxlock originally owned by Carl Akeley, who collected for the American Museum of Natural History in the teens and twenties, and later owned by John Dugmore, a famous Kenya hunter who was one of the early pioneers when Botswana opened.

time-consuming business. It's no easier today than it was a century ago, and there are far fewer men alive in the world today who can do it.

Double-rifle actions, too, have changed very little since the black-powder days. Toward the end of that era, double-rifle design pretty much evolved into two basic types of actions, sidelock and boxlock. The sidelock was and is a "fine gun," technically not all that much more expensive to create but requiring much more difficult finishing and inletting, plus offering the characteristic side plates as perfect vehicles for embellishment. The boxlocks, though expensive when compared to single shots or magazine rifles, were and are "working guns," plainer and less expensive.

Theoretically, the sidelock is the stronger of the two. The reason is that the boxlock's moving parts must be inletted into the steel of the action from underneath. In the sidelock, the breech is left more solid and the moving parts are affixed to the right and left sides of the action. With older steels, the original Anson & Deeley boxlock action occasionally failed in early Nitro Express doubles, which operated at much higher pressures than any black-powder gun. Better steels and better ammunition were probably the primary cure, but improvements such as stronger "third fasteners" helped. Today it is fair to say that the sidelock has no practical strength advantage over the boxlock.

Sidelock doubles have long been a favorite vehicle for the world's best engravers to display their art. This Rigby sidelock was engraved by Lisa Tomlin, whose animal scenes are considered among the finest in the world.

Sidelock guns are generally either bar-action or back-action. The "bar" of a double is the solid portion of the action underneath the barrels, the portion that contains the hinge pin and the locking lugs. In a bar-action sidelock, the mainsprings are in the front part of the side plates, essentially adjacent to the bar. In the back-action sidelock, perfected by Holland & Holland, the mainsprings are to the rear, and thus more integrity is maintained in the bar. Most older sidelock double rifles, with their higher pressures, are of the back-action type, while fine shotguns are often bar-action sidelocks. Today, with modern steels and more precise machining, there is little practical advantage between the two.

The sidelock must be made essentially by hand, while a basic boxlock action, if not mass-produced, can at least be produced on a larger scale. Westley Richards had its own hand-detachable boxlock design, but most of the gunmakers (even the top names) offering boxlock doubles (and they all did) purchased their basic actions "in the white." Webley & Scott made a great many of these actions, and you can find Webley actions on boxlocks by Holland, Rigby, Westley Richards, et al. Only slightly less common is what is often called a "trade action." A bit different from the Webley, this Birmingham-made action also appears in guns from a variety of makers. It is believed that these actions were turned out on a cottage-industry basis by a number of Birmingham craftsmen, and then sold to the trade "in the white" as were the Webley actions.

Whether sidelock or boxlock, the double rifle locks up via lugs—the "lumps" on the underside of the barrels near the breech. Sliding underbolts, originally designed by James Purdey, fit into recesses in these lumps, thus locking the action when the barrels are closed against the standing breech. On firing, the action naturally flexes and attempts to open. All doubles flex slightly during firing, and when this flexing goes too far, an obviously unsafe condition occurs. That's what happens when a double "goes off the face." To prevent this, most double rifles have some form of third fastener at the top of the standing breech. This could be some form of Greener crossbolt, or a doll's head, an extension of the barrels that, on closing, drops into a fitted recess at the top of the standing breech.

The big Nitro Express cartridges work at what is, for modern smokeless cartridges, very low breech pressures. In recent years, with our much stronger and more consistent modern steels, doubles have been built for a number of modern cartridges, including the current version of the .375 H&H (much stouter than the old .375 Flanged Magnum) and the .458 Winchester Magnum. However, this is not a strong action design by bolt-action standards, and there are limits. I have heard of doubles being made for the .460 Weatherby Magnum, a cartridge that achieves breech pressures in excess of 50,000 copper units of pressure (C.U.P.), a good 25 to 30 percent more than any Nitro Express cartridge. Most reports indicate that such guns "go off the face" after relatively few firings, and that should come as no surprise. While nobody tends to want a double rifle without a third fastener, in real terms most such devices are more cosmetic than effective. Over the long haul the only way to make sure a double won't come off the face is to keep the pressure down!

Although extremely complex to make and thus expensive, the double rifle is a very basic tool. Few bells and whistles can be added to it, but there are several variations that remain points of argument for double-rifle men. They are: single or double triggers, automatic or nonautomatic safety, and ejector or extractor.

The question of triggers is the simplest. Actually, very few double rifles have been built with single triggers; the double trigger is most common and most traditional. In theory, one of the advantages of a double is two completely independent actions in case one fails. This advantage, if it really exists, is somewhat negated by a single trigger. On the other hand, hunters who haven't grown up with double-trigger guns may never learn to shift their finger back for the second trigger. If that's a problem, a single trigger is the only answer. I started using a double-trigger side-by-side shotgun for quail hunting when I was sixteen, so sliding my trigger finger back to that second trigger seems perfectly natural. My dad, on the other hand, never used a double-trigger until he was in his forties and tried to use one of my guns. He never, ever got the hang of it; a shotgun with a double trigger was no better than a single shot in his hands. The choice is pretty much a matter of personal preference, but you'll have trouble finding a vintage single-trigger double rifle. If a single trigger is your preference, be aware that

Although there are trends, a double rifle can take almost any form. This is a strange one, an Austrian made hammer gun chambered to the very American .45-70 cartridge . . . and it's fitted with a detachable scope. Very unusual!

you'll lose the ability to have constant and instant availability of either softpoint or solid bullet. That's a real advantage, a wonderful capability, and it's one I've needed and used several times, particularly with buffalo.

More to-do is made over the question of an automatic safety. An automatic safety is basically a sliding shotgun-type safety, seen on 99 percent of all double rifles, that automatically moves to the "safe" position when the opening lever is activated. John Taylor made a fuss over this, believing it was a dangerous feature that could, in a heated moment, get you killed if you reloaded quickly and forgot about the safety when you closed the rifle.

Tony Sanchez-Ariño, on the other hand, made a most rational case for the automatic safety in *On the Trail of the African Elephant.* He believes that sliding the safety forward to "off" as you bring the rifle up should be second nature, and indeed he's correct: Putting the safety forward should be every bit as automatic, or reflexive, as shifting your finger to the rear trigger after firing the first barrel.

I must admit that I have disconnected the automatic safety on my own double rifles, a simple matter. But that act now requires the opposite reaction: After firing and loading, I must be always aware of the need to move the safety to the "on" position if I'm not going to fire again. This is an inherent problem with the double that must be taken into account; it's either fully loaded or fully unloaded, with no "halfway measure" such as a loaded magazine but an empty chamber. If loaded, only that mechanical safety stands between you and an accidental discharge. Well, as I said, I've disconnected the automatic safety on my doubles, but I pay close attention to having that safety in the proper position, and I watch where the barrels are pointed.

To me, it's not important whether a double rifle has ejectors or extractors. Some of the old-timers, Taylor included, wanted nothing to do with ejectors; the theory was that the metallic "ping" when the rifle was opened did more to pinpoint the hunter to dangerous game (especially elephant) than the actual sound of the rifle. That argument really doesn't hold water today, since no sportsman has either the opportunity or the desire to wade into an elephant herd with the intention of dropping as many as possible before they spook. Regardless of who's really right, the ejectors must have won; a double rifle in any caliber is worth quite a bit more with ejectors than without.

However, from a user's standpoint, I don't think it matters a tinker's damn. With the low pressures associated with Nitro Express cartridges, extraction is a breeze; there's little expansion of the brass, and empties simply fall out of the chambers. All it takes to get the cases out of a nonejector double is a flick of the wrist, turning the gun out and down. The empties fall out, and you can stick two more in just as fast as you can with an ejector double. Personally, I prefer a nonejector; I feel I can reload it just as fast, without looking down. That hippo bull I mentioned earlier was caught away from the water in the Selous Reserve. Oddly, in that area it isn't unusual to find them in heavy thorn at midday, miles from water. I was determined to kill him with a body shot from my .470, not the easy brain shot. We got the job done, but I was dumping cartridges in and out, and ejectors wouldn't have sped up the process. Considering the price of new cases, I'd just as soon not have had to rummage around in the grass ten feet away to find my brass when it was all over.

The foregoing paragraphs were written a long time ago, when vintage rifles were plentiful and new doubles were scarce. Today this is reversed, and I must admit I've gotten spoiled. The double rifles I've been using most recently have ejectors, and I have come to appreciate their speed and convenience. I don't think I've forgotten how to dump empties out of an extractor gun, but if I went back to a nonejector I'd have to do some serious retraining!

When the German firm of Heym, a good gunmaker, first offered its Model 88B in .470, I got hold of one. It had what seemed to me a marvelous piece of engineering, a little lever at the base of the fore-end that switched the extractors to ejectors and back again. Great idea, but unneeded moving parts are an invitation to disaster. I got four shots out of the rifle before that switch broke, leaving me with

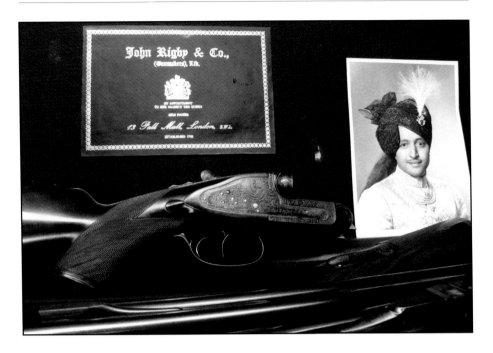

This beautiful Rigby sidelock was commissioned by the Maharaja of Surguja in 1936 and delivered in 1939. It is the only double rifle Rigby ever built in .416 Rigby, and was used by the maharaja to take many of his more than 1,200 tigers. The rifle is currently owned by American Bill Jones, who used it in Botswana in 2008 with its extra set of barrels in .470.

one barrel that ejected and one barrel that didn't. Since then, Heym has dropped that feature. Some of the least expensive new rifles, like the Krieghoff and Merkel, are extractor guns only; most of the more costly doubles are customarily offered with ejectors. Ultimately I still think it doesn't make much difference, but you must become familiar with whichever you choose.

Barrel lengths on most doubles run from 24 to 28 inches. Although the latter figure sounds long, remember that 28 inches is a normal barrel length for a double shotgun; a double rifle with 28-inch barrels will be shorter than most bolt-action rifles with 24-inch barrels. The 28-inch barrels were more popular early on, while shorter barrels are likely to be found on later guns. But you never know. I had a wonderful Wilkes .470, a very old rifle, with 24-inch barrels. It handled like a dream, but so do doubles with 26- and even 28-inch barrels; the differences aren't significant. Optimally, I tend to prefer 26-inch barrels.

Sights normally will be some kind of standing leaf on a quarter or full rib, with or without folding leaves. For my money, the folding leaves are useless on large-caliber doubles. My Andrews .470 had one standing and three folding leaves marked for distances out to 300 yards. So what? I can't see well enough to use a double's bold bead and coarse V much beyond 100 yards, and I doubt if many people can. The main thing is to make sure the first leaf, the one you'll really use, is standing and not folding.

Once in a while you'll find a big double with a flip-up aperture sight or fixtures for a claw scope mount. Depending on who wants the rifle, such features may add or detract. Truth is, anybody sees better and shoots better with a scope. But a scope seems so out of place on a good double that I've never been attracted to one with mounts. That doesn't make much sense, though, because a good low-power scope enhances a double's usefulness immeasurably. In more recent years, as it became increasingly difficult for my eyes to resolve open sights, I've spent a lot more time with doubles mounted with low-power scopes. They still look weird, but optical sights work just as well on doubles as on any other action type!

A great many doubles were more or less standard "over-the-counter" rifles, perhaps more than you might think. But many were indeed made to customers' specifications. Most will have some degree of cast to the stock, and a few have very odd dimensions. Keep in mind that all of this can be fixed; cast can be added or taken off easily, and a comb can always be reshaped or lowered and a too-long stock shortened. However, a comb that's too low or a stock that's too short might need replacement. It can all be done, but the degree of fixing required can ruin any collector value. Also, any and all work on double rifles is very expensive, and there aren't a lot of gunsmiths who can do it right.

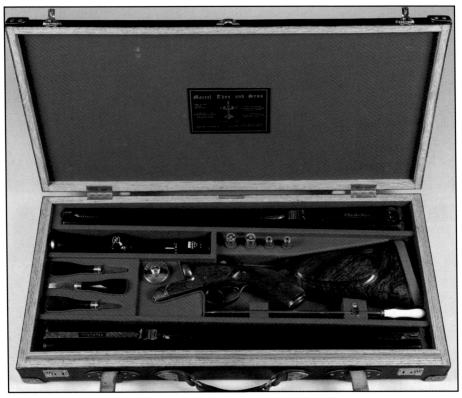

The .600 Nitro Express was fairly uncommon, probably because of both gun weight and caliber. This sidelock .600 by Belgian maker Marcel Thys is extremely unusual because it has a scoped set of spare barrels in .375. (Photo courtesy Holt's Auctioneers)

The crucial thing about a double that's to be used, not just purchased to look at, is that it must fit, properly and perfectly. If it doesn't, fix it, whatever it takes. The double's stock in trade isn't accuracy or firepower. Rather, it is two shots, delivered faster than anything else can deliver them, and gun fit must be right. When the double rifle comes to the shoulder, the sights should be an unneeded redundancy. The rifle should already be there, perfectly lined up. If the sights aren't on when you throw the rifle up, that double simply isn't right for you. Or you aren't right for it.

The Double Rifle Today

Chapter 16

The double rifle could well have died away. Winchester's .458 Magnum, introduced in the excellent Model 70, then the world's preeminent bolt-action rifle, came out at the most opportune time imaginable: 1958, just when Kynoch was discontinuing virtually all the big Nitro Express rounds. Only a few made it into the 1960s, and by 1967 Kynoch was out of the ammo business altogether.

Slowly, as existing stocks of ammo dwindled, the grand old guns were sold or shelved. Many found their way into the hands of American collectors, and it was in America that double rifles got a new lease on life. As mentioned earlier, with Barnes bullets and R.C.B.S. dies, handloaders could keep shooting the big doubles. And then Jim Bell went into business with new brass and ammo.

Economics dictate that the double rifle will never be as common as the bolt gun in Africa or anywhere else. However, the resurgence of the double rifle is one of the biggest changes in "safari rifles" in the past two decades. When I wrote my first African book, *From Mt. Kenya to the Cape,* I stated that I had seen just seven double rifles in use in Africa. Several of those had been in my own hands! By the time I wrote the original *Safari Rifles,* doubles were again in relatively common use—but nothing like they are today!

More new doubles are being built right now than have been for many years. In 1989 Holland & Holland's Russell Wilkin told me his firm had more doubles under construction than at anytime since World War II, including Bill Feldstein's double .700! Fast-forward almost twenty more years, and Holland and Holland is still making doubles. So are a few other classic British firms, including Purdey and Westley Richards.

During those twenty years the double-rifle business changed. One could argue (and it will spark an argument) that the English "best guns" are still the best. Certainly they are the most expensive, and carry some of the longest delivery lead times! However, the real resurgence of the double rifle is not based around the

Andrew Dawson and Paul Smith, partners in Chifuti Safaris, pretty much represent the status of doubles today. Andrew uses a vintage .470, while Paul carries a new Krieghoff in .500. In recent years Krieghoff has probably made as many doubles as any company in history.

handful of best-quality sidelocks, regardless of where produced or who made them. The primary changes are threefold: First, and this is important, the worldwide inventory of serviceable and available used double rifles has just about dried up. Rifles from the classic era (call it before World War II, although that is also arguable) are now at retirement age. This doesn't mean such rifles aren't serviceable, but every year fewer of them remain so. Prices have skyrocketed in the last few years—that is, if you can even find one!

The second change is that the English gun trade no longer dominates the double-rifle business. Today many more doubles are being made in continental Europe and the United States, with multiple makers on both sides offering multiple grades from very basic to highly embellished. This leads to, but is not exactly the same as, the third primary change. Thanks to modern manufacturing techniques, primarily (but not exclusively) CNC machining, reliable working double rifles are now comparatively inexpensive and extremely available. A shocking number of good gun shops will have boxlock doubles from makers such as Heym, Krieghoff, and Merkel available right over the counter. Butch Searcy in Boron, California, has made hundreds of serviceable boxlocks.

No double rifle is inexpensive in the way that a production bolt action can be, but all of these rifles are available for somewhat less than a top-grade custom bolt action, and at this writing basic models of all the guns mentioned (and there are others) cost considerably less than the prices decent vintage boxlock doubles command. It is these rifles that are most often seen in the hands of modern professional hunters, and it is these rifles that are seeing the most use in Africa.

In my first two decades of African hunting it seemed that the American client was the most likely to be carrying a double rifle. Because of the cost and availability of ammo, professional hunters were most likely to carry a bolt-action .458. Today this has changed dramatically. Thanks to Federal, Kynoch, Westley Richards, and semicustom firms like Superior, ammunition for .470s and .500s is more available than ever before, and all calibers are available with a bit of effort. Many older professional hunters have returned to the double rifle, and many younger PHs have embraced them. Doubles of all kinds are once again prevalent, and are being used by younger PHs who can probably afford them the least but believe they provide the kind of life insurance they must have.

In May 2007 I was in Chifuti Safaris' camp in the Zambezi Valley, doing our annual TV filming. Let's count the doubles present. Professional hunter Andrew Dawson had his great old William Evans .470. PH Paul Smith had his Krieghoff .500. PH Mike Payne also had a Krieghoff, his in .470. PH Ivan Carter had his Heym .450-3¼". Among the clients, I had my American-made Rigby .450-3¼". My partner, Dave Fulson, had his Butch Searcy .470. Jeff Wemmer had a beautiful, almost new Purdey sidelock in .470 and another American-made .470 as a spare. This number, eight, exceeds the number of doubles I saw in the field during my first ten years of African hunting! Jeff Wemmer's Purdey was the only sidelock; all the rest were boxlock "working" guns. It is probably equally interesting to note that only one of these rifles, Andrew Dawson's William Evans, was an "old" rifle. All the rest were relatively new. This is still a lot of doubles present in one camp, but as a microcosm I think it does present a reasonable picture of double rifles today.

Twenty years ago .470 Nitro Express ammo was just becoming readily available, and double rifles in .458 Winchester Magnum were relatively common. Fortunately this has changed. As I wrote then, and will write again now, proper double-rifle cartridges have rimmed cases. This is because the double rifle has relatively weak extraction, and the extractors/ejectors need that rim to grab hold of and push. There have been many clever accommodations with spring-loaded plungers that slip into the extractor groove on belted rimless and rimless cases. They work well, but all are subject to eventual or periodic failure. This is not altogether because of the design of these extractors, but more a simple matter of physics. Most belted rimless and rimless cartridges are designed to operate at higher working pressures than the big-case rimmed cartridges for double rifles. This is because bolt actions (and single shots) can handle higher pressures but doubles cannot. Add a complex and not especially strong extraction system to the occasional sticky case and you have a recipe for disaster.

This is not a big problem with smaller-caliber doubles intended for nondangerous game, but it's a huge concern for a large-caliber double designed almost solely as a stopping rifle for the big nasties. I note that there are still quite a few doubles offered in .375 H&H, and a couple chambered to .416 Rigby. I guess it depends on what you intend to do with them, but in my view these should be avoided. And with today's availability of good rimmed cartridges intended for doubles, their existence is unnecessary. Most available is .470, and it remains the most common. Second most available right now is .500 Nitro Express. Either is a great choice for a big-bore double. Hornady's reintroduction of the .450-3¼" should bring this one back, and it's another great choice. If a smaller, more versatile cartridge is preferred, Krieghoff's .500/.416 is available. Recoil is similar to the larger cartridges, so Hornady's .450/.400-3" makes sense and is now being chambered by most modern makers. The rimmed version of the .375 H&H, the .375 Flanged, is not as available as any of these, but it is available (from Superior and others), and some new doubles are being chambered to it. The other large Nitro Expresses are also available, so we really are now in a time when there is no reason for a double rifle to be chambered to anything other than a rimmed cartridge.

Double rifles, even today's more or less production doubles, aren't like factory bolt actions. There aren't all that many of them and they aren't readily available, especially the made-to-order rifles. So no writer can have even passing familiarity

Left, .450/.400-3"; right, .450-3¼". It is still a .470 and .500 world, but other double-rifle cartridges are coming back. Hornady is making new loads for both of these cartridges, and most double-rifle firms have agreed to chamber to them.

The double rifle will remain expensive because of the vast amount of handwork required. Sometimes you get lucky with the regulation, but other times it takes hours and hours of trial and error to get it right.

with all the doubles currently available, and it would be absurd for me to pretend to. For instance, I have never fired a new Holland & Holland or a new Westley Richards, and Jeff Wemmer's Purdey is the only relatively new English rifle I've ever seen in the field. I have also not had an opportunity to use the new Blaser S2 Safari double rifle. (I've examined them and they look good, but I haven't shot one.) So I won't presume to comment on what I don't know about, but I will offer some notes on doubles I have spent some time with.

There are some very inexpensive doubles out there in smaller calibers (such as .45-70), some of which are not actually regulated. Right now the least expensive traditional big-bore double (meaning .375 H&H and larger, and barrels regulated to shoot together) is the Merkel Safari. This is a very sound and very basic double rifle. It is a plain gun with plain wood, but the examples I have seen are well regulated and exceedingly sound. At just over ten pounds it is perhaps a wee bit light for the big cartridges, with the recoil further accentuated by a European-style stock with (to my taste) a bit too much drop. In other words, it kicks a bit more than it has to! But it's a wonderful value.

It is probable that more Krieghoff double rifles have been made and sold in the last few years than all the rest. It is as close to a production gun as a double rifle can be, but all that I have seen have been extremely well regulated. The current stock design seems to me a bit straighter than when the firm first introduced this rifle, which is a welcome change. It is also a wee bit on the light side, but Krieghoff will mitigate this with mercury-tube recoil reducers if desired.

I used a .500/.416 a few years ago when I hunted water buffalo and banteng in northern Australia. At first I was pretty upset with the rifle because it shot horribly with Krieghoff-supplied ammo. Just by chance, my buddy Chub Eastman, then of Nosler Bullets, was going on that hunt with me. Nosler had just introduced its 400-grain .416 Partition, so I had Larry Barnett at Superior cook up some .500/.416 ammo using that bullet. Lo and behold, the accuracy problem was purely the ammo. With Superior's loads that rifle, which had a detachable 1.75–5X Leupold, printed both barrels exactly together at a full 100 yards. It was one of the most accurate double rifles I have ever used!

Both the Krieghoff and the Merkel are extractor guns. This doesn't bother me in the least, and it helps keep the cost down. The Krieghoff, however, has a different cocking mechanism than most doubles. (It is no longer unique, since the Blaser has much the same system.) What appears to be a traditional tang-mounted safety is actually the cocking lever. Push it forward and it cocks the springs; push forward

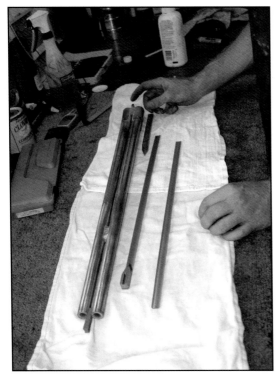

Little has changed about a double rifle in many, many years. Joining the barrels is still a painstaking process. Like all rifles, accuracy depends on the quality of the barrels. But, unique to doubles, it also depends on how perfectly the barrels are joined.

Dave Fulson's double is a boxlock .470 by Butch Searcy. Butch has undoubtedly made more doubles than anybody else on the North American continent, and his sturdy, attractively priced rifles must be given much credit for the resurgence of the double rifle.

again and release and the action is de-cocked. This means that, unlike most doubles, the Krieghoff can be carried loaded but uncocked, in an absolutely inert and safe state. This is clearly a wonderful feature, especially with that over-the-shoulder, barrels-forward "African carry" that is so comfortable with a double rifle. I like this safety feature because with that carry it is very difficult to always ensure that the barrels are pointed safely, especially when walking single file.

That said, it takes some getting used to. Much more thumb pressure is required to cock the action than to release a traditional shotgun-style safety catch. In Cameroon in '06 my rifle followed me by several days, so outfitter Antonio Riguera was kind enough to loan me his Krieghoff .500. We were hunting bongo with the Pygmies and their dogs, and when my bongo bull jumped, pandemonium set in. Following the chase, we ran hard through the forest for several hundred yards. So when the dogs got the bongo stopped and we pulled up, I was huffing and puffing and sweating like a pig. I got the rifle up, but my sweat-slick hands fumbled the cocking lever. I had to take the rifle down and exert concentrated pressure, and then I shot the bongo. Had it been a charging elephant or buffalo, I'd have been run over.

Again, it just takes some getting used to. PH Paul Smith carries his Krieghoff every day, and I've been in camp when he has stopped two close-range charges.

An engraver at work at Heym. The skill of a master engraver is truly amazing to me, and of course engraving ultimately becomes a large part of the cost of a highly embellished double.

Releasing the cocking lever is second nature to him. On the other hand, I use other doubles and double shotguns with traditional safeties, so it stands to reason that it would take me some time to become completely comfortable with this system.

Heym was one of the first European companies to seriously market a big-bore double, the Model 88-B. In recent years the company languished a bit on the American market, but now it has come back strong with a plain (no-engraving) "PH" model that is nicely priced. The Heym is an ejector gun with cocking indicators, and its chamberings include .375 Flanged, .450/.400-3", .500/.416, .450-3¼", .470, and .500, perhaps the greatest array of chamberings of all the "production" doubles. I used a couple of different Heym doubles back in the 1980s, a .470 on a rhino hunt and a .500 on an elephant hunt in Mozambique. They handled nicely and were well regulated. I actually purchased the first Heym "PH" in .450/.400-3" that my family and I could share.

Butch Searcy was perhaps the first American shop to successfully produce and market American-made double rifles. He has made as many double rifles as anyone alive, from boxlocks to very nice sidelocks, and the price and availability of his rifles have had much to do with the double rifle's renaissance. I have never owned a Searcy rifle, but almost everybody who has them swears by them. The most common are very basic boxlocks, plain but hell for stout. However, he has made some very nice rifles. In June 2007 I hunted in Botswana with Johan Calitz, a longtime buddy of Butch Searcy. I was carrying an American-made Rigby boxlock; Calitz was carrying an extremely

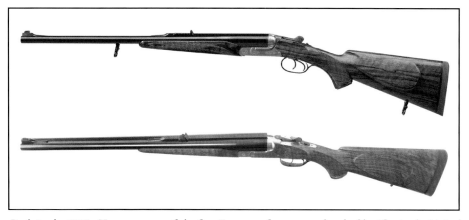

Back in the 1980s Heym was one of the first European firms to market double rifles in the United States. Today they offer custom doubles in calibers from .22 Hornet to .600 Nitro Express. Their "standard" boxlock rifles are Model 88B (top) and the new PH Model (below). The PH is a plain rifle available in a variety of calibers, including .450/.400-3" and .450-3¼".

nice Searcy .470 sidelock. It's a statement that we were both using American-made doubles, but it's also interesting that my Rigby was the plain rifle while Calitz's sidelock .470 was beautifully engraved and absolutely spectacular!

It is probably no secret that Rigby's American proprietor, Geoff Miller, is one of my best friends in the world. So I have used his rifles quite a lot. Long before Miller got involved with Rigby, I used his prototype Rogue River .470 in both Australia and Zambia. Miller is an old benchrest shooter and an accuracy freak, and he goes to great pains to regulate his doubles as well as they possibly can be. That Rogue River rifle shot extremely well. (It still does, now with more than two thousand rounds down its barrels.) He has carried this tradition forward with the Rigby rifles his firm now makes. The Rigby boxlock is sort of a new grade of "best-quality" boxlock rifle. All are made to order, with good wood, match-grade barrels, and numerous options in finish, engraving, sights, and so forth. A boxlock like this is considerably more costly than the plainer, more production guns previously discussed, but it is a true custom double. Rigby also makes gorgeous sidelock doubles that, in my view, rank right along with all the other top names as "best guns." I've used new Rigby rifles in .470, .500, and .577, but my personal Rigby double is a boxlock .450-3¼", light and trim at 10½ pounds. It fits like a glove, and I've taken several elephant with it in the last couple of years.

There are many other makes with which I have only passing (or almost no) familiarity. Some came and have gone, like the Dutch-made William Douglass boxlock. Others are still coming, like the Blaser and Dakota doubles. And there are perhaps dozens of small (and large) shops in England, Belgium, France, Austria,

For some reason scopes are still not common on double rifles. I understand they aren't traditional, but they work. This new Rigby .450/.400-3" is accurate enough for just about any hunting one would care to do.

Germany, Spain, and Italy producing doubles. I have examined many fine Ferlach doubles, and am especially impressed with Herbert Scheiring's work. Also in Ferlach, Fanzoj produces wonderfully traditional-looking doubles, and I suppose if you wanted the best of the best in the entire world you would look to Peter Hofer. George Sandmann at Empire Arms is importing Dumoulin doubles, and there are Chapuis, Marcel Thys (not currently made), and many more. I'm sure that doubles are being made by many small shops that I have never heard of, and by the time these lines are read, there probably will be many more.

Just keep in mind that not all doubles are created equal. It is relatively easy to put together a double that is spectacularly beautiful. This is a matter of fit and finish and the hands of a fine engraver. It is not quite as simple to build a double that will shoot straight and provide the absolute reliability that is its heritage and hallmark. I have seen beautifully engraved and quite expensive sidelock doubles that were so poorly regulated that hitting a barn door would be difficult. I have seen other expensive doubles that had extraction and ejection problems, and I have seen beautiful wood break at the wrist under recoil.

Remember two things. First, the regulation is extremely complex. A double will never be a real tackdriver in the American sense of the word, but a poorly regulated double will have trouble giving barn-door accuracy. Second, the double is not a strong action—it simply must be well made or it isn't safe to fire. So beware of "great deals," and always obtain a guarantee that allows you to shoot the rifle before you're stuck with it! And, since the embellishment is a large part of the cost, especially with sidelocks, keep in mind that price doesn't necessarily equate to either accuracy or reliability!

The new-gun market is one subject, and the used-gun market is quite another. It's a basic decision a hunter must face when he contemplates acquiring a big double. This decision is easier than it used to be, simply because you may desperately want a classic rifle—but you may not be able to find one. If you do, expect to pay more than you will pay for a comparable new gun. This is especially true in the boxlock market. Twenty years ago a boxlock .470 in good condition commanded a premium price of about $12,000. Today you can more than double that if you can find one (regardless of make). A lot of new boxlock .470s, with new barrels and modern steel, are available for much less. Even .450/.400s (from good makers in good condition), once a real bargain, have escalated toward the $20,000 mark, sometimes beyond. Today there are no bargains, and very few guns are available.

In November 2006, while attending the Grand National Quail Hunt, I visited George Caswell's shop in Enid, Oklahoma. George has long been the premier dealer in vintage double rifles, so I was excited to cruise his inventory. There was no inventory! In years gone by Caswell would come to the Safari Club Convention with dozens of great old doubles. In 2006, on the eve of convention season, he had perhaps a half-dozen in stock (some were really choice). He lamented that supplies had just dried up, and his primary business was turning to shotguns.

There aren't many pitfalls to buying vintage doubles, just so long as, even in today's grossly inflated market, you don't pay a great deal more than you should. First, check the barrels. They'll show wear, and some wear is acceptable. Cordite burns very hot, and there will be some erosion in well-used guns. But the rifling should be bright and fairly sharp. The best way to spot serious wear is to see if the left barrel—the second barrel, which isn't fired nearly as much—looks a whole lot better than the right barrel. If the difference is noticeable, you'd best group the rifle before you bite.

Next, check the proof marks on the flats of the barrel. They're confusing, but make sure it's proofed for a full Nitro charge. *Cartridges of the World* will give the original cordite charge of a Kynoch factory load. Black-powder guns later proofed for Nitro will most likely not have been proofed for a full charge.

Finally, unless you're buying the rifle from a reputable dealer, arrange to have a gunsmith take a look to make sure it hasn't come off the face. If it has, it can probably be fixed, but that might be expensive. Incidentally, if the barrels are worn out, consider it a wall-hanger. It would have to be a very fine gun from a "name" maker to be worth rebarreling, and you don't just willy-nilly rebore a double as you might a bolt gun.

The rules of shopping for used doubles haven't changed much, except that prices are now frightening and there are far fewer to choose between. Boxlocks will tend to

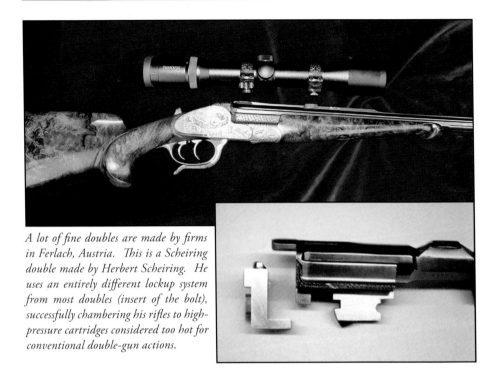

A lot of fine doubles are made by firms in Ferlach, Austria. This is a Scheiring double made by Herbert Scheiring. He uses an entirely different lockup system from most doubles (insert of the bolt), successfully chambering his rifles to high-pressure cartridges considered too hot for conventional double-gun actions.

be "working guns," while sidelocks will tend to be "fine guns." Rifles in .470, .500, .577, and .600 command premiums in exponential escalation, but with ammo now available, even the least desirable calibers (like .475 Nitro Express) are priced along with the rest. Ejector guns are more expensive than extractor guns, and so forth. But, the name inscribed on the barrel still makes the most difference of all. If it happens to say Holland & Holland, add a whole bunch. If it says Rigby or Westley Richards, add a slightly smaller bunch. If it says Purdey, add a whole lot more. If it says Woodward, God help you. William Evans and Jeffery rifles are also escalating in value today. But unless you're a collector, don't get hung up on names. Once you get past the premium names, you aren't into second-class rifles. Most of the name makers made a fair number of second-class (meaning plain, not poor quality) rifles themselves.

There were dozens of small English makers, good 'smiths who just never hit the big time. Their rifles are good, but even today are less costly than the name rifles. Webley and Scott, Grant, Lang, Boswell, Wilkes, Thomas Bland, Thomas Turner, Hollis, Fraser, George Gibbs, Charles Lancaster, Dickson, Tolley, Greener, Manton, Cogswell & Harrison—Lord, who have I missed? There were dozens of small makers in both London and Birmingham, but after two world wars and the Great Depression many records were lost, and it's unlikely that a complete listing exists anywhere. The best old rifle I ever owned was a plain .470 boxlock made by C. W. Andrews, an almost unknown maker. I should have kept that one—as I remind its current owner when I see him at every SCI convention. And, of course, don't forget that a number of very fine rifles have no name on them at all. Virtually all the top makers produced rifles for the Army & Navy Cooperative Stores, Ltd. This co-op furnished rifles (and everything else under the sun) for soldiers and sailors at affordable prices. They were the epitome of the good, sound, working gun. Anybody, the name makers included, may well have made them.

Sidelocks are in another world. The sidelocks were generally the makers' "best" guns, and show a good deal more of the individual maker's taste and innovative touches. Many of the smaller makers didn't produce sidelocks at all but sourced their Webley or trade actions and assembled, barreled, regulated, and finished their boxlock doubles. Those that did make sidelocks generally made good ones. As works of art, they're worth every penny they cost. In terms of function, however, you won't get any more out of them than you will from a boxlock costing half to a third as much.

It's worth repeating here that proper fit is more important with a double than with any other type of rifle since the double's most important job is to deliver two shots almost simultaneously, to stop a serious charge when the chips are down. To do that reliably, it must fit its owner like an extension of his arms and eyes.

The double rifle is Gregory Peck in *The Snows of Kilimanjaro,* Stewart Granger in *King Solomon's Mines* and *The Last Safari,* Robert Redford in *Out of Africa;* it's Ernest Hemingway, Robert Ruark, and J. A. Hunter. The big double symbolizes the grand tradition of African safari. But is it really a sensible choice for today's hunter? It would be foolish to suggest that anyone really needs a double rifle to hunt Africa; many of the great old-timers used magazine rifles exclusively, and many modern PHs still do. Harry Manners never found the .375 in a bolt-action rifle wanting, and Commander Blunt stayed with his .416 Rigby throughout his career. Many top hunters switched back and forth; Hunter loved his double .500s, but for control work he was more likely to use the .505 Gibbs. Samaki Salmon, too, used magazine rifles for control work, a pair of .416s; for ivory hunting, though, he used a pair of .470 doubles. For the sportsman who has no need or desire to take a large number of animals at one sitting, it pretty much comes down to personal preference. However, it would be just as absurd to suggest that a double is not a sound choice as it would be to suggest it as the only choice!

The double does have very real advantages. It's short, it's handy, and its big Nitro Express cartridges are unquestionably adequate. A good double handles like a dream, points naturally, and, no matter what, nothing is faster for a second shot. It's also important to note that the second shot comes with absolutely no extraneous motion or noise. Now, even with much practice, the third shot from a double will come more slowly than from a magazine rifle. However, when that third cartridge is placed in a double's chamber, the fourth goes in right alongside it. I would submit that a double is just as fast for the fourth shot as any magazine rifle—and faster by far than a three-shot magazine rifle.

The double rifle also has serious disadvantages. The first is cost. Even the plainest production boxlock will cost at least ten times what an equally plain production bolt-action .458 Lott will cost. If you can't afford one, don't despair; they're great fun to own and shoot, but they aren't ten times better than a bolt gun!

Yet another disadvantage is the fact that a double rifle is a very basic tool. Like a shotgun, it is what it is and there's little that can be done to change it. A bolt-action rifle can be fine-tuned, accurized, scoped or unscoped, and its ammunition can be carefully tailored for the exact job at hand. Unless you're willing to go to extremes of trouble and expense, as the double rifle comes into your hands, so it shall remain. The bullet weight and load for which it was regulated, unless you're lucky, is probably the only load that will deliver any real degree of accuracy.

The double's barrels are regulated for a certain bullet and a specific charge of powder, and with that load its barrels will shoot together, more or less, if the maker put in the time. I have done some of the regulation shooting for Rigby, and it is incredibly time-consuming. (Also downright painful with the big cartridges!) Modern nuances like laser boresighting and precise micrometer measurement give good starting points, but then you get to the vagaries of individual barrels. Once in a while I've seen barrels come out of the shop that need no further regulation, but these are rare. If adjustment is required, it's a matter of heating the solder, moving the wedge, letting it cool, shooting, and doing it again—and sometimes over and over again.

That said, this business about doubles being inaccurate is largely a myth. It depends on the skill and patience of the regulator. That Krieghoff I mentioned was amazing. Joof Lamprecht had a Heym in .300 Winchester Magnum that was also as accurate as most bolt guns, as was an old Rigby .450-3¼" owned by Tom Siatos. Rigby has a .470 rifle it built for "Tech" Komoto that is stunningly accurate, consistently printing both barrels exactly side by side, touching. Komoto took the rifle on what he believed would be his last elephant hunt, and when he returned he brought the rifle back to Rigby, saying, "You will probably never build another double this accurate, so I think you should keep it here at the shop." It resides in a place of honor under a ninety-nine-year lease agreement!

Such rifles prove it can be done, but they are exceptional. Acceptable accuracy is George Caswell's "minute of orange" at fifty yards, and sometimes "minute of grapefruit" is about all you can get. Keep in mind that the exact loads for which older doubles were regulated haven't been loaded for fifty years or more!

Rifles like this Krieghoff .500/.416 put to bed the myth about double rifle accuracy. They vary, but I've seen a number of double rifles by Krieghoff, Heym, Rigby, and others that provided this level of accuracy.

How big a problem is that? Are doubles actually all that finicky? Well, it depends on the rifle. Getting the barrels to shoot together is a matter of barrel vibrations and harmonics plus that slight degree of convergence of the two barrels. There's nothing magic about Kynoch bullets and cordite powder. As in getting bolt-action rifles to shoot tiny groups, everything interrelates. Bullet weight and bearing surface are important, but velocity is the most critical factor. If you can match the velocity of the original regulation load, then the results should be similar.

The Australian Woodleigh bullets (and excellent bullets they are!) are very similar to Kynochs in profile and bearing surface, and they generally match in weight. So they are usually at least the starting point for finding a load that will regulate in an older rifle. With modern rifles, you need to know if the rifle was regulated with Federal, Superior, Kynoch, or whatever. Some rifles will be forgiving, some will not. Remember that the double rifle's center of gravity lies between the barrels, so the right barrel kicks right and the left barrel left. Barrel time is critical, so slower loads will tend to spread, and increased velocity will bring the barrels together until they cross, which is not desirable. So if your barrels are crossing, you need slower loads; if they're spreading, you need a bit more velocity.

All smokeless powders get a bit "hotter" as temperatures increase, but cordite was more sensitive to temperature changes than our modern powders are. In the old days hunters often found their doubles "crossfiring" at relatively close range when they used cordite ammunition in Africa's equatorial heat. In some cases, "tropical" loads were offered with a slightly lower powder charge designed for use at higher temperatures. Later on, it was common for large-caliber doubles to be specifically regulated for use in warm climates.

In his *Notes on Sporting Rifles,* Sir Gerald Burrard advises: "This crossing of the shots is a very common fault in very hot climates . . . The only plan to advise is . . . to have the rifle regulated in England so that the two barrels shoot a little away from each other at 100 yards . . . As a general guide it may be taken that the barrels of double cordite rifles of round about .470 bore should be made to shoot from 4 to 6 inches apart at 100 yards in England. It will then be found that in the hot climate they will shoot so close together that it will be impossible to distinguish their groups under practical sporting conditions."

With older rifles the flats of the barrel will tell you what bullet weight and charge of powder your rifle was regulated for, but the inscription won't tell you whether it was regulated for the tropics or for England. In other words, you've got a bit of a grab bag on your hands. With so many fine new doubles regulated for modern ammo—and for less money—this in itself is justification for considering new rifles over old ones. But the old rifles are classics, and some of us will always prefer them. If you're in that boat, you will have to solve the ammo problem for yourself.

Original Kynoch ammunition is getting too old to trust in the field and really should be relegated to collectible status. Modern factory ammo is generally loaded to original Kynoch velocities, so it may work. If it doesn't, handloading (or custom loading by someone like Superior's Larry Barnett) is necessary. Some bore diameters will be very limited in bullet selection; others, like .458 and .475, have a rich array. Be careful of all homogeneous alloy bullets in double rifles, especially older rifles. These bullets do not compress like jacketed bullets with lead cores, and may cause dangerous pressure spikes. Be equally careful of powder and load selection. There is now pretty good data out there, but make darn sure you know what you're doing if you are handloading for any double, but especially older guns.

It isn't really all that bad; most doubles regulate more or less readily with handloads of the approximate original bullet weight and a powder charge that yields something close to original velocities. But there won't be a lot of combinations that work, and it can take a good deal of hit-and-miss to find the best solution.

The cases are very large, needed for the bulky cordite. But with modern powders, the case capacity is far more than needed. For this reason it's important to use extremely bulky, slow-burning powders. The older references suggested IMR 3031, and it will work. However, this powder is much too fast for my taste. I

I have long been a fan of the .450-3¼" because its straight case allows better load density and can be put on a slimmer action than the family of cartridges based on the .500 case. I like it even better now that Hornady has a modern load.

have had better luck with IMR 4831, a slower, bulkier powder that uses much more of the case. Even then, sometimes it's necessary to use a bit of polyester fiber on top of the powder. With the larger cases, I have experienced erratic ignition without a bit of filler. The late Jack Lott, a real authority on doubles, used a light cork overpowder wad. I've used Jack's wads—he showed me how to make them—but I've found it easier to put a half-grain of polyester pillow stuffing over the powder. Be advised, though, that nothing is noncritical with these cartridges, and the rifles that fire them will not handle extra pressure with the ease of a bolt action. Once I got a little heavy-handed with the pillow stuffing, and pressures went up alarmingly.

More recently I have gone almost exclusively to Alliant's RL15 powder. A conversion rate of 1.16 times the original cordite load should come very close. For the .470, for instance, the original load was 75 grains of cordite. 1.16 times 75 equals 89.25, and I have yet to see a .470 that wouldn't regulate at something very close to this load. I've used the same conversion on other Nitro Express cartridges with generally good results—and I have not found overpowder wads or filler necessary with this powder.

You won't find much loading data available for Nitro Express cartridges, but it's better than it used to be. Don't do a lot of freelance experimentation, and proceed to full loads very cautiously. If such care is taken, you really can't get into trouble, but once you find a load your rifle will regulate with, you're all finished experimenting.

The double rifle is not for the accuracy freak, and certainly not, generally, for the handloading experimenter. There's lots of experimentation to be done in finding a good load, but once it's found, that's it. On the other hand, relatively few hunters are serious ballistic tinkerers. All the double asks is that she be fed a diet she likes, and it isn't really all that difficult to comply these days.

Accuracy? Well, you aren't going to make a long-range rig out of a big double. But the double's inaccuracy is generally exaggerated out of all proportion. No doubles can offer consistent minute-of-angle accuracy—but they're all minute of buffalo or elephant. They have the capability to put those big bullets where they're needed, when they're needed. And they're also a joy to own and shoot. Yes, a good double is a viable choice for today's African hunting. Africa is a feeling as much as a place, and a big double takes you back in time to the Africa you've read and dreamed about all your life. That's an equally good reason to use one. And make no mistake: There are still times when that instantly available second barrel will save the day. And your hide.

The Bolt Action:
A Historical Perspective

Chapter 17

In 1890 Oliver Winchester's lever actions were the best-known and most-respected repeaters in the world. By the time the Spanish-American and Boer Wars had ended, about 1902, the bolt action had taken over, perhaps not in America but in Africa and the rest of the world.

The first turnbolt rifles were black-powder guns, the classic form being the Model 71 Mauser firing the 11mm (.43-caliber) Mauser cartridge. But smokeless cartridges were right around the corner, and the first turnbolts to catch the eyes of sportsmen fired smallbore cartridges: the 6.5x53R Mannlicher-Steyr and later the 6.5x54 Mannlicher-Schoenauer, the Mausers in 7x57 and 8x57J, and Britain's Lee-Metford .303. Hunters had seen the black-powder expresses fail miserably on large game, but now the long, heavy-for-caliber, fully jacketed bullets for these military cartridges gave the penetration that heretofore required an 8-bore cannon.

The rifles were also incredibly cheap, especially to English sportsmen accustomed to paying for individually crafted arms. In 1892, when Austria's Steyr began selling its 6.5x53R Mannlicher on the civilian market, the cost was about 80 shillings, or $16. An Englishman could purchase a used Martini-Henry for a bit less than that—but not much else! Although this passage has been oft quoted, the great sheep hunter, St. George Littledale, summed things up nicely in a letter written in the 1920s:

> In 1895 Sir Edmund Loder gave me a Mannlicher rifle, bayonet and all, complete, on the eve of my starting for Tibet. Had only time to have sighting altered. On my protesting that I had a room full of rifles and did not want any more, all he said was, "Try the Mannlicher," and like Lily Langtry and the soap, I have used no other since.

From today's perspective, it seems amazing that turn-of-the-century British hunters were so quick to adopt the smallbore bolt action. It was a radical shift, especially for the staid Englishmen. However, the Englishmen who went out to Africa weren't the stodgy noblemen from smoke-filled clubrooms. They were rebels, reckless and often resentful, and many of them had little to lose. If titled, they were often the second and third sons, and more than a few left scandals and unpaid bills behind them. Others were gentlemen of the highest order, but driven by a thirst for adventure that set them apart from their fellows in old England. It was people like these who had built one of the world's great empires from a tiny island nation, and it shouldn't be surprising that they would try something new—especially if it fit their budgets!

Whether the bolt action happened to be a 6.5, a 7mm, a .303, an 8mm, or even an American Springfield or Krag, to understand its rapid, complete, and euphoric acceptance you must understand the arena into which it came. Velocities were low; bullets were soft lead or, at best, hardened lead; smallbores began at .40-caliber and ran to .577. The bullet performance and penetration we take for granted were unknown; the only way to reliably and consistently drop really large game was to flatten them with raw power—which also flattened the shooter. The writings of even the hairiest-chested of the early hunters are filled with references to the sometimes disastrous effects of recoil.

Smokeless powder had existed in experimental form for some time, but until now it had been impractical as a propellant for bullets. The black-powder expresses were already at the upper limits of velocity that the existing projectiles would stand. Smokeless cartridges simply could not exist without a bullet hard enough to be

Left to right: .303 British, .318 Westley Richards, .350 Rigby Rimless Magnum. Contrary to popular belief, it wasn't big cartridges like the .416 Rigby or .505 Gibbs that made the bolt action's reputation. It was military cartridges like the .303 and the 6.5s, and then sound sporting cartridges like the .318, .350, and .333 Jeffery—long before there were big cartridges available.

I had a Westley Richards .318 for some time, which I used to take this impala. It was truly a great rifle, with a 28-inch barrel and leaf sights out to 600 yards! Despite all that business about the 7x57, it was the .318 that yielded Bell's largest bag of elephants.

This is one of just twenty-odd original George Gibbs .505 Gibbs rifles. Like the .416 Rigby (except more so), the legend of the .505 Gibbs far outstripped its actual use. This is Richard Harland's rifle; his friend Barrie Duckworth has the consecutive serial number .505.

driven at such unprecedented velocities. Which came first, the chicken or the egg? Who knows? But it's a fact that the first practical smokeless cartridges came out about the same time as the first jacketed bullets, the late 1880s. A Major Rubin of the Swiss army is credited with inventing the jacketed bullet, initially a lead core sheathed in an alloy of copper and nickel ("cupro-nickel"). Just a few years later, that lead core was sheathed in steel, and then gilded with nickel—essentially the same formula for the "steel-jacketed solids" we use to this day.

The year 1888 saw the introduction not only of the 8mm Mauser ("J" bore, technically a 7.9mm) but also of the .303 British. The .303, with a wonderful 215-grain roundnose jacketed bullet, was introduced as a black-powder cartridge, using a compressed "express-type" load to push that bullet at 1,850 FPS. When the switch to smokeless was made in 1892, the velocity was increased by only 120 FPS.

The Mauser and Mannlicher cartridges all developed somewhat higher velocities, and the European rifles were stronger than the British Lee-Metford. Even so, all of these new smallbore military rifles with their jacketed bullets offered a whole new world of penetration, accuracy, and flat trajectory. And more: The rifles were wonderfully light, especially the little Mannlicher 6.5s. Recoil was nonexistent, and the great clouds of smoke were no more. The early military rifles were mostly

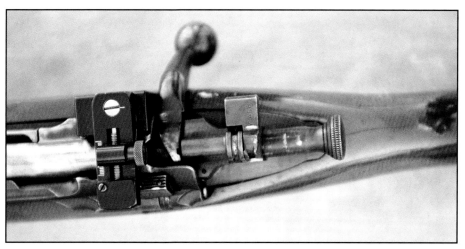

The American Springfield is just a knockoff of the Mauser action. Ultimately the U.S. had to pay Mauser a royalty!

designed to handle charging or "stripper" clips, so not only were they repeaters but the firepower they offered was awesome.

Each of these smallbore bolt actions had its fans, and in truth all of them, given good bullets, were probably just about equal. The 6.5mm, firing those pencil-like 160-grain bullets, may well have given the very best penetration of the whole lot, although the 7x57 with its original 173-grain bullet is hardly a slouch. But the .311-caliber .303 British with 215-grain bullet was and is a real killer; likewise the 8mm Mauser with its original 226-grain bullet. H. C. Maydon swore by his "7.9" Mauser; Stigand, Tarlton, and many others swore by the 6.5, or .256; and Bell loved his .275 Rigby. But the soldiers, hunters, and adventurers who relied on the Lee-Metford .303 can't be forgotten. The .303 was admired by the likes of Selous and Frederick Burnham, and it was a .303 that Lt. Col. J. H. Patterson used to clean out the Tsavo man-eaters.

Perhaps the most anemic of the early smokeless military cartridges was the rimmed 8mm Lebel adopted by France. According to Tony Sanchez-Ariño, it was the favorite of French ivory hunter Theodore Lefebvre, who is believed to have shot seven hundred elephant with his Lebel, never finding it lacking!

The first really successful smokeless-powder bolt action was the German Model 88, variously called a Mannlicher and a Mauser but actually the product of neither designer but rather an amalgamation of the ideas of both. Although chambered for the still-excellent 8x57 (technically 7.9mm with the earlier .318-inch bullet), this wasn't the rifle that caught the world's eye, possibly because, like many military rifles, it wasn't available on the civilian market.

Some of those old rifles really shoot. This is a left-hand-converted R. F. Sedgely Springfield, with original barrel and original aperture sights. And yes, if you know how to use them, aperture sights are incredibly precise.

I used the Sedgely Springfield to take this kudu in South Africa. It was really fun; I felt just like Papa Hemingway with his prized Griffin & Howe Springfield!

One of its variations, manufactured by the Steyr works in Austria, was. This was the Model 1892 (and 1893) Romanian military rifle, using the same basic action but chambered for the 6.5x53R cartridge. Called the Mannlicher or Mannlicher-Steyr, this was the first of the 6.5s to see use on African game. By today's standards the action is a bit weird. The bolt head is a separate piece from the bolt body, although the forward opposing locking lugs at the front of the bolt body are pure Mauser. The extractor, affixed to the bolt head, appears to be weak and is very small—but I've never heard of extraction complaints with this rifle.

The cartridges were loaded in clips, similar to the charging or "stripper" clips that would continue in vogue for many years. However, with the Model 88 and its derivatives, including the 6.5mm Mannlicher-Steyr, the clip and its cartridges were inserted into the magazine box from the top. The clip remained in place while the spring-loaded follower fed the cartridges up one at a time. As long as there were cartridges in the clip, it remained in place; when the last cartridge was fed into the chamber, the clip would drop out through an opening in the bottom of the magazine.

The clip-loading feature was obviously very fast, but if a sportsman didn't have any clips or if he lost them, the rifle became a single shot. Other than the apparently weak extractor, it was a sound and strong action—but it had no facility to vent gases away from the shooter in the event of a ruptured case head or other catastrophic failure.

The later Mannlicher-Schoenauer rifle was developed at Steyr in 1900. Adopted as the Greek military rifle in 1903, chambered for the rimless 6.5x54 Mannlicher-Schoenauer, the rifle was introduced to the sporting marketplace about the same time. Ballistics were essentially identical to those of the 6.5x53R Mannlicher-Steyr, which became known as the "old" 6.5. The action, too, was very similar, in that the bolt assembly was the same, including the detachable bolt head and small extractor. However, the Mannlicher-Schoenauer did away with the Steyr clips, using instead the rotary-spool magazine, which would become the Mannlicher-Schoenauer hallmark from then on.

The top of the receiver was slotted to receive charging clips, essential on a military bolt action, but the clips weren't required for operation and could be discarded. The spool magazine was and is a very fine system; it allowed for unbeatably smooth feeding, and the spool held the cartridges firmly in place and prevented softpoints from deforming in the magazine. Over the years, a great many sporting rifles

were made around this action, and in its original 6.5 chambering it was a favorite among Africa's early smallbore fanatics.

The British Lee-Metford is in many ways a strange action. Never particularly strong (though plenty strong enough for the mild .303 British), its locking lugs are located about halfway down the bolt body. The Metford designation refers to the shallow, segmental Metford rifling, which was found to wear much too quickly with smokeless loads. In 1895 the deeper-grooved Enfield rifling was adopted, and from then forward the rifle was known as the Lee-Enfield.

Perhaps the most famous of all .416 Rigby rifles is the one that Harry Selby used for decades. It now lives in America and, like Harry himself, is retired.

With production ceased in 2006, I suppose the original Winchester Model 70 is now part of bolt-action history—although the Model 70 will certainly be back. My vintage Model 70 is a weird left-hand conversion, but it's now on its second barrel and I still love it.

The basic action was the creation of American designer James Paris Lee, and for a time Remington offered "Remington-Lee" sporting rifles around an earlier version.

Although never available in any chambering other than .303, the Lee-Metfords and later Lee-Enfields saw wide use throughout Africa. The ten-shot magazine capacity was extremely desirable—if not to the hunter, certainly to the soldiers who carried it through two world wars and hundreds of colonial skirmishes. When C. H. Stigand was killed by Dinka spearmen in Sudan, it was reported that the ground around him was littered with cases from his .303. Other than firepower, the Lee-Enfield was in few aspects the equal of the Mauser action that followed it by just a few years. Even so, it was a fixture throughout the British Empire for generations, and Lee-Enfields are still seen all across Africa to this day.

Peter Paul Mauser, who must rank with John Moses Browning as one of the greatest of firearms designers, had been working for years to improve his Model 71 black-powder bolt action. Between 1888 and 1896, every year saw a new Mauser action designed for rimless, smokeless cartridges. Each one was adopted by one country or another: the 1889 Belgian, 1890 Turkish, 1891 Argentine, 1892 Spanish (introducing the 7x57 cartridge to the world), 1894 Swedish, 1895

"Original" and very faithful to the old design, Mausers are now more readily available than since before World War I. Mauser themselves offer a full line of Mausers true to Peter Paul Mausers design, as do other manufacturers, including this lovely Express Mauser from Heym.

Chilean, and 1896 Swedish (again). Then, in 1898, Mauser's bolt action reached what is considered its ultimate design in the Model 98 German Mauser.

The basics of the action are a one-piece bolt body with two massive, forward, opposing locking lugs and a third safety lug farther back. The famed long Mauser extractor of spring steel is attached to the bolt by a collar, and the fixed ejector is on the left side of the receiver. When the cartridge feeds up out of the magazine, the extractor holds it securely until the bolt is moved to the rear. The ejector then passes through a slot in the right locking lug and bolt face until it contacts the case head and flips it to the right and out.

The military Model 98 action is slotted for charging clips, and the left side of the receiver has a semicircular cutout, the thumb slot, to facilitate clip loading. The bolt has openings to direct escaping gas in the event of a ruptured case, making it a safer action than most designs that preceded it.

Over the years, with numerous modifications—many simply cosmetic—the Mauser-type action, characterized by dual opposing locking lugs, long extractor, and fixed ejector, would dominate the sporting-rifle world as well as the military. Both the Springfield and the Pattern 14 (or 1917 U.S.) Enfield were basically modified Mauser actions. So was the pre-'64 Winchester Model 70. So, today, are the many Mauser and Model 70 clones: Dakota, Granite Mountain, Empire, and more.

Dozens of firms have made commercial Mauser actions, in America as well as all over Europe. Initially only the standard-length 8.75-inch action was made, but by 1902 "magnum" Mauser actions 9.25 inches in length, capable of handling larger cartridges, were available. Initially, too, the rifles were commonly available only in their military chamberings, which accounts for the almost instant success of the 7x57 and 8x57.

The days of the smallbores were numbered, however. By the time George Grey was killed while using a .280 Ross, in 1911, the demand for more powerful bolt actions had already begun. John Rigby, Mauser's British agent, chambered magnum Mausers modified with slant-box magazines to the .400/.350 Nitro Express as early as 1902, and a few Mausers in .500-3" Nitro Express were also made. This may not have been satisfactory to John Rigby, a most savvy engineer, because he introduced his rimless .350 Rigby Magnum in about 1905, and a few years later developed his signature .416 Rigby. In 1908 Westley Richards, unable to obtain magnum actions, introduced its revolutionary short-case .425. For those who believe our short, fat, rebated rim cartridges are new, take a look at the .425. Its long neck is archaic, but it was the first rebated rim cartridge. The .404 Jeffery, introduced in 1909, is a very tight fit for a standard action, but can be made to fit. In 1912, when Rigby's magnum Mauser monopoly ended, the .416 Rigby and .375 Holland & Holland joined the .425 and .404.

Now, for the first time, hunters who preferred magazine rifles—or who couldn't afford a double—didn't have to rely on a smallbore. The British, of course, weren't alone. In Europe the 9x56 and 9.5x57 Mannlicher-Schoenauer; the 9x57, 9.3x57, 9.3x62, and 10.75x63 Mauser; and the 9.3x64 Brenneke were all available well before World War I.

Many of Africa's greatest hunters came to rely exclusively on bolt actions: Walter Bell, Harry Manners, Pete Pearson, David Blunt, and more. Others, like John Taylor, remained staunch double-rifle men. However, most hunters who preferred doubles, including Taylor himself, also used the cheaper, lighter, bolt-action rifles extensively, often saving the doubles and their much more expensive ammunition strictly for close-cover work.

The advantages of the bolt-action rifle were readily apparent at the turn of the century, and they're the same advantages the turnbolt offers today. I've recited the litany of cost, weight, and repeat firepower—but, in truth, other repeating action types could compete in all these areas. However, no other repeating action to this day has been effective with the powerful, high-intensity cartridges readily available in bolt actions.

Thus, one of the turnbolt's great advantages is strength. Yes, a bolt gun can be blown up—but every other action type known to man will give up long before a turnbolt does. Part of that strength, too, is in the great camming power the bolt exerts during primary extraction. In the tropics, stuck cases were an age-old problem in single shots, doubles, and even the few lever actions that found their way to Africa. In the very worst of situations, you might have to beat on the bolt handle to get the action open, but it takes more than hot weather to put a bolt gun out of service.

It was obvious, too, that the rigid bolt action offered accuracy previously available only in single-shot rifles—and it offered this accuracy with flat-shooting cartridges such as the world had never seen. Some traditionalists clung to their doubles, but by World War I you'd have been hard-pressed to find an African hunter who didn't appreciate the bolt action's virtues.

Elmer Keith with the epitome of a classic Mauser-action rifle from the Hoffman Arms Company, this one chambered for the .400 Whelen.

Because so many bolt actions began life as military arms, the tradition of customizing them started early. Theodore Roosevelt himself had a modified Springfield on the 1909 safari, custom-stocked and sighted to his specifications and undoubtedly one of the first Springfields so modified. I actually held this very rifle at the Springfield Armory Museum when they were celebrating the centennial of the 1903 Springfield. It had simple open sights and a clean, plain sporting stock, and it spoke historical volumes. It revealed a surprise, too. Roosevelt's rifle has generally been referred to as a .30-06. It actually is not! It was a 1903 model chambered to the original .30-03 cartridge, and it was never modified!

At first, such "sporterizing" had the very simple goal of reducing the weight and perhaps the length of the military rifle. Later, as scope sights came into vogue, bolt handles and flag safeties would require modification to allow scope mounting. And of course, from the very start, discriminating sportsmen wanted wood and metalwork far superior to that which was suitable for a military arm.

In America the New York firm of Griffin & Howe, still turning out fine work today, was one of the pioneers in custom bolt-action work. Hoffman Arms was another, as were Charles Newton's rifles, made by three successive companies in Buffalo, New York, until the Depression finished them forever. Another early

Although well known for his love of the .270 Winchester, Jack O'Connor favored using large-caliber, classic guns such as the .416 Rigby with a magnum Mauser action when it came to dangerous game, as can be seen with this buffalo he shot in Zambia.

"custom firm" was R. F. Sedgely of Philadelphia. His rifles were sort of "blue collar" compared to Griffin & Howe, but the metalwork was wonderful and they shot wonderfully. He was perhaps one of the first to offer left-hand conversions. They were regularly catalogued, but it was a lot of work with little demand, and he might have actually made as few as five. Retired Ventura County Sheriff Larry Carpenter found one for me. It's a magnificent piece of work, and even with its original aperture sight it still groups under an inch. I took it to Africa one year, and when I took a kudu with it I felt just like Papa Hemingway!

The availability of Continental bolt-action rifles took a downhill turn during and just after World War I, but recovered rapidly. During World War II, however, the devastation was almost complete, and from 1939 onward the true commercial Mauser action would become ever more scarce. It's most unfortunate, because some of those commercial Mauser actions are the finest sporting-rifle actions the world has ever seen. Among the most prized are double square-bridge actions, wherein both receiver rings are flat on top, ideal for a variety of detachable and nondetachable scope mounts. Also seen are single square-bridge actions, wherein only the rear receiver ring is flat. And of course there are dozens of standard actions of all variations from many makers. As we know now, thanks to CNC technology almost any variation of a Mauser action is again available. But both original and essentially custom Mauser actions come dear today, the action alone worth at least double the price of most production bolt-action rifles.

To the average American the loss of the Mauser action is not so severe. Starting in 1936, the Winchester Model 70 was available in .375 H&H, and for many years American interest in any other large-bore cartridge languished. After all, America's most popular rifle was chambered for Africa's most popular general-purpose cartridge, and what else mattered?

After the war, the great Oberndorf Mauser was no more, and in fact any Mauser action was in short supply. A few F.N. (Fabrique Nationale, Belgium) actions were available, including Browning's fine line of bolt-action rifles based on this action. A very few French-made Brevex magnum actions trickled in after 1955, and copies of Mauser actions were made in such diverse places as Japan and Spain. But the great days of the Mauser action seemed to have ended, and the postwar "modern" bolt actions began to take over.

Bolt Actions Today

Chapter 18

In the last two decades things have changed, and are changing yet again as these lines are written. For many years the Mauser controlled-round-feed action was very scarce, and the hunting world was dominated by modern push-feed actions from Remington, Savage, Weatherby, and others. An almost lone exception was the Winchester Model 70, and in 1964 it became a push-feed action as well. The "pre-1964" version became an almost instant collectible, but over time the Mauser cult, and the cult of controlled-round-feed, persisted. Eventually Winchester returned to a long extractor and controlled-round-feed with its Model 70 Classic action. But, as we know, in a move that stunned the shooting world, Winchester closed its New Haven, Connecticut plant in 2006, ceasing production of our beloved "Rifleman's Rifle." As these lines are written in late 2007, the worm has turned yet again: The "new" Model 70, now manufactured by F.N. (no stranger to bolt actions!) has just been announced. I haven't actually seen one, but I know it to be a "true" Model 70, a Mauser clone with long extractor, fixed ejector, and control-round-feed.

Although the original Ruger Model 77 had a long Mauser extractor, it was a push-feed action. When the change was made to the current Model 77 Mark II, Ruger waffled a bit on this issue, but the current Model 77 Mark II rifles are controlled-round-feed with fixed-blade Mauser ejectors. The actual Mauser action has also enjoyed a considerable resurgence in popularity. During the seventies and eighties, the Yugoslavian Mark X Mauser was extremely popular. It was then available both in action-only form and as complete rifles, including the attractive Whitworth. The fall of the Iron Curtain opened up some markets, but the breakup of Yugoslavia ended the availability of the Mark X for some years. Today the excellent CZ action, fondly referred to in Africa as the "Bruno" from its origin in Brno, Czech Republic, is readily available and amazingly affordable. This action was always considered rough but hell for stout. The latter still applies, but current CZ rifles are smoother and better finished all the time.

The final iteration of the Model 70 in .375 as made by Winchester. This remains a classic modern bolt action . . . with much of its design going back to the nineteenth century.

What was once the Yugoslavian Mark X is manufactured in what is now Serbia. In 2006 Remington jumped on this bandwagon, importing finished rifles as the Remington Model "798." This is a clever play on numbers, using the "7" that has long denoted Remington centerfires, while the "98" refers to the Mauser 98. The 798 as currently imported is a bit rough on the exterior, but the ones I have used are very smooth (pure Mauser) and shoot straight. I used a left-hand prototype (which may or may not ever be marketed) in Namibia in 2007, and it was a real joy. Both the CZ and the Mark X are essentially faithful Model 98 Mausers, differing primarily in that each has thumb safeties to the side and rear of the bolt, rather than traditional cocking-piece safeties.

There are also new "Model 70-type" modified Mauser actions from Kimber and Dakota on the American market. Kimber (of Oregon) went under in the late eighties but was restarted with manufacturing in upstate New York. Initially it concentrated on Colt 1911 handguns but has been back in the centerfire market for several years. In 2007 the firm introduced the Caprivi, a wonderfully appointed .375 with all the bells and whistles expected of a classic African bolt action: good iron sights, excellent wood, matte blue, extended magazine box, the works. Dakota, too, has had its ups and downs after the death of its founder, Don Allen. As these lines are written the company is undergoing a reorganization. Hopefully it will win through, because the Dakota Model 76, though now much more costly than it once was, is a fine action and Dakota knows how to build great rifles.

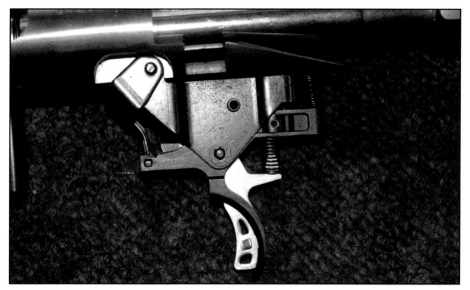

*One of the strong suits of the bolt action is its adaptability to a really good, clean, crisp, adjustable trigger.
This is the Savage AccuTrigger, an innovative trigger that offers a wonderfully clean squeeze.*

Then there are beautifully finished, very faithful, and far more expensive "true" Mauser actions now being manufactured on both sides of the pond: American Mauser actions like Granite Mountain and Empire, and European actions from small makers like Reimar Johansen . . . and from Mauser itself. Faithful? Mauser once again makes its Model 98 in standard and magnum size, using Peter Paul Mauser's original drawings. There are many others as well, some made one at a time and some genuinely manufactured. These actions are expensive, especially the magnum-size actions, but the demand seems to continue to escalate.

All that is well and good; all the actions mentioned, plus the basic Model 1898 Mauser—of which many thousands are still in use—are very fine. However, the majority of bolt-action sporting rifles in use today are neither Mausers nor Mauser derivatives. Mind you, there were always non-Mauser actions: Enfields, Mannlichers, Krags. But the first modern non-Mauser actions began making their appearance just after World War II. One of the first to become really popular was the Remington Model 721, a rifle that, with few changes, became the Remington Model 700, still one of the world's most popular sporting rifles.

The Remington action does use the massive Mauser dual opposing locking lugs, but its extraction/ejection is totally different. For one thing, the bolt face is an unbroken circle of steel surrounding the case head. Now, that's clearly a good idea, and it's a concept found on most commercial actions today. It's safer and stronger,

Today's bolt actions are an eclectic mix of push feeds and controlled-round feed actions. The Model 700 is a modern push feed, but it remains one of the world's most popular bolt-action rifles.

and, in these product-liability-conscious days, these factors must be of primary concern to manufacturers. Unfortunately, Mauser controlled-round feeding is not possible unless the bottom part of the bolt face is left open so that the cartridge can slide from the magazine up against the bolt face. The extractor of most such actions is a thin, C-shaped, spring-loaded clip fitting into the rim of the bolt face, and most modern ejectors are spring-loaded plungers on the opposite side. (For a full discussion of controlled-round feeding, see chapter 19.)

As the postwar decades rolled by, these and similar concepts gradually dominated the bolt-action world. The traditional Sako, for instance, has an anti-bind device on the bolt that looks like a long Mauser extractor but is not; the Sako extractor is a sturdy hook, inletted into one side of the bolt face. It works, but it is not a Mauser extractor. The newer Sako Model 75 is an even more radical departure, with three locking lugs versus Mauser's two.

As noted earlier, Bill Ruger achieved a compromise with his original 1968-vintage Ruger M77. It did have a classic long Mauser extractor, but the ejector was the plunger type on the bolt face, and the cartridge head was encased by steel. When feeding, the cartridge was pushed ahead of the Ruger bolt, not gripped by it; the extractor was beveled to snap over the case head as the round chambers and the bolt goes home. Apparently Ruger, the greatest American firearms genius since John Moses Browning, believed the people had spoken on this issue, because he was still fully in command at Ruger when the Mark II went to controlled-round-feed and the Mauser fixed-blade ejector.

Many modern actions use the Mauser dual opposing locking lugs, but an increasing number do not. A different concept is the Weatherby Mark V, using a large-diameter bolt with nine locking lugs machined from the forward portion of the bolt. Extraction/ejection devices are the modern type. It is often argued that manufacturing tolerances are such that it's rare for all nine lugs to actually bear, but the Weatherby is still one of the strongest actions.

There have always been a few rear-locking bolt actions around; in recent years the Remington Model 788 was a good American rear-locking bolt action. Austria's Steyr-Mannlicher SL series is a fine European rear-locking bolt action. Extremely smooth and reliable, the SL locks up with six lugs just ahead of the bolt handle. This rifle is a modern descendant of the Mannlicher-Schoenauer, and it retains the butterknife handle that always set the Mannlichers apart.

Unfortunately, the M-S rotary magazine was long since replaced with a detachable plastic rotary magazine. It works and, with its modern space-age materials is darn near indestructible.

Personally, I've never understood what place a detachable magazine has on a hunting rifle. They are one of my pet peeves, just something else to look after and possibly lose. However, at least some of the people have spoken on this issue as well, because detachable magazines are extremely common today. Many models, such as today's Remington M700 and Savage 110, are available in both detachable and nondetachable versions, and there are others, like the Browning A-Bolt, which has a detachable magazine that clips to the upper surface of the floor plate, so you can use it or not as you choose.

There are lots of ways to make a bolt-action lockup. Rear-locking actions like the discontinued Remington 788 and Steyr-Mannlicher are rarely seen today, but there are other good ways to skin the cat. As noted, Weatherby uses a unique nine-lug locking system, while three-lug actions like the Sako 75 are not uncommon. Sako's TRG action also uses a three-lug bolt, as does the brand-new Icon from Thompson Center. I have used the Icon in both prototype and production versions, and it's amazingly smooth and, with a very rigid action, inherently extremely accurate.

Another unusual European bolt action is the Sauer, imported into the United States some years ago as the Colt-Sauer, again imported in the late 1980s by Sigarms as the Sig-Sauer, and currently available as the Sauer Model 202. It has a very complex action that achieves lockup via retracting lugs in the bolt body. This makes it one of

PH J. P. Kleinhans and Wayne Holt with a good Mozambique sable, taken with the synthetic stocked "Alaskan" version of the Ruger Hawkeye in .375 Ruger. Today many people prefer synthetic stocks, and most popular rifles are available in both wood and synthetic.

the smoothest of all bolt actions, but the bolt has some thirty parts, three times more than the 98 Mauser. That isn't in itself a drawback, but it does make it expensive and complex to manufacture.

Then there are the Mauser 03 and Merkel KR-I, both featuring six-lug, rotating bolt heads. These two rifles are quite different, the Mauser more traditional in looks and the Merkel more modern. Both, however, have the same intent: an interchangeable-barrel rifle, with the bolt head also interchangeable so cartridges of different case-head diameters can be used. This is also one of the beauties of the Blaser R93, which is a very fast, straight-pull design. Straight-pull bolt actions like the Lee and Ross weren't uncommon a century ago, but today a straight-pull bolt is unusual. The Blaser is so different that, in the rifle world, it is almost like the Glock in the pistol world: There are "Glockophiles," and there are those who love 1911s and hate the polymer-framed pistols. There are "Blaserophiles," and there are those who love Mausers and hate anything new. Unarguably, the Blaser works, is accurate, and is undoubtedly the fastest bolt action on the market. These rifles will be discussed in greater detail later along with other switch-barrel and takedown designs.

There are, of course, a great many more bolt-action rifles from many more makers. But few of them differ from those mentioned in any significant way. More important to this discussion is how today's (and, for that matter, yesterday's) bolt-action rifle fits in as a safari rifle.

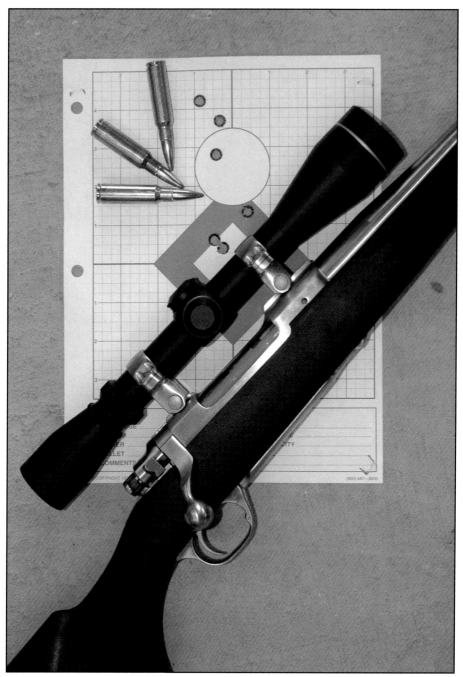

The bolt action can be chambered to myriad cartridges, and new developments keep coming. This is an initial prototype of the .338 Ruger Compact Magnum (RCM). This is the first factory round to be "spun off" the .375 Ruger case—but it won't be the last!

Custom gunmakers do a brisk trade with "high grade" bolt actions with considerable embellishment. This is a new "best quality" Rigby express rifle based on a big Mauser action.

The advantages of the bolt action have been covered: strength, accuracy, and relatively low cost. Of equal significance is the bolt action's ability to be chambered for almost anything. The limitations are the length of the magazine box, the length of the bolt, and the diameter of the bolt face, but in practical terms these restrictions are minor. For instance, every standard-length Remington Model 700 ever made is long enough to accommodate a .375 H&H. And that means it will handle the .416 Remington or .458 Lott.

The standard Ruger Model 77 will not accept .375-length cartridges, which was part of the impetus for Hornady and Ruger to create the .375 Ruger. Now they can offer that level of power in their standard action, and also in their left-hand action. I jumped the gun on this deal. Ruger came on as a sponsor for our *Tracks Across Africa* television show. I needed to use a Ruger, but I don't like to hunt dangerous game with a right-handed rifle (although I will when I must). So I had Arizona gunsmith Don Golembieski rebarrel a left-hand Model 77 in .300 Winchester Magnum to the wildcat .416 Taylor. The rifle was wonderful; it shot well and fed like a dream—but if I'd waited less than a year, the .375 Ruger would have been a reality. At this writing Jon Sundra (and undoubtedly others) have necked the .375 Ruger case up to .416, and I assume some version of .416 Ruger (or Hornady) will be a reality long before this edition is out of print.

At somewhat higher cost, though still a bargain, Ruger also has its Model 77 Mark II Magnum, a big action currently chambered to .375 H&H, .416 Rigby, and .458 Lott. I suspect we'll see other chamberings eventually, including the .404 Jeffery (which has actually been catalogued by Ruger in the past but as of 2007 has not yet been manufactured).

The bolt action's versatility in accepting a variety of cartridges is important because it means an entire battery can be constructed around one action, with

Roy Weatherby sparked the first magnum craze about 1950, and their bolt-action rifles and Weatherby Magnum cartridges remain fine choices. This is a dangerous-game version of the Weatherby Mark V, with good iron sights, detachable scope, chambered to the .375 Weatherby Magnum cartridge.

identical functioning and safety position. Or, for the price of a new barrel, an existing bolt action with which you're completely familiar can be turned into a rifle capable of handling any African game. For instance, an Africa-bound acquaintance of mine rebarreled a pet .300 Winchester Magnum to .458; he thought he'd be better off with a familiar rifle of long-accustomed stock dimensions, and he certainly wasn't wrong in his thinking. The switch-barrel concept extends this versatility. Switch-barrel bolt actions tend to be more costly than standard production models, but compare the cost against additional pairs of barrels for a double rifle!

Virtually any action type, including the double, offers adequate accuracy for most field shooting. Even so, the bolt action, with its stable one-piece stock and rigid lockup, is easily the most accurate action type we have today. (I'm not forgetting single shots, which can be exceptionally accurate but are more limited in their uses; single-shot rifles will be discussed in chapter 20.) In some African hunting situations, every bit of accuracy you can get your hands on is to the good. Whether it's the mountains of Ethiopia or South Africa's Eastern Cape, the deserts of Botswana and Namibia, or the short-grass plains of Tanzania, average shots can be well over two hundred yards. Honestly, African professional hunters have seen so much bad shooting by clients that they are paranoid about allowing long shots. So there is little genuine long-range shooting, as many Americans know it, but in open country shots can and do stretch out to three hundred fifty yards or so. Animals

For hunting nondangerous game in unfamiliar country it is still pretty hard to beat Roy Weatherby's flagship, the Mark V rifle in .300 Weatherby Magnum. OK, I didn't need a cartridge like that for this Vaal rhebok—but it was a tough shot and I did need an accurate, flat shooting bolt action.

such as greater kudu, oryx, mountain nyala, and zebra present a very large vital zone to shoot at. Animals such as springbok, bushbuck, Vaal rhebok, and mountain reedbuck certainly do not. The hunter needs not only the accuracy of a bolt-action rifle but also the flat-shooting cartridges that the bolt action handles best.

When setting up a bolt action for African hunting, the first consideration is likely to be choice of cartridge. I can't disagree with that, but we've covered cartridges thoroughly in the first part of this book, and later on we'll discuss specific cartridge choices for various types of game. Here we're talking about the basic rifle. And indeed the bolt-action rifle can be chambered so it will serve as a light rifle, a medium, or even a heavy. And with a careful choice of both cartridge and bullet, it might well be the only action type that can adequately serve as a complete, all-round safari rifle.

Regardless of the intended use of the bolt action, there are some basic considerations. I prefer the traditional nondetachable box magazine. Detachable magazines have some advantages, one being that the rifle can be completely unloaded and completely loaded very rapidly. To each his own; some of the world's best and most accurate bolt-action rifles today are cursed (or blessed, if you happen to like them) with detachable magazines.

My favorite is the traditional Mauser-type box magazine that must be fed from the top. Should you run the magazine of such a rifle dry while shooting at game (I'll admit that I have on a few occasions!), it's very fast to single-load through the top. Some detachable-magazine rifles have partially enclosed ejection ports that simply weren't designed for top loading, and inserting the one cartridge that you desperately need might be a real struggle.

A couple of my favorite rifles have blind magazine boxes with no floor plate. This setup has the wonderful advantage of absolute reliability; there is simply no chance of the floor plate dropping open at the wrong time, because it doesn't exist. However, I don't prefer this arrangement—for two reasons. First, with a floor plate that can drop open, you can quickly unload the rifle without running the cartridges through the chamber. That's a very minor advantage, but more significant is that you can easily access the magazine box for cleaning. In swampy country or forest, or during the rains, it's common to get the rifle absolutely soaked, and in the plains and desert you get it full of fine dust and sand. I've found it far more functional to be able to get into the magazine box and really clean it out after a day's hunt.

Whatever magazine system your bolt action has, it is extremely important for it to be 100 percent reliable. Cartridges must feed from the magazine into the chamber each and every time you work the bolt, and well before taking the rifle hunting you must investigate each and every potential problem area.

At its best, the bolt action is a marvelously reliable tool. It would be nice if every bolt action came from its maker in such a state. Realities are different. Most of today's rifles are mass produced, and sometimes they have problems. Unfortunately, all too many hunters place childlike faith in their rifles without checking out all the potential trouble spots. One self-inflicted wound we have right now is that it is difficult to make the newer short, fat cartridges feed really smoothly. Fortunately, none of them is intended for dangerous game!

It's a traditional pre-hunt ritual to sight in the rifles, but all too many of us do that sighting-in by single-loading into the chamber. That's the first "no-no." Do your sighting-in and practice sessions with a full magazine, and you'll be surprised what you might learn. Over the years, I've taken delivery on three large-caliber bolt-action rifles that wouldn't feed from the magazine. These were rifles intended for use against dangerous game, and they might well have gotten someone killed.

Such failures generally have simple causes. It could be a follower spring that's too weak to push the cartridges up, or one that's too strong and makes the cartridge literally jump out of the magazine. It could be feed rails that are too narrow or too wide, or shaped slightly incorrectly for the cartridge. Failure to chamber smoothly can be caused simply by a rough spot at the chamber mouth. Lord, I've had them all!

A feeding problem, time permitting, can be turned over to the service department of the rifle's maker, which will undoubtedly make it right. Generally, though, this is nickel-dime stuff that I've turned over to a local gunsmith. Such things are so commonplace that they're almost part of the breaking-in ritual of a new rifle—but if you don't catch them until the first day of a safari, shame on you!

I used the new Kimber Caprivi in .375 H&H to take this beautiful gemsbok in Eden in northern Namibia. The Caprivi is a fine example of a "semiproduction" bolt action offering all the bells and whistles one might expect in an "African express rifle."

Detachable magazines detaching, or floor plates dropping open under recoil, is also fairly commonplace. You often won't discover these problems unless you do your practice shooting with a full magazine; it often takes tension on the follower spring to create the right conditions. Most professional hunters can tell you about clients whose cartridges went "bombs away" on the first shot at a buffalo. It's serious, shockingly common, and absolutely ridiculous that it wasn't caught on the range back home.

I had one rifle that was prone to do this, a very expensive European rifle. The maker was happy to fix it, and it never happened again. Usually the cure is a stronger catch spring, but in extreme cases a beefier catch is needed. If that takes more engineering than is financially sensible, then a simple field expedient is to weld the magazine box shut!

Of course, the bolt-action rifle must not only feed each and every time but must also extract the fired case from the chamber and eject it clear of the action when the bolt is pulled to the rear. Problems in these areas are rare, but they do happen. I mentioned that I owned a Westley Richards .318 Mauser for some time. When I first took it to the range, I discovered that it wouldn't eject consistently; about half the time the fired cartridge just lay in the raceway when the bolt was pulled back. The culprit was a worn ejector, and fortunately my good friend Jack Lott had a spare Mauser ejector right there in his range kit. It took two minutes to slip it into place, and the rifle never gave me another problem. On older rifles, worn extractors are also a potential problem. Again, none of this is serious—if you catch it before you go hunting.

Yet another problem area for bolt actions, especially those chambered for the powerful cartridges often taken on safari, is in the reinforcement given to prevent the stock from splitting under recoil. The forces of recoil may be tough on one's shoulder, but they're pure murder on a riflestock, particularly in the fragile areas around the action inletting and the slim pistol grip. Again, it would be nice if you could purchase a rifle over the counter and never have to question its reliability. But you can't, especially not with rifles in the .375 and .458 class.

Optimally, a powerful bolt-action rifle will have a recoil lug on the barrel and will have the stock reinforced with crossbolts, generally ahead of and behind the magazine box. The stock must be slightly stress-relieved at the tang; the thin pistol grip simply must not be allowed to accept the full forces of recoil. Unfortunately, many manufacturers, including some of the majors, understand completely how to build accurate, reliable, functional rifles—but they don't understand how to build heavy rifles. All too often, the recoil reinforcement on heavy-recoil rifles is either inadequate or just plain wrong.

Many years ago a well-respected manufacturer started offering a safari-type rifle with all the bells and whistles—classic English lines, quarter rib with express sights, the works. It was a beautiful rifle, but the bedding was a nightmare. The recoil lug on the barrel wasn't bedded tightly into the stock and thus did no good. The crossbolts were properly placed, but were D-shaped; the flat side of the D should have been placed facing forward to offer a flat area to bed against and accept the force of recoil. They had been installed backward so the recoil came against the rounded side of the bolt. I don't know if the stock would have split; we never gave it a chance.

It was a simple matter to reverse the bolts and bed both them and the lug in tightly with fiberglass bedding compound. Yes, the factory should have done that—but don't leave it to chance. The first order of business, upon purchasing a bolt-action rifle that has a fair measure of recoil (let's say from the .300 magnums upward), should be to pull the action out of the stock and check the recoil reinforcement. If you don't know what you're looking at, take it to somebody who does.

If you don't check it out, you're inviting disaster. If you're lucky, the stock will split on the range in the first few test firings. More likely, though, it will split in the field after varying conditions of wet and dry have swollen and shrunk the stock and changed slightly the way the action fits it. On my own rifles, I always check and, if it seems called for, rebed or add reinforcement. But in my job as a writer I often test various manufacturers' rifles. On a couple of occasions I've sent them back with split stocks and a note of apology. One of the great attractions of synthetic stocks is, of course, insurance against swelling, shrinking, warping, resultant shifts in bedding, and the possibility of breakage. Good synthetic stocks (which are discussed in chapter 22) are stable and virtually indestructible.

In later chapters we'll discuss scopes and sights in more detail, but here it should be said that the bolt-action rifle is the ideal vehicle for telescopic sights. The action rings provide ideal platforms for scope mounts, and the scope can be mounted low over the receiver without interfering in loading, firing, or cycling in any way. A heavy rifle may be preferred with iron sights; that's a matter of personal preference. But most bolt actions are simply incomplete without a good, well-mounted scope—and that, too, is one of the bolt-action rifle's great advantages. In at least 99 percent of all hunting situations, a scope sight allows the shooter to see better and hit better. The stock of a bolt action, if properly shaped, will be conducive to fast, accurate shooting with a scope.

The last two items to be discussed regarding bolt-action rifles are triggers and safeties, and to some extent they interrelate. Unlike other action types, the bolt action is well suited to an adjustable trigger that can be fine-tuned to the shooter's preference. When it comes to very precise shooting, nothing is quite as critical as a crisp, clean, relatively light trigger pull—so this is yet another advantage of the bolt action.

In today's atmosphere of product-liability paranoia, this advantage has been largely lost; most bolt actions come from the factory with horrible trigger pulls of five and even six pounds, about what you'd expect on a double rifle or a lever action. Fortunately, most

Empire Rifles' Legacy bolt action is an extremely attractive custom rifle offering innumerable options—but also attractively priced, especially considering the quality.

bolt-action triggers can be adjusted. However, this is not a job for you and me. The problem is that the lighter the trigger pull, the closer you are to an accidental discharge. Most bolt-action triggers can, in complete safety, be adjusted to pull of 3 to 3½ pounds, about right for a hunting rifle. A competent gunsmith should do the job.

Safeties and triggers interrelate because most bolt actions today have trigger-blocking safeties. Personally, I don't like them and don't trust them. The old Mauser-type flag safety was, to my mind, much more positive; it had nothing to do with the trigger, but instead positively locked the striker. The old three-position Model 70 safety is of this type. So is the safety on the Ruger Model 77 Mark II. Many other bolt actions can be modified by the installation of this type of safety, and I have done so on several rifles.

However, it must be remembered that any safety is a mechanical device, and therefore I refuse to fully trust any safety. In most of my hunting I never carry a cartridge in the chamber unless I'm anticipating a shot momentarily. And it should go without saying that a firearm carried in a vehicle should never have a cartridge in the chamber. However, walking about in the African bush is a bit different: You just never know what you might encounter. Under many circumstances over there, it could be almost foolish to not have a cartridge in the chamber. A close-quarters charge by a buffalo carrying a grudge along with a poacher's musket ball isn't impossible, nor is it unlikely to step around a bush and come face to face with the kudu of your dreams. But if a rifle is to be carried with a round in the chamber, some reliance must be placed in the safety.

There are several considerations here. First, the safety must work. Test it thoroughly on the range, making certain the rifle does not fire with the safety engaged. With the rifle unloaded but cocked, it's a good idea to bounce it around a bit, dropping it on its recoil pad. If the striker falls with the safety engaged, you have a very serious problem that must be corrected. In Mozambique in 1989 my hunting partner and I chanced across a fine lion. He had never shot one and wanted it badly. When he slipped his safety the rifle fired, fortunately into the ground. Just as fortunately, the lion—just thirty yards away—went in the other direction. No harm done that time, but a rare opportunity lost.

You should check the safety's position. It must be accessible to the thumb so you can slip it readily while you're bringing the rifle up. However, it must engage positively and be in such a position that it's protected from brush and twigs while you're carrying the rifle, whether in your hands or slung over one shoulder.

I had a prototype of a left-handed .375 one time. It was a lovely rifle, and in its right-handed version the sliding thumb safety was on the right side just behind and well protected by the bolt handle. In the left-handed version they switched the bolt to the left side, but the safety remained on the right. Now it was unprotected, and when I slung the rifle over my left shoulder (as lefties are most likely to do), the action of walking rubbed the safety against my side. After a dozen steps, that rifle would be off safe every time.

I don't believe a slung rifle should ever have a cartridge in the chamber; if you're carrying a loaded rifle, you must have the direction of the muzzle under complete control at all times. This is impossible when it's slung over the shoulder. Reality, however, is that out of convenience most of us do this at least some of the time. So this is a good example of a design problem in safety placement. The point is to pay attention to the mechanical safety, and if the way you carry a rifle tends to expose the safety catch, you'd better think about a different safety or a different rifle. And that's yet another wonderful advantage to a bolt-action rifle; if you want a Mauser or Model 70-type safety, it's generally simple and inexpensive to so modify your rifle.

Perhaps, when it comes right down to it, of all the bolt action's advantages, the greatest is that it can so readily be adjusted, fussed with, and modified to exactly suit its owner's tastes and its intended purpose. Double rifles are made from scratch, largely by hand. But no action is altered, improved, and customized as much as a turnbolt. From a simple sporterizing of a military rifle to a full-out custom job costing as much as any double rifle (sometimes more), individually crafted bolt actions run the full gamut. The custom-gun business has never been better, with the best craftsmen commanding top prices and staying booked up months and even years ahead. On the other hand, it isn't essential to spend a lot of money to get a serviceable bolt-action rifle. Modern factory bolt actions are truly wonders of accuracy and reliability. But that isn't exactly new; St. George Littledale discovered exactly the same more than a century ago.

A Question of Extractors

Chapter 19

The factory-made bolt-action rifle is a sound, dependable, downright cheap piece of equipment. If the owner wants to, he can invest a great deal of money in select walnut, engraving, and other embellishment; he can also spend a lot of money for a custom-made or custom-modified action, a select barrel, and the services of a "name" custom gunsmith in putting it all together. The end result will be a pleasing piece that may suit its owner's tastes much better than any factory rifle. It may even function a bit more smoothly than an out-of-the-box production gun, and it just might shoot a bit better (it darn well should!). But the dollars spent for a full-out custom bolt action as opposed to the cost of a production rifle of identical caliber and utility quickly reach diminishing returns in terms of increased performance. Today's factory bolt actions are just plain good rifles.

Yes, as mentioned in the previous chapter, you may want to spend a little bit of time and money in bedding, trigger adjustment (or a replacement trigger like the Timney or Canjar), and even smoothing of the action and adjustment of the follower, follower spring, and feed rails. But that's all nickel–dime stuff compared to genuine custom work.

None of this is meant to say there's anything wrong with a custom rifle. I have several factory rifles that have been extensively customized, perhaps enough to qualify as custom rifles, and I have a couple of full-out custom jobs. I love them, and I have a lot of confidence in them. The value of confidence is beyond price, but factory rifles have gotten so good that they're pretty hard to beat. I have a pure factory over-the-counter Savage 116 in .30-06. It came as a "package rifle," meaning it had an inexpensive Simmons 3–9X scope already mounted. This rifle has produced multiple groups better than a quarter-inch, and with a 180-grain Barnes Triple Shock it will do everything a .30-06 should be asked to do. I have one or two rifles that might do better on a given day. My 8mm Remington Magnum,

I am left-handed, and until recently most left-hand actions have been push-feeds. I have used Weatherby, Savage, and Remington push-feeds all my life, and I have complete confidence in them. This is my custom 8mm Remington Magnum on a Model 700 action, one of my favorites, shown with a huge Kalahari gemsbok.

stocked in English walnut and sporting a really good Pac-Nor match-grade barrel, has done much better. But not every day.

Geoff Miller at Rigby built that 8mm when his shop was still Rogue River Rifleworks. He's an accuracy freak through and through, and he also rebarreled a Model 700 for me to his favorite cartridge, the .300 H&H. That barrel is also a really good Pac-Nor, and it has produced a 1½-inch group at 400 yards. But it won't do that every day, either. It drives Geoff crazy when I come back from the range with a spectacular group shot by a production rifle costing a fraction of what his beautiful rifles bring. But that's reality. Factory rifles are so good that any real gains above their performance are at best incremental, and almost never exponential.

That said, we Americans are freaks for accuracy and velocity. In any hunting field in the world, reliability is more important than either of those factors. I think this is especially true in Africa, since long-range shooting is rare and Africa holds the bulk of the world's supply of game that can still trample or eat you. Both of those rifles just mentioned are built on Remington Model 700 actions. I have used Model 700 actions in various chamberings—the .375 H&H, .375 Remington Ultra Mag, .416 Hoffman, .416 Remington Magnum, and .458 Lott—to hunt the full gamut of Africa's dangerous game. I have also used Weatherby Mark Vs in .375 Weatherby, .416 Weatherby, and even the massive .460 Weatherby. Since I'm a lefty it shouldn't be surprising that I so often choose Remington 700 actions, or for that matter the Mark V; both actions have long been readily available in left-hand

For a push-feed to work properly and consistently the rails must "release" the cartridge at the proper point. If the follower, follower spring tension, or the rails aren't quite right for the cartridge, jams are inevitable—but when everything is right the push-feed works perfectly.

versions. However, an awful lot of right-handers choose these actions, plus the post-'64 Model 70, the Sako, the Savage, the original Ruger 77, and the list goes on.

What all these actions have in common is that none offers controlled-round feeding. This, plus the long extractor, was one of the great strengths of the Mauser design. It carried over into the Springfield, 1917 Enfield, pre-1964 Model 70 Winchester, and a few other actions. Much is made of this feature. In recent years it seems that what we'll call "CRF" (for controlled-round feeding) has won, at least so far as dangerous game is concerned. The last Model 70s produced by Winchester were CRF, the Ruger M77 MK II is CRF, and look at all the Mausers, Mauser clones, and Model 70 clones now available. CRF is definitely in, and there are enough actions available that the choice can readily be made (even if you're left-handed). To hear some writers tell it, you're absolutely taking your life in your hands if you hunt dangerous game with anything but a CRF action—which means a Mauser or its derivatives, nothing else.

First let's define controlled-round feeding. When a cartridge is fed from the magazine of a Mauser action, its rim is pushed up between the bolt face and the extractor, where it is held firmly and "controlled" as the bolt carries—not pushes—it forward into the chamber. It is able to do so because the bottom portion of the bolt face is not encircled by steel; it's open, and as the cartridge comes up out of the magazine, its rim slides into place and is held by the long spring-steel extractor.

It is said that a controlled-round-feed action, based on military rifles, will feed upside down and sideways. Yes, that's true . . . so will a good push-feed action like this Remington Model 700. Try it!

There are tremendous advantages to this system. The Mauser-type action, for instance, will feed reliably upside down, sideways, any which way. (However, let me clue you in on a little secret: A Remington Model 700, and most other push-feed actions, will also feed upside down. I've tried it; so should you if you don't agree!) But there is another advantage: With a CRF action, if your bolt movement is interrupted partway, the cartridge remains held in place until you resume; it cannot and will not be jarred out of place.

In contrast, the more modern action types, with the Remington 700 as a prime example, push the cartridge ahead of the bolt and into the chamber. The cartridge actually lies there loose and is held by nothing; the bolt merely shoves it forward, and as it chambers fully, the extractor snaps over the case rim.

There are disadvantages to this system. It may work, but is not as positive when upside down or sideways. Push-feeds do work best with the force of gravity in a favorable up-and-down position. It seems to me that this handicap may be much more significant in a military rifle than a sporting rifle, but many writers and professional hunters dismiss out of hand any action that lacks CRF. Again, more significant to me is that a push-feed action works best when the bolt movement is smooth and constant. If you hesitate halfway and anything happens, like an unexpected jar, the cartridge can slip out of position and fail to chamber.

Regardless of who is correct, many people prefer controlled-round-feed actions—and many are available. This is the Remington Model 798, based on the Serbian-made Mark X Mauser action. Simple, reliable, and very faithful to Peter Paul Mauser's great creation.

What the newer type of action gives you is strength and, in the event of a case failure, safety. The bolt face is encircled by a ring of solid steel, which encircles the case head when a cartridge is chambered. Controlled-round feeding, to exist, must leave part of the case head exposed.

Rarely is there a clear-cut disadvantage or advantage to either system, but it must be recognized that modern actions are stronger than any Mauser—and if an action is going to blow, a Mauser, Springfield, Enfield, or even pre-'64 Winchester will blow long before a Remington 700, Weatherby Mark V, Savage 110, or similar modern action. And the older action will probably blow with more disastrous results for the shooter.

Such catastrophic failures are incredibly rare, and with safe handling procedures that avoid barrel obstructions, and sane reloading procedures that eliminate overloads of wrong powders, they're almost impossible—but the very real safety margin of the more modern designs must still be accepted. On the other hand, the Mauser action has been adequately strong for generations; its inherent weakness must be considered just as theoretical a disadvantage as its ability to feed better upside down is an advantage.

The Remington Model 700 pictured is a state-of-the-art, left-hand stainless and synthetic rifle from the Remington Custom Shop, chambered to .300 Remington Ultra Mag. Yes, it's a push-feed, and it works just fine.

Controlled-round feeding does have another disadvantage. Single-loaded cartridges must usually be fed down into the magazine; if simply pushed into the chamber, the extractor may not snap over the head and allow the bolt to close. A worn extractor or one that has been beveled to allow it to snap over will work. But you'd better know what you're dealing with; on a true Mauser, a single-loaded cartridge must be fed all the way down into the magazine. With the modern action designs, a single cartridge can simply be dropped into the raceway and the bolt slammed home. If you've fired your last shell and you need one more shot, you're likely to be grateful for every millisecond you save!

The long Mauser extractor is yet another much-touted advantage of Mauser-type actions. It is important to note that this long extractor doesn't necessarily mean CRF. The original Ruger M77, for instance, does have the long extractor but does not have CRF; the extractor is beveled so it will snap over the case head as the bolt goes home, but it does not control the cartridge until that moment. I do like the strength of the Mauser-type extractor and the great purchase it has on the cartridge rim. On the other hand, I have never seen a Remington Model 700 (or a Savage 110, or a Weatherby Mark V, or a post-'64 Model 70) fail to extract.

Once again, the advantages or disadvantages seem more theoretical than practical. I will admit that I have had far more feeding issues with push-feed actions.

The CZ action is another modern Mauser action, incredibly strong and available in several powerful chamberings. Today you can get a Mauser or Mauser-type action if you prefer . . . and many people do.

Especially with the fat new cartridges, feeding problems seem almost normal today, but they are usually easily fixed by a little work on the rails or magazine box. In my experience, once a push-feed action is right, it is extremely reliable. But the current discussion is about extraction, and I have yet to have a push-feed fail to extract, either on the range or in the field. And with all the load development I've done, there have been more than a few loads that were a bit too hot!

On the other hand, the only genuine extraction-related failure I've ever seen was on a very nice F.N. Mauser .375. The rifle is mine, but Paul Stockwell was using it on a Botswana buffalo one day. He was still white as a sheet when he sheepishly handed me the now-useless rifle.

He and his professional hunter, Mark Tout, had found a nice buffalo bull and Paul had shot it badly. They followed it up and found it lying in high grass, facing away. Paul shot again, trying to break its neck, but missed the bone. By now the buffalo had had enough; he launched into a full charge from close range, and Paul worked the bolt.

Paul is a big, strong guy, half again my size and a serious weightlifter. He was also terrified, as anyone would have been. All I can figure is that he worked the bolt with an incredibly powerful jerk. The long, foolproof Mauser extractor separated from the bolt collar, jamming the rifle completely and hopelessly with a fired cartridge in the chamber. The odd thing is that there was nothing structurally wrong with the rifle or any of its parts, but it certainly failed. And, Murphy being the optimist he is, when something goes wrong it goes wrong at the worst possible moment.

Well, that example isn't meant to imply that Mauser actions are prone to failure. Of course they aren't. But neither are the more modern actions. What type of bolt action, then, is really the most reliable and the most desirable for African hunting?

Cameron Hopkins, left, used an old Ruger M77, a push-feed, on this hunt in Mozambique. His partner, Greg Rader, used a M77 Mk II, a controlled-round-feed rifle. Hopkins actually prefers the older version because he likes the sliding tang safety, not because he cares about whether or not it's push-feed!

All things being equal, I'd have to give the nod to CRF, especially with all the actions now available from Dakota, Kimber, Ruger, Mauser, CZ, and so many others. But I wouldn't pick them by a significant margin. Just because I'm a lefty, a great majority of my bolt actions will continue to be Model 700s, Mark Vs, and Savages. And if I were a right-hander who was comfortable with any of these actions, I wouldn't consider making a switch. Provided the rifle has been properly and carefully checked for all phases of feeding, firing, extracting, and ejecting, there's no reason for a sound rifle of any action type to fail in the field. Push-feeds are more finicky, but if you don't check them out before your safari, shame on you! Once a rifle is working properly it should continue to do so, and rightfully can be expected to do so. Of course, any mechanical device made by man can fail. If a failure occurs, well, I believe it can happen to a true Mauser, one of its copies, or any other action with just about equal odds.

Single Shots and Others

Chapter 20

It would be easy to get the impression that only bolt actions and double rifles are suited for African hunting. The bolt is the most common action in use in Africa, and the double rifle is perhaps the most classic. But it would be both misleading and unfair to exclude the other action types: single shot, lever action, slide action, and semiautomatic. All of them are perfectly suitable for at least some applications, and African hunting, with the exceptions of her largest game, isn't significantly different from any hunting anywhere else. Let's take a look at the other action types and see where they might fit in.

Single Shots

The last half of the nineteenth century was the golden age of the single-shot rifle. In the Africa of a century ago, the .577/.450 Martini-Henry was the most common rifle, and it performed far beyond its apparent ballistic capabilities. It was the Martini-Henry that won the day at Rorke's Drift—and lost it at Isandhlwana—and it was the Martini-Henry that the early settler–hunter was most likely to carry. In America the trapdoor Springfield in the somewhat less powerful .45-70 was the most common rifle of the day, so popular that it retains a following to this day.

In both Europe and America, however, there were a number of fine single-shot breechloaders that were far superior to these simple military actions. In America the powerful black-powder single shot was the buffalo hunter's choice. The Sharps was the most famous, but there were many others. Some made it into the smokeless era, examples being the Remington rolling block and the Winchester Hi-Wall (now offered in modern form by Browning). The British and Europeans had a number of fine actions as well, the most famous of which was the Farquharson.

This action was the creation of Scottish gamekeeper John Farquharson, but the rifles were initially made by Bristol gunmaker George Gibbs. A Metford-rifled

Many of us thought Bill Ruger was crazy when he introduced the ultimate "retro rifle," his Ruger No. 1 single shot based somewhat on the old British Farquharson action. Crazy like a fox! The Ruger No. 1 is one of the best-looking factory rifles ever produced, and over the years has garnered a following bordering on a cult.

Gibbs single-shot, black-powder, caliber-.461, Farquharson action was Frederick Selous's favorite rifle well into the smokeless era.

In the latter part of the nineteenth century, Gibbs had the exclusive on the "Farky" action, but in 1895, just when smokeless powder was coming into its own, the original patent expired and several top British gunmakers began building rifles on Farquharson-type actions. The rifles did not do well in the smokeless era. They were much less expensive than double rifles, but unfortunately they were more expensive than European-made bolt actions. They also lacked the bolt action's camming power for primary extraction, and for that matter had less extraction power than a double, wherein several pounds of barrels act as the opening lever. In the earliest days of smokeless, when weak black-powder cases were being used, the Farquharsons acquired a reputation for failure to extract, and it was a reputation from which they never recovered.

The Farquharson action is one of the strongest in the world, and with modern cases there's no reason to fear extraction problems. Today, the few rifles still in circulation are highly prized, nearly as valuable as double rifles. Although relatively few were made, they were chambered for virtually any Nitro Express cartridge you

A single-shot rifle is well suited to a wide variety of African hunting, including hunting leopard over bait. There will be just one shot, and it better be right! With the Miller Arms .30-06 that one shot worked just fine.

can think of. The most common are probably .450/.400-3¼" and .450-3¼", but you'll see them all the way up to .600 Nitro Express.

In recent years a few modern Farquharson actions have been built. Australian John Saunders of Century Arms/London Guns in Melbourne built a matched pair of .600 Farquharsons. Once separated, these are now back together as a pair and live in the United States. A few more have been built on a custom basis in England, Europe, and the United States. The Farquharson falling block was also the basis for the most popular single shot of all time, the wonderful Ruger No. 1, and for one of the most elegant single shots of all time, the Dakota Model 10.

When Bill Ruger introduced the No. 1, the world thought he was crazy. If he was, he was crazy like a fox; the No. 1 has been among the great firearms success stories in the postwar era. With some modifications, the Ruger action is a Farquharson falling block; the underlever cocks the internal hammer and drops the massive breechblock to expose the loading port. It's a very safe, very simple action—and one of the strongest the world has ever known. It's available in several variations and almost every conceivable modern chambering up to .458 Lott.

Mechanically similar, the trim Dakota Model 10, a custom rifle, has also been chambered for darn near anything you can think of. However, no matter how

This is the first buffalo taken with Hornady's reintroduction of the .450/.400-3" Nitro Express cartridge. This picture does bring out one important point: If you are going to hunt buffalo or other dangerous game with a single shot, don't hunt alone!

strong the actions are, all single shots have a relatively weak extraction system, again without the mechanical leverage of the bolt action. This means that, like double rifles, they are at their best with rimmed cartridges. Dakota Model 10s, which are extractor guns only, have been chambered to a wide array of rimmed cartridges. Other than aftermarket work, however, there has been a dearth of big-rimmed factory cartridges suitable for the Ruger No. 1.

That said, Ruger extractors and ejectors work wonderfully with rimless and belted rimless cartridges—but reliability is enhanced with a rimmed case. This worm is starting to turn. Handloaders learned a long time ago that in the Ruger action, the old .45-70, absent a magazine and with lots of strength, could be hopped up very near .458 Winchester Magnum performance. A next and most wonderful step was the odd mating of the Ruger No. 1 to Hornady's reintroduction of the rimmed .405 Winchester. Without concerns over cartridge overall length or action strength, in the Ruger single shot the .405's 300-grain bullet can be traded for a 400-grain bullet, and velocity easily increased to match the .450/.400-3" cartridge. My daughter and I shared a Ruger No. 1 in .405 in Australia, and with it, using heavy loads, she took a fine Cape buffalo in Zimbabwe in 2006.

I used a Dakota Model 10 in .375 Dakota to take this ancient dagga *bull in Zambia's Kafue region. I thought I was fast on the reload, but in this situation nobody could have been fast enough. Fortunately the one shot went in the right place.*

The next step, now accomplished, was for Ruger to chamber the No. 1 in Hornady's reintroduction of the .450/.400-3". I must admit that this was at least a little bit my idea. Custom gunsmiths have long rebored, rebarreled, and/or rechambered Ruger No. 1s to the old Nitro Express cartridges. However, the action size is pretty much maxed out with the .450 case head. You can fit the .500-based cartridges (.470, .500, .500/.450, .465, etc.), but to do so requires considerable work in hogging out the bottom of the action, and the extraction/ejection system has to be completely revamped. Cartridges based on the basic .450 Nitro Express case work perfectly with relatively little modification. So the .450/.400-3" is a perfect fit, not only for the rifle but for the performance it offers at such a modest price in recoil. Hornady has now announced reintroduction of my favorite double-rifle cartridge, the original John Rigby .450-3¼" Nitro Express. It's possible that I had something to do with urging them into this. It's also possible that they leaked the information, but not to me. Before I even knew they were doing the cartridge, Heym announced the .450 as a chambering in its "PH" model double. At this writing Ruger is mum, but I'm confident it will chamber the No. 1 to the .450-3¼". This will effectively max out the Ruger action as far as cartridge size is concerned,

One thing about a single shot is that it does make one very careful with that first shot. This is an impala taken for leopard bait with the Miller Arms .30-06.

a perfect fit. And handloaders will quickly discover that, with that long case in an indestructible action, original Nitro Express ballistics can easily be exceeded.

Two other very fine modern American single shots are readily available, the interchangeable-barrel break-action Thompson/Center, and the Browning Model 1885. And then there are a wide array of excellent reproduction Sharps, high-walls, low-walls, Remington rolling blocks, and break-open actions, plus a fair smattering of custom single-shot actions. Many are chambered to .45-70 and larger black-powder cartridges. With the right loads, the right bullets, and the right mind-set, any of these could take buffalo and some could handle elephant, but only the T/C is available in modern "African" chamberings, including the .416 Rigby. Note, however, that the T/C is not only extractor only but is also an exposed-hammer design. These features combine to make it very slow for the reload. This is not a show-stopper, but don't use it alone!

There are also several excellent modern European single shots, mostly break-open designs. Perfect examples are the Blaser K95 and the Merkel Stutzen, both truly wonderful little guns. In keeping with the European concept of a single-shot "stalking rifle," there are no rifles on Earth handier and sweeter. Like any accurate single shot chambered to suitable cartridges, they would be ideal for a vast range of plains-game hunting—but both are maxed out at 9.3x74R (also a chambering in the Ruger No. 1). This means that they simply don't have the horsepower to be both street-legal and safe for the full run of dangerous game.

The single-shot action has a lot of appeal. It's simple, reliable, and accurate, and the one-shot concept is attractive to sportsmen. I've used single shots—T/Cs, Rugers, Dakotas—in various calibers for quite a variety of hunting in both North America and Africa, and I like them a lot. When I wrote the first edition I must admit that my African use at that time had been confined to plains game. Since then I have taken a couple of buffalo with a Dakota Model 10, and a whole bunch more with a Ruger No. 1. I also used a Miller Arms (a subsidiary of Dakota) falling block on my 2005 Zimbabwe leopard. My basic opinion of single-shot rifles hasn't changed, but perhaps has been tempered by use.

"Fine though a single shot may be, it does present problems, especially for hunting dangerous game. The attractive and sporting one-shot concept is a concept that can get you killed when the chips are down—or, at best, make your professional hunter join in when perhaps he wouldn't have needed to." I put these words in quotes because they are from the original edition. I had it right. Read that again, because it remains a hundred percent accurate. These days we're spending a lot of time in Zimbabwe's Sapi Safari Area, east of Mana Pools National Park, mostly with PH Andrew Dawson. Some years ago a friend of Andrew's was killed by a buffalo in this area. He was using a single shot, and when they found his body his rifle had been fired. Nothing else is known.

For the professional hunter a single shot is just plain silly. For the client it's not quite so silly so long as you know what you're getting yourself into. The hunting client is not alone, so there is backup available. An experienced, cool professional hunter will not fire unless it seems absolutely necessary. But when his client is using a single shot he is much more likely to fire a backup shot than if the same client were using a double or magazine rifle. Again, I have now taken numerous buffalo with a single shot. Once, only once, a backup shot was fired while I fumbled the reload. It probably wasn't necessary; the first shot was fine, and the buffalo was outbound rather than inbound. However, I expect my professional hunters to use their judgment, and I don't personally care if they make the call that they should shoot; my ego is not as important as the lives and limbs of my trackers and PH (not to mention my own!). Anyway, that was the only time a PH fired a backup shot while I was using a single shot—not that it mightn't have been a good idea on other occasions! In several cases the country was so thick (or other buffalo so closely pressed around the target animal)

The Ruger No. 1 in .450/.400-3". To me this is an ideal cartridge for the Ruger No. 1, and an equally ideal cartridge for buffalo. One Hornady solid went through both shoulders and exited, and the bull was down before I could reload and fire again.

that nobody could get off a second shot. In other cases the first shot looked good enough, and the country was open enough that we could see the buffalo and watch it go down—or it was so open that I was able to fire a second shot.

A good, practiced hand with a single shot can get off a second shot very quickly. The routine is to carry an extra cartridge between the fingers of your nonshooting hand, just as you would with a double, except that more than one is superfluous. Fire, drop the lever, and insert a cartridge. This can be done in less than three seconds, without looking at the action. Sometimes that second shot can be fast enough to prevent the escape of a wounded animal. And sometimes not. When you are carrying a single shot, you must accept that the one shot is all you might get! No matter how much you practice and how fast you are, if you are shooting a single shot there will be many situations in which no human being can reload fast enough. In the case of a charge, forget it. One shot is all you have.

Most of the time, that one shot is enough, but when you need a follow-up it won't be there. Now, that does tend to make you very careful about your shot placement, which is certainly to the good. Unfortunately, with the largest of game it doesn't wash. With carefully placed brain shots, one-shot kills on elephant are common—but if the brain is missed, albeit by only a hair, follow-up body shots must be taken instantly or it's a lost animal. So, again, when you use a single shot you should not be alone, and you must not be sensitive about your PH doing his job.

My own experience with buffalo has resulted in dismally few one-shot kills, perhaps 30 percent excluding neck shots. It isn't that the first shot isn't fatal—eventually. Rather, it's that the buffalo is such a strong animal. Most of the time he's going to run, and I'm not willing to bet a dangerous tracking job on the exact placement of that first shot—or the performance of the bullet. With a double or bolt gun, the first shot can be backed up immediately, even if it's only insurance. With a single shot, your professional hunter has a decision to make just as the bull reaches cover. If I were that professional hunter, I'd shoot if my client couldn't.

On cats, well, it depends; I'd certainly use a single shot for baited lion, but I don't think I'd want one on a tracking hunt or when following up a wounded animal. For baited leopard, no problem. The one shot is all there is, and an accurate single shot would be just the ticket. I had wonderful confidence in the accurate .30-06 I used in 2006 . . . but I switched to Andrew Dawson's spare bolt gun during the follow-up! For plains game, regardless of size or conditions, again no problem. As is the case anywhere else, availability of just that one cartridge makes you very careful, and that is not a bad thing.

There is one additional characteristic of the single shot that needs to be taken into account. Like a double, a single shot is either fully loaded or fully unloaded. If you're carrying it in a vehicle or on horseback, you have no choice: The rifle must be empty. That's not a huge problem, but it does mean you must have cartridges very readily accessible. Cartridge loops on a shirt work well, but many experienced Ruger fans carry a couple of cartridges in a Velcro carrier on the wrist of the nonshooting arm. That's fast. In the field, again, the rifle is either loaded or unloaded. Most of the time it will be loaded, but if you're climbing in tough country, for safety's sake you'll have to unload it.

"For the reasons stated, I see the single shot primarily as a light rifle or, at most, a medium. But it sure would be fun to take a single shot .450/.400 after buffalo." I wrote that sentence eighteen years before Ruger chambered the first No. 1 to .450/.400. Now that I've done that, I must report it was as much fun as I'd envisioned, and I'm sure I'll do it again. But I won't do it alone!

Lever Actions

The lever action seems to be almost exclusively an American passion; Sako's short-lived Finnwolf is one of very few European lever guns. In America the lever action remains a traditional choice. Tubular-magazine lever-action rifles from

Donna used the Thompson/Center Encore in .30-06 to take an impala in Tanzania. Although superb for plains game, exposed hammer designs like this are slow to reload and easy to fumble, so regardless of the chambering they are questionable for dangerous game.

Winchester and Marlin define the term "deer rifle" for a great many hunters, and the rotary-magazine Savage 99 was another American classic. Winchester's wonderful rotary-bolt Model 88, long discontinued, was actually Winchester's third-most-popular lever action (following the '94 and the '92). In recent years Browning's BLR hasn't set the world on fire, but it's a fine rifle and has its following.

The lever action, despite its popularity, has some problems. The first is strength. Traditional rear-locking lever guns like tubular-magazine Winchesters are more than strong enough for the woods cartridges for which they're chambered, but they simply won't handle high-intensity modern cartridges. The Winchester 88, Finnwolf, and Savage will—but they're restricted to short-case cartridges. Only the Browning has been lengthened to handle standard-length modern cartridges.

Tubular-magazine rifles were designed to handle only roundnose or flat-point bullets. Since the cartridges rest nose to primer in the magazine, detonation can and has occurred with sharp-point bullets. Hornady's "Lever Evolution" ammo with compressible polymer tips solves this age-old problem, but any given load, no matter how well engineered, will not be accurate in all rifles. The flat-points are extremely effective on game, but trajectories suffer. The Winchester 88, Finnwolf, and Browning use staggered-box magazines, while the Savage had either the

A big-bore lever action like the Marlin .45-70 is a fine brush gun, whether in North America or Africa. This one is a real beauty, customized with peep sight, low-power scope, and long eye relief scope, and it shoots wonderfully.

traditional rotary magazine or a detachable box. All of these will function perfectly with aerodynamic spitzer bullets.

Another problem is inherent with the lever, though, and that's weakness of primary extraction. The camming power of the bolt action simply isn't there. The Browning is the strongest of the bunch, but it just isn't smart to use heavy loads in any lever action. Factory loads are fine, of course, but you must exercise restraint with handloads.

The only catastrophic failure I've ever had in the hunting field was with a Savage 99 in .308 Winchester. I hit a blesbok a bit too far back, and the rifle seized up tight as a drum. I couldn't open it, not even by beating on the lever with a rock in my frustration. Eventually we got the animal, but only after I ran a mile back to the truck for another rifle. It was my fault; I was using fairly stiff handloads, and it was a hot day.

The only lever action that achieved some measure of greatness in Africa was the Winchester Model 1895. Its chamberings included the .405 and .35 Winchester, both loaded for some time by Kynoch, plus the .30-40 Krag and .30-06. The rifle was apparently not very satisfactory in .30-06; sticky extraction wasn't uncommon. However, for many years it was the most powerful American production rifle in its

I took my Winchester Model 88 in .358 Winchester to Zambia in 1996. I didn't actually use it as much as I intended, but it worked just fine for zebra and this impala.

.405 WCF chambering. This was Teddy Roosevelt's "lion medicine," and it was also a favorite of Stewart Edward White and Charles Cottar. Cottar, the first American to become an African professional hunter, used it throughout his long career in Africa. He died with it in 1940 after failing to stop a charging rhino.

Browning's recent (and faithful) reproduction of this rifle has also seen use in Africa. Larry Potterfield of Midway used his lever action .405 on a recent safari, taking both lion and buffalo with Woodleigh bullets. He had no problems, and I had no problems using 300-grain grain Hornady bullets on Australian water buffalo. Today's bullets are a whole lot better than those available to Roosevelt and Cottar, but the 300-grain .411 bullets necessary to fit the Model 95's magazine box are still very light for caliber. I think Roosevelt had it dead right when he called it "lion medicine," and extreme care should be taken if this cartridge and its 300-grain bullets are used on buffalo.

While the Model 95 Winchester is the rifle that comes most readily to mind when we think of lever actions in Africa, other classic lever actions were also occasionally used. In the black-powder era Winchester repeaters were often seen on the African frontier. Some volunteer contingents were armed with Winchester .44-40s during the Zulu Wars, and lever actions were well represented when Cecil

Rhodes's Pioneer Column went north in 1890. They saw action in the Matabele uprisings, and during the Boer Wars as well.

I have seen a few Winchester 94s in use as "camp rifles," and a few Americans have occasionally taken lever actions on safari. As mentioned earlier, James Mellon had a .358 lever action in East Africa, and fellow left-hander Col. Charles Askins used a then-new Winchester Model 88 in .243 in Kenya in the late 1950s. I had high hopes for that ill-fated Savage 99, but shot little game with it before it jammed. It was out for the count for the rest of the trip. I took a Model 88 in .358 to Zambia in 1996, and it worked just as well in African thornbush as it does in North America.

In spite of its minimal recent history, there's no reason not to choose a lever action in a suitable caliber as a light safari rifle, and a Savage 99, Browning, or Winchester 88 (if you can find one!) would make a marvelous general-purpose thornbush rifle in .358. Well, OK, there is one consideration: At this writing South Africa's increasingly draconian gun laws specifically prohibit lever actions (and slide actions, and semiautos!). Generally, the lever action will not be as accurate as a bolt action or single shot, but it is certainly accurate enough for most field shooting, and the odd rifle will surprise you. Marlins tend to be accurate, and the new .308 Marlin Express will do everything any .308 Winchester bolt gun will do. I have a plain old Model 94 Trapper (the short-barreled version), and its accuracy is amazing. My Model 88 in .358 is a custom job built by Rigby's Geoff Miller, and it's a real tackdriver. Customizing and accurizing the Model 88 is one of his pet projects, and he knows how to make them talk.

The lever action's primary utility in Africa is for plains game and perhaps leopard. It occurs to me that a fast lever action would be just the ticket for hunting leopard with hounds. Other than the .405, however, there are few options for using a lever action on the big stuff. The obvious choice would be a Marlin 1895 in .45-70 or .450 Marlin. These rifles (and other .45-70s) have been used to take quite a few buffalo in recent years, so of course it can be done. The Marlin action won't handle the same level of loads that the Ruger No. 1 will, but you can still get reasonably close to .458 Winchester Magnum performance.

The most important caution is choice of bullets. Most .45-70 bullets were not intended for use on game as large as buffalo. And because of the possibility of detonation, I would be scared to death to use even a flatnose solid in a tubular magazine. I would lean toward hard-cast bullets in the 400-grain range, like the heavy loads Randy Garrett offers. I have never taken a Cape buffalo with a .45-70, but a few years ago I used hard-cast bullets loaded to about .45-90 performance to take a huge bison bull. Bison are not as aggressive as African buffalo, but they're

A pet project of Rigby's proprietor, Geoff Miller, is customizing the Winchester Model 88. He really makes them shoot, and for we downtrodden left-handers such a rifle offers a wonderfully ambidextrous option.

a whole lot bigger. Those hard-cast bullets at no more than 1,500 feet per second sailed right through and exited!

Slide Actions

The slide action is yet another American exclusive. Years ago there were pump rifles from a variety of makers, but today there are just a handful. The Remington dominates, but the Browning BPR is a fine rifle. The slide action's chief use, to my mind, is among casual deer hunters who prefer slide-action shotguns. It makes sense, of course, to use the action you're most familiar with. Traditionally, slide actions have been close-cover whitetail rifles. They can certainly be accurate, and both the Remington and Browning are chambered for wonderful general-purpose cartridges such as the .270, .280, .30-06, and .35 Whelen.

I'm not a fan of the slide-action rifle, but hunters who use them swear by them. I've seen a couple in Africa, and there's certainly no reason not to use one. They are very fast, perhaps the fastest repeating action, and the modern rifles are very reliable. If they have a drawback, it's simply that they are not available in serious African cartridges. But for a light rifle, if that's what you happen to shoot best—or handle most comfortably—stick with it! That is, if you can: The slide action is also currently specifically prohibited in South Africa.

Semiautomatics

In general, the same things said about slide actions apply to semiautomatics. Most of the sporting semiautos have been chambered in .308, .270, .30-06, and so forth. The Browning BAR is also offered in belted magnums up to .338, which makes it a pretty serious contender as a medium rifle for Africa. Jack Lott once rebarreled a Browning to .458, and it worked like a charm. It was accurate, too.

The semiauto does have a couple of serious drawbacks. First, it is not authorized for sporting use in all African countries, so the legalities must be checked out. Second, the semiauto will be most reliable with factory ammo; it isn't an action for the serious handloader. Finally, though, there's a functional problem. The semiauto cannot be babied; to make certain the first round is chambered and the bolt is fully seated, that bolt must be released and snapped forward, not "ridden" home. That's a noisy procedure. Therefore, like the single shot and the double, the semiauto is either fully loaded or fairly useless, and if it isn't loaded, it cannot be loaded quietly. Personally, I wouldn't have one in Africa, but I'm a bit old-fashioned. No appropriate semiautos are available for hunting dangerous game (that custom experimental Browning is the one exception I'm aware of). But for a light rifle, or even a medium, if it's legal and that's what you shoot best, there's no reason not to take it along.

Double or Magazine?

Chapter 21

The question isn't new, and certainly it's been addressed, and addressed well, by more experienced hands than mine. But the question remains: Given that the double rifle is such an African classic, is it really preferable to a bolt-action repeater?

In preceding chapters we've looked at the strengths of the double rifle: reliability, balance and quick-pointing nature, and instant availability of the second shot. We've also acknowledged its weaknesses: high cost, relative inaccuracy, limitation of sighting equipment, and weight. We've examined the bolt action in the same manner. Its strong points are strength, reliability, accuracy, and its ability to be adapted to any situation in terms of variety of chamberings and sighting equipment. In truth, the bolt action has few weaknesses, but it generally doesn't come up as quickly as a double, and certainly isn't as fast for the second shot. Or are these claims valid? It's time to look for a verdict if such can be found. Which is better for African hunting: double or magazine?

Although the question has been answered many times over the years, it's arguably a ridiculous question because there can be no definitive or objective answer. Double-rifle fans will always be in the minority, though extremely self-righteous. Bolt-action fans will be in the majority. But a significant percentage of this group will secretly, in their heart-of-hearts, covet doubles and wish they could afford them. Neither group is right or wrong; whatever rifle a person happens to shoot best and be most comfortable with is the right choice, provided only that its caliber is at least reasonably suitable for the intended game. On the other hand, the preceding statement, however true it may be, is of no earthly use to the hunter who is trying to assemble a safari battery. If he's a beginning hunter, it's a bewildering situation. And if he's an experienced hunter in, say, North America, it's even more bewildering. After all, African game has such a legendary reputation for toughness. And it has long been in vogue among some writers (and purveyors of hunting DVDs to portray the African bush as chock-full of things waiting to bite, gore, trample, and eat you.

Gun fit is more important than action type, and if you get a normal shooting opportunity like this it doesn't much matter what you're using, provided the gun fits you and you know how to use it.

It would be easy to get the idea that the garden-variety whitetail, elk, or sheep rifle is useless in Africa, and that a whole battery of doubles is called for. That's ridiculous. Africa does have thick-skinned, dangerous game, obviously absent in North America, and thus there are some peculiar requirements for firearms. But an entire new battery is rarely called for, and while a double may be desired, it's hardly a requirement.

In a later section of the book we'll look at specific rifles and rifle types for various classes of African game, and we'll also look at sensible batteries for various types of safaris. In many cases a double rifle may be a part of such a battery. But, under any circumstances, is a double actually better than a magazine rifle?

First we have to go back to our classifications of African rifles: light, medium, heavy, and so forth. The classic double is a heavy rifle. However, a great number of fine doubles have been built as light rifles. The late Robert E. Petersen, my longtime boss, loved small-caliber doubles. Among his collection he had .22 rimfires and Hornets from "name" English makers, and in recent years Peter Hofer built him a fantastic miniature double in .17 HMR. Geoff Miller at Rigby built him a mismatched pair of light doubles, a .22 Hornet and a .225 Winchester. I shot both of these guns, and they were wonderfully accurate. Over the years quite a number of doubles have been built to rimmed cartridges like .22 Savage Hi-Power, .240

Left to right: .405 Winchester, .450/.400-3", .416 Remington Magnum, .416 Rigby, .416 Weatherby Magnum. There are suitable cartridges available for most action types, so it isn't a matter of power.

Flanged Nitro Express, .246 Purdey, .275 Flanged Magnum, 7x57R, 7x65R, Super .30 Magnum Flanged, .303 British, .30-40 Krag, and God knows what else.

Bob Petersen had a ball scrambling through the chaparral shooting ground squirrels with his little doubles, but I don't think anyone (even Petersen) would argue that a double is a better varmint rifle than an accurate bolt gun. On the other hand, if you have a double in a versatile light or medium caliber, there is no reason not to use it as a light rifle. However, there are plenty of reasons it's still not the ideal light rifle, certainly not as good a choice as a bolt action in similar caliber. We're talking rifles of relatively low recoil, so the added gun weight of a double offers no advantage. We're also talking about a rifle that will generally be used at a variety of ranges, sometimes at small targets. So the accuracy limitations of most doubles are a real disadvantage. The light rifle will also be used on a wide variety of game, at a minimum from duiker up to possibly kudu. Because the double's barrels are regulated for a specific load, the flexibility of using different bullet weights and styles for different game is lost.

Finally, unless a double was originally built with claw-mount fixtures for attaching a scope, it will be inordinately difficult and expensive to scope it. If it's a vintage gun, modifying it in any way may reduce its collector value. A light rifle without a scope is extremely limited.

On a charge things change. Gun fit is still critical, but there is no substitute for the quick one-two punch of a double rifle. On the other hand, it's the PH who is most likely to face this situation, not you or me as the hunting client.

The rapid second shot of a double is an advantage in any hunting, it's true, but with lighter game, often shot at longer distances, it's not as significant. The truth is that as a light rifle, a double is at best a curiosity or an eccentricity. At worst it could be a significant disadvantage. It will do the job, of course, but not as well as an accurate bolt action of similar caliber.

There are also a great many fine doubles in medium calibers, both my "light medium" classification, running between .30 and .375 caliber, and the .375 itself. Although the .318 Westley Richards is a rimless cartridge, a number of doubles were so chambered. Most of these were built by Westley Richards, but Jack Lott had a wonderful Holland Royal so chambered, and he used it extensively on several African trips. There were also doubles for such excellent cartridges as .333 Flanged, .350 No. 2, .400/.350, .360 No. 2, and the European 9.3x74R. All of these cartridges are relatively similar in that they fire long, heavy-for-caliber bullets at fairly moderate velocities (in the case of the .400/.350, as low as 2,000 FPS; for the .318 and .333, up to 2,400). Slightly more powerful is the .369 Purdey, and most powerful of this group is the .375 Flanged Magnum (the rimmed version of the .375 H&H, traditionally with slightly reduced loads to keep pressure down). Today, with better ejection/extraction systems for rimless or belted rimless cases, a new "medium" double is almost certain to be either .375 H&H (belted) or 9.3x74R.

This group of cartridges actually represents a wide selection of good double rifles to be used as African mediums. The older cartridges, especially the .333 Flanged,

As much as I love a double, if the range is such that I need to take a rest, I am much more comfortable with the accuracy of a bolt action.

.350 No. 2, and .360 No. 2, are quite good, can be reloaded, and can generally be had relatively inexpensively in vintage doubles. The 9.3x74R is probably the most common and can be had in both older "working" doubles and new guns at modest prices (as such things go). For all practical purposes, the .369 Purdey (firing a .375 bullet), .375 Flanged, and .375 H&H are close enough ballistically that there's little to pick from. This means that whether your tastes in a medium run toward the .35 Whelen–.338 group or toward the .375 H&H, equivalent doubles are available. The question is, do they make sense?

To some extent, the answer depends on the intended purpose of your medium rifle. The limitations are the same: No double-rifle cartridge offers the flat trajectory of a .338 Winchester Magnum, .340 Weatherby, 8mm Remington Magnum, or .378 Weatherby Magnum. Nor does a double in any caliber offer either the accuracy or load flexibility of an equivalent bolt action. Often, however, the medium rifle isn't expected to reach out as far as the light rifle—and its targets are usually larger. In my view, a medium should surely be scoped, so an iron-sighted medium double is just as much an eccentricity as a light double. But if scoped, a very strong case could be made for a medium double, especially for use in thornbush or forest.

Such a gun would usually be heavier than a like bolt action, but not unbearably so. It would not be as accurate or as flexible—but it would offer that ultra-fast second shot, and it would be used against larger, tougher game where that fast second shot is ever more critical. There are even some applications in which such a double would be superior to a bolt action. Situations that come to mind include hound hunting, whether for bushpig or leopard, and any forest hunting where shooting distances are close and an instantaneous second shot would be a huge advantage.

I can imagine few all-round lion guns better than a scoped double .375, likewise for eland. In the former case, no shot over 150 yards will be taken—ranges will probably be half that—so the double's relative inaccuracy isn't a concern. In the latter case, with eland, a somewhat longer shot might be taken, but the vital area is huge and so again accuracy isn't a major concern. In both cases, however, that instant second shot could be very important. If a medium is to be used on buffalo (in most countries today only the .375 would be legal), the double's instant second shot is needed. However, on buffalo I would submit that pinpoint shot placement, while always essential, becomes ever more critical when you reduce power—so only a scope-sighted, accurate medium double would be acceptable.

As I've said, in some applications a scoped medium-caliber double would be extremely useful. However, the classic medium rifle is not a double; it's an accurate, scoped magazine rifle, probably in .375 H&H. There are good reasons for this. Under most conditions, the medium rifle may be used for antelopes large and small, and while it may be called upon for a snapshot at close range, it could also be asked to reach out and touch a record kudu at three hundred yards and more.

I think a medium-caliber double would be a lot of fun on safari, and in specific instances might well be the best thing going. The very fact that it is a somewhat special-purpose rifle, however, is the strongest argument against a medium double. On safari the medium bore is the jack-of-all-trades, the most general-purpose rifle in the battery. In spite of its virtues, even a scoped medium double is not as versatile as its bolt-action brethren. It won't usually be as accurate, cannot reach out as far, and will not have the flexibility of loads.

I doubt if many readers will argue with the foregoing; light and even medium doubles are somewhat unusual. I have corresponded with an American diplomat-hunter who shoots a .360 No. 2, and I've encountered a smattering of 9.3x74R doubles plus a couple of .375s. Jeff Wemmer of Texas Hunt Company has a .369 Purdey—but because of its lack of versatility he didn't bring it to the Zambezi Valley when we hunted together. That's about it. Most of the double rifles being made today, and most of the older guns still in use (possibly with the exception of the ubiquitous 9.3), are large-caliber rifles. There are exceptions. Virtually everyone who makes doubles offers a .375, either flanged or belted (Heym offers both). They are effective, and make excellent low-recoil options. But the classic form of the double has evolved into a heavy rifle—a charge-stopping big bore designed specifically for the largest and most dangerous game in the world.

Such a rifle is chambered for a variety of cartridges ranging from .450-400 through .700 Nitro Express. It will be heavy, perhaps 9½ pounds at a bare-bones minimum up to more than 20 pounds for a .700. A very rare big double will be fitted for claw scope mounts, but the typical arrangement is open express sights: a shallow standing V rear with or without additional folding leaves, usually on a quarter rib, and a bold ivory or brass ramp-mounted bead front with or without a hood.

As the big double evolved, so did the big magazine rifle, first into "large mediums" like the .425 Westley Richards, .404 Jeffery, and .416 Rigby, and then into ultra-powerful rifles like the .505 Gibbs and .500 Jeffery. Ultimately, economics would virtually kill the double, and the inexpensive American-made .458 Winchester Magnums would dominate. In recent years the large-caliber double has again come back strong, although it has never been and probably will never be as popular as the bolt action. Through it all the controversy has never died: Which is the best stopping rifle for dangerous game, double or magazine?

Even though so little dangerous-game hunting exists today, this is hardly a silly controversy. After all, if you fail to stop it, one serious charge in a lifetime is one too many! If one or the other type were indeed a clear-cut better choice, then it would be foolish not to have the very best in your hands when the chips are down.

When speaking of heavy rifles, we're talking about serious charge-stoppers, rifles you would prefer to have when going after a wounded lion, and rifles that will both open and close the ball game with elephant, rhino, and buffalo no matter what happens.

It could be argued that the .375 is the minimum, and of course it's available in both action types. Personally, I would argue that the .450/.400 is the minimum in a double, while the .404 Jeffery and the current standard loading of the .458 Winchester Magnum are the minimums in bolt actions. But whatever arbitrary minimum you set, there's absolutely no question that adequate cartridges—nay, more than adequate cartridges—are available in each action type. So, given that both doubles and magazine rifles have the power needed, let's examine again the advantages and disadvantages of each, and see if any conclusions can be drawn.

A great advantage to the bolt action is said to be its low cost, while the double's high cost is always listed as its first disadvantage. For this discussion, I think we need to throw that one out. After all, here we're talking about the most specialized rifle of all: the one you will rely on to save your tail. Cost should not be an object when one's life is at stake. Also, it should be mentioned that at the top end bolt actions aren't necessarily less expensive. The highest-quality custom bolt actions cost considerably more than basic working doubles. Yes, perfectly serviceable and reliable bolt actions can be had for a great deal less than any serviceable double. But let's not consider here whether the rifle is affordable or not. Let's decide which is best.

One situation where there is no compromise is elephant hunting. For me there is no substitute for a double rifle . . . but if you use one you simply must practice firing both barrels in sequence, then reloading quickly.

Yet another "failing" of the double rifle is said to be its extreme weight, and I would like to throw that one away as well. Yes, a double has weight; 10½ pounds is a good average for rifles between .450/.400 and .475. The .500s usually weigh more. The .577s and .600s usually weigh a lot more. We'll leave them out of this; they are indeed too heavy to carry all day! The average heavy-caliber bolt action might weigh a pound less than a comparable double, and obviously magazine rifles can be built much lighter: I had a .416 Hoffman in a fiberglass stock that hardly weighed 6½ pounds. It was a joy to carry, but it kicked way too much! And that's the point: The price paid in light weight is recoil, and so long as gun weight isn't unreasonable, the extra ounces will make the rifle steadier in tired hands and make the second shot quicker after recovery from recoil.

One of the most-cited inadequacies of the double is lack of accuracy. True, by bolt-action standards the average double is not accurate. However, we're not talking about popping woodchucks at 400 yards. We're talking about getting a bullet into the vital zone of an unwounded elephant, buffalo, or rhino at some maximum distance well under a hundred yards, and about stopping a charging animal at some distance between the muzzle and, say, twenty yards. When it comes to light and medium rifles, I'd be the first to say that the double rifle's level of accuracy creates a serious handicap. But for a heavy rifle, don't be absurd! A well-made double in reasonable condition, with a good load that's at least close to the regulation load, should be able to put two shots from each barrel into a cantaloupe at 100 yards. As we've discussed, some doubles do much better, but what difference does it make? Minute-of-cantaloupe is more than good enough, and any double worth owning will provide that level of accuracy.

However, sighting equipment is the most significant factor in the accuracy you can realize from your rifle, regardless of what it might be capable of doing. Sighting equipment can be the same for the two types, but generally is not. The bolt action, especially a large medium like the .416 (Rigby, Remington, Weatherby, et al), is likely to be scoped. A .458 Lott may be scoped. A large-caliber double is only rarely scoped, although it could perhaps be argued that more should be. Regardless of how accurate your rifle is, most of us are pretty much at our effective limit with open sights long before a hundred yards is reached. Bolt actions can carry open sights only, and doubles can be scoped. Again, what difference does this make? The primary purpose for a stopping rifle is to stop a dangerous animal at close range, so open sights shouldn't be a big handicap.

Quick-handling abilities are said to be a great strength of the double. Now, any rifle taken after dangerous game should fit the shooter; an ill-fitting heavy rifle of any type is lunacy. A well-fitting bolt gun that comes up to the shoulder smoothly with the sights aligned can be very fast. However, I submit that no bolt action, regardless of fit, will be as fast as an equally well-fitting double. The double comes up like a fine quail gun; it will usually be shorter than a bolt gun and has a perfect center of balance that puts a lot of weight between the hands. It also has the heavy barrels forward and the broad sighting plane.

In the last moments of a determined charge, you'll be shooting your rifle as if it were a shotgun, and indeed you'd better be. In that extreme circumstance, nothing is like a big double that fits properly. The sights are there, but only the subconscious is aware of them; the rifle acts as an extension of the eye and hands, and if you take time to concentrate on the sight picture you'll be overrun before the shot is fired.

On the other hand, at any significant distance beyond bayonet range, even during the initial moments of a charge, it's critical that the sight picture is proper and the sights centered on the right place. If you need to use your sights at all, any optical sight, whether aperture or scope, is faster than any open sight. Period.

To understand this radical statement, it's essential that you understand how the eye works. With an open sight, you have three objects in three planes: the rear sight, the front sight, and the target. The eye cannot focus on all three, so it shifts back and forth. The target must obviously be clear, and younger shooters may be able to keep the front sight almost in perfect focus as well. The rear sight will be blurry for everyone, and as eyes age and become less flexible, the situation worsens. Aperture sights operate in just two planes; the rear ring is supposed to be ignored while the eye automatically centers the bead. A scope operates in just one plane; all that's necessary is to concentrate on the target and superimpose the reticle on the point you wish to hit. Like it or not, optical sights are faster than an iron sight can possibly be at any distance at which you need to use sights.

The late Finn Aagaard was one of the few African professionals I know who really believed this. He went to a scoped .375 many years ago in Kenya, and found that even at very close range he was much faster and more efficient than he'd been with iron sights. Here in the States, he set out to prove his theory. He set up a range with life-size animal silhouettes at various distances, and virtually every visitor to the ranch took part in the testing. With a stopwatch, starting from a "Go!" with the rifle at port arms and ending with the shot, Finn timed a number of shooters with open sights, scopes, and apertures at various distances. Although I took part in his experiment, I don't have his exact data, but nobody, close or far, was as fast or as accurate with iron as they were with a scope, especially a low-power scope with a broad field of view.

The one thing he didn't test (at least in my presence) was short range—last-chance-to-stop-him range. We're talking a matter of just a few feet. At such ranges sights become superfluous and gun fit is everything. A well-fitting bolt gun would do it, but here, and perhaps only here, the handling abilities of a double could save the day.

What am I saying? If a double were scoped, everything would be even up. But few doubles are scoped, while bolt actions can be scoped with ease. The potential accuracy of either type is adequate for dangerous game at all distances at which they should be shot, but a scoped bolt action will stand most hunters in better stead in all circumstances except a close-range charge. In that circumstance, a bolt gun will of course do the job—but the handling abilities of a well-fitting double will do it better.

The double's fast second shot is indeed an advantage that can't be questioned. However, in elephant-culling operations magazine rifles have been the most common tools. Professional hunter Barrie Duckworth, who is just a few years older than I, shot very close to one thousand elephant during control operations with the then-Rhodesian game department. He used a pair of Mannlicher .458s and had a loader behind him carrying the second rifle. Many hunters with the largest total bags (and remember, culling means eliminating entire herds, not selective shooting) used pairs of magazine rifles. For shooting numbers of elephant, there's little question that a pair of four- or five-shot magazine rifles offered more firepower than a pair of doubles.

However, the selective ivory hunter or the professional hunter backing up a client isn't concerned about large bags, nor is today's sportsman. He's concerned about anchoring his chosen animal. Here the fast second shot of a double can come in handy. The double's third shot will be slow, while in a magazine rifle it's ready and waiting. Take your pick. In a bad moment, I'd prefer a second shot instantly available to a third shot more or less available. I have done quite a lot of elephant hunting in the past couple of years, and my opinion on this today is even stronger than it used to be. So I'll phrase it more strongly: Trophy elephant hunting (as opposed to culling) is one situation where the double rifle is far superior to the magazine rifle, and a scope is absolutely unnecessary. Proper shots at elephant are close enough (and the target is plenty large enough) that a scope is silly, just something to add gun weight and catch on brush. Thirty-five yards is a very long shot on elephant. In 2007 alone I took four elephant well inside of twenty yards, two within ten yards.

You don't need a scope for that kind of shooting, but you might well need a second shot. One of the most difficult shots in the hunting world is the frontal brain shot on an elephant. Head angle is everything—and even if you get it exactly right there is always a chance that the bullet won't penetrate deep enough, or won't hold its course. When a brain shot fails, things happen very fast, and you must do something very fast. Until you've been there, it cannot even be imagined how quickly an elephant can turn his backside to you, or get behind brush, or be shielded by another elephant. Elephant hunting is a rare situation where your ability to use a second shot quickly may well be more important than the first shot. Nothing is faster than a double for that second shot that might be needed to save your life, or to prevent the loss of a wounded animal.

Of course, the second shot in a double is instantly available, with no movement whatever. The proper operation of a bolt action keeps the rifle at the shoulder while the bolt is being worked, but there must obviously be movement. The more rapidly the second shot is needed, the more violent that movement must be. A double must be taken from the shoulder to reload for the third and fourth shots, while the magazine rifle can stay in position until it's empty. The double can be loaded very quickly, of course, but if more than two shots are required, the nod has to go to the bolt action.

Almost as much has been made of the reliability of the double's second shot as its speed. I have trouble with that. I've used bolt actions all my life and have yet

The fact that this tuskless elephant fell on its knees indicates a brain shot, but that's only part of the story. My frontal brain shot at five yards failed, but as the animal turned I fired the second barrel for a side-on brain shot. This was possible only with a double rifle; nothing else is fast enough for the second shot.

When my .416 was delayed enroute I borrowed outfitter Antonio Riguera's Krieghoff double in .500-3". In the for

...ble is wonderfully comforting—but also useless for a duiker or bushpig across a clearing or standing on a forest road.

to "short-stroke" one and thereby fail to pick up the cartridge from the magazine. Yes, mechanical failures can happen. And yes, bolt actions can fail to feed, and the magazine boxes can drop open, and the sky can fall. But all of that should be taken care of long before the rifle goes to the field. New double rifles, too, can have breaking-in pangs. I've had ejectors fail and stocks split. And old double rifles can suffer broken springs and broken firing pins.

One significant advantage of the double is that few mechanical failures short of something really catastrophic will affect both barrels and both locks. I would rate a good, modern bolt action as every bit as reliable as any double ever built. But either can fail, and if a double fails, you're generally left with at least a single shot. A bolt action will usually be easier to fix, but until it's fixed you're left with a club.

A more important facet of reliability may well be maintainability, and here the simple bolt action has a significant edge over most doubles. With a single screwdriver it's easy to pull a bolt action out of the stock, and without tools most bolts can be stripped for cleaning and lubrication. In wet weather a double gets just as soaked as any bolt action, but it's a lot harder to do something about it. If the double is one of the relatively few "best" guns, with hand-detachable sidelocks or Westley Richards's hand-detachable boxlocks, you can at least take care of the all-important locks. With nondetachable locks you have to pray a little, and with any of them, removing the buttstock is a chore. Now, it does take a lot to put a double out of action. But I have carried doubles through driving rainstorms on late-season and early season hunts, and every time, I cry a lot inside as I watch rivers of rain sluice down over the action.

Silence of operation is a definite advantage of the double, but these days I'm not sure how significant it really is. The ivory hunters who used doubles often used them without ejectors, and then, not only was the second shot available with no noise but so was the third, fourth, or however many were possible. The theory was that the clatter of a bolt action (and the "ping" of a double's ejectors) did more to pinpoint the hunter than the report of the rifle. With a double's silent operation, some of the old-timers felt larger bags were possible.

These days, that seems a very obscure point. I do like a double's instant and silent second shot, and I like having it with no motion. I have, I'll admit, blown my first shot at an animal and had him stand for a second. That instantaneous, silent second shot with a double can save the day, and it just might make a difference. But not enough difference to make a big deal out of.

One of the most significant advantages of a double rifle, as far as I'm concerned, is one that is rarely mentioned: instant choice of bullet type. It's pretty much the same deal as a double-trigger, double-barrel shotgun offering instant choice of shot size and choke, except that with a rifle the choice is either solid bullet or soft, one in each barrel.

Professional hunter Gordon Cormack, regrettably recently deceased, in a story written for South Africa's *Man/Magnum* magazine about backup rifles for professional hunters does mention this as an advantage but suggests this was primarily "useful for right and left on lion and elephant!" Well, Gordon's a good hand, and this was a marvelous article. He was good enough to send me an initial draft, and we're in agreement on most things. (Good thing, since he has much more experience!) But I suspect he doesn't see this to be a real advantage, and I do. On elephant, no, it's not an advantage; you'll be loaded with solids only. Likewise on rhino. And if you're hunting specifically for lion, you'll be loaded with softs. But for buffalo, or for just kicking around in the bush, I like to load a double with one of each.

Of course, that's because I much prefer expanding bullets for the first shot on buffalo. Those who don't will fail to see any advantage, and well they shouldn't, since it doesn't exist for them. For me, I know I can kill a broadside or facing buffalo more quickly with a softpoint, and in a herd, if I put the bullet on the shoulder it isn't likely to go clear through.

That's the nifty thing about a double: If the angle isn't quite what I like for a softpoint, that solid is right there in the next barrel with no movement whatever. I can remember a couple of buffalo that presented nothing but an angling shot at the end of tough tracking jobs, and the solid did the job when the softpoint may have been questionable. Which, I suppose, is a good argument for sticking with solids altogether on buffalo. But a softpoint in the rib cage just works so well that I hate to give up on them—so long as I can hedge my bets with a solid next door!

In a kind of reverse situation, in 1988 I was buffalo hunting with a .416 Rigby bolt action when we bumped head-on into a nice lion. In those innocent days I wasn't exactly hunting lion, but I had a lion on license. The decision was made with no discussion, but the first shell, my softpoint, misfired. Now, that's a rare occurrence, but it can happen with anything. Had I been carrying a double, I suppose I still would have had to shoot the lion with a solid, since the one softpoint was the one that misfired. But Lord, how I wished for my .470 while I was oh, so slowly working the bolt to get rid of the bum cartridge!

A last comparison, rarely made but important, involves safety. As I mentioned in an earlier chapter, a double shares an inherent safety problem with the single shot in that it's either fully loaded or unloaded. I don't know about most hunters, but with a bolt action I habitually empty the chamber when I'm negotiating tough country, carrying the rifle slung, or just in general

In Boddington on Buffalo I used a Rigby double .470 and a Dakota .375. Ideally it would be nice to have both action types available, because both have their strong points.

when I feel action isn't imminent. It's just as easy to do that with a double, but now you've got a completely empty and thus completely useless rifle. In Africa I fear the common solution is to leave it loaded.

Now, if the chamber is loaded, a bolt action is no different from a double. Only two things stand in the way of disaster: safe gun-handling procedures and, as a backup only, a mechanical safety. Safeties on doubles are pretty good, I guess—but some are better than others. Double interrupting sears, for instance, are more foolproof than simpler safeties, and the Krieghoff cocking system is the most foolproof of all. Whatever, I don't completely trust any mechanical safety, but the ones I trust the most are the striker-blocking types found on Mausers and Mauser derivatives. The best solution is to keep the chamber empty unless it really needs to be loaded (meaning that the bolt action, with its loaded magazine in reserve, is a better option) and, of course and always, to keep the rifle pointed in a safe direction.

One of the big problems with doubles—which are normally carried loaded—is the so-called "African carry." It's a neat way to carry a rifle, especially a double. Barrels are grasped in one hand or the other, and the flat of the action just ahead of the trigger guard is nicely balanced on the shoulder. It's comfortable, and it goes back to the days when the tracker/gunbearer would walk ahead of the hunter with the rifle so carried; then all the hunter needed to do was reach forward to grasp a ready rifle. Problem is it's too comfortable, and everybody started doing it. When the guy carrying a rifle in that fashion isn't first in line, the rifle winds up pointed at the man in front of him.

A professional hunter friend of mine had a double .500/.465 go off when carried in that manner. The bullet went through the legs of both trackers in front of him. One was injured just slightly, but the femoral artery of the other was severed and he bled to death. My friend and he, incidentally, had grown up together, and though their colors were different, they were lifelong friends and hunting companions. It has been a tough thing to live with.

Obviously, something snagged the trigger, but was the safety also knocked off somehow or did it fail? Who knows? It wouldn't have happened had the barrels been pointed in a safe direction, but the "African carry" is a way of life, and it's a bad habit that doubles seem to promote. I carry them that way myself, but never if the bush is too thick to offset myself from the guy in front of me enough to get the barrels pointed well to one side! Safety rules simply must not be ignored. It seems to me that in terms of safety, the double may not be well suited to the inexperienced or extremely nervous hunter. But of course no rifle of sound design is inherently unsafe, and I'm certainly not suggesting the double is.

Can a bottom line be found? All things being equal, the average sportsman on the average safari will get the best service from a scoped bolt action. He can hit better with it, plain and simple, and hunting is a game of shot placement first and foremost. On the other hand, the man who chooses the bolt gun will not have the instant second shot, nor, in my opinion, will he have quite as reliable a last-instant shot.

Now, anyone can benefit from a quick second shot—but anyone is also better off with a perfectly placed first shot. And since nobody wants to get trampled, gored, tossed, or mauled, anybody can benefit from a better last-instant chance. However, let's face the facts. From the hunting client's viewpoint, if things go sour, chances are it's the professional hunter who will clean up the mess. Not only is it his job, technically and legally, but he's also better prepared to handle it—or should be. So it would seem that the man who could best benefit from using a heavy double is the guy who can probably afford one the least: the professional hunter in the field. Sounds logical, but there's a fly in the ointment here. If things get really bad, the professional hunter may have to shoot a nasty off the end of his gun barrel. But before things reach that point, generally there's been another opportunity to settle things, and that's before the animal gets into the thick stuff in the first place. Perhaps, just perhaps, it's as important for the professional hunter to be able to place his bullets in an outbound wounded buffalo at 100 yards or a fast-vanishing lion at 150. It's food for thought.

Which do I think is better? The jury is still out. I think, all things considered, that a scoped bolt action is the most practical, except for elephant. For that game, nothing beats a big double. But even if a scoped bolt action is a better all-round choice for a heavy rifle, the tremendous pleasure I get from carrying and shooting a classic big double more than outweighs any slight impracticality. They're a joy, and while I have passed mine off to the tracker in favor of a scoped bolt gun on several occasions, in very close cover there's never been any question about which gun to carry. Maybe that's the answer: The rifle types are so different that each has its place. Or perhaps, as they've said since about 1910, it really does come down to personal preference.

Stocks, Takedown Rifles, and Recoil Reducers

Chapter 22

Stocks

The purpose of a gunstock is twofold: first, to provide a platform on which the working parts of the rifle perform their functions, and second, to fit the rifle to the person who will shoot it and assist him in hitting what he shoots at. Some stocks are incredibly beautiful while others are, well, something less than that. But if a stock performs those basic functions, cosmetics really don't matter in any practical way.

Of the many dimensions that go into making a stock fit properly, the two most critical seem to me to be length of pull and height of comb. Length of pull is basically the straight-line distance between trigger and butt, and this dimension determines proper positioning of the rifle on both shoulder and cheek. Something between 13¾ inches and 14¼ inches is about right for most adult shooters. I happen to be about five feet nine inches. As much as I hate to admit it, this puts me a little below average height for an American male today. Apparently the factories don't know the current statistics, because the average factory pull of about 13¾ inches happens to fit me perfectly. Arm length and build make a difference, but in general if you're shorter, this measurement may be too long. If you're taller, this "Joe Average" stock will almost certainly be too short. This dimension, by the way, is for a bolt action; a twin-trigger double barrel requires a bit longer length of pull to the front trigger. Fortunately, length of pull is the easiest stock dimension to correct. A stock that's too long can easily be shortened, while a stock that's too short can generally be lengthened by a thicker recoil pad or by a spacer or wooden shim between butt and pad.

The desired height of comb depends largely on personal preference, shooting style, and sighting equipment. Americans, for instance, are usually taught to shoot with the cheek (about midway between jaw and cheekbone) firmly welded to the rifle's comb. Europeans, on the other hand, tend to shoot with head more erect and

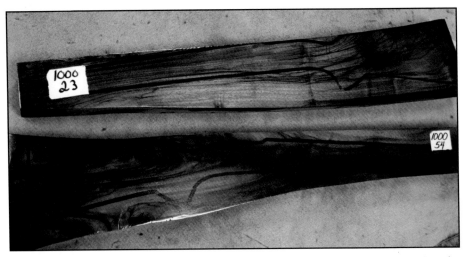

To me few things are more beautiful than really fine walnut crafted into a gunstock. But world supplies are dwindling and costs have escalated dramatically. Good gunstock wood like this now brings a minimum of $1,000.00 for a raw blank.

cheek contact much closer to the jawbone. The typical European stock therefore has a much lower comb than most American stocks.

A stock designed for use with iron sights must have a substantially lower comb than one intended for scope use since most scopes are mounted about 1½ inches above center of bore, while iron sights are less than half that distance above.

Neither the American nor the European style of shooting is right or wrong, but it's very difficult for an American to modify his shooting style to comfortably handle a European-style stock—and vice versa. And although many detachable scope mounts work extremely well, it is virtually impossible to design a stock that is really right for both scope and iron sights. Almost invariably, a decision must be made regarding which is the primary sight and which the auxiliary. Even then, a compromise must be achieved if a rifle wears both scope and iron sights, provided the iron sights are more than merely cosmetic.

All too often I have seen rifles with good detachable mounts that come up perfectly with the scope in place—but when the scope is detached it is impossible to get one's face down far enough on the stock to actually see the rear sight.

That fiberglass-stocked .416 Hoffman I've often mentioned was a classic example. It had wonderful iron sights and detachable scope mounts. The height of comb was perfect for a 3X scope in those mounts; it came up on target like a dream. However, when I took the scope off, I couldn't see the iron sights at all. No matter how hard I scrunched my cheek into the stock, it was just too high.

A custom walnut stock requires extensive and costly handwork—and the finished result is actually fairly fragile. Synthetics and laminates are more durable as well as cheaper.

Eventually I decided I might well want to use irons with the rifle, so Chet Brown switched stocks for me, installing one with a lower comb. With walnut, of course, it's usually no great trick to lower a comb and refinish the wood. It is much more difficult to raise a comb without hurting a rifle's looks!

Drop at heel is the distance the heel, or uppermost portion of the butt, lies below centerline of bore. Depending on the relationship between heel and comb, this dimension also determines the sighting equipment and shooting style for which the rifle is best suited. More importantly, drop at heel will give a good clue about how the rifle handles recoil. A lot of drop—take the old Model 1895 Winchester as the worst example—and you're sure to have a horribly kicking rifle, especially if the butt is narrow and, worse, has an old-fashioned crescent shape.

The American classic style of stock has very little drop at heel and a straight comb, with or without cheekpiece. For me this stock style handles felt recoil extremely well, and it is definitely my preference, especially if the comb is gently rounded and the butt is broad and flat to spread out the kick. The concept behind this style of stock is to bring recoil back in a straight line, and the butt will ride high on the shoulder. The cheek will slide along the stock. (If you don't believe that, shoot a rifle with a fiberglass stock of classic configuration that has lots of recoil and a very rough

Laminated wood is probably the strongest of all gunstocks, almost as impervious to the weather as synthetics. Laminates are also generally the heaviest stocks, but this isn't always a bad thing since a bit more gun weight is the easiest way to attenuate recoil.

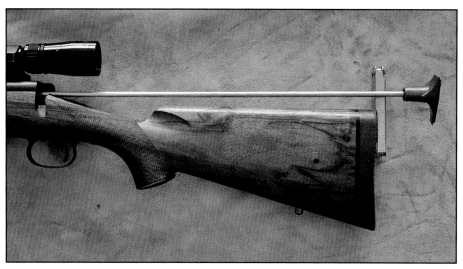

In terms of stock style, I tend to like the "American Classic" style with a dead-straight comb. Everybody is different, but for me this stock design brings recoil straight back and is most comfortable.

krinkle-paint finish. I guarantee you'll lose some skin on your cheek and then reach for the sandpaper to smooth the stock where the face makes contact.)

I prefer this classic stock; the clean lines appeal to me, and I like the way such a stock comes into my shoulder. However, we aren't all the same. Various degrees of Monte Carlo comb are also quite popular. With the Monte Carlo style, the comb is fairly high and slants forward while the heel drops away from the comb and thus rests lower on the shoulder. This is a concept long promoted by Roy Weatherby. His theory was absolutely correct: During recoil, the forward-slanting comb slides away from the face. Over the years, I have done quite a lot of shooting with the biggest Weatherby Magnums, the .378, .416, and .460, all rifles with very heavy recoil. Unquestionably the Weatherby stock style gets the recoil away from your face.

Of course, recoil is recoil, and it is an equal and opposite reaction. In my experience, classic-stocked rifles kick the face a bit harder and the shoulder a bit softer; Monte Carlo stocks are the other way around. Take your pick, based on what feels best to you.

Cheekpieces, as far as I'm concerned, are just a few ounces of ornamental wood. Rollover cheekpieces are several ounces of ornamental wood. A well-designed cheekpiece looks good and feels good, but so does a well-shaped comb sans cheekpiece. Again, your pick should depend on what feels best to you. Thumb-hole stocks aren't for me; I'm a lefty, and I've seen so few I could use that I have no feeling for them. They are very steady for offhand shooting, and they do take a fair amount of recoil into

One advantage to a takedown rifle is that it can be fitted into a short, handy "shotgun-style" gun case. It does reduce the attention a bit, but these days you simply cannot forget to declare a firearm!

the shooting hand. My only problems with them are, to be honest, I abhor their looks and I find them too slow to get into action. But one man's meat is another's poison.

The classic gunstock material is walnut, and the relative merits of American, English, French, Bastogne, Circassian, etc., could be discussed endlessly. The problem with pretty stocks is that the lovely figure denotes weak places in the wood. The ideal stock for a rifle that will see hard use (and especially a heavy-recoiling rifle) will be straight-grained through the action area and the pistol grip, the weakest part of any stock. A little figure in the butt is nice, of course, but with a hunting rifle go for strength first.

I've had several (yes, by now, several) gunstocks broken during transit on airlines; several more have cracked and been repairable, and I've seen a couple just snap off when the hunting car hit a bump. It's disconcerting, and also a good argument against a one-rifle battery. Generally, a careful inspection will reveal hairline cracks before the damage becomes catastrophic, and that should be part of any pre-hunt ritual. Cracked stocks can often be filled and strengthened with epoxy and bedding compound, and drilling and pinning can make a stock stronger than it ever was. I have had three pet guns that were repaired by pinning with dowel rods seated in epoxy: a Remington Model 700 in .30-06, the stock of which snapped off at the wrist; my pet left-hand-converted pre-'64 Model 70 in .375, which developed a serious horizontal crack in the butt; and a favorite Model 12 skeet gun that had the toe of the stock broken clear off. All repairs are virtually invisible, and all are at least as strong as they ever were.

Unfortunately, repairs are tough or impossible to make in the field. A little baling wire and a lot of duct tape may make a temporary fix, but it's far wiser to inspect rifle stocks carefully before going afield! Most (not all) catastrophic stock failures give a little warning.

With bolt actions, recoil reinforcement needs to be given special attention. Much as I hate to say it, don't trust any manufacturer to have it right; nothing will split a stock faster than an improperly bedded recoil lug or a tang that isn't stress-relieved.

Pistol grips are very much a matter of personal preference. I like them thick enough to offer some strength, but not so thick that you can't wrap your hand comfortably. The classic style is for the grip to be "laid back," curving back gently so the knuckle of your second finger is well away from the trigger guard. This can be taken a bit too far, but that depends on your hands. The current Dakota stock, for instance, has a pistol grip so laid back that it is almost straight, and I have a bit of trouble getting my finger properly on the trigger. Such a design would undoubtedly be perfect for people with larger hands.

Fore-ends, too, are a matter of personal preference. I prefer them rounded and not too thick, while others prefer a beavertail. That's all inconsequential. More important is that the forward sling-swivel stud on a heavy-recoiling rifle (let's say above .375) must be barrel-mounted ahead of the fore-end. My right index finger (remember, I'm a lefty) has the scars from a stock-mounted swivel to prove this! Another option, of course, is a flush-mounted stud arrangement.

Incidentally, the sling and its swivels are a much-ignored piece of equipment that I find of critical importance. Whatever style of swivels and studs you choose, they must be properly and firmly installed—and checked religiously. When a sling swivel lets go (or a sling breaks), the rifle is sure to careen off your shoulder backward and land on the scope or sights. The ever-present possibility of this happening is yet another argument for never carrying a slung rifle with a round in the chamber.

In the nearly twenty years since I wrote *Safari Rifles,* synthetic stocks have become ever more popular, until today I honestly believe synthetic stocks outnumber wood stocks. I used to think they were the ugliest things in the world, but they're so darn practical that I've almost grown to like their looks. The various synthetics will never rival a lovely piece of walnut for sheer appeal. However, they're sturdy, durable, and stable. They won't warp in wet weather or crack in dry. They won't change point of impact, and they won't turn white after a rainstorm. In most cases a synthetic stock is stronger than any walnut stock. It is not automatically true that synthetic stocks

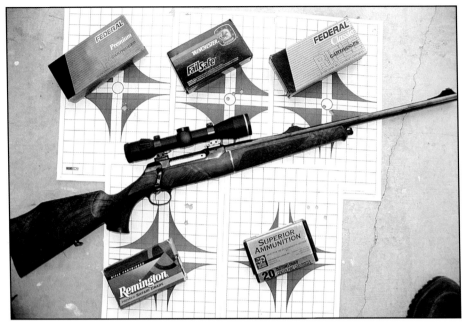

It is more difficult to make a takedown rifle really accurate, but it can be done. This takedown Sauer Model 202 in .375 H&H is one of the most accurate .375s I have ever used.

are lighter than wood. This depends on their construction; some are hollow—foam-injected and reinforced, while others are solid material. It also depends on the wood and how trim the stock is cut. But synthetics are usually a bit lighter. This makes them great to carry—just keep in mind that lighter rifles will kick more.

Despite the strength and stability of synthetics, my strong preference is for walnut stocks in Africa. This is purely and solely because they are more traditional and look better in the photos, not for any sensible reason! The majority of African hunting is done during the African winter, when the weather tends to be dry and dust is the worst hazard to the rifle. On the other hand, there are exceptions! All mountain hunting is hard on walnut stocks, and forest hunting is hard on everything.

In 1997 I took a beautiful new London-made .416 Rigby to the C.A.R. on a bongo hunt. I'd waited three years for the rifle and this was its maiden voyage! It survived a few showers and I dutifully cleaned it every night. All was well until the day of the bongo. We shot him at midday, and were still taking pictures when it began to rain. It rained buckets all the rest of the day and deep into the night. I know this because it was near midnight when we finally stumbled out onto the forest road where we'd left the truck, and it was nearly dawn by the time we cut our way through downed trees back to camp. That evening I noticed (with horror!) that the stock was completely and hopelessly split behind the tang. Good walnut has no place in the forest!

Another alternative that has come on strong in the last two decades is the laminated stock. Laminates are actually the strongest of all gunstocks currently available, stronger than either solid wood or synthetic. In wet weather the finish may become a mess and water may work into some of the layers, but a laminated stock is almost as stable as synthetic. It is also generally the heaviest option. This is not altogether a bad thing, since the easiest way to attenuate recoil is with gun weight! Modern laminates are available in a variety of colors, including "wood grain" that you have to look at awfully closely to tell it isn't solid wood. So, if you like the warm look of wood (like I do) but also like strength, stability, and ability to withstand abuse, laminates offer a wonderful option. Serengeti Rifles in Kalispell, Montana, just made me a beautiful .264 on an old Parker Ackley action, and it has a laminated stock that looks so good you have to look really close to see that it isn't a solid piece of fine walnut. I envisioned this more as a sheep rifle than an African rifle, but it would look just fine in the Serengeti or on the Kalahari.

Takedown Rifles and Switch Barrels

These days many of us are trying to travel as unobtrusively with firearms as we can. Obviously we have to declare them, but a common theory is that we don't have to put neon signs on them. I know some guys who have big stickers on their gun cases like "Acme Irrigation Equipment" or "Smith's School of Music." Maybe that helps, maybe it doesn't. Publisher Ludo Wurfbain made an observation that "Oversize baggage seems most likely to go astray." Unfortunately, a case that will hold a full-length rifle is almost by definition "oversize." One answer is rifles that take down (or break down), reducing the length by half. A lot of duffel bags are now either made with integral hard cases for takedown guns or are capable of accommodating such cases.

All double rifles break down, so there is no need to carry them in a full-length case. The obvious challenge is that most bolt actions do not. But some do. Takedown repeaters are hardly new, but it seems their numbers are growing. Some gunsmiths specialize in interrupted-thread custom bolt actions that can be taken down. Both Winchester and Savage used to offer takedown lever actions as a factory option, and today Browning's BLR is available as a takedown model. Good examples of modern takedown bolt actions include both the Blaser and the Merkel KR-1, which are extremely modern actions, and more traditional models like the Dakota Traveler. While falling-block single actions are usually not takedown models, most break-open guns are, just like break-open shotguns and double rifles.

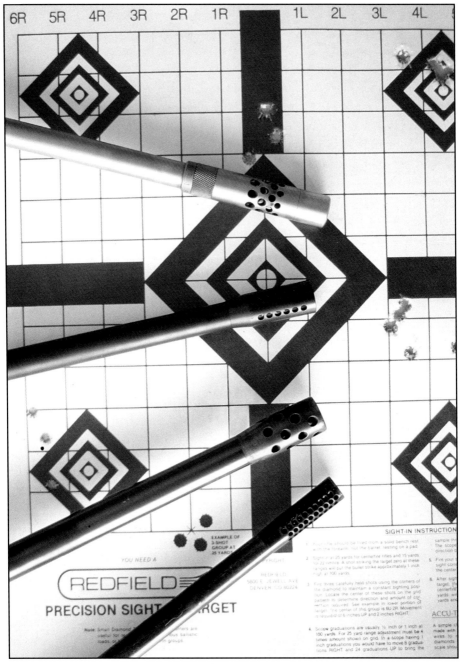

Muzzle brakes come in all sorts of different shapes, styles, and hold arrangements. All work wonderfully well in attenuating recoil—but all are much noisier than a plain barrel. Especially in Africa, where there are always trackers standing nearby, I consider a muzzle brake an absolute last resort in resolving intolerable recoil.

To be perfectly honest, I have rarely gone this route, but there is no reason not to. From a pure engineering standpoint, there is usually no significant weakening of the action. The adage that two-piece stocks are not as accurate as a solid piece of wood does hold some water, but I have seen too many stunningly accurate takedown rifles to put full credence in this. Not too long ago I had a Merkel KR-1 in .375 H&H, and it was probably one of the most accurate .375 rifles I have ever fired. A takedown .35 Whelen (on a Mauser action) built by Todd Hansen of now-defunct Norsman Arms was also incredibly accurate, and repeatable no matter how many times you took it apart. So a well-made takedown will certainly be adequate for any field shooting, and there are advantages to cutting down the size of your luggage. If you own a double rifle, you already have one takedown rifle, so it makes a lot of sense to mate it with a bolt action that will also break down. I have often said I'd like to have such a rifle, but to this day I have never owned one. Don't ask me why!

Part and parcel of a takedown rifle is that it will often accept different barrels chambered to different cartridges. A switch-barrel rifle is an extension of the takedown concept, but it is not the same thing. This is an extremely seductive idea. For instance, you could have a Blaser with one barrel in .300 Winchester Magnum and another in .375 H&H, and you'd have a complete safari battery. It's a great concept. But I'm not sure it's quite as good as it sounds on safari.

The Blaser R93 is another inter-changeable barrel rifle that has inter-changeable bolt heads so different barrels firing cartridges of radically different dimensions can be used on the same stock and action.

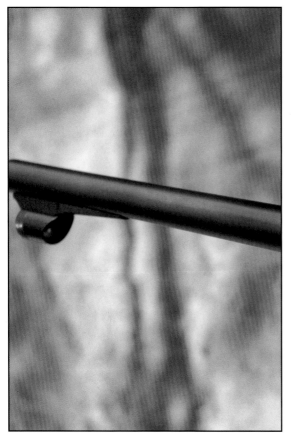

On any rifle with heavy recoil the barrel-mounted front sling swivel isn't just for looks. On a rifle of .375 or greater in power a forward sling swivel mounted on the stock can seriously injure your supporting hand if you don't hold the rifle just right.

Here's what I mean: One of the wonderful things about Africa is the almost endless variety. You never know what a given hunting day will hold. So how do you know which barrel to put on the rifle when you leave camp? Obviously you don't. There are some admirable purists among both professional hunters and their clients who will steadfastly hunt just one species at a time. Most will concentrate on key prizes, but might be willing to deviate from the game plan if and when an exceptional opportunity comes along. When that happens, you will use the rifle you are carrying, or perhaps the spare rifle carried by a tracker. Only rarely will there be time to switch barrels and make a perfect plan. Even the feasibility of this depends on the system. If the barrel carries its own scope, then it's just a matter of switching barrel-and-scope assembly (and making sure you have the right ammo). If the scope is on the receiver and you're only switching barrels, then you probably must re-zero as well. So I think in most cases planning to switch barrels during a hunt is folly.

As we will discuss in detail later in the book, if you take just one rifle on safari, it must be capable of handling any and all game you expect to hunt. In a switch-barrel, the barrel chosen should be similarly capable of handling anything you might encounter. There are two great reasons for taking two rifles. The first is so that you have available rifles and cartridges more ideally suited for a wider range of game. A switch-barrel could accomplish this, provided you understand that there will be

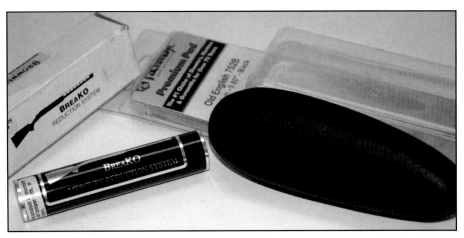

A first step to softening recoil is a good modern recoil pad of shock-absorbing polymer. If that doesn't work, consider adding more gun weight—including a mercury piston in the butt like the BreaKO recoil reducer. These things really work, but they do add about fourteen ounces each.

times when you have the wrong barrel attached. The other reason for two rifles, however, is so that you have a spare in the case of a mechanical failure or something catastrophic like a broken stock. With a switch-barrel you have two barrels, but only one action and buttstock, so you don't actually have any backup.

I do like the switch-barrel concept, but I see it as most valuable from season to season, not within a single hunt. For instance, you could have a switch-barrel rifle with a 7mm Remington Magnum barrel that you use in North America, and then you could put a .375 (or .416 Remington or .458) barrel on the same wonderfully familiar action and use it in Africa. I feel exactly the same way about double rifles with extra sets of barrels in different calibers.

Mitigating Recoil

Very few of us really like recoil, and all of us have limits to how much recoil we can withstand. There's another aspect to this: If you go beyond your personal threshold of sustainable recoil, either too far or too often, your shooting will suffer, perhaps forever. It's easy to acquire a flinch, but it's the very devil to get rid of it. So let's discuss briefly the various means to attenuate felt recoil. First, recoil is simply an instance of Newton's law of equal and opposite reaction. Its force depends primarily on weight and speed of projectile and gun weight. And everybody has his or her own level of recoil tolerance. A nine-pound .375 H&H developing something like 45 foot-pounds of recoil energy might be too much for some folks, while others (damn

A problem with any switch barrel is knowing which barrel to have in place on a given day! We went to northern Namibia expressly for a Damara dik-dik, so I put the .22 Hornet barrel in my Thompson/ Center, and it worked perfectly.

few others!) can handle the 100-plus foot-pounds of a .460 Weatherby Magnum or .577 Nitro Express with no problems.

Gun weight is very significant, and can go far toward reducing recoil energy and thus felt recoil. In fact, one of the easiest ways to reduce recoil is to simply add gun weight. The .458 Lott I cobbled together in the mid-1980s came out a bit too light and it was really punishing. Jack Lott himself hogged out a stock recess in the butt and several smaller recesses in the fore-end channel, and we filled them with molten lead, adding about two pounds. Sure, I had to carry that extra weight—but it made the difference between a shootable rifle and a rifle that was too much to handle.

Numerous makers are now offering mercury pistons as a more or less standard option. These actually have a two-fold benefit. First, they add weight. The "BreaKO" piston is the one I'm most familiar with, and a standard-size BreaKO weighs fully 14 ounces. Second, as recoil moves the rifle rearward, the mercury in the piston (mercury is very heavy) moves forward. It essentially retards rather than reduces the recoil impulse, spreading it out over several additional milliseconds. The effect is very noticeable. One thing to keep in mind: A mercury tube in the butt will alter the "feel" of the rifle, changing a perfectly balanced rifle to an odd "butt-heavy" feel.

Stock style is just as important as weight, perhaps more so. A broad comb and a broad butt really make a difference, not in recoil energy but in how it affects you by spreading it out over a larger area. A-Square's "Coil-Chek" stock is perhaps the ultimate in recoil-attenuating design. Very heavy, almost clubby, his rifles are indeed the softest-recoiling big guns I've ever fired. A-Square achieves this by building them heavy, with a broad comb, massive butt, and almost a target-style pistol grip that brings some of the recoil into the shooting hand and wrist.

These days, there are also a number of excellent add-on devices that really help. Pachmayr's Decelerator recoil pad is just one example of modern polymer recoil pads that soak up one heck of a lot more kick than traditional rubber. Just forget those handsome checkered-steel buttplates on hard-recoiling rifles; they look great but increase recoil and, worse, tend to slip off the shoulder at the worst moment.

Other options are muzzle brakes and muzzle-venting systems, of which many are available today. Best known of the venting systems is Larry Kelly's Mag-Na-Port venting. It greatly reduces muzzle jump, keeping the rifle off your face and thus significantly reducing felt recoil. Muzzle brakes are almost legion in the design and pattern of the vents. They all work, and the better ones genuinely reduce felt recoil by as much as 40 percent.

So why doesn't everyone use one? Well, one of the disadvantages of any muzzle brake or, to a lesser degree, barrel-venting system is a tremendous increase in muzzle blast. Now let's put that in the African context. One or two trackers walk ahead, then comes the PH, and then you, the client. You come to the edge of a little clearing, and the lead tracker spots a world-record crested gazork. He sets up the shooting sticks, and he and his colleague fade two steps to the right. The PH takes a look and nods and takes two steps to the left. You place your rifle over the sticks, shoot the gazork, and blow out the eardrums of your entire hunting team. Some professional hunters have enough bookings that they simply will not allow muzzle brakes in camp, and I do consider the devices a hazard in African hunting.

That said, they have their uses. Many brakes today can be removed. So you can use them while practicing, but take them off before you go hunting. If you do this, make sure you check zero; some rifles change zero when a brake is attached or detached, and some do not. Now, muzzle brakes work. If you use one, spend some time on that all-important sight-in day explaining the potential problem to both your PH and your trackers, and take along some extra earplugs. I have used them in Africa, but I have now lost so much hearing that I don't use them at all anymore. Kick is something we all must come to grips with, difficult though it is. None of us like to admit that our guns hurt us. It takes objective self-evaluation, but it is essential because if recoil is hurting you, it will hurt your shooting. If you feel you need a muzzle brake, then you might want to consider preferable alternatives, such as adding gun weight or going to a lighter cartridge you can handle without a brake.

Iron Sights

Chapter 23

The open express is the classic African sight, defined by a fairly shallow V rear sight, usually with a bead front. Unfortunately, problems are associated with such a sight. For starters, an open sight is optically the least efficient kind there is. Since big-bore rifles have come into vogue today, decent iron sights, including the "express" type, are much more readily available than was the case just a few years ago—but very few manufacturers offer open sights that are rugged and visible. Perhaps most important, using iron sights is nearly a lost art today.

Express sights are part of Africana, but shooting well with them takes a great deal of practice—and even for accomplished users they have limitations. Most of us are children of the scope era, and after years of using telescopic sights you do not suddenly wake up one morning and find yourself proficient with open sights. Since the eye cannot focus sharply on front sight, rear sight, and target all at once, something will be out of focus. If the sight is used correctly, it will be the rear sight that "fuzzes out," and the degree to which it's blurry depends on the age of the shooter, his visual acuity, and the spacing of the rear and front sights on the rifle.

All open sights function essentially the same way, although the variations are nearly endless. The classic American rear sight is a buckhorn or semi-buckhorn, and sights with U-shaped notches are also common. The broad, relatively shallow V, generally used in conjunction with a fairly bold front bead, is probably not as precise as many open sights, but its purpose is to allow you to get on target with instinctive speed. The object is for the eye to position the top of the front sight in the bottom of the rear sight, and then, maintaining this sight alignment, place the front sight on the desired aiming point.

To those of us who grew up with scopes, this is a complex operation. To those who grew up knowing nothing but iron sights, this is simply the way to shoot. Shooters accustomed to iron sights can indeed work wonders with them. The problem is that iron sights take serious practice to master, and there are some pitfalls.

The most important rule about iron sights is that we children of the scope era won't suddenly wake up and find ourselves proficient with them. If you even think you might have to use iron sights you simply must practice with them—a lot!

For one thing, consistently good shooting with iron sights depends heavily on stock fit; if the gun is cheeked ever so slightly differently from one shot to another, the sights may not align in the same way.

In poor light, iron sights are hard to see and the tendency is to see too much bead or post and shoot high. Likewise, if you shoot in haste it's easy to fail to get the bead all the way down into its notch or V. Iron sights work on the principle of the eye being able to center the front sight properly in the rear sight. Strong light from either side confuses this issue, shadowing one side of the front sight and creating a false center. This will throw the shot to one side or the other—and it takes very little aiming error to place the shot off by a matter of feet. A sight hood reduces this problem, but in very poor light it may make the front sight more difficult to see.

In spite of the difficulties involved, open sights have provided good service for many generations, and still do today. Although my first shooting was with U-notch open sights on a .22, I pretty much grew up with scopes. Only as an adult have I spent a lot of time really working with iron sights, and it's amazing what you can do with them.

My Westley Richards .318 had the 1920s version of precision long-range sights. The rear sight was one standing leaf and four folding leaves marked—somewhat

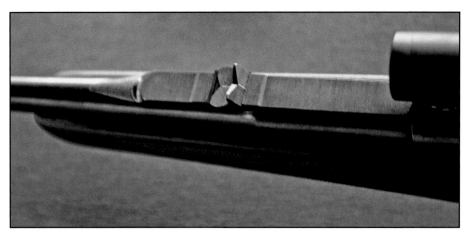

This is a typical British-style open V-express rear sight. It is not particularly precise, but it is about as fast and visible as an open sight can be—and also nearly indestructible.

optimistically, I suspect—for distances out to 500 yards. The front sight, protected by Westley Richards's patented folding sight protector, was a tiny silver bead. I had trouble seeing it in good light, let alone bad. This is another pitfall of the iron sight: As the front sight gets smaller, the aiming point becomes more precise and less of the target is obscured, but aiming becomes slower. I never had the nerve (or the eyesight) to try the 500-yard leaf on that rifle, but I did shoot targets and game out to 250 yards. It was difficult, but possible.

Even so, for most of us the iron sight is a short-range proposition. And the classic African express sight, with its broad, shallow-V rear and bold bead up front, is not well suited to precision work (which, for open sights, we'll define as anything beyond 100 yards). So most of us need to make a conscious compromise between precision and fast acquisition. For me the right-size front bead is ³⁄32-inch, a size that even in my mid-fifties I can still pick up very quickly. But I wouldn't pretend to tell anyone that I could use such a sight much beyond a hundred yards under the very best of conditions. Trust me, getting to that point has required frequent practice for many years!

All too many hunters, like me, are accustomed to hunting almost exclusively with scopes. When we get ready to go to Africa, we put together iron-sighted heavy rifles and go charging off without fully understanding the capabilities of the sights—and our capabilities and limitations with them. Practice is really the key, plus an understanding that it doesn't take much aiming error for a shot to go incredibly wild. I've personally missed whole buffalo inside of seventy-five yards by not hauling the front bead of my .470 all the way down into its notch. With a well-fitting

Front sights are always a tradeoff between precise aiming (small) and rapid acquisition (coarse). New wrinkles include fiber-optic front sights, which are amazingly visible.

rifle that comes up with sights aligned and on target, the open express sight makes snapshooting at very short range almost as fast as with a low-power scope. When precise aiming is required, it is unquestionably slower and a whole lot less precise.

However, the open sight does have its advantages. Properly built, it's extremely sturdy, almost damage-proof. In very close cover the low, snag-proof profile is a blessing, while a vine-snarling scope is a dangerous curse. And in the final instant of a determined charge, when the rifle must be pointed like a shotgun rather than aimed, a scope is just a nuisance.

Yet another benefit of open sights—in fact, for general use perhaps their greatest benefit—is that they're totally weatherproof. Modern scopes from reputable manufacturers almost never fog; it's a possible danger but very remote. On the other hand, surprisingly few raindrops on either lens of a scope will obscure vision sufficiently to make the scope useless until it's wiped clean. Scope caps of some type are a quick fix, but they take time to remove. Even peep sights, of which we'll speak in a bit, can be rendered useless by water droplets gathering in the aperture. They can be blown clear in an instant, but any time lost at all can be serious when the trophy of a lifetime presents a quick glimpse—not to mention the consequences of a waterlogged sight with dangerous game at close quarters. The open sight may be the least precise and most limited in range, but it's always ready.

A little-discussed problem with iron sights today is that relatively few are any damn good. I said that good open sights are incredibly rugged—but there are a lot more bad ones than good ones! It's a scope world, and iron sights—particularly on American production rifles—seem to be present strictly as ornamentation. I've

Really good open sights are rare on American factory rifles. This is the rear sight on the new Ruger M77 Hawkeye "African" rifle, a very simple and very strong sight.

had a couple of American iron sights and one European iron sight fall completely off rifles during recoil. If an iron sight is to be used, it must be absolutely sturdy and reliable. It should be bump-proof and knock-proof, and it must not have a folding leaf as the primary sight. Murphy being the optimist he is, if that sight can be accidentally folded down it will be, and at the worst possible moment. One of the changes to Ruger's new Hawkeye African and Alaskan models is a really good and very rugged standing rear sight mated to an equally good front sight with a bold bead, a much better arrangement than Ruger has supplied for many years. I'd like to think this is a good sign. All too many factory iron sights are obviously not intended for actual use!

Additional folding leaves of greater height for greater distances are all right, I suppose, but for most of us they're an anachronistic ornament. The primary iron sight simply must be a standing, solid affair. I find the British shallow V the simplest and fastest type of rear sight, though perhaps not the most precise. But whatever type you prefer, it should have some device to make it fast and easy to center the bead in the bottom of the V or notch. A silver, platinum, or gold centerline is traditional with English sights, and it works. My Dumoulin .416 Rigby had a gold triangle, apex pointing up, at the bottom of the V. It was extremely fast; the front sight was a gold bead, and the eye naturally nestled the bead against the apex of the triangle.

The best placement for the rear sight is a fair distance down the barrel. This somewhat reduces the problem the eye has focusing on rear sight, front sight, and target; the closer the rear sight is to the receiver, the more pronounced this problem is and the longer it will take to achieve proper sight alignment. Note that this is yet

The front sight on the Ruger Hawkeye is a very visible ³⁄₃₂-inch bead on a raised ramp. For my eyes this is the perfect size for a front sight, the proper compromise between visibility and precision.

another compromise. The longer your sight radius (distance between front sight and rear sight), the more precise your aim—but the more difficult it is for your eyes to resolve proper sight alignment. Most barrel-mounted iron sights are in a good position, perhaps five to six inches forward of the receiver. Eight inches would be better still, especially for shooters with older eyes. This reduced sight radius will magnify any slight aiming error, but an open sight simply must be fast, so the eye's limited ability to focus in different planes needs all the help it can get!

Quarter ribs are, in concept, sound bases for rear sights. They provide a flat, nonglare sighting plane (and of course, they look great on a rifle!). However, beware of quarter ribs that are primarily cosmetic. The best are milled along with the barrel blank, and they're tremendously expensive. The worst are poorly soldered or brazed onto the barrel, and may not be nearly as stable as they look. Quarter ribs that are there for looks may also be too short, placing the rear sight just three or four inches ahead of the receiver. That's great for a shooter in his twenties, but could be a serious handicap for a shooter in his fifties.

To my mind, the very best open sight is the simplest one of all. A solid (or solidly attached) quarter rib is great, but so is a standing leaf dovetailed into place and peened slightly to keep it there. Rear-sight bases that are screwed into the barrel are fine, too, but the more pieces that must be attached to other pieces, the weaker the sight is. I prefer a rear sight to be nonadjustable: installed with a very shallow V, drift-adjustable for windage, then filed to the desired zero by shooting, filing, and shooting.

Front sights, too, should be carefully scrutinized before being considered for serious use. All too many are fragile affairs, and some are impossible to see in poor

The New England aperture sight has different size apertures, which is another tradeoff: The smaller the aperture, the more precise; the larger the aperture, the more rapidly you can acquire the target. Elevation on this fixed sight is adjusted by using a higher or lower front sight.

light. The classic English sight is an ivory bead, but a brass bead works just as well for me, especially if it's filed just a bit so that it slants forward to prevent reflection. In Cameroon in 2006 one of the rifles I borrowed while mine was delayed was a "company rifle," a Winchester Model 70 in .416 Remington Magnum. The only modifications were a better and stronger express rear sight and a red, fiber-optic front sight. I was amazed at how well it worked. One morning I made a truly spectacular shot on a little Peters duiker, a small antelope, at well over a hundred yards. I doubt I'd have connected with a conventional bead front sight.

Sight hoods are certainly desirable. Not only do they guard against light distortion but they also protect the rather fragile front sight. However, I have seen few that would stay on during heavy recoil, and I've lost a whole bunch of them! A little quick gunsmithing can fix that, of course. To be honest, I've generally taken them off and thrown them away in disgust about the third time they kicked loose—that is, if I didn't lose them altogether. But if you use a naked front sight, you must pay attention to it. After any possible knock, take a hard look at it and make sure it's straight!

Although it's an iron sight, the aperture or peep sight is a vastly different animal from the traditional open sight. Technically, it's actually an optical sight in that the eye automatically centers the tip of the front sight in the center of the rear opening or aperture, where the light is the strongest. There is no focusing problem, so the aperture sight is both faster and more precise than the open sight. With a big opening (like, for instance, the opening that's left when the eyepiece of a typical

Like open sights, peep sights require practice—but they are much more precise than any open sight, and with practice generally faster.

aperture is removed and thrown away) and a bold front sight, the aperture sight is possibly the fastest close-range sight of all. This is more or less what is referred to as a "ghost ring" aperture: a very large rear opening that is almost subliminally visible. Of course, this is another compromise; the larger the aperture the faster it is to use—but the less precise!

If there's a problem with peep sights, it's that they're so rare today. In years gone by, flip-up peep sights were often affixed to the rear bridge of a bolt action, or even to the cocking piece of a Springfield or Mauser. If you read your Hemingway you will hear Papa extol the virtues of the peep sight on his beloved Griffin & Howe Springfield, and I have such a sight on my own Sedgely Springfield (and on some of my lever actions as well). But they are no longer common in Africa.

Michel Mantheakis of Miombo Safaris is one of just two professional hunters I have ever seen use an aperture sight. He has one on his Dakota in .450 Dakota Magnum, and he uses it well. Just before our safari in October 2006 his previous client wounded a lion. They finally spotted it in a donga, possibly three hundred yards away, and it was moving out again. Mantheakis held plenty high and got another bullet in it, and they were able to recover it. Hemingway himself couldn't have done better! Michel admitted that his front bead covered "acres of ground around the lion," but he made the shot. He probably wouldn't have even tried with an express sight! The other was David Lincoln in April 2008. Lincoln had a sturdy "peep" on his .416 Rigby.

Michel Mantheakis is among few PHs I know who prefer an aperture sight. His big Dakota, on the tripod behind us, has a rear sight with aperture protected by stout wings like the old 1917 Enfield, virtually a bulletproof sight.

A few custom makers will fit an auxiliary peep sight to the rear bridge of one of their rifles, but not many. George Sandmann of Empire Rifles is strong on aperture sights, either as auxiliary or primary, and I have used a couple of his rifles so fitted. For my eyes these sights were so much easier to use that this is the way I'm having Gun Creations sight my .404 Jeffery.

The peep sight removes most of the potential pitfalls of the open sight. You are much less likely to fail to center the front sight properly, and it's certainly faster. However, iron sights, even good ones, are often used as auxiliary sights on scope-sighted rifles. Failing a custom arrangement of some type, this is almost impossible with a peep sight.

On over-the-counter rifles, peep sights are extremely unusual today. Lyman still makes some good ones, and various options are available from Brownell's and New England Custom Guns. I've long been a fan of peep sights on tubular-magazine lever actions, and I've had no trouble shooting game with such rigs up to about two hundred yards. But it always depends on what you're used to, or how much you're willing to practice. I've used aperture-sighted military rifles enough to know that precision shooting is possible at very considerable distances. Using aperture sights, I qualified Marine Corps "Expert" throughout my career, shooting at ranges up to

This Empire rifle is fitted with a very clever aperture sight from New England Custom Guns that fits into the rear scope base.

five hundred yards. However, I can't say that a commercial aperture sight is any more rugged than today's scopes, which makes it questionable why one would pick an aperture over a low-power scope except in very limited applications.

Whether it's an aperture or open sight, the real weakness is quickly seen—or not seen—in poor light. The best English guns (and a few modern custom rifles) often have a second, fold-up sight bead, a huge ivory bead referred to as a "night sight," designed for short-range use in fading light. Such a device is some help, but not much. Long before it's too dark to shoot with a decent scope, front sights just disappear. And long before that, the sight picture becomes vague and serious aiming errors are likely.

Iron sights have their places. As I said earlier, there is really no utility to using a scope to hunt elephant. If you get your shot at twenty yards, it will do no harm, but you don't need it. If you get your shot within ten yards, which is common, the "tunnel vision" we tend to get when aiming through a scope could hinder you. Through a scope at very close range you may not see much more than a wall of gray, making it difficult to pick out the exact aiming point that you must find—and you may miss subtle movement, whether of your elephant or of other elephant that may be threatening your life while you're concentrating on your chosen target.

There are other applications, such as hound hunting in close cover and any forest hunting (especially in the rainy season), for which iron sights are superior. I often use them for hunting buffalo. This is partly because I like to use iron sights and partly because I have used them long enough that I have a fair amount of confidence. But please keep in mind that I have taken many buffalo. I will probably never see a better buffalo than I have already taken, and it doesn't bother me if I don't get a shot on a given day.

When we were filming *Boddington on Buffalo,* Andrew Dawson and I talked about the issue of scope sights versus iron for buffalo. Andrew carries his Express-sighted William Evans .470 every day, and he's delighted when a client brings a fine double. But he summed it up very nicely: "If a client has an open-sighted rifle, that's just fine with me, but I know we'll have to get close. The average client must understand that if he chooses to use iron sights, he may well be giving up 60 percent of his potential shots." That's a lot to give up, and since Murphy's Law applies, some of the best bulls you will see are almost certain to be among that 60 percent.

Iron sights have their place, and on an African medium or big bore they should certainly be present (and sighted-in) for auxiliary use if needed. With very few exceptions, irons will be the sight of choice for African professional hunters, and with a lifetime of practice these guys can use them. But for most of us, and for general hunting use, iron sights don't hold a candle to a scope. So let's turn next to scopes and mounts for African hunting.

Scopes and Mounts

Chapter 24

Telescopic sights have been with us for much more than a century, but as little as a generation ago scopes were a bit fragile and all too susceptible to fogging. Serious hunters avoided them like the plague. Those days are long since past. Today's high-quality telescopic sight is rugged and reliable, virtually impervious to the elements, and as shockproof as a Timex watch.

American hunters have long since accepted this truth and have almost universally embraced the scope sight. I can count on my fingers the open-sighted centerfire rifles I've seen in North American hunting camps in the past thirty years. Many have been peep-sighted lever actions that I've carried myself, but to those you can add a couple of lever-action .30-30 camp rifles, a couple of weathered Savage 99s, plus a couple of iron-sighted .338s and .375s carried as backup by Alaskan guides. And that's about it.

Yet in the same period I've seen a host of iron-sighted rifles in Africa. Most were in heavy calibers, and many were carried by hunting clients, not by professional hunters. If the scope sight has been accepted as the best possible sight for North American hunting, I fail to see why so many hunters turn to iron sights when they head for Africa. Except for shooting in a driving rainstorm, or for elephant hunting, I can think of almost no instance in which an open sight is preferable to a scope. Finn Aagaard, mentioned earlier as one of the few professional hunters I have known who was a dyed-in-the-lens scope user, summed it up nicely: "In order to achieve shot placement, I preferred clients to use a scope-sighted .375 H&H for dangerous game. Scopes should be not over 4X, and 2.5X is fine."

Within rather broad parameters, the caliber used is never as important as the placement of the shot. Shot placement with a scope will be more precise than shot placement with iron sights. End of discussion. You can't shoot better than you can see, and with a scope you just plain see better.

I will admit I like iron sights on a heavy rifle. This may be a bow to traditionalism, or simply a quirk of my nature. But I don't shoot better with them, nor do I shoot

There is no question that you can shoot better with a scope. This .375 Weatherby was the only rifle I had on this Cameroon hunt, and I needed it for small duikers and big buffalo. A 1.75–5X scope was a good compromise for everything.

faster. I just happen to like them for certain limited applications. And I would be the first to tell any hunting client that iron sights will get you into trouble more quickly than anything I know of.

For one thing, they are extremely limited in range. It would be nice if all buffalo could be shot at forty yards, but you'd be surprised at how often a seventy-five- or one-hundred-yard shot is called for. Many of us just can't handle such a shot with open sights. If we can, our shot placement will not be as precise as with a scope. As I said in the last chapter, professional hunter Andrew Dawson actually put a number on it for me. He believes the client who chooses iron sights for buffalo gives up fully sixty percent of his potential shots.

The scope's tremendous ability to gather light is another significant advantage. For use on lion or leopard over bait, an open-sighted rifle is not only hopeless, it's downright dangerous. My old friend and filming partner Tim Danklef was responsible for doing the research for a book he, Dave Fulson, and I coauthored on leopard hunting. After a few weeks of digging through old books, he was perplexed. There was very little early mention of leopard hunting, and most leopard taken seemed to be incidental or by chance encounter. After a few more weeks he reached the conclusion that baiting for

It was getting very dark when Donna shot this lovely leopard, shown with PH Dirk de Bod and his friend, Jack the Jack Russell terrier. She had a 2.5–8X scope on her .30-06, and it must have been bright enough because her leopard was dead under the tree.

leopard was, though not unheard of, most unusual until after World War II. If you think about it, that's when telescopic sights came into common use!

Leopard are almost always taken at last light; the target is small and shot placement must be perfect. Baited lion are usually taken at dawn. Either way, a good, light-gathering scope is essential. If the lion is tracked up, once again a scoped rifle is the best choice. When you close with the lion, you will often need to make out tawny hide against golden grass, or a piece of shoulder through heavy thorn. The scope sight will give you the best chance for a good, undisturbed shot before you get too close. With dog hunting there's room for argument, but I vote for the scope because, while you might get a shot much closer than you'd like, there's at least an even chance you will get a clear, clean opportunity that is too far to handle with iron sights. And then you have a missed opportunity, a missed shot, or a wounded cat.

If you're after a wounded cat, it's a toss-up. In the case of a charge, a perfectly balanced open-sighted rifle might be the best equipment—but only if the shooter is perfectly comfortable with iron sights. And if we're honest with ourselves, few of us are. The thing to remember is that charges only happen when somebody screws up. The chances for such a screw-up are greatly reduced with a good scope sight—and that's a fact. Even during the follow-up of a wounded animal, a charge is fairly

In 2007 Trijicon added a cross-hair reticle with tritium-lighted center to their AccuPoint line. Just as I was finishing this book I had a chance to try several prototypes and I liked them. What the tritium means is that you have a lighted reticle without the batteries.

unlikely provided everyone goes very carefully on full alert and takes full advantage of any opportunity for a shot before a charge occurs. Those opportunities may be fleeting, almost always in shadowed cover, and are invariably best exploited with a scope-sighted rifle.

In addition to the optical factors that make a scope so much easier for the human eye to use, there's another aspect of scope use—a rarely mentioned aspect—that might be the most important of all the scope's attributes. Much African hunting is conducted in thornbush of varying density. Brush eats up a bullet like you can't believe. With a scope you have a much better opportunity for picking a clear path for your bullet.

There was a time when I wouldn't have believed unseen sticks and vines would turn a heavy bullet, but it's happened to me too often to question. The first time it happened I was hunting buffalo along Zimbabwe's Bubye River. We closed in to about sixty yards in thick thorn, and I let drive with a 500-grain .470 solid at a buffalo's shoulder. The animal dropped as if pole-axed, and although I was delighted, I recognized that such a reaction to a shoulder shot was most unusual.

The thing is, it wasn't a shoulder shot. The bullet had centered the neck, about three feet to the left of my aiming point. And it had entered sideways, leaving the

I used this Leupold VX-7 in 2.5–10X, the latest generation of Leupold's great riflescopes, to take this Grant gazelle. Scopes like this are not compact and are costly, but the optics are truly awesome.

exact profile of a .470 solid. We found a freshly bullet-clipped sapling about halfway between the dead buffalo and where I'd knelt to fire. I would have sworn the path was clear, and it was a good thing the bullet didn't deflect in the opposite direction.

In 1988 Paddy Curtis and I closed in on a big buffalo herd in Tanzania's Selous Reserve. We picked out a decent bull, and when he turned broadside I fired a very careful shot from my .470. The herd ran, of course, but there was no sound of the bullet hitting, no reaction, and, on inspection, no blood. I asked Paddy what had happened, and he shrugged. "I dunno. I saw a leaf fall."

We walked the ground, and there was a pencil-like vine neatly severed by a bullet just a third of the way toward the buffalo from where I'd fired. It doesn't take much. Later during that same trip I had a 400-grain .416 Rigby softpoint fail to make it through light brush that screened a zebra. That time it was obvious—a branch fell, but before it hit the ground the bullet had raised a huge cloud of dust at the stallion's feet.

Now, that zebra was partially obscured and I knew it. I might have gotten a bullet through and I might not have, but I doubt that a scope would have helped. With both of those buffalo, though, a low-power scope might have helped me pick a clear path. But that isn't a certainty. Again in the Selous Reserve, in 2000, I hit a

Some African hunting is done at night, especially for the smaller night predators. A bright scope is essential, and to that I added a SureFire torch with a pressure switch taped to the fore-end.

branch with a scoped .375 Remington Ultra Mag and missed a buffalo clean. I've been lucky; these deflected bullets haven't given me wounded buffalo to chase. But it could have happened, and that isn't my idea of fun.

The choice of scopes for African hunting is really quite simple. In North America extremely powerful variables are the rage today, but they really have no place in African hunting. In many areas there are no opportunities for genuine long-range shooting. Even where the country might allow it, African professional hunters have seen so much terrible shooting (by clients like you and me) that they are downright paranoid about allowing long shots. So any low-power scope of good quality will do the trick. For use on a light or medium rifle in open country, a fixed 4X will probably do everything that needs to be done. That said, it is a variable-power world, and for smaller antelope in bigger country a bit more magnification is wonderful. The 3–9X scope is the most popular scope in the world today, and it is just as ideal in Africa as everywhere else. Somewhat smaller scopes like 1.5–6X or 2–7X are also good choices, and there is very little real utility for a scope greater than 3.5–10X. Once in a while, for a longish shot on a small antelope, the highest power setting is nice to have. But you simply must have a low-range setting that is low enough to allow fast shooting at very close range.

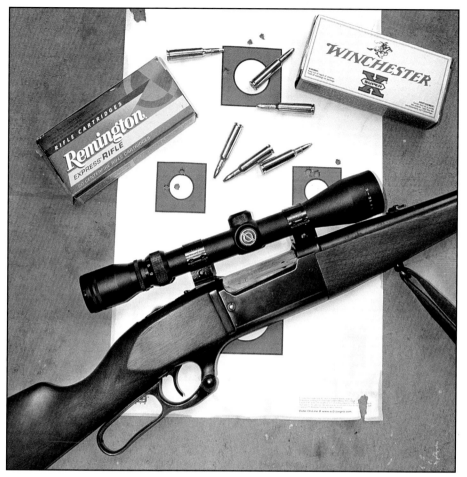

The good old Weaver scope mounting system is not exactly beautiful, but it is incredibly rugged, still a very sound system.

Whatever range of power you have available, it is extremely important to remember to leave the scope on a moderate setting—no more than 4X in close cover, no more than 6X in open country.

On a .375 (or a .416 intended for general purposes) I prefer a low-range variable: 1.75–5X, 1–4X, possibly a 1.5–6X. I have used a number of these scopes from a variety of makers, from premium-quality brands like Schmidt & Bender, Swarovski, Zeiss, and Leupold's top-of-the-line LPS and the new VX-7, to moderately priced scopes from Bushnell/Bausch & Lomb, Burris, and Nikon. It's only fair to say, however, that the most popular dangerous-game scope in Africa is Leupold's light, compact 1.75–5X Vari-X III. If you put a scope on a big bore, whether double or

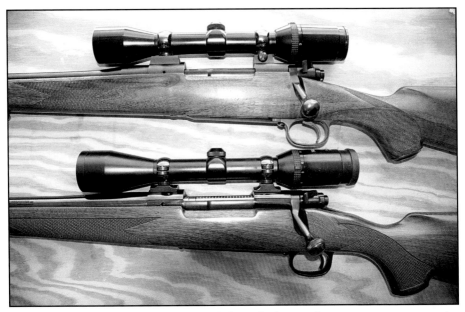

Top, the old Redfield-type mount, now made by multiple manufacturers, is a great system that incorporates windage on the mount. However, in my experience it tops out at maybe the recoil level of the .375 H&H. Leupold's dual-dovetail mount, below, is very sleek and considerably stronger.

magazine, then you want the lowest-range variable you can find. But keep in mind that recoil is a great enemy of the riflescope. It takes a very good scope to withstand the pounding of a .458 Lott or, worse, something like a .500 Jeffery.

Much more important than magnification is the need for absolute reliability in both the scope and its mounts. I have my favorites, but I won't pick favorites here. I've seen failures by any scope you can think of, including my favorites. I will say you get what you pay for, and your chances of failure are less with a top-quality scope. The best course is to look at several brands and buy the scope that seems to suit you best.

One thing you must pay special attention to is eye relief. This is the distance your eye must be from the scope to achieve a proper sight picture. It becomes very critical on rifles above, say, .270 Winchester in recoil levels: Too little eye relief, and your scope will hit you between the eyes every time you pull the trigger. It's painful, messy, and the fastest way I know to develop a flinch. Of course, if you're talking about really serious recoil, you need lots of eye relief.

Exactly how you mount the scope also has bearing. I had a Leupold 1.75–5X on a .375 Weatherby that I took to Cameroon. That scope has as much eye relief as any scope on the market, and it's a fine choice for the heaviest-recoiling rifles. But you must mount it far enough forward so that you're using all the eye relief. On

There is more than one way to skin a cat. Red-dot sights are popular in many shooting disciplines, and they work. This BSA sight on a shotgun would be very fast for stopping a charging leopard—and I know a couple of guys my age who have put such sights on double rifles.

this particular rifle the mount arrangement didn't allow that, and the scope was just a wee bit farther back than necessary. It hit me a couple of times off the bench, so I should have been warned. But I honestly thought I could stay away from it in field positions. On safari it hit me almost every time I squeezed the trigger. I got cut three times before finally, toward the end of the safari, pulling the scope off in disgust. At that point the only major license I had left was a buffalo, and we had been very close to most of the buffalo we had passed.

Murphy lies in wait for the unwary. Within hours of pulling off the scope and checking the iron sights, we got on the kind of buffalo I was looking for, and the shot was quartering away slightly at eighty yards. With the scope I'm reasonably certain I would have killed him. With the iron sights I hit a bit forward, and we tracked a wounded buffalo. We got him, but that unpleasant exercise was not necessary.

Very few scopes, including some of the most expensive ones, offer enough eye relief for rifles with heavy recoil. In this particular arena American scopes tend to be a bit better than some of the best European scopes—but the newer European models are getting better all the time. It doesn't make much sense for me to tell you how much eye relief you need; it depends on your shooting style and the amount of recoil you're contending with. But I suggest you try to buy a scope that appears

The classic form of the double rifle is with iron sights only, but a double benefits from a scope just like a bolt action. This Krieghoff has the European-type swing-off detachable, an expensive mount that works very well.

to have a clear picture a minimum of three inches from your eye. Then mount it as far forward as you can get it and still achieve that clear picture. Finally, no matter how much it hurts, get the rifle out to the range and shoot the hell out of it from all positions. If your scope is a "lemon," that fact will generally make itself known during the first fifty shots. If the scope hits you once, it's possible you aren't holding it properly. Wipe off the blood, grit your teeth, and try it again. If it hits you again, get rid of the scope and get one with more eye relief.

I have a bad habit of "crawling" the stock, and I often get nailed right between the eyes by riflescopes. That's usually my fault, and I always feel stupid when it happens. But over the years I've had scopes that simply didn't have enough eye relief. Two were .300 magnums, both topped with expensive scopes that were optically magnificent but just didn't have enough eye relief. I wound up replacing those marvelous scopes with scopes that were optically inferior but allowed me to use the rifles without bleeding to death. Another horror story involves a .340 Weatherby that, because I was short on time, I didn't sight in for myself (for shame!). This one had a scope with a neoprene ring around the "cutting edges." As the late Bob Milek said, "It doesn't cut you—it just bludgeons you to death." This one did. Every time I squeezed the trigger, the scope cracked me squarely between the eyes. I had it on a moose hunt, and it was cold—Lord, did that hurt. Again, it wasn't the rifle's fault—but I got rid of the whole works as soon as I got back.

It should be obvious that such ridiculous problems are easily avoided by spending time on the range before the hunt. If the scope touches you at all, there's something

A Rigby .416 I owned in the nineties had a very good custom detachable mount that was absolutely repeatable. Mounts like this are frightfully expensive and perhaps overkill—but on a hard-recoiling rifle there is no such thing as a mount too sturdy.

wrong. It could be in your shooting style, but it's just as likely to be lack of eye relief. Whichever it is, it must be taken care of before your safari.

Scope mounts are the subject of much debate, and the question most often asked is whether they should be of the detachable type. Personally, I like to have iron sights on scoped rifles, especially rifles of medium bore and larger. However, I view those iron sights as auxiliary sights, to be used only in the event of scope failure. I do have detachable mounts on several rifles, but the only time I have detached a scope in favor of iron sights was on that one safari in Cameroon.

Still, there is little point in having iron sights unless you have detachable mounts so you can use the irons if you want to . . . or need to, as in when a scope fails. Twenty years ago I wrote that I didn't trust detachable mounts because, at that time, I had experienced a lot of trouble with them. Times have changed. Detachable mounts are much more popular today, and there are many good ones from many makers. The most universally respected, I think, are the Talley mounts, but other good detachables include Warne, several models from Leupold, and the German EAW and Bock mounts. The strongest is probably the European claw mount, which is absolutely rigid but fantastically expensive. The same could be said for the many one-of-a-kind detachable mounts made by a number of American custom gunmakers.

Again, recoil is the enemy. Almost all detachables will hold up well at the .375 H&H's level of recoil. The .416s and .458s need stronger mounts, and very, very few mounts have a chance of holding up on a .460 Weatherby or .505 Gibbs. In all cases it is essential that the mount be assembled absolutely correctly, with all parts fitting

Nice waterbuck. Nice scope cuts, too! This scope, a Leupold 1.75–5X, had plenty of eye relief, but the scope mount didn't allow the scope to be far enough forward. It cut the hell out of me multiple times. Eye relief is essential, and it's equally essential that the mounts allow the scope to be far enough forward so you can stay away from it.

properly. Even then, this business of taking scopes off and putting them back on willy-nilly is, as far as I'm concerned, an invitation to disaster. If a mount is detachable, that's nice—but if one of my rifles is scoped, then the scope is the primary sight and it is going to come off only if there's a problem. If the mount isn't detachable, then I make sure my kit contains whatever screwdrivers are needed to remove the scope.

As far as nondetachable mounts go, there are many wonderful systems. The old Redfield mount has the advantage of windage adjustment on the mount. I have this type of mount on perhaps the majority of my "deer/sheep/goat" rifles, but I don't think it's strong enough for heavy-recoiling rifles. Leupold's "dual dovetail" mount is incredibly strong and also sleek. More important than the mount itself is that it be properly installed—tight screws Loctited into place, and surfaces that fit properly (with additional work if needed).

Iron sights are a perfectly viable alternative if something goes wrong with a scope—but perhaps a better hedge against disaster is a spare scope, already set in rings and, if possible, more or less sighted in. Hunters accustomed to scopes will find iron sights a damned poor substitute if something happens to their one and only scope.

Almost standard today as a detachable mount is the Talley system. I have used them on many rifles. So long as they are assembled correctly they are strong and repeatable up to almost any sensible level of recoil.

I usually have auxiliary iron sights on a rifle, and I often carry a spare scope—especially if I have just one rifle and no spare. The likelihood of using such fallback substitutions is extremely remote. I have had scopes "crap out," it's true, but usually on the range and almost never on a hunt. But then I spend a lot of time on the range. If you've had the rifle on the range several times and it's holding its zero, your chances of scope trouble are extremely remote.

Scope reticles are largely a matter of personal preference. The "plex"-type cross hairs, with thick outer wires and a thin center, are the most popular today. This type is my favorite as well; I find it very fast in low light, yet the thin inner wires allow precision when you need it. In close cover or on moving game, a bold dot with cross wires is nice, but for general use I prefer the "plex." There are now several "dangerous-game reticles" that tend to draw your eye toward the center. They are fast at the close ranges for which they were designed—but at longer range will tend to obscure more of the target. As with so many things, this is a compromise.

Illuminated reticles have become much more popular in recent years, with almost every major manufacturer offering them. I tend to like to keep things simple, so I have used them very little. However, on a baited leopard hunt in 2006 I used an illuminated-reticle Swarovski scope. The leopard came at the very last possible shooting light. When it gets dark you lose the reticle first, especially against a dark animal. I have to admit that lighted reticle was wonderful, and it made what could have been a very difficult shot quite fast and simple. A lighted reticle is good for any dark animal in poor light or heavy shadow, so it wouldn't be all bad for buffalo, either!

During the last couple of seasons I've done a lot of hunting with the Trijicon AccuPoint scope, which is an altogether different concept. Trijicon makes the ACOG scopes used by our military; the AccuPoint takes the same concept of a tritium aiming point fed by fiber optic, the level of brightness adjusted by a sunshade on the ocular bell. The reticle itself is just a post, with the tip either red or amber tritium. Honestly, after a lifetime of using cross hairs, it took some time to get used to the post. I'm used to it now, and that glowing post is the fastest reticle I have ever used. I used it on leopard with dogs, buffalo, and on a wide variety of plains game. It is not a long-range reticle; at distance the post starts to subtend too much of the animal, and holdover, if required, is almost impossible to judge. But with practice it is superb out to, say, 250 yards, which certainly covers the vast majority of all shooting in Africa. I would like to see the tritium center (which requires no batteries) mated with a cross hair, and I'm sure this version will exist by the time these lines are read.

There are other options as well. A couple of friends of mine (in my age group, darn it), Joe Greenfield and his buddy, PH Joey O'Bannon, have admitted their eyes can no longer handle iron sights. The Swedish Aimpoint system uses a centered red dot, and it has proven effective in virtually all shooting disciplines for fast, short-range use. Those two guys have fitted their doubles with Aimpoints, including a gorgeous vintage Rigby double. It looks sacrilegiously weird, but it works! Bushnell's Holo-Sight is another option. If you can't use iron sights and you don't want to use a scope, there are options out there.

Shotguns on Safari

Chapter 25

The late Bob Brister, longtime shooting editor of *Field & Stream,* was one of America's greatest authorities on shotgunning. He was also the finest wingshot I've ever seen in action. Several years ago, on a sort of bet, he killed a Cape buffalo very dead with one Brenneke slug from his Perazzi bird gun. No, a 12-gauge isn't an ideal buffalo gun—but the lethality of the shotgun cannot be argued.

A good thing that is, too, because in a couple of out-of-the-way African countries, firearms importation restrictions are such that hunting is "shotgun-only." Morocco is primarily a bird-hunting destination, but there are good numbers of wild boar and they can be hunted only with shotguns. The West African nation of Liberia, currently closed, has been open off and on and is primarily known for its incredible variety of forest duikers. In dense forest the primary hunting technique is to call the little animals, much as we would call foxes or coyotes. Under such conditions the borrowed, buckshot-loaded shotguns with which hunters are supplied are nearly ideal. However, Liberia also holds a few bongo and some dwarf forest buffalo. I'm told that carefully smuggled Brenneke slugs will do the trick, though I'm not certain I want to see for myself!

Slug-loaded shotguns are used to harvest hundreds of thousands of white-tailed deer annually—and not a few black bears and wild hogs. In brushy country a well-sighted slug gun would be absolutely deadly for most African game. Except for special situations such as Liberia, though, I can't see any reason to use a shotgun for the general run of African game. On the other hand, it strikes me that the shotgun has four primary and very real uses on the average safari: Bird shooting, taking small antelope at close range, keeping on hand in case a dangerous snake is encountered, and following up wounded leopard.

The most obvious is for bird shooting. We'll discuss that topic last and start with the shotgun's use on wounded leopard. This is a traditional use for a shotgun, the old formula being a double-barreled shotgun loaded with SSG, the English

There's nothing like an hour or two at a water hole when the sand grouse are coming in—and also nothing harder to hit in my entire wingshooting experience!

Some very specialized hunts are best done with shotguns. Adrian Ford, left, has a special pack of terriers that hunt only blue duiker. That's outfitter Larry McGillewie behind me, and I used his over/ under shotgun, a wise choice for this little antelope.

equivalent of 00 buck. A few hunters prefer that combination even for wounded lion. Wally Johnson Sr. was quoted as saying that a hunter with a buckshot-loaded shotgun is as safe from a charging lion "as a baby in its crib."

The key to buckshot use is that the animal must be ever so close. At twenty-five yards, the distance from which a charge might well originate, a full load of buckshot may or may not do much damage. At the muzzle, the result will be certain and devastating. Many top professionals still swear by the shotgun, but I had one dismal experience and don't want another. In 1992 I wounded a leopard and we took the spoor at dawn, hoping to find him dead. A false charge at midmorning dispelled that notion. At midday the track led us into a narrow triangle of tall grass, nurtured by runoff from a big monolith.

I had the shotgun, Russ Broom's over/under loaded with good American 00 buckshot, so I went into the grass with old Jack, a Bushman tracker. The leopard was lying in an unseen erosion ditch, fortunately steep-sided on my side and gently sloping on the other. The cat came out under my feet, roaring like thunder, but because of the steep bank he had to take a couple of outbound leaps before he could

Johan Calitz had a beautiful pair of Westley Richards 20-gauge guns that we used in the Okavango to shoot some francolin. Don't count on the "camp shotguns" looking like these!

turn. I hit him twice with buckshot, from about eleven yards and again at seven. I saw the charges hit, understood I had done nothing, and had just time to realize the gun was empty and this was going to hurt. Then Russ, standing by to my right, stopped the cat cold with his double .500. I concede that if I had waited until the last instant the buckshot would surely have worked—but I guess I lack the cool, because I thought that cat was plenty close. No more buckshot on leopard for me!

A few years ago Robin Hurt, a great professional hunter, was terribly mauled by a leopard. He always carries a double .500, but on that day, to follow the wounded cat, he traded it for a 12-gauge. He maintains that if he'd kept his rifle the cat wouldn't have touched him. Maybe, maybe not; not all charges can be stopped. But no more buckshot on leopard for Robin, either.

Still, the shotgun is a traditional choice and will be used (though never again by me!). A double-trigger, double-barreled 12-gauge, relatively short in the barrels and with open chokes, would be my choice for this kind of work. If possible, I'd want it in 3" magnum, 3½" better still—every bit of shot you can get into the shell is to the good. I would personally not care to trust an automatic; I shoot birds with them, but birds don't have sharp teeth and long claws, and I have yet to see an automatic that never jammed.

Professional hunter Russ Broom and his dad, Geoff Broom, do use automatics for backup on leopard. Theirs are probably the ultimate charge-stoppers, a pair of

Some PHs prefer slugs to buckshot when going after wounded cats. Given a choice, I know I would!

20-inch-barreled Ithaca Mag 10 Roadblockers, the police version of the company's now-discontinued 10-gauge automatic. Using 3½" shells stuffed with 000 buckshot (.36-caliber pellets), both Russ and Geoff have stopped enough leopard to have total confidence. As for me, I just don't have that kind of faith in an automatic. Others do. Alain Lefol keeps a pair of Benelli autoloaders in camp, and of course the Benelli is legendary for its reliability.

If I were to use a repeating shotgun, I would opt for a slide action. In experienced hands the pump is just as fast as an automatic (actually faster!), and I have more faith in its reliability. There is also a subtle aiming advantage. When the slide is worked to chamber the second and subsequent rounds, the final action pushes the slide forward to close the breech on a fresh shell. That pushing action is toward the target, and I believe this motion of the supporting arm creates a natural pointing action that does not occur with any other action type. Of course, as an American I'm very familiar and comfortable with the all-American pump gun. Most people from other countries are not. And, as noted in a previous chapter, semiautos are not allowed in a number of African countries, and South Africa currently excludes slide actions as well.

Whatever shotgun is chosen, it simply must fit well and point naturally. A charging cat must be hit, and hit squarely, to be stopped. At the close ranges you're dealing with—feet, not yards—there's very little pattern spread, and no margin for

In 1992 I wounded this leopard and went into long grass after him with a buckshot-loaded 12-gauge. Never again! After the shotgun was empty and the cat seemed unaffected, Russ Broom saved my tail with his double .500.

error. In fact, you're actually delivering a ball of shot, at most a few inches across. In terms of pattern, at such distances the shot charge from a shotgun offers little advantage over a single rifle bullet. That isn't the reason the shotgun is preferred.

Rather, it's because the shotgun's fast-handling abilities and lack of sights are better suited to the instinctive shooting essential to stopping a close-range charge. And because the combined impact and instantaneous energy transfer of nine or a dozen soft lead pellets do more damage to a soft-skinned animal like a cat than a single rifle bullet possibly can. But only if it's close. The greatest danger in stopping a charge is to fire too quickly, and that's especially true with buckshot. Penetration is sketchy. That leopard I failed to stop had the majority of pellets from both charges just under the skin, with no evidence that any had actually penetrated! Most leopard charges are launched at very short range, so this isn't as big a problem as with lion. However, if buckshot is to be used on a lion charge, the shot simply must be held until the very last second or it will not have the needed effect.

Incidentally, said effect of close-range buckshot is quite unbelievable. A friend of mine had a client wound a leopard, and he followed it up with SSG. The cat came

In Central Africa shotguns are often used when calling duikers. This is a red-flanked duiker that came to the call. He was taken with several pellets of No. 4 buckshot from about a dozen yards.

from very close in, and my buddy hammered it right off the muzzle. His client was most upset over the condition of the pelt, while my buddy was much more relieved over the intact condition of his own hide. It's actually quite a simple matter to avoid pelt damage from buckshot—just don't wound a cat in the first place!

Aside from stopping things that bite and claw, a shotgun is also nearly ideal for the very small antelopes in close cover. It would be useless for game such as steenbok, Vaal rhebok, oribi, and klipspringer; you'd never get close enough. But for hunting forest duikers and, in much thornbush, dik-dik and grysbok, a shotgun makes sense. In heavy brush, hunting such tiny animals differs little from hunting cottontails or jack rabbits, and a shotgun gives a slight edge. In recent years I've used the shotgun for blue duiker in South Africa's coastal thorn, and also for small night predators like the African wild cat. One advantage is that the shotgun will do far less damage than a high-velocity centerfire rifle. Personally, though, I'd stay away from the larger buckshot for such things, instead using No. 4 buck or BB. The obvious fallacy is that many of the smaller animals are taken by chance encounter, and you will use whatever happens to be in your hands. But when hunting these

A couple of years after we shot a cobra with it, I used the same Benelli to shoot some waterfowl on the edge of Lake Chad. A short-barreled camp gun like this is great for snakes and OK for duikers, but it made a terrible goose gun!

small creatures specifically, whether calling duiker in close cover or hunting South Africa's blue duiker with terriers, the shotgun is a fine choice.

I'm terrified of snakes—especially some of the snakes found in Africa. In the bush the best thing to do with snakes is leave them alone, but in camp a shotgun seems to me the best means for dealing with the odd mamba or cobra that comes calling. In Central African Republic we used one of Alain Lefol's short-barreled Benelli autoloaders to deal with a huge forest cobra.

A couple of years later I used the same Benelli to hunt waterfowl in the marshes near Lake Chad. Which brings us to bird shooting, and an interesting point: There is usually a shotgun in camp if you want to do some bird shooting. (Enough shells to get serious about it is another issue altogether.) However, the "camp shotgun" may not be your idea of the perfect bird gun! Alain's short-barreled Benelli, for instance, was perfect for snakes and not bad for dumping duiker, but it wasn't much of a duck gun! The Roadblocker 10-gauges used by Geoff and Russ Broom are marvelous for stopping a wounded leopard, but not my cup of tea for francolin or guinea fowl!

Bird shooting either for sport or for the pot is far and away the most common use for the shotgun on safari—and in the right place at the right time, African bird hunting is unequaled. Several species of dove and wild pigeon abound, as do the snipelike sand grouse. Tasty francolin come in several varieties, ranging from quail-size to nearly as large as a hen pheasant. And then there are the guinea fowl, both crested and vulturine—strong runners, fast flyers, and a great addition to camp table fare. Waterfowl, too, are abundant in some areas—spurwing and Egyptian geese and a wide variety of ducks.

In some areas at certain times of the year, game birds are few and far between. But in most safari areas it's no great trick to have an afternoon of fine bird shooting anytime you feel like it. The problem is always time, and that's why I'm ambivalent about taking a shotgun on safari. The bird shooting is there—but I don't go to Africa to hunt birds. The use you will get out of a shotgun in exchange for the hassle of dragging it 20,000 miles really depends on you—on how serious a bird hunter you are, and how serious and difficult the primary objectives of your safari may be.

I have taken a shotgun on several safaris and hardly had time to use it. On the other hand, I've not taken one on other trips and wished desperately that I had one with me. Such has been the case every time I've been in Masailand, truly a bird paradise. I have never taken a shotgun there and probably wouldn't have had much time to use it . . . but that depends on how serious you take your big-game hunting as opposed to your bird shooting. Masailand is a bird paradise, abounding with francolin of at least three different species, and both crested and vulturine guinea fowl. The one time I would have had time to indulge, there was a shotgun in camp but only a double handful of shells. The last couple of years the parts of Namibia I've been hunting have had excellent hatches of both francolin and guinea fowl, and I've done a little shotgunning with borrowed guns. Botswana, too, especially the Okavango, is a bird hunter's mecca.

The issue is whether you should take your own shotgun or not. In most hunting camps there will be a well-worn shotgun of some persuasion, but shells are likely to be scarce. Last year in Botswana, after we got our elephant, Johan Calitz took us up to the Okavango. One morning he put on a "driven shoot" for francolin, sharing his beautiful pair of Westley Richards 20-bores with plenty of shells—but don't count on that happening in every camp!

Here's the way I recommend playing the shotgun angle: Evaluate your interests and desires. If you're a serious bird hunter, and if you're willing to sacrifice some hunting time for some shotgunning, by all means take your favorite bird gun along to Africa. I would especially recommend this for longer safaris and for one-hunter/one-professional-hunter ("1x1") arrangements, in which time tends to be less critical (and is not shared). After a major animal is taken, it's nice to rest for a day, and there's no better way to rest than by a water hole with a shotgun in hand!

If you don't much care about bird shooting one way or the other, don't bother dragging a shotgun all the way to Africa. You won't use it unless you make yourself use it. I do recommend, however, that anyone going on safari take at least one box of shotgun shells, if not two, provided the gun permit and importation regulations in your destination country will allow it. Make them 12-gauge, 2¾", high-base No. 6 shot. This versatile load will do for almost anything. If you're leopard hunting, whether you take a shotgun or not, make sure you stuff at least one five-round packet of fresh buckshot loads in your kit. You'll hope nobody needs them, but take them just in case.

If you plan on doing some serious bird shooting, you can't possibly bring along enough shells. So you'll need to arrange beforehand for your outfitter to have a supply on hand. In South Africa or Namibia you won't have any problem finding shotgun shells, but elsewhere in Africa expect them to be magnificently expensive and probably damn hard to come by. And if you don't make very specific arrangements ahead of time, expect them to be nonexistent.

In all the time I've spent in Africa, I must confess that I've done relatively little bird shooting. It always seems more important to spend one last evening looking for a buffalo, kudu, or whatever. But that's a very personal choice, and for hunters who really want to enjoy Africa, a bit of bird shooting adds memorable spice to any safari.

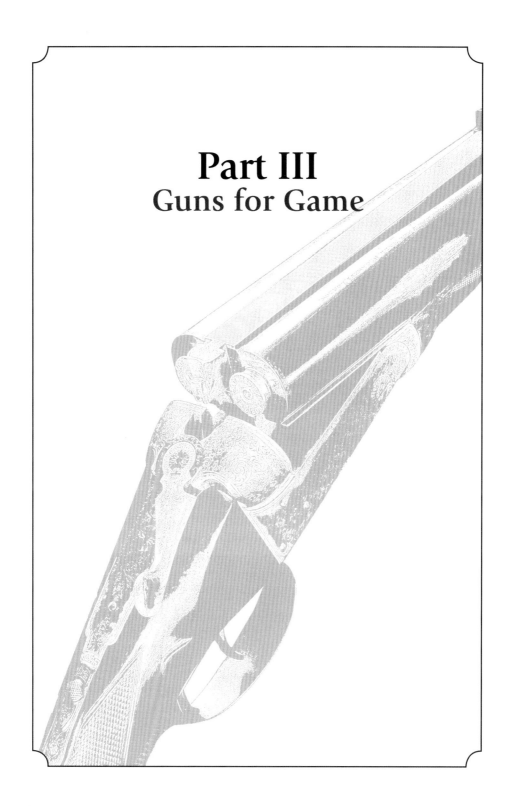

Part III
Guns for Game

Light to Medium Plains Game

Chapter 26

We have discussed in some detail a great many cartridges well suited to African hunting and have taken a hard look at rifles chambered for these cartridges. Now it should be possible to match these tools more specifically with their appropriate jobs by examining the rifles and their cartridges that are best suited for hunting various types of game.

It's important to understand there are no absolutes in this discussion, and what works extremely well for one person may be a disaster for someone else. The best rifle is the one that gives its user the most confidence and maximizes his (or her!) shooting ability. By definition, if the hunter gets his game without wounding, with no horror shows, then the rifle and its cartridge were adequate—at least in that person's hands. But if the hunter does not get his game, was it the fault of the rifle or the shooter?

There is a broad range of rifle/cartridge suitability for any type of African game. An unusually skilled marksman may use a cartridge much smaller than the generally accepted norm—and might do very well. Someone who is a very good hunter, and thus able to consistently close on his game, may use a cartridge much larger and more limited in range than is common for a given type of game. Regardless of generally accepted parameters and any "expert" advice, it is always all about shot placement and bullet performance—the cartridge chosen and the rifle it is fired in are not nearly as important as the person's ability to use it. So I would never question an experienced hunter's choice. On the other hand, few of us are widely experienced with African game. For that matter, considering today's short seasons and low bag limits, few of us are particularly experienced in shooting game of any type.

Genuine experts may read this book, and I hope they enjoy it. I also hope they don't find grievous fault with its ideas and opinions on African rifles and cartridges. But whether they agree or not, they've already made up their minds—and so long as their choices work, they're dead right. On the other hand, the hunter contemplating a first or second safari, or even the old hand planning a trip to an unfamiliar part

Within sensible parameters, hunting Africa's smaller plains game isn't about power—but it could be about accuracy. The oribi is an open-country animal that often requires a longish shot. A .270 Winchester was just fine.

of Africa, may find some real value in this discussion—while bearing in mind that the suggestions are general guidelines, not absolutes. Nor, I hasten to add, are these guidelines mine alone. To a degree they're based on the experience of seventy-five African hunts. But to a larger degree they're based on correspondence and campfire discussion with a great many professional hunters—the real experts. These ideas are not new, nor should they be; smokeless cartridges have been used for well over a century in Africa. Today's hunter is not only well served by paying attention to that century of experience—he's foolish if he ignores it.

Let's begin by defining what I call "light to medium" plains game. This is the huge class of antelope and wild swine that run the gamut from ten-pound dik-dik up to four hundred-pound hartebeest and waterbuck. It's a vast group, and so diverse that it would be ridiculous to lump them together as a single category that can be perfectly matched to a single small selection of rifles and cartridges. However, as many as a dozen of these animals might be hunted on the same safari—and opposite ends of the spectrum might be hunted on the same day. In Masailand or Ethiopia, for instance, you might scour dense cover for lesser kudu in the mornings and evenings—and spend the midday hours out on the plains looking for an exceptional gazelle. In the Okavango Delta or Zambia's Bangweulu, you might comb the reeds for sitatunga—but wind up taking a four-hundred-yard shot at a lechwe. In South Africa you might hunt bushbuck in dense cover in the morning and springbok on open plains in the evening.

Even if we exclude the really large plains species and all the dangerous game from this discussion, the game within this "light to medium" group varies so much in size, habit, and preferred habitat that it would be almost impossible to come up with one rifle/cartridge combination that would be truly suitable. And yet that is what we must try to do, for it is almost never practical to have on safari more than one rifle that will be used for this type of game.

Now, from safari to safari, that single rifle may not be the same one; the plains-game rifle chosen for the Kalahari or Masailand may not be the best choice for the thornbush of Zambia or Zimbabwe. But on one safari, regardless of how many areas are to be visited, any single rifle must cover a very broad range of game that will be taken under widely varying conditions.

It would be a lot of fun to come up with the ideal rifle/cartridge combination for each specific African species. For instance, for Vaal rhebok, spooky little antelope that inhabit South Africa's highest mountains, the lightest, fastest, flattest-shooting, most accurate rig I could come up with would be perfect. A light-barreled .22-250 firing bullets of about 60 grains would be nice, and I'd probably top it with a 10X varmint scope—provided the wind didn't blow. But since those mountains are often windy, maybe I'd want something like a very fast 6.5mm that would carry a bit better.

And then there are springbok and the gazelles. Power isn't important, but, depending on the terrain, you want plenty of reach. Something ranging from .243 or 6mm Remington up to .240 Weatherby, .25-06, or .257 Weatherby would be close to ideal. You'd want plenty of scope, but not too much since mirage and heat waves could be a problem. A variable with a powerful upper end would be good, perhaps a 3.5–10X or even a 4–12X.

The bushbuck is one of my favorite antelope to hunt, and I've been fortunate to hunt a half-dozen different varieties. All are found in heavy cover, and the purest and most enjoyable form of hunting them is still-hunting. They're tough for so small an antelope—and they can be downright dangerous. Great fighters, they've ripped open many a hunter who approached too quickly. I can't imagine a better bushbuck rifle than a lever action in .35 Remington, .358 Winchester, or even .444 Marlin, topped with a bright, quick, low-power scope. That said, I have never hunted bushbuck with such a rifle, because it is impossible to take rifles on safari that are perfect for just one of the many smaller antelopes that might be encountered.

Tom Fruechtel is ready to take this lesser kudu while PH Andy Wilkinson judges the horns. An awful lot of shots at African antelope are much like this, not especially far, but often with a time factor: Pretty soon this animal is going to run.

The same sort of rifle would be ideal for bushpig, but if dogs were being used you might want to leave the scope off. The warthog, on the other hand, is more often seen at a greater distance—and he must be hit hard and anchored lest he make it down a burrow before expiring. (Considering the crawly things that might also inhabit pig holes, you wouldn't catch me digging around in one!) Something fast, flat, and hard-hitting is good warthog medicine; you could make a good case for a .270.

Then there are the heavyweights of this group: the hartebeest, waterbuck, and lechwe. All of these are likely to be shot in open country at long range; a scoped .300 magnum would be hard to beat. And yet in the same size category you have the cover-loving nyala. I can't imagine anything much better than a .35 Whelen.

Since you can't take a half-dozen rifles on safari—and even if you could, chances are you'd have the wrong one in your hands most of the time—the name of the game must be versatility. And to obtain that versatility some compromises must be made. Your plains-game rifle will almost certainly be needlessly powerful for the smaller antelopes, and its sighting equipment probably won't be perfect for everything.

However, it must be powerful enough for the largest game you will use it on, and it must shoot flat enough to handle any terrain you think you might encounter.

Later on we'll discuss building specific African batteries. Here, though, it's important to understand that the less broad your spectrum of game and/or terrain, the more you can indulge in specialized rifles. For instance, if you're planning a typical hunt in Namibia, you know all your hunting will be in relatively open thornbush, desert, or mountains. In other words, your shots will be longer than they would be in Zimbabwe's heavier bush. On most Namibian safaris you will not be hunting any dangerous game, so your battery need not include charge-stoppers. For such a hunt it would be wonderful to take an accurate, scope-sighted .243, 6mm, or .257 Roberts. A rifle like that would be great fun to use for springbok, impala, duiker, and blesbok. But such a rifle would be marginal at best for the full spectrum of plains game; you would still need a rifle that could handle hartebeest plus kudu, gemsbok, zebra, and perhaps eland. The rifle suited for such game would duplicate the .243 in that it would also have to be accurate, flat-shooting, and scope-sighted. But obviously it would be much more powerful, perhaps a .300 Winchester or Weatherby, 8mm Remington Magnum, or .338.

There's no harm in such duplication—but in safari batteries that must contain specialized rifles for the dangerous game, you generally can't afford the luxury. Dangerous-game rifles, by their nature, must be somewhat specialized, while the plains-game rifle must be highly versatile, covering the broadest spectrum of game possible.

The rifle chosen for this work might be asked to punch a bushpig at ten yards, or a tiny steenbok at a hundred, or a hartebeest at three hundred. The first chore requires little more than some measure of raw power, but the second dictates accuracy, while the third calls for flat-shooting capabilities.

Depending on the cover, a lever action in .308 or 7mm-08 might be a good choice. Certainly a modern single shot would do the job. The general preference for this kind of work, however, is a bolt action. The accuracy is there, as is the bolt action's reliability and strength. And, of course, it's available in a host of suitable chamberings.

Choice of caliber is important, but there are many good ones. Choice of scope is perhaps just as important. Again, versatility is the key. This is a rifle that might be asked to reach out a long way—but it also might need to handle a point-blank chance encounter in heavy cover. A skilled marksman will do just fine with a garden-variety fixed 4X scope. However, this rifle really screams for a top-quality variable. Power ranges like 2–7X, 3–9X, and 3.5–10X are just right. The power ring should be kept low, no higher than 4X, most of the time—but if you need to

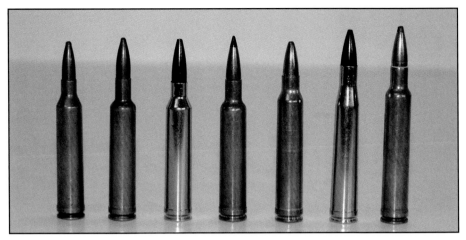

Left to right: .264 Winchester Magnum, .270 Weatherby Magnum, 7mm Remington Magnum, 7mm Weatherby Magnum, .300 Winchester Magnum, .300 H&H Magnum, .300 Weatherby Magnum. You don't have to have a magnum to hunt even the largest "medium" plains game, but in open country a flat shooting cartridge may offer the added confidence needed on longer shots. Any of these are fine choices.

make a longish shot at a smallish antelope, the needed magnification is there when you want it. And it helps.

I just flipped an old notebook open to 1977, the year I hunted in Kenya. On that trip I used two rifles. The larger, a .375, was to be used for lion, buffalo, and eland. The light rifle was used for everything else, and there was a tremendous variety of everything else. My notebook tells me that with that light rifle I shot a running warthog at 10 yards, a dik-dik at 100 yards, a steenbok at 200 yards, a waterbuck at 275 yards, a gerenuk at 300 yards, a duiker at 40 yards, a bushbuck at 60, a hartebeest at 400, and so forth.

The rifle was topped with a 3–9X Redfield scope (times were different then; this was the first scope I'd ever owned with such a large range of magnification!), and you can bet it was cranked up all the way on the longer shots—and on the smaller antelopes. The rifle was a plain out-of-the-box Ruger Model 77, but it seemed to be a magic wand—if I waved it in the general direction of an animal, he fell over dead. The cartridge was hardly anything unusual or hot-rock: the good old .30-06, with handloaded 180-grain Nosler Partition bullets.

The .30-06 has not been my only choice for a light safari rifle, but it has remained my most consistent. It isn't the flattest-shooting cartridge, but it offers the wonderful intangible of near-perfect bullet performance. This is because of its relatively mild velocity, and because most .30-caliber hunting bullets are designed for optimum performance at .30-06 velocities.

Light to Medium Plains Game

Over the years I have used many "light" rifles on safari. In consistently open country, a good light rifle could be the almost defunct .264 Winchester Magnum (or another fast 6.5mm). When I was a kid I thought the .264 was a magic stick. I haven't used one for years, but if you study the charts, the long-for-caliber, aerodynamic .264-inch bullets really do have a lot to offer (as the old-timers and modern 1,000-yard shooters understand). Serengeti Rifles built me a .264 on a P. O. Ackley left-hand Santa Barbara Mauser action, and I expect it will see use in Africa, if not exactly on the Serengeti. Or a .270 (Winchester, Winchester Short Magnum, or Weatherby Magnum). Or almost any of the 7mms, from the 7x57 up through the 7mm magnums; or a .308 or .30-06. The .300 magnums, in my view, form the upper end of the "light rifle" arena. They are, all of them, wonderfully versatile and tremendously effective; with proper bullets they will go well beyond what I think of as light to medium plains game.

The "fast .30s," the .30-caliber magnums, have their place and are possibly the most versatile of all plains-game cartridges. I have personally used several, from the great old .300 H&H through the .300 Winchester Magnum and on up to the .300 Weatherby Magnum and .300 Remington Ultra Mag. Unfortunately, the magnum .30s have a fair amount of recoil and darn few people shoot them really well. No .300 magnum substitutes for good marksmanship. If you shoot a .300 well, then it will serve you well. If you don't, and there are all too many of us who don't, forget it. You'll do much better with a .270, .30-06, or 7mm of some persuasion.

All of these are good, and as I've grown older and gained more experience—not only in hunting but also in observing others hunting—my appreciation for these cartridges has continued to grow. There are places where you really need a fast cartridge with some punch, and we will discuss them. But for most African hunting you need a cartridge you can shoot well that will deliver consistently good bullet performance. For me, absent special circumstances, the .30-06 has remained the light rifle I keep coming back to. It has enough range for most African situations, is

Left to right: .30-06, .25-06, .270 Winchester, .280 Remington, .35 Whelen. Depending on the game and the country, any of these cartridges based on the parent .30-06 case might be ideal for light to medium plains game.

The hartebeest is at the upper end of "medium" plains game . . . and perhaps the 7mm-08 is a bit on the light side. But not if you know the rifle and have confidence in it. That's PH Corne' Kruger on Erindi, with my daughter Brittany.

easy to shoot well, and there are few things you cannot take with a 180-grain bullet from this cartridge.

I had it right in 1977, I had it right in between, and I have had it right the last few seasons when the .30-06 has been my primary light rifle. However, I must say that I am by nature a heavy-rifle guy, and I have learned a lot from several female hunters. The ladies like performance, but they aren't crazy about recoil. As mentioned in an earlier chapter, my old friend Debra Bradbury has taken all game short of buffalo with her whacked-out old Model 70 in .270 Winchester. She knows it, and it works for her.

My elder daughter, Brittany, has reinforced the lesson. She started with a .260 Remington, and then we got her a Kimber 7mm-08. Like the old 7x57 (another of my favorites), the 7mm-08 has the moderate velocity that yields consistently perfect bullet performance. As a very new hunter she worked wonders with that rifle on her first safari. I tried to step her up a bit, but she does some modeling and one scope cut was enough. She loves her 7mm-08, end of sentence. It loves her, too. On our 2007 safari she was shooting better than ever, and everything fell to that deadly (in her hands) little rifle. Sure, it has limitations, but so does she. She doesn't

Shooting smaller antelopes is more about accuracy than power. Regardless of what rifle you're shooting, when you start your hunt don't overlook the essential step of verifying your zero!

take long shots, and when she shoots, things fall down. Shot placement and bullet performance transcend paper ballistics.

Now, Donna is a different kettle of fish. Although also a relatively new hunter, she is not particularly recoil-sensitive, but gun fit is critical. She loves that wonderful 7x57 that Todd Ramirez built me, but, for our television series, "sponsor guns" are essential, and we can only take so many guns to Africa. So we tried sharing a left-hand Ruger M77 in my first love, the .30-06. Turns out the stock was a bit too long for Donna, so we trimmed it just a bit. I can still use it just fine, and now it fits her perfectly. She works wonders with it.

The .30-06 is not exactly the flattest-shooting cartridge out there, but since she didn't waste her youth reading gun magazines, Donna doesn't worry about such things. With no ingrained bad habits, she is dramatically steady and, for reasons I can't fathom (but are probably due to lack of the macho gene), frighteningly calm when shooting at game. We were stalking a springbok in Namibia with our friend Dirk de Bod when we just plain ran out of cover. The ram, a great ram, was bedded with a bunch of ewes, and they started to get up and move out. We were out of options, and the rangefinder said 317 yards. This is a long shot on a small antelope like a springbok, with anything. It is a very long shot with a .30-06.

A super blesbok, taken with PH Styger Joubert in northwestern South Africa. There's a point: The blesbok is an extremely common animal, but nobody will see many of this quality. Make sure your rifle is accurate and zeroed properly so you can capitalize on opportunities.

The rifle had a Leupold scope with the Boone and Crockett reticle with additional hash marks below the horizontal wire. We had never practiced together using these stadia lines (because I didn't think Donna was quite ready for that), but I happened to know that the first stadia line was "on" at 300 yards. The grass was too high for anything steadier, so she was on the sticks. The ram got up last and, walking and stopping, moved slowly to the right. We had a most amusing conversation.

"OK, you see the stadia line right under the cross hair?"

"The what?"

"That little half line right below the intersection."

"Oh, that. Yes, I see it."

"All right, when the ram stops, put that little half line exactly where his black side stripe stops on his shoulder."

"OK."

Two seconds later the ram stopped, the rifle went off, and the distant springbok dropped long before we heard the bullet hit. Now, this proves nothing, really, but illustrates several things (beyond a great truth I have learned: Women listen better than men!): First, if you know how to use it, the .30-06 shoots plenty flat enough for almost all African hunting. Second, whether it's you or the coach, understanding

I used a .375 Ruger with 270-grain bullets to take this fallow deer in the mountains of South Africa's Cape province. Nope, I didn't need that much power—but at 250 yards I needed to know the rifle would do the job. It did.

where to hold and holding there are more important than the trajectory of the cartridge you are using. Third, and by far the most important, regardless of the rifle and cartridge you shoot, confidence combined with bullet performance is what puts trophies in the salt.

Of course, the .30-06 is a bit more gun than is really essential for my "light to medium" classification. One could argue, with justification, that such a shot would have been easier with a fast .25, 6.5, .270, or even 7mm—with less recoil. However, a problem with my "light to medium" classification is that African plains game goes on up from springbok and doesn't stop with waterbuck-size animals. It keeps on going, up through tough game such as oryx, sable, and wildebeest to 600-pound kudu and roan, on up to 800-pound zebra, all the way to eland bulls weighing a ton. Properly chosen, the light rifle can handle some of these chores, and perfectly used (with the right bullets), it can probably handle them all—but it is not ideal. So let's turn now to rifles and cartridges for the largest plains game.

Large Plains Game

Chapter 27

Dangerous game gets, if you'll pardon the pun, the lion's share of the glory and the press. And, as I've said, the smaller plains species comprise the greatest percentage of the bag. Nevertheless, the large plains species are serious business. A few animals in this group—specifically sable, roan, and oryx—can be dangerous when wounded, but only if the hunter makes a foolish and too-hasty approach. The seriousness isn't from potential danger, as it is with the Big Nasties. Instead, it comes from two other considerations.

First, this group contains some of Africa's most desirable and most difficult-to-obtain prizes. Included are the ultra-rarities like bongo, Derby eland, and mountain nyala, each of which may be the sole objective of a lengthy and expensive safari. Also included are prizes less rare but every bit as desirable for their sheer beauty and majesty: greater kudu, sable, roan, common eland, oryx. Members of this latter group may or may not be a safari's single goal, but in areas where they occur they will invariably be very high on the list. And then there are fairly common animals that are big and strong, like wildebeest and zebra.

These animals vary considerably in toughness: Pound for pound, members of the oryx clan are amazing for their ability to take punishment. Wildebeest are, in my view, the toughest of all, while greater kudu, though larger, are relatively soft for their size. That said, the only African animal I have lost in many years is a greater kudu, hit fairly and knocked down with plenty of gun. He got up again while we were running to him, and that was the last we ever saw of him. I think he would have been my biggest kudu, but I don't know that for certain, any more than I know exactly what I did wrong. I hit him with what is actually a big gun for his tribe, a 286-grain bullet from a 9.3x74R, but obviously I didn't hit him where I intended. As always, shot placement is more important than what the shot is made with.

Animals like the kudu, roan, sable, and the great prizes are big enough to be most unforgiving of poor shot placement or unsatisfactory bullet performance—

It isn't necessary to define "large plains game" precisely. You'll know it when you see it! I think the zebra, at maybe 800 pounds, is definitely there . . . and look how this massive eland bull dwarfs the zebra! That is "large plains game." (Photo by Dirk de Bod)

and all are uncommon enough and/or sufficiently difficult to hunt that multiple opportunities on one safari are rare. In other words, you can expect just one opportunity at a really good trophy of any member of this group. Both you and your rifle and cartridge must be up to the task.

Also included in this group are some animals that, while hardly rarities, are some of Africa's toughest, which is a second important consideration in selecting appropriate rifles and cartridges. I'm thinking particularly of wildebeest and zebra, but it occurs to me that giraffe should properly be included as well. The toughness of the wildebeest is legendary; it seems they have a "slow" nervous system, and while they're hardly bulletproof, they do seem impervious to shock. Zebra are often underrated both as a game animal and in terms of difficulty to put down—except by those who have experience with them, of course. Professional hunters seem to lament over running gun battles with wounded zebra more than with any other species. Why this should be I'm not altogether certain. The zebra is big, strong, and very tough, and that's a partial answer. I think there's also something in the natural camouflage of the stripes that confuses the aiming point. In

Giraffe are rarely taken as trophies, but they occasionally must be culled. This is a massive bull taken on Lemco in southern Zimbabwe, and this is one "large plains animal" that should be taken with a very big gun. I used my .416 Taylor.

any case, shot placement and bullet performance must be near perfect on Africa's striped horses.

The giraffe is hardly a hunting trophy, but they are overpopulated in some areas and must be harvested. The skin is beautiful, and a standing mount, though not hard to obtain, is a marvelous accent to a trophy room—a tall trophy room! And the very size of the giraffe makes it a wonderful meat source that should be utilized. It goes without saying that on such a huge beast, shot placement is critical. Attempting to cleanly drop one of these seemingly gentle giants with a body shot is quite a trick! Also, getting close enough for proper shot placement on an animal that can look down through the bush and see you clearly is an interesting little trick! Head shots, though tricky, are certain when done correctly, but for a body shot you'd better get it right (higher and farther forward than you might think) and you'd better use a big gun!

We can leave the giraffe out of the normal safari mixed bag, but zebra and wildebeest will often be included. Unlike hunting the more glamorous of the large plains species, it's usually not terribly difficult to get a shot at an acceptable specimen of either wildebeest or zebra. But when you get that shot, you'd best do it right or you may wind up with a long, drawn-out mess on your hands. Remember that wounded animals will almost always be counted on your license, and even if they aren't, you're obligated to follow as long as any chance remains for recovery. I lost nearly two days of hunting one time when a partner wounded a wildebeest. We eventually got the animal, but timing on a safari can be critical. Perhaps the time spent on that wildebeest is what prevented me from getting a leopard that trip—or my partner from getting a roan.

You'll note that so far I've been speaking of bullet placement and performance rather than caliber. There is such a thing as an inadequate caliber, to be sure. But regardless of caliber, the bullet simply must be properly aimed so as to reach the vitals—and it must be constructed well enough so it can reach those vitals.

We are fortunate to have wonderful bullets available to us today. The over-the-counter stuff is damned good, as are component bullets from major manufacturers. Even if you don't handload, the "super bullets" we have like Barnes Triple Shock and Swift A-Frame are available in loaded ammo from one manufacturer or another. If you're bound and determined to use relatively light rifles on animals in this "large plains game" class, you need the world's best bullets. They are so good they can, in effect, take a cartridge a step up into another power class.

Even with the best bullets in the world, there are limits. The various 6mms and .25s simply should not be used on the likes of wildebeest, zebra, oryx, and sable. But

Donna, Brittany, and I with Donna's huge blue wildebeest. In my opinion the wildebeest is Africa's toughest antelope, and the odd thing here was that Donna's shoulder shot with her .30-06 dropped him in his tracks. As Joe Bishop always tells me, "Boddington, it's all about shot placement."

with carefully selected bullets and a cool marksman willing to wait for a good shot, cartridges such as the 6.5s, .270s, the 7mms, and the nonbelted .30s can do a great job. I've had one-shot kills with the 7x57 and .30-06 on zebra, wildebeest, oryx, and sable with no problems whatever, and likewise with the 7mm Remington Magnum. And I've had the same species require multiple hits from a .375. No two animals are alike in their reaction to receiving a bullet—but if that bullet is properly directed and makes its way to the vitals, the eventual outcome is certain.

My own experience aside, this is yet another lesson I have learned from the ladies in my life. Women listen and tend to be calm. They may not like recoil, but they tend to do more with less. I have seen the diminutive .260 Remington drop wildebeest like the hammer of Thor, and what daughter Brittany has done with her beloved Kimber 7mm-08 continues to amaze me. She has confidence in it (and it alone at this writing) and has used it to effectively take large game such as kudu, oryx, wildebeest, and zebra with no problems. She even used it to take a very fine eland bull with a tiny 140-grain Nosler Partition. Donna, on the other hand, is equally happy with her .30-06, which is a lot more gun than a .260 or 7x57. She has used it to flatten, really flatten, kudu, wildebeest, zebra, and also a big eland bull. Again, shot placement is far more important than what the shot is placed with!

Still and all, when we get into this class of very large and/or very tough plains game, I prefer a bit more power than the .30-06/7mm magnum and lighter cartridges

Brittany used her 7mm-08 to take this gemsbok from about 250 yards, a very long shot for a big, tough antelope like this. Once again, it's all about shot placement and bullet performance, rarely about raw power.

can deliver—provided one can shoot a bigger gun equally as well. I should say, too, that I'm not overly sensitive to recoil, and I'm a trophy hunter. I believe in shot placement, but proper shot placement can come from almost any angle if the cartridge, the shooter, and the bullet are up to the task. If I have an opportunity to take a very fine specimen of the animal I'm hunting, I want to be able to take the shot even if the angle is less than optimal.

I think this is a reasonable mind-set, but power alone isn't enough; you must be certain of your bullet as well. In the Central African Republic in 1994, on my second attempt, I finally got a shot at a Derby eland. He was quartering away. This is far from ideal on eland, but it wasn't all that bad an angle, not even close to a "Texas heart shot." I was shooting a .375 with the then-experimental reissue of the Nosler Partition in that caliber. I took the shot . . . and we got the eland six hours later, at the end of the longest day in my hunting career. I had the line, but the bullet expanded prematurely and failed to penetrate. That bullet was toughened up thereafter and there is now nothing wrong with the large-caliber Partitions—but at that time it wasn't quite right. Sometimes it's part of my job to test bullets, but that isn't your

Remington Ultra Mag with a 200-grain Swift A-Frame on this beautiful southern roan, taken in Namibia.

Regardless of size, the mountain nyala is "large plains game" because of the importance of the shot. Again, though, confidence is critical. I wouldn't use a 7mm on this animal, but Joe Bishop did because that's what he has the most confidence with. Obviously it worked!

job. Rely only on slugs that are known to work, and even then understand that any bullet made can fail. Better to hold the shot unless you are certain!

The various .300 magnums are excellent tools for the larger antelopes, especially with the great bullets we have today. The old .300 H&H remains popular in Africa, but the Winchester, Weatherby, Remington Ultra Mag, the short magnums, and Lazzeroni's fast .30s will do just as well or better with today's great bullets. The last time I took a .300 Weatherby to Africa, I loaded 200-grain Nosler semispitzers as fast as I could push them, and it was an absolutely devastating rifle. In recent years I have gone back to the .300 H&H, and in Africa I have used 200-grain Sierra bullets. Yes, they're soft—but extra bullet weight makes up for construction, and few bullets are as accurate. But even with a rifle of unquestioned adequacy and a bullet of known properties, you never know for sure what's going to happen when you squeeze the trigger.

Once I got a chance shot at a roan in the hills far above the Luangwa Valley. A herd crossed in front of us, running hard, then stopped on a burned-off slope 200 yards away. We picked out the bull, and I dropped into a sitting position and fired as quickly as I could. Absolutely nothing happened. The animal had been quartering away, and now he took one small step and quartered to me. I shot again with the same hold, and he broke into a heart-shot death run, folding up within sixty yards. Funny thing is, the wound channels from the two 200-grain Noslers crisscrossed in the heart.

In spite of that roan's refusal to succumb to the inevitable, the .300 magnums with good, reasonably heavy-for-caliber bullets (180 grains at a minimum) are magnificent choices for the large plains game—especially in open country. Nobody could argue rationally against their use, except possibly on eland.

Ideally, though, I prefer to go up another step to the .325 Winchester Short Magnum, 8mm Remington Magnum, 8x68S, and the fast .33s such as the .338 Winchester Magnum, .340 Weatherby Magnum, and the .338 Remington Ultra Mag. The flat-shooting capabilities are so close to the .300s as to be indistinguishable, and yet the added frontal area and greater bullet weight combine to offer a very real advantage in killing power—if not in energy on paper.

For the American hunter, I think the .33s are the most sensible choices, since the bullet selection is easily the best. That said, my personal pet is the long-unloved 8mm Remington Magnum. It shoots flatter than the .338 Winchester Magnum, but doesn't kick nearly as bad as the .340 Weatherby and its ilk. I have used my super-accurate 8mm Remington Magnum in Zambia, Zimbabwe, South Africa, and Namibia, and it was the only rifle I took on my second Ethiopian safari in 2000 and to Chad in 2001. Honestly, the 8mm Remington Magnum was a concession to mortality; I had a great .340 Weatherby Magnum that I used on several safaris, but it was the only rifle I took on my first Ethiopian hunt in 1993. I shot it almost every day, and ultimately decided it was more gun than I was comfortable with! But all of the cartridges mentioned, plus several others of their ilk, will perform perfectly on Africa's largest plains game—and offer a marvelous level of versatility that a lighter rifle cannot deliver.

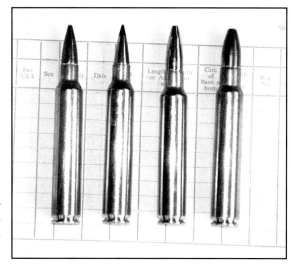

These are the long-cased Remington Ultra Mags, left to right: 7mm, .300, .338, and .375 RUM. Depending on your preferences, with the right bullet any of them would be just fine for "large plains game."

I think the waterbuck falls into "large plains game." I used my Remington M700 with a 200-grain Sierra for this big bull.

My longest shot on African game—a mountain reedbuck at well over four hundred yards—was made with a .338 Winchester Magnum. A bit of luck was involved there—bad luck for the reedbuck and good luck for me. Six years later, in the same mountain range with a different rifle also chambered to .338, I made what I think was my best shot on African game—a single well-considered shot at a tiny Vaal rhebok at something over three hundred yards. Neither of those animals, obviously, is part of our "large plains game" group. But on the two trips where those shots were made, the same .338s accounted for wildebeest, gemsbok, sable, zebra, and kudu. And another hunter borrowed one of the .338s to use on a lion—which it handled very nicely.

I have personally never shot an eland with a .338, but I have seen them shot very satisfactorily with that caliber, and I have "bracketed" the .338 by taking eland with both my 8mm Remington Magnum and a .340 Weatherby Magnum. In some areas you may have a minimum legal caliber of .375, but with good bullets, all of these "mediums" will surely handle eland. There is no question that in a pinch, the cartridges in this class could do the trick nicely on buffalo. Come to think of it, one of the few absolute knockdown one-shot kills I have made on buffalo was done with a .338 Remington Ultra Mag and a 250-grain Swift A-Frame. However, eland (and giraffe) are technically "large plains game." Buffalo and lion are not. In some countries the .375 H&H is the minimum allowed by law for all these diverse species.

As much as I love the 8mm and the .33s, it would be difficult to pick any of them over the .375 for all-round use in Africa (as has been the case since 1912). I have used a .375 to shoot most of my eland, and additionally many zebra, wildebeest, kudu, oryx, my best sable, and a whole host of lesser animals—not to mention buffalo, lion, and such.

The .375 H&H and .375 Ruger will not shoot as flat as the 8mm Remington and the faster .338s, certainly not as flat as the .300s and the likes of the 7mm magnums. The very fast .375s, like the .375 RUM and .375 and .378 Weatherby, will—but only at a fearsome cost in recoil. But the .375 will shoot adequately flat for almost all African hunting. It will absolutely flatten game, and it has plenty of wonderful bullets available.

Over the years I have used many .375s, and the last couple of seasons I have spent a lot of time with the .375 Ruger. It is magnificent, and I predict it will have "legs" in the marketplace. But there is still nothing wrong with the great old .375 H&H as the utility hitter. In 2007, in northern Namibia, I spent two weeks hunting with Kimber's Dwight Van Brunt and the new Kimber Caprivi. It was not the first time, but it was the first time in a long time, that I had done a complete safari with just a .375 H&H. Old lessons are often the best—once again I was struck by the wonderful versatility of this old-timer. I used it for elephant and leopard, both at close range. I used it for very long shots on gemsbok and kudu, and for an even longer shot at the best springbok I have ever had a chance at. With a solid, I even used it to take a fine steenbok. And in one of its most classic uses, I took a superb eland bull. Much of this game is outside the scope of this chapter. Some of these animals, like the springbok and steenbok, are not the most ideal use for a .375. But I hope you get the point: As has been the case since 1912, the .375 is excellent for the largest plains game, and can cover many other bases as well. In Africa versatility is important because of the range of game that might be encountered.

A rifle for large plains game need not be a tackdriver; animals in this group present a large vital zone. However, the rifle cannot be inaccurate, since several of these animals are commonly taken at longer ranges. It absolutely must be scoped, not only for taking gemsbok across an open pan but also for picking out an aiming point on a black sable in black shadow. Again, though, we're dealing with large animals. A simple, rugged, fixed 4X scope is a fine choice, and other good options include variables in the 1.5–6X or 1.75–5X range.

The most logical action choice for such a rifle is the bolt action, its caliber determined somewhat by the terrain and the upper end of game size and toughness.

Jack Atcheson Jr. (and his dad, Jack Sr.) are .338 men. Regardless of the game, they believe in .338s and make them work. Jack Jr. took this fantastic sable in Zimbabwe's Matetsi region with, in this case, my left-handed .338 I had loaned him.

For instance, in very open country with almost no chance of using the rifle on dangerous game, a fast .30 might be a great choice. Add eland, and a fine choice might be a "medium" from a fast 8mm to a (rare) fast .35. But if eland is a primary quarry and the rifle might be employed against buffalo or lion, then one of the .375 cartridges (H&H, Ruger, or Weatherby) would be a better choice.

The Ruger single shot is available in several chamberings that fit nicely into our "large plains game" arena (as are the Dakota Model 10, T/C, and other modern single shots). This might be the most natural habitat of a single-shot African rifle, rather than for use on dangerous game. In thicker cover, a very good case could be made for a scoped double, a .375, 9.3, or perhaps an old-timer like the .360 No. 2. However, if the same rifle is to be used on smaller plains game, as is often the case, then the accuracy of a bolt action or single shot might be called for.

The various .416s available today all shoot plenty flat enough to be considered for use on large plains game, and with its great velocity the .416 Weatherby could legitimately be considered a long-range cartridge. The over-.40s would obviously be effective on eland. There is, however, no real reason to look beyond the .375 for use even on the largest of plains game. And under many, perhaps most, circumstances, the hunter will be better served by a lighter, faster caliber.

Leopard

Chapter 28

The leopard is part of Africa's Big Five of dangerous game, but this is because he is truly dangerous, not because he is big in the sense that a rhino, elephant, buffalo, or even lion is. When selecting rifles, cartridges, and especially bullets for leopard, it's important to keep in mind that although he is a deadly efficient predator, the leopard is a small animal.

A big male will weigh 150 pounds, about the same as a large impala ram. I suspect most leopard taken by hunters weigh a bit less, say 120 to 130 pounds. An occasional monster leopard is taken, of course. My hunting partner, Ron Norman, shot a very big male late one evening on the Sabi River in Rhodesia. They couldn't find it before it grew dark, so had no choice but to look in the morning.

The cat was still alive when they found it, but very sick, and it had bled tremendously. On hunter/rancher Roger Whittall's grain scale, the cat weighed 225 pounds, one of the heaviest verified leopard I know of. A leopard like that is a virtual freak of nature, a huge specimen—and is still a good deal smaller than a big Rocky Mountain mule deer or an average black bear. And it's clearly much smaller than even a modest lion, let alone a Cape buffalo.

Now, I'm not sure there's such a thing as being overgunned, especially on animals that can hurt you, your tracker, or the next local who happens along. But with leopard it's easy to be over-bulleted—a tough bullet, designed for animals several times larger, may just burn through a leopard, doing little damage. That's fine if the hit is perfect; a leopard succumbs rapidly to a well-placed heart or lung shot (what doesn't?). But if the hit is off by just a bit, he'll show some of the nine lives for which cats are famous.

I'm not very proud of it and I've rarely mentioned it, but this is a good place to bring up a most painful memory: I lost a leopard back in 1979. Barrie Duckworth and I had put up a machan for a cattle-killing cat, and in the full moonlight a magnificent leopard sauntered into the clearing. I could see him well against the

This is a big leopard, but on the grand scale of things even a big leopard is not a particularly large animal. This old leopard with zero body fat weighed a bit over 150 pounds. A monster leopard might weigh 200 pounds, not as much as a big whitetail.

Left to right: .270 Winchester, 7x57, 7mm Remington Magnum, .30-06, .300 Winchester Magnum. If local laws require larger cartridges, obey the laws. If they don't this is the class of cartridges I think is perfect for leopard. Mate them with a relatively quick-opening bullet, place your shot, and your leopard will be dead under the tree.

short brown grass, and the .375 absolutely flattened him. We slapped each other on the back, then waited a few moments. Nothing.

We were halfway out of the machan when the cat woke up, and before I could climb back up and bring my rifle to bear, he was gone. We never found him. The blood petered out in a couple hundred yards, and the brush was thick. We even tried the old trick of driving cattle through the area; they'll spook at the scent of wounded leopard every time. But that leopard had kept on going.

It's obvious that I could have, and should have, made a better shot. But, all things considered, it's also likely that the big .375 bullet burned through without opening up, passing close enough to the spine to momentarily knock the cat down and out. I'm not altogether certain what bullet I was using. I do know that American Airlines threw a fit over the amount of ammunition (and reloading components) in my bags, most of it for the beleaguered Rhodesians. Almost all of my own ammunition was left sitting at the ticket counter at LAX, and I managed to buy a box of RWS .375s in Bulawayo, loaded with the hard TUG bullet. I also scrounged a handful of .375s from professional hunter Hilton Nichol. My own .375 ammo had been loaded with 270-grain Hornady roundnose bullets, pre-InterLock. That bullet would have opened. The TUG bullet, ideal for very large game, would not have.

The shot at a leopard should be the easiest in the hunting world. You have a steady rest, you aren't out of breath, the distance is known, and the target is stationary. So why is it so difficult?

The .375 H&H is a great African rifle, to be sure, and it is probably used by more hunting clients to take more leopard than any other single cartridge. There are reasons for its widespread use, some good and some not so good. In some countries .375 remains the minimum caliber allowed by law for use on all dangerous game. Compliance with local law is a very good reason to use it. Another reason is less logical: The leopard is a dangerous animal, and the .375 fires a big bullet that should do a bang-up job of scotching the potential danger. That doesn't wash very well. Consider that an impala or gazelle shot with a .375 is likely to have two small, neat holes, little interior damage, and will probably carry on for some distance before falling over. A leopard is essentially the same size and provides the same resistance to the bullet.

Most of the foregoing words were written twenty years ago. I did pretty good, considering that, honestly, I had a whole lot less experience with leopard then than I do now! I remain convinced that, though the .375 may not be "too much gun" for leopard, most .375 bullets are not designed for leopard-size game. In the several Zambezi Valley areas where we do so much of our filming for *Tracks Across Africa*, the outfitters have a combined quota of more than twenty leopard. The areas are good and they get most of their cats, but once in a while a leopard is wounded. Most of these are recovered, but occasionally, perhaps once a season, a cat is wounded and lost. I pay attention to these things, and in the last couple of years the only two wounded and lost leopard were both shot with .375s.

Obviously, shot placement counts, and if a leopard (or anything else) is lost, shot placement wasn't very damn good! But my partners Tim Danklef and Dave Fulson

Donna used her .30-06 with standard 180-grain Hornady bullets to drop this fine Namibian leopard dead under the tree.

have attended many more leopard hunts than I, and they maintain the leopard is a fairly soft animal. A hit a bit far back and he is still usually recovered—if the bullet opens up. The .375 bullets designed for much larger animals often don't. My own experience bears this out, not only that never-to-be-forgotten lost cat of nearly thirty years ago but also a much more recent experience.

I was hunting in Namibia's western Bushmanland with Jamy Traut, and a beautiful tom leopard jumped onto the branch at 5 P.M., bathed in gorgeous slanting sunlight. This was on the "Kimber Caprivi" safari I mentioned earlier, and I was shooting Federal Premium's 300-grain Trophy Bonded Bear Claw. In good light and with apparently plenty of time, I brought the vertical cross hair up the back line of the foreleg one-third into the chest, then moved the intersection a bit right into the shoulder and squeezed the trigger.

I expected the leopard to collapse onto the branch and thump to the ground under the bait. Instead, as I came back from recoil I had a glimpse of the cat exiting the field of view high and left, as if launched from a cannon! When a cat exits the tree under its own power, it is a bad sign. Even so, I was very sure of the shot and expected we would find him piled up at the end of his trajectory. Nope. So we went into the thin yellow grass that suddenly didn't seem so thin at all! He'd gone only

The real problem with leopard over bait is the tension builds almost unbearably as time passes. When the leopard comes into the tree the adrenaline rush is incredible—but this is the time to stay calm and steady and place the shot.

twenty yards and was stretched out dead in mid-flight. The shot placement really was textbook perfect, with caliber-size entrance on one shoulder and matching exit on the off-shoulder. I am convinced that given that shot, a lesser, smaller cartridge with a bullet designed for smaller game would have dropped him under the tree.

If the .375 is the minimum caliber allowed by law, by all means it should be used. If it is the only scoped rifle you have available, by all means it should be used. But if leopard is on the menu, if possible avoid the really tough 300-grain bullets designed for optimal performance on buffalo and eland. At a minimum take a handful of 270-grain bullets, or even a few of the lighter bullets you can push fast, like handloaded 235-grain Speers or 265-grain Nosler AccuBonds. These will expand, even in leopard. Yes, I'm now being inconsistent because I've said you don't want the confusion of multiple bullets for a given cartridge. The leopard is a special case. When you have a cat feeding and have built your blind, you will (or you certainly should!) verify your zero at the exact distance from bait to blind, so it's no great trick to sight-in with a special leopard load chosen with expansion as a primary criterion.

If the local game laws don't obligate you to use a .375 or larger, consider using your light or medium rifle. Again, the leopard isn't a large animal. Good professional

PH Jamy Traut and me with a nice tom leopard taken over bait in western Bushmanland, northern Namibia. I used a .375 H&H, which worked fine—but I'm certain the cat would have dropped more quickly with a lighter cartridge and a faster-opening bullet.

hunters like Harry Selby and Joe Coogan are perfectly comfortable using the little .243! Typical "light rifles" like .270 Winchester, any of the 7mms, and any of the .30-calibers with good expanding bullets will typically expend more energy inside a leopard-size animal than a larger caliber. With similar bullet placement they will dispatch the animal more quickly. Forgetting for just a moment that screwing up on a leopard can be extremely hazardous to your health, there is no question about the adequacy of .270s, 7mms, and .30-calibers on 150-pound animals.

I shot my first leopard (that I recovered!) on the point of the right shoulder with a 210-grain Nosler from a .338 Winchester Magnum. The bullet exited the left hip, and the cat dropped without any further movement. Even that is way overgunned. When we did the *Boddington on Leopard* DVD, I chose a single-shot .30-06 and used the 180-grain Swift Scirocco, not the Swift A-Frame that is generally a better African bullet. But not for leopard. This cat was taken with a lung shot, the safest shot and the largest target. Lung-shot leopard always run, but not far. We found him about thirty yards into very dark and very scary bush.

A short time after I shot my Bushmanland leopard we were elsewhere in Namibia hunting with Dirk de Bod. He got a leopard on bait for Donna, and she dropped it stone-dead under the tree, just the way it's supposed to be done. She used her Ruger

Hunting leopard with hounds is a bit different. The cat is keyed up, and if he spots you during the approach a charge is extremely likely. I used my .416 Taylor with a big roundnose bullet, which may be a bit of overkill. On the other hand, the leopard went down on the spot with no damage to man or dogs.

M77 .30-06 with a 180-grain Hornady InterLock bullet. When it comes down to it, though, any discussion of adequate cartridges for a 150-pound animal is almost ridiculous. Any centerfire will do the job. It's really a question of bullet placement, and since most leopard are taken over bait, that bullet must often be placed by making your shot in the poorest light imaginable. A good scope is thus almost more important than the caliber of rifle. Keep in mind, however, that you can wound a leopard with any cartridge and any bullet, so shot placement remains the key. I wounded my leopard in 1992 shooting a .300 Weatherby Magnum. It wasn't altogether my fault; we had moved the blind and failed to clear the shot properly, and my bullet struck an unseen branch. But he was still wounded, and we didn't get him until noon the next day after the scariest, hairiest few hours I have ever spent.

Ranges are generally very short. Fifty yards is about average, and a hundred yards would be an unusually long distance from blind to bait. The leopard may come at four in the afternoon, and on occasion he may turn out to be a morning feeder. But most of the time, if he comes in the daylight at all, he will come in the very last twilight. The best bait arrangement will silhouette the feeding cat against the sky to maximize whatever light remains—but don't count on this! The best insurance for leopard is the brightest scope that can be had.

Magnification isn't important. In fact, considering the short range, it isn't particularly desirable—and low-power scopes tend to gather more light than those with higher magnification. Although they're very large and clumsy, the German scopes with 56mm objectives, made for shooting boar at night, are the ultimate for leopard hunting. I must admit I don't like them; they must be mounted so high that I find them most uncomfortable to shoot with. But they sure do gather light. A good compromise is a 30mm tube, which (given equal quality) gathers more usable light than the standard American one-inch tube.

Consider a lighted reticle. These really help focus the aiming point in poor light.

In some areas it is legal and widely accepted to shoot leopard after dark with an artificial light. If it's legal, I don't have any problem with the practice. Game laws usually develop for practical reasons, and the practical reality is that in ranch country, where night hunting is usually legal, leopard have been hunted hard for a century and almost never come to bait in daylight. Night hunting does change the shooting situation markedly. Lack of light isn't a problem, but when the torch comes on, the shot must be taken quickly—and of course it still has to be in the right place. Again, a low-power scope with a highly visible reticle is the way to go.

Other options for hunting leopard include tracking. This is very rare today as it requires not only unique soil conditions that will show the track of such a small animal but also the services of highly skilled trackers, and trackers of this level are a vanishing breed. But it is done, and these hunts often end in charges. Dog hunting was popular in East Africa in Roosevelt's era, and is coming back in southern Africa today. At this writing using hounds for unwounded leopard is illegal in South Africa and on government land in Zimbabwe, but is widely practiced in Namibia and on private land in Zimbabwe, and is occasionally done in Mozambique. These hunts, too, often end in charges.

I am not altogether certain what the best choice of arm would be for either situation. If you knew for certain you were going to take your leopard in a charge at the end of such a hunt, then you might carry a 10-gauge loaded with 000 buckshot! But you don't know that, and you really don't want that as the outcome! In a tracking hunt there is very likely to be a shot before the leopard is pushed as far as he will go. In a hound hunt things happen fast, but there are usually opportunities before you get too close and trigger a charge—and some percentage of the cats tree, just like a mountain lion.

I have done two hound hunts for leopard. One was in South Africa, where we used dogs to recover a leopard another hunter wounded; the other was on Erindi in Namibia. On that South African hunt I carried my old .375 with a low-power scope. The dogs were fighting the leopard in a little patch of brown grass. We

A follow-up is different yet again. Some PHs prefer buckshot, I don't—but whatever you're carrying, you must hope the leopard is dead, because no animal in Africa is more likely to hurt you than a wounded leopard.

approached, and our outfitter, Abie Steyn, made eye contact with the leopard. It was a huge tom, and it came like a bullet. Steyn made a brilliant shot with his .470 at a matter of feet, hitting the cat just slightly off-center in the chest with a 500-grain softpoint. All this did, apparently, was turn the cat slightly. Tim Danklef, carrying a .30-06 with too much scope, fired from the hip as the cat squirted by close enough to touch. Until this moment I was behind Steyn and Danklef, totally out of danger but blocked. When the cat passed Tim, I was clear and I got in a lucky shoulder shot that stopped the action.

There are lessons here. First, although a leopard is not big, when full of adrenaline he can be very hard to stop! Second, whatever rifle you choose, it must handle well enough to allow a fast, accurate shot at extremely close range. The dichotomy is that the same rifle should allow a shot out to at least fifty yards, so that such a situation can be prevented if the occasion arises.

When I did my own leopard-with-dogs hunt on Erindi, I chose a bolt-action .416 Taylor with a big, roundnose softpoint, and I used a low-power Trijicon scope with the tritium post. My leopard was a big old tom, and he fought the dogs on the

On a follow-up you must carry whatever you can shoot "fastest and best." I finished this charge with a very lucky shot with my old .375, a gun I've known long and well.

ground for quite some time while we maneuvered for a shot. For several seconds I had him frontally at maybe twenty-five yards, but there were dogs right behind him so I couldn't shoot. PH Corne' Kruger and I stood motionless, and I was certain we would get a charge. Then the cat turned slightly and moved, and in a few seconds I got a clear broadside shot at twenty yards. The big bullet worked perfectly, and the cat dropped to the shot.

All that said, I am not necessarily advocating such a big gun for this kind of leopard hunt. Corne' Kruger and his brother Nick have done many leopard hunts with dogs, and they carry light rifles for backup—sometimes as light as a .243, more frequently a 7mm. They believe them adequate to stop a leopard and capable of reducing the problem of overpenetration (at least on a frontal shot), which endangers the hounds. Perhaps the most important thing in fast-breaking hunts, whether tracking or with hounds, is the ability to acquire the target and get the shot off quickly—and it still must be accurate. So gun fit and fast, certain sights are far more critical than choice of cartridge. If I ever do it again I would stick with the

Trijicon scope—it is the fastest sighting device I have ever used—and I'd make sure the rifle fit me well enough so I could use it like a shotgun if I had to.

One additional point worth mentioning: I shoot a scoped rifle with both eyes open, which is why I am able to use a low-power scope in very fast, point-blank situations. Most of the time iron sights would be just fine if you are proficient with them, but I know I shoot more quickly and much more accurately with a low-power scope, even at very close range.

When it comes to following up a wounded leopard, tradition suggests that a shotgun loaded with coarse buckshot is the way to go. As discussed in chapter 25, I don't think this is the best choice—but if a shotgun is used, the shot must be held until you are very close.

Realistically, most of the time your professional hunter will wield that shotgun. Whether you accompany him on the follow-up is entirely up to him; if he says no, don't take it personally. Properly, it's his job—and it's generally a one-man job. He simply can't be worrying about anything except the leopard; any distraction and somebody is more likely to get hurt. He must make the call based on his own experience, his assessment of what lies ahead, and his judgment of your abilities. If he asks you to go with him, take it as a compliment and by all means go—understanding you may be sorry you did! Just mind that you don't shoot anyone in the melee. That's the real danger of following a wounded leopard—or, for that matter, any wounded animal.

The best course of all is to make absolutely certain the shot is placed well the first time. If it's placed right, it really doesn't much matter what rifle you used—and there won't be any argument over who carries the shotgun for a follow-up. Instead, you can all gather around and admire one of Africa's most magnificent creatures.

Lion

Chapter 29

For me, the lion is the ultimate African trophy. Of the entire Big Five (or Big Six or Big Seven if you like to count hippo and/or crocodile), he's the only one of which I'm unashamedly terrified. With all the rest, I'm more than willing to concede a healthy measure of caution and respect. But the lion makes my palms sweat and my chest go cold.

I'm not altogether sure why this should be; quite possibly it has nothing to do with the animal at all but rather with something deep in my own psyche. All children have nightmares, and in some kids' bad dreams they're chased by monsters, spiders, the neighbor's dog, you name it. As a child, John Wootters had bad dreams of elephant. He doesn't know why, but he knows he grew up with a pathological horror of pachyderms. He finally cured it when, as a middle-aged man, he shot a fine tusker. I'm not conscious of a deep-seated childhood fear of lion—but I do know that I'm afraid of them today.

I hunted lion for 105 days, over the course of several safaris, before I shot my first one. During those hunts I had plenty of time to think about my fear, and I had a number of close encounters with lionesses and maneless males. Since then, I've shot several more—certainly more than my share, and enough that I don't care if I ever shoot another. The fear has never gone away, and I've decided it isn't a bad thing. It doesn't seem to prevent me from getting the job done—and the heightened sensations when I'm in close contact with the great cats are a palpable thing.

On the other hand, it isn't necessary to be as frightened of lion as I am. It's merely damned important to treat them with plenty of respect. A lion is most unlikely to weigh 500 pounds outside of a zoo; a mature wild male lion is more likely to weigh 350 to 400 pounds—which is still a lot of cat. He may or may not be the king of beasts, but he is the king of African predators, with no enemies save man. Sometimes timid by day, he is bold by night and twilight, and he may or may not have learned to fear humankind; if he just came from a park, he may hold people in contempt rather than fear.

If you get a shot like this at a lion, life is pretty simple . . . but don't count on it. In hunting areas lions that look like this don't wander around in the open in broad daylight. (Photo by Dirk de Bod)

As Africa's cattle-raising human population burgeons, its lion country is shrinking, with ever fewer good areas, fewer lion on quota, and shocking prices that keep going up. I was fortunate to do quite a lot of lion hunting in the seventies and eighties, so I feel for newer hunters who, for good reason, don't know if they will ever have the opportunity. One answer has been captive-reared lion, a practice once common in Namibia (now illegal there) and still widely practiced in South Africa. At this writing is appears this will be either curtailed or made subject to severe restrictions by 2008. These hunting politics are beyond the subject of this book. I personally have no interest in taking a captive-reared lion under any circumstances—but I've had my chances. There are pros and cons, but one thing is clear: These captive-reared animals have no fear of man whatsoever. Hunting them on foot, which has long been a legal requirement, is almost certainly more dangerous than hunting a wild lion!

The lion is amazingly fast, and as unpredictable as a house cat. Often he seems cowardly, but if he's hurt and he knows what hurt him, he may decide to do something about it. If he comes, only death will stop him. The leopard, even if badly wounded, has a tendency to leap in, do damage, and dash away, or hop from one to another of a hunting party. He will often inflict horribly painful but somewhat superficial wounds on several people, eventually giving someone an opening to finish the job. The lion, if he can, will finish what he starts, and he's armed with the equipment to make very short work of a puny man.

Left to right: .375 H&H, .375 Ruger, .375 Weatherby Magnum, .375 Remington Ultra Mag, .378 Weatherby Magnum. Technically a wild lion is generally a 400-pound (tops!) animal, so a .30-caliber is plenty of gun. Realistically, given what a lion can do to you, I think the various .375s are just exactly perfect.

Lion are generally taken in one of three ways: over bait, by tracking, and during chance encounters. In the first instance—and sometimes during chance encounters—the lion is generally undisturbed and unaware, and may be taken successfully with a relatively light rifle. A .300 with a 200-grain bullet, a .30-06 with a good 180-grainer, a 7mm with a 175-grain bullet, even a .270 or 6.5 with heavy bullets, will without question do a number on a lion. But in most countries the legal minimum for hunting lion is .375—and there are lots of good reasons.

Although raw power will not make up for poor shot placement, there are varying degrees of good shot placement. A light rifle leaves no margin for error, even on an undisturbed cat. And a cat with his adrenaline up must not be merely killed; he must be stopped.

Regardless of minimum-caliber rules, a few lion are taken annually during chance encounters while the hunters are carrying light rifles. A lion asleep on an anthill or strolling across the veld is no real problem to knock over, and as hard as good males are to come by, few professional hunters would sacrifice a golden opportunity because of a few thousandths of an inch in bore diameter. Most of the time, if a decent stalk is possible and the client shoots reasonably well, there's no problem.

Should a problem arise, however, the light rifle isn't enough gun to keep you out of trouble. It wasn't for George Grey nearly a century ago, and it isn't today. Truth

Dirk de Bod and me with a spectacular old lion taken on the edge of Etosha National Park in northern Namibia in 2007. A "problem lion" permit came up suddenly and I used what I had, a .300 Remington Ultra Mag firing 200-grain Swift A-Frames. It worked just fine, but I would always prefer a bit more gun.

is, I'm not altogether certain the great .375 is enough gun if things go completely to hell—but it's a giant step in the right direction.

The .375 H&H is the classic lion gun. It's available with wonderful bullets, and it's perfectly at home with a low-power scope for early morning or late evening shooting. However, I should say that, except for brain shots, I have yet to see a one-shot kill on a lion with a .375. I have seen one-shot kills with .416s and .458s.

Even so, the .375 (and I'll include the near-identical 9.3x64 as well as the faster .375s and .378) is the traditional choice for lion hunting—and it's a good one. Accurate, easy to shoot, and plenty adequate in power, the .375 is just plain hard to beat for the big cats.

A rifle for a baited lion should without question wear a scope. The vast majority of baited lion are shot just as dawn breaks, after the pride has fed most of the night and is lounging around with full bellies. Shortly after dawn—or, with hunter-wise animals, a bit before—the pride will steal into heavy cover to sleep off their meal. The idea is to shoot the lion on the bait, undisturbed. A scope that gathers in plenty of light is an absolute must.

We had a pride feeding on a hippo along Zambia's Luangwa River. Before dawn we stalked carefully in to a wall of grass about thirty yards short of the hippo carcass. When we arrived, it was still too dark to see, but the lion were there—we could tell because the hyena were standing off a little way making a tremendous outcry.

This lion knows you are there, and until he either stands or tries to leave there is no shot. So you wait . . . and you'd better be ready! (Photo by Dirk de Bod)

Finally it started to gray up just a little. Professional hunter Bill Illingworth removed a plug of grass and took a careful look, and on his signal I did the same. Directly in front of the bait, just twenty-five yards from us, lay a lion and lioness—both just dimly seen forms. It was still too dark, but shooting light was just minutes away. I waited, and when the light changed almost imperceptibly I slowly moved the .375 into position. But it was already too late; the lioness remained where she had been, motionless—but the lion was gone. Sometimes, as then, getting a lion or not getting a lion is a matter of being able to see to shoot just a few seconds earlier.

In a baited situation, it's possible that a heavier rifle might flatten a cat with more authority than a .375—but there's really no reason for a larger rifle, especially since few hunters shoot larger rifles well enough to have any business tackling lion with them. In a chance encounter, all the recommendations in the world are useless; fate alone dictates what rifle you're carrying. That's why, if lion is on the menu, I never get very far from a .375. It will do everything a safari rifle needs to do on the various plains species—and if you happen to run into a good cat, it will handle that as well.

A tracking lion hunt is a different situation. Sometimes you can follow the tracks to the pride's lying-up place, find the male, and get into shooting position without the animals being the wiser. All too often, though, the lion become aware they're being followed before you're able to close the deal. Then it starts getting dangerous because the big cats don't like to be pushed around.

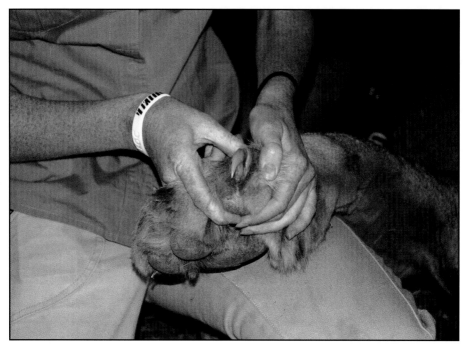

A lion's claws are like poisoned stilettos, and the lion knows how to use them. I am personally more afraid of lions than all the rest put together . . . which adds a very special thrill to a lion hunt.

In Botswana, where tracking lion hunts were the norm, a hunter or two seemed to get hammered every year. Elsewhere, a hunter being mauled is a much rarer occurrence. I've heard it said, "Botswana lion are especially cheeky," but I don't buy that—a lion is a lion. Rather, I think it's the danger inherent in tracking.

A scoped .375 is a perfectly acceptable rifle for a tracking hunt. A scoped .416 might be a better choice yet. In Masailand in 1988 I bumped into a wonderful lion while buffalo hunting with a .416 Rigby. Quarters were awfully close, and I was happy I wasn't carrying a lesser rifle. But if I were to undertake a serious tracking lion hunt, I think I'd carry a big double loaded with softpoints on which I knew I could rely. In the thick cover lion generally lie up in, chances of a shot beyond eighty yards are remote—and the chances of a shot at a quarter that distance are very good. A scope is a definite aid in picking out a tawny form in yellow grass, but when things happen with lion, they happen very fast. The fast second shot from a double could be important. Let's put it this way: The next time I walk into lion at fifteen yards, I want a big double in my hands!

Pretty much the same goes for following wounded lion. With a scoped rifle, there might be a better chance of picking out a hidden lion and getting off a shot before he

Lion

Zimbabwean PH Cliff Walker with the lion that badly mauled both he and his client before succumbing. Cliff normally carries a double .577, but he was in Ethiopia and, because of gun permit issues, carried a borrowed .375. With his own big gun maybe he wouldn't have been touched, but who knows?

charges or moves on. But in the event of a charge, you want all the raw power you can muster. I would choose a double, since I have one and I'm comfortable with it, but a big-bore bolt action in experienced hands is every bit as effective.

Choice of bullets for lion merits a short discussion. It should, obviously, be a softpoint. A solid will deliver the penetration you want, but the lack of shock and tissue damage can get you dead. The lion is not a huge animal, so the softpoint need not be as heavily constructed as it should be for buffalo. However, the lion's shoulder bones are relatively stout, and they can eat up a bullet that's too soft, is pushed too fast, or malfunctions. And it happens.

My longtime boss at Petersen Publishing, Ken Elliott, had a factory .375 softpoint blow up on a lion's shoulder some years ago. I haven't exactly had a bullet fail, but I had a funny thing happen several years ago. I shot a lion in the head at extremely close range with a .375, and of course it killed him very dead. Good thing it was a head shot, though; the bullet vaporized in the skull—no exit, and it didn't penetrate beyond the back of the head.

Bullets I like are Winchester Power Points, Hornady InterLocks, and Remington's Swift A-Frame in factory .375, and Federal's Woodleigh and Trophy

399

We were tracking a buffalo herd in Masailand in 1988 when this lion appeared out of nowhere. My open-sighted .416 Rigby worked just fine, but in general you definitely want a scoped rifle for lion, both for low light and to properly pick out a tawny animal against yellow grass.

Bonded Bear Claw loads are excellent as well. With component bullets it's hard to make a mistake. Nosler's new .375 is great, and there aren't any flies on component bullets from Barnes, Hornady, Sierra, and Swift.

Today the choice is almost as robust in .416 and .458, with offerings dropping off quickly for the other big bores. But there are plenty of good bullets. Day in and day out, though, you can't go wrong by hunting lion with a good .375 that you shoot well. But I do believe the .416s are a bit more effective. If you shoot a bigger gun well, there's absolutely no reason not to use it.

By 2007 it was nineteen years since I had taken a lion, or even seriously hunted them. In the C.A.R. in 1996 we ran into two nice males hunting together. It was an open area, meaning lion were on license with no quota, and I could have taken one quite easily. But it was a pure chance encounter, and the shot would have been from the truck, a very poor way to take such a fine animal. So I passed. Within a few short years thereafter quotas dropped and prices skyrocketed, and I came to think of that incident as the last chance I might ever have to take one last lion. Secretly, however, I did want to take one last lion, and, rifle nut that I am, I sort of hoped I might do it with a double rifle.

Lion

Now he's turned away and there's a bit of brush in the way. Unless things get better this is a "no shot" situation . . . but in today's Africa a chance at a lion like this is so rare that this is a tough call. Bigger is definitely better, but you still must place the shot!

The days of lion suddenly becoming available on safaris not booked specifically for lion are pretty much over, but even today you never know what might happen in Africa. Donna had just taken her leopard at Onguma Ranch, on the eastern edge of Etosha, when one of the property owners came up from Windhoek. He had just come from the game department and had been issued two "problem lion permits," which, in Namibian lexicon, meant that a lion taken on such a permit was fully exportable. This area had a definite lion problem, with tracks everywhere—and some of those tracks were huge. PH Dirk de Bod and I jumped on one of those permits.

I didn't have a double rifle, or even a big rifle at all. The rifle I had was a .300 Remington Ultra Mag. The legal minimum for lion in Namibia is .30-caliber. I could have borrowed resident PH Danny Bartlett's .375 or Dirk's .416, but these were right-handed guns. I did have 200-grain Swift A-Frames, so although this last lion wouldn't be taken with a big double as I'd imagined, I was in business.

There is a fourth option for lion hunting, and that is calling. If the lion comes to another male's roars, he must imagine that an intruder is encroaching on his territory and thus he comes looking for a fight. We found a huge, lone track, hung a bait, and gave a series of roars to let him know. He answered immediately, so we

401

PH Paul Smith and Texan Hayley Killam with a wonderful Zambezi Valley lion. Mrs. Killam used a .375, always and forever the very best choice for lion.

stood in the blind for nearly an hour until he sauntered into the clearing, cautious and on full alert. After nearly twenty years the old fear was still there, but I never questioned the adequacy of the .300. He paused about twenty-five yards from us, quartered, and stared through our souls with his yellow eyes. I shot him on the point of the shoulder, and the bullet exited behind the off-shoulder. Other, unnecessary shots were fired, but he traveled just a few yards and lay still, a beautiful old lion that will almost certainly be my last.

Buffalo

Chapter 30

In the Swahili of East Africa they call him *m'bogo*. In most of southern Africa he's known as *nyati* or, the way it's actually said, *inyati*. Hunters generally just call him "buffalo," but they're usually referring to the southern Cape buffalo, largest of the several African buffalo. This is the one that is hunted throughout southern and eastern Africa. Somewhere in Sudan, a subtle transition begins; the buffalo begin to get smaller in both body and horn, and an occasional animal is red rather than black. Hunting them is the same, but we call these animals "Nile buffalo" rather than Cape.

Farther west still, across the savanna zone that separates the Sahara from the forests of West and Central Africa, is found what used to be called the northwestern buffalo. These animals are smaller yet in both body and horn, with the percentage of red versus black buffalo increasing as you travel from east to west. They get smaller, too, as you move west, so in recent years Safari Club International has classified the savanna buffalo of the C.A.R. as "Central African savanna buffalo," while those from northern Cameroon westward are called "West African savanna buffalo." Whatever you call them, these animals are a true transition from the familiar Cape buffalo to the largely unfamiliar and quite different dwarf forest buffalo. Found strictly in the forest zone from West Africa south to Angola and across the Congos into the forests of the extreme southwestern corner of the C.A.R., the dwarf, or red forest, buffalo is about half the size of a southern Cape buffalo; a forest bull might weigh 700 pounds, while a Cape buffalo bull will weigh 1,500 pounds or more.

Few hunters know the forest buffalo. I have hunted him several times, but I apparently don't know him well because I've never gotten a shot! It's said that what they lack in size they make up for in shortness of temper. This is also said about the savanna buffalo to the north, which I have hunted successfully in both the C.A.R. and Cameroon. Short their temper may or may not be, but in the dense forests they inhabit, the ranges they're shot from will be very short indeed. "Savanna" is a

As Ruark put it, the Cape buffalo looks at you like you "owe him money." Unprovoked charges are extremely rare, but once you open the ball game you must be prepared to finish it.

subjective term. The so-called savanna zone of the C.A.R. and Cameroon, where most hunting is conducted today, is technically Terminalia forest. In my experience it is simply less dense than true forest—but still thicker than most areas where southern buffalo are hunted. In spite of the regional differences in size, I would rate the caliber requirements for buffalo the same across the board, since thicker cover means closer encounters and definitely adds to the danger.

Hunters with far more experience (and others with much less!) than mine have often rated the buffalo as the most dangerous of Africa's big game. All of the Big Five (plus hippo) certainly have the potential to be very dangerous. Which of them is the most hazardous to hunt is a very subjective ranking dependent mostly on one's own experience. My belief is that in order to properly express an opinion you should have extensive experience with them all, and under a wide variety of conditions. J. A. Hunter, for instance, had the right to an opinion. (He rated the leopard as the most dangerous.) Some few modern professional hunters may have both an opinion and a right to express it. I have an opinion, but I will tell you up front that I don't think I have the experience to authoritatively express it. Nor do I believe any other current writer does. I can only say that I am most frightened of lion, but in the close cover where today's elephant are mostly hunted, I think they must be considered the most dangerous. As much as I respect the buffalo and enjoy hunting him, my own experience doesn't show him to be nearly as dangerous as lion or elephant, or nearly as likely to hurt you as the leopard.

Though I have now shot several dozen buffalo, I have not had a major problem with one. Lion, yes; leopard, yes; elephant, many times. Buffalo, never a genuine serious charge. Yet it happens. Every year at the conventions I talk to a couple of guys who caught charges on their very first buffalo. Their experience was different than mine has been, and their opinion of the danger of hunting buffalo is probably also different. I have seen the results of mishaps with buffalo. When I was hunting in the Chobe area of Botswana, a group of citizen hunters followed us on the spoor of a buffalo herd, proceeding on after we had taken two bulls. A couple of hours later, they carried their leader into our camp after he had been almost fatally gored just under the heart. Most of the time you cannot get into trouble with a buffalo if you place the first shot correctly with an adequate cartridge propelling a good bullet. The local hunter just mentioned hit a buffalo somewhere with a .30-06 softpoint, then got hammered on the follow-up.

The .30-06 is well below Botswana's minimum of .375 for buffalo. This is the general rule in most African jurisdictions, which suggests it is probably a pretty good rule of thumb! Since this is usually the law, and since it is part of a licensed professional hunter's credo to enforce game laws, this further suggests that most buffalo are shot with adequate calibers. Which, in turn, suggests that most problems with buffalo are caused by poor shot placement. Unprovoked charges do occur. In Tanzania in 2006 a buffalo came out of nowhere and killed my old friend and Canadian outfitter Bob Fontana. Since that buffalo wasn't recovered, it is impossible to say what caused the incident, but I believe strongly there had to be something wrong with that buffalo. Perhaps he had been wounded previously, perhaps he was wearing a snare, or perhaps another buffalo had gored him.

Sensible buffalo cartridges start at .375, either the H&H, left, or the new .375 Ruger. This is not where they end, but the .375 is enough gun, and for many people it is all the gun that can be handled with the accuracy that is required.

If all shots at buffalo were like this, very close in open country, then any rifle from .375 on up would be just fine. Truthfully, this is a rare opportunity at a shootable bull. Usually there's more brush, and sometimes it's a lot farther.

In the Selous in 2000 hunting partner Chub Eastman was in the back of the hunting car when they rounded an antheap. A buffalo bull charged out of nowhere, and Eastman had the presence of mind to grab his rifle and fire down at the buffalo, into the neck behind the head, before it struck the truck. The buffalo dropped and slid in, its nose coming to rest under the truck. This buffalo had a serious and festering wound in one of its haunches. Things like this happen, but they are rare. Buffalo are big and strong and can be very dangerous, but I think their reputation as "black death" or the devil incarnate is overrated. Hit them well with enough gun and they will die. Even if you don't hit them well, a charge is not a certainty. Some wounded buffalo will indeed find a nasty patch of bush and circle to wait for you. I cannot tell you how common this is, nor can anyone else—but not all buffalo will do this. I don't always shoot perfectly, and I have wounded buffalo—but I have never had one charge. Partly this is because good trackers and a very careful follow-up can often end things before a charge is launched. Partly it is because not all buffalo are disposed to kill you. Many just want to get away. In my experience in many African camps a wounded buffalo is far more likely to get away and be utterly lost than to charge!

This is yet another good reason you want to hit a buffalo right the first time, and with something that will do the job. That and one more thing: I lost the first

406

Often, in a herd, you just can't get as close as you would like. If this bull was just a bit older this would be an ideal opportunity . . . but for most people this is a bit too far for open sights. Generally speaking, you will kill more buffalo and bigger buffalo with a scoped rifle.

buffalo I ever shot at. Film partners Tim Danklef and Dave Fulson both lost buffalo early in their careers. Today, as we bring in sponsor reps to film for our TV show, I have noticed that somebody loses a buffalo every season. Call it one in ten, which I consider a very high loss rate. At the same time, genuine charges hardly occur one in twenty. For better or worse, with a television camera rolling you have instant replay capability, so you can see what happened. We have had several instances where, after that first shot (which may have looked OK but clearly wasn't as OK as it looked), follow-up shots could have been fired but were not. There have been a couple of instances where follow-up shots were fired but either missed or were ineffective. Once in a while there simply is no opportunity for additional shots, but here's the takeaway: The first shot is important, but if it doesn't have its intended effect, second and subsequent shots may be even more important! Unless the buffalo drops and stays down, you have no certain way of knowing if the first shot went in the right place and the bullet did its intended work.

It's been more than thirty years since I lost that first buffalo. Ever since then, I've kept on shooting, provided the target is clear and the buffalo is still on its feet. I have been criticized for showing multiple shots at a buffalo on television and in DVDs, but I truly believe this is the smart money. I expect a professional hunter to

Joe Bishop took this bull in Mozambique with his Sako .375. Joe is a fine shot, and he called his frontal shot a bit to the right. He was correct: His shot was no more than two inches right of center, and this bull got up when we approached and gave us a helluva fright!

use his judgment, and if his experience and instinct tell him he should fire a backup shot, then he'll get no grief from me. However, it's also worth noting that it has been many years since any professional hunter fired a shot at one of my buffalo. This is not because my first shots are always perfect—they are not; rather, it's because I practice working a bolt and using the second trigger on a double, and I consistently back up my own shots. So I think the proper approach for buffalo is threefold: First, use an adequate rifle and a good bullet. Second, wait for a good presentation and place that first shot as well as you can. Third, don't rest on that first shot. If an additional shot is safe and available, keep shooting.

I have never shot a buffalo with a caliber smaller than a .338. Because of its greater sectional density (weight in relation to diameter), with equal construction a .338 will always penetrate better than a .375. I am often asked about 220-grain .30-calibers, .33s, and .35s for buffalo. If it were locally legal I would have no real qualms about shooting undisturbed buffalo in open country with anything from a 7x57 on up—provided, that is, that the bullet was heavy for caliber and was either a reliable solid or an extremely tough controlled-expansion softpoint, and that I could be absolutely certain of shot placement. Also provided I had a much bigger rifle for any follow-up that might be necessary. I find this a silly discussion, however, because in most jurisdictions such shenanigans are illegal.

PH J. P. Kleinhans and Ken Jorgensen with a great Mozambique bull, dropped on the spot with a 270-grain softpoint from Jorgensen's .375 Ruger. The .375 is enough gun—but the shot must be correct.

Game laws tend to exist for good reason, especially in Africa, where the safari business has been just that, a business, for many years. For instance, in most areas where it is legal to hunt leopard at night, it is almost impossible to get them on bait in daylight! For many decades the accepted minimum for Cape buffalo, both by tradition and by local law, has been the .375 H&H or its equivalent. This minimum is based on many decades of experience, and I believe it to be a sound and sensible minimum.

Actually, it can be singularly uneventful to kill an undisturbed, unwounded buffalo. And that's the way it's supposed to be. All too much is written—and, these days, shown on video—of buffalo charges and derring-do. Some first-time clients, believing all that bunk, are downright disappointed if they don't get charged at least once. Keep in mind, first, that charges rarely happen unless somebody screws up badly, and second, that it's the professional hunter's job to keep things like that from happening. Third, always understand that no matter how good you are, not all charges will be stopped!

Yet with buffalo there is that special spice of potential danger—and it's very real. Once you open the ball game with a Cape buffalo, there are just three options. You will finish it, he will, or he will get away. I can recall two buffalo in recent years that I messed up on, one in the Selous in 1994 and another in the Zambezi Valley in 1999. Murphy's Law applying, other buffalo were too close in the Selous

Art Wheaton, PH Cliff Walker, and me with a nice buffalo dropped on the spot with a single 250-grain Swift A-Frame from a .338 Remington Ultra Mag. With a good bullet, perfect shot placement, and a wee bit of luck, buffalo can be taken with lesser calibers—but it's a very bad idea!

incident, and the other time the brush was too thick to get in a second shot. We followed both buffalo forever, not so far in distance but an eternity in time. Both of them circled this way and that, and either one could have and perhaps should have charged and tried to settle the score. Both times I fully understood the danger, but I also understood that as the hours passed, the chances of a wounded and lost animal increased. In both situations, by the time we finally caught up and finished the job, I was mentally begging for a charge to bring things to an end! In my view, it is far better to open and close the game neatly and efficiently, with minimum mess and fuss. That requires calm, deliberate shooting and careful shot placement, nothing more and nothing less. And make no mistake: If you screw it up, things will get very exciting in short order, and they can get extremely messy besides.

Undisturbed, a buffalo will succumb to a heart or lung shot from a .375 (or a .30-06, for that matter) just like any other very large animal. Typically he will receive the bullet and run like hell until he runs out of blood. The problem comes if that first bullet fails to either wreck the heart or thoroughly perforate both lungs. Then, with adrenaline pumping, that placid, grazing beast becomes another animal altogether. In fact, from my experience, he becomes the toughest animal on earth, pound for pound, to bring down.

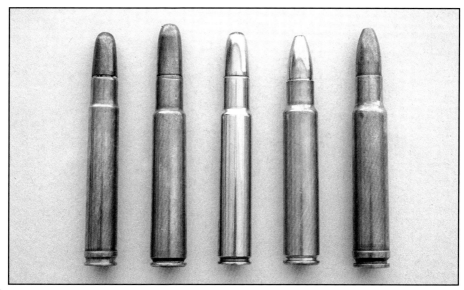

Left to right: .416 Remington Magnum, .416 Rigby, .416 Dakota, .416 Meteor, .416 Weatherby Magnum. Ideally and optimally, I do believe the various .416s are the perfect medicine for buffalo—but only if you can handle the recoil, which is a bit more than the .375 delivers.

That's why it's wisest to use a totally adequate rifle for the first shot on buffalo. If that first shot doesn't do what needs to be done, the next half-dozen might not, either. The literature of Africana is full of tales of buffalo that took a dozen .375s, .416s, .458s, .470s, and such to bring down. It happens, there's no question about it. But it cannot happen if the first bullet does its work. And that's why, regardless of the cartridge chosen, it must be remembered that shot placement remains the critical issue on buffalo—as much as on anything else and perhaps more so. And even though subsequent shots may seem only to add fuel to the fire, I remain convinced that backup shots are important. It is extremely rare for a buffalo to charge upon receiving that first bullet, well placed or not. Typically they will turn away and head for thicker cover, where you do not want to follow them if you don't have to. That's why I like to back up a good softpoint with a solid for second and subsequent shots. Much of the time that backup solid goes up the tailpipe, and when you find your buffalo dead you can learn whether it was necessary or not.

At this point I must admit that I'm ambivalent about choice of rifles for buffalo. I have hunted them with a wide assortment of rifles ranging in caliber from .338 to .500 Nitro Express and in foot-pounds from the .375 H&H up to the .460 Weatherby. There is a big difference between hitting a buffalo with a .375 and hitting one with a .416. Given identically good shot placement in the chest, the animal usually won't go as far when hit well with the .416. And there's an equally big difference between a .416 and a .470, .500, .458 Lott, or .460 Weatherby, etc.— provided the shot placement is equally good.

There's the rub: The strength of a buffalo is unbelievable, and a poor shot with even the largest of sporting rifles is just as big a disaster as with a popgun. Given a good hit, the more powerful rifles will achieve quicker results, but without good shot placement, raw power counts for nothing. I guess. I mentioned a buffalo I wounded in the Selous in 1994. We had tracked a group of bulls for a couple of hours, and we caught them in thick, green bush. A nice old bull stood framed in an almost square window, but just as I finished the trigger squeeze, he started to move. I knew before the bullet left the barrel that my quartering-away shot was just a bit far back. The window closed, and there was no second shot. We tracked him for four hours through patch after patch of really nasty cover. When we caught him he was still on his feet, but very sick. The shot had gone exactly as I'd called it, catching just one lung. The rifle was a .450 Rigby Rimless Magnum with a 500-grain Woodleigh bullet. I do not suggest that power makes up for poor shooting, but if I'd been shooting a lesser rifle, I believe the outcome might have been different, either a lost buffalo or a charge in very thick cover.

For general use, the buffalo rifle should be scoped. Shots at fifty yards in heavy thorn are average, but shots at a hundred yards across openings aren't unusual. And even in the thick stuff, you're trying to pick out an aiming point on a black animal in black shadow. The scope will help. The heavy rifle is often unscoped, and whether it is or not, the average guy just plain shoots better with a scoped .375 than with a bigger rifle, like it or not. As I mentioned earlier, my friend and frequent PH Andrew Dawson put a number on it: He loves to see open-sighted big bores on safari because he loves getting close to buffalo, but he reckons the average client armed with an open-sighted rifle gives up 60 percent of potential shots that a client using a scoped rifle would be able to take.

If I'm serious about buffalo hunting, I like to carry an open-sighted heavy rifle myself, but I'll ask one of the trackers to carry a scope-sighted .375, all set to go with a softpoint on top and solids underneath. Quite often, we've caught a herd in an open glade, and the shot's been farther than I cared to try with open sights. If you're hunting lone bulls or a small bachelor herd, it often isn't a problem to close in, so long as the wind is steady. But in big herds it can be almost impossible to get as close as you'd like—and even if you do, the bull you want is apt to be on the far side of the herd.

That's when it's nice to be able to hand off the big gun for an accurate, scoped .375. You take a good rest, wait until the bull stands broadside, make sure there isn't another buffalo behind (this, too, is easier with the scope), and place the shot just so.

I enjoy hunting buffalo with a double rifle, and I recommend their use. Just make sure you understand you are giving up a fair percentage of potential shots because with any iron-sighted rifle you must get closer.

Keep in mind, however, that I'm fairly comfortable with iron sights and I love the big bores. I usually have one or another big double or bolt gun that I'm just itching to use! So that's me, but me doesn't have to be you. If you're carrying a scoped .375 or .416, you really don't need a bigger gun for buffalo, and you actually can handle any shot that comes along.

As far as shot placement goes, there are very few options for "just so." Neck and brain shots are far too tricky and should be avoided. The classic is the broadside heart/shoulder shot, right up the center of the on-foreleg one-third into the chest. A good softpoint with this shot will surely break the on-shoulder and take out the top of the heart. A solid or really good softpoint from a powerful rifle could break both shoulders. The lung shot is equally good, and although it will not break the shoulder, in my experience a perfect lung shot with a softpoint may well take effect more quickly than a heart shot. Even in relatively thick cover, I have seen a number of buffalo go down within sight to a well-placed lung shot. Instead of the center of the foreleg, come up the rear line of the foreleg one-third to one-half of the way up into the body. In all cases stay away from the top half. As Andrew Dawson says, "There isn't much up there," and if you choose the lung shot, stay very tight on the rear line of the foreleg.

Quartering-to shots are excellent, but quartering-away shots are dangerous. A very shallow angle is fine, but if there's any chance of catching paunch, you need to wait for a better presentation. As I've written elsewhere, on quartering shots (to or from), the best trick I know is to find the sliver of light between the front legs, divide that light vertically, and come up one-third into the body. Frontal shots are also very good—but make sure you're steady. If you slip to one side or the other, you will catch just one lung, and that is not enough.

Wherever you choose to shoot your buffalo, it's critical that you hit him right. I've traded a big open-sighted rifle for a smaller scoped rifle too often to recommend the former without some reservations. The .375 is, I think, a very sensible minimum—and a bigger gun, if you can handle it, will provide more impressive results. But if you choose a bigger gun, it, too, should wear a scope if your goal is to take the very best buffalo you can find in the time you have. The hundred-yard shot, or the shot in heavy shadow, is just too common to overlook, and an open-sighted rifle is a poor choice for such shooting. And of course there's also the problem of picking a path through brush with open sights. As I mentioned in a previous chapter, no matter how big the bullet may be, it doesn't take much brush to deflect it. All that said, however, if your goal is to have the best possible experience from your buffalo hunt, and if you're willing to sacrifice some potential inches of horn for excitement, by all means use an open-sighted big bore. You'll have to get close, and that's at least half the fun of buffalo hunting.

I've had wonderful fun hunting buffalo with various big doubles; as Ian MacFarlane told me one day, "You just feel good about shooting something with a rifle like that." But if I had to pick a perfect rifle for hunting buffalo, it would be a double from .450/.400 up that wore a claw-mounted scope.

I have used single shots for buffalo, and they're fun, too. Again, it depends a bit on your mindset. Even with the very best shot placement, only through blind luck will a buffalo go down on receiving a single bullet. Instead, he'll typically turn tail and head for heavy cover. Often, in a herd situation, there will be no chance for a second shot—but there might be. No matter how fast you think you are, only rarely will there be enough time to reload a single shot and get in another shot yourself. Which means your PH must use his judgment and do his job, and you must allow him to. I'm OK with that.

My second choice, after a scoped double, would be a scope-sighted magazine rifle in one of the .416s, or perhaps the great old .404 Jeffery. But if you're even slightly recoil-sensitive, stick with a .375. On buffalo, the biggest bullet in the world won't do you a damn bit of good if you can't put it in the right place.

Elephant

Chapter 31

Times change. Just twenty years ago, when I was writing the original version of this book, it seemed almost certain that elephant hunting would soon be a thing of the past and Africa's remaining elephant might hang on in a few well-patrolled national parks. In the mid-1980s organized ivory poaching was indeed reducing Africa's elephant at an alarming rate. The great beasts were virtually eradicated across most of Kenya, Zambia's Luangwa Valley, and much of Central Africa. Continent-wide, however, the elephant was never in as dire straits as antihunters would have you believe (and many still believe). At the low point, probably 1988, there were believed to be 700,000 wild elephant remaining in Africa. This was not an endangered population, although elephant were certainly locally threatened in many areas.

Still, the hue and cry did bring on the international ban on ivory trade. This, plus rigorous and often brutal enforcement, actually did put the brakes on ivory poaching. In the last twenty years the African elephant has made a dramatic recovery. At this writing about 1.3 million wild elephant are believed to exist in Africa. Some countries, especially the southern ones that never had a huge poaching problem, are now grossly overpopulated with elephant. These hulking animals are slow breeders, so recovery is slow—especially in the areas that were most heavily poached. But elephant are today recovering almost throughout sub-Saharan Africa. Considering the habitat and crop damage that a surfeit of elephant can wreak— not to mention the stark reality that in a Third World economy wildlife must pay its way in order to be tolerated—right now there is perhaps a stronger conservation and management imperative for hunting the African elephant than for any species on Earth save perhaps the white-tailed deer!

Recognizing these things, the "ivory ban" from the very beginning allowed exemptions for sport-hunted ivory for personal use. These exemptions remain in effect, although the U.S. Fish and Wildlife Service tends to impose more rigorous standards than the international body. At this writing American hunters can import

Cleanly taking an elephant is not difficult. The simplest shot is to follow the crease behind the on foreleg up to the top, about a third into the chest. You can shoot right there, or move slightly right onto the shoulder. Either way, with a good solid this elephant will die. A scope is not needed for such shooting.

sport-hunted ivory from Botswana, Namibia, South Africa, and Zimbabwe without a special importation permit, and Tanzanian ivory with a U.S. importation permit. Adding countries has been slow, but at this writing elephant hunting is also open in Cameroon, Mozambique, and Zambia and undoubtedly will reopen in other countries. Every year more permits are available, and with more competition I am even seeing the prices for elephant safaris come down. Elephant hunting is a true growth industry, and one of the real bright spots in both African hunting and the conservation of Africa's wildlife.

I will now let you in on a little secret. When I wrote *Safari Rifles,* I had relatively little actual experience with elephant hunting. I had taken a few, but I was no expert. At the time, with elephant hunting seemingly on the way out, it didn't seem to matter too much. I freely admit that I am still no expert. There are men still living who, in the days when culling was widely practiced, shot elephant into the thousands. And there are professional hunters who grew up shooting ivory to supplement their livelihood, and who have guided hunters to elephant in the hundreds. I do not claim such expertise. On the other hand, I have done quite a lot of elephant hunting in the last few years, and for darn sure I know more about it now than I did twenty years ago!

The brain shot we all hear about is much trickier, especially the frontal brain shot because the attitude of the head is everything. You must visualize the ear holes (which are not actually visible frontally) and shoot to "break a broomstick between the ear holes." In this photo, with the head very straight, eye level is about right.

Elephant hunting is one of the most specialized pursuits on Earth, and a hunt for good ivory is one of Africa's most difficult quests. This, too, is a sign of changing times. In the vastness that is Africa there may be pockets of really heavy ivory, but right now there is no place open to hunting where a given hunter has even reasonable odds of finding a bull carrying hundred-pound tusks. Part of the reason is that in the wake of the ravages of the 1980s, many recovering herds are still young. More importantly, the reality is that the countries where most elephant hunting is done today never produced heavy ivory in any frequency—which suggests the genetics or the soil minerals simply aren't there. Modern elephant hunters have, of necessity, lowered their standards. A seventy-pounder was always a good elephant but today is considered a great elephant. Most bulls taken as trophies carry much lighter ivory; a fifty-pounder today is yesterday's seventy-pounder, and in some areas forty-pound tusks are as good as it gets. This is all OK because the real trophy of an elephant hunt is the memory of tracking the great beasts, getting close, and making a good shot on the world's greatest game.

Well, OK, elephant hunting is truly addictive, and most hunters who have experienced it do rate the elephant as the world's greatest game. But this point can

The side-on brain shot is simpler. Find the earhole and aim perhaps a hand's breadth—no more—in front of the bottom of the earhole.

be argued. What cannot be argued is that the elephant is the world's largest game! Even so, elephant do vary considerably in size. The elephant of southern and southwestern Africa, from western Zimbabwe through Botswana, Angola, and northern Namibia, stand fourteen feet at the shoulder and are believed to weigh as much as 14,000 pounds. I have hunted elephant in the Hwange Park region of western Zimbabwe, in Botswana, and in northeastern Namibia, and these animals are huge. Zambezi Valley elephant tend to be a bit smaller in the body, with big bulls having somewhat smaller tracks. This carries through into much of Mozambique and on up into extreme southern Tanzania. A bull I shot in 2006 on the Tanzanian side of the Ruvuma River was, at least to my eye, essentially the same size as a good Zambezi Valley bull. Entirely different are the elephant of the eastern coastal regions; the elephant I've hunted in Tanzania's Selous Reserve are little more than half the size of Botswana elephant, certainly no more than four to four and a half tons for a big bull. I'm told that the forest elephant of Central Africa, too, are small in the body, but I've never seen one on the ground. I have had close encounters with elephant in dense forest, and however big they really are, they look plenty big up close and personal!

Elephant habitat, too, varies. In the 1980s what little was left of elephant hunting was generally conducted in the densest cover imaginable, where the harried

Is your frontal shot fully frontal? If it isn't, you must keep in mind that the brain lies at the very back of the skull, so the bullet must angle in. This one is tricky, with the correct spot just to the left of the eye. Personally, I'd let him turn for a straight shot.

animals had retreated. This has changed somewhat today. Nowhere in Africa can you rely on shooting your elephant in open grasslands like the old-timers so often did, but cover does vary. Northern Namibia tends to be more open than Botswana, and Botswana and western Zimbabwe tend to be more open than the *jess* of the Zambezi Valley. Tanzania varies radically. The thicket lines of the Selous Reserve are as thick as anything I've ever been in, while the more prevalent *miombo* forest is relatively open. Far to the northwest is the forest, and most shots are measured in feet, whether we're talking bongo or elephant.

The cover to be hunted and the size of the elephant you are hunting both impact the best choice of rifles and cartridges, at least in a theoretical world. For instance, in most areas the same legal minimum for buffalo also applies to elephant, namely the .375. This arrangement is simple and convenient, but keep in mind that a small-bodied elephant is five times the size of a buffalo, and a really big elephant could be ten times larger! I'm not sure any hand-held rifle has the power to "shock" an elephant, so elephant hunting is a game of precise shot placement. I submit, now that I have a fair amount of experience, that the frontal brain shot on an elephant is quite possibly the most difficult shot in the hunting world.

A scoped .375 is the most versatile of safari rifles. Easy to shoot, it promotes ideal shot placement. On the other hand, while an elephant is not unduly impressed by foot-pounds of energy, it is absolutely essential that the bullet penetrates, whether into the chest cavity on a heart/lung shot or into the brain on a head shot. A good .375 solid will definitely penetrate on a body shot and on a side-on brain shot. Most of the time it will penetrate on a frontal brain shot—but not always.

This is something I have learned in recent years. On any frontal brain shot the attitude of the head is extremely important because the brain lies toward the back of the head. When the head is up, you must shoot a bit farther down the trunk, and thus you need more penetration. When the head is down, you shoot higher, above the eyes, and less penetration is required. At, say, fifteen yards a frontal brain shot is fairly simple and easy to visualize. But at three or four yards, when the elephant is towering over you, you must shoot well down the trunk to have the right line to the brain. Add to this the huge bulk and massive head of a southern African giant, and you must ask your bullet to penetrate a couple of feet of soft tissue before it ever starts to penetrate that honeycombed skull.

I have taken elephant with a .375, and most of the time it will work. I have also seen it fail to penetrate, or fail to hold its straight line, on frontal brain shots. Since this is the shot you must make in the final moments of a charge, I do not believe any .375 is the best choice for elephant hunting. This is one situation where the extra-heavy bullets, 350 and 370 grains, may have some utility, obviously if available in well-constructed solids.

Elephant hunting is also one instance in which I believe there is no benefit to using a scope, and in fact it could be a detriment. Elephant are often taken at very close range. My own closest shot has been four yards, and I've taken the majority at ten to fifteen yards. You don't need a scope for that kind of shooting. Now, I am left-eye dominant and I shoot left-handed. I keep both eyes open when shooting with a

Left, .450/.400-3", right, .404 Jeffery. The .375 has taken far too many elephant for anyone to knock it, but to my thinking these two old ".40+" cartridges represent the absolute minimum for serious elephant hunting. With modern bullets and loads they will handle any shot, and offer surprisingly mild recoil.

Jim Hall, Ivan Carter, and I pose with Jim Hall's Zambezi Valley bull, cleanly taken with a .416 Rigby. The various .416s offer marvelous penetration, and are a bit easier to shoot than the big bores. Jim's bull dropped to a side-on brain shot, and we're certain he never heard the rifle's report.

scope. So I don't lose my peripheral vision with a scope nearly as badly as do people who must close one eye. Even so, the most dangerous thing in elephant hunting is often not the elephant you're shooting but other elephant you may not even be aware of. The tunnel vision that is part and parcel of shooting with a scope can get you killed. Also, when you are very, very close, the elephant may seem like a wall of gray. In order to shoot you must pick the correct aiming point, and any magnification at all can make this more difficult.

I have taken numerous elephant with scoped rifles, and probably will again—but they are not ideal, especially up close.

What about longer shots? Well, elephant hunting is a bit different from most pursuits. Elephant have great hearing and one of the keenest senses of smell in the animal kingdom. I am not altogether convinced that their vision is all that poor. Rather, it seems to me that their other senses are so acute that they just don't rely heavily on their eyes. You must have the wind right and you must be quiet, but if you do these things you can get quite close to elephant. And you should. Getting close to these great beasts is part of the thrill, and it's also a practical imperative because the shot placement must be exactly right. Close, of course, is a relative thing, but there is no hundred-yard shooting at elephant. Forty yards is considered a very long shot, and twenty-five to thirty yards is not considered "close."

Having read much too much Bell, everybody wants to make a brain shot. The brain shot is very tricky, and despite all the old writings, I have seen few elephant actually stunned or knocked down by a near miss to the brain. The more common reaction is instantaneous and rapid flight, and if a well-placed backup shot isn't fired immediately, the most likely result is that your elephant will never be seen again. My opinion is the brain shot is a very bad idea for inexperienced elephant hunters. (Read your Bell one more time: He recommended that novices not take brain shots.) If it's taken, the shot needs to be close and the elephant should be in

Left, .450-3¼" Nitro Express; right, .458 Lott. If you're serious about elephant hunting, I believe the collective wisdom of the old-timers remains valid. The best medicine is a true big bore like these, from .450 caliber on up, and delivering a minimum of 5,000 foot-pounds. But that's true only if you can shoot the big guns well. Otherwise, consider something in the .400 to .416 class.

I used a scoped .375 on the Namibian "problem elephant," taken with PH Jamy Traut. In really open country a scope is not a hindrance, but my first shot was in thick stuff at maybe five yards, and at that range tunnel vision from a scope complicates things.

an open enough spot so that, should the brain shot fail, a backup shot can surely be taken (by either you or your PH). A low-power scope does indeed make it easier to place the brain shot, especially if you aren't confident and competent with iron sights. However, there should be limits. Twenty-five yards is a very long distance for a brain shot, probably too far. Within twenty yards (preferably well within), provided other elephant aren't too close and the cover isn't too thick, the brain shot might be viable. If you've practiced a fair amount with your iron sights, you should be able to handle such a shot.

The heart or lung shots are the easiest to visualize. The elephant has a distinct crease behind his foreleg. For the perfect lung shot with a broadside elephant, just come up that crease to where it ends, about a third up into the chest, and squeeze the trigger. For the perfect heart shot, also use the crease, but from where it ends come (right or left, depending on how the elephant is standing) into the center of the shoulder. At very close range this shot is easier with iron sights because you can see the whole elephant and gain perspective. Even at forty yards, a very long shot at an elephant, iron sights should pose no problem. Their other advantage is that in

We talk too much about the brain shot. It's tricky, with a high chance for failure. This Tanzanian bull didn't even think about it. I found the shoulder and gave him both barrels, and he didn't go far.

walking about twenty yards from us, with dark approaching. A brain shot would have been silly and I

those last few silent moments when you close on your bull, any appendage added to a rifle's profile is just a menace to snag on vines and branches.

Again, I've gained a lot of experience on elephant in the last few years. I've made brain shots and body shots, and I've had brain shots that succeeded and others that failed. Especially on a frontal brain shot, there are no guarantees. If it works, the brain shot is the most spectacular sight in the world. The back legs buckle first, and the entire mass of elephant collapses immediately, almost before you are out of recoil. If it fails, on the other hand, you also know that almost instantly! And then you'd better do something very fast. In elephant hunting the ability to quickly fire an equally well-placed backup shot may be just as important as your ability to fire that first shot. You don't need a scope. You don't necessarily need a double, either. But you must spend plenty of time on the range practicing firing and firing again. If you choose a double, practice the reload as well!

My best elephant was taken in Botswana with Johan Calitz in 2007, a wonderful old bull with beautiful, thick ivory. We had worked him for nearly an hour trying to get a shot. He knew we were there, and instead of running he kept to very thick cover. Finally he had enough and came toward us, not really a charge but threatening. This was the chance we wanted, but he was a monstrous bull, and at six yards I had the worst possible angle for a frontal brain shot. My Rigby .450-3¼" barely rocked him, and I knew instantly I had failed. This time, as we learned later, I had the line but the bullet just didn't go far enough. Right then things were happening fast. As he turned I fired my second barrel into the shoulder, and this would eventually have done the trick fine. But I broke the rifle, managed to get in one cartridge, and just as he vanished into the brush I broke his spine with that third shot. Total distance covered was maybe fifteen yards, total time not three seconds.

As I've said, the .375 is the legal minimum, and it will work most of the time. Come to think of it, even the big bores won't work all the time. There is a big difference between skull size on a cow elephant and skull size on a bull, even before you get to regionally different sizes of elephant. I have used the .375 and would again, but I would much prefer the old East African Professional Hunters' Association minimum of .40-caliber.

Before discussing the exact rifles and cartridges I consider most appropriate for elephant, let's again revisit the premise, because elephant hunting really is different. It starts with a good solid. Effectively killing an elephant is all about penetration into the vitals, nothing more and nothing less. I have personally seen an elephant killed very dead by a 510-grain softpoint from a .458. This was a fluke shot up into the throat as the elephant towered almost straight overhead, demonstrating. I'm also reasonably certain that careful shot placement with really tough modern bullets like the Barnes Triple Shock and Swift A-Frame would be effective most of the time. With elephant, though, "most of the time" isn't good enough. You want either a traditional steel-jacketed solid or a modern homogeneous-alloy solid.

Then you want a heavy-for-caliber bullet that will maintain straight-line penetration. And you want to push that solid bullet fast enough so that deep penetration is assured. All things being equal, the faster the bullet the deeper it will penetrate, and the least resistance it encounters the deeper it will penetrate. There are compromises to be made. At the turn of the century most ivory hunters had experience with low-velocity black-powder cartridges firing lead bullets. Penetration was sketchy, because even hardened lead bullets might deform, velocity was low, and the large-caliber bullets, although they delivered heavy blows, encountered great resistance and slowed down quickly. When smokeless powder was new, these guys discovered that long, heavy-for-caliber, small-caliber bullets like the 156-grain 6.5mm, 173-grain 7mm, 220-grain .30-caliber, and 215-grain .303 (.311) penetrated like crazy. Over time, however, it also came to be understood that these slender bullets occasionally bent and ran off-course, delivering little energy. I think there are good reasons either .375 or .40-caliber has been considered minimal for generations now.

However, their concept of small caliber (which means little resistance) and high velocity isn't all that bad. John Taylor wrote that the .450/.400 delivered more penetration than any of the big Nitro Express cartridges. This actually makes sense. The velocity was the same as the bigger cartridges, roundabout 2,100 FPS, and the 400-grain bullet was long and heavy-for-caliber—but the (nominally) .40-caliber bullet encountered much less resistance than a .458- or .475-inch bullet at the same velocity. Today I think the .450/.400, now resurrected by Hornady and Ruger, once again makes a very sound minimum for serious elephant hunting. This puts the similar (with standard ballistics) .404 Jeffery in the same league.

The various .416s are possibly even better, although they have more recoil. The 400-grain .416 bullet is plenty long and heavy for caliber, and a .416 bullet encounters less resistance than the larger-diameter bullets of a true big bore. Add to this the .416's greater velocity: The Rigby and Remington are about 2,400 FPS, and others like the .416 Weatherby Magnum are faster. I have taken elephant with the .416 Hoffman (wildcat forerunner to the .416 Remington) and .416 Rigby, and I have seen a number of other elephant taken with various .416s. It is my opinion that any .416 with a 400-grain solid at something approaching 2,400 FPS will penetrate better on elephant than any big bore at the Nitro Express standard velocity of 2,150 FPS. This may or may not be true, but I do know that a well-placed .416 solid will penetrate and kill an elephant from any sensible angle. The only downside is that its smaller-diameter bullet definitely doesn't deliver as

Elephant in the country most suited to the body shot
Even here, on an open grassy plain, the brain shot is to be preferred
if the hunter can get to within thirty or forty yards

This original drawing from the master, W. D. M. Bell, shows the proper aiming point for the shoulder/heart shot.

heavy a blow as a bullet from a .450-caliber or greater rifle. Experienced elephant hunters maintain that the true big bores are thus better for stopping a charge. I don't honestly have enough experience in stopping elephant at close range to confirm or deny this, but I tend to agree.

Since John Rigby brought out his .450-3¼" Nitro Express in 1898 its ballistics have remained the standard for a big-bore stopping rifle: a bullet of 480 to 520 grains in weight, between .450 and .488 in caliber, at a velocity of about 2,150 FPS, yielding around 5,000 foot-pounds of energy. In this class the .458 Winchester Magnum (with full loads) is the most popular bolt-action cartridge, while the .470 Nitro Express is the most popular double-rifle cartridge. However, all of the various Nitro Express cartridges between my .450-3¼" and the .475 No. 2 (and No. 2 Jeffery) and .476 Westley Richards should be considered too similar to argue about. I have only taken one elephant with the .500 Nitro Express, but those who use it a lot maintain (and I agree) that its heavier 570-grain bullet of larger diameter deals a noticeably heavier blow. However, since its velocity is the same and its larger diameter means more resistance, it probably doesn't penetrate much better.

All of these cartridges are extremely effective under most circumstances. I tend to prefer them because I like double rifles, and because they are all a sensible mixture

The deadliest and most humane method of killing the African Elephant is the shot in the comparatively small brain contained in his gigantic head

This Bell sketch shows the frontal brain shot. I hate to disagree with the master, but I think the artist or editor did him a disservice. With the head attitude up like this, the aiming spot needs to be dropped a few inches. You must visualize the actual ear holes, which at this angle are below the eyes.

of adequate power with manageable recoil. However, it is occasionally whispered that their velocity level may not be quite enough to ensure adequate penetration. As I said, my .450-3¼" failed to penetrate on a frontal brain shot on my Botswana elephant. PH Johan Calitz, who primarily uses doubles in .470 and .500, probably has as much experience with these Botswana giants as anyone alive—and he likes to get close. He maintains that he has seen similar failures to penetrate adequately with all the Nitro Express cartridges between .450 and .500. He doesn't worry about it unduly, because it doesn't happen all the time and he feels the blow delivered is sufficient to turn a charge. And, of course, as a staunch double-rifle man he is instantly prepared with the second barrel if needed.

It seems generally agreed, however, that in order to get consistent penetration at all angles on all sizes of elephant, the prescription is a couple hundred feet per second more velocity. For exactly this reason, in recent years my old friend Geoff

Donna Boddington used a Heym PH in .450/.400-3" to take this lovely Botswana tusker in April 2008. This cartridge is probably a sound minimum for modern elephant hunting, offering superb penetration and very mild recoil. She used Hornady's new load with their "DGS" (Dangerous Game Solid).

Broom has put away his double .500 and is using instead the .450 Dakota. He uses heavy 600-grain bullets at perhaps 2,250 FPS and maintains that the added sectional density together with the higher velocity enable him not only to penetrate any elephant's skull from any angle but also, on the going-away backup shots a PH must sometimes make, to literally penetrate an elephant's body from end to end. Michel Mantheakis uses exactly the same cartridge and load, but he's a lifelong bolt-action man, so his "upgrade" was from a .458 Winchester Magnum.

There are several large-case "fast .450s," including the .450 Dakota, the almost identical .450 Rigby Rimless Magnum, and the .460 Weatherby Magnum. However, my old friend Jack Lott would be delighted to see that his .458 Lott has become the "standard" in this power level. The Lott is not as fast as the three others mentioned but doesn't lag by much. It is offered in factory rifles from CZ and Ruger, among others, and has the case capacity to easily achieve 2,300 FPS with a 500-grain bullet. Note: At just 150 FPS faster than standard .458 Winchester Magnum or Nitro Express velocities, it kicks a whole lot more. But that extra velocity does make a difference in penetration.

Yet another step up is to the .505 Gibbs and .500 Jeffery, both somewhat resurrected at this writing. Loads vary, but both push heavier .50-caliber bullets at something between 2,300 and 2,400 FPS. So will George Sandmann's .505 Empire, still in development at this writing, and so do other wildcat and proprietary .50-caliber cartridges. The rub, if there is one, is that the fast .450s and the .50s are truly ferocious in recoil, so rifles must be quite heavy to be manageable. My friend Jim Crawford used a .500 Jeffery by Rigby for the 2006 Tanzanian elephant safari we shared. He has learned to shoot that big rifle quite well, but he took his elephant on the twentieth day, and I didn't envy his carrying that twelve-pound rifle all day every day!

The ultimate step up is to John Taylor's "ultra-large-bores," the .577 Nitro Express, wildcat .577s like the .577 Tyrannosaur, and the .600 Nitro Express. And I suppose, since it exists, the .700 Nitro Express must be included. Of these, I think the .577 in a double rifle still makes a fair amount of sense. In a double of adequate weight, recoil is heavy but not beyond reason. The primary problem with all of these, however, is that the rifles they are chambered to must of necessity be too darn heavy to carry all day. I'm in pretty good shape, but I've done enough tough elephant hunting that I know I don't want to do it! There is also the "R Factor," recoil. Some people can learn to shoot these cannons, but many cannot. Even if you can, the issue of recovery time between shots is perhaps as critical as the actual recoil itself. The big guns will absolutely stop any elephant with any sensible shot—but they are too much of a good thing for me!

Specific only to elephant, I have just given a slightly different spin to the old double versus bolt-action debate. Because bolt actions are stronger, they can be chambered to faster, more powerful cartridges than the double rifle's classic Nitro Express rounds. So does that mean the bolt action is a better choice? If you are most comfortable with a bolt action, then indeed it does. I'd start with the .458 Lott as a near-perfect elephant cartridge in all ways. Come to think of it, I'd stop there, but there's much to be said for the raw power of the big .50s.

For me, however, I believe the instantly available second shot, with no sound and no movement, gives the nod to the double. In any determined charge by any dangerous beast, that second shot could save your life. But, again, elephant hunting is different. I know of no other form of hunting in which that second shot is more important, or more likely to prevent the escape of a wounded animal. No matter what happens, if you know how to use your double, you will almost always have available that split second needed to fire that second barrel. And no matter how fast you are, there is not always time with a bolt action. On body shots the one-two punch of a double is fantastic. On brain shots, well, I've conceded that once in a while, particularly up close on a big-bodied and big-headed bull, there can be failure to penetrate. However, on all brain shots the larger and more common problem is simply missing the brain. Either way, things happen very fast, and only a double rifle is consistently fast enough to give you the second shot needed to save the day.

At this writing I can say that I have never lost, or even had to track, any of the elephant I've shot. I can also say that I've messed up my share of brain shots! In 1992, in Russ Broom's concession near Lake Kariba, a cow-elephant herd killed a villager who was trying to protect his crops. A "PAC" (Problem Animal Control) permit was issued, and PH Rory Muil and I went after them. I was shooting a .416 Rigby, and we caught the herd just below a little knoll. Rory and I were on the summit, so I was shooting downhill, a most odd angle. I flubbed the brain shot, and the whole herd was instantly in motion. In just an instant the stricken animal would be covered by another cow. I knew I'd messed up and I saw it coming; I slam-fired the .416 somewhere into the shoulder. It wasn't a good shot, but it worked well enough for us to catch up quickly and finish things with a good brain shot (as opposed to the bad one I'd just made). I'm very fast with a bolt action, but a double would have given me additional split seconds to be surer of the second shot.

Recently I was hunting with Ivan Carter, a great elephant hunter. I had a tuskless permit, and after an hour of cat-and-mouse in thick *jess* I got a frontal brain shot at something absurd like four yards. The frontal brain shot is incredibly tricky, and head angle is everything. The only way to do it right is to visualize a broomstick

A fine Botswana tusker taken by Bill Jones with his Marcel Thys .577, using Woodleigh solids loaded by Superior. The .577 is probably the largest cartridge that makes any real sense for modern hunting.

between the ears and shoot to break it—and even then you can mess it up because it seems unnatural to fire as far down the trunk as you sometimes must. This animal's head was up and I shot a bit too high. Instantly she was in motion, but this time I had my double .450. As the head came around I fired the second barrel just ahead of the ear hole, and she collapsed onto her knees. The time between the shots was less than a half-second, and only a double allows such a fast recovery.

The closer the cover the more valuable a double rifle becomes. As I've said, I haven't hunted forest elephant, and since ivory from the forest zone currently isn't importable, I may never. But I've run into elephant several times while hunting other forest game, and it really is one of the most dangerous situations in the hunting world. A big double provides better insurance—and a sleek, short double is also easier to carry through the thick tangles. In more open country the bolt action's faster cartridges and superior accuracy seem to give it a logical edge. But since there are no long shots on elephant, the point seems moot.

In Tanzania in 2006 it was my seventeenth day before we found the kind of elephant we had hoped to find. Dark was coming soon, and the bull herd was moving out for its nightly raid on orchards of ripening cashews. More than a dozen bulls were lined out on an elephant path through burned mopane, and the bull we wanted was in the lead. This was no time for finesse; we trotted along an adjacent elephant path until we caught up and passed, then we converged. With a moving elephant and darkness coming soon, I gave no thought to a brain shot. I stepped in front and fired both barrels into the shoulder from about twenty-five yards. The bull was obviously hit hard, but he recovered and turned back on his trail. I ran across the angle, reloading, and gave him both barrels into the other shoulder. He went down in another ten yards. In that open ground I could have done just as well with a bolt action, but I seriously doubt I could have fired four shots any faster.

There are exceptions, like Geoff Broom, who has switched from doubles to bolt actions; and there are diehard bolt-action men like Michel Mantheakis and Barrie Duckworth, who have used a bolt action all their lives and are unlikely to switch. But over the last few years, as doubles and ammo for them have become more available, I believe a majority of professional hunters who seriously hunt elephant have gone to double rifles. I think they're right, but that doesn't mean (at all!) that you must have a double to hunt elephant. In fact, unless he is willing to take the time to really learn how to use a double, the first-time elephant hunter might well be better off with a more familiar bolt action. Certainly the power is there, and a bolt action with a detachable scope is clearly a more versatile tool. Overall, however, I believe firmly in the double rifle as the best choice for elephant hunting. Calibers we can argue around the campfire, but I don't think it matters too much. The .500-3", now readily available, is probably the best, but there's nothing wrong with a .470, or my .450, or any of the old calibers. For that matter, a soft-recoiling .450/.400 or versatile .500/.416 is perfectly adequate for any elephant that walks. Power is pure insurance on elephant, and shot placement remains the most important consideration.

Other Heavyweights

Chapter 32

J ust in my time Africa has changed, then changed again, and undoubtedly will
continue to change. When I first hunted Kenya, elephant hunting was closed
but black rhino remained open (with a thirty-five-day minimum safari to obtain a
license). It was the same the first time I hunted Zambia, although I don't recall the
minimum requirement to obtain a black rhino license (I do know it was above my
pay grade). At that time taking a white rhino was unthinkable, though that would
change quickly. Hippo were taken primarily for lion bait, but were rarely considered
a trophy animal.

The collapse came very quickly for the black rhino. In the 1970s, in good
rhino country, it wasn't uncommon to spend a lot of time dodging them. This was
a common form of exercise while hunting buffalo and bushbuck up on Mount
Kenya! In just a few short years they were almost gone. Roger Whittall and I ran
into a rhino track up from Cabora Bassa in Mozambique in 1988 and we were
amazed. In 1992 Russ Broom and I came out of a leopard blind in the dark and
ran straight into a black rhino. It was a rare encounter, but a scary one. The rhino
gave its distinctive *whoof* and crashed off in an uncertain direction. We scattered like
quail, and had a time regrouping and reorienting ourselves.

The South Africans, and later the Namibians, did a wonderful job bringing back
the white rhino. The first modern hunting took place in the 1970s, but it was a few
years later before Americans could bring in rhino trophies. I remember being offered a
white rhino back then—at the same trophy fee as for a nyala! When white rhino became
importable to the United States, the trophy fees skyrocketed, and with little change have
continued to escalate ever since. I took a beautiful white rhino up in the Palala River
country in 1986, and the trophy fee was about $5,000. That was a lot of money to me
back then, but today you'd have to add a zero, and I'm not sure that would be enough!

In the same two countries, South Africa and Namibia (and in special situations
in Zimbabwe), they have also done a great job with black rhino. Both South Africa

Those were the days! Although there is once again a very small quota for black rhino in South Africa and Namibia, realistically the hunting is not as it used to be. The chances of needing to stop a rhino charge today are very, very slim.

and Namibia now have extremely healthy populations, with bulls dying of old age every year. CITES (Convention on International Trade in Endangered Species) has rewarded these efforts by authorizing both South Africa and Namibia very small quotas of black rhino, subject to very rigid conditions (essentially, a targeted bull must be known to be old and infirm!). At this writing Namibia has not actually utilized any of her allocation, but a very few black rhino bulls have been taken in South Africa. U.S. Fish and Wildlife Service does not allow importation yet (and may not), but this reflects another sea change: Absent American hunters, these black rhino are still commanding six-figure prices! Russian sportsmen took the last two I know of, definitely a sign of changing times.

Traditionalists will argue that only the black rhino counts as part of the "Big Five," while the larger but more docile white rhino does not. I'm not sure whether this line of thought is based on snobbishness or "sour grapes" mentality, but I think it's silly. Unfortunately, the circumstances are such that I'm afraid setting out to take

White rhino are grazing animals that tend toward more open country than the black rhino, which is primarily a browser. Even so, the idea is to get close, and a rhino's poor eyesight allows it. So the best rifle is definitely an open-sighted big bore.

the Big Five today is also a bit silly. (But then, if you count the white rhino, I've got mine, so I certainly have no right to throw water on your hunting dreams!)

What I mean by this is that all rhino hunting today is at best a pale shadow of what it used to be, much the same as with hunting the American bison today. Some white rhino are taken in large parks and private reserves, and it can take quite a while to find them. My white rhino was an old bull with a penchant for breaking fences, and it took the best part of two weeks to find the correct one. But while the ivory ban has greatly reduced the market value of ivory, and thus reduced the poaching, the value of rhino horn for dagger handles, poison-proof cups, and aphrodisiac remains strong in some parts of the world. Today's rhino populations are monitored and guarded, so any rhino hunt must be regarded more as a collection than a hunt. Honestly, the other dangerous game offers much more genuine adventure, mostly at significantly lesser cost.

A popular option today is the "green" or darting hunts for rhino. Although my opinion is extremely unpopular, I have misgivings about this practice. If there is a biological or management necessity, such as to collect data, relocate, or harvest the horn (and thus eliminate value to poachers), great. But I worry about starting down the slippery slope toward "catch-and-release" hunting, and of course there are risks associated with darting. Absent a genuine need, it seems to me that if a species is truly threatened or endangered, it should be left alone to breed. If there is a surplus, then

The only rhino I have ever shot and probably ever will shoot was taken in northern South Africa in 1986. I used a Heym double in .470, and of course it worked perfectly.

it should be harvested as hunters always have. On the other hand, that's just me. It's much the same as with the captive-reared lion being "hunted" today. I understand the desire to have a close encounter with a rhino. I'm fairly certain I will never hunt a black rhino, but I had the chance to hunt white rhino when it was affordable, and I certainly can't fault today's hunters who have the same desire.

The hippo has changed dramatically in status in recent years. Part of this, I think, is that ever-shrinking quotas (and ever-escalating costs) have placed greater value on every animal available on any given safari. Safari Club International has had much to do with increasing this recognition. For instance, we didn't used to consider animals such as hyena and crocodile as sporting trophies at all! The hippo is huge, the second-largest land mammal after the elephant. He is generally fearless of man and can be very aggressive; under the right (or wrong) circumstances he is very possibly the most dangerous of all the big stuff. Certainly he is believed to cause the deaths of more rural Africans than all the rest of the land mammals put together.

This is partly because the hippo's habits put him in direct conflict with rural people. The hippo is a grazing animal that tends to spend its days in a water sanctuary but its nights grazing on land—sometimes far from water, depending on available food. In the morning the hippo starts to work his way back to his river, lake, or

The hippo seems a placid beast, and in his water sanctuary he generally is—provided you keep your distance. On land it's a different situation, with few animals more aggressive by nature.

pan . . . and rural Africans also tend to go for water in the mornings. Conflicts are almost inevitable.

If you are on land and the hippo is safe in his water sanctuary, there is almost no danger at all, but you don't want to get between a hippo and his water. Come to think of it, you don't want to get in the water with these hulks, either! Give them their distance and they're usually OK, but it isn't uncommon for hippo to attack boats that come too near. In 1985 Jack Atcheson Jr. and I were hunting in the Okavango with Ronnie MacFarlane. We poled a dugout canoe, called a *mokoro*, up a channel until it opened into a lagoon. At the far end of that lagoon there was one hippo, maybe two hundred yards away. Ronnie stopped the canoe and stabilized it as the hippo dipped under the water. Okavango hippo, protected for many years, are fearless and often aggressive, so he was being careful, including exchanging his pole for his Ruger .458.

A few seconds later we saw reeds moving in front of us, sort of like an inbound torpedo. Jack and I were sitting in the thwarts, with absolutely no place to go. The hippo boiled up at Ronnie's feet, nothing but a huge pink mouth and gleaming teeth. He fired once, straight down from the hip, and the lagoon became very quiet. We poled to the nearest island and sat for a long time. I believe this was the closest call I have ever had with an African animal.

Steve Hornady took this hippo with a brain shot from the first Ruger No. 1 chambered to his reintroduced .450/.400-3" cartridge. If a brain shot is possible, then a scoped rifle is the best choice. If a body shot is needed, a scope won't help—but you'd better have a big gun loaded with solids!

Recognizing both the size and potential danger of hippo, the African Professional Hunters' Association a few years ago formally created the "Big Six," including the hippo with the traditional Big Five of leopard, lion, buffalo, rhino, and elephant. I think this is appropriate, and certainly there are many more opportunities to hunt hippo today than will ever again occur for rhino. Since our current subject is rifles and cartridges for African game, the hippo is actually far more interesting than either rhino!

All three are genuine heavyweights. The black rhino, though more aggressive by nature, is much smaller than the white rhino. Call him 3,000 pounds, or twice the size of a Cape buffalo. The white rhino might go two and a half tons, while a big hippo bull is probably three tons and more. All three are clearly thick-skinned game, and the proper bullets should be well-constructed solids. The legal minimum for this class is usually .375, sometimes extended to include the 9.3. I'm real comfortable with a .375 for buffalo, and certainly you can kill any of these animals with a well-placed .375 solid. Stopping a charge is another story, and in my view bigger is definitely better.

Rhino have keen senses of smell and hearing, but very poor eyesight (if anything, worse than elephant!). So it is generally possible to get the wind right and stalk fairly close. In the old days, when black rhino were hunted in

This was my shooting position when I shot my big crocodile. I used my old .375 with a 1.75–5X scope. I believe choice of cartridge was good, but if I had it to do over I'd use a bigger scope, because even at 70 yards the intersection of the cross hairs covered everything I needed to hit!

hilly and scrub desert country, an argument could perhaps have been made for a scoped .375 or .416, at least for starters. Though black rhino were once quite plentiful, long-horned rhino were always prized, and it might have made sense to have a rifle that would allow a longer shot if that was what a really big one presented. Today there is no reason for that at all, and the nature of rhino hunting is such that part of the satisfaction should be derived from getting close and doing it right. I used a Heym double .470 for my one and only white rhino, and I believe this is a natural use for any big double from .450/.400 upward. Likewise, any bolt action from .404 Jeffery upward would be a fine choice, but if scoped I'd take the scope off and use iron sights for this one.

Hippo hunting is considerably different. Twenty years ago I wrote, "In the water, the hippo is hardly a game animal at all; he is most susceptible to a brain shot from a very light rifle, and his chief value is for use as a huge lion bait. On land, however, the hippo can be a most dangerous and extremely exciting animal to hunt." Well, I was close, but I didn't have it exactly right, certainly not from today's perspective. It is not much of a hunt to take a hippo in the water. Certainly there is no danger whatsoever (provided you do it right). It is much more exciting to

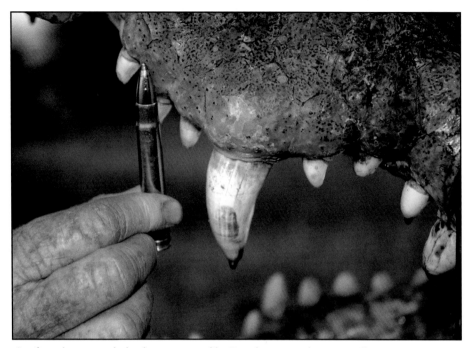

One fact to keep in mind when hunting a crocodile: Every big croc is at least potentially a man-eater!

take a hippo on land, where they will readily charge. However, there are significant differences in the two approaches, and both have their places.

The problem with hunting hippo on the ground is they cannot always be found on dry land in daylight. In some areas, such as the Selous Reserve, it seems fairly common to track hippo away from water and find them sleeping in the bush at midday. But in other areas, such as the Zambezi and Luangwa Valleys, this is almost unheard of. As the dry season progresses, you may find hippo isolated in ever-shrinking pans, where they can also be very aggressive, but the big numbers will be in the big rivers and lakes most of the day. A lion hunter may still want a hippo for bait, quickly, without great concern for size. However, trophy fees are considerably higher today, and the hippo has become an important trophy animal with quotas generally limited.

In other words, if you wish to take a hippo you probably want one with the best tusks you can find. The best way to find a big hippo is to go for the numbers. In the last few years I've spent a lot of time in the lower Zambezi, and I know a great deal more about hippo now than I used to. Shooting "any hippo" in the water is quite easy (if you do it right the first time). A brain shot is almost mandatory because that is usually all you have to shoot at. The skull is actually quite fragile, and while the proper choice is probably a scoped .375 or .416, hippo can be effectively brained with much lighter cartridges. (Any 180-grain .30-06 will do it nicely; it's what happens if you miss the brain that you need to worry about.) The hard part is judging them, whether on land or in water. If the latter, it can be equally difficult to get close enough to make that perfect brain shot.

We have spent hours studying pods of hippo in the Zambezi, trying to get clues as to which ones are bulls and which bull is largest. Once in a while you'll get a good yawn and you can see the tusks, but you might wait all day and never see this. Then they go under water and mix up, and you must start all over again. Most clues are subtler. Sheer size and size of head are good clues. Perhaps the best, requiring both time and experience, are the "bumps" on the side of the snout. These are actually callused receptacles for the major lower tusks, so prominent bumps mean bigger teeth. By the way, this is not a perfect science. Even after hours of careful study it is quite possible to get it wrong and wind up with a huge cow instead of a bull!

Once a hippo is selected, getting a shot may mean more hours of slithering through mud trying to get close enough for a shot. The actual shot isn't difficult. From the side the sweet spot is right below and a bit forward of the base of the ear; from the front the hippo actually has a visible depression above and between the eyes that makes a perfect aiming point. But you must get close enough to be sure. In pans or very shallow water you might be able to correct a mistake, but in a flowing river a wounded hippo will almost surely be lost. So there are three important points: Taking a hippo in water is not unsporting. It is probably the best way to take a good trophy, and it is definitely a game of cool marksmanship. How far to shoot depends on the circumstances and the hunter, but generally you want to close within a hundred yards. Paul Smith and Andrew Dawson actually drag along the Texas-made VRS (Versa Rest System) on both hippo and crocodile hunts; a steady rest makes a huge difference.

On land, or in small pans, hippo hunting is quite a different game. Note, however, that it is not as selective. You may run into a huge bull, but many of the lone hippo you run into in potholes far from big water are younger bulls forced out of the pods. From a distance you can attempt to size them up and pass, but once you get close you may well be committed, because on land or in little water hippo tend to be very aggressive and will charge readily. This proclivity has enabled a couple of very exciting DVDs in recent years. A hippo is more likely to charge than anything else!

In the charge they are so huge that the vulnerable brain shot remains the best, especially at very close range. However, like all brain shots, the target is small and, on a moving animal, tricky. I do not recommend running around looking for such encounters, because not all charges can be stopped. But if you spend enough time around hippo you will get some very serious charges. If the brain shot works, it's lights out. If it doesn't work, or if you go for a body shot, then you confront several tons of muscle covered by thick hide and fat, a classic bullet sponge. So there are truly two types of hippo hunting, on water and on land, and two types of hippo rifle. For the former, a scoped .375 is fine, but a scoped .416 would be better in case the brain shot fails.

I was with Steve Hornady when he took the first animal with his new .450/.400-3" load. It was a scoped Ruger No. 1 single shot, and his brain shot was perfect. But when a brain shot fails, things happen awfully fast. Especially in big water, you want to be able to back up your shots quickly to prevent the loss of a wounded animal. So I'd have to give the nod to a bolt action. On land, however, you want the biggest rifle you can shoot well. I would lean toward an open-sighted double in .450 or greater, but if you prefer a bolt action, that's just fine. The last hippo I shot was with a big Ruger in .458 Lott, and of course it worked perfectly.

The hippo will never be regarded as the grand game animal that the elephant is and the black rhino was, but he is definitely a greatly underrated prize. Seeking a big bull is an extremely interesting hunt in itself, but if you catch one resting in thornbush in daylight or lounging in an evaporating mud hole, he can give you a wonderful adventure you will never forget. Stalk in close with a big rifle—and be ready.

It occurs to me that in the original *Safari Rifles,* and so far in this book, I have almost completely omitted mention of crocodiles. This is as good a place as any, because a big crocodile is a true "heavyweight," a really good one in the 14-foot class or larger easily weighing a ton and more. A crocodile like this may be seventy or eighty years old, usually with plenty of "hunter education" and exceptionally keen senses. In my view the crocodile is the most difficult of all animals to stalk, and poses one of the most difficult shots in African hunting.

This last is because the crocodile is an aquatic creature. He can be properly judged and effectively shot only when he is out of the water. During the warmer midday hours crocs tend to come out and sun on banks, beaches, and sandbars. Depending on the situation, they can be stalked. They can also be baited into very shallow water or up onto a bank. Either way, the crocodile is a reptile with a slow nervous system. A fatal heart/lung shot will kill him, but that isn't good enough. The crocodile must be anchored on the spot; one flick of the powerful tail and he'll be in the water, and then all you have is an expensive splash. The only real options are the brain shot, essentially right under the bony "horns" at the rear of the skull, or a perfect spine shot. The spine is a slightly larger target; on a broadside crocodile you aim a few inches behind the end of the mouth in the horizontal center, right behind the smile.

Dave Fulson and PH Dominique Marteens with a huge Mozambique crocodile. This croc was up on the bank with a full-grown bushpig in its mouth. Dave used a .375, and at 150 yards, a very long shot, he took the safer, but still difficult, spine shot.

Accuracy is the most essential element. Even at that, a shot much past 100 to perhaps 150 yards is foolish—but that depends on your equipment. I made a brain shot on a huge Zambezi crocodile in 2005. The distance was only 70 yards, but I was using my old .375 with its 1.75–5X scope. The intersection of the cross hairs covered everything I needed to hit, and I rate it one of the most difficult shots I've ever made. The best situation, to my thinking, would be a .375 with a more powerful scope than is usually used on that type of rifle. If I had it to do over again, I would probably choose a lighter rifle if the lighter gun carried a more powerful scope! I have seen crocodiles anchored very effectively with 7mms and .30-calibers . . . and I've seen them lost with .375s. More than anything else I can think of, this is a game of perfect shot placement. The brain isn't much bigger than a golf ball, and the larger target, the spine, isn't as big as a softball. A near miss may or may not give time for a backup shot, so you have to be very steady and very certain both of the hold and of your rifle's zero—and you have to do it right.

Rifles for Desert, Savanna, and Thornbush

Chapter 33

Hunters who have not yet been to Africa tend to envision either Tarzan's jungle or the endless cinematic plains of Robert Redford and Meryl Streep's *Out of Africa*. Africa doesn't have true jungle, but it does have vast forests, denser than anything Johnny Weissmuller encountered in his *Tarzan* movies. And it does have broad short-grass plains and vast deserts. However, the reality is that most African hunting, the normal safari for a varied bag, is conducted in neither extreme.

Savanna woodland is a term for plains interspersed with hardwood cover and thornbush. The more open hunting areas are likely to be this kind of country, good examples being Masailand; Ethiopia's Danakil; the extreme northern C.A.R. and Cameroon and southern Chad; the region surrounding the Okavango Delta; and quite a bit of Namibia. Other areas, such as northern South Africa and most of Zimbabwe and Zambia, are thicker with fewer openings, and we call this kind of country "thornbush." Properly it is woodland characterized by the dominant tree: In the south it's "mopane woodland." In Zambia it is more properly called Brachystegia woodland, and on up through southern Tanzania it's called *miombo* forest. Far to the north, above the forest zone and below savanna woodland and true savanna, is a vast belt of Terminalia forest. All are characterized by a hardwood forest of small to medium trees, with a varying understory of thornbush.

In some areas the woodlands—thornbush, if you will—extend for miles without a break. More frequently, though, the sea of brush is broken by waterways with even denser riverine growth or ridiculously open flood plains. There are natural clearings, too. Sometimes they're huge, sometimes very small. In the early season, high grass chokes open areas, but later the grass will be burned and the game will flock to the new green. The terrain may be very flat, but more often it's broken by the typical African kopjes, rocky hills that make wonderful vantage points. Sometimes these hills are full-fledged mountains with their own microcosms of habitat.

While adequate power for the game you're hunting is always a consideration, a lot of great African trophies offer very small targets. In more open country, rifle accuracy is an important consideration, whether you're hunting springbok in South Africa or a Thomson gazelle like this in the short grass savanna of Masailand.

Even the deserts are less open than you might imagine; most of the Kalahari, for instance, is a sea of low brush. Perhaps the most open country I've seen in Africa is the windswept Karoo of South Africa's Cape Province—and even here you will find low brush and the occasional hill mass.

In a typical general-bag area in Ethiopia, Tanzania, northern C.A.R., Zambia, Zimbabwe, Botswana, South Africa, or you name it, the vegetation varies from relatively thick cover to fairly open and back again. And while it could be consistent either one way or the other, it's likely to change back and forth in the space of a few kilometers.

African professional hunters rely heavily on shooting sticks, especially in more open country. Using them properly is almost critical to success, so learn how to use them at home, on your own range.

Take the Selous Reserve of southern Tanzania, for instance. Much of it is relatively open *miombo* forest, with little understory and good visibility. But the Selous is cut by monstrous belts of near-impenetrable thicket, seeming to follow almost imperceptible shifts in elevation, and here visibility quickly dwindles to zero. And there are also vast open areas, too big to be called clearings and almost big enough to be called plains. Masailand is much the same, with savanna woodland varying tremendously in visibility over short distances. In the course of a day you could switch from terrain that calls for long-range shooting to terrain that calls for "average" shooting, and then into thickets where any shot at all would leave powder burns. The Zambezi Valley is known for its *jess* thickets, truly horrible, nasty tangles. Some Valley areas have a lot of *jess* and some much less, but all will also have broad flood plains along the big river, and many miles of relatively open mopane woodland. Some, like Dande and Chewore, have very significant hills.

It's the thornbush, woodland, plain, and even desert regions of Africa that hold the continent's great variety of game. The forests, swamps, and mountains are interesting—but the hunting is mostly very specialized and the species more limited. In the thornbush and savanna, it's the subtle and constant variation of

448

In thicker country a rangefinder isn't needed, but in open country it can be a godsend. I'm getting steady on a springbok in northern Namibia, a small target, while PH Jamy Traut gives me the range.

vegetation and terrain that has created habitat for Africa's fascinating mixture of diverse species.

Country like this is not particularly hard on a rifle. Most safaris are conducted in the long dry season, when unseasonable rain is only a remote possibility. Rust will form, but it will be from perspiration, not precipitation. A constant problem is dust, fine red dust and fine white sand that will filter into a rifle's action. Normal daily maintenance will keep a rifle working, but without it, the grit could keep an action from closing when you need it most.

But if such areas demand only minimal maintenance, they demand the utmost in performance. In the morning you may shoot an impala for leopard bait at seventy-five yards. In the afternoon you may chance across a wonderful sable standing on the far side of a broad *dambo*—and the only shot you have is three hundred yards. In between, you may chance across buffalo, steenbok, lion, duiker, eland, reedbuck, warthog, zebra, and more. The distances may be from a few yards to as far as you are comfortable shooting, and the game may be placidly grazing or heading for the thick stuff as fast as it can get there.

Versatility is the key: Within reason, the rifle you're carrying should be able to handle almost anything the area you're hunting can throw at it. One rifle doesn't have

In thornbush country there may be targets of opportunity, and you will use the rifle you are carrying. If that rifle is a scoped .375, you can handle almost anything you might encounter.

to do everything; there's always a place for that ultimate specialist, the dangerous-game rifle. The problem with such thinking is that your heavy rifle could be miles away in the Land Cruiser when you need it most.

If dangerous game is on the menu, the rifle you regularly carry when you leave the vehicle should be able to handle it in a pinch. That doesn't mean you won't find uses for the ultra-accurate flat-shooting smallbore; but the smallbore, just like the heavy rifle, is specialized. The heavy rifle won't reach across a big clearing—and a very light rifle won't stop a buffalo. In thornbush and savanna, the most important rifle—the one you'll carry most and, on a typical safari, harvest the most game with—must be versatile.

Its caliber depends on you and the kind of game you're spending the most time hunting. It might be a .375, what I call the ultimate compromise cartridge. If it is, you are ready for anything. But a large number of modern safaris are for plains game only, so you may not need a .375. Instead you might choose something on the order of a .338, on the upper end of the game ladder and not quite so versatile as a .375, but more or less able to handle anything that comes along. At an absolute minimum it could be a 6.5mm, .270, 7x57, 7mm magnum, .30-06, or any of the

After more than thirty years of African hunting I still believe the great old .30-06 to be one of the most versatile of all African cartridges, especially in thornbush country where really long shots are rare. I took this beautiful sable in Mozambique.

magnum .30s. If it is, and you're a good shot and you pick your bullets with the utmost care, you may be able to handle anything that comes along. Many hunters have. But you might also give serious thought to having a tracker carry a heavier rifle just as a matter of course.

A lighter rifle, such as a 6mm, a .25, or a hot .22 centerfire, may well have its place—but it will not do as the only rifle available to you, whether you're in the hunting vehicle or on foot. Nor, incidentally, should an open-sighted heavy rifle be the only rifle available to you—unless, in either case, you have decided to make that particular outing a specialized quest for the type of game either rifle is suited for. Today, few safaris are lengthy enough to allow that kind of luxury.

A wonderful lion I took with Russ Broom back in 1984 was actually shot during a chance encounter. I had a lion on license and we had some baits out, but I wasn't really hunting lion and didn't expect to shoot one. Fortunately, the lightest rifle I had was a .375, and when this magnificent lion appeared I was ready. Had I been carrying a light rifle, there might have been time enough to switch guns. Or, had I shot him with a light rifle, I might have gotten away with it. I guess it was the reverse in 2007, when Dirk de Bod and I had one of Namibia's rare "problem lion permits"

This is a huge Sahara dorcas gazelle, taken on wide-open flats in central Chad. The only rifle I had was my 8mm

Remington Magnum, clearly more power than needed—but I did need its accuracy and flat-shooting capabilities.

In really open country a faster magnum might give you more confidence. I used a .300 Remington Ultra Mag to take this warthog on an open pan about 300 yards away. In Africa this is considered a very long shot!

come into our hands. The largest rifle I had with me was a .300 Remington Ultra Mag. No .30-caliber has ever been my idea of ideal lion medicine, but I had good Swift A-Frames and plenty of confidence. It worked just fine, but had I had even the most remote idea that such an opportunity would come along, I would have brought a bigger gun.

Such unexpected opportunities are rare today, but part of the magic in Africa is that you really don't know what a given safari—or even a hunting day—might bring. Over the years, I've shot a great many gazelle, springbok, warthog, impala, and even pygmy antelope with rifles far larger and more powerful than necessary. Overkill isn't the worst thing that can happen, so long as the rifle you carry has both the accuracy and the flatness of trajectory to make careful shot placement practical over the full spectrum of hunting ranges your area might offer. And, quite obviously, you must be able to shoot your chosen rifle. If its recoil is too much for you to handle, whatever capabilities it might have are useless. Remember, too, that an African safari is not an elk hunt in the Rockies that might conclude with just one shot being fired. On the typical plains-game or general-bag safari you will shoot your rifle every day. If it's pounding you on a daily basis, your shooting will suffer.

This is a hard lesson to learn, and it's important that you objectively try to analyze what works best for you, without focusing too heavily on what seems to work for me or anyone else you read. Here are a couple of examples of mistakes I have made: I love the .375, and I truly believe it remains one of the most versatile of all African calibers. However, as I mentioned above, depending on what you're hunting you may not need a .375. Typically, we put low-range variable scopes on our .375s, and they are certainly appropriate. But I have been in many situations when the .375 with its low-power scope was the only rifle I had available for plains game. That's just fine in the generally heavy thornbush of Zimbabwe, but in more open country such as Namibia or the Eastern Cape, a .375 with a low-power scope makes routine shots at various antelope much more difficult than they would be with any favorite deer rifle topped with a 3–9X variable.

If you take a .375 into relatively open country you might consider increasing its versatility with a slightly more powerful scope. These days 1.5–6X scopes are increasingly common. On plains game they do offer more capability than variables that "max out" at 4X to 5X—without reducing the rifle's effectiveness on dangerous game. In Namibia in July 2007 and again in Masailand later that year, I used Leupold's new 30mm-tube VX-7 in 1.5–6X on two different .375s. The capability was just fine on buffalo, elephant, and leopard, and equally fine on game ranging from steenbok and springbok on up to kudu, gemsbok, and eland at widely varying ranges.

I am also a big fan of the fast .33s, and for many years I honestly believed "the faster the better." I took a .340 Weatherby Magnum, a marvelously capable cartridge, as my only rifle on my first Ethiopian safari. It was a fine choice for mountain nyala, a tough hunt that usually boils down to just one chance. But then we went up to the Danakil to hunt a wide variety of plains game, and I had to shoot that cannon every day. The fun wore off very quickly! That is an important point. The kind of country we're talking about holds a wide variety of game, and usually a considerable density. You will shoot your plains-game rifle literally every day, sometimes several times—so it had better be something you're comfortable shooting and shoot well!

It goes without saying that the typical rifle for bush and savanna will be scoped, and it will probably be a magazine rifle. It could be a single shot, and it could even be an exceptionally accurate scoped double. It could even be a lever action, slide action, or semiauto in appropriate caliber—but it will probably be a bolt action, neither too large nor too small in caliber. Such a rifle will be the basic gun in your battery for a general-bag safari. It may be backed up by a heavier rifle or a lighter rifle, or both; we'll discuss safari batteries in more detail later. First, though, let's take a look at rifles for Africa's more specialized hunting.

Rifles for Forest, Swamp, and Mountain

Chapter 34

A hunt in Africa's thornbush and savanna could well be a specialized quest. Any serious cat hunt is specialized, and a veteran hunter may return to a specific area to concentrate on a big kudu, an extra-special buffalo, or some other animal found locally in exceptional quality. But most safaris to general-bag areas are just that: Hunts intended for a general bag, with some priorities usually established for animals that will occupy the bulk of the time.

In contrast, safaris to Africa's forests, swamps, and mountains are usually very specialized, single-purpose hunts, with one or two unique species of game as the only objects. Such hunts might be very long, for instance a three-week safari to the forests of southern C.A.R. or Cameroon strictly for bongo. Or they may be very short, perhaps conducted as a side trip to another safari. A good example would be a few days up at Bangweulu trying for a sitatunga, while the bulk of the safari would be spent in the Luangwa Valley or Kafue; another would be the three-day hunts (now closed) up on the slopes of Mount Meru for suni and Abbott duiker—a highly specialized endeavor but usually conducted as part of a general-bag Masailand safari. Or, as occurs in almost any Masailand concession, a few days up on one of the many tall *oldonyos* (mountains) for bushbuck, bushpig, or buffalo.

Such specialized hunting situations exist from one end of Africa to another. They include mountain nyala hunting in the forests and heather of Ethiopia's high country, sitatunga hunting in any one of a dozen African swamps and river systems, and any forest safari at all, regardless of the primary game. Even hunting the elusive little Vaal rhebok in the mountains of South Africa is a highly specialized undertaking, although it is usually conducted as just part of a more general South Africa safari. Although it takes place in areas that hold quite a lot of other game, hunting the Derby eland is just as specialized as a bongo hunt—though altogether different. And in today's market any elephant hunt, whether in forest or thornbush, is one of the most demanding and specialized safaris of all.

The forest is probably the most challenging of Africa's habitats—for both hunters and their equipment. Even on a dry day everything will get soaked, and constant gun care is required to stay ahead of rust. This may not be the place for a fine double.

For most of us, African hunting follows a fairly predictable path. We start with plains-game or general-bag safaris, working our way up to the more difficult prizes. When I wrote the original *Safari Rifles,* I had done an awful lot of general-bag hunting but was just starting to scratch the surface of the more specialized (and generally more difficult) hunting areas. In the years since then I have done multiple safaris (each) to Cameroon, the C.A.R., and Ethiopia, a long safari to Chad, and several more elephant safaris. Which, I guess, is one way of saying I know a great deal more about this stuff now than I did then!

Whether it's an elephant hunt in the Zambezi Valley, a mountain nyala hunt in Ethiopia, or any of the safaris in Central Africa, there are several common characteristics. First, most "specialized safaris" are very hard on both people and equipment. The mountains can be constantly wet and are usually cold. The forests are often wet and extremely hot, and biting insects are much more of a problem than on the average safari. Swamps are not only wet, but add leeches and the threat of bilharzia. The Derby eland country is blessedly dry, but Equatorial heat is incredible and the distances to be covered on foot are often daunting. My personal vote for Africa's most physically demanding safari is not bongo, not elephant, and not mountain nyala. It is a tracking hunt for Lord Derby giant eland. Yet the animals found in these inhospitable regions are among Africa's greatest prizes, and generations of hunters have found them worth whatever travails their pursuit requires.

Such quests test both stamina and psyche—and can literally eat up a good rifle. Serious rust can be an overnight problem, and in swamps and forests you can forget about a walnut stock's lovely finish. After a few days it will be a uniform scaly gray. And this brings us to a second characteristic generally common to this kind of safari: The areas are remote and hard to get to, with few roads, and you can expect much of the hunting to be done on foot. Most of the time you must get by with just one rifle. If you take two, the second serves primarily as a spare and is often left in camp.

For myself, on this kind of safari I do not take two rifles. In large part this is because charter aircraft are almost essential to reach the remote areas we're talking about. Space and weight are thus at a premium and are probably better used for things other than an extra rifle that I always fervently hope won't be needed. At this writing I have taken four safaris in the C.A.R., three in Cameroon, two in Ethiopia, and one in Chad. I took just one rifle on each of these. I'm going to Cameroon again in just two months, and again I will take just one rifle. This is quite a concession, especially if you understand not only that I'm a rifle freak but also that I make part of my living writing about the rifles I use! It should go without saying that the rifle you choose needs to be ideally suited for the game and conditions, and damn well better be a hundred percent reliable!

Life on such safaris isn't the luxury vacation a general-bag hunt sometimes is. The country is more remote, and the supplies are scanty and harder to replenish. Food might be terrible and not overly plentiful. (Honestly, though, such conditions are rare. African outfitters do a great job—but once in a while supplies run low!) Again, hunting will most likely be on foot, and some nights may be spent on a track. Daily maintenance takes on new dimensions: maintaining aching muscles and feet raw from immersion; ritual inspections for leeches and insect bites; and cleaning, lubricating, and thorough inspection of the rifle so it will be ready when you finally get a shot.

Some hunters might leave these last chores to the PH, who will probably delegate them to his trackers. Perhaps that's all right; considering the cost of most specialized African hunts, it's unreasonable to expect the client to sit up late punching the bore of his rifle. But he'd damn well better inspect his rifle and his ammunition carefully each and every day. The more specialized the hunt and the more elusive the animal, the fewer and farther between are the opportunities. It's always important that a hunter be absolutely certain his rifle will function. This is a "duh!" on dangerous game, but on these specialized hunts there will be few opportunities, and everything (including lots of sweat and a huge financial commitment) may rest on just one chance. These specialized hunts can be murder on a rifle, and failure to clean and lightly lubricate each day and inspect your ammunition could result in a failure when that one and only chance comes. Sometimes, like when you stumble into camp late, it's hard to do.

Regardless of what you're hunting in the forest there is always the chance for a close encounter with an elephant or Rigby. Since then I've stuck with a .416—but I'll never again carry a really good, expensive rifle.

a buffalo. On my first forest safari I took a .375, but when I got this bongo on my second trip I carried a .416

Mountain hunting is mountain hunting, requiring climbing and, occasionally, very long shooting. This is a typical situation for hunting mountain zebra in Namibia.

But you might have been drenched with rain or half-submerged in flooded plains all day, and by morning you can have a serious and lasting rust problem on your hands. If your rifle fails you when you need it, it's nobody's fault but your own.

Sometimes a little casual inspection reveals some interesting things. My good friend Jack Lott was hunting gaur in Southeast Asia. One day he discovered wasps busily building a nest in the muzzle of his .458, turning it into a pipe bomb. Our publisher, Ludo Wurfbain, has done a number of "do-it-yourself" safaris in the forests of Cameroon. Typically he carries a synthetic-stocked .416 Remington, a very good choice. Despite daily maintenance and inspection, one day he discovered that his safety catch was solidly rusted in the "safe" position. In other words, the rifle could not be fired. Ludo has taken a lot of dangerous game with this rifle, and once it saved his bacon when a hippo charged out of nowhere. But suddenly it was useless. It took three hours of soaking in oil to break the rusted safety free.

I've had my own gun problems in the forest. In 1997, on my second bongo safari, I took a brand-new .416 Rigby, one of the last English-made Rigby rifles. It was about noon on one of the best hunting days of my life when I shot my first (and best) bongo, and we had just finished all the chores when it started to rain. It rained sheets and buckets the rest of the day and far into the night, and it was nearly dawn

Donna used the Ruger 77 in .30-06 to take this excellent Vaal rhebok. Truthfully, the .30-06 was a bit outclassed by the distances. If we ever do this hunt again I would prefer something lighter and flatter-shooting with a bit more scope!

before we finally got back to camp. I dried and oiled the rifle as best I could, but by that evening the stock was completely and hopelessly split behind the tang. OK, it was probably fitted poorly in the first place—work out of England was pretty sad in those days, and that rifle was nothing but trouble. But that situation left behind some obvious lessons about really nice rifles on really tough hunts, and choices between synthetic and walnut!

Although the maintenance requirements become more stringent as the hunting becomes more specialized, the choice of rifle should get easier. Quite simply, the rifle chosen should be whatever rifle is best for you for hunting your primary quarry. "Best for you" implies some caliber suitability, of course, but also a comfort level. The rifle chosen for a specialized hunt must be adequate for the main prize—but it must also be a rifle you are thoroughly familiar with and in which you have total confidence. Chances are you'll need both the confidence and the familiarity when your chance comes.

It must also be suitable for the conditions of this specialized safari. For instance, most would agree that a scoped .375 of some persuasion is the natural choice for a Derby eland safari. Such a rifle is adequate for the primary game, ideal for the kind of shots that are most likely, and also adequate in power to handle other game that

Lechwe hunting, too, often requires a fair amount of wading through swamp and muck. These are good places for synthetic stocks and rustproof metal finishes.

might be encountered, such as lion and savanna buffalo. You could make do with a .416, and you could get by with a fast .33, but any accurate scoped .375 is certainly in the ballpark. If you go hunting for mountain nyala, think about hunting elk in high alpine country. You need reach, and you need some punch. I chose a .340 Weatherby on my first mountain nyala hunt, and it was fine. I took my pet long-barreled 8mm Remington Magnum the second time around, and it was even better. You could certainly use a fast .30 or even a 7mm magnum and you'd be just fine—but if you also intended to hunt Nile buffalo or lion on that same Ethiopian safari, then you'd need to choose a bigger rifle or take a second rifle.

Now, when you get to the forest, things change a bit. The bongo is a big, blocky forest antelope, but he's not as heavy as a kudu. My concept of the perfect bongo rifle would probably be a short, light carbine in something like .350 Remington Magnum. Perfect for bongo, yes, but not a suitable forest rifle! In the forest you can run into trouble with an elephant or a forest buffalo at any given moment, and you must carry enough gun at all times. Period. So a .375 H&H should be the absolute minimum on any forest safari. Shooting distances are short, so trajectory matters not at all, and whether to use a scope or open sights depends a bit on you. I am more comfortable with a scope, and while I haven't needed one for bongo, I've been glad I had a scope for other forest game.

Hunting aoudad in the mountains of Chad is just like any other sheep or goat hunting anywhere in the world (except it's a bit hotter than most places). You must find the animal, and then you must get to him.

I carried a .375 on my first forest hunt and was comfortable with it, but I have carried .416s ever since. Typically I'll put a softpoint on top, but I put solids underneath. I'm not at all certain what good this does me; if you get into elephant trouble in the forest, it can happen so fast and so close that it's really unlikely I'd ever have time to cycle out the softpoint and get to the solid. But at least it makes me feel better to load up that way.

The concept of a safari battery may still apply, of course. On most elephant safaris there is some other game, and a second, lighter rifle is usually taken along. Some of my partners and camp mates in Cameroon and the C.A.R. have taken a second rifle, so it isn't a hard-and-fast rule that you must get by with just one. However, the rifle you choose for your main quarry is likely to be the only one readily available at any one time. Remember, chances are your hunting will be on foot. You could have a tracker carry a second rifle, but there's little point. You won't be doing much random shooting until you have taken the main prize, whatever it is. Also, encounters in the forest are so fleeting that there is rarely opportunity to switch back and forth.

In swamp country you do need to worry about hippo, but the primary swamp game is sitatunga, and you need to be able to reach out a bit. I am unabashedly afraid of hippo,

The only rifle I took to Chad, where I shot this Barbary sheep, was my 8mm Remington Magnum. Of course it worked, but in retrospect I should have taken a lighter rifle that would have been easier to carry.

but I think it's best to figure the professional hunter has to deal with this problem. If you're hunting sitatunga, you need to carry something relatively fast and flat-shooting. I've been pretty lucky with sitatunga, and I've taken them with a .270 Winchester, .300 Winchester Magnum, my old 8mm Remington Magnum, and a .338. Anything in this range that wears a good scope and shoots straight would work, but in the swamps I would strongly recommend synthetic stocks and rustproof metal finishes.

Much as I love double rifles, I'd have to think hard before taking one into forests or swamps, even though the ability to keep a softpoint in one barrel and a solid in the other offers excellent insurance. There's too much damage that can remain hidden if you submerge the action. My .416 didn't arrive with me for a Cameroon forest hunt in 2006, so outfitter Antonio Riguera was kind enough to loan me his Krieghoff double .500. I was as careful with it as I could be, but the forest is just plain hard on nice rifles, and with most doubles you can't readily strip down the action and make sure there's no hidden rust forming. I would also not take a double on a mountain hunt. Mountains are often rainy, and even if they're forested the relief can mean very long shooting. That's not the double's strong suit.

Depending on the game, a mountain rifle might range from a 6.5mm on up to the fast .33s, but you definitely want a good, clear scope and a flat-shooting cartridge. It's understood that all forest hunting is specialized . . . but so is all mountain hunting! If you go to Ethiopia for mountain nyala, you're going to put some serious thought into your

Perhaps the ultimate mountain hunt in Africa is hunting mountain nyala in Ethiopia's high country. The animals are big and tough and the higher slopes are brushy. You need reach and power—but you don't want a rifle that's too heavy to carry.

rifle and cartridge, because that mountain nyala is to be the primary goal on a long and expensive safari. But the same thought process applies to all mountain hunts.

This was sort of thrown in my face this past summer on a Vaal rhebok hunt. I regard the Vaal rhebok as South Africa's top trophy, a wonderful little animal that offers one of Africa's relatively few true mountain hunts. I'd failed to get one a couple of times, but I shot a very good one in the eighties, a long and lucky shot with a .338, and I got an even better one in 1992 with Noel Ross, shooting a .300 Weatherby Magnum. Both of mine were taken on one-day hunts, so I don't think I had a proper appreciation for this great little trophy. In 2007, fifteen years later, PH Russell Lovemore took us back to Noel Ross' place to film a Vaal rhebok hunt. I figured I had already taken my share, so Donna would be the hunter, but it really didn't matter who was doing the shooting. We caught three days of horrible wind, and it was just plain tough.

The .30-06 is one of the most useful plains-game cartridges around, but in those big mountains I felt like the .30-06 was badly outclassed. On the fourth day the wind calmed down and Donna shot a wonderful Vaal rhebok, but if we ever again do such a hunt I will choose something that shoots flatter, and I'll add a bit more scope! Come to think of it, since then Match Grade Arms built Donna a .270 that fits her, and it would have been a much better choice. Again, all mountain hunting is specialized, no matter what else you might be doing on that particular safari.

Many of these specialized hunts are ideal uses for synthetic stocks and rustproof metal finishes. I was slow to embrace these things. Synthetic doesn't have the warmth of a fine piece of walnut, and matte blue appeals to my eye better than stainless. However, I've ruined a lot of good wood on tough hunts, and I've seen too much rust on fine metalwork. On my first bongo hunt I took my old left-hand-converted Model 70 in .375. The stock turned an ugly gray and the action got rusty, but that wasn't so bad because it's a battered old rifle anyway. My partner, Sherwin Scott, took a beautiful David Miller .375, and we both cried a bit as the rust formed around the gold inlay and the figure disappeared on the beautiful walnut.

However, the primary reason to choose synthetic stocks on tough hunts isn't for cosmetic reasons but because they are stable. They can't shift zero on you, and they're stronger than wood. As discussed in an earlier chapter, laminates are yet another option that is stronger and more stable than solid wood. There are a lot of interesting sheep and goats in the world that aren't all that large in the body, so mountain hunting is my primary intent for a laminate stock .264 just built by Serengeti Rifles. But for serious wet weather, I would go with synthetic.

Rustproof metal finishes (and rustproof metals) have tremendous value for wet-climate hunting. No, they aren't nearly as attractive as old-time rust bluing. But under rough conditions you can watch the finest rust bluing turn to red rust in hours. Stainless steel isn't entirely rustproof, but it resists far longer than carbon steel. Metal finishes like the old military Parkerizing and modern Teflon coatings also work wonderfully. Keep one thing in mind: The best anything can offer is resistance to rust. The only real proof against corrosion is care and cleaning, and on many of these specialized hunts you're going to have to do some serious cleaning and maintenance each and every day. That means you must take cleaning gear with you! These days I carry a little Otis cleaning kit with me, no bigger than a fist and very light. On these tough hunts, especially when it's wet, it doesn't matter how tired you are. You have to make yourself pay attention to your rifle every evening, so it will be ready when you need it. Remember, another characteristic of these very specialized hunts is that you may get only one chance!

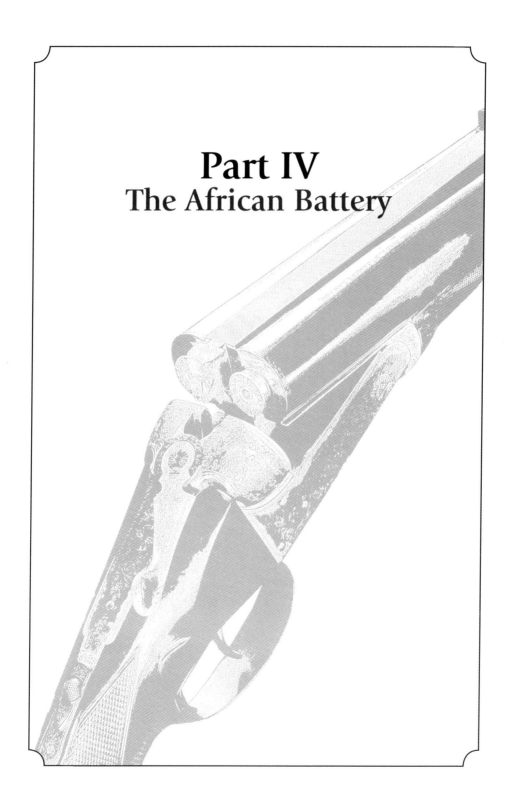

Part IV
The African Battery

The One-Rifle Safari

Chapter 35

There's a saying in the whitetail woods: "Beware the one-rifle hunter." The hunter who shoots just one rifle season after season will come to know that rifle like an extension of his body. If he hunts a good deal, or if he practices as much as a hunter should—or both—he will become exceedingly confident in and deadly with that one rifle. This is just as true in Africa as anywhere else. There will be no confusion over which rifle to reach for, and no confusion over ammunition.

It's a concept that makes sense, no doubt about it. The problem is that African game varies tremendously in size, and the hunting conditions can vary widely even within a limited geographic area. Limiting oneself to a single caliber simplifies many things—but it does severely limit one's choice of rifles and cartridges. And it means compromises must be made, for it's obvious that no one cartridge is particularly well-suited for the entire range of African game from dik-dik to elephant.

It should be just as obvious, however, that if only one rifle is available, that rifle will be used on the entire spectrum of game to be hunted, and the rifle and the cartridge it fires must be chosen with extreme care.

If the game to be hunted runs the full gamut from dik-dik to elephant—or, to be more reasonable, from duiker to buffalo or impala to lion—then the choices are very limited. First and foremost, on any one-rifle safari the rifle chosen must be fully adequate for the largest game that will be hunted, especially if that largest game happens to be dangerous. Adequacy on the upper end must come first—but it would also be nice if the rifle were accurate enough for the smallest antelopes, flat-shooting enough for the longest likely shot, and portable enough to carry all day.

If dangerous game such as lion, buffalo, or elephant will be on license, you have to stretch your imagination to find more than one candidate: the .375. The 1912-vintage .375 H&H remains the most popular in its class, as well as the most "shootable." Faster options include the .375 Weatherby Magnum, .375 Remington Ultra Mag, and .378 Weatherby Magnum; just note that as you move

Although it's nearly a century old, there are still few choices other than the .375 H&H for a one-rifle safari. On this hunt in Zimbabwe a Dakota .375 accounted for grysbok and buffalo . . . and was ready for anything in between.

During the development and early marketing of the new .375 Ruger, Steve Hornady made two one-rifle safaris checking out the new cartridge. This was the first buffalo to fall to the .375 Ruger, and it did just fine on everything else.

up the velocity scale from .375 H&H, recoil goes up in equal measure. The new kid on the .375 block is the .375 Ruger, a bit faster than the H&H but, perhaps more important, able to be housed in a .30-06-length action (meaning a shorter, lighter, and less expensive package). No .375 is perfect for elephant, and they are not the best thing going for shots past 300 yards. But they will do it all, and while there are a few other choices for a one-rifle safari that includes dangerous game, there may not be any better choices.

The European 9.3x64 could certainly be an alternative to the .375, but for a full range of game I can't envision any smaller cartridge being chosen. I can envision a larger cartridge for a one-rifle safari, especially if the cover tends to be thick and dangerous game is high on the hunter's want list. All of the low-.40 cartridges fit in nicely, from the .404 Jeffery on up to the various .416s. Depending on the velocity, these cartridges may not have energy levels as high as the faster .375s, but I guarantee their heavier bullets of larger diameter will hit harder and thus are better suited for the largest game. The obvious drawback is they are not quite as versatile. Well, OK, a fast .416 like the .416 Weatherby shoots flatter than most .375s—but you have to be awful tough to shoot it as well!

In the forest you may want to go heavier than a .375—but you probably still need a scoped rifle with some versatility. This Peters duiker was taken with my .416 Taylor scoped with the Trijicon AccuPoint, a fine choice for a one-rifle forest battery.

It goes without saying that such cartridges are needlessly powerful for anything but the dangerous game—but as I've said before, there are worse things than overkill (if overkill even exists). I can't see using a cartridge larger in bore diameter than a .404 (bullet diameter .423-inch) or a .416 as a one-rifle battery—unless, of course, the hunt is strictly for elephant. But a scoped .416 could do everything, and do it well.

Years ago, the only rifle I took on a Botswana safari was a .416 Weatherby when the cartridge was first introduced. It performed admirably, but I should say that it was a short hunt with limited objectives—mainly buffalo and a couple of head of plains game. Still, that .416 was all I needed, and as short as the hunt was, another rifle would have been nothing but excess baggage. On my first forest safari I took my old .375. Like most journeys into totally unfamiliar country, it was an eye-opener. I didn't get a bongo, but I did get some great consolation prizes, like giant forest hog and buffalo. I realized that I didn't need the range of even a .375, and it was so thick that a bit more gun could be handy.

On my second forest safari I took a .416 Rigby. Par for the course, the only shot I got was at my bongo. (It worked fine.) In 2006 I took a Ruger M77 rebarreled to .416 Taylor on a forest hunt in Cameroon. The rifle was delayed in transit, so by the time I received it I had already taken my bongo with Anthony Riguera's double

.500. Late in the hunt, however, I took a fine yellowback duiker that presented a rare 200-yard shot down a forest road. The .416 was topped with a Trijicon scope with lighted tritium post. That's a pretty fancy shot with any .416 firing a 400-grain roundnose bullet, but it worked just fine!

Two of the final chapters of this book are devoted to a survey sent out to several hundred licensed African professional hunters. That survey could well be the most valuable part of the book, since the professionals not only know what works for them but their lives depend on their clients' choice of arms and their skill in employing them. You will note that the results of the 2007 survey differ somewhat from the 1988 survey; however, both surveys provide extremely valuable advice. Twenty years ago, fully 75 percent of the professional hunters surveyed listed the .375 H&H as their own personal "all-round" choice, and 65 percent suggested it as the rifle they would recommend to their clients as a one-rifle battery. I think this reflects a sea change in African hunting that has occurred in the last twenty years. Back then, at least a small majority of African safaris included at least one member of the Big Five. Today many more safaris are conducted across Africa—possibly 20,000 hunting safaris annually—but the vast majority are "plains-game safaris," meaning that no dangerous game is on the dance card.

Any one of the several .375 cartridges available today makes a wonderful one-rifle safari battery if buffalo, lion, or perhaps eland are on the menu. As much as I love the .375, it actually has been my one-rifle choice on only a few occasions. At this writing I have made three safaris into the "Derby eland country" of northern C.A.R. and northern Cameroon. Twice I carried a .375 Weatherby Magnum, and once a .375 H&H. I'm headed back to northern Cameroon in March 2008, and I intend to take my .375 Ruger. In these situations the hunting is tough and charter flights are usually included. It isn't convenient to take more than one rifle, and the game list includes not only eland and savanna buffalo but also other big, tough antelope like western roan and western hartebeest. This is .375 country, and few other choices make much sense to me.

Interestingly, I'm writing these lines near Lake Natron in Tanzania's Masailand, and the only rifle I have with me is my .375 Ruger—but for different reasons. I'm on a short safari with buffalo as the primary quarry. I might take a gazelle or an impala, but it just didn't seem to make sense to bring more than one rifle. As always, a good .375 will do the job, and makes sense if the game includes buffalo along with other game.

Today there are many more safaris that don't include buffalo and other big nasties than those that do. If thick-skinned dangerous game isn't to be hunted, then there is absolutely no reason for a rifle of .40-caliber or larger. I do believe strongly that the

Kirk Kelso with a very nice West African savanna buffalo, dropped in its tracks in northern Cameroon with a single 270-grain Barnes Triple Shock bullet from his .375 H&H.

eland is in .375 territory, but if eland is not on your safari wish list, then there's no real need for a .375. I also recognize that it's extremely arguable whether you really need a .375 for eland. I have taken eland, or seen them taken, quite effectively with various .30-calibers, my 8mm Remington Magnum, and various .33s. They work just fine. If eland is a primary goal, I'd recommend a bit more gun than a .30-caliber, but I concede you don't absolutely have to have a .375. Of course, a .375 works just fine for the average plains-game safari—but a lighter, easier-to-shoot .300, .30-06, or 7mm magnum, or even a .270, would better serve most hunters.

All too many hunters seem to drag along a .375 or heavier rifle "just in case." Believe me, in today's Africa, if you haven't specifically booked a hunt for lion, buffalo, or elephant, the chances of just running across such animals and being able to legally capitalize on the opportunity are extremely slim. They are not "nonexistent," although I used that word in the first edition. The proof was the "problem lion permit" I was offered in Namibia in 2007. That wasn't exactly a one-rifle safari. I actually had my choice of three: I had a Remington M700 in .300 RUM, Donna had the Ruger .30-06 we often share, and Brittany had her Kimber 7mm-08. Obviously I chose the .300. My other option was to borrow a more suitable rifle, an increasingly attractive alternative that we will discuss in a bit.

The thing about taking just one rifle on safari is that, barring big surprises, that rifle must still be adequate for the full range of game you intend to hunt. Chances are your favorite elk rifle (if not deer rifle) will be up to the task. And you'll probably shoot it well, just as you do at home. I do believe in the toughness of African game, and, as I'm often accused, I stand guilty of tending to go heavier rather than lighter in calibers and bullets. As mentioned earlier, my old friend Debra Bradbury takes only her well-worn Model 70 .270 wherever she goes. She knows the rifle, and it works for her. Also as mentioned earlier, my daughter Brittany has great faith in her 7mm-08 (and, at this writing, not much faith in anything else!). In her hands, that little rifle with a 140-grain Nosler Partition took down a huge eland bull as cleanly as you please.

Unfortunately, guys like me know too much about bullets and ballistics and such, and I simply cannot bring myself to place such faith in as light a rifle as a .270 or any 7mm for a one-rifle safari battery. Once more, with foot-stamping for emphasis: Shot placement and bullet performance are always more important than exact caliber, velocity, or foot-pounds of energy—at least within very broad ranges of suitability. But you, and I, must choose rifles and cartridges we are comfortable with for the full range of game we intend to hunt. With decreasing baggage allowances and increasing paperwork, taking just one rifle is ever more seductive.

I've talked about the occasions when I chose a .375, and on those hunts it made sense. On other safaris there was no reason for a .375, but I still wanted

On my first forest safari I used my old .375 H&H, and I was fortunate to get a rare opportunity at a giant forest hog.

Any scoped rifle could have handled the shot, but I'd have been up a creek with an open-sighted big bore.

plenty of power. As I wrote earlier, on my first Ethiopian safari I took a .340 Weatherby Magnum. This was an ideal choice for mountain nyala, but it wasn't much fun to shoot every day in the Danakil. On my second Ethiopian hunt, in 2000, I took only my 8mm Remington Magnum. This is a heavy rifle with a long barrel. Performance is similar to the fastest .33s, but recoil is noticeably less. The only shot fired on that safari was at a wonderful mountain nyala, a tricky neck shot that I could have taken with many lesser calibers but would have attempted only with a rifle I trusted as much as that 8mm, built for me by Rigby's Geoff Miller.

I used the same rifle a year later in Chad. It was a real pain carrying it in the Ennedi Mountains, and clearly I didn't need that level of power for aoudad or dorcas gazelle. But it was a long safari, and I wanted to take only one rifle. Eventually we would wind up down on the Bahr Aouk River, where we would hunt korrigum, the giant topi, and where I hoped we might find western roan. Something larger than a .30-caliber made sense to me on that safari. Honestly, however, when you settle on a one-rifle safari and it's clear you don't absolutely have to have a .375 or larger, your own comfort level becomes extremely important. Joe Bishop and I hunted together on both those Ethiopian safaris. I, the large-caliber, heavy-bullet guy, used a .340 Weatherby and an 8mm Remington Magnum. Joe used his battered old Sako in 7mm Remington Magnum and certainly did as well! Lest I be branded a big-bore maniac, on another South African safari I took only a Remington M700 rebarreled to .300 H&H. With 200-grain Sierras it worked wonders on everything from mountain reedbuck and warthog to waterbuck and greater kudu, so it was truly an ideal one-rifle battery.

What about taking along your favorite rifle and planning to borrow a "heavy" if needed? There are good points and bad points to such a plan. In my experience, professional hunters may or may not have the best equipment available. Rifles and ammunition are hard to come by in Africa, and a professional hunter might have very fine rifles or he might have tired old relics. I wouldn't take it on blind faith that a PH will have a spare .375 or larger available. On the other hand, if he says he has an adequate rifle, I'd bank on it. He's banking his life on its proper functioning. And, as traveling with firearms becomes ever more difficult, more outfitters are making sure they have suitable firearms available for hire.

The obvious disadvantage to borrowing a heavy rifle is that you'll be using an unfamiliar rifle. However, if you aren't taking your own heavy rifle, it's likely you either don't have one or you don't have one that you're totally familiar with. I suggest that you are better off borrowing a heavy rifle from your hunter than purchasing one especially for your safari—unless, of course, you are willing to spend the time and

If there is no dangerous game on the list the one-rifle battery can be revised. I took my 8mm Remington Magnum to Chad, maybe not a great choice in the mountains but just perfect for game like this western greater kudu and korrigum.

energy to become totally familiar with your new heavy, and to shoot it enough to work any potential bugs out of it.

As I've mentioned, "over-the-counter" heavy rifles are notorious for feeding problems and splitting stocks. A "camp" rifle may not be pretty, but odds are good that the bugs were worked out many safaris before. If you plan on borrowing a rifle for the two or three shots you might fire at dangerous game, then your one rifle can be whatever rifle you shoot best.

Incidentally, if you plan on using a professional hunter's rifle for anything, find out what the caliber is and bring along a couple of boxes of ammunition if you can. In today's Africa, do not try to sneak anything in! If you can bring ammo, this will ensure that you have enough and that it's fresh. Insist on burning up some of that ammo sighting in your borrowed gun and becoming familiar with it.

Since most gun cases are built for two long arms, taking only one rifle makes it extremely convenient to pack along a shotgun. If things break right, there might be time for some spectacular bird shooting. Or you might have to make time—or you

On my first Ethiopian safari in 1993 I took only my .340 Weatherby Magnum. It was perfect for mountain nyala, but really gave me a pounding when I used it every day in the Danakil. This is a great beisa oryx.

might not use the shotgun at all. Chances are, though, that it will be a handy thing to have, if only to shoot a few guinea fowl for the pot. On that trip to Botswana, I threw in a 12-gauge over/under and two boxes of shells in addition to the .416 Weatherby Magnum. We didn't have time for serious bird shooting, but we did wind up with some most welcome guinea fowl, francolin, and even a few doves for the pot. If you really aren't a bird shooter but some birds to eat sound good, consider filling the other half of your gun case with a .22 Magnum or .22 Hornet.

As discussed in chapter 22, a switch-barrel rifle—essentially one rifle with multiple barrels in different calibers—is an extremely versatile choice for a safari battery. I have personally decided that for me a switch-barrel rifle isn't the answer, not even a double that allows the switching of barrels in seconds. The problem is that no matter how you slice it, only one barrel and one caliber will be available for use at any one time. At least some of the time, it's not going to be the one you want. For instance, one time I took a Thompson/Center with a .22 Hornet barrel and a .270 Winchester barrel. The Hornet barrel was so handy for steenbok and such

On my second mountain nyala hunt I took only my 8mm Remington Magnum. It was a bit heavy in the mountains, but I drew a tough shot on this wonderful bull, and I was happy for its accuracy as well as its power.

that I actually used the .270 barrel only once. Mind you, that wasn't the only rifle available. If it had been, then the .270 barrel would have been in place all the time and the .22 Hornet barrel would never have been used! But if you choose a switch-barrel, give some thought to the applications of each caliber—and what must be done to switch them out. If the scope is on the barrel, then so long as each barrel has a scope sighted-in, there is little delay. But if the scope is on the receiver, as is the case with most bolt-action switch-barrels, then you must re-zero every time you switch, and the actual utility seems very limited to me.

An inherent problem with using one rifle for all of your big game, whether a switch-barrel or just one rifle of any type, aside from the compromises involved, is that there is no backup whatever. Your professional hunter will have some kind of rifle, should yours fail—but you can't rely on the presence of an extra rifle, let alone its reliability. Rather, if you decide on just one rifle, you must bank on your chosen arm being able to get you through the entire trip.

483

An excellent Lord Derby giant eland, taken in northern Cameroon in March 2008. The rifle is a .375 Ruger with a 300-grain softpoint. A scoped .375, whether the old H&H or a faster cartridge, is almost the only sensible choice for this very specialized safari.

You'll want to go over it with a fine-tooth comb, carefully examining the stock for signs of minute cracks. You'll want to disassemble it completely and examine all the springs and parts—and if you aren't sure what you're looking at, ask a good gunsmith to do so. The sighting equipment requires special attention; the scope mount and scope-ring screws need to be checked over and Loctited into place, and there simply must be auxiliary sighting equipment. Optimally, you'll have iron sights on the rifle and an extra scope already set in rings. And, of course, you'll have the full range of ammunition, both solids and softs as applicable. The solids are useful not only for the largest game but also for the smallest—if you know exactly where they shoot.

As mentioned, two of the last chapters in this book will be devoted to the "professional hunter's survey" I did in 1989, and a new one done in 2007. It's worth noting here that nearly 70 percent of the professionals recommended ".375" as their choice for a one-rifle safari battery. I put this in quotes because most didn't specify which .375 cartridge. Those who did overwhelmingly said ".375 H&H." In fact, there was only one specific mention of another .375, which stated ".375

Ruger." Several recommendations for a one-rifle safari stated ".375 or .416." Four professional hunters—Johan Calitz, Robin Hurt, Stephane Ndongue, and Joe Wright—recommended only the .416 for a one-rifle safari battery. In explanation, Calitz, Hurt, and Wright tend to concentrate on dangerous game, while Ndongue is primarily a forest hunter. Other recommendations for a one-rifle battery were for smaller cartridges—a couple for 7mm and a dozen for .30-calibers. Understandably, these came primarily from professionals who concentrate on plains game.

The one-rifle safari has merit, and I would never argue against it. It's simplicity itself—but it does require serious compromise on one end or the other. Unless there is serious justification, I'm too much of a rifle nut to limit myself to just one. So let's look next at two-rifle batteries.

The Two-Rifle Battery

Chapter 36

Ihave implemented a "one-rifle battery" on several occasions, always for what I considered good reason. Truthfully, however, I have never been comfortable with just a single rifle on a hunting trip a long way from home, especially a trip as lengthy and requiring as much shooting as the typical African safari. The likelihood of a gun becoming inoperable or a stock breaking beyond field-expedient repair is remote, but such things do happen (and I've had them happen). Of course, part of the whole deal is that I'm a rifle nut. And part of the attraction of African hunting is the rich variety of game. You can make do with one rifle, but one size doesn't fit all, so the compromises are huge. Part of the fun of any safari, at least for me, is in the anticipation and preparation—a large portion of which involves planning the perfect rifles and loading or sourcing the perfect ammo for the game I intend to hunt.

Admittedly, I've gone much too far on several occasions; at least twice I've taken four rifles to Africa, and more than once I've taken three rifles and a shotgun. If a nonhunting companion is traveling with the hunter, it's no problem to haul two gun cases. However, it's important to point out that traveling with more than three firearms is not only an incredible nuisance but might also be illegal. Unless you secure an export license, you cannot leave the United States with more than three firearms of any one type. That means up to three each of rifles, shotguns, and handguns—but not four rifles under any circumstances.

Seems like a strange law, but it does allow hunters to take plenty of guns—actually, more than you need or can look after, and, given today's shrinking baggage allowances, more than you want to haul. Whether or not you plan to take a shotgun, two rifles comprise a sensible battery for most modern hunting safaris. In these days of shorter, more specialized safaris and reduced bag limits, the old rule of "two's company and three is a crowd" really does apply. I have a couple of cases that will hold three firearms, but most hold just two. By using a large duffel bag and a two-gun hard case, it's practical to go on safari with just the

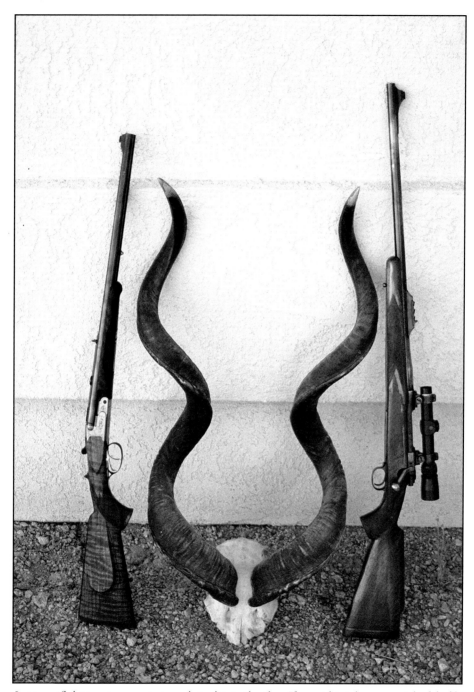

In a two-rifle battery, to some extent one choice dictates the other. If you wish to take an open-sighted double, for instance, your second rifle must be very versatile—like a scoped .375. If you want to take a really light rifle, like a .243, then your heavier rifle must also be very versatile . . . like a scoped .375.

On this safari my light rifle was a .270 Winchester, ideal for a wide variety of plains game, including this sitatunga, taken near Zambia's Lake Bangweulu.

two pieces of luggage, plus a carry-on camera bag that will also hold a change of underwear and other essentials. In this fashion, with just the two bags to check, overweight charges are usually less or can be avoided.

Under most circumstances, two rifles are also plenty to look after and use. Having two different rifles means each one can be slightly more specialized than the single rifle for a one-gun safari. However, part of the reason for carrying two rifles instead of one is so you'll have backup available if either rifle develops an unsolvable problem.

One way to do this would be to pack two rifles of identical caliber. John Taylor suggested that an ideal battery, to him, would be two Westley Richards .425 rifles, one bolt action and one double. This would give him a double, which he preferred for thick-cover work, and it would give him the accuracy of a bolt action for hunting in more open country. Best of all, he would need to worry about just one caliber of ammunition.

It seems a strange idea at first glance, but perhaps is not all that strange. One common caliber of ammunition would be nice, and it would be nice, too, to know that either rifle was perfectly capable of handling anything you came across. A pair of .425s (one of the few cartridges that were made in both double and magazine form) would be hard to come by today, but a double .375 backed up by a bolt action would be very possible, if expensive. For that matter, a matched pair of bolt-action

In this two-rifle battery I backed up the .270 Winchester with a scoped Dakota Model 10 in .375 Dakota. Between the two I was ready for anything.

rifles in .375 or one of the .416s wouldn't be a totally ridiculous choice, though the only purpose would be backup in case of mechanical failure.

I suspect most hunters (me included!) would opt for a two-rifle battery that included two substantially different calibers. This allows a bit more specialization, which means that one of the rifles will probably be better for smaller animals and/or longer ranges, while the other will be of heavier caliber for much larger game. One caution is to avoid too much specialization in a two-rifle battery. For instance, there are uses for a scoped .25-06 in Africa and also uses for a double .577 . . . but the two together would make an absurd battery! A better plan is to have some degree of overlap so that each rifle could, in a pinch, take the place of the other—not only in case of a mechanical problem but in case you happen to be carrying the wrong rifle at the right moment.

There are endless permutations of two-rifle batteries, and their choice can be greatly simplified by two hunting partners pooling their batteries. For instance, on a 2x1 safari where each hunter will be shooting buffalo, it might be advantageous to share a heavy rifle. On a Zambian safari, my own battery was comprised of a scoped .300 Weatherby and an open-sighted .460 Weatherby. But I knew my partner had a scoped .375, and I used it on several occasions. Obviously, if both parties have

Overall, and excluding some very special situations, the .30-06 is my favorite for a light rifle. It will handle pretty much the full run of plains game at most ranges to be encountered.

rifles they want to use, there's no reason to share—and mixing and matching is not practical if each client has his own PH.

It's easy to have too many rifles, but it's also possible not to have enough. On a Botswana hunt many years ago, Paul Merriman, Paul Stockwell, and I hunted on a 3x2 basis. The two Pauls each had a light rifle and planned to share a .375 among them. I had a .318 Westley Richards bolt action, a .470 double, and a scoped .375. First the stock of Merriman's .30-06 shattered. Then the extractor broke on their shared .375, and they were nearly out of rifles. I gave them my .375, which worked just fine. But if I hadn't had three rifles, it might have been an awkward situation. By the way, this was more than twenty years ago, and it was the only time I have seen multiple rifles out of action on one safari. So this kind of mess is very rare, especially with proper preparation—but Murphy's Law always applies, and such things can happen.

In a two-rifle battery the choice of the two rifles depends very much on the game to be hunted. If no dangerous game will be available, things are simplified considerably. However, it seems to me that at least one of the two rifles should be very versatile, able to handle all the game to be hunted under all the conditions anticipated. For instance, let's go back to our pet .25-06. That's a fine, flat-shooting cartridge, and it would be useful for a wide variety of plains game, especially in open

On this safari in northern Namibia I had a .30-06 and a .375. There is quite a bit of overlap between the two, and that isn't bad. When I saw a nice kudu it didn't really matter which rifle I had in my hands, in this case the .375.

country. But it would be very marginal for anything larger than waterbuck, and useless for dangerous game. If matched with an open-sighted .577 double, you'd have two very specialized rifles—and absolutely nothing that would make sense for kudu, zebra, eland, sable, roan, wildebeest, and so much more. But if you matched up your .25-06 (or .243, .270, 7x57, .280, etc.) with a scope-sighted .375, you could get effective use out of both rifles.

On the other hand, you may have a heavy rifle that's a real prize, perhaps a vintage double or a customized bolt action. So long as your safari includes one or more of the Big Five, there's no reason not to take your heavy. After all, that's what it's for, and if you can handle the recoil and place its bullets where they'll do some good, no lighter rifle will be as effective.

So take your big bore, but with the understanding that it's the most specialized of rifles. In today's Africa you may use it only once or twice in the course of an average safari. And since you'll have limited use for the big bore, your other rifle will have to serve for everything else. That means the second rifle will have to be very versatile, but will also have to be on the heavy side. It must serve for the larger plains game, perhaps for lion and leopard, and for the smaller plains game as well, and that's a tall order.

Tom Fruechtel with a very nice gerenuk taken in Masailand. His light rifle is a .30-06, versatile and flat-shooting enough for most situations.

A good match for an open-sighted double or big-bore bolt action is obviously a .375, and there are few other choices. The fast .33s are possibilities, likewise the rare fast .35s (like the .358 Norma Magnum or wildcat .358 Shooting Times Alaskan). But an open-sighted big bore, though indispensable when you need it, is so limited that you are almost obligated to back it up with the most versatile of African calibers, the .375 (or its European counterpart, the 9.3x64).

In 1983, as I mentioned, I took the .300 and .460 Weatherby Magnums as a two-rifle battery. But I knew my partner would have a .375, and I used it several times. The next year I went back to Zambia, but I was hunting alone. Again I took just two rifles: an open-sighted .458 Lott bolt action and a scoped .375 H&H. In terms of game bagged, that was one of my most successful safaris. I got my best lion, a great buffalo, my best sable, my best eland, my best reedbuck, and my best hartebeest. I also got a wonderful Kafue lechwe, shot at over 400 yards, and a good oribi, shot at 125 yards. In the course of the entire safari I carried the .458 Lott three times. The .375 did almost everything, and did it all well. I could just as easily have left the .458 at home—but I enjoyed carrying it, and I was glad I had it. A flatter-shooting light or light-medium rifle might have been more useful on some of the longer shots, but we did just fine with the .375.

When I went on my first safari, I didn't own a heavy rifle. I did own a good .375, a rifle I'd hunted with considerably in the Rockies. For a second rifle I took a .30-06, but I actually expected to use the .375 most of the time. It didn't happen that way. I carried the .375 when hunting lion, buffalo, and eland; the .30-06 was used for everything else with near-perfect results. I couldn't have done without the .375, and indeed, when we got into some heavy cover with a wounded buffalo, I wished for a much bigger gun. But if I'd shot the .375 a bit better when I had the chance, there would have been no need for anything larger.

That was more than thirty years ago now, and I guess things have come full circle. Thanks to our *Tracks Across Africa* television series, the last few years have been extremely Africa-intensive, with multiple trips required. Generally I have carried a .30-06 and a .375. On a couple of occasions, I've brought my double .450 and backed it up with my .375 Ruger.

These are not the only approaches, and possibly not the very best. Many years ago, back in 1985, I carried a .338 Winchester Magnum and a .416 Hoffman—both bolt actions, both fiberglass-stocked, both scoped. This was an unusual hunt in that it started in the Okavango Delta, where I hunted leopard, buffalo, and sitatunga; moved on to an elephant hunt in the Matetsi area; and finished up in South Africa's eastern Cape, where I hunted (for the third time) and finally shot a Vaal rhebok. That hunt covered not only a diversity of terrain but also a wide variety of game. The .416 was used only on buffalo and elephant—but it was most welcome. The .338 handled everything else with wonderful efficiency.

As much as I love the big boomers, I believe the most ideal two-rifle battery will not include a rifle that's too specialized. The .338 and .416 combination, or something along those lines, may well be one of the very best batteries available. It could be a .416 Rigby, a Remington, or a Weatherby. Or a classic .404 Jeffery or .425 Westley Richards. Or a .450/.400, either a double or a Ruger No. 1—provided either is topped with a low-power scope.

The lighter rifle wouldn't have to be a .338, but for the most versatility and efficiency it should shoot flatter than a .375 and be somewhat more powerful than a .30-06 or 7mm magnum. Other good choices would include the 8mm Remington or any of the other fast .33s. A .300 magnum would fill the bill, especially with well-constructed, heavy bullets. However, I truly believe something a bit larger is more ideal. In 1999 I did another multi-country safari, first in Zimbabwe's Zambezi Valley and then moving to Namibia. I took a scoped .416 Rigby and my 8mm Remington Magnum. The .416 was used on both buffalo and elephant in the Valley, and in Namibia the 8mm handled gemsbok and kudu with equal efficiency. This is obviously not a battery I have stayed with, but as a gunwriter I don't always get to make my own choices (or use my own rifles). I still think something like a .338 and something like a .416 make the most versatile and sensible two-rifle battery.

Tom Fruechtel backed up his .30-06 with a scoped .375, just fine for buffalo.

I wish I could say my survey of professional hunters agreed with me, but in truth it did not. Twenty years ago, only my old friend Ray Millican, professional hunter in Zambia, stipulated the .338 and .416 for a two-rifle battery. I knew he would. Earlier, we were chewing the fat at a convention, and he stated that the .338 and .416 made the most versatile and sensible two-gun battery. I replied that the only thing that might be better would be the .340 Weatherby in place of the .338, if one could handle the extra recoil. I guess Ray and I are a quorum of two; no other professional hunter who suggested specific two-caliber batteries mentioned the .338 and .416 together. In the more recent survey Ray Millican remained almost alone, joined only by my friend Pete Kibble, who is also a staunch .338 fan. The more recent survey did reflect the resurgence of the .416: Votes for a .416 as the heavy rifle of a two-rifle battery lagged only slightly behind the .375—but almost all PHs who recommended a .416 as the heavier of a pair recommended a .30-caliber as the lighter. Still, votes for a .30-caliber paired with a .375 remained strong. Note that this is what I started with, and what I most frequently use today! The .375 could be equally well paired with a .270 or 7mm. What is important, I think, is that the light rifle of such a pair be something familiar and comfortable as well as versatile. Most of the time I have paired a .375 with a .30-caliber, my choices ranging from .30-06 to .300 Weatherby and including .300 Winchester Magnum and .300 H&H. However, I have also paired a .375 with a .270 Winchester, a 7x57, a .280 Remington, and a 7mm Remington Magnum. Take your pick!

Here, unfortunately, is where theory and reality probably diverge a bit. In theory, if you're after thick-skinned dangerous game, you are far better off with something on the order of a .416 than a .375—if you can shoot the bigger gun equally well. And there's the rub. Most people can learn to shoot a 9½- or ten-pound .375 H&H or .375 Ruger. Many people either cannot or do not take the time to learn to shoot rifles with higher levels of recoil. Terrible shooting by all too many clients is the reality that professional hunters must deal with—and it's up to them to clean up the mess. Theoretically, a bigger hammer is usually better—but you and I must separate theory and reality and be objective about our own capabilities, our own recoil limits, and how much time we are willing to invest in shooting practice. These days very few professional hunters carry rifles as light as the .375 for their own backup use— but the .375 remains their overwhelming recommendation to their clients because they know most people will shoot it better!

In addressing a two-rifle battery, most professional hunters include dangerous game in their thinking. Most of my own safaris in recent years included buffalo or elephant somewhere along the way, so I tend to think the same way. Once again, it's important to remember that the majority of modern safaris are for plains game only. As with the one-rifle battery, this changes things. If you aren't hunting lion or buffalo (or anything bigger), you don't need a .375 (or anything bigger). This gives you the great luxury of being somewhat more specialized in your choices. For instance, if you wanted to take your pet .25-06, or .243, or even .22-250, you certainly could, and you'd enjoy using it on the smaller antelope. You'd just need something a bit bigger for the larger antelope and zebra.

Except for the .22 Hornet (for obviously specialized uses), I have personally never taken a rifle smaller in caliber than .25 to Africa, but I've used borrowed .243s on several occasions. Depending on your preferences and the range of game to be hunted, the lighter rifle of a pair could be anything you want it to be, just so long as the heavier rifle is big enough for the largest game to be hunted. But since this is my book, I have some obligation to offer some recommendations, don't I?

I think the fast mediums have a natural position as the heavy rifle of a two-rifle plains-game battery. I recognize that I'm one of the last people in the world still championing the 8mm Remington, but I've used both it and various .30-calibers enough to believe that the 8mm's larger bullet diameter makes a difference, whether we're talking elk or Africa's larger antelope. Europeans who use the 8x68S tend to agree. I have also used the .325 WSM in Africa, and it's a great cartridge for large plains game.

The only rifle I brought was a scoped .375, but on a "two-by-one" hunt it's possible to mix and match. My partner had a .30-06 and I borrowed it to take this Grant gazelle because of its 2.5–10X scope.

OK, so I've touted the unloved 8mm one more time. Now I'll admit that the fast .33s are even better. For a two-rifle plains-game battery I don't think there is a better "heavy rifle" than a .338 Winchester Magnum, .340 Weatherby, or .338 Remington Ultra Mag, the choice primarily depending on how much recoil you are personally comfortable with. The .338 Winchester Magnum is fairly mild, kicking somewhat less than a .375 H&H (depending on gun weight), while the faster .33s, though marvelously effective, pound you pretty hard.

Again, the lighter rifle could probably be your favorite deer rifle. If that's a .30-caliber, fine, but when I have carried a medium bore I've generally gone a bit lighter with the second rifle.

Combinations I have personally used included a .260 Remington with my 8mm, 7x57 with .338 Winchester Magnum, and .270 Weatherby Magnum with .340 Weatherby Magnum. The potential combinations are endless, of course, but the rules don't change: The heavier rifle must be powerful enough for the largest game to be hunted, and versatile enough to handle any likely shot at that animal. Provided those conditions are met, the second rifle can be highly specialized or extremely versatile. Just make sure you can shoot both rifles well!

The Three-Rifle Battery

Chapter 37

The classic African battery has traditionally consisted of three rifles: light, medium, and heavy. This concept originated in a different world, when hunters traveled to Africa by slow-moving steamer and the average safari stretched into months. With trips of such duration and magnitude, the amount of allowable baggage wasn't as critical as it is today, and certainly there was much more shooting to be done than on the modern safari.

For his 1894–1897 safari, covering on foot some 4,000 miles of Africa, Edouard Foa chose a black-powder 8-bore double as his heavy rifle, a pair of .577 Express black-powder doubles for the "medium," and a smokeless .303 Lee-Metford as a light rifle. All served him well.

Just a few years later, the new .450-class Nitro Express cartridges would replace the big 8- and 10-bores, and even smaller smokeless cartridges would supplant the old black-powder Expresses in the medium classification. The light rifle, well, as such it hardly existed before smokeless powder, unless you'd consider such as the .577/.450 Martini a smallbore!

In 1909 Theodore Roosevelt's primary battery took the classic three-rifle form: His .30-06 Springfield was a light rifle, his Winchester Model 95 in .405 was a medium (his "lion medicine"), and his Holland & Holland double .500/.450 handled the largest game. His son, Kermit, was similarly armed, except he had a Rigby .450-3¼" as his heavy rifle.

Similarly, the great American hunter/author Stewart Edward White stayed with his Springfield .30-06, Winchester .405, and Holland double .465, not only in the years before World War I but also on his last safari in 1925. Pioneer photographer Martin Johnson's battery, used from 1921 to 1935, was almost identical: a .30-06, a .405, and a .470 double by Thomas Bland.

Hemingway's 1935 battery was a departure. He had a 6.5mm Mannlicher, his famous and beloved .30-06 Springfield of course, and a big double in .470, but none

Three-rifle batteries bring an awful lot of guns into camp. The concept remains sound, but only for longer safaris with a wide range of game. Even then, you should give hard thought to whether you really need all three.

of the three rifles was a classic medium. In 1952, however, Robert Ruark's battery was perhaps the classic three-rifle armament. He had a Remington .30-06, presumably a Model 721; a Winchester Model 70 .375; and a Westley Richards .470 double. He also took along a .220 Swift, but found it unsatisfactory and quickly gave up on it.

Ruark's first safari, so ably recorded in *Horn of the Hunter,* was typical of the day: a lengthy, freewheeling affair that wound its way across much of Tanganyika. The bag included two lion, a great leopard, some marvelous buffalo, plus waterbuck, oryx, and the typical East African plains game. They did not hunt elephant, and were unlucky with both rhino and kudu. But all three rifles got substantial workouts.

About five years later, my uncle, Art Popham, made a thirty-day safari into Tanganyika on a collecting expedition for the Kansas City Museum of Natural History. Not as leisurely as the Ruark safari, his adventure got right down to business: He shot the usual two lion, buffalo, an 80-pound elephant, and the full range of plains game. His battery consisted of two Winchester Model 70s, one in .300 Improved and the other in .375 Improved (respectively identical to .300 and .375 Weatherby), and a big double. Unfortunately, there was no ammunition for the double, and information on the big Nitro Express cartridges was extremely sketchy in America in those days. It was a .450 of some type, but the only ".450 Nitro

In a three-rifle battery the light rifle is usually the one that will see the most use. For most of us, a favored deer rifle like this .30-06 will be just fine, with the classic battery rounded out by a medium like a .375, plus a big bore.

Express" cartridges they had split badly. I suspect they were trying to shoot .450-3¼" cartridges in a .500/.450 or possibly .500/.450 in a No. 2 chamber. Anyway, he took the rifle to Africa hoping to find ammunition in Nairobi or Arusha. No such luck, not even in 1957. The heavy rifle was thus useless, but the .375 served with perfect satisfaction on buffalo and elephant.

The three-rifle concept has great merit, especially if you follow the classic model of the "light, medium, and heavy." On the one end you have a very specialized, short-range, charge-stopping big bore; on the other end you have an accurate, flat-shooting, low-recoiling light rifle. And in the middle you have a versatile medium bore, a rifle that will be perfect for lion and very large antelope, and can serve in a pinch for both the largest and smallest of game.

The medium, the general-purpose rifle, is the mainstay of a three-rifle battery. The most logical choice is a .375, but if a lot of heavy game is to be encountered, a .416 or similar rifle could serve. Whatever the caliber, the rifle must be scope-sighted, and of course both solid and softpoint ammunition must be available.

The heavy rifle could be a double or a magazine rifle, whichever the hunter prefers. It should definitely be of .450 caliber or larger. Traditionally, such a rifle is

The medium rifle of a three-rifle battery should also be fairly versatile, and it may well see a lot of use. Perhaps my .30-06 would have been more ideal for this lechwe—but I was carrying my .375 Ruger and it worked just fine.

open sighted, but there's no reason it shouldn't wear a low-power scope and good reasons it should. It is the rifle that will be used the least, but when it's used the stakes are highest. So it must be selected with care—it must fit the shooter perfectly, and it must be in perfect working order.

The light rifle could be anything from .243 up to .338, but its most likely and most sensible calibers lie between 6.5mm and .300. It will be scope sighted, and it must be accurate and flat-shooting. It is probably the rifle that will be used the most, but depending on the range of game and the hunter's preferences, that honor could go to the medium. The light rifle will surely be used on a variety of game at a variety of distances, and it should be in a caliber as versatile as possible—and one with which the hunter is familiar and comfortable.

I have used Ruark's battery of a .30-06, .375, and double .470 on a couple of occasions, and that's a wonderful mix. I've also replaced the .30-06 with 7mm or .270, and the .375 with a .416, always with equally good results. In recent safari seasons I've gone back to the .30-06. Instead of a .375 H&H I've been using the .375 Ruger (take your pick), and my current double is a Rigby .450-3¼". Again, take your pick!

There are problems with a three-rifle battery, the main objection being that three rifles add up to a lot of weight to haul around. Many "two-rifle cases" of generous

An open-sighted big bore like my Rigby .450 is perhaps the most specialized of all rifles. There's nothing wrong (and much right) in including such a rifle—especially in a three-rifle battery, where the other two can add all the versatility you need.

dimensions will handle a disassembled double plus two scoped bolt guns—but such a setup will push the fifty-pound-per-bag limit, and you do not want to exceed that magic number. It isn't entirely a question of overweight charges (which can be horrible). If you break the baggage limit, your bags have an exponentially better chance of not making it to your final destination with you. Often, two gun cases will be required to house a three-rifle battery, so the hunter traveling solo is asking for a monstrous overweight baggage charge. Of course, if you will have two gun cases anyway, you might as well haul along a shotgun! Obviously, two hunters traveling (and hunting) together, or a husband/wife or other family team, can easily mix and match batteries and bring two gun cases. Better questions are: Do three-rifle batteries still have validity in today's Africa, and are they worth the extra hassle?

Twenty years ago I concluded this chapter by being very hard on three-rifle batteries. Specifically, here are some comments by experienced PHs who did not recommend three rifles. This is what the 1988 survey found for the three-rifle block:

George Hoffman wrote, "Too many—you never know which one to use! Better the third gun be a shotgun or .22."

Cotton Gordon said simply, "Two is enough."

Depending on where you're headed, you might want either the light or the medium rifle to be something extremely flat-shooting with a fairly substantial scope.

Finn Aagaard said, "Not necessary. A .22 rimfire or varmint rifle if he likes."

Franz Wengert wrote, "Anything more than two guns is a headache."

In the last twenty years the average safari has gotten ever shorter. With fewer hunting days and ever-shrinking quotas and resultant bags, African hunting is more specialized than ever. I'm sad to say that George Hoffman, Cotton Gordon, and Finn Aagaard are all gone today, and Franz Wengert sold his safari company and is currently retired. But all four were absolutely correct in the context of the average modern hunting safari. They were correct in the late 1980s, and they are much more correct in the new millennium: For safari batteries, two is company and three is a crowd.

At least most of the time. Rifle cranks like me can always come up with reasons to take rifles on safari, but on the average modern safari of ten days or even two weeks it is unlikely that more than two rifles are needed, and a third rifle might not be used at all. On the other hand, subtle changes over the last twenty years have brought some renewed validity to the classic three-rifle battery. One is the resurgence in popularity of the double rifle; another is the tremendous increase in elephant hunting. Any big bore, regardless of action type, is a very specialized rifle—but a big gun remains the most appropriate choice for a serious elephant hunt. Unless you're going on safari for just an elephant, nothing else, a true big bore is a horrible choice for a one-rifle safari. So you must mate it with something extremely versatile, like a scoped .375 or perhaps a .416. Now you're set for elephant, buffalo, hippo, even lion . . . but if the bag includes a fair selection of plains game, then you might add an accurate, versatile, easy-to-shoot light rifle. And we're right back where we were in Ruark's day!

The professional hunters I surveyed in 1989 had a wide divergence of opinion about a three-rifle battery, but some 60 percent made specific recommendations. Darn few were alike. There were several votes for a .30-06, a .375, and a ".400-plus," and a couple more for a 7mm magnum, .375, and .458. Several suggested a .300 magnum plus a .375 and .458, and a couple more recommended the .243, .30-06, and .458. One recommended a .270, an 8x68S, and a .458. Soren Lindstrom declined to recommend a second or third rifle, saying that if the hunter had a .375, nothing else was necessary.

Mike Rowbotham, at that time having had thirty-seven years in the field, personally used a .275 Rigby, .300 H&H, .338, .375, and .470 double for the various types of game. He recommended that clients bring, as a three-rifle battery, a .275 (meaning, I assume, a 7x57), a .338, and a .458 with handloaded ammunition. Mike Carr-Hartley, another pro with vast experience, recommended a 7mm magnum, a .375, and a .458—but added that, if available, a double of .470 or similar caliber was preferable.

Interestingly, the results of my 2007 survey were a bit different. Only 25 percent of the professional hunters who responded were emphatic in saying "no" to a three-firearm battery (as opposed to nearly 40 percent in 1989). Once again, however, actual recommendations were all over the map, with only about 25 percent recommending our classic "light, medium, and heavy" battery. However, a surprising number recommended my "ultralight" category in a three-rifle battery—for example, a .22 Hornet with a .300 and a .375; a .223 with a .300 and a .458 Lott; several recommendations for a ".22" mated with various combinations, such as .270 and .375, .30-06, and ".375-plus;" and even one recommendation for a .22 along with a .375 and a .470. There was also a recommendation for a .25-06 mated with a .300 and a .375. And once again the .243 garnered a couple of recommendations as the lightest rifle of a three-rifle battery: a .243 mated with a ".30-caliber and a .375 or .416," and a .243 mated with a .300 and a .416.

This is well-considered and valuable input. However, I have to hold to the premise that no modern safari absolutely requires three rifles. On safaris of two weeks or less, it's generally silly to take more than two. On the other hand, the three-week "general bag" safari isn't dead, and true big bores are far more popular today. Also, much more value is placed on the pygmy antelopes

The third gun in a three-firearm battery doesn't have to be a centerfire rifle. In terms of weight and baggage allowances, three guns are three guns, so depending on what you wish to hunt, a shotgun or a .22 might be good additions to a two-rifle battery.

today than was the case twenty years ago. Depending on the mix of rifles you wish to use (and the mix of game), a three-rifle battery may make a lot of sense, especially on longer safaris. But this isn't universal. For instance, last year I did a three-week elephant safari on the Ruvuma River. Donna had a full license as well, and we took three rifles among us: my double .450, a .375 Ruger, and a .30-06 we could share. An elephant hunt can be quite specialized and time intensive. The double worked just fine on a great tusker. The .375 was used along the way for a lovely kudu and a couple of duiker. The only animal taken with the .30-06 was an impala, and it would obviously have made more sense to leave it at home!

However, the three-rifle battery does have a place, and most of the time I've been grateful for all three when I've opted to take that number—and when the safari bag has been close to what was anticipated. However, this is a lot of rifles to look after, and a lot of rifles to use on the average safari today. Again, a three-rifle battery makes sense only on a lengthy safari, and even then only if a large variety of game will be hunted—multiple members of the Big Five, and a significant range of plains game.

On the shorter, more limited hunts most common today, the opportunity to use three rifles will generally not present itself, and the last thing you want is confusion over which rifle to reach for. I have carried heavy rifles to Africa and never fired them once, using the medium instead when the opportunity occurred. By the same token, I've carried light rifles all the way to Africa and never fired them, either, again using the medium instead—not because I needed to but because it was the medium I was carrying when I might have used the lighter rifle. If you decide on a three-rifle battery, understand that you may have excess-baggage charges to deal with, and that at least one of the three rifles may see extremely limited use. And then, if you're on a lengthy safari and can justify it, and if you're a rifle nut like me, you'll probably choke it up and take three rifles anyway!

The Professional's Choice in the Good Old Days

Chapter 38

Writing this book (now twice) has been quite a project, albeit an enjoyable one. From the start, I knew it would be presumptuous if all the ideas were my own—and such folly would negate any real benefit the book might have. Fortunately, the community of currently active professional hunters was most generous with its opinions on African rifles, both in 1989 and today, in late 2007. In the next chapters we'll look at both the rifles they use personally and their recommendations to clients. Here, I thought it would be interesting to take a historical look at the batteries that served sportsmen in the early days.

Some of the old-timers were ivory hunters. Others were sportsmen and women in the modern context, while others were explorers, adventurers, naturalists, or soldiers. A few emerged as "professional hunters" as we know the term today. But all had considerable experience shooting game in an Africa that will never be seen again.

The people we will look at here hunted Africa from the earliest days through World War II. Very few of these hunters, if any, are alive today. Fortunately, many of them left behind written records, part of the impressive body of African literature that still stirs our imagination. Usually the old-timers tell us what rifles they used, because their firearms were among their most essential tools.

There's another marvelous reference, long out of print, by S. R. Truesdell: *The Rifle—Its Development for Big Game Hunting.* In it Lieutenant Colonel Truesdell takes old-time gunwriter Ned Crossman's advice to heart: "After all, the digest of the experience of a hundred men—picked men, not chaps who once killed a buck in the Adirondacks and know all about game rifles, is the best way to reach an intelligent decision."

Truesdell gathered up the experiences and choices of arms of more than a hundred (170, to be precise) extremely experienced hunters, many of whom were still alive at that time. Included were American buffalo hunters, early African explorers, ivory hunters, colonial administrators, missionaries, the great turn-of-the-century sheep

A classic three-rifle battery from years gone by: Westley Richards .318, John Rigby .416, boxlock .470 by C. W. Andrews. Now, in truth, relatively few of the old-timers would have owned such an august battery! Most of them used what they had, and by our standards today many did extremely well with "inadequate" arms.

hunters, and even familiar names such as Jack O'Connor and Elmer Keith. In the text he discusses the rifles and cartridges as well as the experiences of those who used them, and he provides fascinating tables that list the names, hunting experiences and locales, and batteries of his chosen experts.

The way Truesdell saw it, between the early nineteenth century (when rifled arms came into widespread use) and World War II, the use of hunting rifles could be divided into four eras: from about 1834 to 1874, the time of the large bores; from 1875 to 1892 (coinciding with the British Express rifles), the era of the medium bores; from 1893 to 1905 (the infancy of smokeless powder), which he reckons as the time of the smallbores; and from 1906 to 1946, when the high-velocity smallbores held sway. It's a most interesting premise and a fascinating book. I hope someone resurrects and reprints it for today's hunters. I'd also like to know what Truesdell would have made of the last sixty years of sporting rifles!

In any case, this excellent reference provides a marvelous thumbnail sketch of the rifles used and preferred by widely experienced hunters the world over. Most of this material is, of course, available in books written by the individuals themselves (which means that if you want to obtain the same information, you must face the enjoyable but time-consuming task of reading 170 volumes, as Truesdell undoubtedly did).

Truesdell's African experts start at the beginning, with Capt. William Cornwallis Harris, whose 1835–36 South African expedition was perhaps the first safari in the modern sense. Harris relied primarily upon a double-barreled, muzzleloading 8-bore, and he had trouble with the largest animals—as did all hunters until the advent of the reliable penetration afforded by jacketed bullets. William Cotton Oswell followed hard on Harris's heels, hunting from 1837 to 1852. His two favorite arms were a smoothbore double 10-bore by Purdey, of course a muzzleloader, and a rifled 12-bore by Westley Richards.

The wild Scotsman, Roualeyn Gordon Cumming, wandered and hunted in southern Africa from 1843 to 1848. His favorite arm was a muzzleloading 12-bore double by Purdey, but he also used a huge 4-bore single shot along with several other big muzzleloaders. This passage, from his *Five Years Hunting Adventures in Africa,* is not atypical of the lengths to which the early hunters had to go to kill the largest African animals: "Having fired thirty-five rounds with my two-grooved rifle . . . I opened fire upon him with the Dutch six-pounder . . . and when forty bullets had perforated his hide he began for the first time to evince signs of a dilapidated constitution."

Earlier I referred to Sir Samuel Baker's "Baby," a 2-bore that fired a half-pound explosive shell. He actually used the cannon very little, however, relying

Philip Percival, "dean of professional hunters," as a young man. Percival started out with the light rifles that were available to him, but as he grew older he advocated heavier rifles, and as president of the East African Professional Hunters' Association was largely responsible for Kenya's ".40-caliber minimum" for thick-skinned game.

An older Philip Percival with Ernest Hemingway, 1934. On this safari Hemingway used a 6.5mm Mannlicher, his beloved .30-06 Springfield, and a big double that he hated. Percival was the model for the professional hunter in The Short Happy Life of Francis Macomber, *which immortalized the .505 Gibbs.*

mostly on 8- and 10-bore muzzleloading doubles. Later on, he was one of the first of the famed African explorers to rely on a breechloader, a .577 black-powder double made by Holland & Holland. However, he believed strongly that a .577 was a light rifle, only for thin-skinned game. He died in 1893, still maintaining that a double 8-bore was the only medicine for the largest game.

William Finaughty, hunting from 1864 to 1875, was another hunter whose career saw muzzleloaders replaced by breechloaders. He eventually gave up on the 4-bore single-shot muzzleloader in favor of a breechloading 12-bore double. Arthur Neumann, one of the great ivory hunters, had an unusually long career; he hunted elephant from 1868 to 1906, thus seeing the transition not only from muzzle to breechloading but also from black powder

J. A. Hunter, right, and client with a great elephant from days gone by. Hunter is perhaps best known as an advocate of the .500 double rifle, but he also used bolt actions, especially for elephant control work.

to smokeless. He finished his career using a double .450-3¼" by Rigby and a .256 Mannlicher as a light rifle. However, unlike so many turn-of-the-century hunters who swore by the 6.5mm or .256, Neumann never used it for elephant. Perhaps that was because, back in 1896, he was almost killed by an elephant after his .303 Lee-Metford failed him. His .450 was one of the first to see service in Africa, and he swore by it.

Frederick Courteney Selous hunted for ivory in his earlier days, using a beast of a muzzleloading 4-bore single shot that he came to hate. It's fair to say that later on he was more of an explorer, writer, and naturalist than an ivory hunter—but he was always hunting, often for the British Museum. He saw the changes that Neumann saw, and was almost as quick to adopt the new smokeless cartridges. In the middle years of his career, his favorite rifle was a Gibbs-Farquharson .461; he preferred its accuracy to the brute force of the big bores—and he still preferred it after the Nitro Expresses came into being.

While relatively few men were "professional ivory hunters," a great many early settlers, farmers, and professional hunters augmented their income by hunting elephant and selling the ivory, as shown here in this picture of an early ivory market in Kenya. That's J. A. Hunter in the center.

Around the turn of the century, Selous had Holland build him a single-shot .303, virtually identical to his old .461, and this also became a much-used rifle. Like virtually all the turn-of-the-century hunters, Selous used a .256 Mannlicher extensively. For his last East African hunting, just before World War I, he used a .375 Holland & Holland, a rifle worlds removed from the single-shot 4-bores he started with. Of these newfangled little guns Selous said, "Had I only one of these rifles in my early days, I would have shot thrice the number of elephants I did."

In the 1890s the most common batteries were a mixture of black-powder and smokeless arms. Edouard Foa's heavy 8-bore, medium .577 Express, and light .303 formed a very normal mixed battery—at least until confidence in the new, fast-moving smokeless cartridges grew. Lt. Col. H. G. C. Swayne, who hunted in Somaliland between 1884 and 1897 (and is immortalized by the Swayne hartebeest subspecies) used 8- and 12-bore Paradox guns, the ever-present .577/.450 Martini, and later a .303—but his primary arm was a black-

J. A. Hunter (in the vehicle) and client with a very big leopard. Interestingly, prior to World War II there are very few references to baiting for leopard. This apparently only became a preferred technique after telescopic sights came into common use.

powder .577 by Holland. The .577 was perhaps the only caliber that was revered in both black-powder and smokeless form. As a black-powder cartridge it had enough bullet weight and caliber to get the job done, albeit with little to spare. When it was transformed to a smokeless cartridge, it became hell on wheels!

On his earlier trips Edward North Buxton used a black-powder double .500 Express almost exclusively, but by 1893—very early in the smokeless game—he had added a .256 Mannlicher, unquestionably the 6.5x53R Mannlicher-Steyr, to his battery. This very quickly became his only rifle.

Sir Edmund Loder (the Loder gazelle of North Africa bears his name) started his career in India and Sumatra with 8- and 12-bore doubles by Reilly. Later he gave up on the big guns in favor of a .450 Express, but by the early 1890s he was sold on the .256 Mannlicher; it was the only rifle he used on his 1906–1907 East African safari.

Around the turn of the century, the smokeless era had well and truly taken hold and black-powder rifles were vanishing from the scene. Maj. C. S. Cumberland started his hunting career in Asia with a 12-bore double, but when he hunted East Africa in 1911 he used a double .500 by Henry, a smokeless gun, and a .303 Lee-Metford.

A very young Harry Selby and Robert Ruark with some great ivory at the Mount Kenya Safari Club. With a career spanning from 1945 to the present, Selby is one of very few professional hunters who has seen it all from the great old days to now.

The Rev. William Rainsford, an American Episcopalian clergyman from New York, was quite a hunter. On his earlier trips to the western United States he used a .50-110 single-shot and a double 8-bore by Rigby (unusual in North America!). He preceded Roosevelt to East Africa, not once but twice between 1906 and 1909. His battery, like Roosevelt's, was the classic three-rifle arrangement: a .450-3¼", probably by Rigby, as a heavy; a .350 Rigby Magnum as a medium; and a .256 Mannlicher as a light. Like many hunters before and since, he got the most use from his medium and was lavish in his praise of it.

Richard J. Cunninghame and Leslie Tarlton were contemporaries in the Kenya Colony; Cunninghame settled there in 1889 and hunted until 1924, Tarlton from 1891 to 1926. Both were early settlers, sport hunters, commercial hunters, and professional hunters. Both undoubtedly started with black-powder arms, but both eventually became fans of Holland's .500/.465 and, a

Leslie Tarlton was the founder of Newland and Tarlton, thought to be the first East African safari company. He was a founding member of the EAPHA and a professional hunter on the Theodore Roosevelt safari in 1909.

Phil Percival, together with John Hunter, was one of the few PHs to gain fame as a PH before WW II. He was considered the dean of the professional hunters of East Africa.

seeming contradiction for English colonists, the American .30-06. Tarlton, one of the greatest of all lion hunters, also favored the .275 Rigby (7x57) and .350 Rigby Magnum.

Although Truesdell properly assigns the period from 1893 to 1905 as the time of the new smokeless smallbores, hunters who used the little 6.5, 7x57, .303, and so on exclusively were somewhat rare. On the other hand, such rifles were used extensively on a tremendous variety of African game. Often the light rifle's use was accidental, in that it was the rifle the hunter customarily carried, while a tracker carried the heavy rifle. When an opportunity for a shot arose, it was sometimes more expedient to shoot than to switch guns—and it was discovered that the light rifles, with long, heavy-for-caliber solid bullets, performed surprisingly well. Also, as Finn Aagaard noted, not very many early settlers had what we today might think of as "suitable" rifles for Africa's largest game. They used what they had, most often a military caliber, and they worked amazingly well. But very few of the serious professionals actually relied on the smallbores; Bell was a notable and outspoken exception, and C. H. Stigand was another.

In 1946 Sydney Downey founded the firm Ker and Downey (with Donald Ker), which became the preeminent safari outfitting company after WW II. He's shown here with a dik-dik shot by Jack O'Connor.

Richard John Cunninghame was one of the PHs on Kermit and Theodore Roosevelt's safari in 1909. Here he is seen with a hippo shot by a member of the Roosevelt party.

Sir Alfred Pease hunted in North Africa in the early 1890s, then in East Africa between 1896 and 1924. His .256 Mannlicher was indeed his most-used rifle, but he also used Jeffery rifles in both .333 and .404, a .350 Rigby, and a 10-bore Paradox. Naturalist John G. Millais, on the other hand, used only his .256 Mannlicher on his many expeditions between 1893 and 1924.

Maj. P. H. G. Powell-Cotton was another who used a Paradox gun—they were actually very popular. But for light game he relied on his .256 Mannlicher. He wasn't necessarily a smallbore addict, however; for his Central African hunting between 1902 and 1904 he used a double .450/.400 on most of his heavy game— and a tracker carried a double .600 by Jeffery for use in tight spots.

Denis D. Lyell, who hunted in Africa and wrote about it extensively between 1897 and 1920, was another vociferous smallbore advocate. He had a .404 Jeffery, but on the whole much preferred a 7.9mm Mauser, .275 (7x57), or .256 Mannlicher. Lyell was much more experienced with the largest game than most hunters of today, but he didn't have anything like the experience of a James Sutherland. Sutherland, as we've seen earlier, used the .318 and also the 10.75 Mauser, but for elephant he came to rely on a pair of double .577s. With them he had one of the longest careers of any of the serious ivory hunters, from 1896 to 1932.

The American naturalist Carl Akeley hunted and collected throughout East and Central Africa between 1896 and 1926; he died of fever and was buried in the Belgian Congo. His battery developed into a .256 Mannlicher as a light rifle, a 9mm

Baron Bror von Blixen-Finecke possibly was the first PH to specialize in taking hunters after large ivory. He was relatively unknown to the modern hunter till the movie Out of Africa *made him famous. If it were possible for a posthumous career to take off like a meteor, his would be it.*

Mauser as a medium, and a double .470 for his heavy. Later he seems to have given up on a medium, using mostly a Jeffery double .475 No. 2 in addition to his William Evans .470. That particular William Evans .470 has had quite a career, and today is carried by Zimbabwe professional hunter Andrew Dawson. Akeley also used three fairly similar light rifles: a .275 Hoffman, a 7.9mm Mauser, and a .30-06.

Maj. C. H. Stigand, killed in action in Sudan in 1919, was a courageous and well-liked officer who served primarily in Africa from 1899 until his death. He was definitely a smallbore man, preferring his .256 Mannlicher, although he did have a double .450 available for backup.

A. Blayney Percival, author of *A Game Ranger's Notebook,* was another .256 man. He also had a double .360 and a double .450, but he wrote, "I shot most of my lions, say forty, with the .256. I do not remember exactly, but I feel sure that two-thirds of the lions did not need a second shot; if one did, it usually meant several more. When hunting alone I seldom fired till I had a lion just how I wanted him, and I shot to put him out of business. Softnose bullets I gave up long ago except for small stuff or in heavy rifles."

John Taylor will always be known as the person who gave the hunting world African Rifles and Cartridges, *one of the most sought-after books on the subject ever. It has been in print off and on since 1948.*

Teddy Roosevelt, naturalist J. Alden Loring, and Richard J. Cuninghame, with a bull elephant shot in Meru, Kenya, in 1909.

Col. J. Stevenson Hamilton, a contemporary of Percival, shot an enormous number of lion—perhaps more than even Tarlton. He apparently used a .303 Lee-Metford for much of his lion shooting, which definitely qualifies him as a smallbore man. However, he also used a .350 Rigby Magnum, and for larger game both a .416 Rigby and a double .577.

Marcus Daly, hunting between 1897 and 1936, was a magazine-rifle man. He much preferred them to doubles, doing most of his later hunting with a 10.75 Mauser and a .416 Rigby. He did not believe in the smallbores for elephant, feeling that they were adequate for brain shots on undisturbed game but not for use in thick cover.

The Hungarian Kalman Kittenberger, author of *Big Game Hunting and Collecting in East Africa*, 1903–1926, used Mannlichers in 6.5, 8, and 9mm, and Mausers in

7x57 and 8x57. He seems to have preferred the 8mm and 9mm magazine rifles, but he also relied on a Holland double .465 for the largest game.

American Charles Cottar, one of the most colorful of the early professional hunters, plied his trade in Kenya between 1902 and 1940. He never lost his love for the .405 Winchester, but he also had a double .470 by Rigby, a .35 Newton that he used extensively, and a .250 Savage for light game. He also, at least according to legend, used the incredibly anemic .32 Winchester Special to take virtually all species of African game when he first arrived.

Maj. H. C. Maydon, whose marvelous *Big Game Shooting in Africa* remains a valuable reference three-quarters of a century after publication, was primarily a smallbore man. He used a .470 double extensively on his first safari to Portuguese East Africa, but after he acquired a 7.9mm Mauser, his .470 became a seldom-used backup.

Capt. A. H. E. Mosse, who hunted in Somaliland for five years, 1907 to 1912, had a three-gun battery: a 12-bore Paradox, a double .450/.400 by Watson, and a .318 Westley Richards magazine rifle. He did not hunt elephant, but, unlike his smallbore contemporaries, he relied on his .400 double for most of his lion hunting.

On their 1909 safari, Kermit Roosevelt's battery was similar to his father's. For a light rifle both had a .30-06, and for a medium a .405 Winchester; only Kermit's heavy differed in that it was a .450-3¼" by Rigby. Like his father, he used the big double but little, relying mainly on his .30-06 and .405 Winchester.

George Agnew Chamberlain, another visiting sportsman who hunted in Portuguese East Africa between 1909 and 1923, used a .450 double by William Evans and a .470 by Churchill. He had a .256, but his favorite light rifle was a .318 Westley Richards.

American naturalist James L. Clark, best known for his *Great Arc of the Wild Sheep,* hunted and collected extensively in Africa. He used a number of rifles, but his Springfield .30-06 and William Evans .470 double remained his two mainstays. Another American author, Edison Marshall, also used a two-rifle battery on his 1929–1930 safari. Unlike most Americans, he eschewed the .30-06, using instead a 9.5mm Mannlicher and a .470 double.

Dr. Richard Sutton, surgeon and naturalist, hunted widely in both Africa and Indochina. His favorite rifle was a Holland double .465, which he used essentially as a medium. His "heavy" was heavy indeed, a double .577, while as a light rifle he used a .30-06. Later on he turned to a 9.3x62, but rarely used it in place of the .465.

After the death of her father, Vivienne de Watteville carried on with their joint expedition in East and Central Africa. Though a petite woman, she had no problems with her .416 Rigby, which she used extensively. Her light rifle was a .318 Westley Richards.

Capt. E. T. L. Lewis, hunting in East Africa between 1924 and 1928 and later in India, is one of the few who used what we would consider today an ideal three-rifle battery: His heavy was a Holland double .465, his medium a .375 H&H Magnum, and his light a .303 Lee-Metford. Perhaps surprisingly, his favorite rifle was the big double—but he made no bones over being a double-rifle man.

Count Vasco da Gama wandered and hunted throughout French Equatorial Africa for nearly two years during the late 1920s. Apparently a man of some means, he tried out a variety of rifles, including doubles in both .577 and .600. He found them obviously effective, but too heavy to carry and with so much recoil that the second shot was too slow. Much better as a stopping rifle, he reckoned, was the Holland .465 that he settled on, but he was actually more of a smallbore magazine-rifle man, preferring to use a .275 Rigby Mauser, a 7.9mm Mauser, or a 9mm Mannlicher.

A list of this sort—the choices of the old hands—could go on almost forever. Such a study is fascinating, but its value to today's hunter is somewhat limited, for two reasons. First, many of the rifles and cartridges used before World War II are no longer available, or available only with extreme difficulty. If they were better than modern counterparts, pursuing them would be worthwhile at all costs, but with the possible exception of some of the big Nitro Expresses (which are relatively available), this is hardly the case. We have excellent modern cartridges chambered in modern rifles fully capable of handling any game that walks. Second, African hunting conditions aren't the same today as they were back then.

It would be nice, even from purely historical interest, if some kind of consensus could be gleaned from the study of the rifles and cartridges chosen by the old-timers. But even that seems impossible; they were as human as we are, and their choices, recommendations, and biases were based not only on what worked for them but also, at least to some degree, on what was available to them at the time. Some of them favored smallbores, some big bores; some used doubles while others preferred magazines. It will be always thus. As Mark Twain observed, "It is difference of opinion that makes horse races."

Let's leave the past now and take a look at the rifles and cartridges of today's experts—the professional hunters still in the field.

The Professional's Choice, 1989

Chapter 39

A t this stage in the revision of this volume I was driven to a most difficult decision. Back in 1988 and 1989, long before Al Gore invented the Internet and when few people had FAX machines, I conducted a survey of professional hunters in the field, primarily through international "snail mail" using the mailing lists of the International Professional Hunters' Association (IPHA) and "country" professional hunters' associations. It was a brutal process, but the results were wonderful. As we know, I have just conducted a new and very similar survey with a similar number of respondents. The decision was whether to simply replace the 1989 survey with the one for 2007 or somehow try to blend the results.

Ultimately, I decided to do neither, but to let each stand alone. If this volume has the same shelf life as the original, there will come a time when 1989 was a long time ago. Right now, however, many of the comments from 1989 remain extremely valid. Many of the professional hunters who responded are still in the field. Some were reached with the second survey and responded again, but some did not. There may also come a time when commentary and recommendations from the 1989 survey will have historical significance, so the wisest course seems to be to allow the bulk of the 1989 survey to remain, with minimal additional comment as appropriate.

My opening to this survey remains valid: There are African professionals who happen to be firearms enthusiasts and may experiment year in and year out with various guns and loads. In that profession, though, such a man is rare. Most PHs lack the time, budget, or inclination for such experimentation. Africa being Africa, they also have limited availability and selection. The pro is likely to find what works for him and stick with it.

On the other hand, the professional sees it all in the long procession of clients' rifles that show up in his camps. He gets to see what works and what doesn't, to a degree unmatched in the hunting world. In now seventy-six safaris I have shot and seen shot a great deal of African game, and I've done it and seen it done

Roger Whittall and me "on the ivory trail." OK, I'm not on the trail at all, but this was Roger's season's worth of ivory back in 1989, the last year Mozambique ivory was allowed into the U.S. Whittall's rifle is a back-action sidelock Holland & Holland in .500/.465.

with a wide variety of rifles, cartridges, and bullets. It is perhaps true today (not in 1989!) that I have more experience than some younger professional hunters, and certainly true that I have hunted a greater cross-section of Africa than most. But the real hands-on experts remain the African professional hunters, and if you take input from more than a hundred professionals in the field, you have an immeasurable wealth of knowledge and experience.

Realizing that professional hunters are busy men—and most of them abhor correspondence—I kept it short, just a one-page fill-in-the-blanks form. I asked how long they'd been in the field and what type of country they hunted: plains, desert, thornbush, forest, swamp, or a combination thereof. Then I asked which of the Big Five, if any, they hunted.

The next set of questions asked for the professional's own choice of rifle for use on light plains game, medium plains game, large plains game, lion, leopard, thick-skinned game, and all-round use. Following that, I asked for specific recommendations to clients for a one-rifle safari, a two-rifle battery, and a three-rifle battery. Finally, I asked whether the client should bring a shotgun, and I also invited further comment, hoping that those who had more to say would take the time to do so. Many did, and some of these extra comments, for which I'm most grateful, may be the most valuable tidbits in this entire volume.

The responding professional hunters ran the gamut of the industry. Perhaps the largest number of them operate in South Africa, which doesn't surprise me since that country hosts something like 50 percent of all of today's hunting safaris. Zimbabwe had the next highest number, also not surprising. The third largest geographic grouping, however, had Kenya postmarks. A few of these hunters were retired, while most were operating in Tanzania—but as a group the old Kenya hands were extremely well represented in the 1989 survey. By 2007 this had changed dramatically. There were other dramatic changes as well, and I think many readers will have fun comparing the two. You will find the 2007 survey in the following chapter, and insofar as possible I will keep the same format to simplify this comparison.

The senior professionals to respond in 1989—Tony Henley and Harry Selby—each had forty-four years in the field at that time; the junior man had but two. Collectively, the respondents represented more than 1,800 years of African hunting, with an average of sixteen years per man. These figures are humbling, representing vast experience with African game. For interest's sake, the 2007 survey, with a slightly smaller sampling, actually indicated a longer average of 19.5 years per respondent!

The faces of Africa have changed a lot since that 1989 survey, and many of my old friends are now gone. Among them, Lew Tonks, a great Eastern Cape outfitter.

I've had a wonderful time writing this book, and I believe its ideas are sound. However, if a choice should be made between my ideas and the ideas of professional hunters in the field, whether in 1989 or 2007, my recommendation would always be to go with the real experts! On a daily basis, their reputations, livelihood, and very lives depend on sound choices in rifles and cartridges.

I expected most safaris to be conducted in thornbush, followed by plains, and this proved a good assessment. Interesting was the fact that desert, swamp, and forest habitat seem to be hunted about equally, but with much less frequency than plains or thornbush. Most respondents hunted a variety of habitat, and most hunted one or more of the Big Five. I was amazed at the number of hunters who seek lion, but even more surprised by the percentage that have experience with rhino and elephant.

Personal Choices

It goes without saying that the rifle a professional hunter chooses for himself might not be one he would recommend to a client; like most of us, professionals are prone to use old favorites. And since they live in Africa, they have occasion to use rifles that are perhaps more specialized than they might advise a client to bring. I asked for personal choices in seven areas.

Light Plains Game

Like most of the game categories that follow, this one was purposely vague. My idea of light plains game may or may not be the same as it would be for the professionals, and what really mattered to me was what they considered an adequate rifle for the light plains game of their own areas.

Of all the dozens and dozens of truly fine "deer-class" cartridges that would fill this need, only nineteen cartridges were mentioned. They did run the gamut. French hunter Pierre Caravati, a professional for thirty-two years, uses his .460 Weatherby for everything, including light game. Campbell Smith, on the other hand, a ten-year professional in several southern countries, specifically limited "light plains game" to duiker, steenbok, and such, and stated his choice was a .22 Hornet.

In terms of numbers, the .243 Winchester was a surprising winner with thirty-two specific mentions, followed by the .270 with 28, the 7mm magnum with thirteen, the .30-06 with twelve, the .300 H&H with nine, the 7x57 with nine (Mike Rowbotham had the distinction of being the only respondent to call this cartridge the .275 Rigby!)—and on down from there. Perhaps the most interesting choice, to

I did some of my early South African hunting with Raymond Theron. Raymond was killed by a buffalo in 2006.

my mind, came from my old friend Joof Lamprecht, who hunts in Namibia. In that open, arid country, where springbok are often taken at extreme range, his choice as a light rifle was the .264 Winchester Magnum. Although unusual in Africa and underrated in America, that's an excellent choice.

Medium Plains Game

This category, though also vague, was perhaps clearer to the respondents than the previous one. It obviously stops short of eland, but could be taken to include animals well into the quarter-ton category. Just fifteen cartridges were mentioned in this group, the largest being Pierre Caravati's .460 Weatherby again. The smallest was .243, but only three respondents still clung to such a light rifle.

The most common choice by far was the .30-06, with 33 mentions. The 7mm edged the .300 H&H by three—twenty-five mentions to twenty-two—while the .270 came up a close fourth with twenty-one. Notice that if you took the twenty-two .300 H&H entries and added eight votes for the .300 Weatherby and five for the .300 Winchester, you'd have an overwhelming amount of support for a "fast .30" for use on medium plains game. There were also a few scattered mentions of the .338 and 8x68S. I would have expected both to come in a bit stronger, likewise

Michel Mantheakis was among relatively few professional hunters who responded to both the 1989 and 2007 surveys. In 1989 Mantheakis worked for Luke Samaras and carried a .458. He has long since headed up Miombo Safaris, and although still a bolt-action man he has upgraded to a .450 Dakota.

the old 9.3x62, which had but one vote. Interesting to me was the fact that opinion was hardly divided at all in this category; to me, there is little difference in effect on game between the .270, 7mm magnums, .30-06, and .300 magnums—and these cartridges collectively comprised about 75 percent of the responses in this category.

Large Plains Game

This category seemed clear in that it would have to include eland, roan, sable, bongo, zebra, and such—whatever happens to be the largest in one's hunting territory. I was therefore surprised to see three respondents hanging in with the .243 in this category. However, that doesn't mean those professionals hunt eland; more likely, the largest plains game they personally hunt is greater kudu for meat—and the .243 is a favorite among South African kudu hunters willing to pick their shots.

Except for another lone respondent who stuck with his .270, most of the respondents made a shift here to heavier calibers. Fully fifty-eight chose the .375, way up from just four for medium game; but the .300s stayed strong—an aggregate of forty-one. The sudden strength of the .375 is telling; that's clearly the firearm of choice among a majority of professional hunters for use on the

South African PH Noel Ross with a fine Eastern Cape kudu. Noel Ross is the king of Vaal rhebok hunters. I hunted "Vaalies" with him clear back in 1992, and again in 2007.

largest plains game. Many of those who recommended the .300s, incidentally, specifically stated that they use 200- or 220-grain bullets.

Lion

It's important to keep in mind that this question concerned the rifle the professional uses himself, not the rifle he recommends for his client. Some PHs are or were farmers, and have had occasion to shoot lion—while others manage to fit in a private safari of their own between clients. So in some cases the rifle suggested is what would be used when the pro is actually hunting lion; in others it would be a rifle used strictly for backup and thus might be heavier in caliber.

Some respondents specified one rifle for personal use and another for backup. Gary Baldwin of Hippo Valley Safaris, Zimbabwe, for instance, uses a .375 on lion for his own hunting but for backup carries a double .470. Surprisingly, nineteen different calibers were mentioned for use on lion. With few exceptions, however,

One's first professional hunter usually sets a mark that cannot be beaten. Mine did! This is Willem van Dyk in 1977. After Kenya closed he hunted in South Africa for many years. He's now retired, and his son is a professional hunter.

there were just a couple of votes per caliber. No surprise was that the .375 got about half of the total votes, sixty-six. Next was the .458 with fifteen, followed by the .416 Rigby with ten. There was one vote for the .270, four for the .30-06, two for the 7mm magnum, and six for the .300 H&H.

Everything else was up into the medium-bore class or larger. Four double-rifle cartridges were mentioned: the .500, the .470, the .500/.465, and the .475 No. 2. More surprising to me was that four wildcat cartridges were mentioned: the .450 Ackley, .450 Watts, .416 Hoffman (three votes), and the .510 Wells.

It seems that a majority of professional hunters feel the .375 is enough gun for lion under most conditions, while a very few rely on picking their shots with smaller cartridges. Peter Johnstone, for instance, reported that he has shot sixty lion himself and another fifty to sixty with clients. He prefers a .30-06 for his own use, but admitted that the .375 is better. Still, some prefer bigger guns, all the way up to the .500s.

"Googee" Wahib, a Nairobi-based professional with over twenty years' experience, was one of few who listed a buckshot-loaded shotgun for wounded lion. Several hunters, however, did mention specific bullet designs. Most often mentioned were

Noslers, Swift A-Frames, and Bear Claws. I find it fascinating that such relatively new designs as those last two have found such rapid acceptance in Africa.

Leopard

Only 12 rifle calibers were mentioned, but a number of hunters did list their choice as a buckshot-loaded shotgun. A couple of those specified the 3½-inch 10-gauge! Among the rifle calibers, the .375 again ruled the roost. However, several respondents made the notation that this was the minimum caliber required by law, thus perhaps not reflecting a true preference. Interestingly, only four votes came in for cartridges larger than the .375: Caravati's ever-present .460, of course, plus a .416 Hoffman, and three votes for the .458. Second in votes to the .375 was the .300 magnum, followed closely by the .30-06. A number of professionals specified low-power scopes of high quality— and the general message of the additional written comments was that accuracy and exact shot placement are far more important than caliber where leopard are concerned.

Thick-Skinned Game

Here, finally, the light rifles are all weeded out. No caliber under .375 H&H was mentioned, but sixteen larger cartridges were. Most commonly used is the .458 Winchester Magnum, and that should be no surprise—it's the most commonly available, and the rifles are the most economical. However, as I mentioned earlier, a good number of those relying on the .458 specified handloaded ammunition.

Second most popular was the .375 H&H—gain no great surprise. The rest of the choices are a real grab bag. Fully nine of the old British cartridges were mentioned, including eighteen .416 Rigbys and fifteen .470s. There were also doubles in .450-3¼", .475 No. 2, .500/.465, .500, and .577—plus two .500 Jeffery bolt guns and three .404s. I was very surprised not to see a .505 Gibbs listed by anyone, but I must say there are a lot of classic old guns still in action. Many, of course, are in the hands of the old guard, like Tony Henley and his Holland Royal .465. The big wildcats were almost as well represented, with two each using the .458 Lott, .450 Watts, and .450 Ackley; and three using the .416 Hoffman.

All-Round Use

This was a tough question, and a number of respondents said so. What, for instance, does "all-round use" mean? Perhaps a useful rifle to be carried around in the truck just in case? Or did I really mean one rifle that would do it all? Was I including

In 1979 I was Barrie Duckworth's first client, right after he left Rhodesian Parks. Barrie has become one of Zimbabwe's most respected outfitters—and he still prefers the .458 Mannlichers that he used in his culling days.

or excluding dangerous game? As before, I wanted the respondents to take it any way they wanted to, but I also wanted just one rifle mentioned for whatever they considered "all-round" use. That really cut down on the number of cartridges—only twelve were suggested, and only seven of these got more than one vote.

Most of the professionals must have had dangerous game in their general hunting category, because the .375 was the overwhelming choice (eighty-one mentions), with nothing else making even a close showing. In second place was the .416 with seven votes. However, several professionals specified one rifle for personal use and another for guiding. Rudy Lubin, longtime professional hunter in Central Africa, suggested a .375 for his own use but a .416 Rigby when he was with a client. Thirty-two-year veteran Cotton Gordon, one of few Americans to do really well in African professional hunting, uses a 7mm magnum for his own hunting—but carries a .458 when he's with clients.

There were a couple of other interesting choices. German professional hunter Franz Wengert, for instance, uses a 9.3x64. And of course there were a couple of guys who carry their heavy rifles for everything. By and large, though, after all these years it seems that the .375 H&H is still hard to beat as that elusive, perhaps imaginary "all-round" rifle.

Recommendations to Clients

Since it's almost impossible for a hunting client to bring more than three firearms to Africa—and more than two can be most inconvenient—for this section

I abandoned the game classifications and simply asked, "What rifles do you prefer your clients to bring on safari?" Then I asked for recommendations for one rifle, two rifles, and three rifles, with blank spaces left for each. Some of the respondents made recommendations for one-, two-, and three-rifle batteries. Others made suggestions in one or two but not all categories. A great many of the recommendations to clients differed from the hunter's personal choices.

One Rifle

Approximately 90 percent of the respondents suggested bringing just one rifle—not necessarily as the only or best option but as a viable option for their clients. Only ten cartridges were mentioned—and the only one with more than a handful of votes was, naturally, the .375 H&H. A very distant second was the .30-06, followed by ".300 magnum" (exact cartridge unspecified). Several light cartridges were mentioned. In most of these cases, a close look at the survey revealed that these professionals had but limited hunting for dangerous game—perhaps only leopard. In other words, there wasn't a real need for a dangerous-game rifle. Other cartridges mentioned were the .270 Winchester, 7mm magnum, 8x68S, .416 Hoffman, .338, 9.3x64, and .416 Rigby. A close look suggested that the PHs who selected light cartridges did mostly plains-game hunting, while those who chose heavier cartridges hunted in dangerous-game areas.

Two Rifles

More recommendations were made here than in the two other categories, and several respondents left the two others blank. It's interesting to note that all the cartridges recommended are commonly available—no obscure wildcats and nothing obsolete.

The vast majority recommended two-rifle batteries consisting of a reasonably heavy rifle and another of somewhat smaller caliber. The suggestions for a light rifle were extremely diverse, although mostly within the same basic power range. On the other hand, just three calibers were cited as a second, heavier rifle: .375, .458, and .416 in that order of popularity. In combination with the .375, most respondents suggested a .270 Winchester, .30-06, 7mm magnum, or one of the .300s. Several didn't specify an exact cartridge, writing down instead something like ".270-.30-06-7mm + .375."

Finn Aagaard added the .280 Remington to that mix, but he was the only one who mentioned that particular cartridge. For some reason, this truly excellent

Zimbabwe PH Angie Angelloz and me with a magnificent Zambian buffalo taken in 1996. Angie was one of the finest young hunters I ever had the honor to hunt with but, like many, he has since gone on to other pursuits.

cartridge has remained more or less an "American" round, while the very similar .270 has really established itself in Africa. I guess the same could be said of the wonderfully versatile .338; it did much better in the survey than the .280, but not nearly as well as I would have expected.

Aside from the .270 to .300 range of cartridges, little else was recommended as a second rifle. Interestingly, there were five votes for the .243 in combination with the .375. I'd never considered such a battery, but that's not a bad combination at all: the pleasant-shooting little .243 for camp meat and lighter plains game, and the .375 for everything else. Three professionals, on the other hand, recommended the .338 in combination with the .375. This is a battery whose utility eludes me. The two cartridges are both superb, but so close in trajectory, energy, and penetrating powers that I'd prefer two rifles in either chambering to both of them. Most suggestions for a second rifle in concert with a .416 or .458 followed right along—in other words, something between a 7mm and a .300. In this case, there were no votes for a .270,

Rudy Lubin is another extremely experienced professional hunter who responded to both surveys. In 1989 he was hunting exclusively in the Central African Republic. He remains one of the leading PHs in the C.A.R., and has since hunted in Tanzania and elsewhere.

Joe Coogan and Harry Selby on safari. In 1989 Coogan, who apprenticed under Selby, was hunting in Botswana, but he would soon come to work with me at Petersen Publishing. Later he would do several seasons in Tanzania. Selby did fifty-five full seasons as a professional hunter, a mark that is unlikely to be equaled.

so it appears that those who like heavier rifles on the upper end like heavier rifles on the bottom end as well.

Three Rifles

Oh, boy! This one turned out to be a real can of worms, with very little consensus and some 30 different recommendations to sort through. As I reported in my own chapter on three-rifle batteries, mixed in with the recommendations for three rifles were a number of strident comments against a three-rifle battery. Many of these hunters stated flatly that three guns are too many to look after and use, or that deciding which to use is too confusing. As I mentioned, Franz Wengert called three rifles a "headache." Gerry Gore, who hunts in both South Africa and Botswana, said of three-rifle batteries, "God preserve me."

When two rifles were all that would be available, the .375 was the overwhelming choice as the heavier one. However, when three rifles could be chosen, a much larger percentage—in fact, a decided majority—recommended that one of them be over .400 in caliber. Several wrote it just that way, suggesting that the third rifle be "any .400-plus," or words to that effect. A number specifically suggested one of the .416s or the .458. And for the first time in recommendations to clients, suggestions of double rifles began to appear. Two recommendations favored the .470, and a couple wrote in the .458, then added "if available, a double over .450 is preferable."

The .375 was the most common choice for a medium bore—but not by as great a margin as you might think. A surprising number of hunters suggested that the medium should be a .300, .338, or 8x68S. In these cases the lighter rifle was often much lighter, a 7x57, .270, or .243, while the heavy rifle could be a .416, .458, or .375. The light rifles ran the gamut from .22 Long Rifle to .300 magnum.

My idea of the "classic" three-rifle battery—comprised of something in the .270 to .300 class, the .375, and a big gun—was certainly present in the survey. Although the results were so varied as to be bewildering, this was probably the most common recommendation. The second most common variation, however, listed the .243 as the light rifle. And, often enough to take into serious consideration, the .375 was either listed as the heaviest rifle or ignored altogether, in which case a .300, .338, 7mm, or .30-06 was listed as the medium rifle.

A number of hunters suggested that the third firearm be a shotgun. This brings us to the final questions of the survey, which asked whether a client should bring a shotgun, and whether one was kept in camp. The answer to the former was about six to one in favor of clients bringing shotguns. Only three respondents didn't keep a shotgun in camp, and several added that they also kept a .22.

Additional Comments

A great many respondents took the time to add comments on their own choices of rifles and observations on what has worked best for their clients. This unsolicited information sometimes ran into several pages. It was generally valuable and always fascinating. Space precludes quoting every comment by every professional, but what follows, in no particular order, is some of the most interesting information and opinions from professional hunters all over Africa. Note that these comments are a snapshot in time, specifically 1989. Some of the names were famous then; some have become famous in the years since. Regrettably, many of these professional hunters are deceased or retired . . . but others are still in the field, and you will note in the next chapter that some of them added comments in the 2007 survey.

Kenyan Mike Carr-Hartley has hunted Tanzania, Sudan, Kenya, and Zambia since 1962. He was one of the hunters who suggested that the heavy rifle should

John Kingsley-Heath hunted in both East Africa and Botswana extensively. He was once severely mauled by a lion but returned to hunting quickly. He guided many famous hunters of the twentieth century, such as Jack O'Connor. Here he is depicted with Eleanor O'Connor, Jack's wife.

be, "if available to client, a double of .470 or such caliber." He also suggested that if the heavy rifle is a .458, the ammo "should be handloaded and beefed up as factory loads lack punch."

An American who has become a legend in Africa, former Colorado outfitter Cotton Gordon, has thirty-two years in the business. He specifically recommended that his clients bring a 7mm or .300 magnum plus a .375, and then stated, "Two [rifles] is enough!" He also wrote that he keeps a shotgun in camp because he prefers "that clients not have to bring three firearms."

Alex McDonald, now retired after twenty-five years of experience, suggested "a .22 rimfire is good for practice, game birds, and curing a flinch." He went on to say, "Bullet placement is the main criterion. Clients should practice a lot before a safari and know their rifles intimately. Bullet construction (and not so much caliber) is the second most important factor. No caliber ever went out there and killed an animal; it's the bullet that does this and it must be good—but it cannot do its job if placed incorrectly. Practice is essential." Amen!

Gary Baldwin of Hippo Valley Safaris in Zimbabwe had the following excellent advice: "Positively only one weight of bullet for each rifle. Different weights only cause confusion. Take into account re-zeroing your rifle when assessing the amount of ammo to take on your hunt."

With fifteen years as a professional hunter and another dozen years hunting on his own before that, Farouk Qureshi, an East African pro, prefers his .460 Weatherby Magnum for heavy game, stating: "I have also used the .30-06 on all plains game and the .458 on Big Five. I used to carry a .450 Straight double [.450-3¼"]. The .450 was better than the .458, but I gave it up due to ammo problems. Now I use the .460, which was assembled by a friend on a Mauser action. I find it to be the best of all. The .30-06 is the best plains-game rifle. I have used a lot of different calibers during my hunting career, such as .275, 7x64, .470 DB, .500 DB, and .416 Rigby. I sold these last three due to expensive ammo."

A ten-year veteran hunter in Zimbabwe, Clive Lennox is another who recommends handloaded .458 ammo rather than factory loads. He went on to say: "We find the .375 to be the most versatile of all calibers. However, not all Americans like to shoot the .375 as it is considered to be slightly heavy for the average American game. We tell clients to bring the rifle they are comfortable with and, most of all, familiar with."

Stephen J. Smith's outfit, Hunt Africa, is a new South African concern, but Steve has been involved in African hunting for thirty-one years and has a wide variety of experience. He writes: "I shot my first buffalo in 1954 and have been hunting ever since. I used a .30-06 and a .470 double for years, then a 9.3 Mannlicher-Schoenauer and a .458. From experience with clients, I reckon that the .338 will handle everything from duiker to buffalo, and from there up the .458 is ideal. It's best to have the least number of guns in your truck. So a shotgun (12-gauge) plus .338 plus .458 is what I have always recommended. A factor often overlooked is the availability of ammo! Both .338 and .458 can be purchased from Nairobi to Cape Town. My favorite double is the .577, but where can you buy ammo—and the price!"

With 30 years' experience covering the full range of African species, J. H. Swanepoel uses light rifles (.270 and .30-06) for most of his own hunting but carries a .458 or a .460 Weatherby when backing up clients. He had this to say regarding recommendations to clients: "Any rifle my client prefers. After all, it's his hunt; nine times out of ten it's not the caliber that counts but bullet placement. The client usually dreams of that hunt with his rifle, not the professional hunter's rifle."

Ray Millican, now hunting primarily in Zambia, offered this: "People may query why I use preferably .375 H&H for leopard. Well, when shooting a lighter caliber, if you don't hit a vital spot you could lose your cat. He may take off, and

Tony Sanchez-Ariño has now hunted more than fifty years in Africa, and he remains active today, mainly as a PH on elephant hunts. He has seen the great herds of pachyderms of the post-WW II era greatly diminished in such places as Sudan, but, conversely, he now feels that there is a great elephant revival taking place south of the Zambezi River.

on average the light factor is diminishing rapidly. Quite possibly you'll have to continue the next day. Our friend the hyena comes across your leopard and all you end up with is pieces. I think the last time we had a chat, we were unanimous about the .338 and a .416 as an unbeatable combination."

South African Carl Labuschagne of Wagendrift Safaris has experience with all of the Big Five, and he was the only man who personally used a rifle as big as the .577 double, which he loads for and uses extensively. For a one-rifle client he recommended ".375 H&H Magnum with a quick-detachable scope (Kimber mounts)."

One of the all-time greats, Tony Dyer hunted professionally from 1947 to 1961, and since then has been keeping the lion properly thinned on his farm well up on the slopes of Mount Kenya. He shoots a pre-'64 Model 70 in .300 H&H rechambered to .300 Weatherby for all plains game and leopard, a .416 Rigby for lion, and a .375 H&H for all-round use. He wrote: "The .458 used to be good, but not anymore. I will be rebarreling my .458 to .375 H&H. The .416 with all the new ammunition is superb."

A veteran of more than fifty years of African hunting with a personal bag exceeding eight hundred elephant, Tony Sanchez-Ariño is one of the most experienced of the modern-day hunters. For thick-skinned game he personally uses a .416 Rigby, a .500 Jeffery (magazine rifle), and a double .465. However, like almost everyone else, he recommends the .375 for all-round use. Perhaps surprisingly, Tony's recommendation for clients is a two-rifle battery: "One in the .300 class plus the .375 H&H Magnum with a good scope."

George Hoffman, who developed the .416 Hoffman and still swears by it, advises his clients to bring only two rifles, a 7mm magnum and a .375 or .416. Three rifles are "too many; you never know which one to use. Better the third gun be a shotgun or .22."

Among his many clients, sixteen-year veteran Don Price is pure gold. A Zimbabwean, he's been hunting in Zambia for several seasons and is now in Tanzania. For his own use he's a .470 and .416 Rigby fan, but he suggests a .375 for his clients—or a .30-06 and a .375. He says he "still feels clients should stick to one rifle and get really good with it—ideally the .375 H&H with solid ammunition."

My old friend Finn Aagaard, former Kenya professional hunter, had this to say:

1. No cartridge has the power to flatten an animal in his tracks regardless of where hit. Penetration and shot placement are the two absolutely essential factors. If you achieve them, then caliber, etc., aren't terribly important, within reason.
2. In order to achieve shot placement, I preferred clients to use scope-sighted .375 H&H for dangerous game, while I backed them up with .458.
3. I believe the fad for bad-mouthing the .458 is mostly hot air and blaming cartridge/gun for own failures. Apart from some lots of bad ammo, I have never been able to detect any difference in the field, on game, between the .458 and .500/.450, .465, .470, or even the .500 N.E.

Doug Kok, a thirteen-year veteran, stated: "I prefer a client to bring a lighter rifle if he is scared of recoil. I would rather have a lighter rifle and a confident client than a heavy rifle and a flincher!"

Campbell Smith, with a decade of experience in southern Africa, uses a .450 Watts personally for heavy game. He excludes the .458, stating that he wants "something firing a 500-grain bullet with velocity more than 2,150 FPS and not more than 2,300 FPS." He mentions the .458 Lott, .450 Watts and Ackley, .460 G&A, and .470. He was also one of the few to specifically recommend bullets, suggesting Nosler, Swift, and Bear Claw for softpoints and Hornadys and Monolithics for solids.

Rudy Lubin, with seventeen years of hunting in the C.A.R., Sudan, Gabon, and Cameroon, hunts tough country almost exclusively on foot. He recommends: "No sophisticated rifle for African hunting. Better use well-known and widely used

Brian Marsh (left, with publisher Ludo Wurfbain) was one of the earliest professional hunters to set up shop in Zimbabwe. He remained active in that country for years, but later hunted professionally in other countries, such as Botswana.

ammunition. In case you lose them, the PH can help you. There are very few gun shops in these countries."

Rudy also recommended solids only for the very small antelopes, plus elephant, rhino, and hippo. He feels that all the rest, including buffalo, are better shot with softs.

Hunting several areas in southern Africa, Francois Loubser offers a wide assortment of game in a wide variety of terrain. He had a number of excellent comments, and I hope he'll forgive me for toning them down a bit for public consumption:

> The reason I appear so adamant about the use of the 7mm magnum is the fact that everybody—man, woman, or child—can handle this caliber. It really doesn't matter whether you call it a Remington, a Weatherby, or a 7x61.
>
> The two major reasons for lost trophies are most definitely: (1) Too much gun—a gut shot with a .300 Winchester Magnum does not kill like a lung shot with a 7mm; (2) bad bullets—thank St. Hubertus for people like Jack Carter of Bear Claw fame and Lee Reid, who gave us Swift bullets. When you're shooting at a trophy that costs $$$$, why worry about a $2 bullet?

I would like to add that I do not always understand the choice of scopes. If you have an $800 rifle with the latest junk scope, held together by junk mounts, you have in effect got a $40 rifle—but the cost of the safari is the same.

The 9.3x64 is hell on wheels. If someone will make us some tough bullets, it will be my preference over the .375 H&H.

Another widely experienced professional hunter who did some magnum-bashing was John Brelsford, currently hunting South Africa and Zambia, formerly Gabon and Tanzania. He commented: "A client who can use any of the [fast] magnums consistently well is a rarity. I have personally never had one. Their shooting might start off well, but by the end of the safari it has generally deteriorated to a terrible extent, with the client developing a flinch. I think certain types of clients who are attracted to the super magnums are possibly inherent bad shots, hoping that the extra power will make up for accuracy, or rather lack of it."

To a large degree Harry Selby is responsible for keeping the .416 Rigby alive. He didn't choose it for all-round use, citing the .375 instead, but he added: "Of all the big-bore cartridges available, I think that the .416 Rigby is totally outstanding. Great penetration and knockdown; with modern powders its performance is unique." While his peer, Tony Henley, is a double-rifle man, Harry prefers bolt guns because "doubles don't shoot straight enough."

Another living legend, with twenty-seven years in the field, Robin Hurt's personal heavy rifle is a double .500. For his clients he recommends a .375 for one rifle, adding a 7mm Remington Magnum for the second and a ".450-plus" as a heavy rifle. He suggested that the heavy not be a .458: "Lacks penetration." Robin also commented that most clients can't shoot well with calibers larger than .375.

Ian Wilmot of East Cape Trophy Safaris generally recommends the .270 Winchester and .300 Winchester Magnum, stating: "I have grown up in the Eastern Cape, which as you probably know has a wide variety of terrain with genuine long shots often taking place, hence the flatter-shooting calibers over the 7x57, .30-06, etc. In the bush, though, I really advise these slower calibers. The lightest bullet in .300 must be 180 grains in my opinion. In the .270, 130- or 150-grain."

Tony Tomkinson has nine years' experience as a professional, mainly in Zululand, and before that was a game ranger for sixteen years. In the latter occupation he was involved in some large-scale culling operations, and he had some extremely interesting observations:

In my experiences both as a professional hunter and a game ranger, where in the latter case I took more than 20,000 head of game during cropping operations,

Tony Tomkinson (right) has hunted for decades in Africa, and among his many clients was H.I.H. Prince Abdorreza, the brother of the last shah of Iran.

I have found that within reason it is very often not the caliber or rifle type which is of importance but rather bullet weight and design.

It is those badly angled shots where the whole bit of bullet performance comes into play, and accordingly when advising my clients I stress that preference should be given to bullet design that will hold up when hitting bones, etc. Here the Nosler Partition bullets and custom-made H-Mantel bullets certainly have a bit of an advantage over the conventional types.

During 1982 to 1984 I was involved with the annual removal of 150 hippo from the Lake St. Lucia Game Reserve where I was warden in charge. During this period I was able to evaluate bullet and rifle performance on thick-skinned game pretty thoroughly as most of these animals were shot on land at night in circumstances that forced us to use body shots.

First, the rifles we used were .30-06, .375, .338, 9.3x64, .400/.350 Rigby, .450 No. 2 Nitro Express, and .470 Nitro Express. Second, none of the rifles used resulted in immediate kills unless the spine or central nervous system was destroyed. In all cases, lung- and heart-shot animals covered between 75 and 200 yards before becoming immobilized.

By virtue again of bad angles, we finally settled on calibers that would give us the best penetration. Accordingly we ended up using the .30-06 with 220-grain full-metal-jacket bullets for daytime shooting, i.e., head shots, and .375 full-metal-jacket bullets for night work. Our second choice on night work was the .458 Winchester Magnum.

I'm sure you will probably raise an eyebrow on our nonselection of the British calibers; however, we only had Kynoch full-metal-jacket ammunition available, and on a number of occasions these solids became misshapen or broke up completely on striking heavy bone.

Based on the above experiences, I personally now use a .458 Lott with solids for dangerous game and a .300 H&H Magnum with 220-grain full-metal-jacket bullets for backup on plains-game hunts.

Mark Tout, an energetic young professional with nine years of experience in South Africa, Botswana, and Zambia, had this to say about bullet performance: "In my experience as a PH I reckon there is not such a big problem of clients using inappropriate rifles but rather having unsuitable ammunition and even more a lack of capability in using the rifle they bring—especially in offhand shooting conditions."

Another old friend, Peter Johnstone, longtime proprietor of Rosslyn Safaris in the Matetsi region of Zimbabwe, sent me a very long letter with his questionnaire. I'll never forget the beautifully battered pre-'64 Model 70 he carried when he backed me up on my first elephant, and apparently that rifle is just Peter's style. According to him, "Using one rifle has a great advantage in that the hunter becomes very familiar with it, shooting the ordinary animals, and therefore when he comes under emergency conditions he can handle and shoot his rifle without any problems."

Discussing personal favorites, he says:

In the late 1950s I had a team of hunters shooting zebra, wildebeest, giraffe, kudu, and eland using the 9.3x62 with 286-grain solids. This provided penetration at all angles and plenty knockdown power. We also shot some elephant, mainly cows and young bulls.

My next favorite rifle is the 7x57mm. The one I had was deadly accurate; I could brain-shoot antelope out to 100 yards, and buffalo bulls at a few yards were great fun. I preferred the long roundnose, solid bullet. When I see a client with a 7mm magnum, I shudder; it's all noise and blast and deflected bullets!

The .30-06 is an exceedingly good rifle which has done me very well over the years. With my .30-06 I've shot many lion, leopard, antelope, also some buffalo bulls, giraffe, a moose, a grizzly, Dall sheep, caribou, ibex, red deer . . .

The .375 is the greatest rifle, and that's really the only one necessary for a client to bring for big-game savanna hunting. To be responsible for the care, safety, and shooting of one rifle is really enough for a client/hunter in Africa.

John Reeve Moller, currently hunting in Tanzania but with experience in Sudan, Zaire, and Ethiopia, in part had this to say:

Harry Selby is considered the dean of the professional hunters today. After losing his double rifle in an accident early on in his career, he got a bolt .416 Rigby and never looked back. This picture was taken in 2007.

This may sound odd to you, but I have never had much time for the .375. I do not advise clients to bring one on safari as I have never been very happy with the results of the factory ammo. My medium-caliber rifle is a .338 Winchester Magnum. I have had it for years, and the results have been very good indeed. I have used it on elephant and buffalo on control work and have never had any problems. I always take it to a lion blind in case of a runner at a distance. However, I also have the .460 with me for anything that needs a bleeding nose at close quarters. For wounded leopard I use a 10-gauge AYA with OO or No. 4 buck. On wounded lion, and of course on other dangerous game, I always use the .460 Weatherby.

Always outspoken—and most astute—veteran hunter Gordon Cormack sent volumes of information, all of it helpful. Among his comments were several that should be passed along:

The trouble with this sort of questionnaire is that circumstances can differ—e.g., a long shot at a lion (150 meters) would be better taken with a .375, 300-grain soft, utilizing a scope sight, than with a .450-3¼" Nitro Express using open sights. By the same token, I would rather use a double .450 with open sights and a 480-grain softnose at close quarters in thick bush.

As one rifle I would take a bolt-action .416 Remington. A client who does not do much shooting would be better off with one weapon being a .375 H&H. Bullet weights are important, and the heavier the better, especially with grass and bush in the way.

Finally, I was most honored to receive a nine-page letter from Ian Henderson, a twenty-eight-year veteran who, together with Brian Marsh as Henderson and Marsh Safaris, was one of the pioneering outfitters in what is now Zimbabwe. I wish I could reproduce his comments in toto; not only is he more experienced than I, he's also a fine writer. Here are some of his comments:

In general I would recommend the heaviest weight of bullet for the caliber in question, viz. 220 grains for .300 H&H and 300 grains for .375 H&H. This gives the best sectional density, which is of vital importance for penetration. That is why the solid in both cases is available only in the heaviest bullet weight.

Also in general, one must use the heaviest bullet and caliber with which one can shoot with accuracy. Put another way, a small caliber in the right place is far better than a large caliber in the wrong place. . . . Flinch is an insidious fault and far more prevalent than realized, a subject deserving of far more attention than it receives at the moment.

Ian chose the .375 H&H for large plains game, stating: "Probably the most popular weapon in this category. I have, however, found it somehow lacking in knockdown effect. I would actually prefer to use a .416 or .404, which I cannot fault, but because of the availability of ammunition becoming more difficult (and expensive), the .375 remains the obvious choice."

For lion he chose the .470: "Once again, I would prefer to use a .404 or .416, but as lion are often hunted in thick bush and may be wounded, the .470 double is the obvious choice, especially as I already have the rifle and it fits me. Any other heavy double is as suitable."

Ian goes on to discuss, at length and with great clarity, the perennial problem of velocity versus bullet performance. Like most African professionals of vast experience, he isn't overawed by velocity but demands penetration above all else. He'll willingly accept velocity, mind you—but only if he can also get penetration. Finally, he concluded with his "dream battery":

> Over the years one builds up a particular respect for certain calibers. Though not spectacular in any sense, they perform consistently and just do what they are supposed to do. No doubt I am also influenced by the store I place in sectional density. Thus if I had to change and put together a battery that I find appealing to me, I would choose:
> 1. 6.5mm firing a 160-grain bullet (soft- and hardnose).
> 2. .333 Jeffery.
> 3. .505 Gibbs.
> What a combination! No finer could I imagine.

After all these years, with all of our brave new cartridges, perhaps we haven't progressed much beyond the infancy of smokeless powder. Or, to put it another way, in the last eighty-odd years we haven't come up with a better solution than to use a long, heavy bullet at moderate velocity. Or have we? There may never be a consensus on calibers, but the professionals agree on this: Whatever rifles and cartridges work best for you, give you confidence, and perform consistently because you shoot them well—those are the ones to use on Africa's game. And now we shall see how opinions have changed in the last twenty years!

The Professional's Choice, 2007

Chapter 40

G iven the wonders of Internet communications, I expected it to be much simpler to gather in a meaningful survey than it had been nearly twenty years earlier. It might have been faster, but it was not easier! I think this is partly because African hunting is genuinely more popular than it ever has been before. Business was brisk in 2007, and I needed to gather the results and meet a deadline before the season was fully concluded in many countries. Too, life today seems to move faster than it did twenty years ago. Lord knows I'm a lot busier, as are the many professional hunters now operating in multiple countries. I am grateful to the hundred-odd professionals who found time to respond—and especially grateful to their organizations—the African Professional Hunters' Association and the country PH associations of Namibia, South Africa, Tanzania, Zambia, and Zimbabwe—for helping me get the word out. Also, for the excellent response from Tanzanian PHs I owe a special note of thanks to Corne' Oelofse, Tanzania Game Trackers' manager in Arusha. She was tireless in her efforts to get surveys from every PH she could find!

The results were, in a word, fascinating. As you will see, there were significant differences between the 2007 survey and the one that preceded it in 1988–1989. Back then the .416 was just starting to make a comeback, and I was shocked at the support shown for the .416 in this survey. I was also surprised at how much stronger the support was for the fast .30s. Although I did ask the question, I was also surprised at how many professional hunters mentioned specific bullets. I must wonder if support for faster cartridges is based at least somewhat on the better bullets we have available today?

On the other hand, I was equally surprised at increased support for several old-timers, including the 7x57 and the 9.3x62. Now that ammunition is much more readily available, I was not surprised to see a stronger showing for double rifles and double rifle cartridges . . . but I was surprised by the strong showing

Guav Johnson, like many young professional hunters, hunts multiple countries. He's a Zimbabwean and spends several months there, but he also hunts both the savanna and rain forest of Cameroon, and has spent some time in Mozambique. No professional hunter I know puts as many hunting days per year as Guav Johnson.

of other old-timers, including the .404 Jeffery, .500 Jeffery, and .505 Gibbs. Of course, my old friend Jack Lott would be pleased at the strong show of support for his namesake, the .458 Lott.

In general the format of the 2007 survey was similar, although I let this one run to two pages. I asked for each PH's name and company name, number of years as a professional, and the country(ies) in which he operates. Then I asked the same question about the type of terrain he operates in: desert, thornbush, forest, swamp, mountains, and "combination." Adhering to the APHA's guidelines, I asked if he hunts any of the Big Six of elephant, lion, leopard, buffalo, rhino, and hippo.

Now we get to the meat. I asked for personal choices in the following categories: light plains game, medium plains game, large plains game, leopard, lion, thick-skinned game, and all-round use. I asked whether he prefers iron sight, peep sight, or scope, and (new to this survey) I asked for "any comments on personal preferences in bullets."

The next section, part 2, was "Recommendations to Clients." Again I asked for suggestions for one-, two-, and three-rifle batteries, and whether clients should

I've known Michel Mantheakis of Miombo Safaris since he was a very young hunter. A seasoned veteran and successful outfitter today, Mantheakis remains a bolt-action man to the core.

bring a shotgun. Also new to this survey, I asked about choice of scopes and choice of bullets, whether he preferred solids or softs for buffalo, and the number of cartridges to bring on safari. I also added a space for "Any comments on pre-safari practice/training" and of course invited additional comment as well. As before, these comments in both categories are some of the most valuable tidbits you will find in this book!

The professional hunters who responded represented a marvelous cross-section. The junior man, South African Willem O'Kelly, had just one year as a pro in the field (although more than a quarter-century of hunting), while the senior respondent, the redoubtable Fred Duckworth, has been hunting for fifty-five years. He was followed by Robin Hurt with forty-four years' experience, and several others were in the high thirties and low forties The average was 19.5 years, a tremendous amount of experience.

Virtually every African country that has been open to hunting, either present or recent past, was represented. The largest number of PHs to respond hunted in South Africa, which follows because South Africa has the largest hunting industry and the largest number of licensed PHs. Zimbabwe and Tanzania followed in a tie. It is notable that these days a great many respondents hunt in several different countries. As for habitat types, this question, unfortunately, proved silly. Thornbush and plains were most common, but all other habitat types were well represented, and almost every respondent hunted a "combination" of habitats.

Personal Choices

The specific question was "What rifle do you use (or prefer) for your personal use" for the various types of game. The way this was taken probably changed with the various categories. For instance, most professional hunters have occasion to shoot various antelope for the pot, and it isn't often that backup is required on "light plains game." On the other hand, with quotas as they are today, relatively few PHs have the opportunity to hunt lion for themselves, so backup is what concerns them the most. Anyway, here are the rifles and cartridges today's professionals carry for "personal use" (whatever that might be).

Light Plains Game

Eighteen cartridges were mentioned, with no clear winners. The .243 was not as strong as it was in 1989, losing out by a slight margin to the .270 and .30-06, which (in that order) were the two most-named cartridges in this survey. The 7x57 was strong. Of historical interest, in 1989 Mike Rowbotham was the only PH to refer to the 7x57 as the ".275 Rigby." In 2007 Robin Hurt picked up this torch, and while the 7x57 has come back (tied with the .300 H&H at twelve mentions), this time Robin was the only PH to use its old English designation of .275 Rigby. Support for the 7x57 increased, but relatively few professionals seem to have clung to the .300 H&H. The .300 Winchester Magnum tied the 7x57 in this category and remained prominent throughout the survey. In this category the 7mm magnums were weak, and remained weaker throughout this survey than they were in 1989.

The versatile .375 received seven votes, and it's worth mentioning here that a .375-caliber cartridge was invariably described as ".375 H&H" or just ".375." Only twice in the entire survey were other .375 cartridges specifically mentioned, two PHs naming the new .375 Ruger. There was some support for the .308 Winchester, and several PHs preferred .22 centerfires for "light plains game"—the .222 Remington, .223 Remington, and .22-250 were all specifically mentioned. And then there were single votes for a "6.5mm" (exact cartridge not specified), the .25-06, the .257 Weatherby Magnum, the 8x68S, and the 7x64, and two votes for the 6x45.

The strength of the .30-06 didn't surprise me, but the number of votes for the .270 did. In this survey these were the clear winners, receiving respectively twenty-one and eighteen mentions. I was also surprised at the lack of support for the 7mm magnums—but throughout the survey the fast 7mms were not nearly as prominent as they were in 1989.

Medium Plains Game

Again, my categories were undefined and purposely vague. We could probably agree that springbok and gazelles are "light plains game," but I left it to the individual to decide where "light plains game" stopped and "medium plains game" started. The PHs were clearly thinking bigger, because we lost all the .22 centerfires and the .243, and we almost lost the .270 Winchester.

Only thirteen cartridges were mentioned in this category. The .375 was the clear winner right up until the last groups of responses came in—and then the .30-06 surged ahead with twenty-four mentions. The .375 and the .300 Winchester Magnum tied for second, with twenty-two mentions each. However, if you add seven votes for the .300 H&H and five votes for the .300 Weatherby Magnum to support for the .300 Winchester Magnum, you have tremendous support for a fast .30 for "medium plains game." And if you add in the .30-06 and six mentions of the .308 Winchester, you have overwhelming support for .30-calibers in general.

The 7x57 remained fairly strong, leading the "7mm magnums" (exact cartridge never specified) eight votes to seven. Though never as strong as I think it should be, the .338 was stronger in this survey and especially in this category, also with seven mentions. Everything else was very much the personal choice of just a handful of PHs: six for the .270, a couple for the 8x57, two for the 9.3x62, and one for the 8x68s.

Large Plains Game

This category is somewhat easier to define. It may not be clear where "medium" stops and "large" starts, but this category must include animals such as kudu, roan, and zebra all the way up to eland. Only thirteen cartridges were mentioned, and most of the PHs were thinking heavy. Nearly half chose the .375, but a considerable number (eighteen) recommended a .300 magnum (in most cases the exact cartridge was unspecified). Interestingly, support for the .30-06 here dropped to just three mentions, but there were still eight votes for

Richard Harland, a fine author in his own right, is a legend in Zimbabwe as both a game ranger and professional hunter. Like many with culling experience he is a bolt-action man, shown with his beloved original George Gibbs .505.

the 7x57 and five for 7mm magnums. A few stepped up even farther, with nine votes for the .416, while one PH carried his .460 Weatherby for "large plains game." I expected a stronger showing for the .338, but just six PHs chose it—plus Robin Hurt and South African PH John Oosthuizen named the .340 Weatherby Magnum. The grand old 9.3x62 was in there with four votes (but, oddly, none for the much more powerful 9.3x64). One PH stuck with his .270 and another with his .308 Winchester, and that was it—except for South African PH Mark Dewet, who specified heavy bullets for .30-calibers and also (in my view wisely!) named the .35 Whelen for large plains game.

My guess is that most PHs were thinking "eland" and recommended a .375—but this wasn't universal at all. The guys from Ethiopia were thinking "mountain nyala" and envisioning longer shots in the mountains. They wanted a fast .30-caliber.

Leopard

Here we had a wide range of opinion, all the way from the .243 Winchester to the mighty .500 Jeffery. Fully eighteen cartridges were represented, including several votes for the 3½" 10-gauge! Most common was the indefatigable .375

Andrew Dawson of Zimbabwe's Chifuti Safaris carries his William Evans double every day of his working life. This rifle was owned by Carl Akeley and John Dugmore, and was even used briefly by Peter Capstick.

with thirty-six mentions—although several PHs specified that this was the minimum legal requirement where they hunt. Clearly represented, at least to me, was a split vote: Some PHs were literally answering the question, which was what they would personally choose for leopard. Others, just as clearly, were stating what they carry for backup.

For instance, Joe Coogan wrote that the only leopard he took for himself was cleanly dropped with a .243. This preference follows naturally from his old friend and mentor Harry Selby. In his East African days Selby often loaned his accurate, easy-to-shoot .243 to clients for use on leopard, writing me once: "Of the 103 leopard taken by my clients in East Africa, the majority were shot with my .243." Namibian PH Corne' Kruger, with whom I did a hound hunt for leopard in 2006, has often used his little .243 for backup—but he actually prefers a 7mm Remington Magnum.

Although it is clearly an assumption, I suppose that those who use the big guns are speaking about backup. Again, several specifically stated "3½-inch 10-gauge." Jaco Oostuizen, hunting in South Africa and Botswana, recommended a 12-gauge for backup. But, as mentioned earlier, this is also a split vote. Robin Hurt, who was badly mauled after failing to stop a charging leopard with a 12-gauge, specifically recommended against using a shotgun for wounded leopard.

I was surprised at the amount of support for the .375. As I said in chapter 28, if this is the legal minimum, go with it, but given a choice I much prefer a rifle chambered to a lighter cartridge firing bullets designed for leopard-size game, preferably with a bright scope. Many PHs seemed to agree, but in fairness a large number of the real experts don't agree with me. However, if you take all the light cartridges mentioned—.243, .270, .300 H&H, .308, 7mm, .30-06, and .300 Winchester—and add them up, you do have an aggregate of thirty-nine mentions, which exceeds support for the .375. There were also a few votes for the .338 and one for the 9.3x62. Completing the picture were a wide scattering of big bores, which I firmly believe were named with follow-up in mind, not for the first shot on an unwounded leopard.

Lion

This one was easy. Only sixteen cartridges were mentioned, with the majority of opinion going to the .375. Again, many respondents did not name a specific .375 cartridge, but those who did named the .375 H&H, with no other .375 cartridges identified. The .416s followed, but distantly: Thirty-eight mentions of the .375 to twenty-one for the .416. Again, only rarely was a .416-caliber cartridge specifically named. If it was named, the .416 Rigby was the overwhelming choice. A few respondents suggested lighter cartridges: Specific mentions came in for the .300s (six), .7mm (four), .30-06 (three), .308 (one), and 9.3x62 (one). These fifteen votes for cartridges below .375 surprised me, but I am guessing these are PHs' personal choices for lion, not what they would recommend for you and me, and probably not what they might carry to back up a client.

Quite a few more named big bores, eight cartridges from .458 Winchester Magnum all the way up to .505 Gibbs, for a total of twenty-eight. As with leopard, although possibly to a lesser degree, this result almost certainly represents a split between PHs who are thinking about actually shooting a lion and PHs whose intent is to back up a client or conduct a follow-up.

There is no question about the ability of a well-placed 7mm or .30-caliber bullet to kill a lion—but stopping a charging lion is something else again. With this in mind, there was one vote for a buckshot-loaded 10-gauge for lion, this made by Fred Duckworth, whose experience throughout Africa cannot be questioned. The shotgun is not as traditional for lion as it is for leopard, but his is not a unique choice. The late Wally Johnson Sr., for instance, once stated that with a buckshot-loaded 12-gauge you were as safe from a lion as "a baby in its crib." A 3½" 10-gauge with modern loads, like OOO buckshot, would

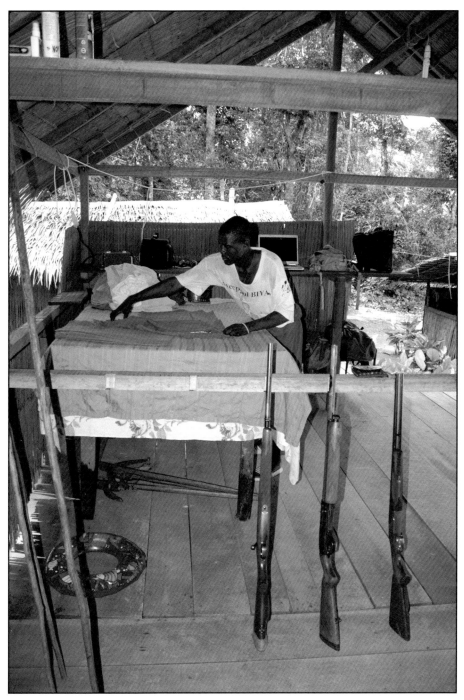

While relatively few PHs suggested their clients should bring shotguns, the majority stated that they always kept a shotgun in camp.

obviously be much better than any 12-gauge load. I lack the experience to offer substantive comment, but I can say that you'd better be very cool and wait until the last possible moment!

Thick-Skinned Game

The big-bore rifle is the tool that professional hunters carry every single day of their working lives, at least in dangerous-game areas. In the last couple of years there were a couple of bad accidents (meaning human deaths) with elephant, and in three cases I know of, the PH's heavy rifle was either left in the truck or wasn't readily at hand. So the PH's backup rifle is a serious tool, and in this category I believe the responses mostly reflect the rifle the PH carries not only when hunting elephant, rhino, buffalo, or hippo but also the one he'll carry—fully loaded—whenever any of these animals are in the area.

There are many viable big-bore cartridges, and a great many of them were represented in our survey results. Here, for the first time, the .375 started to fall by the wayside. Also for the first time in either survey, a double-rifle cartridge came up the winner: the .470 Nitro Express, with fully twenty mentions. The .416s outweighed the .375 by fifteen to ten. Come to think of it, the .458 Lott beat out the .375 as well with thirteen votes. And although the .458 Winchester Magnum is clearly not as popular as it once was, it tied the .375. Again, relatively few respondents specifically named a .416 cartridge, and most that did named the .416 Rigby. One professional hunter, Andre Roux of Central Africa fame, named his .416 Taylor. I, too, have used it; it's an excellent wildcat based on the .458 Winchester Magnum necked down, but is not often seen today. The .416 Remington Magnum was specifically mentioned a few times, but since most PHs simply said ".416," I took the liberty of lumping all .416s together.

There were no votes for cartridges lighter than .375, and other than those mentioned, nine other big bores were specifically named. I think this reflects the greater availability of both ammo and rifles today, in both doubles and bolt actions. The .500-3" Nitro Express was strong with seven mentions—but the .500 Jeffery was stronger with eight. The .460 Weatherby Magnum received five mentions, and there were five votes for the .450-3¼" and four for the .505 Gibbs. The .450 Dakota was named by two PHs, and there was one mention apiece for the .425 Westley Richards, the wildcat .450 Ackley, the .450 Rigby Rimless Magnum, the .475 No. 2 Jeffery, and the .450 No. 2 Nitro Express.

The fifteen cartridges named thus represent an interesting and eclectic mix of old, new, standard, wildcat, and proprietary cartridges. Obviously all of those

Johan Calitz, South African by birth and longtime Botswana PH and outfitter, has probably guided more hunters to big Botswana elephants than anyone else. He is a double-rifle man, using an eclectic mix of .470s and .500s from both American and British makers.

named are suitable. Interestingly, in this survey there was no mention of cartridges larger than .50-caliber, although I know a few are still out there. Zimbabwean PH Cliff Walker, who actually hunts all over the place, carries a double .577, but unfortunately my survey may not have reached him. Since ammo is much more available, I was surprised that more rimmed Nitro Expresses weren't mentioned. It has clearly become a .470 and .500 world, with just a scattering of other cartridges still in use. Of course, this survey isn't definitive. We had five .450-3¼" rifles mentioned, one .450 No. 2, and at the last moment John Abraham added his .475 No. 2 Jeffery—but there are definitely other doubles still in use. For instance, I know that well-known PH Jeff Rann carries a .500/.465, as does my old friend Roger Whittall, and so forth.

The .470, no surprise, is easily the most popular double-rifle cartridge today. The rifles encountered are a mixture of old and new. Andrew Dawson of Chifuti Safaris in Zimbabwe has a beautifully refurbished William Evans .470. The rifle is a plain boxlock, a classic working gun with an unusual legacy. It was originally owned by American Carl Akeley, who collected for the American Museum of Natural History early in the twentieth century. Later it was owned by well-known professional hunter John Dugmore. Dugmore, now retired in Maun, Botswana, was one of the Kenya hunters who went south in the 1960s. Dawson bought the rifle from Dugmore and had William Evans clean it up. Mike Payne, also hunting for Chifuti Safaris, carries a .470 as well, his a new Krieghoff.

Dawson's partner, Paul Smith, also carries a Krieghoff, but his is in .500-3". Although lagging far behind the .470 in popularity, the .500-3" was well represented. Its users include Robin Hurt, Harpreet Brar, and Antonio Riguera. My favorite, the .450-3¼", is still out there in greater numbers than I would have thought. PHs using it included Ivan Carter and Wayne Williamson, and it was the favorite of my old friend Gordon Cormack (who, regrettably recently passed away)—but all the other big rimmed cartridges seem to have fallen by the wayside.

This is not the case with the older British rimless cartridges designed for repeating rifles. While most PHs simply wrote ".416" without stating the exact cartridge, the .416 Rigby was almost the only .416 cartridge specifically identified. It is definitely the most popular .416 and easily the most popular "large medium." This I expected. Very few respondents specifically cited the .416 Remington Magnum, which got just a couple of mentions. Given the limited availability of both rifles and ammo, I did not expect to see as many PHs using the .500 Jeffery (eight) and .505 Gibbs (four). Clearly these big cartridges have made a significant comeback. Richard Harland, Barrie Duckworth, and Kevin Robertson all use .505 Gibbs rifles, while Rudy Lubin, Simon Evans, and Andre Roux (among others) all use the slightly more powerful .500 Jeffery. Zambian PH Strang Middleton made the only mention of the .425 Westley Richards. This cartridge has become a rare bird, so I was a bit surprised to see it mentioned at all. But the biggest surprise was no mention of the .404 Jeffery, especially considering the numbers of rifles I know are out there, with plenty of ammo available. Andy Wilkinson carried a lovely .404 when I hunted with him in Masailand in 2007, but, interestingly, it wasn't in his survey as his primary personal preference.

All-Round Use

This was another of my purposely vague categories, my intent being that each respondent make of it whatever he wished. Perhaps I should have spelled it out more carefully, because several PHs either didn't respond or questioned the question, writing in comments like, "I'm not sure what this means." Most apparently took it exactly the way I do: Maximum versatility for the widest

Today most professional hunters recommend a good expanding bullet for the first shot on buffalo, followed up by solids. Many stipulated that softpoints must be used when hunting in herds, for the obvious reason of avoiding overpenetration.

variety of game. With this in mind, a majority abandoned their favored big bore! More than half of those who answered this question (47 of 89) chose the .375. The second most popular choice was the .416 with fifteen mentions. The only other mediums mentioned at all were the 9.3x62 (five) and the .338 (four). So among African professional hunters the .375 remains the versatility champion. In general I assume bolt actions here, but one PH, Jurgen C. Schlettwein, specifically cited a double, stating, "There is only one all-purpose rifle: a double in .375 H&H."

Most of the remaining responses named a big bore, with nine cartridges between .458 Winchester Magnum and .505 Gibbs mentioned. This is probably the professional hunter's "carry rifle," the rifle he carries for backup and other emergencies virtually every working day. In that context "all-round" has a different meaning! Peter Butland (eight years as a PH but fifty years of African hunting), for instance, wrote, "I use a .416 Rigby for all backup."

Three professionals cited .30-calibers: Julian Mavrey (.30-06) and Andrew Pringle and Chris Bruster (.300 magnum). This is not an anomaly. All three are South African professionals who hunt primarily plains game, so their definition of "all-round" doesn't extend to the dangerous game. In that context a versatile .30-caliber makes sense to me!

Sights

For professional hunters it's still an iron-sight world! The vast majority of respondents (seventy-four) cited irons as their preference. However, a significant number (forty) also checked the "scope" column, almost always with a caveat such as, "for plains game." Only ten professional hunters marked "scope" without also marking "iron sights." Most of these gentlemen are primarily plains-game hunters, so their choice of a scoped rifle makes sense.

For those who hunt dangerous game, iron sights are also a sensible choice. The obvious reason is that their primary use on a rifle is to stop a charge. Not quite so obvious is that a PH might carry his rifle every day of a six-month season and use it only a half-dozen times. As simple and sturdy as they should be, iron sights are more goof-proof than scopes—and also make a rifle lighter and easier to carry. Just remember: This is the professional hunter's personal preference. Many emphatically recommended scoped rifles for their clients!

I did offer an additional option in this survey. As mentioned earlier, my old friend Michel Mantheakis now carries a .450 Dakota with an aperture sight well protected by wings (sort of like a 1917 U.S. Enfield). I was curious to see how many PHs use the aperture or "peep" sights. I was surprised at this result: Fully fifteen PHs circled or checked "peep sights" for their personal use!

Bullets

I undoubtedly complicated a simple question by asking about specific bullet recommendations in two places, first in the PH's personal choice and again in "recommendations to clients." The results differed only slightly; for personal use several PHs prefer European or South African bullets that they know are not readily available to the majority of their clients. So specific preferences included some fairly exotic bullets, several of which I know only vaguely. These included GS Custom, GPA, Rhino, Dzombo, and Stewart. South African PH Siegfried Osmers was kind enough to send me a photo of the Dzombo monolithic solid, made in South Africa.

In the mainstream, there was clear awareness of the great bullets we have available today. The single most cited bullet was Barnes (X-Bullet and Triple Shock), with twenty-eight specific mentions. This was followed closely by Swift A-Frame (twenty-four mentions). Then came the Trophy Bonded Bear Claw (eleven), followed by

The 2007 survey asked for comments on practice and training. A huge number of PHs specifically advised getting shooting sticks and learning to use them. Sticks are an important part of my range gear, and we practice with them every time we go shooting.

Woodleigh with eleven mentions. Other than the bullets mentioned above, the only other specific recommendations for expanding bullets were for Nosler Partitions (five), Nosler AccuBond (two), and Speer Grand Slam (one).

Specific solids were mentioned much less frequently, but those cited were: Monolithic Solids (five), Sledgehammer Solids (five), and Hornady solids (five). Four professionals simply named brands, with two stating Federal and the two others stating Norma. Harry Claassens, a well-respected twenty-two-year South African PH, made this interesting comment regarding bullets: "In the past, many perfectly sound calibers were branded as 'poor' only because inferior bullets used at the time resulted in bullet failure." I agree with this completely. Today we have no "bad" calibers—and there are so many great bullets that there is really no excuse for a poor choice.

Recommendations to Clients

What rifles do you prefer your clients to bring on safari?

As in my previous survey, I asked for recommendations for safari batteries of one, two, or three rifles, then asked "Should your clients bring a shotgun?" Very few professional hunters made recommendations in all categories. Some were very specific, others more vague. Some followed their own personal preferences, but many did not. Here goes:

One Rifle

Almost shockingly, only eight cartridges were mentioned! The overwhelming winner for a one-rifle safari battery was the .375, with fifty-seven mentions. Once again, the majority specifically stated ".375 H&H." Quite a few just said ".375," while two PHs mentioned the new .375 Ruger (as in ".375 H&H or Ruger"). This is not surprising, because I think we've all known for a long time that the .375 remains the most versatile African caliber.

However, things now get interesting! A dozen PHs, including knowledgeable hands like Derek Hurt, Wayne Williamson, Ivan Carter, and Richard Harland, wrote in ".375 or .416." And nine PHs, including such equally knowledgeable hands as Derek Hurt's father, Robin, and Johan Calitz, Joe Wright, and Stephane Ndongue, wrote in ".416" as their choice for a one-rifle safari battery! Those who recommended the .416 (singly or with the .375) were primarily dangerous-game hunters (or, like Ndongue, forest hunters). Taken any way you want to take it, this support for the .416 was amazing, especially since, in the same category, the previous survey turned up just one mention each for the .416 Rigby and .416 Hoffman.

Nothing else was even close. There were five recommendations for the .300 Winchester Magnum, four for the .338 Winchester Magnum, three for "any .30-caliber," two for the 9.3x62, and just one each for the 7mm and .308 Winchester. Note, please, that most of the guys who recommended cartridges less powerful than the .375 are primarily plains-game hunters.

Two Rifles

The greater flexibility of a two-rifle battery really opened up the floodgates. There were twenty-three specific recommendations for two-rifle batteries. Interestingly, the single most common was a ".300 plus .416" with twenty-seven specific mentions. Clearly the thinking here was that with the addition of a lighter rifle, the second rifle could be a little heavier and a little less versatile than a .375. That said, the .375 was hardly abandoned. The second most common was ".300 plus .375" with twenty mentions, followed by ".30-06 plus .375" with sixteen.

No other specific recommendations were even close. However, other combinations that included a .375 as the heavier of a pair included .308, 7mm, .270, .243, ".22 or shotgun," and .338 as the lighter gun. A couple of recommendations had the .375 as the lighter rifle of a two-rifle battery, including ".375 plus .416 or larger" and ".375 plus double." Collectively, the support for the .375 as part of a two-rifle battery was overwhelming, mentioned in fifty-two out of ninety-three responses to this question. Support for the .416 was not weak, with nearly a third (thirty out of ninety-three) of the respondents combining a .416 with something else.

The real winner as part of a two-rifle battery, however, was the .30-caliber. A .300 (generally unspecified), a .30-06, or a .308 (paired with a heavier caliber) were mentioned in sixty-seven out of ninety-three responses! No other light caliber came even close. There were just six specific mentions of a 7mm (cartridge unspecified), five for a .270, and two for a .243. All others were single entries, except for the .338. Again, I remain surprised at the limited support for this useful cartridge among African professional hunters. However, in this part of the survey there were six mentions of the .338. Only two PHs (including, as in 1989, Ray Millican) agreed with me on the wondrous choice of a .338 and a .416! However, Ivan Carter recommended ".338 plus a double," and two PHs (who primarily hunt plains game) recommended the .338 as the heavier of a two-rifle battery, paired respectively with the .25-06 and .270. If a consensus was reached, then, it would clearly be a .30-caliber (either a .30-06 or a .300 magnum) in conjunction with either a .375 or a .416!

Three Rifles

Once again, the three-rifle battery became a bit of a grab bag, with twenty-six separate recommendations, no clear consensus, and only forty-one professional hunters actually recommending a three-firearm battery. Many simply left it blank,

A big difference between this survey and 1989 was the resurgence of double rifles and their cartridges. The .470, right, was far and away the most common, but the much less available .500, left, also garnered considerable support.

while fifteen wrote in "no," sometimes with caveats such as "too many," "too complicated," "baggage allowance too restrictive," and so forth.

Only five recommendations appeared more than once. There were ten recommendations for ".300 plus .375 plus .458," which is actually quite strong support for the most classic three-rifle battery. Other three-firearm arrangements mentioned more than once were: ".270 plus .300 plus .416" (three), ".22 plus .30-06 plus .375-416" (three), ".300 plus .375 plus 12-gauge" (three), and ".223 plus .300 plus .458 Lott" (two).

Interestingly, given the flexibility of a three-gun battery, there was more support for heavier calibers, with thirty-one recommendations for a .416 or larger as part of the trio. These included eight for doubles or double-rifle calibers. This same flexibility showed on the lighter side as well, with twelve suggestions that the light rifle should be a .22, a .22 centerfire, or a 6mm. When you think about it, this makes a lot of sense—but much fewer two-rifle batteries (just three) recommended inclusion of a cartridge of 6mm or less, clearly reflecting the greater flexibility of the three-gun arrangement. In short, the three-rifle battery is far from dead . . . but in today's Africa, support for it is even more guarded than it was twenty years ago.

Should your clients bring a shotgun?

A substantial number of PHs (thirty-eight) simply said "No," with some adding that they always keep a shotgun in camp. A larger number than I expected (twenty-two) said "Yes." Quite a few offered what I call a qualified yes: "Only for birds" (twenty-one); "For duikers and such" (eleven); and, from Fred Duckworth, "Yes—for lion!"

Do you make (or have) specific recommendations on . . .

Scopes

Eight different brands were recommended. Leupold and Swarovski were easily the most mentioned, tied with twenty-nine mentions each. Zeiss followed with twenty mentions, and everything else was way down. There were nine mentions of Schmidt & Bender, three for Trijicon, three for Leica (notwithstanding the fact that Leica hasn't offered riflescopes for years!), and one each for Nikon and Bushnell. One PH specified "illuminated reticle," and Dirk de Bod (primarily hunting plains game and leopard) specified "3–9X42." This question elicited few additional comments, but Mark Dewet added, "I always tell a client to spend more on a scope than on a rifle." (Good advice!)

Bullets

This was the second time I asked for recommendations on bullets, and in general the responses were more mainstream. Once again Barnes Triple Shock X-Bullet was mentioned most frequently (twenty), followed by Swift A-Frame with seventeen. There were nine mentions of Woodleigh and eight of Trophy Bonded Bear Claw. Then came Nosler and Hornady with six each. Monolithic Solids were specifically mentioned three times, as were Barnes Super Solids. Rhino bullets were specifically named twice. Other recommendations were less specific, with eight PHs citing "Federal ammo," two mentioning "Remington," and one stating "Norma." Some professionals were extremely clear in their recommendations. John Sharp, easily one of Zimbabwe's most respected pros, was downright emphatic: "Softpoint bullets must only be Swift A-Frame, Trophy Bonded Bear Claw, or Woodleigh!"

Solid or soft for buffalo?

The majority, forty out of the seventy-five who responded to this question, took the bull by the horns and wrote in "first soft, then solid." Twenty PHs wrote in simply "soft," although some referred back to their bullet recommendations. A surprising number (nine) said something like, "It depends on herd or single bull." The message was: Don't shoot solids in a herd! Louis Venter went a step farther, stating: "Solids are dangerous." John Oosthuizen uniquely wrote, ".375, solid; .400+, soft." There is clearly a lot of awareness of how good our modern softpoints are—but support for using them on buffalo is not universal. Ian Goss, a forty-year veteran hunting in South Africa, Mozambique, and Tanzania, wrote, "SOLIDS!!!" He was joined by five other PHs who still prefer "solids only" for buffalo. Personally, I go with the majority, preferring to start the ball game with a good softpoint, solids thereafter. But the best advice I could offer is: Follow your professional hunter's advice!

Number of cartridges to bring on safari? This one was all over the map! The low number cited was fifteen (specifically for a dangerous-game rifle). The high number was one hundred. The most common responses were "forty per rifle" (twenty-five mentions) and "sixty per rifle" (also twenty-five). Several who cited the higher figures qualified it by saying "for a twenty-one-day safari." A few stated "maximum allowable"—but that could mean by baggage limit or by gun-permit restriction. Either way, the high numbers were often explained by comments like, "in case of scope trouble," or "good to have plenty of practice ammo if 'shooting challenges' emerge."

Left to right: Sissai Shewemene, Col. Negussie Eshete, and his son, Danny Eshete. These three Ethiopian professional hunters are all extremely experienced with mountain nyala. They were universal in recommending cartridges like the .300 Weatherby Magnum for this kind of hunting.

It is not my place or intent to second-guess the PHs, but one comment might be in order: Relatively few professionals actually have occasion to themselves travel by air with firearms. The restriction of "five kilograms" of ammunition per passenger is fairly general among most airlines, and in the post-"9-11" world is much more frequently enforced. Regardless of what a given country's gun permit might allow, this is the weight limit within which to stay. I'll make my own recommendations in the final chapter.

Any comments on pre-safari practice/training?

The 1989 survey contained so many unsolicited comments about shooting and shooting practice that I included this question in the 2007 survey. Almost to a man, every respondent said something about the necessity of practicing and becoming familiar with your rifle. More than forty professional hunters specifically said something about practicing off shooting sticks! If you've followed my stuff in recent years you know I've said in numerous magazine articles that Africa-bound hunters need to get shooting sticks and learn how to use them. I didn't come up with this on my own; it's advice straight from the African professionals!

A large number of pros also stressed the need to get in shape, with a couple dozen suggesting some variation of practicing "running and shooting," the idea being to learn how to get steady when you are slightly out of breath.

Andrew Dawson: "The more fit you are the better you will shoot. Trigger squeeze, squeeze, squeeze."

Doug McNeil: "Practice makes perfect. Get fit for your safari."

Ray Millican: "Practice regularly for at least a month before your safari. Get fit!"

There were an equal number who, in addition to sticks, suggested practicing shooting offhand (or, as they more frequently put it, "freehand").

Doug McNeil: "Freehand and off sticks."

Ian Goss: "We try to get a dead rest, but it isn't always possible. Get used to your rifle and practice freehand."

Andre Roux: "Practice offhand."

Jerome Latrive: "Practice as much as possible off shooting sticks. Know your trigger and learn to shoot fast."

Fred Duckworth: "Absolutely vital to be competent at offhand shooting. Also practice with open sights. No muzzle brakes, please!"

Joe Wright: "Make sure you are familiar with your rifle and practice some snap-shooting at moving targets either side-on or angling away."

Kevin Robertson: "Once you have [your rifle] fitted perfectly, sight in from a bench at the distance recommended by your PH or outfitter. Thereafter, NEVER shoot your rifle off the bench again. To do so will only create a 'flinch from hell.' The shots you'll most commonly take out here will be while leaning up against a tree trunk or branch, off the shooting sticks, or from the sitting position with your elbows resting on your knees. You need to learn how, and practice thoroughly, getting set up quickly for the shot from these positions."

Rudy Lubin: "Practice a lot with the rifles you will use on your safari, in different positions and at different distances, with and without shooting sticks."

Several other comments touched on the value of practicing with a light caliber, another fine idea that I have often written about . . . but didn't come up with on my own.

Dirk de Bod: "Practice a lot with a smaller caliber to avoid flinching. Practice shooting from sticks."

Bert Klineburger: "A hunter does not have to use his big rifle for practice. He can make targets of animal photos and practice with a .22, a .22 magnum, or a .223. Make a tripod and practice shooting off sticks."

Alan Vincent: "Lots of shooting practice, even with a .22."

Any other comments?

This survey, as did the previous, yielded a treasure trove of valuable information. I really appreciate all the detailed comments and wish there were space to include every single word. Most comments, however, took essentially the same track: Get fit, practice sensibly, and one more: Bring rifles you are familiar with.

Howard Knott: "Don't buy a rifle two weeks before the safari."

Ian Batchelor: "Don't bring anything you're scared of."

Ernst Scholz: "Bring only guns you have used a lot and which have been assembled for a long time. All screws should be Loctited into place."

And finally, there were several gems of really good advice:

Wayne Hendry: "Never leave your rifle on the car."

Coenraad Vermaak: "Clients must read, read, read, and practice, practice, practice—especially with a new piece they aren't accustomed to."

Johan Calitz: "Enjoy the hunt and listen to your PH."

Ian Goss: "Enjoy every part of your hunt. Learn new things all the time, and don't 'supermarket shop' your animals."

Stephane Ndongue: "It is very important to be in touch with the PH you will hunt with. Each hunt is different even if the final goal is the same. Your PH is a better adviser than anyone else!"

Doug McNeil: "Good and expensive ammo and scopes are cheap compared to lost and wounded animals."

Ian Batchelor: "The first shot is always critical. Make sure of it. If in doubt, don't shoot."

And finally, from Robin Hurt: "Learn animal anatomy. Learn to squeeze the trigger. Make sure your trigger pull is crisp and not too heavy. Listen to your professional hunter and heed his advice. That is what you are paying him for!"

The Professional's Choice, 2007

Professional Hunter Survey—2007
General Data
Total Number of Respondents: 107
Most Years in the Field: 55
Least Years in the Field 1
Average Years in the Field 19.5

Dangerous Game Hunted:
Buffalo .... 94 Respondents
Lion .... 88 Respondents
Leopard .... 93 Respondents
Elephant .... 86 Respondents
Rhino .... 38 Respondents
Hippo .... 93 Respondents

Professional Hunters' Personal Choices
Light Plains Game

Caliber	#
.270	21
.30-06	18
.243	15
.300 Win. Mag.	13
7x57	13
7mm (Magnum *)	8
.375 *	7
.300 H&H	7
.308 Win.	6
.223	6
.222	3
8x68s	1
7x64	1
6x45	2
6.5 *	1
.257 Wby. Mag.	1
.25-06	1
.22-250	1

* Exact Cartridge Unspecified

Medium Plains Game

Caliber	#
.30-06	24
.375 *	22
.300 Win. Mag.	13
7x57	8
.338 Win. Mag.	7
.300 H&H	7
7mm (Magnum *)	7
.308 Win.	6
.270	8
.300 Wby. Mag.	5
9.3x62	2
8x57	2
8x68s	1

* Exact Cartridge Unspecified

Large Plains Game

Caliber	#
.375 *	52
.300 (Magnum *)	18
.416 *	9
7x57	8
.338 Win. Mag.	8
7mm (Magnum *)	5
9.3x62	3
.30-06	3
.340 Wby. Mag.	2
.35 Whelen	1
.460 Wby. Mag.	1
.308 Win.	1
.270	1

* Exact Caliber Unspecified

Leopard

Caliber	#
.375 *	36
.300 Win. Mag.	18
.30-06	13
7mm *	7
.416 *	5
.338 Win. Mag.	5
10-Gauge Shotgun	4
.470	3
.500 Jeffery	2
.458 Lott	2
9.3x62	2
.300 H&H	2
.475 No. 2 J	1
.450 Dakota	1
.450-3 ¼" Ne	1
.270	1
.243	1
12-Gauge Shotgun	1

* Exact Cartridge Unspecified

Lion

Caliber	#
.375 *	38
.416 *	21
.470 Ne	7
.458 Lott	7
.458 Win. Mag.	6
.300 (Magnum *)	6
7mm (Magnum *)	4
.30-06	3
.500 Jeffery	2
.450 Dakota Magnum	2
.450 3¼" Ne	2
.475 No. 2 J	1
.505 Gibbs	1
9.3x62	1
.308 Win.	1
10-Gauge	1

* Exact Cartridge Unspecified

Thick-skinned Game

Caliber	#
.470 Ne	20
.416 *	16
.458 Lott	14
.458 Win. Mag.	10
.375 *	10
.500 Jeffery	8
.500-3" Ne	8
.450 3 ¼" Ne	5
.505 Gibbs	4
.450 Dakota Magnum	2
.475 No. 2 J	1
.450 Rigby Rimless Magnum	1
.450 Ackley	1
.450 No. 2	1
.425 W-r	1

* Exact Cartridge Unspecified

All-round Use

Caliber	#
.375 *	49
.416 *	15
9.3x62	5
.470 Ne	4
.458 Win. Mag.	4
.338 Win. Mag.	4
.505 Gibbs	3
.458 Lott	2
".300 Class"	2
.500 Jeffery	1
.475 No. 2 J	1
.460 Wby. Mag.	
.450 Rigby Rimless Magnum	1
.450 Dakota Mag	1
.30-06	1

* Exact Cartridge Unspecified

Sights

Type	#
Iron	74
Peep	15
Scope	10
For Plains Game	40

Bullets

Type	#
Barnes X/TS	28
Swift A-frame	24
Trophy Bonded Bear Claw	15
Woodleigh	11
Nosler Partition	5
Monolithic Solid	5
Sledgehammer Solid	5
Hornady Solid	5
"Federal"	2
"Norma"	2
Dzombo	2
Gs Custom	1
Gpa	1
Rhino	1
Speer Grand Slam	1
Stewart	1

573

Safari Rifles II

Recommendations to Clients
One Rifle

Caliber	#
375 *	57
".375 Or .416" *	12
.416 *	9
.300 Win. Mag.	5
.338 Win. Mag.	4
"Any .30 Caliber"	3
9.3x62	2
.308 Win.	1
7mm *	1

* Exact Cartridge Unspecified

Two Rifles

Caliber	Caliber	#
.300 (Magnum *) +	.416 *	27
.300 (Magnum *) +	.375 *	20
.30-06 +	.375 *	16
7mm (Magnum *) +	.375 *	4
.300 (Magnum *) +	.458 Win. Mag.	3
.375 * +	.458 Win. Mag.	2
.338 Win. Mag. +	.416 *	2
.270 +	.375 *	2
.243 Win. +	.375 *	2
.416 * +	.470 Ne	1
.375 * +	"Double"	1
.375 * +	".416 or Larger"	1
.338 Win. Mag. +	"Double"	1
.338 Win. Mag. +	.375 *	1
".30-06/.338" +	".375/.416"	1
.300 * +	.458 Lott	1
.308 Win. +	.375 *	1
7mm * +	9.3x62	1
".270/7mm" +	".375/.416"	1
.270 +	.375 * **	1
.270 +	.338 Win. Mag.	1
.25-06 +	.338 Win. Mag.	1
"Light" +	.375 *	1
".22 Or Shotgun" +	.375	1

* Exact Cartridge Unspecified
** Respondent Specified ".270 And .375" as
Ideal Battery for Female Clients

Three Rifle Battery

Caliber	Caliber	Caliber	#
.300 * +	.375 * +	".458+" *	10
.270 +	.300 * +	.416 *	3
.300 * +	.375 * +	12-Gauge	3
.22 * +	.30-06 +	".375/.416" *	3
.223 +	.300 * +	.458 Lott	2
.300 * +	.416 * +	".470+" *	1
.338 Win. Mag. +	.375 * +	.470 Ne	1
.300 * +	.375 +	"Double"	1
.300 * +	.416 +	.470 Ne	1
.300 * +	.375 +	.416*	1
.30-06 +	.375 +	.470 Ne	1
.30-06 +	.375 +	".416+" *	1
.30-06 +	340 Wby. Mag. +	.375 *	1
.30-06 +	.416 +	12-Gauge	1
".30-06/.300/.338" +	".375/.416" +	".458/.458 Lott/.470"	1
7mm * +	.375 +	".470/.500 Jeffery"	1
.270 +	.300 +	.458 Win. Mag.	1
.25-06 +	.300 +	.375 *	1
.243 Win. +	.300 +	.470 Ne.	1
.243 Win. +	.300 +	.416 *	1
.243 Win +	.300 +	".375/.416" *	1
6mm * +	.30-06 +	.375 *	1
.22 * +	.375 +	.470 Ne.	1
.22 Hornet +	.300 +	.375 *	1
.22 * +	.270 +	.375 *	1

* Exact Cartridge Unspecified

Shotgun

No:	38
Yes:	22

"Qualified Yes"

"Only for Birds"	21
"For Duikers, and etc.	11
"For Lion"	1

Recommended Scopes

Brand	#
Leupold	29
Swarovski	29
Zeiss	20
Schmidt & Bender	9
Leica	3
Trijicon	1
Bushnell	1
Nikon	1

Recommended Bullets

Brand	#
Barnes X/TS	20
Swift A-frame	17
Woodleigh	9
Trophy Bonded Bear Claw	8
"Federal"	8
"Nosler"	6
"Bonded Core Softpoint"	6
Hornady	4
Monolithic Solid	3
Barnes Super Solid	2
"Remington"	2
Rhino	2
"Norma"	1

Solid or Soft for Buffalo?

Recommendation	#
"First Solid, Then Soft"	40
Softpoint	20
"Softs in Herds, Solids on Solitary"	9
Solids only	6

Number of Cartridges to Bring on Safari
(for dangerous-game rifle)

Low:	15
High:	100

Preferred:

40 Per Rifle	25 Respondents
60 Per Rifle	25 Respondents

574

Care and Transport of Firearms on Safari

Chapter 41

Regardless of which rifles you take on safari, they won't do you much good if you don't get them to Africa, through whatever Customs you must pass, and to camp in good working order. Once there, of course, you must keep them working—but that's pretty simple compared to the potential problems that can arise when traveling with firearms.

The foregoing paragraph was written when "9-11" lay far ahead in the unforeseen future. The dastardly events of that day changed all of our worlds, probably forever. It certainly changed the way we are able to travel with firearms. There are more rules and more restrictions, and I tend to think they are getting worse all the time. Of course, it isn't all "9-11" stuff. It used to be very simple to take hunting arms in and out of South Africa. Now the permit application runs for pages and pages, with some of Africa's most draconian restrictions. On the other hand, we Americans don't have much right to complain about any other country's restrictions. We are more or less able to move about with our firearms—but I pity anyone from elsewhere who wants to hunt in the United States. Since 2001 it has been almost impossible for any foreign national to bring a firearm into the United States for any purpose. In fact, right now this situation is so bad that it is almost impossible for Canadians or Mexicans to transit the United States en route to Africa (or anywhere else) with firearms!

There is one small bit of good associated with all this. At least in the United States, where most of us reading these lines start our journeys, the rules are far better understood today. I can actually say that I've had less trouble traveling with firearms since "9-11" than before—and I've had no arguments with either airline representatives or security people. On the other hand, these days it isn't smart to argue with such people!

The first and most important rule is to plan your safari as far ahead as possible, and include your choice of firearms as part of that initial planning. Some countries are easier to get firearms into and out of than others. Right now Namibia requires no prior

The last few seasons I've been using a big SKB gun case. I think modern plastics are as tough as metal, though probably not much lighter. If I'm taking just two rifles I pack all my accessories in the gun case, and the rest in a "compressible" duffel.

paperwork; all that's needed is to register the serial numbers and obtain a permit right at the airport Customs. South Africa has a lengthy application, plus you need a letter of invitation from your outfitter and your own country's gun permit (for U.S. citizens, Customs Form 4457 suffices). Zimbabwe is almost as simple as Namibia, provided your PH is there to meet you with his paperwork. Cameroon is at the other extreme, with unusual amounts of paperwork and a great deal of advance time required to obtain permits. Somewhere in between are Zambia, Botswana, Tanzania, Mozambique, and most other safari countries, all of which require that permits be obtained in advance.

Your professional hunter or outfitter will usually handle all the details of obtaining your gun permits if any are required. Normally, the client's primary function is to list the make, type, caliber, and serial number of each firearm, plus the amount of ammunition to accompany it. The critical detail here is that the serial numbers must be correct. Once declared, don't make any changes! As a writer, with obligations to try out and write about various firearms, I have more than once planned on taking some new rifle that turned out not to be ready at the last minute. Aside from the paperwork hassles of such last-minute changes, which create a professional hunter's nightmare, the risk of not getting your firearms to your final destination is greatly increased. Once you've decided what firearms you're taking and have communicated all the needed information, don't change your mind. This means you must be sure of the firearms you're taking. If a new rifle is in your plans, get it in plenty of time, check it out, and make sure everything works as it should. Then, and not before then, send whatever information is needed.

When you're planning a safari, you should ask your hunter what he recommends in rifles, understanding that he may or may not have any real interest in firearms beyond their efficiency as simple tools. According to my surveys (chapters 39 and 40), the odds are good that he'll simply tell you to bring a .375. That isn't bad advice, but you may or may not wish to follow it. Whether you do or not, at least make certain the firearms you plan to bring are legal. Some countries do not allow semiautomatic firearms, while others prohibit .22-caliber firearms. South Africa currently prohibits lever actions and slide actions as well as semiautomatics! Many countries have specific caliber limitations for use on various classes of game, especially dangerous game.

Handguns can be easily imported into some countries and are totally taboo in others—and this seems to change with some frequency. I don't like to be encumbered by a handgun when I'm hunting with a rifle, so I rarely worry about it. On the other hand, I've done some handgun hunting in both South Africa and Zimbabwe and have enjoyed it immensely. If you wish to bring a handgun, make certain its importation will be legal.

Ammunition can be subject to restrictions, and the exact amount you plan to bring is often stated on the gun permit. In Botswana, Mozambique, and the C.A.R. I have

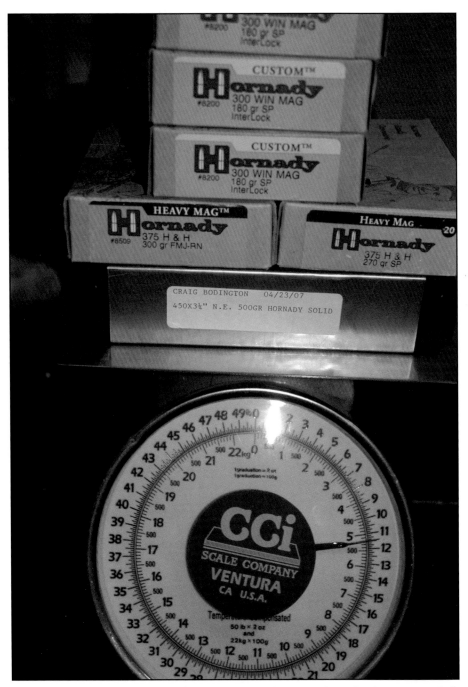

Weight of ammunition needs to be kept to five kilograms (eleven pounds) total. This ammo supply for a three-rifle battery—sixty .300 Winchester Magnum; forty .375 H&H; and twenty .450-3¼"— "breaks the bank" at 11½ pounds.

Let's hope no gunsmithing is required, but just in case make sure you bring screwdrivers that will fit all of your action screws and scope mount screws.

customarily had my ammunition counted on the way in, and in Tanzania you can expect to have it counted both coming in and going out. In rare instances, having cartridge headstamps that don't match the caliber of your rifle can be a real problem. For instance, my .416 Taylor rifle using ammunition handloaded from necked-down .458 Winchester Magnum cases, as absurd as it sounds, is a potential problem. The gun permit says I have a .416 and authorizes the importation of .416 cartridges, but the only ammunition I have is clearly headstamped .458. An alert Customs official may well refuse entry of the ammunition, leaving you up the creek without your paddle and very little recourse.

Such restrictions vary tremendously from country to country, but all that's required is pre-hunt communication and common sense. The second rule is to know the rules—or learn them—and then follow them. These days this is the only way to fly! Aside from gun permits and such, which vary widely from country to country, the basic rules are pretty darn simple. Firearms must be stowed in a hard-sided gun case that locks, and you must declare them. Whether ammo goes separately or with the guns seems to vary a bit. Also, some airlines require advance notification that you are traveling with firearms, and some do not. Some countries require authorization before you can even transit with a firearm. At this writing this is true of the Netherlands (primary gateway from the United States to northern Tanzania)—but the system works and is not a real problem provided you know the rules and follow them.

Airline restrictions on the amounts of ammo they will carry are almost more demanding than African importation regulations. Whichever airline you're flying, make certain you call a few days before your departure and ask someone in a responsible position what the current regulations and policies are for carrying ammunition. Each airline is a bit different, but a standard restriction is five kilograms of ammunition, usually required to be in original factory containers. Less common—though you may run into it—is the requirement for ammunition to be in a separate, locked, wood or metal container.

Five kilograms, or eleven pounds, isn't much ammunition. A reasonable mix of ammo for a classic three-rifle battery might be sixty rounds of .300 Winchester Magnum, forty rounds of .375 H&H, and twenty rounds for a .450-3¼". On my little postal scale, that broke the bank at 11½ pounds! But it's close—if I was taking a 7x57 or .30-06 instead of the .300, I'd be just fine. Although it seems a small point, my recommendation is to avoid exceeding that limit. While it's a good idea to use original factory packaging, the boxes don't have to be full. So if that means taking fifty-two rounds instead of sixty so you can make weight, do it.

As mentioned in chapter 22, traveling with takedown rifles in shorter cases is handy and convenient, and may reduce the scrutiny. But DO NOT attempt to avoid any formalities. Always declare your rifles and your ammo, and keep smiling! I think the best way to ensure that your baggage arrives with you is to avoid short connections. For an international connection, I figure less than two hours is pushing it. Also, avoid overweight baggage if at all possible. With multiple firearms this can be very difficult, but overweight baggage charges can be outrageous, plus extra bags are red flags for delayed baggage.

Always check in early. These days you can expect to be treated professionally and courteously, but expect checking in with firearms to require extra time. And don't forget to get that timeless, priceless little piece of paper from U.S. Customs, Form 4457—simply a standard form for registering articles to take abroad. No copy is kept, so it's a totally meaningless form . . . unless you forget to get one! It takes about two minutes to fill out, and is good for as long you own a given firearm. Optimally, get this form in advance and put a copy in your gun case along with a copy of your passport. Keep the original with your passport, and in many situations you can use it to fill out required forms without needing to dig into the gun case to check the serial number.

There are many good gun cases, and many not so good. I've been through a bunch of them, and it is absolutely amazing to me what the airlines are able to do to a seemingly indestructible case! I'm not convinced that metal is stronger than good plastic . . . nor am I convinced that heavy plastic weighs less than light metal. Just make sure the case closes tightly on all sides, locks securely, and has strong hinges opposite the locks. Far more important, to my mind, than the construction of the

You don't need to bring a complete gun cleaning kit, but you should bring some minimal gear so that you can wipe down and lubricate your rifle daily—and punch out the bore as needed.

case is how it's packed. I've gone through a half-dozen good metal cases in the last twenty years, and in between I've used several very inexpensive plastic cases with equally good results. There aren't any real secrets to packing a gun case except to make certain there's adequate foam or other cushioning material to pad the rifle well and keep it immobile. I often augment a case's padding with rolled up T-shirts or clean socks, especially around the scope. Bolts are a potential problem with bolt-action rifles; if left in the rifle, the bolt can cause a serious bulge, which, if the case is dropped, can result in serious damage. I am fairly certain this is how one of my rifles, a Weatherby Mark V, was shattered inside a good stainless-steel case.

These days I take the bolt out and wrap it in a clean pair of socks. Some guys like to put their bolts in another bag to discourage theft. It's a sound idea, but it would be just my luck for that bag to go missing. I'm knocking on wood as I write this, but to date I have never lost any guns in transit—although I have had several delayed for quite some time. Last year I did lose a duffel bag in transit while my gun case, which had been hand-carried (as the airlines are supposed to do), arrived safe and sound. The ammunition was in the duffel bag, and it was a scramble to find some in Johannesburg. But if the bolt to my .375 had been in that duffel bag, there would have been little point in shopping for ammo!

Once the rifles arrive safely in camp, African hunting is generally not as hard on them as is most American game country. In most areas dust and grit are constant, so regular cleaning is absolutely essential to ensure proper functioning. Rust prevention is also extremely important. In dry weather, sweating hands cause rust overnight, and the effects in wet weather are obvious. Most camps will have a cleaning rod and some oil, but the wealth of excellent gun-care products we have in America is unheard of over there. On my last several trips I've carried a small Otis kit that has literally everything in a fist-size zippered bag—except a jointed cleaning rod, which is a mandatory addition. At a minimum, take a small cleaning kit that includes a good jointed cleaning rod. The flexible pull-through type of rod is fine for cleaning, but if you take a spill and lodge some debris in your muzzle, you simply must have a solid cleaning rod to get it out.

You should also have a good gunsmith's screwdriver that fits the action screws of your rifle so you can pull the action out of the stock in case it gets really soaked—and, of course, screwdrivers that fit the mounts of your scope. Speaking of scope mounts, alternative sighting equipment is absolutely essential. Auxiliary iron sights are one approach, and they'll surely do in a pinch—so long as you've checked them out before the hunt. Another option is to carry an extra scope already mounted in rings that will fit the bases on at least one of your rifles.

In your emergency repair kit, carry along some Super Glue and the best plastic tape you can find. You'll be amazed at what you can do with it. One year I arrived at a deer camp in Georgia at midnight, only to find my riflestock broken in two at the pistol grip. We rustled up some Super Glue and tape, and with liberal doses of each I got the stock put back together. I fired only three shots with it before I sent it in for a new handle. One shot was fired to check its zero, which hadn't changed. The two others were used to take two nice white-tailed bucks with one shot each.

Which brings up one last point about traveling with firearms: Before you leave any airport anywhere in the world with rifles, open the gun case and check them out. If there's damage, you may have a legitimate claim against the airline for repairs. You will have a terrible time collecting, but if you don't check before leaving the airport, you have no chance at all.

OK, that reminds me of one final issue to discuss, which is making a decision not to travel with firearms. Unfortunately, as time goes on I expect the hassles of traveling with firearms to get worse rather than better. This is terrible news for a guy like me, since a large percentage of my writing is about guns rather than strictly about hunting. Unfortunately, it seems we're headed that way, and it is a whole lot simpler to simply leave your own rifles at home. Most African outfitters have perfectly suitable rifles for hire, and in my 2007 survey a couple of professional hunters specifically recommended hiring rifles as a preferable option to bringing them! As much as I hate the thought, hiring or borrowing rifles is a sound option. Certainly it's simpler, although for many of us part of the anticipation of any hunt

Soft gun cases are bulky, but you really need a soft case for protecting your rifle(s) in the vehicle—especially if you bring fine guns! Some outfitters provide these and some don't.

comes from choosing the perfect rifle(s), working up the best loads with the ideal bullets, and of course practicing regularly. And, for rifle nuts like me and many of you, part of the satisfaction is derived from seeing those choices perform as well as we'd hoped. That said, it sure is easier to travel without firearms!

The armament available varies wildly and widely. Chances are you won't be handed a Holland & Holland! But you will almost certainly be handed a rifle that has proven itself serviceable time and again. There are variations on this theme. Most of us have a favorite deer rifle, and that favorite deer rifle will probably be suitable for the majority of the nondangerous species. If you're going buffalo hunting, especially for the first time, you may not have a suitable rifle. You can get one—but it's certainly a viable option to borrow one. In fact, if you aren't sure what to get and don't have a whole lot of time, it could well be better to borrow one. But if you aren't bringing all the rifles you will need, advise your outfitter so he can have rifles and ammo on hand. Of course, if the unthinkable happens and your gun case is delayed or misdirected, he'll scramble a battery and your hunt will proceed—but if you make a conscious decision to hire a rifle, arrange that up front and try to find out what you'll be using.

One important note: Borrowing rifles for the actual hunt does not preclude the necessity for pre-safari practice! As reflected in so many comments from so many professional hunters in my survey, practice is critical. In fact, it may be even more important if your intention is to use unfamiliar rifles! As one PH suggested, if you plan to hire rifles, then spend some time on the range with your buddies and shoot their equally unfamiliar rifles!

I must admit that I have never purposely gone to Africa without rifles. (Other countries on other continents, yes.) So far the pleasure of organizing and using my own rifles has greatly exceeded the pain of increasing paperwork, and I hope that doesn't change. Even so, I have borrowed rifles on numerous occasions, and for numerous reasons. Few African professionals are rifle nuts in the way that many of us are. In some cases this is because the rifle is, to many PHs, a basic tool. More frequently, given limited availability and their own onerous gun-licensing procedures to deal with, they have limited opportunity to try a variety of calibers and bullets. But they know from firsthand experience what works and what doesn't, and it is hardly in their best interests to hand you something that doesn't work! So if you're daunted by the paperwork, jumping on a last-minute opportunity, or feel your own rifles aren't up to the task (or are too valuable to travel with), don't hesitate to hire rifles. This should not be a stumbling block to the grand experience that is safari.

As a final word to this volume, this has been a lengthy discussion of rifles and cartridges suitable for African hunting. At the start I was daunted by the task of updating a book I'd written nearly twenty years earlier. The more I got into the project, though, the more I enjoyed it. There have been no sweeping changes in twenty years, but there have been many new developments, and many subjects that I know more about at fifty-five than I did at thirty-five. The result you hold in your hands is truly a word-for-word revision, more than a third longer in word count, with several times more photographs. I believe the concepts herein are sound, and I suspect they will lead to many campfire discussions for years to come. I am sure many more new developments will take place in the next twenty years, and I'm equally sure there will still be great African hunting and people like you and me who are fascinated by such things.

However, should I be fortunate to live so long, I will be seventy-five in another twenty years. Please don't count on my revising this book again! But let me say in closing that while rifles and cartridges and bullets and sights and their suitability for various types of game comprise a fascinating subject, how well you shoot is always far more important than what you are using. So, whatever rifles you plan to carry on safari, get to the range and shoot. We can (and will) argue the nuances endlessly, and in our differences of opinion we'll have our horse race. But ultimately Walter Dalrymple Maitland "Karamojo" Bell always had it right: Shot placement is, if not everything, at least almost everything.

Bibliography

Chapter 42

Aagaard, F & B. *Aagaard's African Adventures.* Long Beach: Safari Press Inc., 2008.

Aitken, R. B. *Great Game Animals of the World.* New York: The Macmillan Company, 1968.

Askins, Colonel C. *Asian Jungle, African Bush.* Harrisburg, Pennsylvania: The Stackpole Company, 1959.

——. *African Hunt.* Harrisburg, Pennsylvania: The Stackpole Company, 1958.

Barnes, F. C. *Cartridges of the World.* Revised 9th Edition. Northbrook, Illinois: DBI Books, Inc., 2000.

Barrett, P. *A Treasury of African Hunting.* New York: Winchester Press, 1969.

Bell, W. D. M. *The Wanderings of an Elephant Hunter.* Long Beach: Safari Press Inc., 2001.

——. *Bell of Africa.* Long Beach: Safari Press Inc., 1989.

——. *Karamojo Safari.* Long Beach: Safari Press Inc., 1989.

Blixen-Finecke, Baron B. von. *African Hunter.* New York: St. Martin's Press, 1986.

Blunt, Commander D. E. *Elephant.* London: The Holland Press, 1985.

Boothroy, G. *Gun Collecting.* London: The Sportsman's Press, 1987.

Broom, G. and Boddington, C. *A Life On Safari.* Atascadero, California: Mission Trails Media, 2004.

Bull, B. *Safari—A Chronicle of Adventure.* London: Viking, 1988.

Bulpin, T. V. *The Hunter is Death.* Long Beach, California: Safari Press Inc., 1987.

Burrard, Sir Gerald. *Notes On Sporting Rifles.* London: Edward Arnold Ltd., 1958.

Carmichel, J. *Jim Carmichel's Book of the Rifle.* New York: Outdoor Life Books, 1985.

Clark, J. L. *Good Hunting.* Norman, Oklahoma: University of Oklahoma Press, 1966.

De Haas, F. *Bolt Action Rifles.* Northfield, Illinois: DBI Books, Inc., 1984.

Donnelly, J. J. *The Handloader's Manual of Cartridge Conversions.* South Hackensack, New Jersey: Stoeger Publishing Company, 1987.

Foa, E. *After Big Game in Central Africa.* Long Beach: Safari Press Inc., 1986.

Forker, B. *Ammo & Ballistics.* Third Edition. Long Beach, California: Safari Press Inc., 2006.

Haggard, H. R. *She; King Solomon's Mines; Allan Quatermain.* New York: Dover Publications, Inc., 1951.

Harland, R. *Ndlovu; The Art of Hunting the African Elephant.* Harare, Zimbabwe: Ivory Imprints, 2005.

Hemingway, E. *Green Hills of Africa.* New York: Charles Scribner's Sons, 1935.

Hornady Manufacturing, Inc. *Hornady Handbook of Cartridge Reloading; Volumes I and II.* Sixth Edition. Grand Island, Nebraska: Hornady Manufacturing Company, 2003.

Hunter, J. A. *Hunter.* Long Beach: Safari Press Inc., 1999.

Ker, D. I. *African Adventure.* Harrisburg, Pennsylvania: The Stackpole Company, 1957.

Kittenberger, K. *Big Game Hunting and Collecting in East Africa 1903–1926.* New York: St. Martin's Press, 1989.

Lott, J. *Big Bore Rifles.* Los Angeles, California: Petersen Publishing Company, 1983.

Lyell, D. D. *African Adventures–Letters from Famous Big Game Hunters.* New York: St. Martin's Press, 1988.

Matunas, E. A. *Shooting.* New York: Outdoor Life Books, 1986.

Matthews, C. W. *Shoot Better.* Lakewood, Colorado: Bill Matthews, Inc., 1984.

———. *Shoot Better II.* Lakewood, Colorado: Bill Matthews, Inc., 1989.

Maydon, H. C. *Big Game Shooting in Africa.* London: Seely, Service & Co. Ltd., 1957.

Mellon, J. *African Hunter.* Long Beach: Safari Press Inc., 1995.

Nobel. *Sporting Ammunition.* London: Nobel Industries, Ltd., 1925.

Nosler Bullets. *Nosler Reloading Manual Number Two.* Bend, Oregon: Nosler Bullet, Inc. 1981.

O'Connor, J. *The Big Game Rifle*. Long Beach, California: Safari Press Inc., 1989.

Pardal, J. C. *Cambaco*. Lisbon: T. Protasio, 1982.

Patterson, Lt. Col. J. H. *The Maneaters of Tsavo*. New York: St. Martin's Press, 1986.

Popham, A. Jr. *Stalking Game; from Forest to Tundra*. Clinton, New Jersey: Amwell Press, 1985.

Ruark, R. C. *Horn of the Hunter*. Long Beach: Safari Press Inc., 1987.

——. *Something of Value*. Long Beach: Safari Press Inc., 2007.

——. *Use Enough Gun*. Long Beach: Safari Press Inc., 1999.

Rushby, G. G. *No More the Tusker*. London: W. H. Allen, 1965.

Sanchez-Ariño, T. *On the Trail of the African Elephant*. London: Rowland Ward, 1987.

Sierra Bullets. *Sierra Bullets Reloading Manual*. Second Edition. Santa Fe Springs, California: Sierra Bullets, The Leisure Group, Inc., 1978.

Speer Omark Industries. *Reloading Manual Number Ten*. Lewiston, Idaho: Omark Industries, 1979.

Stigand, Capt. C. H. *Hunting the African Elephant*. New York: St. Martin's Press, 1986.

Taylor, J. *African Rifles & Cartridges*. Long Beach: Safari Press Inc., 1994.

——. *Big Game and Big Game Rifles*. Long Beach: Safari Press Inc., 1993.

Truesdell, S. R. *The Rifle—Its Development For Big Game Hunting*. Long Beach: Safari Press Inc., 1992.

White, S. E. *The Land of Footprints*. London: Thomas Nelson and Sons, 1925.

Wright, G. *Shooting the British Double Rifle*. Second Edition. Australia: Arms & Militaria Press, 1999.

Wynne-Jones, A. *Hunting—On Safari in East and Southern Africa*. Johannesburg, South Africa: Macmillan South Africa (Publishers) (Pty) Ltd., 1980.

Index

Index